This major contribution to Ottoman history is now published in paperback in two volumes: the original single hardback volume (1994) has been widely acclaimed as a landmark in the study of one of the most enduring and influential empires of modern times. The authors provide a richly detailed account of the social and economic history of the Ottoman region, from the origins of the Empire around 1300 to the eve of its destruction during World War I. The breadth and the fullness of coverage make these two volumes essential for an understanding of contempory developments in both the Middle East and the post-Soviet Balkan world.

The text of the first volume is by Halil İnalcık, covering the period 1300–1600. The second volume, written by Suraiya Faroqhi, Bruce McGowan, Donald Quataert and Şevket Pamuk, continues the story to 1914. Each volume examines developments in population, trade, transport, manufacturing, land tenure, and the economy, and extensive apparatus and bibliographic information is provided for students and others wishing to pursue the subject in more detail. Both volumes will be fundamental to any future discussion of any aspect of Ottoman history.

AN ECONOMIC AND SOCIAL HISTORY
OF THE OTTOMAN EMPIRE
Volume 1: 1300–1600

خ

AN

ECONOMIC AND
SOCIAL HISTORY

OF THE

OTTOMAN EMPIRE

EDITED BY
HALİL İNALCIK

WITH
DONALD QUATAERT

Volume 1: 1300–1600

HALİL İNALCIK
Professor of History,
University of Bilkent

CAMBRIDGE
UNIVERSITY PRESS

CAMBRIDGE UNIVERSITY PRESS
Cambridge, New York, Melbourne, Madrid, Cape Town, Singapore, São Paulo

Cambridge University Press
The Edinburgh Building, Cambridge CB2 2RU, UK

Published in the United States of America by Cambridge University Press, New York

www.cambridge.org
Information on this title: www.cambridge.org/9780521574563

First published 1994
First paperback edition (see below) 1997
Fifth printing 2005

A catalogue record for this publication is available from the British Library

A note on the paperback edition

An Economic and Social History of the Ottoman Empire was first published in hardback
as a single volume. For its paperback appearance the work has been divided into two,
the original Part I (by Halil İnalcık) constituting the first paperback volume, and Parts
II to IV (by Suraiya Faroqhi, Bruce McGowan, Donald Quataert) and the original
Appendix, now Part V (by Şevket Pamuk) constituting the second paperback volume.
Although the arabic pagination remains continuous between the two volumes, for the
convenience of readers common material (like the glossary and chronology) are printed
in both volumes, and each has its own index.

Volume 1: 1300–1600
HALİL İNALCIK
ISBN-13 978-0-521-57456-3 paperback
ISBN-10 0-521-57456-0 paperback

Volume 2: 1600–1914
SURAIYA FAROQHI, BRUCE McGOWAN, DONALD QUATAERT, and
ŞEVKET PAMUK
ISBN-13 978-0-521-57455-6 paperback
ISBN-10 0-521-57455-2 paperback

Single-volume hardback edition (1300–1914) still available
ISBN-13 978-0-521-34315-2 hardback
ISBN-10 0-521-34315-1 hardback

Transferred to digital printing 2006

CONTENTS

List of maps   *page* ix
List of figures   x
List of tables   xi
Genealogy of the Ottoman dynasty   xiv
Chronology of Ottoman history, *1260–1923*   xv
Preface   xxii
List of abbreviations   xxv
General maps

General introduction   I
Halil İnalcık and Donald Quataert

PART I THE OTTOMAN STATE: ECONOMY
        AND SOCIETY, 1300–1600   9
        Halil İnalcık, University of Bilkent

Introduction: Empire and population   II

    A   THE ECONOMIC MIND   44

    B   STATE REVENUES AND EXPENDITURES   55
1   Sources of revenue   55
2   The state treasury and budgets   77

    C   STATE, LAND AND PEASANT   103
3   State-owned lands (*miri*)   103

vii

Contents

4   Land possession outside the *miri* system   120
5   Land surveying   132
6   The *çift-hane* system: the organization of Ottoman rural
    society   143
7   Settlements   155

D   TRADE

8   İstanbul and the imperial economy   179
9   International trade: general conditions   188
10 Bursa and the silk trade   218
11 Dubrovnik and the Balkans   256
12 The Black Sea and Eastern Europe   271
13 The India trade   315
14 Northerners in the Mediterranean   364
Bibliography   380

List of weights and measures   xxxvii
Glossary   xlv
Index   liii

MAPS

1	The Ottoman Empire, 1300–1512	*page* xxix
2	The Ottoman Empire, c. 1550	xxx
3	Ottoman provinces and vassal states, 1609	xxxii
4	The Ottoman Empire, 1683–c.1800	xxxiii
5	Dismemberment of the Ottoman Empire, 1672–1913	xxxiv
6	Ottoman provinces, c. 1900	xxxv
7	Turcoman İl or Ulus confederations in Asia Minor	33
8	Principal mining sites in Serbia, Bosnia and Macedonia	61
9	State revenues in the early years of Kanuni Süleyman	81
10	Anatolian goods marketed in İstanbul	183
11	Trade routes of the empire	220
12	Venetian sea routes in the Mediterranean in the fifteenth century	318

FIGURES

I:1   Production of leading silver mines in Ottoman Rumelia,
c. 1600   *page* 60
I:2   The development of field patterns   158

TABLES

I:1   The poll-tax-paying non-Muslim population, 1488–91 *page* 26
I:2   Non-Muslim population in Anatolia, 1489   27
I:3   Population growth in Anatolia   28
I:4   *Sancak* population increase in the *liva* of Damascus   29
I:5   Population density estimates of the Ottoman Empire and
      European countries, 1600   31
I:6   Nomad households (*hane*) of western Anatolia   35
I:7   The militia of yörük origin in the Balkans, 1560   36
I:8   Muslim nomads in the Balkans; tribal confederations in
      eastern Anatolia   37
I:9   Poll-tax and principal *mukataas*, 1475   56
I:10 Principal revenue estimates (*mukataas*) in the city of
      Damascus   57
I:11 The main *mukataas* in Hungary   58
I:12 Principal mining areas in the Balkans, 1468–77   59
I:13 State revenues from principal salt works in the sixteenth
      century   63
I:14 Revenue from the poll-tax in 1528   67
I:15 Tribute from Christian states   67
I:16 Tribute of Wallachia and Moldavia   67
I:17 Increases in the rates of poll-tax and *avarız*   70
I:18 The revenue of the Ottoman state as estimated by
      Europeans, 1433–1603   78
I:19 The Ottoman central "budget" of 1527–28   80
I:20 Total revenue of the empire, 1527–28   81
I:21 Estimated annual revenues of European states   82
I:22 Total revenues of the Ottoman Empire by province,
      1527–28   82

xi

I:23 Balance of revenue and expenditure by region, 1527–28   83
I:24 Annual surplus of the revenues of the provinces of
Aleppo and Damascus sent to İstanbul   86
I:25 Main revenue sources in Egypt, 1527–28   86
I:26 Revenue of Egypt in 1595–96 and 1671–72   87
I:27 The Ottoman army, 1473   88
I:28 The Ottoman army, 1528   89
I:29 *Timar* holders and state revenue distributed as *timar*,
1527–28   90
I:30 The number of active *yayas* and *müsellem* soldiers in
Anatolia in 1540   92
I:31 Deficit in Ottoman budgets, 1523–1608   99
I:32 Extent of freehold (*mülk*) and *vakf* lands in the total
budget   129
I:33 A peasant's (*raiyyet*) average *çiftlik* land in *dönüms*   147
I:34 The settlement pattern of the Yeni-İl *kada* in the province
of Sivas   160
I:35 Village formation in Kilia and Akkerman   171
I:36 Provisions arriving in İstanbul by sea   180–81
I:37 Customs duty rates, 1470–1586   200
I:38 Goods sold at Nicopolis town market and dues (*bac*)
paid, sixteenth century   205
I:39 The population of Bursa   225
I:40 Total revenue from the scales (*mizan*) tax on raw silk at
Bursa   226
I:41 Genoese imports from the Ottoman Empire, 1519   227
I:42 Varieties of Western cloth imported to Bursa   236
I:43 Prices of silk purchased by Florentines in Bursa, 1501   237
I:44 Cloth merchants and bankers in İstanbul, Pera and Bursa,
1501–02   239
I:45 Prices of woolen cloth imported from Florence, 1501–2   240
I:46 Prices of pepper and rhubarb at Bursa or Pera, 1501–2   240
I:47 Estimate of the annual import of Persian silk to Europe
in the 1630s   245
I:48 European imports at Aleppo, 1605   245
I:49 Raw silk prices at Bursa, 1467–1646   250
I:50 (a) Prices of various kinds of raw silk, 1482–83 (b) Prices
of raw silk at Bursa during the embargo, 1519   251
I:51 Average prices and price increases in raw silk, 1557–1639   251
I:52 Population of the principal cities in Anatolia and the
Balkans, 1520–30   257

1:53	Ragusan tribute	261
1:54	Annual customs revenue for the port of Dubrovnik	263
1:55	Varieties of woolen cloth imported by Dubrovnik for Ottoman dominions, 1531	263
1:56	The population of Caffa, c. 1520	280
1:57	Exports via Caffa from the northern regions to İstanbul, c. 1470	281
1:58	Goods arriving at Caffa, 1487–90	282
1:59	Customs duties and other dues at Akkerman according to the regulation of 1484	294
1:60	Development of the foreign trade of the city of Brašov, 1484–1600	297
1:61	Pepper prices around 1500	301
1:62	Total textile imports at the ports of Buda and Pest	309
1:63	Textile imports from Habsburg territories and taxation at Estergon and Buda	310
1:64	Total imports of metal goods at the ports of Buda and Pest	311
1:65	Prices of spices and European woolen cloth, mid-fourteenth century	316
1:66	Revenue from the ports of Yemen, 1600	336
1:67	Alum production in western Anatolia, 1547	341
1:68	Estimates of the spices coming to Europe via Lisbon, Beirut and Alexandria, 1497–1513	342
1:69	The price of pepper in Cairo, 1496–1531	344
1:70	Customs dues on Western goods imported at the port of Tripoli, 1571	348
1:71	Customs dues on exports to Europe from Tripoli, 1571	349
1:72	Imports from India to Basra, 1551, 1575	350
1:73	Imports from Iran to Basra, 1551, 1575	352
1:74	English export of kerseys and broadcloths to the Levant	370
1:75	English imports from the Levant, 1588	371
1:76	English silk imports from the Levant	372

GENEALOGY OF THE OTTOMAN DYNASTY

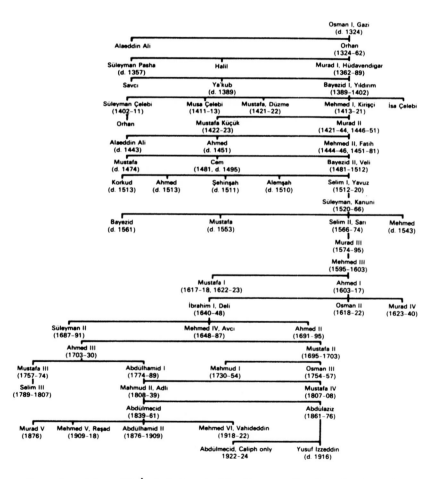

Reproduced from H. İnalcık (1973). *The Ottoman Empire: the classical age, 1300–1600*, London.

CHRONOLOGY OF OTTOMAN HISTORY, 1260–1923

1261–1300	foundation of the *gazi* principalities of Menteşe, Aydın, Saruhan, Karesi and Osmanlı (Ottoman) in western Anatolia
c. 1290–1324	**Osman I**
1324–62	**Orhan**
1326	Ottoman conquest of Bursa
1331	Ottoman conquest of Nicaea (İznik)
1335	fall of the Mongol Empire in Iran
1354	Ottoman occupation of Ankara and Gallipoli
1361	Ottoman conquest of Adrianople
1362–89	**Murad I**
1363–65	Ottoman expansion in southern Bulgaria and Thrace
1371–73	Ottoman victory at Chermanon; Byzantium, the Balkan rulers recognize Ottoman suzerainty
1385	Ottoman conquest of Sofia
1389	Ottoman victory at Kossovo-Polje over the coalition of the Balkan states
1389–1402	**Bayezid I, Yıldırım**
1396	battle of Nicopolis
1402	battle of Ankara, collapse of Bayezid I's empire
1403–13	civil war among Bayezid's sons for sultanate
1413–21	**Mehmed I**
1421–44, 1446–51	**Murad II**

1423–30	Ottoman–Venetian war for Salonica
1425	Ottoman annexation of İzmir and the reconquest of western Anatolia
1439	Ottoman annexation of Serbia
1443	John Hunyadi invades the Balkans
1444	revival of Serbian Despotate, battle of Varna
1448	second battle of Kossovo-Polje
1444–46, 1451–81	**Mehmed II, Fatih**
1453	conquest of Constantinople; fall of Pera
1459	conquest of Serbia and the Morea
1461	conquest of the empire of Trabzon
1463–79	war with Venice
1468	conquest of Karaman
1473	battle of Başkent
1475	conquest of the Genoese colonies in the Crimea
1481–1512	**Bayezid II**
1485–91	war with the Mamluks of Egypt
1499–1503	war with Venice; conquest of Lepanto, Coron, and Modon
1512–20	**Selim I**
1514	Selim defeats Shah İsmail at Çaldıran
1516	conquest of Diyarbekir; annexation of eastern Anatolia; defeat of the Mamluks at Marj Dabık
1517	battle of Ridaniyya, conquest of Egypt; submission of the sharif of Mecca
1520–66	**Süleyman I, Kanuni**
1521	conquest of Belgrade
1522	conquest of Rhodes
1526	battle of Mohács; Hungary becomes a vassal
1529	siege of Vienna
1534	conquest of Tabriz and Baghdad
1537–40	war with Venice

1538	siege of Diu in India
1541	annexation of Hungary
1553–55	war with Iran
1565	siege of Malta
1566–74	**Selim II**
1569	French capitulations; first Ottoman expedition against Russia; siege of Astrakhan
1570	Uluç Ali captures Tunis; expedition to Cyprus; fall of Nicosia
1571	battle of Lepanto
1573	peace with Venice and the emperor
1574–95	**Murad III**
1578–90	war with Iran, annexation of Azerbaijan
1580	English capitulations
1589	Janissary revolt in İstanbul
1591–92	further Janissary uprisings
1593–1606	war with the Habsburgs
1595–1603	**Mehmed III**
1596	Celali rebellions in Anatolia
1603–39	Iranian Wars
1603–17	**Ahmed I**
1606	peace of Zsitva-Török with the Habsburgs
1609	suppression of the Celalis in Anatolia
1612	extension of capitulations to the Dutch
1613–35	rebellion of Ma'noğlu Fahreddin
1618	peace with Iran, Ottoman withdrawal from Azerbaijan
1618–22	**Osman II**
1621	invasion of Poland
1622	assassination of Osman II
1617–18, 1622–23	**Mustafa I**
1623–40	**Murad IV**
1624–28	rebellion in Asia Minor; anarchy in İstanbul

1632	Murad takes full control of the government
1635	siege of Erivan
1624–37	Cossack attacks on the Black Sea coast
1624–39	war with Iran, fall of Baghdad
1637	fall of Azov (Azak) to Cossacks
1638	Ottoman recovery of Baghdad
1640–48	**İbrahim I**
1640	recovery of Azov
1645–69	war with Venice; invasion of Crete; siege of Candia
1648–56	Venetian blockade of the Dardanelles
1648	deposition and assassination of the sultan
1648–87	**Mehmed IV**
1648–51	the child sultan's mother Kösem in control
1649–51	Janissary dominance in İstanbul and Celali pashas in the Asiatic provinces
1651–55	anarchy in İstanbul, Venetian blockade continues
1656	Köprülü Mehmed appointed grand vizier with dictatorial powers
1656–59	reestablishment of the central government's control over the Janissaries and in the provinces
1657	lifting of Venetian blockade
1658–59	reestablishment of Ottoman control over Transylvania and Wallachia
1661–76	Köprülü Fazıl Ahmed's grand vizierate
1663	war with the Habsburgs
1664	battle of Saint Gotthard, peace of Vasvar
1669	fall of Candia, peace with Venice
1672–76	war with Poland, annexation of Kaminiec with Podolia, treaty of Zuravno
1676–83	Kara Mustafa's grand vizierate
1677–81	rivalry over Ukraine with Russia
1681	French attack against Chios
1683	siege of Vienna

1684	Holy League against the Ottomans between the emperor, Polish king and Venice
1686	fall of Buda, Russia joins the coalition; Venetians in the Morea
1687	second battle of Mohács; army's rebellion; deposition of Mehmed IV
1687–91	**Süleyman II**
1688	fall of Belgrade
1689	Austrians at Kossovo; Russians attack the Crimea
1689–91	Köprülü Fazıl Mustafa's grand vizierate; tax reforms
1690	recovery of Belgrade from Austrians
1691–95	**Ahmed II**
1691	battle of Slankamen; death of Fazıl Mustafa
1695–1703	**Mustafa II**
1695	fall of Azov
1696	Ottoman counter-attack in Hungary
1697	Ottoman defeat at Zenta
1698–1702	Köprülü Hüseyin's grand vizierate
1699	treaty of Karlowitz
1700	peace with Russia
1703	army's rebellion; deposition of Mustafa II
1703–30	**Ahmed III**
1709	Charles XII, king of Sweden, takes refuge in Ottoman territory
1711	battle of Pruth, Ottoman victory over Peter I of Russia, insurrection at Cairo, realignment of Mamluks; Shihabi supremacy over Mount Lebanon
1713	peace treaty with Russia: Azov recovered, Charles XII returns to Sweden; introduction of Phanariote rule in principalities
1714–18	war with Venice, recovery of the Morea
1716	war with Austria
1717	fall of Belgrade
1718–30	Damad İbrahim Pasha's grand vizierate

1718	peace treaty of Passarowitz with Austria and Venice: Morea recovered, large parts of Serbia and Wallachia ceded to Austria
1723–27	war with Iran, Ottoman occupation of Azerbaijan and Hamadan
1730	Patrona Halil rebellion; deposition of Ahmed III; end of Tulip period
1730–36	Iran's counter-attack; loss of Azerbaijan and western Iran
1730–54	**Mahmud I**
1736–39	war with Russia and Austria
1739	peace treaty with Austria and Russia; recovery of Belgrade
1740	extension of French capitulations; Ottoman–Swedish alliance against Russia
1743–46	war with Iran under Nadir Shah
1754–57	**Osman III**
1757–74	**Mustafa III**
1768–74	war with the Russian Empire
1770	Russian fleet in the Aegean; Ottoman defeat on the Danube
1771	Russian invasion of the Crimea
1773	Ali Bey's rebellion in Egypt
1774–89	**Abdülhamid I**
1774	treaty of Küçük Kaynarca, independence of the Crimea and northern coasts of the Black Sea from the Ottoman Empire
1783	Russian annexation of the Crimean khanate
1787	war with Russia
1788	Sweden declares war against the Russian Empire
1789–1807	**Selim III**
1792	treaty of Jassy
1798	Napoleon invades Egypt
1804	Serbs revolt

1805–48	Mehmed Ali as ruler of Egypt
1807	Selim's reform program crushed by revolt
1807–08	**Mustafa IV**
1808–39	**Mahmud II**
1808	Document of Alliance
1811	Mehmed Ali massacres Mamluk remnant in Egypt
1812	treaty of Bucharest
1826	destruction of the Janissaries
1832	battle of Konya
1833	treaty of Hünkiar-İskelesi with Russia
1838	Anglo-Turkish Convention
1839	battle of Nezib
1839–61	**Abdülmecid I**
1839	Tanzimat begins with Imperial Rescript of Gülhane
1853–56	Crimean War
1856	Imperial Rescript
1856	treaty of Paris
1861–76	**Abdülaziz**
1875	*de facto* Ottoman bankruptcy
1876	first Ottoman Constitution
1876–1909	**Abdülhamid II**
1878	treaty of Berlin
1881	formation of Public Debt Administration
1885	occupation by Bulgaria of eastern Rumelia
1896–97	insurrection in Crete; war with Greece
1908	Young Turk Revolution and the restoration of the Constitution of 1876
1909–18	**Mehmed V**
1911	war with Italy
1912	Balkan War
1914	World War I begins
1918–22	**Mehmed VI**
1920	establishment of French mandate over Syria and Lebanon and British mandates over Iraq and Palestine
1923	proclamation of the Republic of Turkey

PREFACE

HALİL İNALCIK AND DONALD QUATAERT

These volumes are intended for students and, more generally, the informed reader. They are also addressed to the specialist who should find much new material of interest. The authors are specialists in their fields and of the respective time periods on which they have written. The work was first planned by Halil İnalcık, who then invited the best-known scholars to participate, including Mehmet Genç and Halil Sahillioğlu. Generally, the authors of each chronological section survey political events before proceeding to the study of economy and society.

Some subjects of inquiry were not included either because research materials were lacking or because of space considerations. In the latter case, the authors make references to existing literature to guide readers. Thus, to keep the manuscript within manageable limits, Halil İnalcık left the history of urban life and industry before 1600 for another occasion and provided readers with sufficient bibliography on the subject.

This project was begun in 1985 and, inevitably, there were delays in its completion. Some sections were finished in late 1989 while others were prepared in Spring 1992. In some cases, new publications have appeared and are not discussed. For personal reasons, Mehmet Genç and Halil Sahillioğlu found it impossible to continue. And so, Bruce McGowan assumed sole responsibility for the eighteenth-century section and we invited Şevket Pamuk to write the monetary history. We are very grateful to Professors Genç and Sahillioğlu for allowing us to use their unpublished materials.

We have sought to respect the longevity and complexity of Ottoman history in our spellings of personal and place names and technical terms. Thus, we have used the spellings most appropriate to each particular time period and area. Otherwise, we have sought to use modern Turkish spelling whenever possible. We use the English terms for Arabic, Turkish and Persian words that have come into English. In the text, we have sought to minimize the number of technical terms, but have had to use some to maintain accuracy. Hence, for example, *timar* is preferred to fief.

Halil İnalcık thanks his colleagues for agreeing to participate in this project. He is especially grateful to Donald Quataert for all his labours in helping to bring the project to fruition. In addition, he thanks C. Max Kortepeter for his generosity in taking considerable time to make stylistic suggestions.

Suraiya Faroqhi thanks Rifaʿat Abou-El-Haj, İdris Bostan, Linda Darling, Neşe Erim, Cornell Fleischer, Daniel Goffman, Ronald Jennings, Gülru Necipoğlu, Cemal Kafadar, Heath Lowry and Leslie Peirce. She wishes to thank Halil İnalcık and Donald Quataert for commenting on the manuscript as well as Engin Akarlı, Halil Berktay, and Nükhet Sirman Eralp. And finally, for their help with historiographical issues, she thanks Rifaʿat Abou-El-Haj, Chris Bayly, Huri İslamoğlu-İnan, Ariel Salzmann, Sanjay Subrahmanyam and İsenbike Togan.

Bruce McGowan wishes to thank, above all, Professor Mehmet Genç of Marmara University, who generously shared his expert advice on several historical concepts employed in Part III. The writer is well aware that the fit between this section and others is far from perfect. His own conception from the start was to provide a brief and interesting review of the literature which would be useful for students. The writer is, above all, grateful to have had access to the Regenstein Library of the University of Chicago, the collections of the Oriental Studies Department of the University of Vienna, and the American Research Institute in Turkey.

Donald Quataert thanks Cem Behar, Alan Duben and Judith Tucker for providing manuscript versions of their research findings. He is especially grateful to Tom Dublin for his careful reading of an early draft. Thanks also to the Ottoman reading group of the Fernand Braudel Center and Faruk Tabak at Binghamton University as well as Rifaʿat Abou-El-Haj for invaluable comments on various portions of the manuscript. Binghamton University has been very generous in providing the staff support, without which this volume could not have been completed. Marion Tillis has been the very model of efficiency in typing substantial versions of each of the four major contributions. Faruk Tabak has been invaluable for his editing and proofreading assistance.

Şevket Pamuk acknowledges the indispensable work of Halil Sahilli-oğlu over the last three decades as well as the extensive discussions in the summer of 1990. He also thanks Cüneyt Ölçer, Mehmet Genç, Zafer

Toprak, Yavuz Cezar, İsa Akbaş, Mehmet Arat, Linda Darling, Reşat Kasaba, Faruk Tabak, Oktar Türel and Halil İnalcık.

Halil İnalcık provided the chronology up to c. 1700 while Bruce McGowan and Donald Quataert respectively prepared most of the entries for the eighteenth and nineteenth centuries. Halil İnalcık prepared the genealogical table, the lists of weights and measures and the glossary.

ŝ

ABBREVIATIONS

AA	Auswärtiges Amt
A&P	Parliamentary Papers, Accounts and Papers, GB
AAH	*Acta Historica Academiae Scientiarum Hungaricae* (Budapest)
AAS	*Asian and African Studies* (Jerusalem)
AE	Archives du Ministère des affaires étrangères, Quai d'Orsay, Paris, Fr.
AHR	*American Historical Review*
AIESEE	*Association Internationale d'Études du Sud-Est Européen,* Bulletin
Annales, ESC	*Annales: Economies, Sociétés, Civilisations*
AOr	*Acta Orientalia* (Budapest)
AO	*Archivum Ottomanicum* (The Hague)
AS	Annual Series, GB
ASI	*Archivio Storico Italiano*
Aus	Austria
B	*Belleten* (Ankara)
BAN	Bılgarska Akademia na Naukite, *Istoria na Bılgaria*
BBA	Başbakanlık Arşivi, now Osmanlı Arşivi, İstanbul, Turkey
BCF	*Bulletin consulaire français. Recueil des rapports commerciaux adressés au Ministère des affaires étrangères par les agents diplomatiques et consulaires de France à l'étranger*
BEO	Bab-ı Ali Evrak Odası, BBA
Bel	Belediye, BBA
BF	*Byzantinische Forschungen*

Bl	*Belgeler* (Ankara)
BN	Bibliothèque Nationale, Paris
BN, MS	Bibliothèque National, Paris, MS fonds turc
BSOAS	*Bulletin of the School of Oriental and African Studies*
BS	*Byzantinoslavica*
BSt	*Balkan Studies* (Thessaloniki)
BTTD	*Belgelerle Türk Tarihi Dergisi* (İstanbul)
BuHI	*Berichte über Handel und Industrie.* Deutsches Reich (Germany)
CC	Correspondance commerciale, Fr
CED	*Coğrafya Enstitüsü Dergisi* (İstanbul)
Cev	Cevdet Tasnifi, BBA
CIEPO	*Comité International d'Études Pré-Ottomanes et Otto-manes* (İstanbul)
CMRS	*Cahiers du Monde russe et soviétique* (Paris)
CSP	*Calendar of State papers and manuscripts relating to English affairs existing in the archives and collections of Venice and in other libraries of northern Italy: Venice,* 38 vols., London 1864–1947.
Dah	Dahiliye, BBA
DII	*Documenta Islamica Inedita* (Berlin)
DO	*Dumbarton Oaks* (Washington, D.C.)
EB	*Études Balkaniques* (Sofia)
EI²	*Encyclopaedia of Islam,* 2nd edition
EcHR	*The Economic History Review*
EHR	*English Historical Review*
EUQ	*East European Quarterly*
FO	Foreign Office, GB
Fr	France
GB	Great Britain
GDAD	*Güney Doğu Araştırmaları Dergisi* (İstanbul)
Ger	Germany
HEMM	*Histoire économique du monde méditerranéen, 1450–1650, Mélanges en l'honneur de Fernand Braudel,* I–II, Toulouse 1973
HH	Hatt-ı Hümayun, BBA
HHSt A	Haus-Hof und Staatsarchiv, Vienna, Politiches Archiv (PA), Austria
HUS	*Harvard Ukrainian Studies* (Cambridge, Mass.)
İ	İradeler, BBA

IA	*İslâm Ansiklopedisi* (İstanbul)
IFM	*İstanbul Üniversitesi İktisat Fakültesi Mecmuası*
IHR	*The International History Review* (Canada)
IJMES	*International Journal of Middle East Studies*
IJTS	*International Journal of Turkish Studies* (Madison)
ISN	*Istorija Srpskoga Naroda* (Belgrade, 1986)
JAH	*Journal of Asian History*
JAS	*Journal of the Royal Asiatic Society*
JAOS	*Journal of the American Oriental Society*
JEEH	*The Journal of European Economic History*
JEH	*The Journal of Economic History*
JESHO	*Journal of the Economic and Social History of the Orient*
JMH	*Journal of Modern History*
JOS	*Journal of Ottoman Studies (Osmanlı Araştırmaları)* (İstanbul)
JRAS	*Journal of the Royal Asiatic Society*
JSAH	*Journal of South Asian History*
JTS	*Journal of Turkish Studies*
Kepeci	Kamil Kepeci Tasnifi, BBA
k und k	*Berichte der k. u. k. Österr.-ung. Konsularämter über das Jahr . . .*, Austria
Mal	Maliye, BBA
MD	Maliyyeden Müdevver, BBA
MES	*Middle Eastern Studies*
MHR	*Mediterranean Historical Review* (London)
MM	Meclis-i Mahsus, BBA
MOG	*Mitteilungen zur osmanischen Geschichte* (Vienna)
MOI	*Mediterraneo e Oceano Indiano, 1970*: Atti del VI colloquio Internl. di storia marittima, 1962, Florence
MTM	*Milli Tetebbu'lar Mecmuası* (İstanbul)
MV	Meclis-i Valâ, BBA
PP	*Past and Present* (Oxford)
R	*Review: A Journal of the Fernand Braudel Center* (Binghamton)
RC	*Rocznik Orientalistyczny* (Warsaw)
RCC	Rapports commerciaux des agents diplomatiques et consulaires de France
RCL	*La Revue commerciale du Levant, bulletin mensuel de la chambre de commerce française de Constantinople, 1896–1912*

RESEE	*Revue des Études du Sud-est Européennes* (Bucharest, 1924–42)
RH	*Revue Historique*
RHES	*Revue d'Histoire Économique et Social*
RIR	*Revista Istorica Romana*
RMMM	*Revue du Monde Musulman et de la Méditerranée* (Paris)
ROMM	*Revue de l'Occident Musulmane et de la Méditerranée* (Aix-en-Provence)
RRJTS	"Raiyyet Rüsumu, Essays presented to Halil İnalcık," *Journal of Turkish Studies*, X-XI, 1986
SB	*Studia Balkanica* (Sofia)
ŞD	*Şura-yı Devlet*, BBA
SF	*Südost-Forschungen*
SI	*Studia Islamica* (Paris)
SR	*Slavonic Review*
TA	*Türkologischer Anzeiger, Turkology Annual* (Vienna)
TAD	*Tarih Araştırmaları Dergisi* (Ankara)
TD	*Tarih Dergisi* (İstanbul)
TED	*Tarih Enstitüsü Dergisi* (İstanbul)
THİM	*Türk Hukuk ve İktisat Tarihi Mecmuası* (İstanbul)
TİTA	*Türkiye Iktisat Tarihi Üzerine Araştırmalar, ODTÜ Gelişme Dergisi* (Ankara, Middle East Technical University)
TOEM	*Tarih-i Osmani Encümeni Mecmuası*
TM	*Türkiyat Mecmuası* (İstanbul)
TSAB	*Turkish Studies Association Bulletin*
TTD	Tapu Tahrir Defterleri, BBA
TV	*Tarih Vesikaları* (İstanbul)
Ü	*Ülkü* (Ankara)
UPA	University Publications of America
USCR	Consular Reports of the United States
VD	*Vakıflar Dergisi* (Ankara)
VS	Vilayet Salnameleri
VSWG	*Vierteljahrsschrift für Sozial- und Wirtschaftsgeschichte*
WI	*Die Welt des Islams*
WZKM	*Wiener Zeitschrift für der Kunde des Morgenlandes* (Vienna)
ZDMG	*Zeitschrift für der Deutschen Morgenländischen Gesellschaft*
ZstA	Zentrales Staatsarchiv, Potsdam, Auswärtiges Amt, Ger., former Democratic Republic

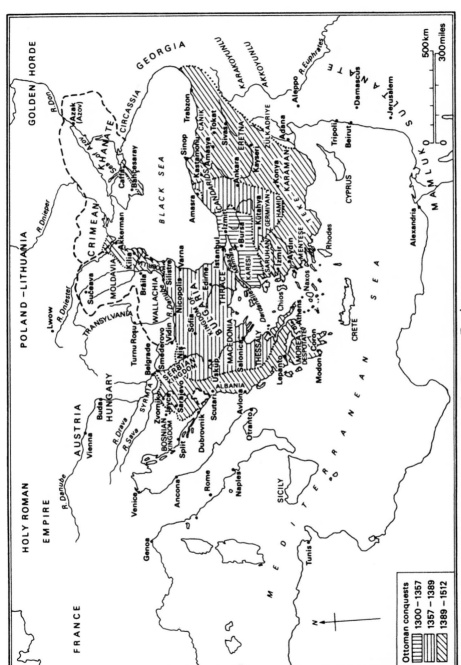

1 The Ottoman Empire, 1300–1512

2 The Ottoman Empire, c. 1550

0		500		1000 km
0			500 miles	

Kazan

Moscow

R U S S I A

N O G A Y S

Aral
Sea

R. Dnieper

COSSACKS

R. Don

R. Volga

Astrakhan

CRIMEAN KHANATE

Azak
(Azov)

MOLDAVIA

Akkerman

Sea of
Azov

CIRCASSIA

KABRDA

C A S P I A N   S E A

Kilia

Caffa

HIA

Suhum

GEORGIA

DAGHESTAN

SHIRVAN

BLACK SEA

Sinop

Trabzon

Erivan

GILAN

Edirne

Istanbul

Erzurum

L. Van

AZERBAIJAN

Tabriz

Bursa

Ankara

Sivas

R U M

L. Tabriz

Kütahya

Kayseri

Diyarbekir

Mosul

Hamadan

Foçalar

ANATOLIA

Zülkadriye

R. Tigris

I R A N

Izmir

Konya

CHIOS

Ayasoluk

Antalya

Aleppo

I R A Q

R. Euphrates

Baghdad

Candia

RHODES

Bandar-Abbas

CYPRUS
(Venice
1570)

Tripoli

Beirut

Damascus

Basra

PERSIAN GULF

Hormuz

S Y R I A

AL - HASA

S E A

Jerusalem

Bahrain

Katif

Alexandria

Cairo

Suez

A R A B I A

O M A N

E G Y P T

Kusayr

R E D   S E A

SHARIFATE OF MECCA

Medina

R. Nile

Jidda

Mecca

Suakin

INDIAN
OCEAN

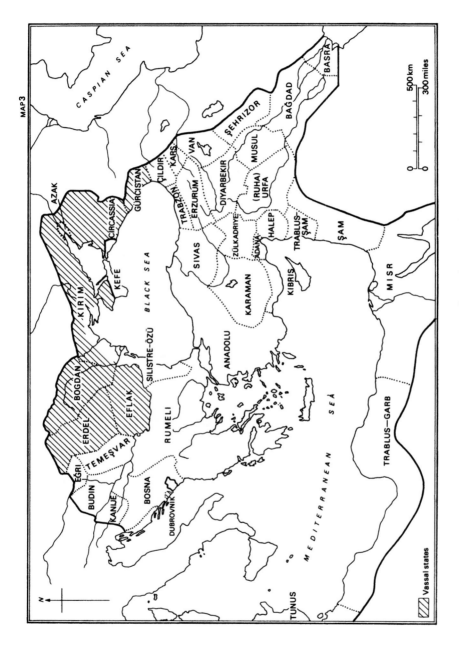

MAP 3

CASPIAN SEA

AZAK

CIRCASSIA

GÜRCİSTAN

YILDIR.

KARS

VAN

ŞEHRIZOR

BAĞDAD

BASRA

KIRIM

KEFE

TRABZON

ERZURUM

DIYARBEKIR

(RUHA)
URFA

MUSUL

BLACK SEA

SILISTRE–ÖZÜ

SİVAS

ZÜLKADRIYE

ADANA

HALEP

TRABLUS-
ŞAM

ŞAM

BOGDAN

EFLAK

ANADOLU

KARAMAN

KIBRIS

MISR

ERDEL

TEMEŞVAR

RUMELI

EĞRI

BUDIN

BOSNA

MEDITERRANEAN SEA

KANIJE

DUBROVNIK

TRABLUS–GARB

TUNUS

N

500 km

300 miles

0

0

▨ Vassal states

3 Ottoman provinces and vassal states, 1609

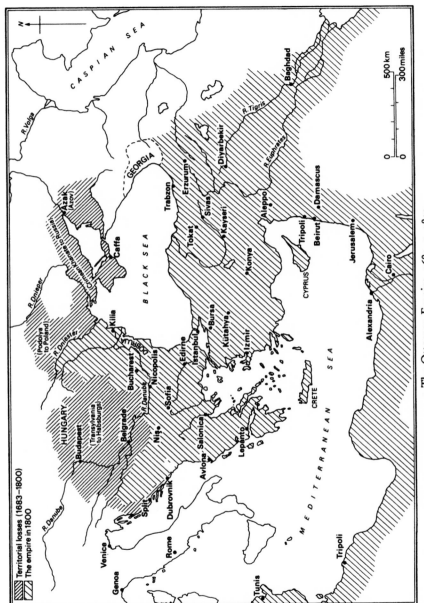

4 The Ottoman Empire, 1683–c. 1800

Territorial losses (1683–1800)
The empire in 1800

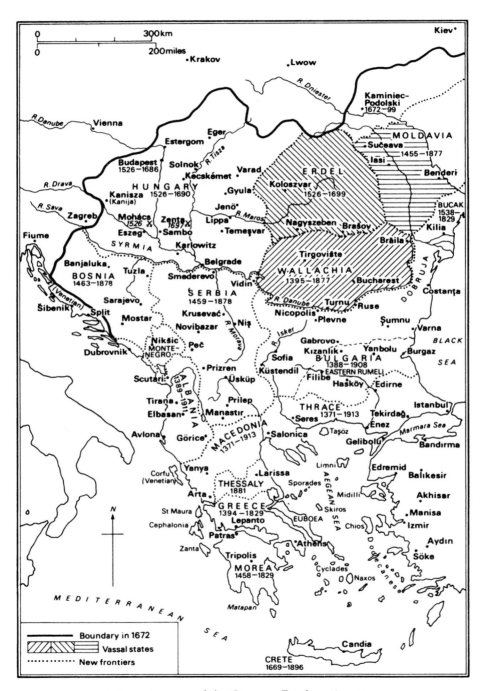

5 Dismemberment of the Ottoman Empire, 1672–1913

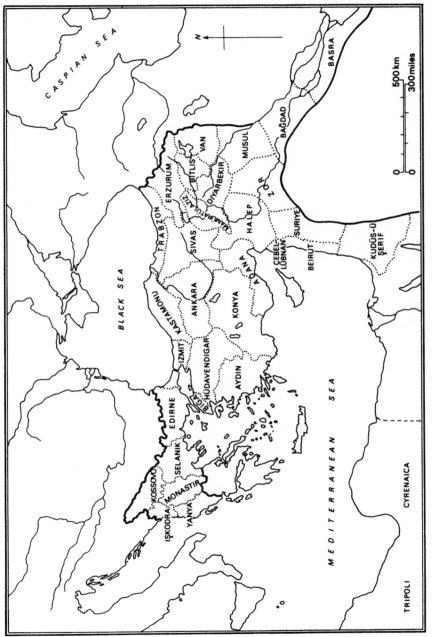

6 Ottoman provinces, c. 1900

⌣̇

GENERAL INTRODUCTION

HALİL İNALCIK AND DONALD QUATAERT

These volumes summarize the field of Ottoman social and economic history and, at the same time, offer new findings and perspectives. They build on a half-century tradition of scholarship and present an area of study still in its infancy. Simultaneously, the various authors offer their own research, pushing beyond synthesis into new inquiries and analyses.

In organizing the six centuries of Ottoman history, the classical period 1300–1600 is taken as a well-defined, distinct period with an autocratic centralist government and a command economy, while in the following "decline" period, underpinnings of this traditional polity entered a process of transformation. The seventeenth century became in fact a period of transition, witnessing thorough-going changes. The Köprülüs' attempt to restore the traditional autocratic centralist system totally failed during the disastrous war period from 1683 to 1699. The eighteenth century saw a radically changed Ottoman Empire with the rise of local powers under provincial notables and "dynasties," decentralized, so to speak. The central government followed "liberal" policies not only in the administration of the empire but also in landholding and economy in general. Also, there occurred a radical change in the attitude of the Ottomans toward Europe and its civilization. The Ottomans, for the first time, now admitted the Europeans' superiority and began to imitate and borrow western ways. This led to increasing Ottoman dependence on Western powers for survival. The nineteenth century witnessed gaining momentum in Ottoman dependence on the West, both politically and economically, and in radical westernization reforms.

In our volumes, these four periods – 1300 to 1600 and the seventeenth, eighteenth and nineteenth centuries respectively – have each been prepared by one specialist independently; but the unity of approach is secured by a common plan presenting the period in its political, economic and social aspects.

The individual chapters are substantially expanded with tables providing detailed statistical data. A genealogical table, general chronology, a list of weights and measures, and a glossary (in transcription) are also included. Bibliographies at the end of each author's section are designed to provide the basic literature on the period discussed. In the books, the authors hope the reader will be able to follow the metamorphosis of an empire as a whole, as viewed in its basic aspects.

Hopefully, our volumes will be invaluable for a time and, by the force of its own syntheses and new research, be superseded in the not too distant future. Their publication makes clear the accomplishments and shortcomings of a maturing field that is exploring the social and economic structures of an empire whose legacy has been overlooked for much of the twentieth century. This neglect has been part of a more general attitude that has ignored the Ottoman influence on the present, however powerful it may have been. The decades-long neglect seems doubly odd since the work of some eminent earlier historians, such as William Langer's *The diplomacy of imperialism* (1935) placed the İstanbul-based empire at the very center of European history (in this case political). Recently, the Ottoman past has begun to receive the attention merited by its actual historical role. Take, for example, the commercial success of the flawed *Peace to end all peace* (1989) by David Fromkin, that examines the Middle East regions of the empire during the World War I period. The accelerating interest in the Ottoman experience should be reinforced considerably by the events of the early 1990s, including those in southeastern Europe and the emergence of Turkey as an international power astride Europe, the Middle East and Central Asia. Empires do fall but the residues of their influence linger on.

Until World War II, studies of Ottoman history dealt almost exclusively with military and political events. This focus generally derived from the emphasis then prevailing in European historiography. More particularly, the Ottomans represented for Europeans primarily a military intrusion, requiring latter-day crusades that haunted the Western memory. After c. 1945, interest shifted to the economic and social aspects of the Ottoman historical experience, in part because of better access to the Ottoman archives. The new focus also derived from the growing emphasis on social and economic history in the West. That is, as before, trends in Ottoman historiography followed those set in other areas of historical research.

Fernand Braudel's *La Méditerranée et le monde méditerranéen à l'époque de Philippe II* (1949) can be taken as a watershed, presenting the Ottoman Empire as an integral part of the Mediterranean world, not only in the struggle for hegemony but also in economic relations. In earlier works, notably in Wilhelm Heyd's classic, *Histoire du commerce du Levant* (1936), the Ottomans' role in Mediterranean trade is viewed solely from its European (in this case, Italian) partner's vantage point; thus, developments affecting their position in the Levant are judged negatively without taking into account positive effects that might have accrued to people in the region itself. Little note was given to the fact that the Ottomans did not aim to destroy the Italian trade in the Levant, but rather sought to control and profit from it, which meant eliminating the Latin domination and exploitation that had been established during the period of Byzantine decline. That is, among its other contributions, this work attempts to present events from the Ottoman perspective. It offers the Ottomans as agents capable of independent and internally consistent actions and not, as had been the case for too long, as passive spectators of a European drama.

Also, it can be said, without exaggeration, that the Ottoman superpower in the East substantially contributed to the shaping of modern Europe. For example, when a decisive struggle developed against Venice and its powerful Habsburg allies who then dominated Europe, the Ottomans did not hesitate to extend the same capitulatory commercial privileges to France, England and the Dutch that it earlier had bestowed on the Venetian Republic. This Ottoman re-orientation proved to be a decisive turning point for the initial mercantilist–capitalist expansion of these rising Western nation-states. (It also, obviously, was important for the Ottoman economy.) From then on, every European country aspiring to mercantilist expansion, as a prerequisite for its economic development, sought these economic privileges from the sultan. The West depended, at least at the beginning, on supplies from or through the Ottoman Empire for its newly rising silk and cotton industries. The first successful chartered companies in the West were the Levant companies.

The Ottoman Empire's economic significance in world trade, so far understated by historians, is dramatized in this study. The various authors, on the one hand, trace trade patterns long forgotten by historians in the West. For example, while the horizontal trade route in the Mediterranean through the Middle East to Venice or Genoa was considered the main trade link with Arabia and India, a vertical south–north international trade route through Damascus – Bursa – Akkerman – Lwow had also developed through Ottoman territories, beginning c.1400. The so-called oriental goods, including spices, silks and cotton goods, reached Poland, the Baltic countries and Muscovy through this route. Further to the east, Hungary and Slovakia through the Danubian ports and Brašov in Transylvania were another market for the south–north trade. At times, Hungary received more spices through this route than through Venice. On these points, Ottoman customs registers were found to have fully supported the findings of Polish, Hungarian and Romanian historians.

The authors, on the other hand, track the shifting importance of the trade in its global context. In the sixteenth century, the Ottoman Empire played a determining role in world trade. The empire's far-flung adventures – on the Volga river, in the Mediterranean, in Azerbaijan and the Caspian Sea, in Yemen, Aden and Diu, in Sumatra and Mombasa – all had economic implications. Ottoman military actions were closely connected with economic – fiscal issues, such as the control of the Tabriz – Bursa silk route, the Akkerman – Lwow route, the Black Sea sources of food and construction materials for İstanbul, and Yemen and Aden for the Indian trade. The battle of Lepanto (1571), and the advent of the English and Dutch in the Mediterranean (1580–90), marked the beginning of the empire's reduction to a regional state. At the same time, the rise of the Atlantic economy, with America's huge supplies of cheap silver, cotton and sugar, and above all Europe's aggressive mercantilism, caused the collapse of the Ottoman monetary system, triggering dramatic changes in the seventeenth century. Subsequently, the relative importance of Ottoman foreign trade to the global economy declined although, after c. 1750, its volume actually rose, especially during the period 1750–1850. International trade rose to greater heights than ever before in Ottoman history. Thus, by 1914, the Ottoman and Western economies were intertwined to an unprecedented degree. But, in terms of economic significance, the Ottomans had slipped from first to second-rate status.

Our examination of foreign trade justifiably stresses the dynamic Ottoman role in the world economy. At the same time, the various authors spend considerable time examining the importance of trade within the Ottoman frontiers, an activity that too often has been overlooked in favor of the foreign trade. To a degree not sufficiently highlighted in the previous literature, this intra-Ottoman trade played a vital role in the economic life of the empire, even during its final years. Overall, tracing the history of these domestic trade patterns over time, an emphasis that derives from our concern to present the story from the Ottoman vantage point, makes apparent their centuries-long continuity. And, as a corollary, we more clearly can see the disruptive impact of the territorial losses of later Ottoman times that diverted, truncated or altogether destroyed well-established domestic trading networks.

Similarly, the authors have placed considerable emphasis on the study of landholding patterns and forms of agricultural exploitation. As a result, a comprehensive picture of the crucial agrarian sector over the entire Ottoman period begins to emerge. We explain and trace the impressive continuity in small landholding patterns while also illustrating how and when large estates did emerge. Generally, we found that over time and space, large estates tended to appear in areas being brought under cultivation rather than on already settled lands. This trend was especially marked in the nineteenth century, when the state settled refugees and reluctant tribes on once nearly vacant lands. In the focus on agriculture, we contribute to a debate that has engaged historians and historical sociologists for the past several decades. The debate centered on the issue of the Ottoman social formation and the utility of the paradigms of Marx and Weber. Some of the research in our volumes suggests limits to the usefulness of these models: the Ottoman village generally was not a self-sufficient social entity independent from the city. A money economy was quite developed in the Ottoman world from an early date, and then expanded considerably in the nineteenth century. Further, small-holdings – not large estates – generated most of the marketed surplus throughout the Ottoman era. Thanks to the meticulously detailed tax and population surveys of the bureaucracy, we now see an Ottoman social formation based on the *çift-hane* in rural areas, a social system that is fully described for the first time by İnalcık in this volume. Indeed, this is the "peasant family labor farm" discussed by A. V. Chayanov as an independent mode of production.

In volume II, our treatment of manufacturing activities during the period c. 1600–1914 (we ignore the earlier period for reasons stated in the preface), extends and sometimes breaks with existing accounts in several important respects. First, the contributions by the various authors collectively offer a comprehensive account that points to remarkable continuities in the loci of manufacturing. In many cases, industrial centers flourishing c. 1600 were still active in 1914. Second, in common with the commercial and agricultural sectors, Ottoman manufacturing is seen to have possessed its own internal dynamics, creatively adapting to shifts in domestic and international conditions. Thus, sometimes new production centers but more often new production methods and/or new products appeared to retain markets or capture new opportunities. And, as in the case of trade and agriculture, the declining political fortunes of the state and the concomitant territorial losses are seen to have played a vital role in the story of Ottoman manufacturing.

In these volumes, much attention is placed on the relations of the empire with the West which intensified after the sixteenth century. The Ottoman state was the first Asian empire to experience the impact of the phenomenal rise and expansion of Europe in the economic and military fields. While the mercantilist West was keenly interested in the preservation and exploitation of this market so vital for its economy, the Habsburg and Russian empires, taking advantage of new advanced war technology, started an aggressive policy for the conquest and dismemberment of the Ottoman Empire. Thus, already in the first decades of the eighteenth century, the so-called Eastern Question appeared in European politics, putting on the agenda the issue of the very existence of the empire. In the new period, European hegemony changed the Ottoman Empire's position from dominance to mounting dependency. In an attempt to find a way out of the crisis, the Ottomans sought to alter first their military, and then their administrative organizations. So, there appeared for the Ottomans what we may call the Western Question, in the sense of a traditional Muslim society trying to determine to what extent it should follow European ways.

These military and administrative changes accompanied and accelerated increasing imports from the West, not only in weaponry but also in the artifacts of everyday life. In the eighteenth century, the substantial reduction in transport and manufacturing costs in Europe led to an unprecedented trade expansion with the Ottoman territories. During the nineteenth century, additional innovations in transportation technologies further changed the face of the land and densities of populations.

A most interesting development in the post-classical period was Ottoman "liberalism" in culture and economic issues. Capitulatory privileges were extended to all European nations. As the authors show, a liberal policy was also manifest in land possession rights, in *vakfs* and tax-farming; these entailed administrative decentralization and brought about the rise of the provincial notables and loss of the central bureaucracy's control in the provinces. In the final Ottoman century, liberalism resumed with the 1826 destruction of the Janissary protectors of guild privilege and the 1838 Anglo-Turkish Convention. Government efforts to direct the economy, after nearly wrecking it in the late eighteenth century, steadily diminished thereafter. In the nineteenth century, however, the state still attempted to intervene and protect. Administrative centralization, marked by a vast expansion in the numbers and responsibilities of bureaucrats, accompanied military changes that resulted in a state apparatus vastly larger and more powerful than that of the previous era. Wars and territorial losses, however, continued to shatter trade networks and forge new ones, profoundly affecting agricultural as well as manufacturing activities in their wake.

In brief, we have attempted to present an interpretation of the Ottoman social and economic reality in its global context from, whenever possible, new perspectives, based on original archival materials and the most recent studies derived from these same sources.

Part I

THE OTTOMAN STATE: ECONOMY AND SOCIETY, 1300–1600

HALİL İNALCIK, UNIVERSITY OF BİLKENT

$$\overset{\cdot}{\frown}$$

EMPIRE AND POPULATION

FORMATION OF THE OTTOMAN EMPIRE

The Ottoman state came into existence around 1300 as a small frontier principality which devoted itself to the *gaza*, Holy War, on the frontiers of the Seljukid Sultanate in Asia Minor and of the Byzantine Empire. Its initial *gazi* frontier character influenced the state's historical existence for six centuries: its dynamic conquest policy, its basic military structure, and the predominance of the military class within an empire that successfully accommodated disparate religious, cultural, and ethnic elements. The society to which these elements gave rise followed in the tradition of earlier Islamic empires, but some of its most unique features were created by the Ottomans themselves.

The Ottoman crossing of the Dardanelles and settlement on European soil proved of crucial importance for the transformation of the Ottoman state from a rather insignificant frontier principality into an empire encompassing the Balkans and Asia Minor. Süleyman Pasha, son of the second Ottoman sultan, Orhan (1324–62), was responsible for the first Ottoman settlement in Europe. He first established himself on the Gallipoli peninsula in 1352 as the ally of John Cantacuzenus, pretender to the Byzantine throne. Two years later Süleyman seized the fortified city of Gallipoli and made it a strong base from which he initiated his conquests in Thrace. He soon attracted Turkish immigrants from Anatolia, landless peasants, nomads, and all kinds of uprooted people seeking a new life on the other side of the Straits. Thus the so-called Pasha *sancak*, which would embrace the entire Balkan peninsula, came into being.

After a precarious period following Süleyman's sudden death in 1357, the conquest of Thrace was resumed with renewed vigor under the command of his brother, Murad, and in 1361 the important city of Adrianople fell to Ottoman forces. The rapid conquest of Thrace caused consternation in Byzantium and in Europe because the European approaches to Constantinople had fallen so rapidly into Ottoman hands. During the period 1362–89, Murad I subdued the greater part of the Balkans north to the Danube and made Ottoman vassals of most of the local dynasts, thus creating an empire composed of vassal states. In 1389, in the battle of Kossovo-Polje, the attempt of the assembled Balkan dynasties to throw off Ottoman domination failed.

Losing his father on the battlefield, Sultan Bayezid I (1389–1402) vigorously took up the reins of government and consolidated his holdings in Anatolia. In 1393, he returned to the Balkans to establish centralized control over the Slavic principalities and to expand further to the north. Bayezid's rivalry with Hungary in the lower Danubian territories and with Venice in the Morea, Albania, and the Aegean resulted in an Hungarian–Venetian alliance against the Ottomans. When Bayezid began his siege of Constantinople, Hungary and Venice succeeded in mobilizing the Crusaders to stop him. But Bayezid surprised and defeated the Crusaders at Nicopolis in 1396. Thus he firmly established Ottoman rule in the Balkans and also gained enormous prestige for himself throughout the Islamic world. Egypt and Syria now believed themselves to be free from Crusader attack. Furthermore, the Ottoman sultan did not hesitate to eliminate the Turkish dynasties of Anatolia in an attempt to incorporate into his empire all lands west of the Euphrates in Asia Minor. As Bayezid strove to expand his territory and to build a strongly centralized state on the model of the classical Islamic states, he unavoidably became embroiled with the native military class in Anatolia who looked to Timur in the east for salvation and protection.

Now Timur, claiming himself heir to the Mongol Empire in Iran, claimed overlordship in all of Anatolia, including the Ottoman state. When Bayezid challenged Timur, he suffered a crushing defeat at the battle of Ankara in 1402, and his empire collapsed. As a result, the Anatolian dynasties reestablished themselves and the vassal states in the Balkans (Byzantium, Wallachia, Serbia and Albania) regained their freedom from the Ottomans.

Civil strife among contending Ottoman princes between 1403 and 1413 slowed greatly the Ottoman recovery in spite of Timur's death in 1405. Nevertheless, stability quickly returned during the reigns of Mehmed I (1413–21) and Murad II (1421–51), because they could build upon the prior solid institutions of the Ottoman state. Those forces – the Janissary army, the *timar*-holding *sipahi*s, the ulema and the bureaucrats – had a vested interest in the revival of the centralized state and, under able leadership, made fundamental contributions to the remarkable recovery of the centralized Ottoman state. The critical juncture arrived when the Ottomans repelled Hungarian Crusader attacks in the Balkans at the battles of Zlatića in 1443, Varna in 1444, and Kossovo in 1448. Clearly the Ottoman forces once again showed their capacity to conquer new territories and this time they planned to conquer the Byzantine capital itself. One should also note that after Timur's blow to the first Ottoman empire under Bayezid I, the center of gravity of the state shifted to the Balkans. From the Balkans, the Ottomans reestablished their domination in western and northern Anatolia prior to the accession of Mehmed II, the Conqueror of İstanbul (1451–81).

Organization of the conquests, the frontier versus the center

During this period of expansion, the administrative set-up largely conformed to the military organization, clearly aiming for a centralized system. *Sancak*s, or sub-provinces, were placed under military governors known as *sancak-begi*s. These *sancak*s became a part of the province of Rumeli (an equivalent of Romania of the Byzantine era), which was in turn governed by a *beglerbegi*, a military commander in charge of all provincial forces, including special frontier units.

The frontier forces, led by *uç-begi*s (*uç* = frontier) were the most active part of the Ottoman army. These *uç-begi*s played a major part in the internal and external affairs of the empire during the period 1360–1453. These forces were organized under hereditary family leaders, with one *uç-begi* on the right wing in the direction of the Lower Danube and Wallachia, one on the left wing in the direction of Macedonia, and one in the center in the direction of Sofia and Belgrade. As the conquests proceeded, the frontier lines in these *uç-begi*s' districts advanced further, from the Balkan range to the Danube, from Thrace to Macedonia and then to Albania and Bosnia, and from Philippopolis to Sofia and Niş.

During the interregnum after the defeat of 1402, effective power in the state passed into the hands of the frontier begs. However, starting with Murad II's (1421–51) assigning of his own men, mostly from among the palace servitors, to frontier commands, centralist policies increasingly became important until they came to predominate under Mehmed II (1451–81). Before the completion of this process, the rivalry grew acute between the frontier forces under hereditary *uç-begis* and the cavalrymen holding *timar*s in the hinterland. In fact, this rivalry helps to explain many of the tensions and upheavals during the period, including the Sheyh Bedreddin rebellion of 1416 which, until now, has not been interpreted against this background. Pretenders to the Ottoman throne also took refuge in the frontier zones, which were always centers of dissension against the central government.

Yet it was the frontier begs who played a crucial role in pushing the Ottoman borders forward during this same period. Under the pressure, many of the Balkan princes and lords readily accepted Ottoman overlordship to spare themselves from the continual raiding of the frontiersmen. Once the lands had become tribute-paying territories, their non-Muslim inhabitants assumed the status of *ahl al-zimma*, i.e., protected subjects of the Muslim state in accordance with Islamic Law.

The transformation from tributary status to total annexation and assimilation into the Ottoman system, that is, being registered as a *sancak*, varied in time with the particular circumstances of each territory. In general, however, the period of transition consisted of first tightening the bonds of vassalage by eliminating local dynasties and refractory elements, and then replacing all remnants of the pre-Ottoman administrative apparatus with the *timar* system, the basic building block of Ottoman provincial administration.

This policy of gradual absorption of occupied territories persisted, as a rule, well into the sixteenth century. The annexation of Hungary is a case in point. Only after an autonomous Hungary was proving unviable, in the face of the Habsburg threat, was the Danube basin turned into an Ottoman province under a *beglerbegi*. Only special conditions enabled certain territories, such as Wallachia and Moldavia, to persist as autonomous entities long past the sixteenth century.

The heritage of the early Ottoman frontiers can also be observed in the peculiar ethnic composition of the Balkans under Ottoman rule. The successive frontier zones in Thrace, eastern Bulgaria, Macedonia and Thessaly in the fourteenth century became zones where Turkish immigration and culture came to predominate, with such frontier centers as Plovdiv, Sofia, Babadağ, Silistre, Vidin, Skopje, Seres, Triccala and Argyrocastron. In these areas the dense settlement of Turkish peasants in the villages followed the same pattern as that of Turkish expansion in western Anatolia, with pioneering dervish hospices (*zaviyes*) and the sedentarization of semi-nomadic Yörük groups.

The conditions of Ottoman expansion in Europe

As indicated, the Ottoman conquest of the Balkans was carried out by stages in the half century 1352–1402. The conquest was facilitated by a number of factors. The Balkan peninsula at this time comprised a patchwork of small states divided among feudal lords or dynasts. The Ottomans exploited the rivalries among these local leaders in order to extend their own control, first as their allies and later as their protectors. Both Hungary in the north and Venice to the south and west also tried to take advantage of this political fragmentation, but since their rule would entail the domination of Catholicism, which regarded Orthodox Christians as schismatics, it was generally resisted by the Balkan population. As the protectors of the Orthodox Church, who accorded its clergy a place in their own state organization, the Ottomans emerged as a Balkan power from the earliest conquests, in spite of the Hungarian and Venetian efforts. Indeed, one can cite many instances of cooperation of local Orthodox priests with the Ottoman state.

In each Balkan state, the local aristocracy and palace generally followed a pro-Western policy. In return for military aid from the West, these privileged elements promised to recognize the supremacy of the Roman Catholic rite. This policy greatly alienated the populace from their feudal lords, and there was always a pro-Ottoman faction among the elite.

It was, however, the social conditions prevailing in the Balkans in the fourteenth century which made the Ottoman expansion possible. With the decline of central Byzantine authority, according to recent scholarship, the holders of large military and monastic estates in the provinces, who had increased their privileges and tax exemptions at the expense of Constantinople or various local regimes, became autonomous in their own regions. To support their tiny feudal states, they tightened their control over the land and peasantry and imposed heavy taxes and labor burdens upon them.

By reversing this tendency toward feudalization of the Balkans, the Ottomans established a strong centralized regime, similar to certain states of Western Europe in the fifteenth century. During this centralization process, the Ottomans restored to state proprietorship, or control, the bulk of the lands found in the hands of local lords or families and monasteries. In many cases, it is true, they reassigned part of these lands to their previous owners, but these local lords were now made Ottoman *timar*-holders under strict state control. To be sure, the Ottoman sultans brought about this change largely because they had created a strong central military force, the Janissary corps, the first standing army in Europe. Under the direct command of the sultan, this corps increased from 1,000 in the 1360s to 5,000 under Bayezid I (1389–1402).

The reassertion of state control over agricultural lands brought with it substantial changes in the circumstances of the Balkan peasantry. Under the new regime, many corvées and other feudal obligations were simply abolished. Taxation and exemptions, the status of groups and individuals, and land titles were all regulated by laws issued by the central government in the name of the sultan. Their administration and execution was entrusted to the district kadis and begs. Under Bayezid I this centralized administration came into full force for the first time. A significant feature of Bayezid's policies was his reliance on the *kuls*, the palace servitors trained to be loyal and efficient instruments of the imperial administration.

Taxation and reaya

Under the Ottoman regime the population was divided into two main groups. The *askeri*, the military or administrative class, performed some public function as the delegates of the sultan and was thereby officially exempted from all taxation. The second group, the *reaya*, the merchants, artisans and peasants (literally "the flock"), pursued productive activities and therefore paid taxes.

The Ottoman system imposed more simplified and initially lighter taxes on the *reaya* than the former Byzantine–Balkan system.

The state also exempted from the extraordinary (wartime) levies, the *avarız*, certain groups of *reaya* who rendered some special service, such as guarding mountain passes and fortresses or contributing special supplies to the palace or army. These groups, known as *muaf ve müsellem* to signify their exempted status, made up a kind of intermediary class between the *askeris* and the *reaya*.

All these groups – the *askeris*, the *reaya* and the *muaf ve müsellem* – were recorded in special registers on the basis of surveys made at regular intervals throughout the empire. However, a certain degree of mobility existed among these groups, making the Ottoman system much less strict than the rigid compartmentalization of a caste system. Indeed, there were recognized ways for *reaya*, both Christian and Muslim, to become military. The *devshirme*, the levy of Christian children, furnished one such opportunity for Christians to join the military class. Also, to ease the effects of their conquest, the Ottomans in the early period often incorporated into their own system pre-Ottoman military groups called *proniar, voynuk (voynik), martolos,* etc. For Muslim *reaya,* it was possible to be enrolled in the military by a special decree of the sultan if, as volunteers on the frontiers, they accomplished some outstanding act of courage.

Nonetheless, the general principle was adhered to that each individual should remain in his own status group so that equilibrium in the state and society could be maintained. It seems that the Ottoman system found its logic in the fact that the state had been established through the efforts of a small professional military group, a kind of warband gathered around its military leader, Osman Ghazi. The dynasty preserved this central position as a keystone of the entire socio-political structure.

As a productive but dependent class, the *reaya,* Christian or Muslim, was obliged to submit to *askeri* leadership and to pay taxes. The ruler, in accordance with ancient tradition, was described as the shepherd protecting his flock, the *reaya,* and leading them in the righteous path. This concept in practice found expression in the many protective measures by which the sultan tried to show his concern for the condition of the *reaya.* As will be noted below, the whole political apparatus was based on this principle; and the Ottoman sultans endeavored to indicate to the masses that the sultan was their ultimate protector against all manner of local abuses and injustices.

The foundation of the Ottoman Empire under Sultan Mehmed II (1451–81)

To Mehmed II fell the responsibility of completing the centralist and absolutist Ottoman system in Anatolia and the Balkans (see Map 1). By taking Constantinople, Mehmed the Conqueror felt that he was the most powerful sovereign in the Islamic world, and he thus challenged the Islamic empires in Iran and Egypt. He also acquired in his own person, immense, unprecedented authority which he used to create the prototype of Ottoman padishah, an absolute monarch in the tradition of ancient Persian kings or Turkish khans.

Claiming that the conquest of the imperial capital entitled him to restore the furthest boundaries of the Eastern Roman Empire, Mehmed II embarked upon a series of expeditions that, in a quarter of a century, resulted in the annexation of Serbia (1459), the Morea (1459), Bosnia and Herzegovina (1463–64), Euboea (1470), and northern Albania (1478–79) in the Balkans; and the territories of the Candarids in Kastamonu-Sinop

(1461) and of the Karamanids in central Anatolia (1468). The southern shores of the Crimea were annexed and the Crimean Khanate was brought under Ottoman suzerainty in 1475. Mehmed's efforts to take Belgrade (1456), gateway to Central Europe, the island of Rhodes (1480) and Italy (1480), failed. Nonetheless, his conquests had made the Ottoman Empire a territorially compact unit between the Danube and the Euphrates, thus reviving Bayezid I's domain, although on a far more substantial foundation. This same expanse of territory endured as the heartland of the Ottoman Empire until the nineteenth century. For this rapid expansion of the empire, the effective use of artillery and the augmentation of the Janissaries from five to ten thousand men must receive much credit. But one should not underestimate the policy of reconciliation (*istimalet*) which Ottoman sultans practiced in newly conquered territories.

In order to resolve the most important problem of all pre-modern empires, notably the formation of a central treasury large enough to finance imperial policies, Mehmed resorted to a number of harsh, innovative financial measures. Its fiscal policies are at the heart of the widespread, and even violent, discontent that marked the end of Mehmed's reign.

İstanbul, the new capital, became the symbol of Mehmed's ambition for a universal empire. Throughout his reign he made every effort to transform İstanbul into a political and religious metropolis, as it had once been in the days of the great Roman emperors. He styled himself caesar and the ruler of the two continents and two seas. He soon forcibly repopulated the dilapidated and neglected city with Turkish, Greek, Armenian and Jewish colonies from various parts of the empire. He also extended his official recognition and accorded high honor to the Greek Patriarchate of İstanbul and later on his successors invited the Armenian Patriarch to take up residence in the city. On the other hand, he reconfirmed the commercial privileges of the Italian maritime states.

In an effort to revive economic prosperity in İstanbul, he built commercial centers – a large covered bazaar in the "old city," and lesser bazaars in the port area (Tahtakale) and in the middle of the city (Fatih). While the population of Constantinople was estimated at between 30,000 and 50,000 just before the conquest, according to a census taken in 1478, it held 14,803 families, perhaps a total of over 70,000 people. İstanbul was to grow rapidly under Mehmed's successors, and one century after the conquest it was the largest city in the Middle East and Europe with a population of at least 400,000. The rise of the Ottoman capital cities,

Bursa, Edirne (Adrianople), and İstanbul, as populous and thriving commercial centers had profound effects on the new economic structure of the Middle East and the Balkans. Even after the rise of İstanbul, Bursa continued to be the main emporium for Iranian silk bound for Italy, and a local silk industry developed there supplying brocades and other silk fabrics to the Ottoman palace and to other markets in the Middle East and Europe.

As a result of the violent reaction against the Conqueror's financial policies, the government of his successor, Bayezid II (1481–1512), assumed a most reconciliatory stance. For example, it restored to their former possessors, whether pious foundations or private landowners, most of the lands confiscated and distributed as *timar* by Mehmed II. The generally peaceful and benevolent reign of Bayezid II witnessed significant internal development. It was particularly under Bayezid that İstanbul was firmly established as an economically viable city. The great expansion of the central treasury enabled the state to reinforce the army and navy, increase the number of Janissaries equipped with handguns, and to construct, with the supervision of Genoese engineers, warships of a size never before seen on the Mediterranean.

Ottoman sea power and imperialism

Following in the tradition of the sea *gazis* or corsairs of western Anatolia, dating back to the early fourteenth century, the Ottoman navy under Bayezid I had already challenged the Venetians from its fortified staging point on Gallipoli. Later, under Mehmed II, the navy played a crucial part in establishing Ottoman domination over the Aegean and Black Seas; and contributed to the war effort against the Mamluks (1485–91) by attacking Syrian coasts. Most remarkable of all, the Ottomans effectively challenged the Venetians on the open sea in the Venetian War (1499–1503).

The contemporary historian, Ibn Kemal, emphasized that the Ottomans had surpassed in power all preceding Muslim sultanates because, among other things, they had turned their state into a formidable sea power in the Mediterranean. In fact, during this first era of Ottoman naval ascendancy, the Turkish sea *gazis* appeared in the western Mediterranean to aid the Muslims of Spain who had appealed to Bayezid II for help. The Mamluks, too, requested Ottoman supplies and experts to rebuild their navy at Suez after their defeat at the hands of the Portuguese in 1509.

The rise of Ottoman sea power in the Mediterranean had far-reaching consequences not only in the extension of Ottoman rule to the Arab lands from Syria and Egypt to Morocco, but also in their expulsion of the Portuguese from the Red Sea. Thus, contrary to popular belief, the ground work for the spectacular rise to world power under Selim I (1512–20) and Süleyman (1520–66) was laid in the reign of Bayezid II.

The caliphate

Until Sultan Mehmed II a kind of solidarity had generally been maintained between the Ottomans and Mamluks in the face of the crusading West and the threat from the Timurids in the east. Rivalry first manifested itself over the questions of suzerainty for the Turcoman principalities in the border zone, the Karamanids, the Zülkadirids and, later, the Ramazanids.

Prior to the Ottoman challenge, the Mamluks had been considered the leading Sunni Muslim power because they had defeated the Mongols, had become the protectors of the Holy Cities of Mecca and Medina and also maintained the descendents of the Abbasid caliphate in Cairo. Careful in their propaganda to distinguish the Arabs from their "Mamluk oppressors," the Ottomans, under their energetic Sultan Selim I (1512–20), decided to end Mamluk rule in the Arab lands.

The Ottomans quickly established their rule in Syria and Egypt following Selim's victories over the Mamluks at Marj Dabık on August 24, 1516, and Ridaniyya on January 22, 1517. The sharif of Mecca, at that moment under the threat of a Portuguese invasion, hastened to recognize Selim's authority over the Hejaz.

A legend, apparently fabricated in the eighteenth century, tells us that Al-Mutawakkil, a descendent of the Abbasids, handed over his rights as caliph to Selim I in an official ceremony. In fact, Selim was quite content at that time to take only the title of protector (or servant) of Mecca and Medina. Although Süleyman I later on styled himself "caliph of all the Muslims in the world," he meant by this to emphasize his role as protector of the Muslim world. Thus, the new Ottoman concept of the caliphate was actually an extension of the original Ottoman concept of leadership in the Holy War (*gaza*). In line with his policy of world leadership, Süleyman tried to demonstrate his role as protector of Muslims all over the world. In 1538 he dispatched a fleet to oust the Portuguese from Diu in India. Upon the appeals of the sultan of Atjeh in

Sumatra, he sent technical aid, and he planned an expedition to expel the Muscovites from the Lower Volga in order to open trade and pilgrimage routes for the Muslims of Central Asia.

After the seventeenth century, however, the Ottoman sultans no longer had the capability to project their power for the sake of Muslims. Instead, they increasingly emphasized their legal rights as caliphs by making reference to the definitions of the caliphate which had been formulated by religious authorities of the tenth century. This emphasis on legality would lead, in the nineteenth century, to a Pan-Islamist movement under Abdülhamid II (1876–1909).

The traditional idea of *gaza*, combat against the infidel, was recast by the Ottomans in the fifteenth and sixteenth centuries to support Ottoman expansion in the east at the expense of their Muslim neighbors. When the Ottomans decided to take action against their Muslim rivals – the dynasts of Anatolia, then the Akkoyunlus, and finally the Safavids in Iran – they accused them of obstructing the Ottomans in the latter's performance of their essential duty, the Holy War against Western Christendom. The Ottomans found additional justification against the Shiite Safavids when the Ottoman ulema readily gave approval for war against "the heretics."

Ottomans and the West

The strong autocratic military state of the Ottomans provided the means by which the Islamic world first resisted and then passed to the offensive against the West. The struggle began on a large scale when the Ottomans, taking advantage of the divisiveness arising from the appearance of Protestantism and national monarchies in Europe, launched a series of sustained attacks against the Habsburgs in Central Europe and the Mediterranean. This resulted in the occupation of Hungary (1526–41), the first siege of Vienna in 1529, and the naval victory at Preveza in 1538. During the period 1528–78, the Ottomans pursued an active diplomacy in Europe, everywhere supporting forces opposed to the Papacy and the Habsburgs, such as the Calvinists in France, Hungary and the Netherlands, the Moriscos in Spain and the rising national monarchies in France and England. In addition to concerted military expeditions, the Ottomans expressed their support by granting commercial privileges to friendly nations (France in 1569, England in 1580, and the Netherlands in 1612). In the long run, these commercial rights gave a powerful boost to those Western economies supported by the Ottomans.

Another pillar of Ottoman diplomacy at this time was to avoid a two-front war. In particular, the empire wanted to avoid a war with Iran when engaged in Europe. This goal was thwarted in 1603 when Shah Abbas (1588–1629) declared war and took back all of the Ottoman conquests in Azerbaijan while the Ottomans were engaged in a long and ruinous war with the Habsburgs (1593–1606). The treaty of Zsitva-Török with the Habsburgs in 1606 is justly regarded as a reversal in the tide of Ottoman fortunes and the beginning of decline. The Ottoman failure meant that a traditional Asiatic culture, even when it had borrowed war technology from the West, was doomed before the rise of modern Europe. It is to be noted that the Ottoman decline was as much the outcome of Western Europe's modern economic system as of superior European military technology. The Ottoman economy and monetary system collapsed in the 1600s mainly because of the aggressive mercantilistic economies of the Western nations that replaced the Venetians in the Levant.

The time of troubles at the end of the sixteenth century – the decline

As factors paving the way for the crisis of the late sixteenth and early seventeenth centuries we can cite the influence of increase in population, Europe's new military technology and the monetary and financial crisis.

Violence had already erupted in Anatolia in the middle of the sixteenth century, notably during the episodes involving the princes Mustafa and Bayezid. Thousands of unemployed Anatolian peasants flocked to the rival princes as mercenaries in hopes of earning military class status under the banner of their victorious prince. Timariot-*sipahi*s who had lost their *timar*s or whose *timar*s had become devalued constituted one of the chief elements of the unrest. In addition, thousands of young peasants, eager to share in the prerogatives of the religious class, filled the religious colleges in towns in Anatolia, but devoted much of their energies to pillaging and despoiling these towns and the countryside. The Balkans had helped to siphon off a good part of the Anatolian population when the frontier zones afforded young men intent on embracing a military career ample opportunity to demonstrate their valor as *gönüllüs* (volunteers). However, in the second half of the sixteenth century, Ottoman expansion in Europe came to a standstill and the organization of *akıncıs*, frontier raiders, collapsed.

In Anatolia, meanwhile, population pressure on the arid Anatolian plateau continued. This pressure has been studied on the basis of Ottoman population surveys, but its precise scale can never be calculated.

After 1578, the wars with Iran stimulated large numbers of young men of *reaya* origin to enroll in the armies. In a sense the wars with Iran and Austria at the end of the sixteenth century were in part a consequence of the growth in population, since it set in motion a variety of social, political and financial pressures within the empire.

In the vast conquered regions of the Caucasus, thousands of *reaya* from Anatolia functioned as timariots or as guardians of fortresses. But, and it is this that Ottoman observers of the decline decry so bitterly, this very mobility irrevocably compromised the guiding principle of the Ottoman system, that of the separation of the *reaya* from the military.

With respect to other causes of decline, Ottoman writers of the period stress the reduced autonomy of the imperial divan and its bureaus, particularly in the wake of the battle waged against the Grand Vizier Sokollu by power groups newly arrived in İstanbul upon Selim II's accession (1566). The traditional independence of the administration, in better times the guarantor of state interests, was restricted by the palace courtiers and other irresponsible people. Thus began the corruption and disintegration of the laws and statutes of the empire, one of the most far-reaching consequences of which was the large-scale transfer of *miri* (state lands) from state control into *mülk* (private proprietorship lands) and *vakf* (pious foundation) status. Also at this time the religious class, ulema, tended to interfere more and more in the administration and in the laws promulgated by the crown. Questions relating to sultanic laws and administrative regulations became increasingly subject to the *fetva*, the official opinion of the Sheyhülislam, head of ulema, in accordance with religious authority. This clerical influence reinforced Sunnite conservatism and severely curtailed the government's freedom of action in response to changing conditions.

The Ottoman writers of that period, then, attribute the decline primarily to the corruption of institutions that had achieved their apogee under the rule of Süleyman the Lawgiver. Unquestionably there is a good bit of truth in all this and modern historians for the most part are in agreement with it. But the Ottoman writers failed to discern all of the contributing causes and to appreciate the true significance of the changes that were occurring in their own time.

Earlier we touched on the problem of over-population while underlining the difficulty of determining with any clarity its consequences. We now turn to a consideration of the military and financial systems, which bear directly on the issue.

The wars with Iran which began in 1578 and lasted intermittently until 1639 should be regarded as one of the principal causes of the decline of the Ottoman Empire. The invasion and occupation of Azerbaijan and Shirvan in the years 1578–90 were highly destructive, not only for the Turkish military structure but also for the Ottoman finances. The occupation troops stationed in these lands constantly had to be reprovisioned from Anatolia. Then, in 1603, the Iranian counter-offensive threw the Ottoman soldiery stationed there completely back into Anatolia.

During the wars against Austria from 1593 to 1606, the need to send into battle infantry troops equipped with firearms resulted in a significant increase in the number of Janissaries (7,886 in 1527 and 37,627 in 1610) and, in Anatolia, in the enrollment of large numbers of sekban mercenaries (mostly of peasant origin) – all with firearms. During interludes of peace when their services were not required, these mercenaries, lacking salaries and employment, roamed the countryside exacting tribute from the Anatolian population. Sipahis, dispossessed of their timars, or no longer able to make a living off them, were among those who joined the armed groups. Known as Celali, these packs of bandits so terrorized the countryside that they were a chief cause of rural depopulation and of the ruin of Anatolian agriculture. As a result, the state was paralyzed just when the Iranians mounted their counter-offensive between 1603 and 1610. At the same time Macedonia and northern Bulgaria experienced similar disorders in which Christian bands took an important part.

The same scenario repeated itself more than once during the wars of the seventeenth century, but particularly between 1683 and 1699. The Ottomans were unable to do without the service of the sekbans and the other variously named armed mercenaries in wartime. To pay them, and the inflated number of Janissaries as well, the central treasury had to search for new sources of revenue. The fact that the Ottomans had been obliged since Lepanto in 1571 to maintain a powerful fleet in the Mediterranean as a counterweight to the allied fleet only added to the financial strain.

After 1590 the treasury suffered huge deficits. In the same period the increase in the avarız (emergency levies) and the cizye (non-Muslim poll-tax) and in the abuses committed during their collection aggravated the discontent of the reaya. The avarız became a tax payable in cash on a regular, annual basis, and its rate continued to rise over the years (40 aspers in 1582, 240 in 1600, 535 in 1681). The cizye, which amounted to 40 aspers per person in 1574, climbed to 70 in 1592, 150 in 1596, 240 in 1630, and 280 in 1691.

A factor with devastating effects for Ottoman financial stability was the depreciation of silver coin, the principal cause of which was the flow of cheap silver from Europe after 1580. Ottoman markets were flooded with European silver and with counterfeit currency. Since the taxes and impositions attached to the *timar* were not raised, their nominal value remained unchanged although their real value had actually fallen sharply. Not surprisingly, the *sipahis* and other timariots tried to make up for their loss in income by inventing new taxes or demanding higher rates on the old from the already hard-pressed *reaya*. The numerous uprisings of the Janissaries during this time also relate directly to their reduced real income and the instability of the currency.

As a result of these upheavals, the Ottoman Empire of the seventeenth century was no longer the vital empire it had been in the sixteenth. The *timar* system, born of conditions peculiar to the Middle Ages, was irretrievably shattered. It had been supplanted by a gun-bearing army of mercenaries and a central treasury shifting to taxes paid in cash. The Ottoman asper was replaced by European currency; and the economy entered the orbit of the European mercantilists.

THE EMPIRE'S POPULATION AND POPULATION MOVEMENTS

Population

The most reliable figures on the Ottoman population of the fifteenth century come from the tax surveys (see below, pp. 133–39) and *cizye*, poll-tax registers.[1] Regarding non-Muslims the poll-tax registers from the Hegira years of 893 to 896 (December 17, 1487 to October 5, 1491) give the data in Table I:1. The total *cizye* revenue for the year 1489 is 32,407,330 *akça* for all groups. The figures comprise *hanes* (households) and widows who inherited their husbands' land. *Hane* does not mean all the people living under one roof but married couples with an independent source of income. Thus, a married son living in his parents' house but with an independent source of income constitutes one *hane*. A household is an economically independent family.

It is, however, not possible on the basis of these figures even to approximate the total non-Muslim population for this period. The non-Muslims subject to the poll-tax were those adult males over 12 or 15 years old capable of sustaining themselves through economic activity. But in rural areas in general the head of the peasant household (*hane*) was responsible for all taxable persons and paid one *cizye* for the household. Also, poll-tax surveys excluded non-Muslims exempt from this tax, namely clerics,

Table I:1. The poll-tax paying non-Muslim population, 1488–91

	Households			
	1488	1489	1490	1491
The Balkans				
Regular *cizye*-paying households	639,119	646,550	621,508	639,387
Groups subject to lower *cizye* rates (Eflaks and miners in the Bosnia, Serbia and Salonica region)	19,079	34,902		34,970
Total	658,198	681,452		674,357
Anatolia	–	–	32,628	–

Source: Barkan (1964).

slaves, destitute people, the retinue of military personnel and sometimes members of Christian militia.

By the date of our survey, the Ottoman territory comprised the Balkan lands north to the rivers Danube and Sava, excluding northern Bosnia and Croatia which were under Hungarian control, and Dalmatia, under the Venetians, including some fortresses and islands in the Greek and Aegean archipelago.[2] The total of the registered non-Muslim households subject to a poll-tax amounted to about 674,000 in the Balkans and about 32,000 in Anatolia in 1491. Assuming after Barkan that the exempted population consisted of 6 percent of the total population with an average household of five individuals, there was a non-Muslim population of about four million in the Ottoman Balkans in the 1490s.

As for Anatolia, the Ottoman territory by 1490 was delimited by a line approximately from Trabzon to the bay of Antalya, leaving out all of eastern Asia Minor. In this region, with a total of 27,131 Christian households, the Trabzon–Rize region, conquered from the Comneni in 1461, was the only one with a compact Christian population by 1490.[3] By contrast, in western Anatolia, which was invaded by the Turcomans much earlier, at the turn of the thirteenth century, the non-Muslim population subject to the poll-tax numbered only 2,605 households, and those in the rest of Anatolia 2,856 (see Table I:2), most of whom were Greeks and Armenians together with small Jewish communities in the cities.

In the period 1520–35, the taxable Christian households in the five Anatolian provinces numbered 63,300 or 7 percent of the total population, while it had been c. 32,000 around 1490. The increase might have

Table I:2. Non-Muslim population in Anatolia, 1489

	Households		
	hane	*bive*	
Saruhan	480	94	Mostly Greeks
Aydın	570	172	
Menteşe	168	51	
Teke	236	33	
Hamid	491	112	
Germiyan	167	31	
Ankara	728	46	Mostly Armenians
Kiangiri (Çankırı)	504	34	
Kastamonu–Sinop	1,253	282	Mostly Greeks
Bigacık	9	—	Greeks
Total	4,606	855	

Source: Barkan (1964).

resulted from a population growth which was a general trend for the period 1490–1535 and less efficient registration, or from immigration from the east. The entire number of Balkan converts to Islam numbered 94 households in the Hegira year 893, and 255 for the years 893–96.[4] The Christian boys levied for the Janissary corps and the palace servitors who would later join the military class after training are not included in this figure.[5] In the period 1520–35 there were in Anatolia only 271 taxable Jewish households and in the province of Diyarbekir 288.

In other words, by the end of the fifteenth century Anatolia to the west of the Euphrates was predominantly a Muslim country settled by immigrant Muslim Turks, or converted native populations. There was no question that widespread islamization had occurred. This was mostly a result of a socio-cultural process during the three centuries of Turkish Seljukid rule.[6] Judging from the Ottoman population and tax registers of the second half of the fifteenth century, western Anatolia had by then been mostly settled by Turcomans.[7]

We do not have data for the Muslim population of Anatolia before the period 1520–35. In this period, according to the calculations of Ö.L. Barkan the taxable Muslim households for the same area in 1490 numbered 832,395.[8] Added to this figure are the military households exempt from taxation which constituted a small group, mostly living in the towns. Through the same surveys, the population growth in the five Asiatic provinces are shown in Table I:3.[9] By 1580, multiplied by five, the population of these five provinces was 6,802,370 as against 4,636,050

Table I:3. Population growth in Anatolia

	Households		
	1520–30	1570–80	Growth %
Anatolia (western Asia Minor)	474,447	672,512	41.7
Karaman (central Asia Minor)	146,644	268,028	82.8
Zülkadriye (Kırşehir–Maraş area)	69,481	113,028	62.6
Rum-i Kadim (Amasya–Tokat area)	106,062	189,643	79.0
Rum-i Hadis (Trabzon–Malatya area)	75,976	117,263	54.0
Total	872,610	1,360,474	

Source: Barkan (1970), p. 169.

around 1490. Here the growth rate varies from 41 to 82 percent according to the particular region.

In reality, households in the towns consisted of three to four individuals and were smaller than those in the countryside.[10] Barkan's coefficient of five for each *hane* or household is discussed by L. Erder,[11] in light of modern demographic theory. Ottoman *hane*, Erder points out, is often purely a fiscal convenience and is not geographically constant. Taking the male population above the age of puberty which is recorded in certain types of Ottoman tax and population registers and using the theory of the relationship of population growth rates and the changing age composition of a population, Erder finds all multipliers are confined to a relatively narrow range of between 3 and 4.

In any case, Barkan suggests that the Ottoman Empire joined the spectacular population growth in the Christian western Mediterranean by an average increase of 59.9 percent in the period 1520–80, which Braudel sees as reasonable.[12] The increase, Barkan adds, was as high as 83.6 percent in large cities. Based on the increase in the number of households, the conclusion must be reliable except for possible small discrepancies in the figures due to the deficiency of successive surveys. In any case, the average household cannot be less than two persons, which gives a population of 1,664,790. Every time we added one person to the household the difference would be a population of about 800,000 higher. So, calculations of population on the basis of taxable households are quite hypothetical. But we are more certain in calculating population increases since our sources use the *hane* household all the time. By 1535, Syria and Palestine, as well as the provinces of Diyarbekir (southeast Asia Minor) and Zülkadriye had been annexed to Ottoman territory. By 1535, the total number of taxable Muslim households in the Asiatic provinces, including Cilicia and the Arab provinces of Syria and Palestine and the

Table I:4. *Sancak* population increase in the *liva* (sub-province) of
Damascus

Year	No. of villages	No. of Muslim taxable households	Annual revenue in millions of *akça*
1521	844	38,672	12.6
1548	1016	63,035	13.6
1569	1,129	57,897	15.8

Source: Barkan (1957).

military personnel, numbered 1,067,355 households, or about 5,300,000
individuals if we apply the same coefficient of five. When Christians and
Jews were added it came to 1,146,697 or 5,733,485.

In sum, Barkan suggests,[13] for the period 1520–35, a population of 12
or 12.5 million in the Ottoman Empire including the population not
entered in the tax registers in the Balkans and Asia Minor. Braudel pro-
poses a maximum of 22 million for the greatest extent of the empire by
the end of the sixteenth century. For the end of the century,[14] however,
Barkan surmises a drastically larger population of 30–35 million; he
estimates a natural growth of 60 percent and adds also the population of
the territories annexed after 1535 (Syrmia, Croatia, Hungary, and Slovakia in Europe; northern Abyssinia, Hejaz, Yemen, Iraq, Al-Hasa, and
the North African coasts).[15] Evidently, Barkan's figure must be exagger-
ated.[16] In our calculations we have to consider also the particular conditions of the Ottoman conquest. In general, there was a regression in
prosperity and population in the newly conquered lands by the Ottomans
as documented in Syria, southeast Asia Minor[17] and Hungary.[18] But when
Ottoman rule was firmly established and order and security came back,
recovery and development followed and the population increased (Table
I:4).

Population pressure

The growing Turcoman nomadic migration into the frontier zone in
western Anatolia was one of the principal causes of the westward drive
of the Turks in the period 1260–1400. Population pressure, interpreted
as economic shrinkage and growing poverty, as a result of the increasing
discrepancy between the population and economic resources,[19] is also
taken up by several Ottomanists as a major issue to explain the crisis and
structural changes in the Ottoman Empire experienced in the period

1580–1620.[20] Several indices were used to determine whether or not real population pressure occurred in that period.

In order to test the hypothesis on population pressure during the sixteenth century in Anatolia, Michael Cook examined demographic and economic data from Ottoman surveys.[21] Earlier studies (in particular those of Akdağ, Braudel and Güçer) had to rely on the contraction in wheat exports, rising prices, shortages and famines in the empire as the main indicators of population pressure. Cook examines the question by investigating the ratio of population to economic resources and whether the ratio changed considerably over a given period of time in selected areas. Studying such related phenomena as unavailability of marginal land, a rise in land prices, an increase in the number of landless peasants and emigration he concluded that "the population growth was more rapid than the extension of cultivation." He also discussed "a demographic saturation under the sixteenth century conditions." Cook suggests figures for the ratio between the population growth and the extension of cultivation as 17 to 12 in the period 1475–1575 using an index with a base level of 10 in 1475. It should be noted that the average peasant household landholding had fallen from half a çift to a third or even a quarter of a çift by the end of the period, in the areas examined. Reduction in size of the family farm is undoubtedly a sign of crisis for the rural population as well as for the çift-hane system (see below, pp. 153–54) as a whole. Cook also draws attention to the fact that food prices rose faster than wages but no statistical evidence is offered. More intensive exploitation of the soil or a shift to more profitable crops are also suggested as indicators of population pressure.[22] Faroqhi concurs with Michael Cook in observing the discrepancy between the population increase and grain production growth. Faroqhi and Erder examined population changes in the areas of Şebin-Karahisar and Kocaeli in two periods.[23] In both cases the authors observe that "some decline of population occurred towards the end of the sixteenth century" and assert that "this was in fact a generalized phenomenon."

For population estimates and changes some unexpected developments have also to be considered. For example, for the sharp increase in total population in the Karahisar area, the exodus of the Christian population from eastern Anatolia as a result of the Celali depredations might be another explanation. Faroqhi also suggests that, despite legal prohibition, there was a trend to subdivide the çift units during the sixteenth century and this may be one of the results of the population increase (Table I:5).

Table 1:5. Population density estimates of the Ottoman Empire and
European countries, 1600 (persons per square mile)

Country	Density
Italy	97
France	86
Low Countries	112
Britain	56
Turkey in Europe (the Balkans north to the Danube and Drava Rivers)	41
Turkey in Asia (approximately Turkey today, excluding Thrace)	20

Source: McGowan (1982), p. 174 n. 3.

Population movements

From the beginning, Ottoman society was made up of immigrants,
uprooted people, pastoralists in search of pastures, jobless soldiers or
landless peasant youths seeking their fortunes and a new life on the
frontier. Early popular Ottoman chroniclers say: "These Ottomans sym-
pathize with uprooted strangers (*garibs*)."[24] Evidently Ottomans believed
that prosperity and expansion of the state revenues were primarily
dependent on human energy and skills. It will be seen that *timar*-holders
or *vakf* trustees encouraged people to come and settle on their territory
since the most important component of means of production was labor in
this rural economy with limitless marginal land available for agriculture.

The Ottomans always welcomed refugees. Tens of thousands of Jews
expelled from Spain, Portugal and Italy came and founded prosperous
communities in towns under the protection of the Ottoman sultans
during and after 1492. Groups of Moriscos expelled from Andalusia in
the sixteenth century were settled in the heart of Galata.[25]

Old Believers from Russia survived to the twentieth century in northwest Anatolia. In the last centuries of the empire, hundreds of thousands
of refugees fleeing from Russian invasions of the Balkans, Circassia and
Crimea were welcomed and settled by the Ottoman government in
Anatolia.[26]

Although usually circuiting in their *yurt*, which is an area with well-
defined summer and winter pasturelands, the pastoral nomads, particularly numerous in the large area stretching from the desert of northern
Syria and Iraq to western Anatolia, sometimes migrated en masse in
search of better pastures when the central government's authority
weakened or when they were pushed by more powerful nomad groups.
Thus, a continuing stream of nomads, mostly Turcomans, but also Kurds

and Arabs, moving from east to west, reached western Anatolia, the
Aegean Islands and the Balkans throughout Ottoman history.

On the other hand, the state's deportation policy, political and social
upheavals such as the Celali depredations and sometimes population pressure in a particular region played a major role in the shifts of population
in the empire. Migrations of pastoral nomads were always particularly
conspicuous in the process.

As was true in the Byzantine and Iranian empires, the Ottomans, too,
applied the policy of forced deportation of population in an effort to get
rid of a rebellious ethnic group or to colonize a particular area important
for the state. We find, for example, the rebellious Çepni Turcomans from
the Black Sea region of Canik settled in Albania in the early fifteenth century, Tatars from the Tokat–Amasya region, in the Maritsa valley, and Turcomans of Saruhan (western Anatolia) in the vicinity of Skopje by the
1390s. A large-scale colonization occurred under Mehmed II when he
deported en masse peasants from newly conquered lands of Serbia and the
Morea, and Turcoman nomads to the villages around İstanbul which had
lost their Greek population during the siege of Constantinople. In 1455, he
also deported all of the Jewish communities in the Balkan towns to repopu-
late and stimulate economic activities in his new capital of İstanbul.[27] He
caused Greeks to settle in İstanbul also from his successive conquests in the
Morea, the Aegean Islands, Trabzon, and certain central Anatolian towns.
Armenians from central Anatolia, the two Phocaeas and Caffa, as well as
Muslims from Anatolia were brought to İstanbul in the years 1459–75.
Selim I brought to İstanbul about 200 households of craftsmen from Tabriz
and 500 from Cairo.

A massive population shift occurred as a result of the upheaval which
the Celali bands caused in Anatolia in the period 1596–1610.[28] In the
contemporary sources the exodus to other provinces as far afield as
Rumeli, the Crimea and Syria was labeled "the great flight." Then, the
government took drastic measures to ensure the return of these peasants
to their abandoned villages in Anatolia.[29]

In 1613 in the wake of the Celali disorders the clans making up the
Boz-Ulus Turcomans in eastern Asia Minor began to shift to central
Anatolia as far as Kütahya, causing great harm to the cultivated lands on
their way.[30] During the seventeenth century, the migration from central
Arabia of the Arab tribal confederations of the Shammar and the Anazeh
to the northern Syrian desert appears to have caused a mass migration of
the Turcoman and Kurdish clans to the central and western provinces of
Asia Minor. We find then Boz-Ulus Turcomans in the Ankara, Aydın
and Amasya–Tokat areas.[31]

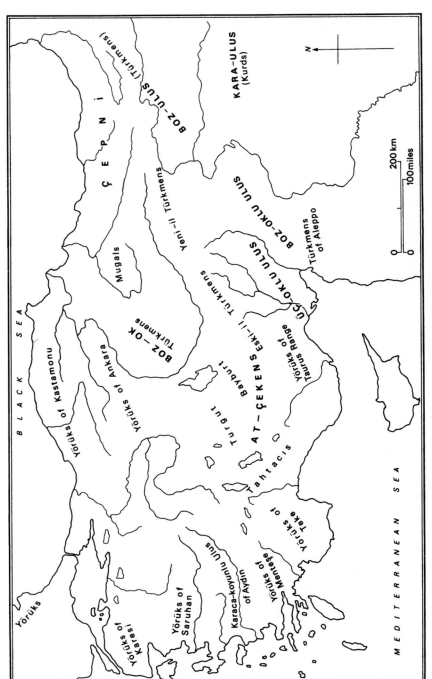

7 Turcoman Îl or Ulus confederations in Asia Minor

Source: Sümer (1949–50), pp. 437–532; *idem* (1967), pp. 199–362

The Turcoman nomadic populations and their economy

The Seljukids of Anatolia representing a centralized bureaucratic state supported the peasantry and the commercial interests against the Turcoman pastoral population. Pushed by the state to marginal lands, the Turcomans were concentrated on the frontier zones and mountain pasturelands of the ranges of the Taurus mountains to the south and the Pontic mountains from Bolu to Trabzon in the north. On the dry central Anatolian plateau from Konya to Ankara there was another Turcoman pastoral concentration (see Map 7). Actually, because of the necessity of the seasonal transhumance between summer and winter pastures, *yaylak* and *kışlak*, the Turcomans took their herds in winter to the lowlands in the valleys of the major river beds in southern and western Anatolia.[32] Ignoring the borders they penetrated deep into the western Anatolia valleys, which were under the control of the Byzantines,[33] from the eleventh century until the time when they conquered and settled these valleys under the *gazi* leaders.[34]

Known as Türkmen, Yörük, or later Kızılbaş,[35] Turkish nomads made up about 15 percent of the population in the Anadolu province in the 1520s (this province stretched to a line between Sinop and Antalya Bay in the west). If we add the *yaya* and *müsellem*, military groups of nomadic origin, the percentage goes up to 27. In fact, the great Yörük concentrations were found in the sub-provinces of Ankara, Kütahya, Menteşe, Aydın, Saruhan, Teke, and Hamid. These seven *sancaks* combined had a nomadic population of about 80,000 households[36] (see Table I:6).

A great number of Turcoman tribes had been there since the first Turkish invasion of Anatolia in the last decades of the eleventh century.[37] Later, a constant stream of nomads, mostly Turcoman, continued to increase the nomadic population in the region.

While the general population growth in western Anatolia from the period 1520–35 to 1570–80 is calculated to be 42 percent, the growth of the nomadic population is 52 percent, a fact explicable by immigration from the east rather than natural growth.[38] Turcoman westward mass migration gained momentum when the Ottomans established a bridgehead in the Balkans in 1352. When Turcoman overseas raids were blocked at İzmir by western Crusaders,[39] that is in 1348, Turcoman migration took a new direction and an exodus began from the Denizli–Aydın–Saruhan region to the Dardanelles, and thence into Thrace and eastern Balkans during the early Ottoman conquests. Ottoman surveys show that this Turcoman mass migration and settlement had a revolutionary

Table 1:6. Nomad households (*hane*) of western Anatolia (Anadolu *beglerbegiliği*) according to the Ottoman survey registers of the periods 1520–35 and 1570–80

Sancak	1520–35	1570–80
Alaiye	227	455
Ankara	9,484	23,911
Aydın	6,692	3,693
Biga	99	2,066
Bolu	461	2,003
Hamid	4,978	11,814
Hüdavendigar	1,600	2,055
Karahisar-Sahib	2,385	1,729
Karesi	—	2,445
Kastamonu	1,248	1,457
Kiangiri (Çankırı)	?	976
Kocaeli	?	?
Kütahya	15,164	23,935
Menteşe	19,219	16,912
Saruhan	6,640	15,072
Sultanönü	255	2,095
Teke	8,816	5,601
Total	77,268	116,219

Source: Barkan (1957), p. 30.

effect on the demography of the eastern Balkans and Thrace. Along with the Ottoman policy of transferring disorderly nomadic groups into the Balkans in order to turkify and secure new conquests, a large-scale voluntary immigration took place during the fourteenth century in the same regions. A detailed map based on Ottoman surveys by Barkan demonstrates this dramatic change in the ethnic composition of the population.[40] As occurred earlier in western Anatolia that was not, to use Speros Vryonis Jr.'s words, "a typical military conquest . . . but an ethnic migration of nomadic peoples of substantial numerical proportions."[41] In the eastern Balkans between the Black Sea and a line of the Mesta and Yantra rivers, Turkish settlements formed the majority of the population both nomadic and sedentary at the beginning of the sixteenth century (Table 1:7).

The Ottoman administration re-organized the pastoral tribes of eastern Anatolia into two large confederations: the Turcomans into Boz-Ulus and the Kurds into Kara-Ulus. Disputes often broke out between the two *ulus*.

By that time the majority of the Turks had already converted to a sedentary life in the towns and villages. Even then, Turcomans were still

Table I:7. The militia of yörük origin in the Balkans, 1560

Under *subaşı* (commander)	Number of *subaşı*	*eşkünci* (soldiers)	*yamak* (assistants)
Salonica (Macedonia, Thessaly)	13	3,000	9,000 (600 *ocak*)
Vize (northern Thrace)	4	525	1,575
Yanbolu (Upper Tunca river)	?	?	?
Naldöken (Eski-Zagra, Filibe)	42	1,715	7,548
Ofçabolu (İştip-Üsküp)	1	485	2,218
Kocacık (Yanbolu, Varna, Shumen)	?	900	2,700
Tanrıdağ (western Thrace, Thessaly)	47 (in 1591)	2,125	14,710
Kesriye (Castoria area)	?	?	?

Source: Gökbilgin (1957).

densely populated on the eastern Balkan range between Aytos (Aydos) and Stara Zagora, and on the Rhodopes between Batak, Haskovo and Komotini. Another Yörük concentration existed in the mountain area north of Salonica. The Dobruja steppe in the north of Varna and Shumen was almost thoroughly occupied by the Yörüks. By contrast in the western Balkans there were only sporadic Yörük groups in the area west of the Mesta and Yantra rivers. They lived on the heights north of Skopje and on the Karatova mountain south of Küstendil. On the other hand, massive Yörük nomad groups were settled in the Maritsa valley between Haskovo and Pazarjık, who were located there in villages and towns by the turn of the fifteenth century. According to the early sixteenth-century Ottoman registers, nomads of the Muslim faith in the Balkans were as shown in Table I:8.

During their seasonal transhumance between the winter pastureland in the Berriye steppe in northern Iraq, and the Bingöl mountains in the north between the Murad and Euphrates rivers the Boz-Ulus tribes had to pay various dues to several local Kurdish lords (Table I:8a). The Ottoman administration abolished these dues and replaced them by a single tax consisting of one sheep for every herd of 300 to be levied for the state treasury at the fording of the Murad river.[42] In İçili, in the heart of the Taurus mountains, Yörüks made up the majority of the population[43] and there was a constant emigration to the surrounding provinces where they were engaged in agriculture in the sixteenth century. They migrated

Table I:8. Muslim nomads in the Balkans

	Households
Yörüks	14,435
Yörüks (militarily organized)	23,000
*Müsellem*s (of Yörük origin)	12,105
Total	49,540

Table I:8a. Tribal confederations in eastern Anatolia

	Households	Sheep	Total tax to be paid (in *akça*)
Boz-Ulus (Turcomans)	7,325	1,998,246	c. 2 million
Kara-Ulus (Kurds)	?	?	c. 1 million
Şam (Damascus) Turcomans	?	?	100,000
Other scattered clans in the province of Diyarbekir	273		14,806

Source: Barkan (1943), pp. 143–44.

to the coastal plains in winter.[44] By 1530 many of them became sedentary or were engaged in field agriculture or viticulture as a supplementary activity.

Nomads and the economy

It is misleading to follow uncritically the judgments of the sedentary people, particularly the bureaucrats of the central administration, regarding the nomads.[45] In fact, Turcoman nomads constituted an integral part of the sedentary society and fulfilled certain functions without which the society could not survive.

The Ottoman state, recognizing this fact, took measures to accommodate the nomads in its imperial system.[46] Each clan was given a *yurt*, consisting of summer and winter pasturelands the limits of which were determined and were entered in the imperial registers. In this *yurt* area, along with animal husbandry, Turcomans were also engaged, though marginally, in agriculture. They reclaimed land in forests or swamps to grow wheat, cotton and rice for their own needs or for the market. Most of the land, for example, in the river valleys in western Anatolia and in lower Cilicia were malaria-stricken swamps left uncultivated. Coming for their winter encampment Turcoman nomads reclaimed part of this land for such cash crops as cotton and rice[47] (see below, p. 162). When they left for summer pastures they stationed watchmen and came back for the harvest. Such temporary settlements turned into small villages over time (pp. 167–71). Ottoman surveys show that in certain western Anatolian lowlands Turcomans grew cotton which was sold to Italians at the ports of Ephesus (Ayasoluk), Palatia (Balat) or on the island of Chios. The total value of the raw cotton purchased by the Genoese there reached the enormous amount of more than half a million gold ducats in the 1450s.[48] Pegolotti (toward 1340) mentions such export items as wheat, rice, wax, hemp, gallnuts, alum, opium, madder-root, valonia and "Turkish silk."[49] In the trade agreements made between the Turcoman emirs and the Italian mercantile states particular reference is made to wheat, dried fruits, horses, oxen, sheep, slaves, wax, hides and alum as export items and to wine, soap, and textiles as imports. Elizabeth Zachariadou's studies[50] based on Latin sources shed light on the economic recovery of western Anatolia under the Turkish emirates, thus modifying the gloomy picture of the complete destruction and decline of the region under Turcoman rule. Over time, under the tolerant emirs, a symbiosis between the Turcomans and the Greek population appears to have been established.

Along with wheat and cotton, the export of carpets became the subject of an international trade and made a tremendous impact on the Turcoman economy and society in western Anatolia.[51] In the 1330s, Ibn Battuta,[52] speaking of Aksaray near Konya, says: "There are manufactured there the rugs of sheep wool called after the place, which have no equal in any country and are exported from there to Syria, Egypt, Iraq, India, China and the lands of the Turks." Later on particularly the Uşak–Gördes–Kula basin in the upper Gediz river became an internationally known center of carpet manufacturing. This unique development was associated with various factors. Geography of the region with the high pasturelands on the surrounding mountains densely settled by the Turcoman pastoralists supplied wool in abundance and cheap as well as skilled labor. Best quality madder and alum for dyeing, the fast running streams for washing the raw wool and finishing the carpets and the Gediz river for transport to the sea offered the ideal conditions. Over time prosperous towns emerged in the basin which were all inhabited by the Turcomans, who spent two or three months each summer on the surrounding mountains.[53]

We have to bear in mind that animal husbandry supplied the foodstuffs and basic raw materials such as wool and hides for urban industries and had a vital economic significance in preindustrial societies in the east as well as in Europe. It is no surprise that wool and hides always came on top of the lists of exports to Europe from Ottoman Anatolia and the Balkans from the fourteenth to the twentieth century (see pp. 263–65).

Another fact about the Anatolian pastoralists is that they monopolized land transportation of the empire not only in the private sector but also in state enterprises. The camel is the most important animal for the Yörüks. Camels were used to carry baggage under difficult circumstances, but the Yörüks also employed them in the transport business and to make money. Considering the importance of the camel, they did not slaughter them for food, and they called them a "major capital" item. Some pastoralists even became capitalists, hiring shepherds to tend their flocks and engaging themselves in long-distance transportation or in the trade of livestock.

In 1555, the Imperial Ambassador Busbecq's remark[54] that the Ottoman Empire came into being thanks to rice and camels reveals to us an important point (rice was the basic food in campaigns because of its durability). The Turcomans bred hybrids using the Arabian dromedary and Bactrian types, which were suited to the Anatolian cold and rainy climate and rugged terrain. Tavernier observed that new breeds employed in the caravan traffic between Tabriz and İstanbul were larger in size and carried more load than the dromedary.[55] They pulled themselves out of mud without difficulty. Anatolia's huge camel population disappeared only in the twentieth century when the railroad network was completed.

The camel was used in the transport of all kinds of heavy equipment, such as arms and ammunition and provisions for the army, as well as for bulky and heavy commercial goods. The camel had a carrying capacity of about 250 kg, twice as much as a horse or a mule, and relatively little cost was involved. The Ottoman army was able to move from the Euphrates to the Danube in one season with all of its heavy equipment and arms. Without the camel, transport costs would have been prohibitive for carrying wheat, flour and barley for provisioning the army and the isolated fortresses. It was no coincidence that in 1399 Bayezid I took away as part of his booty ten thousand camels from the Antalya region. The camel drivers in this area and in western Anatolia were either Turcoman or "immigrant Arabs."[56] In short, the Ottoman armies depended on the camel-driving nomads for their transport and logistic services. It was again for this reason that the Ottomans lacked hard surfaced roads. Although the palace maintained a relatively small number of camels for the transport of the sultan's baggage, they would hire tens of thousands of camels and nomadic drivers for the army during a campaign.

When, under certain conditions, Yörüks were obliged to take up a sedentary life they could do so without much difficulty within a short adjustment period (pp. 170–71). In their pastoral life they often practiced agriculture as a supplement to their economy. Yörük villages are recognizable by being smaller and more primitive than the surrounding larger villages as observed in Deli-Orman and Dobruja or central Anatolia.[57] The Ottoman tax and population surveys of the fifteenth century show that western Anatolia by then had a predominantly sedentary population of Turkoman origin, and thanks to its integration into European trade through its exports of wheat, cotton, raisins, figs, alum, carpets, wool and hides, the area became one of the most prosperous provinces of the empire.

It has been argued[58] that in the sixteenth century rapid growth in the peasant population caused a general expansion of arable lands at the expense of pasturelands, so that the Yörüks had to retire progressively to marginal lands on the higher altitudes. The increasing number of the settlements of agriculturists in forest areas is primarily explained by the same factor. In the sixteenth century, in eastern Anatolia the struggle between the pastoralists and the peasantry became a serious question for the government. When the region, particularly the Erzurum–Pasin corridor, became the passageway of the Ottoman armies, the peasant population abandoned the land and scattered. Then, pastoralists from the south came to use the land as summer pasture. As the government assigned the land as *timar* to *sipahis*, these men brought peasants back and tried to turn the land back to cultivation.[59] Thereupon the pastoralists were forbidden to come and graze their herds. Frustrated by the sultan's order, the nomads threatened to leave the country altogether and go to Azerbaijan under the shah of Iran.[60] In fact, there occurred a continuous flight of the Turcoman clans to Azerbaijan in the sixteenth century.

Seasonal migration of the tribes, mostly of Kızılbaş Turcomans, in search of pastures on both sides of the Ottoman–Iranian border, was one of the main causes of conflict between the Ottomans and Safavids. Because the herdsmen disregarded the political borders, a similar situation existed between Poland and the Ottoman Empire in the same century (see pp. 285–91). In general, western Yörüks in central Anatolia from the Sivas area to the Mediterranean and from the Sakarya valley to the Aydın province, taking advantage of the more favorable climatic conditions, were engaged in agriculture as supplementary to animal husbandry, while tribes in northern Syria and eastern Anatolia were more completely dependent on pastoralism.[61] In general, in order to increase their *timar* incomes, *sipahis* were particularly anxious to convert the pastures reserved for the pastoral nomads into cultivated lands. One of the excuses they employed was the claim that the nomads had abandoned the pasture.[62] In short, the theory of arable land's expansion at the expense of pastureland was a fact of sixteenth-century Anatolia.

Since shifting nomads from one area to another did not usually disrupt tax revenues, a situation which was unavoidable with the peasants, the state employed Turcomans on a wide range of public works. It used them as auxiliary troops in the Balkans (Table I:7), or deported them from Anatolia and settled them in Rumeli in strategically important places along the roads, in the mountain passes, etc. The nomad labor force, in return for tax exemption, was widely exploited in various state enterprises such as mining, rice growing, or training horses for the state. The state also assigned particular groups of nomads to supply regularly the palace or army with certain provisions, such as butter, and bows and arrows.

In their delicate economy, nomads were more susceptible than sedentary populations to adverse factors. An epidemic could wipe out their herds, thus reducing them to utter poverty. Under such conditions, they resorted to brigandage or enrolled in the imperial army as mercenaries for a small salary. Being segmented, unprivileged groups in the Ottoman society, they joined every movement against the established order. Being inaccessible in their mountains, rebellion became endemic with the Yörüks on the Taurus range and among the Albanian tribes in the Balkans. In eastern Asia Minor, where the pastoral economy prevailed, the Ottoman administration tried to compromise with the tribes by respecting tribal autonomy under hereditary chieftains. The taxes, nominal in amount, were collected and delivered by the chieftain, and, in return for privileges, the obligation of military service under hereditary chieftains was required.

Muslim and Christian mountain peoples presented certain common features. As a rule, the imperial administration divided the traditional large tribes into independent clans under chiefs officially recognized and controlled. Although their *yurt* area and the tracks followed in their seasonal transhumance between summer and winter pastures were defined in official registers, conflicts with peasants and administrative authorities were not infrequent. The pastoralists hated the bureaucratic restrictions, the registration and the taxes and, whenever the central authority grew weak, they became restless and out of control.

NOTES

1 Barkan (1964).
2 See Pitcher (1972), map no. XVI.
3 Lowry (1981).
4 Barkan (1964), p. 13.
5 See İnalcık (1965a), pp. 1085–91.
6 Turan (1959); Vryonis (1971), pp. 351–402; Cahen (1988), pp. 162–75, 321–23; İnalcık (1970c).
7 İnalcık (1986a), p. 47.
8 Barkan (1957), p. 20.
9 Barkan (1970), p. 169.
10 İnalcık (1978a), pp. 79–80; Göyünç (1979), pp. 331–48.
11 Erder (1975), pp. 284–301.
12 Braudel (1972), I, p. 398.
13 Barkan (1957), p. 23.
14 Braudel (1972), I, p. 396.
15 Pitcher (1972), map no. XXI.
16 İnalcık (1978a), p. 75; Braudel (1972), I, p. 398.
17 Barkan (1957), p. 25; Cohen and Lewis (1978), pp. 19–41.
18 Káldy-Nagy (1960).
19 Cf. Issawi (1958), pp. 329–33.
20 Braudel (1973), I, pp. 593–94; İnalcık (1978a), pp. 80–83; Cook (1972).
21 Cook (1972).
22 İslamoğlu-İnan (1987), pp. 107–28.
23 Erder and Faroqhi (1979), pp. 322–45.
24 Oruç (1925), pp. 4, 79.
25 İnalcık (1991a), pp. 67–70.
26 Karpat (1985).
27 İnalcık (1973b), p. 225.
28 Akdağ (1963), pp. 250–54; *MTM*, I, p. 82.
29 İnalcık (1965b), pp. 126–27.
30 Güçer (1964), p. 18.
31 Barkan (1955–56), p. 203.
32 Planhol (1958); Hütteroth (1974), pp. 30–40.
33 Vryonis (1971), pp. 143–287.
34 Wittek (1934).
35 İnalcık (1986a), pp. 41, 47.
36 *Ibid.*, p. 45.
37 Vryonis (1971), pp. 223–44.
38 İnalcık (1986a), pp. 45–46.
39 İnalcık (1985a), pp. 197–99.
40 Barkan (1953–54), pp. 209–39; Barkan (1946–50): map.
41 Vryonis (1975), p. 50.
42 Barkan (1943), pp. 140–42.
43 Barkan (1943), p. 52, article 19, nomads made up 54 percent of the total population in Zülkadriye, 58 percent in Aleppo province, and 62 percent in Baghdad province in the period 1580–90, see Murphey (1984), p. 192.
44 Barkan (1943), p. 53, article 23.

45 Vryonis (1975), p. 57, admits that a gradual symbiosis took place between Greeks and Turks.

46 Lindner (1983), pp. 51–74, suggests that the Ottoman state deliberately followed a tax policy aimed at ruining the Turcoman nomads economically so that they had no choice but to become sedentary, cf. İnalcık (1986a), note 67.

47 Soysal (1976), pp. 24–28.

48 Heers (1961), p. 393.

49 Pegolotti (1936), pp. 293–300, 360–83, 411–35.

50 Zachariadou (1983), pp. 125–73, modifies Vryonis' decline theory (Vryonis [1971], pp. 144–45).

51 Due to their artistic designs and vivid colors Turcoman carpets were displayed in European cities on the walls of churches or business offices and copied in the paintings of such masters as Carpaccio, Lotto or Holbein; see Yetkin (1972); Aslanapa and Durul (1972); Rogers (1990–91).

52 Ibn Battuta (1962), pp. 432–33.

53 İnalcık (1986a), pp. 54–55.

54 Foster (1933), pp. 108–10, 241.

55 Tavernier (1970), pp. 36–37.

56 İnalcık (1983d), pp. 263–67.

57 İnalcık (1992b); Tunçdilek (1960); İnalcık (1970b), p. 21.

58 Planhol (1959).

59 *Sipahi*s led the peasants in turning pastures into fields, see Barkan (1943), pp. 27–29, 67.

60 Sümer (1957), pp. 429–47.

61 Sümer (1949–50), p. 516.

62 Barkan (1943).

A   THE ECONOMIC MIND

In the Iranian state tradition the economy was considered exclusively as a means of strengthening the state's finances and thereby the ruler's power.[1] In organizing the empire's economy and trade, the Ottoman regime primarily aimed at accumulating as much bullion as possible in a central treasury. Fiscalism, noted by van Klaveren,[2] is "the endeavour to maximize the public revenues at all times for other than economic purposes"; this indeed was a key principle for the Ottoman Empire.

On the other hand, since military power was believed to be the principal means of securing wealth, military imperialism together with fiscalism formed the basis of the Iranian–Ottoman concept of state, and together they account for the dynamics of Ottoman conquest and the empire-building process. The Ottoman writer Kınalızade (d. 1561)[3] advised Ottoman policy makers that:

> Some authorities confined the acquisition of wealth to three sectors: commerce, craftsmanship and agriculture. However, some legists adding military–political power (*emaret*) cited four sectors. There was a disagreement on which religiously or ethically was the best. According to the Imam Shafiʿi, commerce was the best because it was the Prophet Mohammed's noble profession. But Mawardi put agriculture above the others. Some later authorities argued that so many illegal practices invaded the commercial transactions that a distrust on the origin of the fortunes arose; thus agriculture should have precedence over commerce. In the acquisition of wealth, one should refrain first from oppression and injustice; secondly from shameful activities, and thirdly from disgraceful or dirty occupations.
>
> Craftsmanship consists of three categories: noble, neutral or inferior. The professions of ulema, bureaucrats and soldiers are based on spiritual qualities such as reason, rhetoric and valor respectively and thus make up the noble professions. Usury and the entertainment-oriented occupations are inferior professions. For the good order of the world, all these professions are necessary and it is imperative that each group remain within its

44

own sphere of activities. The middle or neutral professions include agriculture which is necessary for subsistence or the jeweler's work which is not so vital.

In professional activity, Kınalızade pointed out,[4] a craftsman should endeavor to make the best product possible without being content merely to earn his livelihood. While it was necessary, he added, to please the consumer since his satisfaction and prayers are the source of prosperity and salvation in this world and hereafter, it is a waste of time to be too meticulous making luxury goods. It is far better for a Muslim to spend his time in prayers. It is worth underlining Kınalızade's insistence on the significance of agriculture and the maintenance of an ethical approach to economic activities.

These ideas cannot be altogether dismissed as purely theoretical and ethical advice, since they actually influenced the mind and behavior of the Ottoman elite and populace on social and economic issues, a fact for which we have visible evidence in many situations and institutions in Ottoman history.

The priority given to agriculture as the most significant and necessary economic activity is of particular interest. Sultan Süleyman I recognized the peasant as the true benefactor of mankind and expressed his opinion strongly. Along with the notion of enhancing state power the Ottoman polity developed a parallel principle in the *çift-hane* system for the increase of agricultural production and the protection of peasantry (see pp. 143–46).

By contrast, what made western mercantilist power different from the Ottoman state was that the European state gave much weight to industries and manufacture in the wealth–power–wealth equation, so that mercantilism and mercantile classes assumed a leading place in society. In other words, while the West moved toward an economy of national wealth acquired through ever-expanding industries and markets under a capitalistic system, the Ottomans stuck to an imperial policy with emphasis on territorial expansion, along with traditional monopolies in manufactures and a conservative policy in landholding and agriculture.

THE OTTOMAN STATE: A WELFARE STATE

Although it seems contradictory with the goals of a power state, there is in the Islamic state an overriding concern for the well-being of the community which called for an economy of plenty. After all, in the pure

Islamic tradition, the state is considered merely a means to promote the ideology of Islam. Deriving their judgments from Islam's canonical sources with some perspective perhaps from Max Weber, modern Muslim scholars[5] assert that economic activities are determined by the value-system of Islam, whose prime concern is the well-being of the Muslim community as a whole. Criticizing the western concept of *homo economicus*, they point out that the Islamic world-view is based on oneness of this world and the hereafter, since human life is conceived as one harmonious whole oriented towards one ultimate goal, "obtaining the acceptance of Allah." Giving charity to the poor and needy, committing resources for the welfare of future generations and seeking to improve communal life are the real "economic" goals. "Production and profit are not," M. al-Mubarak asserts,[6] "ends but means. The moving force of current systems is profit, but in an Islamic system it is human welfare." But one may, of course, dispute when and where the Islamic theories have been translated into a reality. In fact, the conflict between the Islamic ideal and everyday practice has been an ever-present issue in Islamic societies.[7] Completely ignoring the elaborate non-Islamic taxation found in all of the Islamic states, the orthodox legalistic view also asserts that Islam's fiscal system is based on Islamic charity, "which aims at ensuring minimum means of livelihood to each and every individual" and productive use of economic resources for the material well-being of the community. The basic orientation "is the mutual sharing of the community's income between the affluent and have-nots." But at the same time private property is a religiously sanctioned precept in Islam.

There is, however, a theory propounded by classical Muslim legists which distinguishes *necessities* and *refinements*. So, in practice, they say, while luxury goods, mostly imported by merchants, are not subject to state price controls, necessities and local products in the common bazaar are subject to the close inspection of the bazaar inspector (*muhtesib*) appointed by the state.[8] The maximal price system (*narh*) and the constant inspection of prices and weights and measures in the bazaar as far as necessities are concerned are among the most important responsibilities of the head of the community, sultan or local kadi; in fact, Ottoman sultans took this duty most seriously. One may argue that political concern too may be involved since popular uprisings for bread are quite familiar in Islamic cities. In any case, to prevent shortages in basic needs and to secure an economy of plenty was a central concern of the sultan (see pp. 48–52). Archival evidence indicates that these principles guided Ottoman bureaucrats in all of their decisions concerning economic activities.

In this context, the important place of charity in Islamic Law is revealing. It is the expression of thanks for God's bounties to his creatures. Thus, interpreted within the religious duty of alms giving, or *sadaka*,[9] charity is highly meritorious behavior in Islam. Sultans frequently distributed alms, slaughtered thousands of sheep on certain occasions and distributed them to the poor, sometimes with their own hands. Soup kitchens (*imaret*) were one of the most widespread institutions attached to the religious endowments in cities. Incidentally, Ottoman sultans had difficulty in curbing the influx of beggars into İstanbul during the fasting and charity month of Ramadan. Thousands of "prayer-saying" people (*duaguyan*) in the mosques throughout the empire, in particular in the fortresses on the frontier, formed a regular salaried group in the payrolls of the state. The belief that charity pleases God and brings God's blessings determined Muslim behavior in many basic acts of economic importance in Islamic states, and the Ottomans were particularly zealous in that regard.

Institutions derived from charity played a significant part in redistributing wealth in society. Large groups of the destitute and unemployed in Ottoman cities and towns were maintained through such charity institutions.[10] Thus, a significant part of the fortunes accumulated in the hands of the elite, although sometimes temporarily employed in *commenda* enterprises, ultimately were bestowed on charitable endowments. The economic significance of such institutions is not to be underestimated in Ottoman society.[11]

Unlike market economies, Karl Polanyi points out, economic integration in the so-called "archaic" or traditional societies is regulated under institutional arrangements such as kinship, household, temple or state. In fact, the categories in use in market economies such as profit, wage and salary take on a rather liturgical meaning in Ottoman society. Since redistribution presupposes the presence of "an allocation center," the sultan assumes a fundamental role in that society.[12] Obviously, a pious foundation (*vakf*) in the Islamic state is a primordial institution for redistribution with a basic social and economic integrative function.

On the other hand, reciprocity in the form of exchange of gifts, in particular gifts or *pişkeş* presented to the sultan on special occasions, at the beginning of the New Year festival (*navruz*) or at religious festivals by dignitaries and foreign embassies, was carefully observed by the Ottomans. The economic consequences of this tradition are not to be underestimated. A group of palace artisans (*hiref-i hassa*) was created to prepare imperial gifts in the palace. Periodic distribution of woolen cloth to the Janissaries gave rise to an extensive woolen industry in Salonica and

İstanbul. Gifts, baksheesh and service fees expected by the dependents had a quasi-ritual significance, the neglect of which justified protest or rebellion. Money distributed to all the members of the military divisions and employees on the occasion of the accession to the throne of a new sultan had a tremendous impact on the imperial finances and taxpayers; uprisings of the military in İstanbul broke out when the administration was unable to pay.

Mention should be made of transactions intended purely for profit making, such as investments in *commenda* partnerships (*mudaraba*),[13] a practice approved by Islamic Law and widely followed in the Ottoman Empire. Also, following the widespread practice of credit giving with interest concealed under religiously approved forms,[14] the use of letters of credit (see below, pp. 206–9), the activities of money-changers and a primitive type of banking (*dolab*), the Ottoman economy of the sixteenth century employed some practices basic to capitalist market economies, partly because of the influence of the Italian merchant community at Galata and of Ottoman subjects of Italian origin.[15] But all these commercial devices appear to have remained rather marginal or peripheral since the Ottoman socio-economic structure and mind did not undergo any fundamental change because of these, and no development parallel to what happened in the West occurred in the Ottoman Empire. Obviously, in Ottoman society, the state's control and patrimonial relationships remained an essential mechanism for redistribution. The empire's economy and finances depended fundamentally on state ownership of land and its control of agricultural production, the main source of wealth. Peasant subsistence as well as the maintenance of a large body of the military class was based on a specific landholding system and taxation policy (see pp. 103–7).

AN OTTOMAN ECONOMY OF PLENTY IN THE FACE OF EUROPEAN MERCANTILISM

The nature of Ottoman economic relations with Europe would inevitably undergo some changes with the advent of the Western nations in the Levant, and the capitulatory regime itself would assume a new direction. Western mercantilism based on the concept of national economy, which was conceived and managed as a nation-wide corporation, was an advanced form of capitalism compared to its initial forms in Italy. Mercantilism was in complete contrast to Ottoman notions of economic relations. Western economies took maximum advantage of Ottoman concepts on economy to promote their own mercantilist policies and to develop their capitalistic pursuits.

Mercantilist theories were derived apparently from popular beliefs which circulated in the West as well as in the East,[16] from a common medieval heritage. For example, easterners also believed that political power depended on the extent to which the monarch was able to accumulate gold and silver in a central imperial treasury, so taxpaying subjects should be protected in order to become prosperous and feed that treasury. To this concept, mercantilists introduced a new idea, asserting that gold and silver accumulation depended on a favorable balance of trade through a continuous growth in home industries and in exports. In fact, this very idea would lead the west in the eighteenth century to complete divergence from eastern economies, to the industrial revolution and free market economies.

Both easterners and mercantilists supported the policy of barring the export of precious metals and allowing their free import. The Ottoman state, we know, exempted silver and gold imports from customs' duties and prohibited their export. In the medieval East, a country's prosperity generally was measured by the abundance and availability of gold and silver in the market. Their scarcity, causing hardships in trade and in the payment of taxes, was condemned and attributed to the ruler's covetousness in hoarding gold and silver in his treasury.[17]

On the other hand, in the Ottoman Empire the sultan frequently prohibited the export of grain and raw materials such as cotton, raw wool and hides, a policy advocated by mercantilists in the West also. But the Ottoman government pursued such a policy with the purpose of preventing shortages in necessities for the masses, while in a mercantilist economy the main intention was to ensure cheap labor and encourage industries to produce export items at competitive prices for a world market.

Despite the similarities, the basic difference between the Ottomans and mercantilists was that in the West a nation's economy was conceived globally like that of a corporation, with attention to the aggregate balance in favor of the country and computed in terms of its precious metals or durable commodities. In fact this idea of an aggregate balance of trade first originated in the compact mercantile republics of Italy, which prospered in the Levant trade and later served as a model for the newly rising nation-states in the West. On the other hand, in such a regime, a city's or nation's wealth was also believed to be dependent on its ability to protect trade routes. The key role of sea power in Venetian supremacy in the Levant trade was simply magnified later by Western nation-states, and Ottoman sea communications became dependent largely on Western shipping in the period of Ottoman decline.

It is true that the Ottoman state was vitally concerned for the security of trade routes and sustained a constant struggle against corsairs. Furthermore, state-owned ships were employed in the traffic with Egypt already under Mehmed II.[18] All of this concern, however, was motivated by fiscal interests or the need to ensure adequate supplies in the home market, and, in particular, the provisioning of the crowded imperial capital. Although fiscalism and market supply were also part of Western mercantilism, the idea of an economy as a whole and its protection, in physical or economic terms, against competitor nations never seems to have occurred to the Ottomans before the eighteenth century. Apparently no concern existed for the protection of home industries against foreign products, not even for the traditionally well-established industries such as the Ottoman silk manufactures of Bursa. In fact, the Ottoman "pseudo-mercantilism" (the term van Klaveren used for such economies) was not concerned with whether or not home industries were experiencing a decline as a result of Western mercantilist competition until Western merchants were far advanced in undermining the empire's economy, as became particularly apparent in mass-consumption goods such as cotton cloth in the second half of the eighteenth century (see below, Part IV, Ch. 32). Chiefly concerned with low prices and variety in the market-place, the Ottoman ruling elite rather disapproved of the export of these silk luxury items to foreign lands and encouraged the imports of Venetian, Florentine, Genoese, and later of French silk cloth into the empire under the capitulations. Ottoman silk cloth, cotton goods and mohair made up quite an important part of Ottoman exports to Europe before European industries imitated and superseded the Ottoman products. The Ottomans basically did not interfere in cloth exports because they were produced by a private sector motivated by the desire of profit, and because traditionally Ottomans advocated state intervention only in the trade of necessities. Fundamentally the Ottomans appear never to have developed an economic doctrine, such as Western mercantilism, to regulate the country's economy systematically in its totality. Imports were viewed as beneficial to ensure surplus in the market without any other economic consideration such as a balance of payments, the protection of industrial production or labor by exchanging labor-intensive manufactures for agricultural products. Given this mentality, the Ottomans considered the capitulations or trade privileges beneficial for the empire; such privileges were gladly granted to the European mercantilist nations as serving the empire's interest.

Also, state interventions in the Ottoman Empire, namely regulations for customs and guild manufacture, fixing maxima in prices, market inspection on the quality and measures of goods, monopolies on the manufacture and sale of certain necessities, were different in essence and in intention from the regulation of a mercantilist state. In the Ottoman case, the main concern was always for the fiscal interests of the state and the protection of consumers in the internal market, while in the mercantilist economies economic regulations were determined by a competitive international market. In the last analysis, the rift is linked to the contrast between a social structure which is controlled by an authoritarian ruler in an estate society and a civil society in which the class system and the participation in power of the rising bourgeois class prevailed.[19] To explain the European departure from the medieval economy and its structural differentiation from Asiatic economies, the emphasis should be placed on the fact that fifteenth-century Europe evolved from "a predominantly natural economy to a predominantly money economy," while in the Ottoman East bartering and long-term credit transactions in trade continued throughout the sixteenth century until Western silver coins invaded the empire after the 1580s.

Also, it is to be remembered that, for the Ottomans, wealth was expected to derive from new tax resources in the lands annexed by conquest, not by intensive methods such as maximizing the income from agriculture, industries and commerce through new technologies.[20]

The Ottomans were committed to their old ways, but sometimes for good reasons. The state itself was not directly involved in development projects or reclamation. Reclamation of wastelands was indeed encouraged, but primarily for fiscal reasons. In constructing dams, canals, or artificial ponds for irrigation, the Ottoman state took the initiative only in some urgent cases, and private participation in such enterprises was encouraged mainly for the tax revenues to be gained. In contrast, as argued by economic historians, in Europe, the relatively small-sized state structures, fiercely in rivalry against each other, and also population pressure, led Europeans to intensive agriculture and to systematic efforts for mercantile gains from foreign trade as well as to a more intensive use of labor at home.

To sum up, Ottoman society did not create the conditions leading to a "development, from an agrarian base, of an industrial, commercial and maritime superstructure coupled with an attempt to secure a bigger share in the profits of international commerce for [its] own citizens."[21] The Ottoman government's economic measures were not derived from a systematized and coherent theory as in the West, but, as was true in other areas of activity, it simply followed the long-tested practices and traditions inherited from Middle Eastern society and culture.

Nowhere is the contrast more visible than in the Ottoman customs policy, and in the capitulation regime. The Western mercantile system with emphasis on commercial expansion was closely linked to the Levant trade, and Western monarchies followed Italians in this direction, too. In mercantilist Europe, every national monarchy which aspired to expand its economic base endeavored to have first a capitulation from the Ottoman government and set up its own Levant company. The Levant trade and Levant companies became the necessary corollary for the success of European mercantilism.

There is a consensus[22] that, since the early Middle Ages, the deficit in the balance of trade between Europe and the Levant on the one hand and the Levant and the East (India) on the other became a structural pattern, so that there was a continuous flow of silver from west to east. In the period 1450–1550, when the Levant, that is, the eastern Mediterranean, the Balkans and the Black Sea regions, was unified under a centralized empire and the European economy was in a period of expansion, the flow of precious metals intensified – a phenomenon seen as one of the main motives for westerners to go in search of El Dorado.[23] As India and Iran were dependent on the intermediary role of the Ottoman Empire to replenish their stocks of bullion, Europe, in turn, with capitulations and other facilities to trade in the Ottoman Empire, was able to channel its industrial products to Asia.

MARKET AND ECONOMY

As far as the urban market was concerned Ottoman policy was based on a limited production of goods for a limited market, which required state regulation and constant oversight by a market controller, *muhtesib*. This state official had the responsibility to ensure the regulation and inspection of the price and the quality of goods in the market.[24] The production of luxury goods in this system suited the requirements of a limited market, since a small group of elite, who had accumulated cash for conspicuous spending, was interested primarily in the best quality goods.

There appears to be a contradiction between the restrictive controls and the desire for an economy of plenty. The contrast lies in the difference between an economy of protection and command and that of the *laissez-faire* of a bourgeois society which sought plenty not through regulation but in freedom. Actually traditional societies like that of the Ottomans were aware by experience and tradition that insufficient production leads to higher prices for the consumer, and over-production to low prices unfair for the craftsman; hence, regulation was in the interest of both consumer and producer. Expansion was possible only when giant city markets like that of İstanbul emerged. Thus, traditionally and in general, oriental economies were based on long experience of small towns with limited and static markets where citizen and craftsman alike wanted regulation. In the West, and notably first in Italy, the economies developed on the basis of an ever-expanding market.

In the last decades of the fifteenth century guilds in the great city of Bursa, under pressure from popular demand, ignored the regulations and produced cheaper silks for an expanding market of commoners.[25] The state reacted vigorously and established a new regulation defining the quality and amount of silk and dye which could be used in each variety of cloth. The members of the guilds confessed that there was a demand for cheaper varieties and that the government-appointed market inspector had accepted bribes and had not strictly implemented regulations. Here it is important to note that such a market expansion was observed solely in big cities such as Bursa, Edirne and İstanbul, where a large population created a demand for more and cheaper varieties and the expanding market set in motion economic forces which clashed with state regulations. This case illustrates how the Ottoman economy was bound under the strict control of a strong centralist state to follow a typical medieval economy with a fixed market and production levels. This also explains, I believe, the dichotomy between stagnant Ottoman industries and commerce and the dynamic European market economy which first appeared in Italy and the Low Countries and then in other Western countries. Thus, it was European market expansion and competition which stimulated new technologies producing cheaper and better quality goods.[26] These changes secured Western economic supremacy and the decline of Eastern industries. Ottoman woolen and silk industries and mining were severely affected by the growing import of cheaper Western products at the end of the sixteenth century. It should be emphasized that in economic terms it was the price differential or production costs that were at the root of the divergent economic evolution between East and West.

On the other hand, one might argue that, in the last analysis, these changes had been determined by general social and cultural evolution in the West. Fortunately for the East, Western industrial and commercial supremacy was limited to certain economic sectors, such as woolen textiles and metallurgy, until the Industrial Revolution, at which time the East lost all possibilities of competition in the face of cheaper and better quality machine-made goods in all sectors.

NOTES

1 İnalcık (1973a), pp. 65–66.
2 Coleman (1969a), p. 142.
3 Kınalızade (1284 H/1867), II, pp. 2–4, 8–10, 72–74, 110; III, pp. 6–8.
4 *Ibid.*, II, p. 9.
5 Rehman (1974); Ahmad (1980), pp. 3–18, 119–30, 143–70.
6 al-Mubarak cited by A. Zarqa in Ahmad (1980), p. 16.
7 Kuran (1989), p. 171.
8 İnalcık (1969d), p. 98.
9 Ahmad (1980), pp. 119–30.
10 Yediyıldız (1985); Barnes (1986); Akgündüz (1988), pp. 438–43.
11 Faroqhi (1984), index: *vakf*; Barkan (1955), pp. 289–311; Mutafčieva (1981).
12 Dalton (1968), pp. ix–liv; Polanyi *et al.* (1957).
13 Udovitch (1970), pp. 166–248; Lopez and Raymond (1962), pp. 174–84.
14 Ahmad (1980), pp. 59–84; Barkan (1968), pp. 31–46; Mandaville (1979).
15 İnalcık (1991a), pp. 17–40.
16 Heckscher (1935), II, pp. 26–103.
17 İnalcık (1951), p. 652, note 98.
18 İnalcık (1960b), p. 147.
19 Coleman (1969a), pp. 98–99; Viner (1969), pp. 81–92.
20 The contrast between the two systems is already emphasized by A. Smith (1937), pp. 3, 97.
21 Van Klaveren cited by Coleman (1969a), p. 5.
22 Godinho (1969), pp. 305–15; Braudel (1972), I, pp. 463–75.
23 *Ibid.*, 17–48.
24 See Ahmad (1980), pp. 288–89; Ergin (1922), pp. 334–470, 1754–59; Kütükoğlu (1983), pp. 3–34; Yücel (1988), pp. 19–31, Text 1–153; Barkan (1942b), I, pp. 326–40; II, pp. 15–40.
25 Barkan (1942b), II, pp. 28–31.
26 In 1600, it was a revolutionary new strategy for English cloth merchants to manufacture and sell as cheaply as possible. The result was a five-fold expansion in the production of new draperies between 1600 and 1640, see B. Supple cited by Rapp (1975), pp. 512–13; then the inexpensive and imitative English woolens totally replaced Venetian quality goods in the Levant.

B STATE REVENUES AND EXPENDITURES

1

ġ

SOURCES OF REVENUE

SOURCES OF REVENUE

In all of the provinces, including Egypt, the bulk of the state revenues came from the poll-tax and the *mukataas*, constituting almost 90 percent of the total. A *mukataa* means a source of revenue estimated and entered into the registers of the finance department, each as a separate unit. For the most part they were farmed out to private contractors under a specific tax-farm system. Since *mukataas* included a host of revenue sources, a closer examination is necessary to understand what type of revenues were included in this category. An Italian source, actually a copy of an original Ottoman document, provides an early list of the revenues in detail[1] (see Table I:9).

The table clearly demonstrates that in 1475 Ottoman Rumeli was the center of the empire, providing about 81 percent of the total revenue amounting to 1,769,000 gold ducats, excluding the revenues distributed to the benefice holders (*timar* and *hass*). If you add the benefices distributed in Rumeli and Anatolia to the central treasury funds, the total revenue in 1475 is estimated at around 3 million gold ducats.

The poll-tax, the single most important source of state revenue, amounted to 48 percent of the total budget, followed by mines, mints and salt works, representing 28 percent of the total revenue. At this time in Anatolia, the copper mines of Kastamonu (Küre) are noteworthy; they represent over 45 percent of the total revenue from the Asiatic provinces. The principal zones providing large amounts of revenue to the central treasury were: western Anatolia, a major trade zone with Europe via Chios; Karaman, a zone rich in grain production and the manufacture of cotton goods; the Black Sea trade zone with the port cities of Caffa,

Table I:9. Poll-tax and principal *mukataa*s, 1475 (in thousands of gold ducats)

Rumeli		Anadolu	
Poll-tax	850	Tolls and revenue from salt	
Tolls at Gelibolu and İstanbul	50	works, western Anatolia	32
Customs dues, İstanbul	70	Tolls and tithes, Alaiye	
Customs dues, Gelibolu	9	(Canderone)	12
Salt works	92	Old and new Foça (Phocaea) poll-tax and	
Mints (silver coins)	120	alum revenue	20
Mints (gold coins)	3	Tolls (*bac*) and customs dues	
Mines	120	from silk, Bursa	50
Poll-tax and salt works, Enez	11	Revenue of Kastamonu, in	
Salt works, Salonica	2.5	particular copper mines	150
Revenue, Euboea	12.5	Trabzon, Amasra and Samsun,	
Revenue, Morea	31.5	customs dues	10
Revenue, Avlona	1.5	Revenue, Caffa	10
Grain tax	20	Revenue, Karaman	35
Revenue, Sofia	1	Salt works	12
Revenue, Edirne	12		
Gypsies	9		
Bathhouses	8		
Rice cultivation	15		
Total	1,438	Total	331

Source: Babinger (1957), pp. 62–72.

Trabzon, Amasra and Samsun and, lastly, Bursa, the center of the Iranian silk trade.

The principal sources of revenue at Aleppo were from the minting of coin, the sheep market, the slave market and the silk trade. The silk scales tax superseded all other sources of revenue under Selim II. Along with Bursa and İstanbul, Aleppo was one of the main entrepôts for Iranian silk and the most important export items to Europe (see below, p. 244). What comes as a surprise is that cloth imported from Egypt and Gaza was widely traded in Aleppo. Imperial customs and estate books indicate that Egyptian *alaca* and *kutni* fabrics and linens were in great demand all over the empire including İstanbul, Akkerman and Caffa from the fifteenth century onwards. Aleppo must have been a distribution center of such fabrics for Anatolia and the Balkans. The large amount of revenue from the dye-houses is another indication of Aleppo's significance in textile trade and industries. Customs dues from Europeans were comparatively modest in this list. The reason must have been that, except for woolen cloth and minerals, European imports were limited in Aleppo, and they had to import large amounts of silver in order to purchase

Table I:10. Principal revenue estimates (*mukataa*s) in the city of
Damascus (in *para*)

	1529 for one year	1548 for three years	1562 for three years
Mint	60,000	100,000	288,000
Customs	300,000	222,222	285,000
Silk scales tax	–	118,000	–
Dye-houses	20,000	–	–
Slave market tax	–	27,624	30,000
Market due on spices from pilgrim caravans	60,000	–	2,100,000
Sheep market tax	–	213,312	–

Sources: BBA, Tapu 169 (936/1529); MD 4175 (969/1562); Sahillioğlu (1974), p. 278.

Iranian silk; however, c. 1575 European imports appear to have more than doubled.

In the second half of the sixteenth century Aleppo was to become the emporium for Indian goods, such as textiles, spices and dyes, which arrived via the Gulf and Basra. Imports of musk and rhubarb from China and Tibet must have reached Aleppo either by caravans from Iran or Basra. As in all other big cities in the empire, domestic trade and urban consumption constituted the backbone of economic life, as reflected in the very large revenues from the slave tax and the sheep tax, which almost doubled in half a century.

The large amount of activity at the gold, silver and copper mints of Aleppo is another indication of the major economic role of this city as the center of exchange between Asia Minor, the Balkans and the Black Sea on the one hand, and Syria, Egypt, Arabia, India and Iran on the other. European merchants had to deliver to the Aleppo mint 400 *keylçe* of silver annually as a gift (*pişkeş*). This was probably a custom established under the Mamluks. The *para* circulated in Arab lands was the principal silver coin at Aleppo; and the provinces of Egypt and Syria prepared their budgets in *para* (see below, pp. 86, 87).

Another important source of revenue was the manufacture and the trade in soap in Aleppo. (Compare the *mukataa*s in the city of Damascus shown in Table I: 10.) The *mukataa*s in the province of Hungary were quite different in nature (see Table I: 11).

Together with other sources of revenue the *mukataa*s of the province of Hungary in 1560 amounted to about 4.5 million *akça* or 75,000 gold pieces. This figure was one million *akça* more than the revenue of the previous year. Since Hungary's defense absorbed so much money, some

Table I:11. The main *mukataa*s in Hungary: total revenue in 967
(Oct. 30, 1559 to Sept. 21, 1560) (in thousands of *akça*)

Tax		
cizye	1,797	Islamic poll-tax
tapu	167	Fee paid for possession of state-owned lands
berat	296	Fees paid for diplomas of benefices
kilisa	12	Church tax
pencik	43	One-fifth of slaves captured
beytülmal	469	Properties without heir
mabeyn	28 (in 966)	Revenues from vacant *timar*s

Source: Fekete and Káldy-Nagy (1962), p. 770.

years the central treasury had to supplement the Hungarian revenue by subventions (in 1571–72, 15 million *akça*).[2]

MINING AND SALT PRODUCTION

The empire depended on enormous sums of liquid cash for its centralized administrative apparatus, in particular to create, maintain and lead huge armies to distant fields of action as well as to sustain numerous costly garrisons. In Middle Eastern political theory, the power was believed to rest on the ability of the monarch to ensure a large and steady source of revenue. Liquid cash, gold and silver, the only possible means to accumulate sources of revenue at the center, was believed to be the foundation of a centralized power. The paramount concern of the sultan's bureaucracy was how to bring in and to keep as much bullion as possible in the central treasury, hence the imperial fiscalism.

The mines of gold and silver, as well as the transit centers of international trade producing cash through customs, were the first targets of imperial policy. The persistent Ottoman efforts to get control of the rich silver and gold mines of Serbia and Bosnia had started already under Murad I.[3] These mines, vitally important for Hungary and the Italian states (see below, Ch. 11) were one of the main causes of rivalry between these powers and the Ottomans. In establishing the empire, Mehmed the Conqueror needed the cash from these mines and concentrated his efforts during the first years of his reign, from 1454 and 1464, on controlling these regions. Once they were in his possession, he tried to expand production levels of the mines with the assistance of Serbian and Greek financiers. The annual production of gold and silver of the principal

Table I:12. Principal mining areas in the Balkans, 1468–77 (in thousands of *akça* for three years)

mukataa unit		Tax-farmers
Mines in the districts of Vilk and Laz (Serbia)	8,000 (in 1468)	Yani Cantacuzenus of Novobrdo, Yorgi İvrana of Seres, Tomanin Cantacuzenus of Seres and Palologoz of İstanbul
Mines of Kratova and Sidrekapsı	2,250 (in 1471)	Ali son of Abdullah of Kratova, Yuvan son of Koya, Vuk son of Mladin
Newly operated mines in the province of Hersek	159 (in 1477)	

Note: There were other less important mines (gold, silver, copper, lead and iron) in Bosnia, Trepča and Menlik in the same period (see Map 8).
Source: BBA, MM 176.

mines in the Balkans under Mehmed the Conqueror is shown in Tables I:12 and Fig. I:1.

The Ottomans did not make any basic changes in the production methods or technology in the mines which came under their control in Serbia and Bosnia in the period 1435–65. Their regulations on mines were simply a translation of the pre-Ottoman regulations, in which the original German (Saxon) terminology was preserved.[4] Mining technology was originally introduced by Saxon immigrants to the Balkans in the mid-thirteenth century. The Ottomans grafted their *mukataa* system onto the administrative organization of these mines. They made every effort to exploit them to the full in order to meet their growing need for precious metals, iron and lead.

Following the conquest of Bosnia, those mines which had been abandoned by the Bosnian kings were farmed out to tax-farmers from Dubrovnik, on condition that the gold extracted was to be delivered to the Ottoman mint. The Bosnian mines of Fojnica and Kreševo were particularly rich in silver. At Olovo lead was extracted, in the Srebrenića district silver and lead. In several villages in the district of Hersek and Pavlovići, on the right bank of the Drina and on the river Praca iron mines were operated. Čagnice was the most important center for iron production. The most important silver mines lay in the district of Srebrenića and a very active mint was located in the town.

Salt was not only a necessity in a man's diet, but was also widely used in the empire for preserving fish, beef and vegetables. The Ottoman government organized, according to special regulations, the production and distribution of salt in delimited regions. Salt mines and salt beds

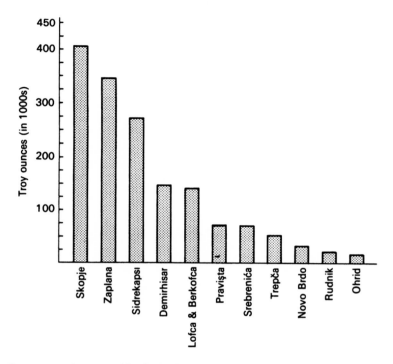

Fig. I:1. Production of leading silver mines in Ottoman Rumelia, c. 1600.
Source: Murphey (1980), p. 79.

were considered state property. However, to ensure the continued supply of this necessary item, the state encouraged private enterprise in the production of salt by recognizing the freehold rights of the privately created salt works. Such enterprises had to deliver, however, the canonical one-fifth of the product to the state.

As was true for most of the state-controlled enterprises, the actual undertaking and management was assumed by private contractors (*amil*) (see pp. 64–66). The entrepreneur was empowered with a special diploma from the office of the sultan, giving him the power to enforce the monopoly. The capital needed for exploitation and management was invested completely by the contractor. In fact, the state closely cooperated with him in finding labor and protecting the monopoly and profits. A salt works operated under a tax-farm arrangement was financially autonomous, having to meet all managerial expenses including wages, staff salaries and repair expenses from its receipts. Because of the insurmountable

8 Principal mining sites in Serbia, Bosnia and Macedonia
Source: Beldiceanu (1964a), p. 310.

difficulties in communication, this type of financial decentralization was followed in all state enterprises.

Under a special regulation, the state assigned the peasant population living within the vicinity of the salt works to various activities associated with the production of salt. The salt works of Ahyolu (Anchialos) on the Black Sea, for example, attracted workers from neighboring areas including Kırkkilise, Rusi-Kasrı, Zagra, Kızanlık and as far away as Filibe (Plovdiv). They acquired a permanent special status as salt workers (*tuzcu*) and enjoyed an exemption from extraordinary levies and services and lower rates for some other state taxes. There were 1,047 peasants registered as salt workers in Ahyolu and 1,546 in Salonica.[5] In some areas, the workers also received a share of the salt produced, ranging from 10 percent to one-third of the total amount. It was an incentive for them to continue working and increase production. Those who fled to escape the heavy work load or low income were forcibly returned. The status of a salt worker was inherited by the sons. Thus, the *tuzcus* shared the same conditions as the peasants registered as miners or rice growers.[6] In salt production areas, production and labor were organized according to a standard regulation applied in such state-run exploitations.

As in rice cultivation or mining, the production units were under the responsibility of the "chiefs" (*reis*), who supervised production and managed the sale of the product to salt traders in the region. Under the supervision of the general tax-farmer, they acted as sub-contractors. There appear to have been local upper-class Muslims or Christians who undertook this business for profit and their title and function was inherited by their sons. In general, the salt produced was sold by the agent of the fisc or tax-farmer. In the years 1492–95 in Ahyolu, each 45 *okka* of salt was sold at 30 *akça*, two *akça* of which belonged to the "salt producers" (chiefs).[7] Since the salt works had to continue their production uninterrupted and the state collected revenues, the population of a salt "region" had to buy a certain amount of salt every three years whether they were in need of it or not. This method was open to various malpractices and caused complaints and resistance on the part of the people. Towns and villages in each delimited "region" assigned to the sale of a particular salt-production site were supplied either by the private salt traders, who had to buy and transport the salt by their own means, or the state organized the transportation and distribution itself. In the latter case, the salt was stored in the state-owned depots in the bazaars of each town and was sold through sub-contractors. Since the salt produced had to be transported to the depots at a reasonable cost, there were special

Table I:13. State revenues from principal salt works in the sixteenth century

Salt works	State revenues (in 1,000 *akça*)
Aydın (1575)	884
Gelibolu (1594)	756
Ağrıboz (1568)	705
Holobnik (Nicopolis) (c. 1580)	630
Menemen (Izmir)	540
İşkodra (Albania, 1580)	531
Vidin (c. 1580)	529
Menteşe (1583)	513
Gümülcine (c. 1570)	450
Adana (Ayas) (c. 1570)	400
Kızılca-Tuzla (Edremid)	383
Ahyolu (c. 1580)	153
Basra	116
Cyprus (1572)	100
Total	6,690

Source: Güçer (1962–63), pp. 130–31.

implications for the transportation of this heavy, cheap commodity. For example, for transport from Kızılca-Tuzla, a salt-production site active since antiquity, the state had organized, under a specific regulation, the "Arab camel drivers" in this region since the fourteenth century. The transport of the annual production of 3,000 tons of salt corresponded to 12,000 camel loads.[8] Granted exemption from extraordinary taxes, Arab camel drivers performed the same transport service in other western Anatolian *sancak*s, including Saruhan, Aydın and Menteşe. In the *sancak* of Aydın, they also carried provisions such as wheat, dried fruits and cotton from the inland areas to the port of İzmir. The government paid a fixed price per camel load, while private interests offered much higher rates for commercial transport. Resistance from the Arabs finally convinced the government to abolish forced service altogether in return for a fixed tax beginning in 1528. In order to realize the profits from the monopoly, the state prohibited, under severe punishment, the consumption of salt imported from other areas. The regulations even authorized the sultan's agent to search private houses for smuggled salt.

The principal supplier of salt for İstanbul was the Crimea. In 1587 the Crimean Khanate exported to İstanbul 41,274 *kile* or 1,000 tons of salt. The responsible Ottoman agent for the transport of this salt was a Greek and most of the shipowners were also Greek captains. The annual net salt revenue for the state treasury amounted to 8.3 million *akça* or about 140,000 gold pieces (see Table I: 13).

By contrast, the rock salt of Wallachia became the object of large-scale trade, provisioning the Balkan cities, including İstanbul. It was also a necessity in stock breeding. Extracted from the salt beds of Telega and Ghitiora near Tirgovište, the salt was brought in carts to certain ports on the Danube. Its sale and distribution were under a state monopoly on both the Wallachian and Ottoman side of the river. Peter the Young (1559–68) is reported to have sold five thousand carts of salt,[9] while in 1583 Voyvode Michnea (1577–83) was to dispatch 2,150 carts to Giurgiu and Nicopolis (one cart carried 1,000 okka or 1,282 kg of salt). Both the Ottoman and Wallachian governments levied customs duties (4 percent at Nicopolis, 5 at Rusçuk) and other dues in cash and in kind on salt at these ports. In addition to the dues, the Ottoman government bought the imported salt at a fixed price (47 akça per hundred pieces at the port of Silistre) and sold it at a higher price, 80 akça.

Ottoman customs agents or tax-farmers advanced large sums of capital mostly in the form of gold to the voyvode of Wallachia to enable him to buy the salt destined for the Ottoman market.[10] Also, private Ottoman investors including leading statesmen and ulema advanced capital to the Wallachian voyvodes for the same purpose. Following the depreciation of the akça in 1584 the rigid Ottoman price policy in purchasing Wallachian salt and Ottoman exploitation of Wallachians through credit dealings were perhaps the real reasons for the subsequent rebellion of the Wallachian Voyvode Michael the Brave, and his attempts to divert the salt trade to other countries. Later, in 1630, the Porte agreed to leave to the new voyvode all of the tax revenue at the Danubian ports in return for an increase of 3 million akça to the Wallachian yearly tribute. Thus, the voyvode took the place of the tax-farmers in collecting duties on Wallachian salt.

TAX COLLECTION IN MUKATAAT (TAX-FARMS)

During an imperial campaign, the chief finance minister in İstanbul had full authority to send orders, to supervise all those involved in collecting taxes including commissioners, tax-farmers and kadis, and to dismiss those failing in their duties. In order to collect the unpaid tax and the arrears owed by tax-farmers or others, a special organization with extensive powers was created. With his sixty men, the chief of the organization, başbakıkulu, had the power to pursue those who failed to pay the tax and, if necessary, to put them in prison on his own responsibility. Under Mehmed II many tax-farmers were imprisoned and some executed for failing to pay their debts. A tax-farmer had to find wealthy sureties when he made a contract with the government. In the contract, he vowed to deliver to the treasury a certain amount of money in regular installments during the time agreed upon, which was usually three years. The tax-farming system[11] was the principal method of revenue collection from the earliest times. The alternative method was to appoint a salaried government commissioner, an *emin*, to do the job of a tax-farmer. Another method to collect taxes was for the sultan to send his servants, *kuls* who were usually members of the cavalry division at the Porte. A tax-farmer or *emin* had extensive powers in collecting revenues and had to make direct regular payments to the local soldiery if so ordered by the sultan. His reports proposing new means to increase revenue from his district were often followed by the central government.

Tax-farmers, *emins* and local kadis were responsible for finding new sources of revenue such as a pre-Ottoman customs duty, mines or any other taxable activity. After the local inquiries had established that the new source was large enough and equitable for the taxpayers, it was registered in the finance books in the central finance department with the estimated amount of revenue as *mukataa*. This process constituted the principal method of creating new sources of revenue for the treasury. The revenue from *mukataas* in the provinces of Rumeli (Balkans), Anadolu (western Asia Minor), Egypt and Damascus amounted to 166.94 million *akça*, or about 30 percent of the total revenue of the central treasury in 1528.

The withdrawal to the ruler's treasury of a huge amount of specie from circulation was always viewed as unjust and unwise in the East.[12] Since the amount of silver and gold in circulation was in limited supply, such a large withdrawal of tax monies caused various disturbances in the market-place and an artificial dearth of money, higher rates of coinage and hardships in payments and transactions. Therefore, flexible financial methods were applied to alleviate the negative consequences. Instead of bringing in all taxes to the central treasury, a decentralized system of collection and payment was followed. Local expenditures, whether for construction work or salaries, were made by a tax-farmer and an *Emin* upon receiving an order of payment sent by the central treasury. The tax-farmers used the payment orders and the delivery documents given by the local kadi to settle their final accounts with the government. This system of transfer[13] saved the finance department from the transport cost of huge amounts of specie and secured quick payments on the spot and a quick return of the specie into the market. By contrast, to carry the treasury in a military campaign required a long train of camels. The transfer method was widely used by the government and the merchants.

The tax-farming system gave rise to a group of financiers and to speculative transactions which had a strong influence on the entire Ottoman economy. The huge tax-farms, such as the customs zone of İstanbul or the silver and gold mines of Serbia, each valued from 10 to 20 million *akça*, called for consortiums of Turkish, Greek or Jewish financiers to manage the tax district, together with wealthy citizens serving as sureties. Italians, either Ottoman subjects or foreign merchants settled in Galata, were also involved in such big tax-farms.[14] The government resorted to the tax-farm or *mukataa* system to levy certain revenues which required rather complicated organizations or were difficult to follow up and collect, such as inheritances without an heir. When sold to private interests such elusive revenues produced maximum yield.

The flexibility of the Ottoman tax-farming system itself facilitated the tax-farmer's task, since he could divide the job on the basis of localities and sell shares to lesser local tax-farmers responsible to himself, who were in a better position to collect such revenues. At the top of the tax-farming hierarchy stood rich bankers in the capital. Wealthy money-changers (*sarrāfs*) played the role of bankers by providing credit to the tax-farmers and becoming sureties for them, thus enabling them to fulfill their contractual obligations to the treasury.

The agrarian taxes to be collected from the lands reserved for the sultan (*havass-i hümayun*), or more exactly for the central treasury, were generally sold as tax-farms to private persons. The viziers and governors for their *hass* benefices and even big *timar*-holders resorted to the same method, or sometimes they employed stewards. Consequently, over half of the public revenues were subject to tax-farming.

THE POLL-TAX

The revenue from the *cizye* or poll-tax in the Hegira year of 894 (December 5, 1488–October 24, 1489) for the entire Ottoman Empire amounted to 30.71 million *akça*.[15] There were 681,452 non-Muslim households subject to the poll-tax in the Balkans. In the "budget" of 1528 the revenue from the poll-tax had increased (Table I:14), and represented about 8 percent of the empire's total revenue. Tribute from Christian vassal states, which were considered as part of the poll-tax and paid in one lump sum, were to be added (see Tables I:15 and I:16).

Table I:14. Revenue from the poll-tax in 1528

	Million *akça*
Rumeli	42.29 (*ispence* included)
Asia Minor and the Crimea	3.76
Total	46.05

Table I:15. Tribute from Christian states

Byzantium	480,000 *akça* or 15,000 gold ducats	vassal, 1371–1453, tributary, 1379–1402
Serbian despotate	50 *vukiyye* of silver, then 40,000 gold ducats raised to 50,000 under Georg Branković	vassal since 1386, occupied in 1439, final annexation 1459
Bosnia		vassal since 1428 conquered 1463
Dubrovnik (Ragusa)	12,500 gold ducats	vassal since 1433
Chios	12,000 gold ducats	vassal since 1413, annexed in 1566
Cyprus (Venice)	8,000 gold ducats	since 1516, annexed in 1570
Venice	10,000 gold ducats	since 1479, not paid after 1481
Holy Roman Empire	30,000 gold ducats	1547 to 1606
Iran	200 bales of raw silk	1618–1624
Muscovy	25,000 roubles	to the Crimean khan
Poland	15,000 gold ducats	to the Crimean khan

Table I:16. Tribute of Wallachia and Moldavia

Wallachia		Moldavia	
Year	Gold ducats	Year	Hungarian florins
1474	10,000		
1535–45	19,298	1538	10,000
1545–60	50,000	1541	15,000
1560–69	48,305	1551	20,000
		1553	30,000
1569–75	99,150	1568	35,000 (in ducats)
		1569	40,000 (in ducats)
1575–84	104,237	1574	50,000

Note: The reasons for increases were: internal struggle for power in the principalities, the periodic augmentation in the rate of poll-tax, increase in the population, and Ottoman financial crises or punishments for insubordination.

1 gold ducat or *sultanin* = 57 *akça* between 1535 and 1560, 59 between 1560 and 1574
1 Hungarian gold piece = 55 *akça* in 1535–60, 57 in 1560–74

Source: Maxim (1972, 1974).

The *cizye* was an Islamic tax paid by non-Muslim subjects which was always collected in cash and placed directly into the central treasury. In the hierarchy of taxes it was the most important "legitimate" (*hak*) tax. Exemption from it or its grant as a benefice was an exception. For a Christian, active military service was one case leading to exemption. In the first centuries, it was collected directly by the sultan's *kuls*, usually by the members of the cavalry division of *sipahi-oğlanları*, who struggled to retain this privilege since they received a fee from tax payers. Farming out the collection of *cizye* to private interests became a common practice from the second half of the sixteenth century.

In classical Islam, jurists set the *cizye* rates at 1, 2 or 4 gold *dinar*s or 12, 24, or 48 *dirhem* of pure silver for the poor, middle class and the wealthy respectively. But the Ottomans adjusted these rates to pre-Ottoman poll-tax levels extant in the conquered countries and levied one fixed rate per household, usually one gold piece or its equivalent in silver coins. This tax was actually less than the equivalent of one gold piece in many areas, 30 *akça* in the island of Thassos and 55 in the province of Bitlis but 80 *akça* in Syria and Palestine (one gold piece equalled 60–70 *akça* in the period 1520–70). In Hungary it was 50 *akça*, but a lower rate of 5 to 25 was applied for the poor in the period around 1560.[16] Considering the liberal policy being pursued with the lower rates, an addition of 10 *akça* was declared at the accession of Selim II in 1566. There were substantial increases each time a new sultan acceded to the throne and in the period of the *akça*'s devaluation during the long campaigns of the last two decades of the sixteenth century.

In order to avoid disputes resulting from the several types of silver coins in circulation, the government declared that it would accept only gold pieces as payment for *cizye*. This created another hardship, particularly for the peasants. Fees for the expenses of the collectors and for registration services amounted to 1/25 of the poll-tax itself. But the imposition of additional exactions was routine.[17] In many instances, particularly with non-Muslim communities in towns or on islands, agreements were made with the finance department to pay the poll-tax in a predetermined lump sum (*maktu*) for the whole community. Collecting it among themselves, usually through the local priest, they were spared from the exactions of the Ottoman officials. Although this method guaranteed a stable revenue source for the government, the poll-tax on newcomers was lost.[18]

A particularly onerous condition for the Christian peasantry in the Balkans came about from the Ottoman practice of imposing collective responsibility on village communities for the poll-tax of fugitives and the dead. Under Mehmed II the *timar*-holder and the villagers were each required to pay half of the poll-tax for fugitives.[19] It later became the sole responsibility of the community. This practice sometimes caused the depopulation and ruin of an entire village. To remedy this situation adjustments were made every three years by counting and registering all adult subjects required to pay this tax and removing the names of the dead and fugitives from the register. The government tried to collect the poll-tax from fugitives by using private tax-farmers who actively pursued them.

It can safely be said that increases and exactions of the poll-tax were fundamental reasons for the alienation of the Christian population from the Ottoman regime from the end of the sixteenth century on. The poll-tax was also responsible for mass conversions in various parts of the Balkans in later centuries.

In connection with the Islamic poll-tax we have also to speak of a customary poll-tax originally of pre-Ottoman origin called *ispence* (from *jupaniča*) in the Balkans or gate-tax (*kapu-resmi*) in Hungary. It was levied at the rate of 25 *akça* without change over the centuries. As a "customary" feudal tax in its origin it was, as a rule, included in the *sipahi*'s *timar* and always levied in cash. The Ottomans introduced this tax in eastern Anatolia in 1540. In the imperial *hass* lands, *ispence* was levied together with the poll-tax for the treasury.

Apparently evasion from the poll-tax must also have been quite widespread. In Hungary the total *cizye* revenue was 1,530,000 *akça* in the Hegira year of 966 (October 14, 1558–October 2, 1559), while in the following year it was 1,797,000 *akça*.[20] It has been suggested that the Ottomans levied the poll-tax at a rate much lower than that stipulated by Islamic Law because many taxpayers were already required to perform extraordinary services. But when pressed by a chronic financial crisis, the government invoked the Sharia to legitimize a rate increase in the tax. The rates for all taxes levied in cash went up further with the addition of fees for collectors and scribes and because gold and big silver pieces were accepted at a rate lower than their actual ratio to the *akça* in the market (generally 2 *akça* less). This measure was introduced probably because of the constant inflation in the *akça*[21] (Table I:17).

PEASANT TAXATION

Taxation had, particularly in the Asiatic empires, a decisive impact on the economy and was the basis of status in rural society (see below,

Table I:17. Increases in the rates of poll-tax
and *avarız* (oarsman tax) (in *akça*)

	Poll tax	*Avarız*
1475	70	
1489	40–70 (Rumeli in general)	
	25 (special groups)	
	25–28 (Albania)	
c. 1500	25–28 (Anadolu)	
1512		12
1537	–	65
1541	50 per household (Hungary)	30
1545	48 (Adana)	
1564	–	80
1566	30 (in general)	
1574	40 (in general)	
	66 (Hungary)	
1592	85 (in general)	160
1593	–	250
1595	140 (in general)	
1603–4	140 (in general)	360

Note: In order to balance the state budget the government
added 45 *akça* to the poll-tax of non-Muslim subjects in
1585.
Source: Akdağ (1949), pp. xv, 553–62; Barkan (1964).

pp. 149–53). It is interesting to note that labor services or their cash
equivalent were interpreted in the sultanic law codes as being derived
from the "slave" (*kul*) or "dependent subject" status of the peasants, or
reaya. As the Islamic Law does not recognize such a principle in terms
of taxation, such taxes were categorized as "customary" or more exactly
"sultanic" or "state" (*urfi*) taxes,[22] as distinguished from the Islamic taxes
which are called "rightful taxes" (*hukuk*). Sultanic or "customary" taxes,
also designated as "dues" (*rüsum*) included occasional dues such as fines,
wedding dues, or fees paid for legal transactions.

Originally, customary-state taxes were those taxes which the conquered people used to pay under the pre-Ottoman regimes. By making
inquiries and using pre-Ottoman laws and registers the Ottomans were
particularly concerned about maintaining all such taxes except for those
which were openly contrary to the Ottoman regime. As was the case in
the *çift-resmi* system (see below, pp. 149–53), many of these taxes were
cash equivalents for feudal labor services owed to the local lord.[23] Thus,
many pre-Ottoman, Byzantine or Balkan taxes, labor services or customary dues were incorporated into the Ottoman tax system in the name of
customary-state dues under the name of *rüsum-i urfiyye* or *tekalif-i
urfiyye*. As far as such taxes were concerned, the general Ottoman policy

was to convert labor services or customary fees due to local lords or officials into state taxes in cash – a necessary policy for a centralized empire replacing feudal local lords in the Balkans. However, it is important to keep in mind that, because of the underdeveloped economy, some labor services had to be preserved, particularly such services as building a house for the *sipahi*, to carry the *sipahi*'s tithes to his barn or nearest market-place, to mow and store the *sipahi*'s hay, to provide straw and firewood and to work on the land assigned to the direct use of the *sipahi*. All such services actually inherited from the pre-Ottoman feudal practices were to continue under the Ottoman regime as necessary corvées to relieve the military from non-military occupations.

These services altogether were called *kulluk*, that is dues owed by the *kul*, "servile class," or more exactly a "dependent peasant," since the Ottoman peasant *reaya* were not considered enslaved. Nevertheless, the fact remains that under the Ottoman *timar* regime, in which *sipahi*s lived in the village and actually controlled the land and taxation, the basic characteristics of a feudal society persisted. The important difference from a Western type of feudalism was that the state abolished all personal dependencies between the peasant and the local military, and land titles, taxation and relations between the *sipahi*s and peasants were strictly regulated by the sultan's laws under the tight control of a centralist bureaucracy (see pp. 108–18). On the other hand, before the Ottomans, under the weakened states in Byzantium and the Balkans, central bureaucracies attempted to fight against the feudalization process except in the regions where the Latins dominated.[24] At any rate, it was because of its customary local origin that the state reserved most of these taxes for the *timar*-holders. Naturally, tithes, which as a rule were collected in kind and constituted at least half of the rural tax revenues, were also included in *timar*s. *Timar*-holders, particularly when grain prices were low, preferred to collect tithes in cash, mainly because they needed as much money as possible during the campaign season when they were away from home. In general, approximately half the *timar* revenues were paid in cash, and the other half in kind. So, a peasant had to convert his surplus produce into cash by taking it to the towns and the rural periodic markets, which assumed a crucial importance in the rural economy.[25] In this regard, small village money-lenders also played an important role.[26] Of course, where it was possible to grow grapes or cash crops, there was more opportunity to gain cash. During the period 1520–80, there was a considerable increase in the number of local markets and their development into important centers in some regions in Anatolia. This development must have been in direct relationship to the general demographic and economic development observable in the imperial survey books. But even during this period, as the local kadi court records show,[27] *sipahi*s and peasants were in constant conflict over taxes and the mode of their collection as well as over matters concerning land titles and transfers. It appears that *sipahi*s were constantly trying to gain more labor services for their farms, pastures or vineyards, and to use the peasants' draft animals for cartage. They also transferred land titles illegally in order to receive extra fees, whereupon the peasants used every trick available to pay less and work less for the *sipahi*. To alleviate the conflict, most of the sultanic law codes were designed to specify the mutual obligations and the local kadi courts performed an important role in enforcing the regulations.[28] During the great crisis of the 1590s in Anatolia this entire mechanism collapsed.[29]

Instead of outright abuse of the tax system, the *sipahi*s used such legitimizing devices as referring to extra taxes as pre-conquest customary dues. In many cases, the administration discovered that such customary dues were abolished under the Ottoman regime or were replaced by new Ottoman taxes. But after a certain time the *sipahi*s revived the old dues and thus were able to impose double taxation. Double taxation also occurred when a new *timar*-holder demanded the taxes and labor services already rendered to the outgoing *timar*-holder. To prevent such abuses, subsequent regulations specified the exact time of the collection of a particular tax. Already in the fifteenth century, in popular works,[30] sharp criticisms were leveled at the state's extraordinary levies and corveés, and the rapacity of the financial administration. Take the following example. "They collect money from people to make state construction works, but they cut the wages of the workers and masons who were forcibly mobilized or forced them to work without pay. This is natural, since the sultan's finances are now under the control of unscrupulous merchant usurers" (here "merchant usurers" are tax-farmers).

TIMAR PREBENDS

Along with the central bureaucracy's interest in acquiring *mukataa* revenues from foreign conquests, there was pressure from the lower ranks of the soldiery to gain *timar* benefices in the conquered lands. This pressure also became a powerful factor in maintaining the conquest policy and can be considered as a part of the Ottoman fiscalism. The pressure was indeed very strong, since it was not only volunteers and raiders on the frontiers who expected *timar*s in the conquered lands, but also, more importantly, Janissaries and other *kul*s of the sultan, as well as the military elite, were impatiently waiting the moment of "going out" of the imperial household and establishing an independent life and family as *timar*-holders in the countryside.[31] The study of the *timar* registers shows[32] that a high percentage of *timar* recipients were of *kul* origin, that is, retainer "slaves" or *kul*s sharing the privileges of their patrimonial military masters. The other groups entitled to *timar*s were members of the pre-Ottoman military class and volunteers. As a reward for valor in a campaign, loyalty or long service, they were given certificates for a *timar* of a certain size; but the actual receipt of a *timar* depended on availability in the provinces (see below, pp. 113–17). Actually, it was a relief for the state to be able to create extra *timar*s in the conquered lands, in Hungary, for example, for the Bosnian *sipahi*s, and in the lands of Zülkadriye and Syria for the *sipahi*s from Karaman. Thus, expansion through conquest provided new sources of revenue in the form of *timar*s and therefore became a catalyst for expansionism. It is said that this policy illustrates, in the final analysis, the military expansionist or so-called "feudal" character of the Ottoman state, which was seeking to find new resources in the form of taxes and tributes through conquest rather than through economic means.

As for the methods of remuneration, *timar* assignment and tax-exemption methods spared the state the expense and delay involved in collecting the revenues and then making payments from a central treasury. Certain distant provinces, such as Egypt, Baghdad and Yemen, were financially autonomous in collecting and spending the provincial revenue and sent a pre-determined surplus to the central treasury (see pp. 83–87). In contrast to the European monarchies, the Ottoman Empire followed essentially a decentralized system in its finances, a situation basically determined by its vast territory and its less advanced monetary economy. During the seventeenth century, a major part of the *timar* revenues in the hands of *timar*-holders were entered in the central treasury as "substitute money" (*bedel*) for exemption from active military service, since the provincial cavalry had become obsolete by that time. In 1699, such revenues amounted to about 15 million *akça* from the four provinces of Erzurum, Maraş, Damascus and Aleppo. Another way to bring the *timar* revenues into the central treasury was to convert them into imperial demesne (*hass*) and to farm them out. On the other hand, in the frontier areas, notably in Bosnia, a different development for big *timar*s and *ziamet*s took place. They were consolidated as hereditary prebends in the possession of local families, *kapitanes*, which gave rise in later centuries to a powerful class of magnates.[33] The Porte yielded to the pressure of these families mainly because Bosnia was on the main defense line of the empire against the Habsburgs.

The *timar*-holders at every level, including the simple *sipahi*, employed agents or surrogates called *kethüda*, *vekil* or *voyvoda* to collect revenues and exercise the delegated powers. Complaints were frequent against the malpractices of these agents. The central government always sought to respond to the malpractices of *timar*-holders or their agents concerning the land and labor of the peasant *reaya* (see below, pp. 171–3).

SALE OF OFFICES, *PIŞKEŞ* AND BRIBERY

In his *Relazione* dated 1596, Venetian Bailo Malipiero[34] concurs with the Ottoman memorialists that high offices were obtained only through huge sums of bribe money – for the grand vizierate 80,000, for the finance ministry 40–50,000 gold pieces. Once in office they redeemed these bribes by taking bribes for other major appointments so that all officials were involved in bribery.[35] This practice became so routine that Evliya[36] candidly gives two amounts for the income of a judge, one with the bribe and the second without. At the bottom of the system those officials in direct contact with the taxpayers used all kinds of devices to extort extra money in the name of a service fee or gift. Besides, it was the legally approved right of an official to receive a small fee for the service he performed for the people – poll-tax collectors and even judges took such fees. Others expected it in the form of a gift or baksheesh. To prevent the abuse, regulations specified the rates for such personal fees or sometimes converted them into public revenue and prohibited personal fees.

As was the case with monarchies in the West, bribery and the sale of offices became part of public administration and a source of public revenue. In the Ottoman Empire, the sale of offices became a widespread practice in the seventeenth century and were given to those who bid the highest amount. Thus, sale of office was considered a kind of tax-farm, which included, over time, governorships and even *timar* benefices. The mentality behind all these dealings was shaped by the patrimonial character of the authority. Authority was considered as a property of the ruler and public service as a privilege. Those who had authority, including a ruler or his delegates, regarded the office as a source of material gain and therefore negotiable for compensation (see above, pp. 47–48). With the

Ottoman state this principle existed from the beginning, when personal service fees were recognized as a legal right. Bribery was considered a crime when the monarch's direct interests were in jeopardy. Since it was hard to make a distinction, the officials involved felt free to exchange favors for profit in any situation with the belief that in the last analysis it was good for the ruler's treasury. Also, *pişkeş*, "an offering made by an inferior as a mark of respect and dependence" was widely practiced in the Ottoman Empire.[37] Every dignitary, including governors, viziers and patriarchs of Christian communities, had to offer to the sultan a *pişkeş*, the amount of which was fixed by regulation. For example, the governor of Rumeli gave 10 thousand *akça*, a Greek Orthodox Patriarch 20,000 *guruş* (mid-seventeenth century) at the time of receiving the imperial diploma which legally validated their authority in the office. Officials of lesser grades paid a fixed amount of money called the diploma (*berat*) fee, which altogether amounted to quite a large sum for the treasury. The sultan reciprocated the *pişkeş* from high office holders by giving a caftan, a horse richly harnessed, a fur coat or a sword, which symbolized the authority delegated and a compensation for their *pişkeş* expenditure. Originally, the exchange of presents, a custom going back to ancient Iran, established the bond of dependency between lord and retainer or vassal. In the later Ottoman Empire, *pişkeş* became a kind of auction and source of revenue for the public treasury.

NOTES

1 Babinger (1957); Majer (1982).
2 Fekete and Káldy-Nagy (1962), p. 772 note 68.
3 Neschri (1987), p. 212, "fifty thousand *vukiyye* of silver given as tribute" (in İdris, only "50 *vukiyye*").
4 Anhegger and İnalcık (1956), nos. 28–35; Beldiceanu (1964), pp. 53–66, 279–307; Murphey (1980), pp. 75–104.
5 Güçer (1964), p. 103.
6 İnalcık (1982b), pp. 59–141.
7 Güçer (1964), p. 137.
8 İnalcık (1983d), pp. 256–63.
9 Maxim (1988), p. 117; Bulgaru (1987).
10 The tax-farmer of Vidin lent 20,000 gold pieces to the voyvode, Peter the Young, see Maxim (1988), p. 115.
11 On *mukataa*, see İnalcık (1969e), pp. 283–85.
12 İnalcık (1951), p. 652 note 98.
13 İnalcık (1969e), pp. 283–85.
14 İnalcık (1967), pp. 153–57.

15 Barkan (1964), *Ek cedvel*; İnalcık (1963a), pp. 563–66; Barkan's calculation includes revenue from *ispence* or *jupanića*, a pre-Ottoman head-tax in Serbia, see Bojanić-Lukač (1976), pp. 9–30.
16 Fekete and Káldy-Nagy (1962), p. 704 note 51.
17 İnalcık (1969b), pp. 283–85.
18 Goffman (1982).
19 Anhegger and İnalcık (1956), no. 34.
20 Fekete and Káldy-Nagy (1962), p. 765.
21 Akdağ (1949), p. 558.
22 İnalcık (1969c), pp. 105–38.
23 İnalcık (1959a), pp. 575–87.
24 Ostrogorsky (1954); Jacoby (1971); Topping (1949).
25 Faroqhi (1979a), pp. 32–80; Asdrachas (1970), pp. 36–69.
26 İnalcık (1993), pp. 161–76.
27 *Ibid.*
28 İnalcık (1975c), pp. 556–62; İnalcık (1975c), pp. 562–66.
29 Akdağ (1963), pp. 171–257; Griswold (1981), pp. 238–39; İnalcık (1975b), pp. 562–66.
30 Giese (1922), p. 25.
31 İnalcık (1973a), pp. 76–88.
32 İnalcık (1954b), index: *gulam*; İnalcık (1954c), pp. 120–22.
33 Filipović (1953–54), pp. 154–58.
34 Cited by Steensgaard (1972), p. 178; on bribery, see Yücel (1988), index: *rüşvet*; Koçi Bey (1939), p. 59; İnalcık (1992c).
35 Naima (1281 H/1864), VI, p. 26.
36 Evliya Çelebi (1896), II, p. 82.
37 İnalcık (1982c), pp. 447–48.

2

THE STATE TREASURY AND BUDGETS

THE CENTRAL IMPERIAL BUDGET

In classical Islam, it was believed that one-third of a peasant's income was the maximum amount which could be collected as tax for the public treasury, one-third was for the maintenance of the tillage and one-third was for the nourishment of his family and himself.[1] A number of the Ottoman balance sheets of state revenues and expenditures are available, the earliest dating back to 1475[2] (see Table I:9). The real purpose of these balance-sheets was to determine whether a surplus was realized. If so, it was deposited in the inner treasury. In fact, Ottoman and pre-Ottoman Middle Eastern states had two treasuries, the reserve treasury preserved in the inner palace under the direct control of the ruler and the current treasury located at the government offices under the joint control of the grand vizier and finance minister (*defterdar*). There were separate balance-sheets for certain provinces to determine whether or not they provided a surplus for the ruler's treasury. The fundamental concern of an oriental ruler was a full treasury under his control as a source of support for his power and authority. For a healthy "budget" Ottoman statesmen expected a surplus after expenditures so that those receiving a salary from the sultan's treasury would not have any concerns about their income.[3]

Any budget surplus, extraordinary revenues such as the sultan's share of booty, confiscated estates, and gifts were preserved in the palace treasury. Consequently it contained not only cash but also jewelry, precious textiles and items such as dresses, silver and gold cups and containers.[4] The inner or palace treasury functioned as a reserve bank for the main current treasury. Loans were made from the former with the sultan's

Table I:18. The revenue of the Ottoman state as estimated by
Europeans, 1433–1603 (in million gold ducats)

Date	Revenue	Expenditure
1433 (Bertrandon de La Broquière)	2.50	
1465 (Chalcocondyles)	8.00 (probably includes the *timar* revenues, too)	
1496 (Alvise Sagudino)	3.30	
1503 (Andrea Gritti)	5.00	
c. 1510 (Spandugino)	3.60	
1512–20 (Mocenigo)	3.13	
1522 (Minio)	3.00	
1524 (Zeno)	4.50	3.00
1526 (Bragadin)	12.00 (central treasury 4.5)	
1527 (Minio)	7.00	
1530 (Zeno)	6.00	4.00
1534 (Ramberti)	15.00 (10m of which in *timars*)	
1553 (Navagero)	7.16	
1554 (Trevisano)	8.19	
1557 (Erizzo)	4.60	
1558 (Barbarigo)	7.74	3.60
1560 (Postel)	12.00 (8 million of which in *timars*)	
1561 (Donini)	4.13	4.10
1584–87 (Bernardo)	9.00	
1592	10.00	
1603 (Knolles)	8.00	

Source: Lybyer (1919), p. 180.

approval in times of shortage to the grand vizier, who gave a written
pledge under his signature as a guarantee for repayment.

The budget can be taken as quite a reliable index for the general condition of the economy. The total revenue of the Ottoman state is estimated
at around 3 million gold ducats by Venetian observers (see Table I:18)
between 1433 and 1522, obviously leaving out the *timar* revenues. Andrea
Gritti's estimate (1503) of 5 million gold ducats must include the latter.
After the eastern Asia Minor and the Arab lands were annexed under
Selim I, the central treasury appears to have risen to about 4.5 million
gold ducats and to 7 or 8 million in the period 1527–1603. Although
Venetians had access to authentic Ottoman sources, wild discrepancies
nevertheless exist in their estimates. The very high estimates for the reign
of Süleyman I of 12 or 15 million gold ducats must definitely include the
timar revenues in addition to the sums in the central treasury. Some of
these observers, Zeno (1524 and 1530), Barbarigo (1558) and Donini
(1561), give also the amount of the total expenditures, which indicate a
favorable balance-sheet for the Ottoman budget in the period 1524–61.

The earliest official Ottoman balance-sheet available goes back to the
year 1527–8, more exactly March 21, 1527 to March 20, 1528 (see Tables

I:19 and 20). Five million gold ducats for the central treasury and 3.6 million for *timar*s in this official source approximate the figures given by the Venetians who served in İstanbul as *bailos* (ambassadors), the closest figure being that given by Trevisano (1554). The revenues of the pious foundations (*vakf*), and of the freehold land properties (*mülk*), which originally belonged to the state, could not be included in the current state budget, but on the other hand various public services such as the construction and maintenance of bridges, hospices, market-places, caravanserais and hospitals were, on a regular basis, funded by the pious foundations. As for the state lands, which were turned into freehold properties, these were mostly required, under the dual ownership system (see below, pp. 126–30), to furnish soldiers to the sultan's army.

Lybyer,[5] who estimated that there were 8 million gold pieces in the current treasury in 1566 and calculated it to be worth less than 70 million American dollars in 1913, declared it "no large sum for so great an empire." Even if we add to it *timar* and *vakf* revenues, which he says probably amounted to about twice as much, the Ottoman state revenues look quite modest. For the sake of comparison, Table I:21 gives a list of the budgets of some European states during this period.

Comparing the regions (see Table I:22), we find that the highest revenue of 198 million *akça* came from the province of Rumeli, which comprised the Balkan lands south of the Danube and Sava rivers excluding Dalmatia, some ports in Greece, but including some northern Black Sea areas in the Crimea. The revenue of Egypt and Syria calculated together at 187 million *akça* comes out a close second to Rumeli, and Asia Minor, with 152 million, ranked third.

While the Arab lands yielded about two-thirds surplus, the coreland of the empire had a deficit of about 10 percent (see Table I:23).

THE PIOUS FOUNDATIONS (*VAKFS*)

Certain construction works were undertaken directly by the state. A vast network for public construction and repair work was organized under the chief architect. In each provincial capital there was a state architect who was empowered, when needed, to mobilize the local masters and work force to build or repair fortresses, bridges, mosques and other public buildings. However, commercial facilities – bazaars, shops, bathhouses and *bedestans* – were built in the cities under the *vakf* system as a source of income to support the religious and charitable complexes. As a rule, all public construction works were supervised by a special agent called *emin*. With alloted

Table I:19. The Ottoman central "budget" of 1527–28: revenues of the fiscal year of 933–34 March 21, 1527 to March 20, 1528 (in thousands of *akça*; one gold ducat = 55 *akça* at this time)

	Poll-tax	*mukataat*	*berat & tezkire*	*beytülmal*	*mabeyn*	Miscellanea	Total
Rumeli[1]	42,291	45,920	1,797	2,939	1,116	0,718	94,781
Anadolu, Karaman,[2]							
Rum and Zülkadriye	3,764	25,603	0.100 (tezkire)	0.447	0.811	3,296	34,021
		2,507 (Kastamonu copper mines)					
Damascus	440	10,485					10,925
Aleppo							13,808
Diyarbekir							7,169

[1] The Balkan peninsula south to the rivers of the Danube and Sava leaving out Dalmatia.

[2] These provinces comprised Asia Minor to the west of a line from Georgia to the bay of Antalya.

Note: The total revenue from these five zones is 160,704,000 *akça*. Egypt has a different structure. Since the imperial revenues from Egypt in terms of *akça* amounted to 116,538,994 *akça*, the total annual revenue accumulated in the central treasury in Istanbul was 277 million *akça* or 5 million gold ducats. The revenue distributed as benefices are not included in this sum. When such revenues, amounting to 200 million, are added the total revenue amounted to 477 million *akça*. The revenues of the *vakfs* and those originally state lands whose revenue went to private persons is calculated by Barkan ([1946–50], XV, p. 277) as 60 million *akça*. In sum, the total state revenues reached 537 million *akça* or 9.7 million gold ducats.

Source: Barkan (1953–54), pp. 249–329, with some alteration.

Table I:20. Total revenue of the empire, 1527–28

Revenue from	in millions of *akça*	in millions of gold ducats
Home provinces, Syria and Egypt, including the imperial *hass*	277	5
timars and *hass* distributed	200	3.7
vakfs and freehold properties	60	1
Total	537	9.7

Source: Barkan (1953–54).

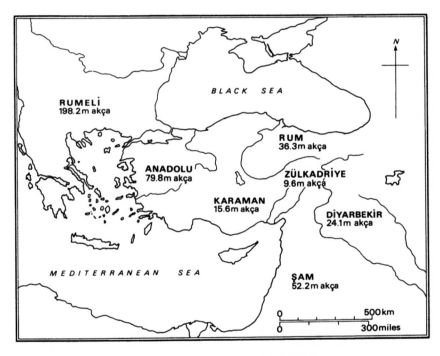

9 State revenues in the early years of Kanuni Süleyman
Source: Faroqhi (1984), p. 290.

funds he was responsible for the organization, supervision and financial administration of the undertaking and at the completion of the work he submitted a full report along with accounts to the finance department. Having a religious connotation, the water systems, with the construction of aqueducts and conduits, were given particular attention. For the repair work of the waterlines, a special agency called *su-yolcuları* was organized,

Table I:21. Estimated annual revenues of European states (in thousand gold ducats)

Italian states, 1492		Other European states, c.1600	
Naples	1,600[2]	Spain (Castile)	9,000
Venice	1,000	France	5,000
Milan	600	Venice	3,900[1]
Florence	300		
Papal state	200		
Genoa	100		
Iran	3,000	(Source: Alessandri [1873], pp. 219–26)	
Byzantium	7,000–8,000 (early middle ages) 1,000 (early fourteenth century)	(Stein [1924], p. 142)	

[1] Venice's annual revenue from its colonies in the Levant amounted to 180 thousand ducats (Pullan [1968], p. 79).
[2] Delaborde (1888), p. 328.
Source: Gregorovius (1891), VII, p. 342; Braudel (1972), I, p. 451.

Table I:22. Total revenues of the Ottoman Empire by province, 1527–28 (in million akça)

Province	Imperial hass	Other hass revenues and timars	Religious endowment and freehold lands	Total
Rumeli (the Balkans)	94.74	92.53	10.88	198.20
Anadolu, Karaman, Zülkadriye and Rum (Asia Minor)	34.01	73.52	22.08	129.62
Diyarbekir (eastern Asia Minor)	7.16	14.29	1.31	22.77
Aleppo and Damascus	24.73	19.83	7.28	51.85
Egypt	116.53		18.92(?)	135.46
Total				537.90

Source: Barkan (1953–54), XV, p. 277.

which was apparently inherited from the Roman–Byzantine tradition. A group of these experts, mostly Greeks, were sent to Mecca and Jerusalem to build the city water system and water conduits. It appears, however, that construction of public facilities such as market-places were undertaken by the state only when it was deemed absolutely necessary for the general improvement, and when they ultimately served the financial interests of

Table I:23. Balance of revenue and expenditure by region, 1527–28 (in million *akça*)

Province	Revenue	Expenditure	Balance
Rumeli, Anadolu, Karaman, Zülkadriye and Rum	294.85	322.13	−27.28
Egypt, Damascus and Aleppo	161.11	61.14	+99.97
Diyarbekir	21.46	20.10	+ 1.36

Note: For comparison of these figures with those from other sources see Barkan (1953–4), pp. 273–76.
Source: Barkan (1953–4), p. 272.

the state. When peasants applied for the construction of dams to regulate the use of lake water in the Konya region, the government told them it was their business, not the state's. In general, many works of public benefit were left to the care of the private endowments as part of the religious charities. The extensive public works to rebuild İstanbul after the conquest by Mehmed II seems to be an exception.[6]

In the province of Anatolia, for instance, out of a total revenue of 79.78 million *akça*, 13.64 million or 17 percent came from pious endowments and freehold arable land owned by private persons.[7] Almost all of this revenue consisted of the same kind of "taxes" as in the state-owned lands. The endowments and landowners simply collected these taxes as rent without being involved directly in the production. All the expenses, including the salaries of the staff and repairs of the following charitable institutions in Anatolia, were met through the endowment funds:

344 large mosques
1,055 small mosques
110 religious seminaries
154 schools for children
626 large and small dervish lodges
45 soup kitchens for travellers and the poor
75 caravanserais

The funds came from the rent of 75 caravanserais, 238 bathhouses and hundreds of other profit generating establishments as well as from endowed villages. There were 3,756 salaried persons in the mosques and 121 professors at the seminaries.

PROVINCIAL BUDGETS

Most of the provinces annexed to the core territories of the empire had an autonomous fiscal organization under the administration of a finance director (*defterdar*) and the general responsibility of a governor-general (*beglerbegi*).

The core territories consisted of the provinces of Anatolia, Rumeli and Rum, roughly the area from the Danube to the Euphrates. The Arab lands, Cyprus and Hungary, annexed in the sixteenth century, had their own provincial budgets. In the latter category all of the expenditures of the province were met by local revenues and the surplus, if any, was sent to the imperial treasury at İstanbul. If there were a deficit the imperial treasury had to match it. The central finance department, however, had, through the provincial *defterdar*, a constant control over the finances of such provinces and received a balance-sheet, often with detailed accounts, at the end of each fiscal year.

This type of financial autonomy gave more independence to the governor-general in Egypt, Yemen or Budin than in other provinces, so that he could face emergency situations at these far-away frontier regions without having to await the decision of the central government. These particular governors, who enjoyed the ministerial rank of vizier already in the sixteenth century, were given supremacy and authority over the neighboring *beglerbegis* in times of crisis. Governors of Egypt were responsible for affairs in the provinces of Yemen and Habesh (northern Abyssinia), and the governors of Baghdad for Basra, the Gulf and the eastern part of the Arab peninsula. The governor of the Aegean Islands held the rank of grand admiral of the navy and the North African provinces of Tunis, Algeria and Tripolitana were under his jurisdiction. However, the fact that the government had constant supervision, through the provincial finance director and kadi, over financial activities, and that the governor-general could at any moment be dismissed from office, does not allow us to speak here of a real autonomy. By contrast, the voyvodes of Wallachia (Eflak), Moldavia (Boğdan) and the republic of Dubrovnik enjoyed complete autonomy in their internal affairs, being obliged only to send an annual tribute at a fixed amount to the sultan. But here too, the sultan could dismiss the voyvode when he failed to send the tribute in time or caused unrest among his subjects by resorting to oppressive methods in collecting the tribute money. In sum, as far as the Ottoman provincial administration was concerned, one may speak of a relative provincial autonomy or of increasing decentralization from the center to the periphery.

Now, let us start to examine some of the budgets of the autonomous provinces with Yemen (for political conditions see below, pp. 331–35). In the Hegira year of 1008, between July 24, 1599 and June 12, 1600, the total revenue of Yemen amounted to about 400 thousand gold pieces and expenditures to about 561,353, with a deficit of 161,353 gold pieces.[8]

The principal sources of revenue were classified as the land tax (*haraç*), making up 49 percent of the total revenue, tax-farms on livestock, bazaar dues, etc., producing 5 percent, and the dues at the ports, about 29 percent.

In Yemen, the exceptionally high percentage of customs dues and other port dues came from the Indian transit trade, although the land tax was the highest, almost half of the total revenue, which was normal for Yemen and the whole empire. The highest figure in the category of miscellania belonged to the profit from the exchange of gold coins for the debased silver coins and the intestate properties.

As was true for the several provincial budgets of the empire, in Yemen too, the greater part of the revenue income went to pay the salaries of the soldiery, a sum of over 15 million *para* or 67 percent of the whole expenditure of the province in 1599. About two million of this amount went to the salaries of the garrison troops placed in thirty-eight fortresses.

The governor's annual salary was fixed at 1,100,000 *akça* (but actually he took about 900,000 *akça* in 1599). A governor's income was extremely high everywhere in the empire, since governors had to maintain quite a large military contingent as part of their household so that they could bolster their authority and respond to emergencies.

In Yemen, the price of the robes of honor given to the native notables or captains navigating in the Indian Ocean amounted to quite a substantial sum – about 1.5 million *akça*. In this troubled frontier province, the annual balance showed a deficit of 6.59 million *para* or 161,000 Ottoman gold pieces in 1600, and the deficit was made up by a transfer of funds from the treasury of Egypt.

Syrian provinces also had autonomous budgets, sending substantial surpluses to the central treasury in İstanbul (see Table I:24). The steady fall in revenue from Syria may indicate a serious economic decline; however, further study is needed to see whether the decrease originates from an increase of local expenditure so that the surplus sent to İstanbul became less. In 1525, out of the 12.6 million *akça* of revenue for the entire province of Damascus, 3.4 million came from the city of Damascus alone. From the sale of potash the treasury obtained 666,666 *para* annually in 1548.

Table I:24. Annual surplus of the revenues of
the provinces of Aleppo and Damascus sent to
İstanbul (in million *akça*)

1547–48	21 (the share of Damascus alone is 13)
1566–67	17
1567–68	17
1582–83	7

Source: Sahillioğlu (1974), p. 500.

Table I:25. Main revenue sources in Egypt, 1527–28 (in thousands of
akça)

	Revenue	Expenditure in Egypt	Surplus
Urban *mukataa*	84,940		
Customs	17,730		
Grain supplies	13,860		
Total	116,530	45,840	70,690

Source: Shaw (1962).

Egypt, too, had an autonomous treasury. Governors collected revenues
and covered expenditure locally in the province and sent the surplus to
İstanbul annually. Egypt's total revenue is shown as 116.5 million *akça*
in the "budget" of 1527–28 (see Table I:25). The 70 million *akça* surplus
equals about 1,200,000 gold ducats. The breakdown of the sources of
revenue of Egypt in 1595–96 and 1671–72 is shown in Table I:26. Land
tax was paid for the most part in cash in lower Egypt. Some land taxes
on cotton, rice and sugar were delivered in kind directly to the imperial
treasury or to the imperial granary.[9] In 1670, 421,514 *ardabb* of wheat
were levied (one *ardabb* = c. 90 liters).[10]

The principal customs houses were located at Suez which was "the
principal entrepôt for Egypt's trade with Yemen, Arabia, India and the
Far East. All the trade between these places and Cairo passed through
Suez."[11] The total annual revenue from the *mukataa*s of customs and
other *mukataa*s attached to them amounted to 16.32 million *para* in the
fiscal year 1595–96.

Fixed miscellaneous revenues amounted to 1,200,000 *para* in 1595–96
and about 17 million in 1671–72.[12] Among the non-fixed revenues, mention should be made of the revenue from the state-owned boats on the
Nile river, which brought in 760,000 *para* as rent in the fiscal year 1595–
96.[13] Variable or non-fixed tax revenues amounted to about 10 million
para in that year and 17 million *para* in the fiscal year of 1671–72.[14]

Table I:26. Revenue of Egypt in 1595–96 and 1671–72 (in thousands of *para*)

Taxes	1595–96	1671–72	
Land tax	44,478	63,093	in cash and in kind
Poll-tax	2,275	2,929	in cash
mukataat			all *mukataas* in cash
Customs, Suez	3,922	4,063	
Customs, Alexandria and Rosetta	5,076	6,322	
Customs, Damietta	1,629	— —	
Customs, Barullos	406	— —	
Customs, Bulaq	1,737	3,240	
Other urban mukataas	3,556	3,685	

Note: 1 *para* = 1.2, later 2 *akça*
Source: Shaw (1962), pp. 71, 108, 110–11, 117, 131, 167, 183, 278.

In sum total, tax revenues demanded for the imperial treasury of Egypt amounted to 69 million in 1595–96 and to 95 million *para* in 1671–72[15] (82.8 and 114 million *akça* respectively).

The principal expenditures of Egypt included salaries (*ulufe*) of the commanders and bureaucrats, religious officers, salaries of the paid troops, and pensions, which altogether amounted to 31.6 million *para* in 1595–96 and 56.4 million in 1671–72. Payments in kind were also made out of the imperial granary in Old Cairo. In the first generation after the conquest, those Mamluk emirs who declared their loyalty to the Ottoman sultan were employed in administrative positions and received regular salaries.[16] Other expenditures such as payments to tax collectors, for maintenance of public works, in particular water supply and canals, and for repair work on public buildings constituted a smaller amount compared to salaries. One major expenditure for the Egyptian treasury was the provisions supplied for the Holy Cities of Islam, Mecca and Medina, and for the annual pilgrimage. This amounted to 4.3 million *para* in 1595–96 and 9.5 million in 1671–72.[17] The *vakfs* of Egypt supplied an additional 3.3 million *para* in cash and 172,583 *ardabb* of grain to the Holy Cities.[18] It is calculated that the annual overall contribution to the Hejaz amounted to 300 or 385 thousand gold ducats toward the end of the sixteenth century.[19] Tiepolo, the Venetian *bailo*,[20] said that the crops of wheat, barley and beans annually delivered to the imperial granary in Egypt were worth 1,200,000 gold ducats. The produce was distributed

Table 1:27. The Ottoman army, 1473

Janissaries	12,000
Cavalry of the Porte	7,500
Timariot sipahis of Rumeli	40,000
Timariot sipahis of Anatolia	24,000
azebs	20,000
Total	103,500

Source: Barkan (1953–54).

to the Ottoman troops in Egypt or sent to the Hejaz and İstanbul as provisions. The expenditures for the imperial navy and other units for the defense of Egypt and Syria were not reflected here.

A significant portion of the imperial revenue was set aside and assigned as *timar* for the members of the imperial navy or for the construction of vessels for the fleets based at Alexandria, Damietta and Suez.[21] The captains of these bases alone received 1,800,000 *para*. Egypt's rich resources and surplus revenue were crucial for the imperial defense finances. In times of shortage, the governor of Egypt, who was responsible for policies and activities in the Indian Ocean, also supplied the province of Yemen through its provincial budget. When in 1573 the governor of Yemen was unable to pay the salaries of the troops, who were putting pressure on him, the Porte ordered the governor of Egypt to send a subvention of 50 thousand gold ducats.[22] After meeting all the expenses and salaries, the province of Egypt sent a half million gold ducats to the central treasury annually, and occasionally also subventions to Hejaz, Yemen and Habesh.[23] It is to be remembered that most of the *mukataa*s came under the control of the emirs (Mamluks) of Egypt through the tax-farming system.[24]

EXPENDITURE FOR THE OTTOMAN ARMY

As seen above, the largest part of the state revenue was reserved for soldiers' salaries. İdris,[25] a reliable source for the early sixteenth century, analyzed the Ottoman army during the campaign against Uzun Hasan in 1473, when the sultan gathered all his forces for this decisive confrontation. His computation is shown in Table 1:27.

In the official list dated 1528,[26] the regular forces numbered about 87,000, of which 37,000 were provincial *timar*-holders, and 50,000 were salaried troops (Table 1: 28). *Timar*-holders had to bring to the campaigns auxiliary troops (*cebelü*) at their own expense. Barkan[27] estimated the

Table I:28. The Ottoman army, 1528

	Number	Salary or benefice in million of akça	
A. Regular army			
The salaried (ulufeli) soldiers			
Divisions of the Porte (Janissaries, sipahis, cannoniers, etc.)	24,146	65.88	
Inner palace servants	2,903	–	
Fortress guards, martalos and navy	23,017	40.13	
Beneficiaries of hass, ziamet, and timar in the provinces	37,741	200.19	Including those timariot sipahis as guards in the fortresses, which numbered 9,563 men
Total	87,807	306.20	
B. Auxiliary troops			
Yaya, müsellems, canbaz, bazdars and Yörüks, Anatolia	8,180	3.08	In 1582, at the abolition of their organization, yaya and müsellem numbered 6,900, canbaz 1,200 (Ayni [1280 H.] p. 45)
Yörüks and Tatars, Rumeli	7,000	?	(Gökbilgin [1957])
Voynuks, eflaks and other Christian soldiers	3,000	?	
Registered akıncıs (frontier raiders)	12,000	?	Their numbers swelled by volunteers in times of large-scale raids
Total	30,180		
Grand total	117,987	309.28	

Source: Barkan (1953–54), pp. 280–329.

number of these *cebelüs* at 60,000 in 1528. In the calculation *azeb*s (see below) were not included.

An Italian source (Bessarion: 1470) and an Iranian source (*Ahsan al Tawarikh*) give a lower figure of 70,000 men, when the irregular forces, the *azeb*s, were excluded. This was a small army by modern standards, but only by considering the extraordinary problems associated with feeding and moving troops into fields of action hundreds of miles away in Hungary, Iran and Iraq can we understand its enormity for the age. For

Table I:29. Timar-holders and state revenue distributed as timar, 1527–28 (in million akça)

Provinces	Hass and timars		timars for garrison soldiers	
	Annual revenue	No. beneficiaries	Annual income	No. soldiers
Rumeli	82.45	10,688	10.08	6,620
Anadolu	35.73	7,536	3.81	2,614
Karaman, Rum and Zülkadriye	33.97	6,518		
Aleppo and Damascus	19.16	2,275	0.67	419
Diyarbekir	14.29	1,071	—	—
Total	185.60	28,088	14.56	9,653

Source: Barkan (1953–54), p. 255.

the Ottoman bureaucrats it was an agglomeration of men "the earth cannot bear."

In 1528, the timariot constituted the largest single division in the Ottoman army. It is clear from Table I:29 that in 1528 prebends bestowed as hass and timar to the military in the provinces (except for a very small number of officials in the capital city enjoying timars) amounted to about 200 million akça or 37 percent of the total Ottoman budget. There were two groups of provincial sipahis enjoying timars, those going on campaigns (eşkünci), numbering 28,088,[28] and those timariots acting as guards in the fortresses (hisar-eri), numbering 9,563 men. Timar-holders collected directly from the taxpayer the taxes and dues assigned to them as timars. Since about half of the total timar income was paid by peasants in kind, about one-fifth of the state revenue, or 100 million akça, was paid in kind. The total expenditure for the regular army, that is, the provincial cavalry and the standing army in the capital, was about 265 million akça (the entire state revenue amounted to 537 million akça), or about half of the entire budget. It should be remembered that members of the standing army received in addition clothing, bonuses on the accession of a sultan, for campaigns and festivals, and special provisions during campaigns, while the provincial cavalry had to meet all of their own expenses, including provisions during the campaigns. Their equipment, auxiliary men (cebelü) and valets (gulam) had to be brought in the number commensurate with the amount of their timars as specified in detail in the regulations.

Also of interest is the respective revenue reserved for timars and the number of timar-holders in each province. Rumeli and Anadolu provinces provided 129 million akça in revenue, which was distributed to about 28,000 men, while in the areas conquered in the sixteenth century about 60 or 70 million *akça* was reserved for *timar*-holders, who numbered about 10,000. This reflected the new trend in the composition of the Ottoman army, giving weight to the salaried footmen (Janissaries) with firearms,[29] as well as the specific conditions of the conquered lands – mostly Arab lands. The salaried (*ulufeli*) soldiers, which included the Janissaries, the six cavalry divisions of the Porte, cannoniers and other specialized corps at the Porte,[30] numbering 24,146, received 65.88 million *akça* yearly or 12 percent of the total state revenue. For the salaries of the guards at the fortresses and of the navy personnel, numbering altogether 23,017 men, was allotted 40.13 million *akça* or 7.4 percent of the budget.

As for the auxiliary troops, they were not included in the proper "military" class and were given no salary or prebend from the state treasury. They earned their livelihood by cultivating land granted to them by the state. In addition, they enjoyed exemption from extraordinary taxes and paid some of their taxes at lower rates. These auxiliary troops consisted of *yaya*, *müsellem*, *bazdar*, *canbaz*, Yörüks, Tatars, *voynuks*, *eflaks* and *akıncı* raiders. Each of these groups was organized under a common system very similar to the Byzantine organization of *stratiots*.[31]

In these auxiliary organizations, each group of 25 or 30 peasant households was registered as a unit (*ocak* or hearth), and five of them were distinguished as "campaigners", usually relatives, with each man taking turns to go on campaign (in actuality the number of households in the unit and of campaigners varied). The campaigner collected for his expenses a certain amount of money, varying from 20 to 60 *akça*, from each of the non-military members or "assistants" (*yamak*) of the unit and from those campaigners who did not go on campaign in that particular year. This money was interpreted as corresponding to the extraordinary taxes levied from ordinary subjects. In the earlier *yaya* registers, a standard peasant *çiftlik* (see below, p. 147) was in the possession of a *yaya* with his assistants, who were usually his relatives, cultivating and living on the same *çiftlik*.

The most important of the auxiliary troops were the *yaya*s and *müsellem*s, the latter being mounted and enjoying further exemptions. A late fifteen-century Italian source[32] describes them as "peasant footmen." Mostly found in western Anatolia and representing a privileged group among the *reaya* with their *yaya* farms and special tax status, *yaya*s and *müsellem*s numbered about 7,000 peasant families (Tables I:28, I:30). In 1574, the *müsellem*s of Kütahya alone, who were drafted for service,

Table I:30. The number of active *yaya* and
müsellem soldiers in Anatolia in 1540

Sub-province (*sancak*)	*müsellem*	*yaya*
Karahisar	98	685
Kütahya	273	641
Hamid	305	473
Biga	50	283
Karesi	–	300
Total	726	2,382

Source: Káldy-Nagy (1977), pp. 276–78.

numbered 821 men. The total number of the households in the units,
however, should amount to over 20,000 men.[33]

Yaya and *müsellem* militia were particularly strong in the areas of
Turcoman-Yörük pastoralists (see above, p. 35). In the mid-fifteenth century, in the sub-province (*sancak*) of Teke, for example, there were 361
head-*müsellems* and 172 *müsellems* registered. The "assistants" (*yamaks*),
who provided campaign contributions, numbered 3,763. Thus, at this
time, the average *müsellem* unit could not have comprised more than
eight members. It should be mentioned that in this period *müsellems*
appear as active combatants equipped with arms and some even wore
armor. Every "hearth" was given a farm (*çiftlik*) varying between 12.5
to 37 acres.

It appears that originally *yayas* were Turcoman warriors who made
up the bulk of the Ottoman army in the first emirate period of the
Ottoman state. Apparently each Turcoman warrior was given a *çiftlik* in
the conquered lands. They made up the principal army of the sultan until
the Janissary corps was created as part of the sultan's household in the
1360s. Then there arose a fierce rivalry between the *yaya* army and the
Janissaries, which affected Ottoman politics in the fourteenth and fifteenth centuries. While the Janissaries and other *kuls* who were dependent on the central bureaucracy joined and supported Murad II and
Bayezid II in their fight for the Ottoman throne, the irregular forces,
principally *yayas* and *azebs*, sided with the pretenders, Prince Mustafa
and Cem Sultan in the years 1421–24 and 1481–82 respectively. Popular
chronicles claim that there were 60,000 *yayas* at the battle of Kossovo in
1389.[34] Over time the *yayas* and *müsellems* lost their original martial
qualities and were employed only at such tasks as transportation or
founding cannon balls. In 1582 the organization was totally abolished.

Barkan[35] calculated that the tax exemptions of the *yaya* and *müsellem* amounted to about 2.65 million *akça* in 1534.

Acquiring the status of *yaya* was apparently quite popular in the fourteenth century because of the substantial benefits. Later, it became quite burdensome when the *yaya*s were required to assist the heavy logistic services for the regular army and, as a result, they began to abandon their *çiftlik*s in order to avoid the service. This appears to have become widespread as early as the fifteenth century. At an inspection in 1466, for example, 260 *yaya*s were found to have deserted their land as against 536 registered *yaya*s in the province of Hüdavendigar.

In the fourteenth and fifteenth centuries under the system of extraordinary services, a kind of militia called *azeb* was called to service from the entire Muslim population. Every household unit as defined in the tax registers had to provide an *azeb* soldier at its own expense. Sedentary populations furnished infantry and nomads provided cavalrymen. According to the chronicles,[36] in 1389 Murad I gathered 40,000 *azeb*s to confront the Serbs at Kossovo. On the battlefield against the Akkoyunlu (1473) there were 18,000 *azeb*s in the army. In 1492, 9,000 *azeb*s were recruited in Rumeli who were well-equipped fighting men.[37] Even under Süleyman I, a contingent of 20,000 *azeb*s was reported[38] to have been levied in Rumeli. *Azeb*s made up an important part of the infantry in the army and were employed as fighting men in the navy.

Also, since Bayezid I's time,[39] the Ottomans recruited militia from among their Christian subjects, who were called *suhra-hor* or *cere-hor* since a fee (*suhra*) was paid for their service. The exemption from this extraordinary service was granted only when a service in another sector, such as mining, was undertaken.

In the fortress garrisons, along with the Janissaries, the cannoniers and other *kul*s, members of several companies were of *reaya* origin. Volunteers or raiders on the frontier were appointed fortress *azeb* with regular pay when a slot (*gedik*) in the cadre became vacant. It was such an opportunity that it lured many jobless young men from the countryside to the frontier areas.

EXPENDITURE FOR THE OTTOMAN NAVY

Naval expenditions represented the most expensive military undertaking for the empire. The government had to build and maintain huge naval forces in the Mediterranean with principal bases at Gallipoli, Galata,

İzmit, Ağrıboz, Sinop, Avlona and Alexandria.[40] Also, in order to protect the coasts, squadrons were stationed at Kavala, Mitylene, Rhodes, Suez and Alexandria. The cost of maintaining a fleet of galleys is estimated at no less than half a million ducats a year.[41] The squadrons which were maintained by the Barbary corsairs in the North African provinces of Tunisia and Algeria at their own expense joined the imperial navy during major naval expeditions. In 1571 at Lepanto 100 ships from these provinces reinforced the imperial navy of 200 ships. In 1539, for a naval expedition to recover Nova (Hercegnovi) on the Adriatic coast from the Venetians, the Porte allotted a total 12 million akça or about 20,000 gold ducats for three months.[42] The fleet consisted of 82 standard war galleys, 58 heavy galleys and 11 light galleys as well as 4 ships for the transportation of cannons. The personnel numbered 27,204 men, 22,538 of whom were oarsmen. The rest comprised the crew, Janissaries (2,958 men) and craftsmen. The wages of the crew and craftsmen amounted to 8,481,880 akça, the cost of the biscuits and water-barrels, 2,294,580, and the bonuses distributed to the Janissaries together with other miscellania to 201,411 akça.

Ship building gave rise to quite sophisticated industries at various naval bases where wood supplies from nearby forests were available, such as Gelibolu, Sinop and İzmit. In the mid-sixteenth century the district of Kasımpasha at Galata with its 123 docks became the center of such industries. Skilled workmen in Galata were then mostly Christians, Greeks or Venetians, while crew and fighting men were Muslims.

The enormous expenditures involved in maintaining a fleet were supplemented by extraordinary taxes and services extracted from the subject population. A fleet of 200 galleys required at least 22,000 oarsmen. The Ottoman galley slaves provided only a small part of those needed; consequently, the sultan ordered every household tax unit to send one oarsman to the navy. Under the guidance of the local kadi, the tax units collected money to hire an available young man, usually a peasant drifter, to serve as an oarsman. In the sixteenth century, each Muslim oarsman was given 106 akça, and a Christian, for the same task, 80 as a monthly allowance. When the government asked for money instead, the tax units had to pay cash, 1,500 per unit in 1551. The crushing Ottoman defeat by the Christian allied armada at Lepanto in 1571 and the great financial sacrifices to protect the empire by building a new fleet[43] signaled the end of Ottoman sea power. Although Andrew Hess,[44] taking into consideration Ottoman successes in the Mediterranean after Lepanto, believes that Ottoman sea power survived the defeat, the financial burden and the advent in particular of the English and Dutch on the Mediterranean (see p. 376) made a recovery of Ottoman sea power impossible.

There was also a state merchant marine, known since Mehmed II's time. Wood and lumber were transported on state-owned ships from Antalya to Egypt and Syria. Twenty-six large ships (*navi*) owned by the state were active in the traffic between Syrian ports and İstanbul by 1553.[45] Navy captains and state dignitaries too owned ships sailing between İstanbul, the Black Sea ports, Syria and Egypt.[46] In wartime such ships were apparently used as transport.

THE IMPERIAL CAMPAIGN: LOGISTICS

William McNeill[47] contrasted two methods of provisioning an army on the move: either "to plunder local food producers by seizing their stocks of grain or animals," or to organize the logistics before the campaign started. The latter was based on the tax and rent system, by gathering food supplies from the peasants and storing them in magazines along the intended route of the march. The first method proved to be self-destructive in the end since the peasants were scattered or unable to continue to cultivate for some time, while under the tax and rent system the peasantry's productivity and the regularity of provisioning of the army were guaranteed.

The Mongols of Genghis Khan and, later, Timur's army were typical examples of the predation method, while the Persian–Islamic imperial tradition typified the logistic system. Under the influence of the Iranian–Seljukid and Byzantine traditions, the Ottoman imperial system developed quite a complex pattern of logistics which attracted the admiration of European observers.[48]

Protection of the peasantry against depredation was discussed by the Ottoman historian Aşık Paşazade[49] (d. 1502) in his chapter on Osman Ghazi. In the sixteenth century, during the joint campaigns of the Crimean Tatars and the Ottomans, serious misunderstandings arose when the Ottoman command prohibited the plunder of tributary or subject people in Moldavia, Wallachia or Hungary. Although booty raids into the infidels' land, interpreted as being ordered and rewarded by God, were systematically organized by the Ottomans, the protection of non-Muslim subjects was guaranteed under the law of Islam.[50] What is more, the Ottoman government believed it was good policy for expanding its territories to promise protection to the "infidels" living on the other side of the frontiers in the Abode of War. Foraging or taking goods without paying while in Ottoman territory was prohibited and was sometimes followed by capital punishment.

However, it was a fact that the corridor zones through which the Ottoman troops passed suffered and tax resources declined. This happened as a result of the provision levies of the government in addition to the occasional forages of the soldiery. To avoid these, inhabitants had no choice but to leave their homes and flee.[51] In 1579, in the campaign against Iran, the corridor of the army's passage had to be changed because on the Ankara route "no settled villages" the official report testifies "were left because the peasants were scattered."[52] The Ottomans could not establish full control over their conquests in Azerbaijan in the period 1587–90 mainly because they became dependent on grain imported from the homeland. A sharp decline in agriculture in the area resulted from the flight of the Shiite population of the region and the exactions which the hungry Ottoman soldiery, without provisions or money, made on the villagers.[53] Using the long-established practice of imposing extraordinary levies (avarız) in times of emergency, the state demanded from its subjects a series of additional services and taxes both in kind and in cash. During war years such unforeseen demands had shattering effects on the rural economy, particularly on the fragile balance of the peasant subsistence economy. Although first applied only during large-scale campaigns, the extraordinary levies were transformed to regular in-cash taxes during the prolonged war period of 1587–1612. Coinciding with the Celali depredations, it became another factor in the ruin of the agrarian economy in Anatolia.

The successful outcome of a campaign depended to a great extent on how well the provisioning of the army and the frontier garrisons was organized. During government deliberations on the opening of a campaign in a particular year, a shortage or abundance of wheat and barley in the country was seriously taken into account.[54] To ensure that armies in motion were supplied with basic foodstuffs and fodder, the Ottomans perfected an elaborate system of logistics.[55] Basically, three methods were followed in procuring wheat or flour for men and barley for animals. First, direct taxes (nüzul), consisting of a certain amount of foodstuffs, were imposed upon household units;[56] secondly, there was an obligation to bring and sell foodstuffs at government fixed prices at pre-determined halting places (sürsat); and thirdly, government purchases were made at locally fixed market prices (iştira). While nüzul was a real tax, sürsat was interpreted by the government as a transaction which formed "an aid" to the army's provisioning by peasants agreeing to sell certain foodstuffs. But for practical reasons, the provisions were actually bought by an army agent at fixed prices and re-sold to the soldiery. There are indications that payments were delayed or not made at all.[57] There were also cases when taxpayers were forced to deliver both the *nüzul* tax and *sürsat* at the same time. The government demanded as a rule that the taxpayer meet the transport expenses or carry *nüzul* levies themselves, which became an extremely onerous obligation for the peasantry. It was the responsibility of the local kadi to collect and organize the transport of the provisions. Kadis had difficulty in fulfilling this task: peasants sought to escape their obligations, since it meant either sharing their family's subsistence or selling the surplus at low prices. The household unit for *nüzul* levies varied from three to thirty households. For instance, in 1579 every levy unit of twenty households had to deliver 25.64 kg of grain.[58] The amount demanded in this case was quite reasonable. Huge supplies, however, were still needed. In 1637, the army needed for its march against the Iranians in Baghdad 13,600 tons of barley, 1,512 tons of flour and 886,000 loaves of bread to be levied from Anatolian and Arab provinces.[59]

As for the origin of these levies (*salgun*, *avarız*), it appears that when the military either arrived or was stationed at a place, food and fodder were demanded from the peasants. This customary due was eventually converted to a regular tax for the prebend-holder under the name of *salariyye* or *salarlık* (dues for the commander) in addition to the canonical tithes. The question of reducing this tax burden to a reasonable rate could be solved by extending it over a large area. But then the question arose of how to collect and transport the wheat and barley to the army or frontier fortresses, because transport costs were prohibitive. Ottoman bureaucrats tried to solve this problem by commuting the tax-in-kind to a tax-in-cash in the remote regions and using the money that was obtained to make purchases in local markets near the passage route of the army, or to stockpile items in the fortresses. Such purchases supplemented the obligatory levies becoming, as Ottoman bureaucrats put it, a source of income and prosperity for the local population. In 1594, *nüzul* was fixed at 2.5 *kile* (c. 64 kg) of grain per household unit or as a cash substitute of 300 *akça* in the district of Rodoscuk.[60] It appears that during and after the long war period from 1578 to 1606 such cash substitutes became regular taxes. Introducing new taxes on the basis of customary practices was a well-known process in the Ottoman tax system.[61]

The stations (*menzil-hane*) along major imperial roads had depots to store grain brought under the kadi's supervision. When the army did not need such supplies, they were sold or distributed to the public in emergencies. When major imperial campaigns were in question large stocks were to be placed in the strategic fortresses near the field of action. Supplies were collected months in advance and transported from regions of plenty, such as Egypt or the fertile Danubian basin, by waterway. For the fighting armies beyond the Ottoman frontiers, provisions were supplied from the depots of such strategically situated frontier fortresses as Van or Erzurum for the Iranian campaigns and Belgrade for the Hungarian campaigns. In times of shortage, the government had access to the grain stored in the depots of hospices, fortresses, or route stations. Despite all the setbacks, the Ottoman logistic system functioned well. Finkel[62] calculated that an Ottoman army of 150,000 men could provide "in an equitable fashion" basic foodstuffs for a march through Rumeli and Hungary. The price of bread was even a little cheaper for the Ottoman soldier than for his European counterpart. But the conditions were quite the reverse in eastern Asia Minor during the campaigns against Iran, especially when the enemy scorched the corridor zones of the Ottoman army. The campaigns against Iran caused widespread discontent in the army and changes in the state's strategic plans.

DEFICITS, EXTRAORDINARY MEASURES

During a war, extraordinary measures were taken to meet the treasury's immediate cash needs, including confiscation of the surplus from the pious endowments, trust funds of minors preserved in the city's *bedestan*,[63] and forced loans from the wealthy. Because of the deficit in the state budget, Sultan Murad III ordered members of the imperial council and governors of the provinces to build galleys at their own expense for the projected naval expedition against Spain in 1590. In exchange they were given certificates for reimbursement from unpaid taxes of previous years. Reference is made to loans from leading merchants during wartime.[64] Before major campaigns, an extraordinary cash tax was demanded from all subjects throughout the empire: for the campaigns of Belgrade and Rhodes a 15-*akça* tax was levied. Already under Süleyman a shortage in public revenues was felt. In 1557, for example, 80,000 gold pieces had to be delivered to the current treasury from the palace. Chronic shortages, however, began during the long war period of 1578–1606 (for budget deficit see Table I:31).

Table I:31. Deficit in Ottoman budgets, 1523–1608 (in thousands of
akça)

Fiscal year	Revenue	Expenditure	Difference
1523–24	116,888	118,783	− 1,895
1524–25	141,272	126,581	+ 14,691
1527–28	277,244	150,228	+127,016
1546–47	241,711	171,872	+ 69,839
1565–66	183,088	189,657	− 6,569
1567–68	348,544	221,532	+127,012
1582–83	313,744	277,578	+ 36,166
1592–93	293,400	363,400	− 70,000
1597–98	300,000	900,000	−600,000
1608	503,691	599,191	− 95,500

Note: Timar revenues not included.
Source: Tabakoğlu (1985), pp. 14–15.

In evaluating these figures, it must be kept in mind that in 1584 the
akça was devalued by 100 percent (see below, Appendix), so that the real
value of the revenue in 1592–93 would, in terms of the *akça* of the
previous period, be only 146,700,000 *akça*. Expenditures in terms of the
old *akça* were 181,700 in 1592. Thus, there was a decrease of 95,878 in
expenditure. However, this decrease did not result in a balanced budget.

It was a long-established tradition in Ottoman financial dealings to
make salary payments according to the Islamic lunar calendar year (354
days). Since in the solar calendar the succession of seasons does not
change, the state fiscal year had to follow the solar year in the collection
of agricultural taxes.[65] This led to a discrepancy in the budgetary account-
ing, especially in salary payments. The salary claim at the end of each
calendar year overlapped by eleven days the solar year. The result was
one extra lunar year for every thirty-two years. In other words, in a
time span of thirty-two years, the salaried could claim payments for
thirty-three years, while the state levied taxes for only thirty-two. Thus,
the state was obliged periodically to make special extra payments. Sahillioğlu believes that this situation was the source of major cyclical crises in
state finances and was responsible for discontent among the salaried soldiery. It should be remembered that the soldiers' salary claimed 12 percent of the entire budget. As Janissary salaries were paid in four
installments each year it would be necessary to make one extra payment
at the end of eight years and four extra payments every thirty-two years.

To cover this huge emergency expenditure the government had to find
new sources of revenue. Failure to pay or to delay a payment led to
Janissary uprisings. Sahillioğlu[66] attempts to explain historically known

uprisings of the soldiery through such failures. If the inner reserve treasury of the palace had sufficient funds, the crisis was met by loans to the government. But during the long wars in the last decades of the sixteenth century the reserves were depleted. Then the government resorted to other measures, such as imposing new taxes, debasing the silver *akça* or starting a war in order to secure booty and land which could be distributed in the form of *timars*. But these measures in turn led to a further destabilization in the peasant economy as well as the country as a whole. Following the sharp devaluation of the *akça* in 1584, the Iranian campaign which started in 1578, instead of bringing in new resources, entailed enormous new expenditure for the treasury and threw the empire into a long financial and political crisis. The soldiery welcomed the opening of a new front in Europe in 1593, but here too it was not a profit producing business as it had been under Süleyman the Magnificent.[67]

NOTES

1 Yahya b. Ādam (1958), pp. 7, 58.
2 Babinger (1957); Majer (1982); for a critical examination of the budget given by Laonicus Chalcocondyles, see Vryonis (1976), pp. 423–32.
3 M. 'Ālī, *Nushat al-Salātīn*, MS Fatih Library, İstanbul 29b.
4 On the dual treasuries in Iran, see Nizam al-Mulk (1893), p. 205.
5 Lybyer (1919), p. 181.
6 İnalcık (1973b), pp. 224–29.
7 Barkan (1953–54), p. 277.
8 Sahillioğlu (1985).
9 Shaw (1962), p. 74.
10 *Ibid.*, p. 80.
11 *Ibid.*, p. 103.
12 *Ibid.*, p. 169.
13 *Ibid.*, p. 178.
14 *Ibid.*, p. 181.
15 *Ibid.*, p. 183.
16 *Ibid.*, p. 199.
17 *Ibid.*, p. 268.
18 *Ibid.*, p. 270.
19 Faroqhi (1990), p. 123; on the expenditure for the extensive public works, including the water-supply system in Mecca and Jerusalem, *ibid.*, pp. 126–62.
20 Cited by Braudel (1972), I, p. 583.
21 Shaw (1962), pp. 134–37.
22 BBA, *Mühimme Defteri*: no. 23, document no. 239 dated 981 H/1573.
23 According to a document in BBA, Fekete Tasnifi no. 1168, in the year 940 H (starts on July 23, 1533), the surplus sent to the sultan was about half a million gold pieces, and consisted of 369,793 new *sultani*, 54,490 old *sultani*

and 72,655 *flori*; in addition 14,000 *sultani* was sent to Mecca and Medina to be distributed among the poor; an additional sum of 25,939 was spent for purchases of spices, drugs, pastes, jewelry and cloth for the imperial palace; altogether a sum of 536,877 gold pieces was alloted to the sultan's treasury and miscellaneous expenses.

24 Shaw (1962), p. 152.
25 *Hasht Behisht*, MS Topkapı Palace Library, Hazine no. 1655.
26 Barkan (1953–54), pp. 281–83, see Table 28.
27 *Ibid.*, p. 256.
28 *Ibid.*, pp. 258–65, finds a few thousand more.
29 İnalcık (1975a).
30 İnalcık (1973a), p. 83.
31 Lemerle (1958), p. 43ff.
32 Angiolello (1909), "*musalem.*"
33 BBA, *Mühimme Defteri*: no. 26, 216.
34 But Oruç (1925), p. 25, mentions the presence of 10,000 *yayas* at this battle.
35 Barkan (1953–54), p. 259.
36 Ten thousand *azebs* from Rumeli, mentioned in Oruç (1925), p. 25.
37 The Anonymous Chronicle, MS BN, 105.
38 Charrière (1848), I, p. 322.
39 Aşık Paşazade (1947–49), p. 70.
40 İnalcık (1965b), pp. 983–87; Imber (1980), pp. 211–82.
41 Imber (1980), p. 218.
42 *Ibid.*, pp. 203–16.
43 İnalcık (1974).
44 Hess (1978); Braudel (1972), II, pp. 1102–6, 1127–42.
45 Alberi (1839–63), III, p. 153, cited by Imber (1980), pp. 57–58.
46 İnalcık (1992b).
47 McNeill (1982), pp. 2–4.
48 Angiolello (1909).
49 Aşık Paşazade (1949), pp. 98–99.
50 qv. "Dhimma" by Cahen, *EI²*, II, pp. 227–31.
51 Güçer (1964), p. 145; Finkel (1988), pp. 130–44.
52 Güçer (1964), p. 145.
53 Murphey (1988), p. 250, List.
54 Güçer (1964), p. 143.
55 For logistic problems in the Hungarian campaign of 1593–1603, see Finkel (1988), pp. 121–208.
56 An *avarız-hane* was a fiscal unit of households organized for the collection of extraordinary levies, see Barkan (1944), pp. 13–19.
57 Güçer (1964), pp. 105–15.
58 *Ibid.*, p. 76.
59 *Ibid.*, p. 100.
60 Finkel (1988), p. 142.
61 İnalcık (1980a), pp. 311–23.
62 Finkel (1988), p. 154.
63 İnalcık (1980d), pp. 2–3.

64 Koçi Bey (1939), p. 46.
65 Sahillioğlu (1970), pp. 230–52.
66 *Ibid.*
67 İnalcık (1980a). In the late eighteenth century it was a rule to add two *akças*, called *tefavüt*, onto each silver *guruş* when the tax-farmers delivered the contracted monies. In 1784 finance officials explained that this was actually to make up for the loss resulting from the use of different calendars in the accounts. Thus, the application of different rates of gold and silver coins for receipts and payments provided a new source of revenue, see the document published by Sahillioğlu (1970), p. 100.

3

⌣̇

STATE-OWNED LANDS (*MİRİ*)

THE ORIGIN AND NATURE OF THE STATE OWNERSHIP OF LANDS

State ownership of arable land was not an Ottoman invention. In Islamic jurisprudence, ownership of land was based in the last analysis on the concept of the conquest and the right of the Islamic community (*umma*) as God's trustees. The concept of the *fay' al-muslimin*, in the sense of making the conquered lands the inalienable common property of the Muslims or the Islamic state, took its definitive institutional form during the first century of Islam under Byzantine and Sasanid influence.[1] These were also known as *haraci* lands, or those lands which were left in the possession of non-Muslims in exchange for land taxes (*haraç*).[2] The Caliph Umar I (634–44) reportedly argued that if the conquered lands, waters, and peasants or serf-tenants were distributed among the conquerors as the property of individuals, future generations of Muslims would be deprived of this source of revenue. Actually, state lands with peasants of similar status had existed in Byzantine Syria and Egypt as well as in Sasanid Iraq. The caliphal decision was simply legitimized by the Quranic verses on *fay'*.[3]

Whenever their sovereignty over a territory was challenged, the Ottoman sultans asserted their rights by saying that they had conquered the land "by force of the sword." The assumption was that the victor acquired an absolute right over the persons of the defeated and over their properties, including the land. In Islamic Law from the Prophet's time, Holy War and conquest (*cihad* and *fath*) had been considered the principles which established the absolute control of the Islamic community over the land and the labor of the men who cultivated it. The imam was free either to eliminate or enslave the defeated or to keep them as tenants on the land in exchange for the regular payment of a fixed amount of ransom (*cizye* or *haraç*).

In fact, the conquerors could not take the place of the indigenous peasant tenants; but, leaving them to continue to cultivate, they acted simply as "rent" gatherers. The treasury of the Muslims (*bayt al-mal al-muslimin*) appropriated such lands with the pre-conquest peasant populations on them as tenants. While the use of the land was left to the farmers, the state retained the *dominium eminens* (*rakaba* or *rikab*), as was stated by the Caliph Umar: "*Rikab* over land always belongs to us." There were indeed urgent practical reasons for the state ownership of land. It was in order to build up a public treasury, to support the army and to defend and expand Islamic territory that the Caliph Umar made conquered lands the common property of the Islamic community or the state. Clearly, the rationale for state ownership of land was presented as the necessity to create a central treasury for the empire.

The *dominium eminens* of the state on conquered lands was sometimes interpreted as a simple right of legal control (*vala'*), in consideration of the fact that the state controlled the land's use but did not in principle actually use it itself. The Ottomans, basically following Islamic tradition, recognized two principles which established proprietorship in land, namely, conquest and reclamation. Conquest gave *dominium eminens* on all lands to the community of the conquerors, the Muslims as a whole, or, more precisely, to the state as its embodiment. The state, then, was the only legitimate authority establishing proprietary rights on land under certain conditions, the most important of which was reclamation. Ownership of the wasteland (*mevat*) was initiated by occupation of the land with the permission of the head of the Islamic community (imam); it was then completed by actual reclamation. The imam's authorization excluded interference by others and established legitimation/legalization of the acquisition. "Pure ownership" (*mülk mahz*) comprised all aspects of disposition (*tasarruf*) in an absolute fashion. But still the state held *dominium eminens* and under certain conditions could abrogate propriet- ary rights on freehold property, or such lands might be turned by its owner into *vakf* in the name of the Islamic community's interest.

Controversy over whether or not the state's legal validation was neces- sary for the appropriation of the wastelands is of particular interest. Most authorities agreed that it was necessary. The underlying argument always was that such lands belonged to God, or to the imam as His trustee, who represented the Islamic community; it was his duty to see that such lands were administered in the way that would best serve the interests of the community and Islamic state, *Din u Dawla* as the Ottomans used to say. Furthermore, authorities such as Shafiʿi, who gave priority to the *umma* (Islamic community) and its welfare in the face of dynastic-monarchical interests, saw no necessity for legalization by the political authority. The theory that the state had the *dominium eminens* of all lands postulated that, without the legalizing power of the state, no possession or ownership could be established. The Ottoman bureaucracy was very strict on this point, so that at the time of land surveys, titles to land in freehold, arable lands and pious foundations were checked carefully by the surveyor; and then a special diploma of the reigning sultan was issued. Thus, the principle of the first occupation did not establish ownership on land; it was the state's *dominium eminens* based on conquest and consequently its validation power that established ownership.

In the Mirror-for-Princes literature of Persian origin in Islam, the fundamental principle which guaranteed the whole politico-social structure was expressed in the maxim: "The land and the peasant belong to the sultan." Found in Nizam al-Mulk's[4] famous treatise on the politics of the twelfth century, and in the Ottoman law codes, the motto actually expresses the foundation of all oriental imperial systems, and this principle always was based on the right of conquest.

In the first centuries of the Ottoman Empire, matters concerning landholding and land taxation were treated as an area of civil administration independent of religious authorities. The state (*miri*) lands, about 90 percent of all the arable lands, were placed under the responsibility of the *nişancı*, a civil bureaucrat, and run according to a sultanic law code drawn up by the civil bureaucracy.[5] It was this law code, actually a combination of Islamic and local practices related to the Roman–Byzantine legacy, which administered the relationships in Ottoman landholding and taxation. In fact, the system was closely analogous to that of previous Islamic and Byzantine states, and there was no reason for the Ottomans to revolutionize tested methods as long as the state received its revenues. Dependent peasant masses provided the basic underlying factor of continuity, producing within the same system but for a new ruling group. On the other hand, it is equally true that the Islamic – and Ottoman – landholding system had its own evolution in relation to changing historical conditions, and it was the task of the jurists to choose and legalize certain practices or principles in response to the requirements of the situation.

It is significant that while systematic Islamic law books had no specific chapter on landholding, jurists wrote independent treatises on the subject in response to the need of the state administration.[6] Actually, these later additions sought to legalize existing or surfacing conventions in the field of landholding and land taxation. As will be seen, Ottoman jurists of the sixteenth century referred to such authoritative books to make the Ottoman rules and practices conform to the Islamic tradition.

A further scrutiny of the nature of state ownership of land in Islam shows that, as in Roman Law, ownership in land presupposed three basic elements, *rakaba* (*abusus* or *dominium eminens*), *tasarruf* (*usus* or possession), and *istiglal* (*fructus* or usufruct). However, in Islamic Law, these three elements were treated independently, each forming a separate object of disposition.[7] The state retained *rakaba* and handed over the rights of possession and usufruct to the farmer as separate elements. Abu Hanifa, making an absolute distinction between *rakaba* (here, ownership) and *manfa'a* (usufruct), went so far as to assert that even by establishing a pious foundation (*vakf*) the original owner gave away only its usufruct and retained the *rakaba*, and so he had the right to abolish the status of *vakf* at any time. When Mehmed II decided to abolish private and *vakf* properties, this principle of inalienability of the state's *rakaba* apparently was employed. We shall see that the right of usufruct was treated as another independent object of transactions, such as sale, mortgage, or transfer by will or inheritance. Thus, it is said that usufruct rights actually entailed a kind of disposition indistinguishable from ownership, a development that occurred during the eighteenth century when possession rights were extended under the dual tenancy (*icaratayn*) system.[8]

Also, in the *tapu* contracts (see below), the transaction usually was called a sale (*bay'* or *satma*) without implying the sale of the land itself but rather the rights of actual possession or usufruct.

Ottoman religious authorities asserted that state lands were those arable lands whose ownership always belonged to the public treasury but whose actual possession and usufruct rights were "fully entrusted" (*tafviz*) to farmers. Also it should be kept in mind that state ownership was applied as a rule to arable lands reserved for grain cultivation, that is, those necessary for basic food production. In legal language arable land was defined as "the land ploughed," "the cultivated land," or "the land for which tithes are paid."[9]

Ömer Lûtfi Barkan[10] saw in the state's right of eminent domain a control system necessary for the maintenance of a specific *military–political regime* by an all-powerful state. Instead, he should have rather emphasized a specific agrarian production mode based on the peasant family farm (see below, Ch. 6).

By insisting on its character as the fundamental legal basis of the whole socio-economic system of the Ottoman – or the so-called Asiatic – empire and the determinant of the "relations of production," the Marxist interpretation of state ownership of land admittedly offers a broader view of its significance and implications. According to the Marxist interpretation of eminent domain, basic taxes paid by the direct producer formed a land *rent* shared by the sultan or dominant class created around him, because "Der Staat ist hier der oberste Grundherr." It has been argued that state ownership of land in the Ottoman Empire (as well as in the Mughal Empire of India) originated from and was based on the right of conquest and served to exploit the direct producers, or to appropriate the surplus product by a military "feudal class." In other words, state ownership in land is seen as a legal device for exploitation imposed by a dominant class on the direct producers. Thus, in Marxist interpretation, it makes no difference whether "the usurper" is a local seigneur-landowner or a centralist state.

Close state control of landholding is also found by Marxists to be responsible for the failure of Ottoman agriculture and agrarian relations to venture into new directions, and thus for the stagnation of the Ottoman economy and society in general. Archival documentation demonstrates that the Ottoman centralist government always vigorously strove to maintain its *miri* system against new developments.

Accentuating Karl Marx's notion that the Asiatic ruler established his *real* and actual ownership on conquered land, the Marxist legal historian F. Milkova[11] sees in the Islamic–Ottoman *rakaba* something more than the *dominium eminens* or *nuda proprietas* of the state. She suggests that the Ottoman state, exercising public authority, monopolized the right of real proprietorship, which is actually the subject of civil law, and thus what the state collected as revenue from land had the nature of simple rent, as Marx and Engels claimed. She argues that the sultan exercised *direct control* through his exclusive right of choosing the use of the land in each individual case throughout the empire. In addition, the state reserved for itself the right to directly exploit mines, forests, and certain other soil resources. Let us add that when the state saw it necessary, as in the case of rice cultivation, it would directly organize even the production process itself.[12] Land tax in the Marxist sense thus is simply a rent. Interestingly, this interpretation agrees in principle with that of the Islamic jurists (see below, pp. 145–53). But, as will be discussed later, the nature of Ottoman state ownership of land can be understood only within the *çift-hane* system.

TYPES OF POSSESSION OF STATE-OWNED LANDS:
TAPULU AND *MUKATAALU*

The state-owned lands are basically divided into *tapulu* and *mukataalu*, the former comprising all lands given to peasants under the *tapu* regulations, and the latter includes those lands leased under a simple rental contract, *mukataa*. The *tapulama*, leasing under *tapu*, giving a specific status to the land, brought it under the *çift-hane* system. The *tapulu* *çiftliks* were family farm units given over to peasant households. The *mukataalu* ones were those rented to any person who, under a rental contract, a lease, paid only a lump sum rent agreed upon (*maktu*) for the tithes. The renters were not liable for any peasant taxes. Here, the specific nature of the *çift-hane* system clearly emerges. While the simple rental contract, the *mukataa*, was freely concluded between the state and an individual, the *tapu* implied a certain status stemming from an original "subjugation" (*kulluk*) which entailed, in addition to the tithes, certain personal obligations such as the payment of the *çift-resmi* or the *ispence* (see below, pp. 149–51). In the case of the *tapulama*, the one who leased the land was a dependent peasant or *raiyyet* (singular of *reaya*), who had to pay all taxes and also provide certain services to the state and *sipahi*. According to an interpretation of the jurists, *raiyyet* belonged to the group of subjugated non-Muslims who were left on lands belonging to the Islamic community or the state.

The lands which were subject to the *tapu* contract were called *tapulu* *arazi* (lands under *tapu*) and were ideally divided into *çiftlik* units. In general, *tapulu* lands included fields for the cultivation of grain, which made up far the greater part of arable land, as well as pasturelands, registered meadows and lands reclaimed by peasants. Vineyards and orchards were excluded from the *tapulu* lands because of their status as private freehold. Vegetable gardens, when registered and taxed in the survey books, were considered among the *tapulu*. In other words, *tapulu* lands were all those arable lands registered in the survey books with fixed tax revenues, and constituted the area of the *çift-hane* system. Sometimes they were called "the land reserved for the peasants" (*raiyyetlik-yer*). The Ottoman law code ruled,[13] "any land that is ploughed is *miri*. It is given under *tapu*. This is the established law." A vineyard or garden automatically became state-owned (*miri*) when ploughed for cultivation, and henceforth paid regular tithes and the peasant taxes.

In addition, those arable lands reclaimed by a peasant within the boundaries of a *timar* automatically became *tapulu* and the *timar*-holder took for himself the taxes applicable to such land. However, as they were sometimes considered as accretions not registered in the original registers, the revenue was claimed by agents of the public treasury. But the Law Maker eventually decided in favor of the *sipahi*, because of their great service during campaigns, and added that the boundaries of *timar*s be clearly distinguished. In general, the state left such windfalls to the *sipahi*s as an incentive to increase the arable lands under *tapu*, and enjoy the extra revenue until the next land survey. In general, the *sipahi* made every effort to unify pieces of land to create a family farm (*çiftlik*), or encourage his peasants to reclaim land within the *timar*.

The eligibility to acquire land by *tapu* was limited to those who could cultivate it and pay taxes, i.e., the peasants (*reaya*). In principle, townsfolk or members of the military class were excluded. When they obtained it one way or another, they were subject to the obligations of peasants and were treated as such. Nomads who were not registered in the state surveys were qualified only for state-owned lands not already given to the villagers under *tapu*. When a family farm land became vacant, first those relatives who had preeminent rights and then the inhabitants of the village were eligible to bid for the *tapu*.

Acquisition of the *tapulu* land was distinguished from that by simple lease contract, purchase or bequest by a simple procedure called *tapulama* or *tapuya verme*. In practice, the *tapu* contract, as found in the court records,[14] was drawn up in the form of a sales contract. In it, the state agent declared that he "sold" the land described with all the pertinent rights and, in return, received the *tapu* payment in cash. Then, the other party declared that he accepted all the conditions. The kadi certified that the entire procedure took place in full accordance with the prescriptions of the Sharia, and the contract was kept in the kadi's register. The usual formula used in such contracts was as follows:

> The reason for the redaction of the document is that Mehmed, holder of the *timar* in such and such a place, expressed his will in the court as follows: I gave the possession of the *çiftlik* situated [within the boundaries described] to 'Ali who is holding this document on condition that he shall cultivate it and collect its produce and pay the tithes and dues each year, and I received from him the *tapu* fee in cash, in the amount of ... *akça*. Then 'Ali accepted the statement.

This contract stipulated nothing about the conditions of possession, the inheritance rights, land use, taxes and labor services, etc. All of these aspects are detailed in the sultanic law codes which are separate from

Islamic Law. The word *tapu* used in the contract implies that either party agreed on all the provisions prescribed in the sultanic laws.

The *tapu* contract gave the parties the legal guarantee to go to court in case a dispute arose about the conditions of possession. Sultanic law[15] confirms the peasant's possession rights as follows: "When the land of a peasant (*raiyyet*) is given into the peasant's possession, no one can take it away from him under the *tapu* law. And once possessed under *tapu*, a land cannot be subject to a new *tapu*."

It appears that most of the time the parties did not need to go to town and pay the court fees, and everything proceeded as required by custom. Therefore, sultanic law recognized that if a peasant held the actual possession of land long enough, and no one disputed it, this constituted legal possession. The relatively small number of formal contracts in the court records suggests that the legal formality was often neglected by *timar*-holders and peasants. Moreover, if a *timar*-holder let the peasant cultivate land without the *tapu* document for some time, successive *timar*-holders could not claim the *tapu* fee.

THE NATURE OF POSSESSION RIGHTS UNDER THE *TAPU* SYSTEM

The peasant's possession right, generally described as *tasarruf*, was further clarified as a *tafviz*. *Tasarruf* means simply actual possession. *Tafviz*, meaning "giving full authorization," actually designated the peasant's independence in organizing the whole process of production. Other portions of the law, as well as the kadi court records, make clear that the *timar*-holder could not interfere in the peasant's cultivation activities except when the peasant diverted the use of the land so that it affected regular grain production or its *miri* nature. From the Islamic Law standpoint, the legal nature of the *tafviz* of state-owned land was a renting of the land. However, a *tafviz* contract did not contain all the conditions of a regular Islamic renting or lease procedure because the peasant was not free to negotiate the conditions of the lease. In the attempt to interpret *miri* land possession in terms of Islamic leasing, contradictions inevitably emerged, since the specific provisions of state ownership originally were determined by a set of empirical rules for maintaining a historically shaped agrarian system, or *çift-hane*.

In possession under *tapu*, the principal rights which established a real ownership were denied. The possessor of state-owned land could not sell, donate, endow, mortgage or leave it by will, or change its original use by turning it into a vineyard or orchard or by constructing buildings on it. On the other hand, possession with *tapu* entailed certain privileges which distinguished it from a simple tenancy, such as the rights of transfer (*ferag*) to another farmer, bequeathing to sons, and preeminent rights of acquisition by wife, daughter and brother.

Now let us examine the reasons why these particular restrictions were made and privileges added in the *tapu* lease. The sale of state-owned land was prohibited mainly because, when sold, the land would then become the object of private ownership with all its consequences. According to Islamic jurisprudence, all debts of a deceased person were paid out of his properties before division of the inheritance. In practice, the court records contain instances when lenders attempted to take the peasant's land for an unpaid debt and to deprive the son of his inheritance. Apparently because such cases became quite widespread, the sultan issued a law, in 1601, that under no circumstances could *miri* land be sold to pay a debt. In particular, Ottoman legists expressed the concern that in such cases, the *çiftlik* units of the peasants would be apportioned among the heirs or buyers and the whole Ottoman tax assessment and prebendal system would collapse. The integrity of the *çiftlik* units was particularly stressed in the Ottoman land laws (see below, p. 148).

However, as Abussu'ud indicated and court records attest, *miri* lands became the subject of sales.[16] Although it was extremely difficult to sell a piece of state-owned land because the local *sipahi* or others had vested interests in keeping its *miri* status intact, there were loopholes and legal devices by which the law could be circumvented (p. 112). Once sold with a court document, land could not revert to its *miri* status, because it became the subject of a sale contract under Islamic Law, which establishes absolute ownership. It required the sultan's radical decision to recover such lands for the state as seen in Mehmed II's land reform.[17] Islamic Law, of course, was supreme, and it was a sin to act contrary to its prescriptions. Thus, in survey books, the registers of the kadis and the records concerning private estates and pious foundations, we frequently find a note emphatically stating that the land in question was acquired through a sale in accordance with Islamic Law. Sometimes the transaction gives the impression of collusion. The same device was widely employed by private interests to convert state (*haraci-fey*) lands into private estates in the early centuries of the caliphate; it was obviously to serve the state that some jurists introduced the rule that any sale of *haraci* lands was contrary to the law and consequently null and void.[18]

The Sheyhülislam Abussu'ud's rulings give the impression that, by the middle of the sixteenth century, the illegal sale of state-owned lands had become widespread enough to cause alarm in government circles.[19] Since the religious courts were instrumental in these sales, the opinion of the Sheyhülislam, the most authoritative religious person in the realm, was needed to stop the practice. Abussu'ud ruled that "the delivery by the kadis of such documents of sale is absolutely null and void." In various rulings he declared these sale documents absolutely against Islamic Law; the question was even asked whether a kadi who issued such a document was liable for punishment.[20] It appears that in most cases a sale of state-owned land occurred because the situation was ambiguous, or it was impossible for the kadi to investigate and establish the true nature of the possession. Of course, bribery or favoritism also played a role. Successive sales of such lands further consolidated the proprietary rights of its owner.[21]

Ambiguity seems to have stemmed mainly from the fact that the transfer (*ferag*) of state-owned land in return for monetary compensation, which was a lawful transaction, also was called a sale. To reduce this ambiguity, the religious ruling required that in such transfers the kadi should specifically state that "the possessor of the land transferred its full possession (*tasarruf*) to so-and-so with the *sipahi*'s permission in return for such-and-such a payment of money; and thereupon the *sipahi* too confirmed it by giving it in *tapu* for such-and-such an amount of money paid as *hakk-ı karar*" (payment for the establishment of permanent possession rights)." Such a formula made it definite that the object of the transaction was not a regular sale with freehold rights but a simple transfer of possession or tenure.

When an influential member of the ruling class entered into possession of land by sale, he usually went also to the sultan to obtain a document granting freehold rights on it in order to consolidate his proprietorship.[22]

In the mid-sixteenth century, Sheyhülislam Abussu'ud (d. 1574), preoccupied with the problem of the state land versus freehold status and taxation, formulated responses (*fetvas*) on the land regime with commentaries based on classical Islamic theory.[23]

Given by the most authoritative religious scholar of the time, his *fetvas* had a decisive effect on the subsequent Ottoman interpretation of landholding and taxation practices in the empire. Abussu'ud's formulation on state-owned land was to be included in the new law codes and survey registers as the ultimate and definitive commentary of the Ottoman land law. Obviously, Abussu'ud's main concern was to give an authoritative definition of the Ottoman *miri* regime and land taxation, in order to stop practices which threatened the landholding system. He pointed out that some judges who were unaware of the *miri* nature of a certain category of land were issuing documents legalizing freehold rights on these lands; this malpractice, he said, had become so widespread that it began to threaten the entire traditional order in the public as well as private sectors. In an effort to provide the religious sanction, he tried to explain the Ottoman *miri* regime within the principles formulated by the great jurists of the ninth century, in particular, Abu Yusuf, the most liberal exponent of the Hanafi school.

According to Abussu'ud, the *miri* meant, in Ottoman practice, the land under the state *dominium eminens*. He asserted that, though termed *öşri*, that is, subject to tithes being in the possession of Muslims, in practice such lands were originally *haraci*. If pre-conquest non-Muslim cultivators were allowed to continue cultivating such lands, they had to pay on their harvest a *haraç* rated from one-fifth to two-thirds, depending on the circumstances. In contrast, those conquered lands which were distributed among the Muslim conquerors, or the lands acquired in peace, rendered only one-tenth (*öşr*). Abussu'ud stressed that all lands in the Ottoman Empire had been acquired by military force so that they were all *haraci* lands, and thus owed a land tax at the established rate of *haraç*. This interpretation was bound to have revolutionary effects on the Ottoman peasantry because, prior to this ruling, the imperial laws had fixed the percentage of the tithe as only one-eighth for lands reserved for grain cultivation. And, as the survey registers show, these laws actually were applied in the conquered lands in the fourteenth (Bithynia, Thrace, northern Greece, Bulgaria and western Anatolia), fifteenth (Albania, Morea, Serbia and Bosnia) and sixteenth centuries. The rate of one-fifth was imposed only in the lands conquered after Abussu'ud had issued his commentary, that is, in Cyprus (1570–71), Georgia (1570) and Crete (1669).[24] In the lands of earlier conquest, tithes at a rate of one-eighth generally were maintained, while the extraordinary taxes (*avarız*) now were more frequently imposed. It appears that, in one way or another, state revenues had to be increased in order to meet the needs of a quickly expanding budget. But at this time, as Abussu'ud himself tells us, peasants who were taking the one-tenth in its literal meaning, disputed even the tithe of one-eighth, and claimed the right to pay only one-tenth.[25] This issue, too, must have caused the government to ask Abussu'ud to issue his responsa on the Islamic basis of the current taxation system.

STATE-OWNED LANDS AND THE *TIMAR* SYSTEM

Timar allotments are delimited following the boundaries of villages, *çiftliks* and *mezraas*. Although *timar* grantees were unable to own or use the land for their own benefit, they were authorized by law to have control of arable lands, vacant or possessed by the peasant *reaya*, pastures, wastelands, fruit trees, forests or waters, within their *timar* territories. *Timar* grantees supervised the manner of possession and transfer of the *tapulu* lands, rented vacant arable lands and collected taxes for themselves from outsiders, using the pastures and waters or cultivating the unregistered lands within the boundaries of their *timar*. Fruits from the naturally grown trees also belonged to them. In brief, one can speak of the "territorial" rights of the *sipahi*s within the boundaries of the *timar*.

The *timar*-holders also had police authority to pursue and arrest wrongdoers in their respective territories. But no penalties, even the smallest fines, could be imposed by them without a prior verdict from the local judge in accordance with imperial penal law. In brief, their duties consisted of protecting the persons and rights of peasants who were assigned to them in their *timar* territory and to join the imperial army during campaigns when called. Higher echelons of the *timar* hierarchy, those in possession of *ziamet*s, were also responsible for maintaining security and consequently shared in the revenue from fines occurring in *sipahi timar*s. However, this situation caused frequent disputes and called for reform. The territories of the *ziamet* holders were immune from the periodic security tours of the governors and their lands formed a privileged category called *serbest*, immune or autonomous.

Already in the surveys under Murad II (1421–51), more than one *sipahi* jointly held a single *timar*.[26] Such *timar*s might have developed out of the government's policy to keep the registered *timar* units (*kılıç*) intact while increasing the number of *sipahi*s. This was also the case when a *timar* was granted to a *sipahi*'s sons in common upon his death. However, in the sixteenth century, joint *timar*s usually were held by non-relatives. On the other hand, *timar*-holders were given shares in various villages to make up their *timar* instead of receiving an entire village. This was a natural outcome of the need to make assignments of various sizes and promotions without being obliged to partition large *timar* units. On the other hand, there is a deliberate policy behind it: to prevent a *sipahi* from acquiring complete and independent control of the land and peasantry of a village in the same fashion as a feudal lord. Likewise, the *hass* lands of the governors lay scattered in various parts of the *sancak*, sub-province, or *beglerbegilik*, province. But in this case there was an additional reason, namely to make the governor equally concerned with all parts of his territory, particularly during his periodic tours for security.

In their control of land and the peasants, *timar*-holders cannot be compared to western feudal lords. They were authorized to collect the assigned tax revenue but had no specific rights to land or peasants except for services defined by the law. They were not landowners, though the laws sometimes conventionally referred to them as the "owner" (*sahib*) of the land or the peasant *reaya*. As state agents, they simply supervised the possession and use of land. But they were expressly prohibited from possessing and cultivating lands reserved for the peasant *reaya*. They could have a *çiftlik* and/or a vineyard and a meadow to satisfy the needs of their families, retainers and horses. In the classical age, it was against the basic rules of the *timar* system to transfer the father's *timar* as a patrimony to a son or sons in common. The latter case occurred in the early centuries of the Ottoman state mainly as a transitory measure, when indigenous seigneurial families were incorporated into the Ottoman *timar* system. In Albania, during the first half of the fifteenth century, when it was a frontier land where Ottoman rule was not firmly established, most ordinary *timar*s were transferred to the sons.[27] Thus, while in earlier times a hereditary principle regarding *timar* transfers seems to have prevailed, with the progress towards government centralization, the non-hereditary principle won out. In fact, the lack of inheritance rights on land and the frequent dismissal from *timar*s is an essential characteristic of the Ottoman *timar* system. This impressed contemporary European observers and was interpreted as the principal reason why the Ottomans did not have a patrimonial feudal system or hereditary landed nobility as in the West. Not only were *hass* allotments held as long as the high office was occupied, but also *timar*s and *ziamet*s were retained contingent upon active service. When dismissed, *timar*-holders lost all rights and control over the land, peasant *reaya* and income. However, they retained the title of *sipahi* and were eligible for another *timar* or *ziamet* on condition that they remain in the military class by participating in the imperial campaigns. This "candidacy" (*mülazemet*) period ended when they proved themselves useful during campaigns and obtained a *timar*. If a dismissed *sipahi* engaged in the occupation of a peasant and failed to do military service for seven years, he lost his title of *sipahi* and all the privileges of the military class. Then, as a peasant (*raiyyet*) he was obligated to perform all subject (*kul*) services and pay taxes.

As a rule, upon the death of a *sipahi* his son or sons were eligible for *timars*, the size of which being determined by the rank and the actual size of the prebend held by the father.[28] But a *sipahi* could also give up his *timar* and ask the administration to assign the whole or part of it to his son or sons.

As seen earlier, there was fierce competition for the limited number of *timars* and this became one of the most important questions for the empire at all times. The number of candidates for a *timar* grew over time, creating a difficult situation by the time of Mehmed II. Initially, candidates were chosen and recommended individually or as a group to the government by the commander under which they served. Upon receipt of the memorandum (*tezkire*), the sultan issued an order that commanded the provincial governor to award the candidate a *timar* within his territory. Such a candidate, "with the sultan's order" (*eli emirlü*) went out and sought a vacant *timar* fitting his conditions. Most of the time the search and waiting was long and success largely depended upon his ability to give gifts and bribes to the governor and his staff.

It is a common mistake to assume that *timars* were reserved exclusively for native Turks or that they constituted the majority. In the Balkans, it is true that Turks fighting on the frontiers, or volunteers or deportees (*sürgün*) from Anatolia received *timars*. But even in this case the system favored patrimonial relationships in the process of being recommended to the government and in receiving a *timar*. A great number of the *timar*-holders were actually the dependent men of the governors.[29] On the other hand, Janissaries, palace gate-keepers, imperial kitchen assistants and others who, after a period of service, were entitled to a "release" from palace service and to receive a *timar* were in a privileged position. Dismissed *sipahi*s anxiously seeking re-allocation, as noted above, also swelled the ranks of candidates. It has been suggested[30] that there was a regular rotation system so that *timar*-holders were "dismissed" after serving a defined period of tenure the length of which, however, varied widely. In any event all these *timar* candidates, while still taking part in the sultan's campaigns, formed a competing group, clamoring for favoritism, patronage and resorting to corruption. It is no wonder that dismissed *sipahi*s are mentioned among the organizers and leaders of the rebels in the reports to the sultan during the terrible Turcoman insurrections in Anatolia in the period 1510–29.[31] The government had to take drastic measures to meet the crisis either by turning existing *timars* into jointly held ones, dividing the *timar*s into shares or creating extra *timar* units through new surveys or by conquering neighboring countries and distributing the land as *timar*s.

On the other hand when the provincial *sipahi*s proved to be inadequate for modern warfare during the war against the Habsburgs in the last decade of the sixteenth century, they were neglected. *Sekban* and *sarıca* mercenary troops equipped with firearms and a considerably expanded Janissary corps increasingly replaced the conventional troops in the battlefields.[32]

Hassa çiftlik

Prior to Süleyman I's time, *sipahi*s were each given direct possession and management of one *çiftlik* land, as well as of vineyards, meadows, fruit trees and flour mills – a pre-Ottoman practice in the Byzantine and Balkan states. This type of possession was known as *hassa*. It was supposed that the *sipahi* could find time and means to manage all these properties through the labor services provided by the dependent peasantry. But, unlike the Byzantine and Balkan *pronoia* holder, the Ottoman *sipahi* had to go on campaign almost every year and had little time to care for these possessions. In addition, the Ottoman regime cut down many of the labor services or converted them into cash taxes. Under the new conditions the *sipahi*s were unable to attend to the exploitation of the *hassa* resources, even when they could rent them to private persons under the *mukataa* or renting system and merely collect the income. Actually, as revealed in the survey books, the Ottoman *sipahi* usually had recourse to the latter method instead of attempting direct management. In other words, this was a development in the direction of further professionalization of the military and its alienation from all types of involvement in production. The renting system as applied to public revenue resources was actually the basic system of exploitation employed by the government and by the members of the elite. From another point of view, the renting system depended on a more progressive monetary economy and the presence of people in the countryside who could pay cash rents. In brief, it can be argued that the Ottoman imperial system signified a more centralist regime with less labor services, or more professionalization in the military class and more peasant independence in the production process.

Whatever interpretation for the spread of the renting method under the Ottoman centralist regime is offered, the fact remained that the *sipahi* proved to be an inefficient manager of *hassa* land and inefficient as well in pursuing the rent for the resources reserved for him. The Ottoman surveyors reported this inefficiency to the central government repeatedly from all over the empire. Possession under renting was considered a better way than possession by *tapu* to guarantee the upkeep of the *sipahi*'s "reserve" (*hassa*) land, meadows, fruit trees or flour mills. When in 1539 this fact was observed and reported by the surveyor in Bosnia, the sultan ordered the abolition of the *hassa* status of such lands, that is, the direct control and renting of the *sipahi* and the "sale" to *reaya* under *tapu*. The same policy was applied in the Hüdavendigar *sancak* in Anatolia in about the same period.

NOTES

1 Abū Yūsuf (1302 H/1884), pp. 28–39, also see pp. 23–27, 52–58; Morony (1981), pp. 135–75; Schmucker (1972), pp. 157–65.
2 Modarressi (1983), pp. 105–51, *haraci* lands of early Islam correspond to Ottoman state-owned lands, see Haque (1977), pp. 92–95, 105, 117–50, 152, 163, 170.
3 Abū Yūsuf (1302 H/1884), pp. 23–27; Lokkegaard (1950), pp. 38–72; Haque (1977), pp. 125–50.
4 Nizam al-Mulk (1962), pp. 19, 29, 41, 53, 59.
5 İnalcık (1975b) and (1975c).
6 For example, Abū Yūsuf (1302 H/1884).
7 Cin (1969), pp. 99–100.
8 On *icaratayn*, see *MTM*, I, p. 52; Akgündüz (1988), pp. 354–99; Kreiser (1986), pp. 219–26.
9 *MTM*, I, p. 87, the law stipulates that "all land that is ploughed and cultivated is absolutely state-owned (*miri*) . . . land which is ploughed and cultivated never becomes freehold."
10 Barkan (1937), no. 49, pp. 33–48; no. 53, pp. 101–16, 329–41; no. 56, pp. 147–58; no. 58, pp. 293–302; no. 59, 414–22.
11 Milkova (1966).
12 İnalcık (1982a).
13 *MTM*, I, p. 51.
14 See the *kanunname* of Zvornik dated 1548, Djurdjev *et al.* (1957), pp. 108–11.
15 Law code of Mehmed II, text 15r.
16 *MTM*, I, p. 51.
17 For the "abrogation" of the *vakf* and freehold status of agricultural lands, see İnalcık (1982b), p. 78; Mutafčieva (1988), pp. 131–35.
18 Haque (1977), pp. 240, 267, 270, 294; Modarressi (1983), pp. 200–2.
19 *MTM*, I, p. 51.
20 *MTM*, I, p. 58.
21 For examples, see Gökbilgin (1952), p. 436; Barkan (1988), pp. 69, 102–3, 233–35.
22 Barkan (1970).

23 See note 19 above.
24 Barkan (1943), pp. 197 (Georgia), 351 (Crete).
25 In the Hungarian provinces tithes were levied exactly at the rate of one-tenth of the produce, see Barkan (1943), pp. 296–324.
26 İnalcık (1954b), p. 15 no. 19; p. 35 no. 78; p. 69 no. 185.
27 İnalcık (1954c), pp. 116.
28 Beldiceanu (1967), 9v–10r.
29 İnalcık (1954b), index: *"gulam."*
30 Kunt (1983), p. 77; Howard (1987), pp. 85–90, 174–75.
31 Uluçay (1954–55), vi, p. 65.
32 İnalcık (1980a), pp. 288–97.

4

☾

LAND POSSESSION OUTSIDE
THE *MİRİ* SYSTEM

DEAD LANDS (*MEVAT*) AND THE SULTAN'S GRANTS OF
LAND (*TEMLİK*)

"Dead" or waste land having the potential to be revived and owned, and mainly used to create estates through a sultan's grant (*temlik*) for the elite, played an extremely important role in the social and economic history of Islamic empires.[1] "Dead" land involved the questions of private and state ownership of land, expansion of arable land and the tax base, as well as a specific type of agrarian exploitation. Thus, from the earliest times, the activity of legists added an important chapter to Islamic Law regarding the problems related to "dead" land. First of all, the state's *dominium eminens* was established by the Prophet's tradition saying: "Verily all uninhabited, uncultivated and ownerless lands are for God and his Messenger."[2] The first controversial question was how to define the "dead" land. Corresponding to *res nullius* in Roman law, it was defined first of all as wastelands such as forests, swamps, marshes and deserts. But some legists added those arable lands which were abandoned by their cultivators and remained uncultivated and ownerless over a long period of time. If, however, the previous cultivators returned before much time had elapsed, they had preeminent rights to reclaim the land. As it placed the extensive lands recorded in the Ottoman land surveys as *mezraa*, deserted, or *hali*, uninhabited, lands in the category of dead lands, the commentary had very important consequences in practice. When applied, it would allow the state to make land grants (*temlik*) of arable land which had been deserted by its former inhabitants to members of the ruling elite. Usually such lands were exploited by neighboring villagers as a kind of reserve land or were inhabited by them or by

wandering peasants or nomads. Sometimes the previous village population even returned. The sultan's grant of private ownership of deserted
and uninhabited lands meant the loss of these advantages for the nearby
villages and led to the exploitation of peasants by landowners, since the
peasants on such lands had to hand over a higher percentage of their
produce as sharecroppers. However, in the Ottoman Empire, in contrast
to the experience of lower Iraq in Abbasid times, such lands were often
settled under conditions of regular tenancy by peasants. Evidently, difficulty in attracting sharecropping workers into the uncultivated lands was
the reason for favoring the peasants in the Ottoman case.[3] One may
speak of the expansion of agriculture and the tax base only in those cases
where estates were created from dead land, forests or swamps.

In principle, the Ottoman sultan granted deserted or uninhabited lands
to individuals when settlement and cultivation was possible only through
this method. Otherwise, in order to obtain revenue from abandoned
lands, the government used the simple renting method (*mukataalı*).
Actual reclamation could precede or follow the imam's permission for
reclamation. Thus the state was in a position to prevent appropriation of
abandoned arable land reserved for the peasantry. In reclamation, real
improvements, such as preparing the land for cultivation, were required
for acquisition; it was not enough just to enclose the land by hedges.

The legists, finding the imam's permission a prerequisite for the ownership of reclaimed land, added arguments of a practical nature, saying that
without a regulatory authority the acquisition of such lands would lead
to constant conflict and even fighting among interested individuals. As
kadi court records show, the appropriation of village commons, pastures,
threshing floor, etc. by notables, at the expense of the peasants, was a
general problem against which the imperial bureaucracies in the Byzantine and the Ottoman empires constantly had to fight.

An analysis of the imperial land grant (*temlik*) deeds can further clarify
the Ottoman notion of landownership. As a rule, the procedure for
obtaining a land grant started with a formal application to the sultan,
directly or through a high dignitary such as the grand vizier or the *beglerbegi*. The occasions for the application varied extensively: in most cases,
the applicant stated that he needed the revenue to establish a charitable
work through a pious foundation – a mosque complex, a *medrese* or
fountain – or, less frequently, for his own benefit and that of his descendants, or to make an addition to an already established property or pious
foundation.

The land applied for had to be defined clearly. The object of a grant was usually cultivated land – a village or villages with its peasants (*reaya*), or abandoned arable land or pastures and meadows, or wasteland, or land reclaimed by the applicant and turned into an estate, or sometimes simply the use of a defined amount of water from the public system.

In the title deed, the sultan conferred ownership on the applicant, recognizing that he deserved such a favor because of his loyalty and his distinguished services. The land granted was delimited carefully in the title deed. Usually, after the official grant, the interested person wanted to be certain of the boundaries and obtained a separate document with their description.

A special document of delimitation known as *sınırname*, in the form of an imperial diploma, was issued; this guaranteed freehold possession of the defined land and prevented any intervention by outsiders, including the local authorities. The grantee's freehold ownership was established on everything within these boundaries, including the arable land, wasteland, hills, forests, rivers, lakes and springs. The state relinquished in favor of the grantee all its rights, including taxes and the right of entry to pursue criminals. A special formula emphasizing this immunity from official control was used, stating that the land was given "in the way of full immunity" (*serbestiyet*) and it was "crossed out from the registers in the state bureaus," and the local authorities or anybody else were prohibited "from setting their feet" on the land.[4]

The full autonomy and immunities pertaining to such lands led to important changes in the Ottoman social and administrative organization. Most significantly, peasants abandoning their farms in their villages tended to come and settle in these sanctuaries. Thus, land grants had the effect of ruining the family farm system on regular state-owned lands. This is why the abuse in granting land by the sultan was vehemently condemned by the bureaucrat-critics. On the other hand, since police forces in the rural areas under the jurisdiction of the local authorities, that is, *sancak-beg*s or *subaşı*s, could not enter these lands, individuals who were pursued for their illegal acts took refuge in them. Because such land grants or *vakf* lands usually welcomed potential labor of whatever origin to expand their cultivated area, disputes arose between their managers and the local administrative authorities. However, in the sixteenth century, this development was not so widespread as to permit us to state that land grants subverted the state-owned land system and gave rise to a class of landowners. Besides, it should be remembered that such land grants were made less frequently from *miri* lands than from reclaimed wastelands.

From the beginning of the Ottoman state, the sultans made land grants mostly to enable the members of the elite to found pious endowments – a purpose made explicit in the grant diplomas. Also one of the most popular kind of land grants were those made in favor of the founder of dervish convents (*zaviye*), which had vital functions in creating Turkish rural settlement in the conquered lands. Under Süleyman I, however, many convents of the heterodox Turcoman *kızılbaş* were closed down and their *vakf* lands confiscated because they had become centers of anti-Ottoman propaganda. But later, again in the reign of Süleyman I, it was admitted that a safe and easy journey, as well as prosperity along the highway to Erzurum in eastern Asia Minor, was disrupted as a result of their abrogation, so a number of them were restored. In any event, early convents and estates/*vakfs* based on property grants were mostly created out of lands reclaimed from swamps and forests.

As stated above, the grant blocked all taxes due to the public treasury, so that a tax collector could not visit the estate or *vakf*. However, it was exceptional that the poll-tax, an Islamic tax paid in cash, also was included. In general, tithes and customary dues made up the income from the land grants. In most cases, the landlord simply sent a steward to the estate to collect the income – the same taxes and dues as under state control. The steward's functions were the same as a *timar*-holder's, that is, to collect the assigned dues, to ensure that peasant families did not alter the status and use of the land, and, to maintain or increase the number of the peasant family farm units.

Except in the case where the land was reclaimed and granted as free-hold, the grantee was usually not directly involved in the production process. In any case, shifts in the status of the villages from *miri* to the private estate/*vakf* or vice-versa did not affect its production organization at the level of the direct producer, or the peasant's obligations towards the landlord or the state.

In the first three centuries of the empire, large land grants often were granted to sultanas or to viziers, mostly to enable them to establish a major *vakf* establishment.[5] For example, in order to enable Sokollu Mehmed Pasha to build a mosque complex in the newly conquered city of Becskerek, several abandoned villages were given as freehold in the 1550s. The powerful Sultana Kösem (d. 1651) constructed a monumental bridge linking northern and central Greece, thanks to the rich *vakfs* in the area, previously granted as freehold by Süleyman I to his daughter Mihrumah and subsequently managed by the sultanas.[6]

In some situations, the grantee might later on request additional rights in the lands previously granted. For example, Hürrem Sultan, the wife of Süleyman I, requested the freehold ownership of six villages which had come into existence within the boundaries of land for which the grant previously had been given to her.[7] During the period 1541–51, the new villages had emerged when a number of peasants from outside settled on her property. In general, the transfer of peasants to such grants or *vakf* lands was not welcomed by the central bureaucracy since it caused harm to settlements under the public trust. In this case, the additional grant was made, but further settlements by outsiders were not allowed, nor could agents of the sultana encourage peasants to come and settle.

The land granted in favor of Grand Vizier Ahmed Pasha in 1554 shows how a freehold property was established out of abandoned lands. Ahmed Pasha requested the *temlik* of the two plots deserted by their peasant populations which he bought from a certain Yahya and, settling his Bulgarian, Hungarian and Serbian slaves, turned the plots into villages with cultivated lands. Since these lands originally belonged to the category of the conquered lands, the *dominium eminens* belonged to the state and a rent always had to be paid to the state treasury. When Ahmed received the grant, that is, the freehold proprietorship, this rent also was granted to him.

In the fifteenth and sixteenth centuries, sultanic grants of state lands to individuals consisted mostly of those lands which were found abandoned and unused. Also, a significant portion of them were merely wasteland (*mevat*). The sultans, or more exactly, the bureaucrat-statesmen, were reluctant to give away prosperous villages with their peasant families to individuals. By granting "dead" land to members of the ruling elite who had the capital to reclaim or revivify abandoned lands or wastelands, new sources of revenues were created and eventually important public services were provided, since most of these lands soon were donated by their owners to charitable purposes through the foundation of religious endowments (*vakf*) – such as the construction of mosques, schools, libraries, bazaars and shops, bridges or fountains.

In reality, the struggle carried on by the central bureaucracy against the greed of the other members of the ruling elite was an eternal question in the Ottoman Empire, as was the case in earlier patrimonial empires. Even as early as the first half of the fifteenth century, and particularly during political crises when the sultans had to make significant concessions to the religious and military elite, a great amount of state-owned lands escaped state control through land grants and *vakf*s.

The fact that the state always retained *dominium eminens* is clearly seen in cases when someone with a freehold grant did not comply with its conditions. So, for example, if he did not cultivate the land for three successive years, he lost his ownership rights. The imam legally could give the land to another person. Thus it was the actual reclamation and cultivation that was the real purpose for land grant and legalized ownership. In the last analysis, ownership of land appears to have been always dependent on the paramount interest of the Islamic community or state. In the Ottoman Empire a revision and "abrogation" of such land titles occasionally was carried out, although the operation always entailed a profound political crisis, as happened in the period 1470–1512 (see below).

Granting of arable lands as private estates goes back to the early Islamic period, when it eventually engendered a similar social transformation. During the first two centuries of the caliphate, a powerful centralist government was able to maintain the integrity of the *haraci*, the state-owned lands.[8] Then, in the subsequent period, the estate system spread both on the reclaimed "dead" lands as well as on the regular *haraci* lands. In other words, in Islamic empires, including the Ottoman, the weakening of the central power entailed a relative dissolution of the classical landholding system.[9]

We have seen that the state's main interest in the granting of land was to bring abandoned or wastelands under cultivation and thus create sources of revenue for public works projects. But an individual's motivation for investing capital to improve such lands was evidently his desire to create a religious-charitable work in the form of a *vakf*, or in most cases to ensure a perpetual source of revenue for his family and offspring under the so-called family *vakf*.

As far as the economic organization was concerned, estates and *vakf*s from wasteland constituted a category which contrasted with the state-owned lands where the peasant family farm under state control, or *çift-hane* system, was the norm. As the above examples demonstrate, in many of the estates land and labor organization were different at the beginning, with wage or servile labor and sharecropping, and sometimes the land would simply be turned into a ranch for breeding cattle.[10]

However, over time, the land and labor organization in many estates and *vakf*s also began to take the regular form of a family labor farm or *çift-hane* under *tapu*. As we have seen, peasant families from state-owned lands often settled on these estates and *vakf*s, and also, because the slave population which settled there was organized as peasant families on the basis of *çift-hane*, they later acquired mostly the status of the regular free *reaya*. Then, the regulations concerning the general status of the peasants and land use were applied as in the state-owned lands, and the same rent/ tax and dues constituted the income. Besides, there was always a chance that freehold and even *vakf* lands would revert back to their original *miri* state. The only significant difference was that the peasantry on the freehold or *vakf* lands enjoyed immunities and better protection. In the private estates or *vakf*s, as well as in the imperial domains, the most interesting feature, from an economic viewpoint, was the fact that the peasants collected a large amount of surplus wheat to export to distant markets in the urban centers of the empire and in Europe. Many of them also were oriented towards the production of cash-crops – cotton, sesame, flax and rice, to mention the most important ones.

Thus, as long as the owners of estates and *vakf*s did not appropriate state-owned lands, they apparently played an important and positive role in the economy of the empire. Being in a position to accumulate cash capital, the ruling elite formed the main group in the society able to invest in and expand the arable lands. In the classical age, those who controlled such estates were the high dignitaries of the central bureaucracy under the direct control of the sultan. This state of affairs was particularly true when grants were made from wastelands, and these sometimes formed important economic projects. However, because of the basic patrimonial character of the state, it was common to find land grants made from lands in good condition, and assigned to the sultan's favorites. In the sixteenth century, such aberrations remained limited as long as the sultan's centralist authority was intact, and conscientious bureaucrats like Celalzade and his disciples used it to preserve the original imperial system. At the turn of the century, the memorialists and counsellors to the sultan[11] bitterly complained of the growing influence of the palace favorites in the government and of the sultan's loss of independence, which resulted in the plunder of the state-owned lands through the awarding of irresponsible land grants.

THE EXTENSION OF STATE OWNERSHIP AND DUAL OWNERSHIP OF LAND: THE *DİVANİ-MALİKANE* SYSTEM

In 1478 Mehmed II ordered that all founding charters of freehold and *vakf* lands were to be investigated and those not meeting the requirements for re-validation should be "abrogated" and re-assigned to state ownership.[12] The justification given for this radical move was that *vakf* buildings in a ruined condition or diverted to other uses were considered to have lost their real charitable and religious purpose, and so the *vakf* lands had to return to state ownership. Every new ruler had the ultimate right to inspect the legality of freehold and *vakf* lands for re-validation. Villages and farms granted by the early sultans must have amounted to a substantial part of total revenues when Mehmed II ordered the revision of all freehold lands and *vakf*s in his dominions. According to the testimony of Tursun Beg, an official directly engaged in the revision, state ownership of over 20,000 villages and farms was re-established.[13]

Practiced by other, earlier Islamic rulers, the state's claim over freehold land and *vakf*s actually was based on the assumption that the eminent domain of the state never became obsolete on arable lands conquered from non-Muslims. On the other hand, the state claimed a "government share" (*divani*), also on the assumption that the peasants, and water used, always belonged to the state. In particular, the peasant's personal taxes of customary origin (*çift*-tax) formed the basis of state taxation. Mehmed II's bureaucrat advisors believed that state lands had escaped state control and served the personal interests of certain "inactive" groups such as retired ulema, dervishes and absentee lords. Small plots granted to dervish convents by early sultans particularly became a target of abrogation. Following the empire-wide revision the sultan distributed "abrogated" lands as *timar*s to the soldiery to expand his provincial cavalry army.

This radical "reform," reminiscent of the confiscation by absolutist Western monarchs of ecclesiastical and feudal lands, triggered a deep social and political crisis throughout the empire. The traditional non-military groups, which suffered most by the abrogation, began to form secret opposition centers, particularly in Amasya around Prince Bayezid and in Konya. Among religious opponents, the Sufi orders, in particular Halvatiyya dervishes, became most active in organizing secret opposition against the "despotic," "anti-Sharia" measures of the sultan, who was rumored to have been misled by evil councillors.[14] At Mehmed's death, the general discontent exploded in a terrible insurrection in which the Grand Vizier Mehmed Pasha was ferociously murdered and Bayezid was brought to the throne instead of Cem, who was supported by the military faction. Under Bayezid II a reaction, rather a counter-revolution, swept the empire and most of the confiscated freehold and *vakf* lands were returned to their former owners by the new sultan, who was highly praised as the "restorer of the Islamic Law and tradition." The land surveys and other documentary collections of this reign attest to the intensity and extension of the restoration. However, it was not universal, and the Conqueror's "reform" survived to consolidate the power of the Ottoman centralist monarchy under his successors.[15]

A more conciliatory device to solve the problem of using freehold lands to secure additional troops was the so-called "dual ownership" (*iki baştan*, or *divani-malikane*), in which the state and landowner shared the surplus of the peasant production as tax or rent.[16] As a rule, Ottoman sultans recognized the land grants previously made by Muslim rulers, while they considered themselves free to bestow such grants in lands conquered from the Christians in the Balkans. Freehold arable land, acquired by grant, sale or inheritance, was quite extensive in the countries which came under Islamic rule before the Ottomans. Thus, in central Anatolia and the Arab provinces, the Ottoman state had to confirm the hereditary freehold rights of the old landowning families. But, at the same time, the state claimed that such lands originally fell into the category of conquered (*haraci*), and that the state, having inalienable sovereign rights over the *reaya* cultivating such lands, had an exclusive right over the state taxes.[17] Therefore, in return for confirming the ownership rights in cases where such rights could not be denied, the state imposed on landowners the obligation to furnish auxiliary soldiers for the sultan's army. However, unlike an ordinary *sipahi*, the landowner could not be dismissed and lose the land when he failed to fulfill the military aid. In such cases he had only to pay compensation. He disposed the land as freehold in all its legal aspects, namely, he could sell, donate, mortgage, and leave to his legal heirs who could in turn partition the land. Thus, private ownership rights sanctioned by Islamic Law continued, which a Muslim state could not ignore.

The owner's share in tithes (*malikane*), as well as the state's share (*divani*), were taken in varying rates according to the fertility of the soil and local custom. State insistence on its exclusive control over the labor of the *reaya* is of particular interest in this case. The private owner might be an individual or a pious endowment, and the sultan might assign the *divani* share to its agents, *sipahi*s or state officials, as prebend, or to any person as a favor. Of course, both the owner's and state's share of the produce always were paid by the direct producer, the *reaya*, separately to the private owner and the state. Most *malikane*s over time were converted into pious endowments; the sultan sometimes added the *divani* portion as a favor to *vakf*s endowed by eminent persons.

When attempting to interpret the second set of taxes, and the obligation to equip an auxiliary soldier for the army, the Ottoman ulema had difficulty in finding a completely satisfactory answer in the earlier Islamic

Table I:32. Extent of freehold (*mülk*) and *vakf* lands in the total budget

Regions	Total revenue (million *akça*)	Percentage of *mülk* and *vakf*
Anatolia (provinces to the west of the Euphrates)	129	17
Rumeli (territory to the south of the Danube)	198	6
Southeast (province of Diyarbekir)	22	6
Syria (provinces of Aleppo and Damascus)	51	14

Source: Barkan (1953–54), p. 277.

religious literature. Abussu'ud stipulated that such lands were a separate category of arable land on which Muslims had full proprietorship, including the right of *dominium eminens (rakaba)*. Thus, the landowner's share is a rent. But earlier practices contradict this interpretation.

The dual ownership system represents an attempt at reconciliation or an intermediary regime between the ownership rights of the local hereditary lords and the Ottoman *miri* system. The concentration of the dual system in the Amasya–Tokat–Sivas district is not accidental. This was Turcoman country, where Ottoman rule established itself only after a long struggle, and where aristocratic families in control of numerous Turcoman clans and a regime of big estates as family patrimony were dominant. During the interregnum period 1402–13, Mehmed I, in his struggle against his brothers, had to make concessions to these local magnates to secure their support.[18] Mehmed I's successors confirmed these privileges in recognition of their service in this critical period. In the provinces further east, conquered under the autocratic Sultan Mehmed II, dual ownership did not exist.[19] Actually dual ownership was a system applied in Islamic lands long before the Ottomans. The Ottomans confirmed it and extended it to the western parts of their empire.[20] It is obvious that under dual ownership the peasant was intensively exploited. Thus, in the course of the sixteenth century, this remnant of "feudal" landownership declined as a result of periodic governmental surveys and the extension of the *miri* land system.

In 1528 the total revenues of freehold and *vakf* lands made up 12 percent, or about 60 million *akça*, of the total imperial revenues of 538 million *akça* (for a breakdown in various regions, see Table I:32).

Historically, from the outset, the paramount question in the Ottoman state was to define, supervise and maintain the status of various types of land. Since the degree of land control determined power relationships between the state and the leading families in the empire, the question of state lands *vis-à-vis* freehold and endowed lands was especially important. We mean not only the newly established Ottoman leading military and ulema families, but also those non-Muslim native seigneurial families that the Ottomans maintained at the first stage of their conquest. The crises between the state and the leading families focused on both control of the land and the peasantry. Land alone did not mean much without productive peasant labor organized as dependent family labor. These crises broke out at times when the state, that is the sultan, with his centralizing bureaucrats, attempted to abolish or diminish the military and ulema class control by re-introducing state ownership of land as a paramount principle against the established rights of private ownership or pious endowments (*vakf*). The signs of such a crisis, historically detectable, are to be found already under Murad I (1362–89) and gained momentum under Bayezid I (1389–1402). The collapse of the first centralist bureaucratic empire which came about in 1402 marked the re-establishment and consolidation of feudal control of land.

As seen earlier, the most dramatic outbreak in the struggle came during the rise of the centralist Ottoman Empire under Mehmed II (1451–81). With the succession of the authoritarian sultans, Selim I (1512–20) and Süleyman I (1520–66), the ever-present question of *miri* versus freehold and *vakf* stirred the powerful military and ulema groups, and then the centralist bureaucracy turned to the same Sharia principles to find support for state ownership over land, or, more precisely, the full establishment of state control on the grain-producing lands and peasantry. Since the usual device through which the state lands escaped were the land sales in the kadi courts, in accordance with the principles of Islamic Law, the state bureaucracy concentrated its attention there. Always a supporter of state policies, Ibn Kemal, the Sheyhülislam under Selim I and Süleyman I, summarized the legal principles regarding state-owned land. "Since neither *timar*-holder (*sipahi*) nor tiller of the land (peasant)," he said, "owns the land itself and its *rakaba* (*proprietas nuda*), they are not allowed to sell it or donate it or make a *vakf*. However, its lease, cession and transfer is permissible; and under the sultan's law the sale of the possession right through cession and transfer in inheritance to the male children is also permitted."[21]

NOTES

1 On *temlik* (*tamlık*) and (*ikta'*) for the pre-Ottoman period, see Cahen (1953), pp. 25–52; Morony (1981), pp. 135–75; *idem* (1984), pp. 209–23; Haque (1977), pp. 254–84; but Ottoman *temlik* is a direct continuation in content

and basic terminology of the Turco-Mongol *soyurghal,* see Subtelny (1988), pp. 479–509.

2 Yahya b. Adam cited by Haque (1977), p. 251.

3 On the revivification of the wastelands, slaves from East Africa were brought to lower Iraq under the early caliphate, while Ottomans employed war captives.

4 The formula used by Muslim bureaucrats is *"mafruz al-kalam wa maktu' al-kadem."*

5 For a collection of *temlik* documents originating in Süleyman I's reign, see MS British Library, Or MS 9503, fol. 2–34.

6 *Ibid.,* fol. 15, dated 961 H/1554.

7 *Ibid.*

8 Haque (1977), p. 250.

9 Termination or weakening of state control on land through *temlik,* leasing or tax-farming entails decentralization in provincial administration, as occurred in the Ottoman Empire in the eighteenth century, see İnalcık (1977b), pp. 27–52.

10 For a similar development under the Abbasids with the prevalence of the *muzara'a* or sharecropping system, see Haque (1977), pp. 310–46; sharecropping was the system particularly practiced on *ikta'* lands.

11 For example, see Koçi Bey (1939), pp. 38–40.

12 On the abrogation of freehold or *vakf* status of arable land under Mehmed II, see İnalcık (1982b), p. 78; Mutafčieva (1981).

13 İnalcık and Murphey (1978), text 18a, but in 169a one thousand.

14 *Ibid.*

15 See İnalcık (1982b), pp. 78–79.

16 The pioneering study in dual ownership is Barkan's (1939), pp. 119–84; see also Venzke (1986), pp. 451–69.

17 On the so-called *urfi* taxes, see İnalcık (1980a), pp. 311–37.

18 *Ibid.,* and "Mehmed I," *EI².*

19 Barkan (1943), index: *"divani," "malikane."*

20 Venzke (1986), pp. 461–69.

21 *MTM,* I, p. 62.

5

ö

LAND SURVEYING

LAND SURVEYING (*TAHRÎR*) AND REGISTERS

When examined carefully, the reports of the intended conquests reveal that the first question for the monarch and his bureaucracy was how much revenue could be derived from the region; and the first act after the conquest was to put down in the registers all possible sources of revenue. In fact, two factors, the prestige of the dynasty and the need for financial gain were the main driving forces for continued Ottoman conquests. These conquests, of course, were supported at the same time by Islamic ideology and the *cihad* legitimation.

The purpose of surveying is made clear in the preambles of instructions to surveyors. It was with the intention, they assert, of protecting the *reaya* against abuses introduced by the local military that the survey was made as a general inspection – an avowed policy with the emphasis on the protection of the *reaya*, that is, the taxable population. But at the same time it was asserted that, as the ultimate goal, the survey sought to record and make available all taxable sources and to uncover evasions, and to inspect all kinds of tax immunities so as to ultimately achieve an increase in public revenues. Throughout the document one can see these two points as the main concern of the administration. In order to make a compromise between these two rather conflicting goals, the sultan ruled that all taxes should be assessed and collected with "justice" under the stipulations of the existing laws and "ancient custom."

In 1574 the surveyor Ömer Beg was praised because he accomplished the survey in perfect justice so that peasants as well as the military who had *timar*s were agreeable to and thankful for his decisions. At the same time it was pointed out that his efforts proved to be advantageous for the treasury.

The first survey of a conquered land was decided when it was annexed to the Ottoman Empire, and the *timar* system was to be established. Thereupon a detailed registration of all sources of revenue was undertaken and the results were entered in a detailed register (*defter-i mufassal*). Then these revenues were distributed among the members of the military class, mostly among those *sipahi*s who had participated in the conquest of the land. The latter usually were *sipahi*s without *timar*s or dismissed *sipahi*s from neighboring Ottoman provinces. Those members of the sultan's standing army (*kapı-kulu* including the Janissaries) who performed well during the campaign were given priority in the distribution of *timar*s.

All this explains the dynamism of Ottoman expansion, with the military anxious to get *timar*s in the lands to be conquered. The survey was a prerequisite to the distribution of revenues among the military. A separate book called a "summary register" (*defter-i icmal*) was drawn up for the distribution. It contained all three categories of prebends – *timar*, *ziamet* and *hass*, indicating the location with a short note about the number of taxpayers and amount of the revenue.

A detailed description of an after-conquest survey can be seen in the case of the survey of Cyprus in 1572.[1] From the correspondence between the central government and those responsible for the survey, we learn that the government was most anxious to win over the peasants and to preserve and, if possible, increase sources of revenue on the island. This concern was spelled out even before the conquest, as we read in an order to the governor of İçili advising him to do his utmost to win the hearts of the masses and to convey the sultan's pledge that if the island is conquered, the native peasant population shall in no way be molested, and that any property which they and their families have owned shall suffer no violation. "It was supposed," a contemporary Western source tells us,[2] "that there were some fifty thousand serfs (*paroikoi*, or *parici*) who would be ready to join the Turks." During the military operations a great number of the peasants on the plain took refuge in the mountains and it was found that seventy-six villages in the Masarea and Mazoto region did not have any farmers. Since their population did not return, the government took measures to settle the land with farmers from Anatolia in order to restore tax resources. Strict orders were sent to the Ottoman agents to give confidence to the Greek serfs. "It is my desire," the sultan said in a firman[3] while the census was in progress,

> to ensure that everybody attend to his daily work and concerns with a
> mind free from discomfort and anxiety, and that the island be restored to

its former prosperity. Those responsible for causing the *reaya* to disperse through oppression and exacting the taxes at an excessive rate shall be chastised.

The survey commenced. "In making the census of the villages and their inhabitants," a Greek source reported,[4]

> he [the Pasha] used the books and accounts of the Latin rulers, to discover how much revenue the island yielded to the royal treasury, *parici* and *perpiriarii*, who were slaves of the chiefs and upper classes who could not own land, and whose very selves and children were their master's property, never ceased to help the Turks, for they hoped under their yoke to find freedom and rest. They made known to the commission of inquiry and to the Pasha the revenues, estates, villages, and even in detail the families in each village and their houses.

The sultan asked whether the inhabitants wished to remain under the pre-conquest statutes or whether they preferred the Ottoman laws enforced in neighboring Ottoman provinces. In the hope of freeing themselves from the condition of serfdom of the Frankish period, the peasants readily accepted Ottoman practices.

According to the instructions given to the surveyor, this is how a registration was made. The sultan appointed a qualified surveyor, chosen from among respectable ulema or bureaucrats with a reputation of being just and honest, by a special diploma which empowered him with all necessary authority, and ordered the subjects and local officials including the kadi to obey and assist him in his task. In the diploma, the procedure to be followed is described in detail. The surveyor started his investigation on the spot, comparing the actual situation with what he had found in the previous survey book. In a village, for example, he invited into his presence the elderly, the *vakf* trustees and the military with all the documents in their hands.

First, the status of each peasant was investigated and taxes connected with *çift*-tax were established. *Timar* or *ziamet*-holders each were to bring their own dependent *reaya* into the presence of the surveyor with the grown-up sons fit for tax liability. Since evasions from registration were quite frequent, *sipahis* were warned to be alert on this matter. Those *sipahis* found responsible for the registration of a minor or concealment of any subject liable to taxation were punished and dismissed, while those *sipahis* who brought to the attention of the surveyor the additional sources of revenue were rewarded. In fact, there were cases of mass flight, particularly among the nomads, to evade registration. Rebellion and attacks on the person of the surveyor have also been recorded. The long

Albanian resistance started following the registration of 1431–32 and continued until Skanderbeg's death in 1468.[5] In 1527 Turcomans killed the surveyor and started an insurrection in a large area from Kayseri to Amasya.[6]

Survey books not only constituted a record and reference to identify the resources to be assigned to the military, but also were a status book for the land and population which determined, until the next survey, the social position and tax liabilities of lands, persons and groups. A person recorded as a married peasant in possession of a farm of a defined size could not escape without penalty his registered status and its attendant obligations. As a rule he could not abandon the cultivation of his land and go to town and acquire the status of townsman. The married peasants in possession of a *çiftlik*, those with half a *çiftlik*, married and non-married peasants with no land or little, were each recorded separately. When the registration of peasants who were classified in accordance with the *çift*-tax system was completed, the surveyor determined the totals of tithes in kind on the basis of production during the previous three years. The value of wheat, barley etc. was computed later when the sultan announced the fixed price of each type of grain for the whole region. Being of great concern and consequence for the state revenues as well as for the rural economy and its population, an average regional price was determined through the local kadi on the basis of prices during three consecutive periods of the year. The imperial diploma ordered that all tax immunities were to be carefully investigated and recorded in the new registers. A particular concern for the central government was to restore deserted villages (*mezraa*) and *çiftlik*s during the survey. Those abandoned were carefully recorded to be auctioned among renters later on.

In order to make peasant farms and individual fields identifiable, their local names were carefully recorded, in some cases with second names. Thus, survey books ensured the central administration a close and effective control of the *reaya* and the peasant farms.

Following the *çift*-tax and tithes, the third category of taxes consisted of dues (*rüsum*) which included taxes on vineyards, grain mills, fullers' mills, beehives, fishing and market dues as well as the bride tax, *tapu* dues and fines. The surveyor was to determine the amount of each in view of the population size and economic conditions.

As for the fourth category of taxes, *avarız-ı divaniyye*, or extraordinary levies for the state, which affected rural as well as urban populations, the surveyor or kadi determined and registered each category of *reaya* separately, as well as those enjoying exemption.

The *reaya* who were permanently required to provide a service for the state, such as working in the mines or on state-owned lands, or as guardians of bridges or mountain passes, were exempt from the extraordinary levies. Wherever *reaya* were found to have abandoned their original land of settlement or service, they would not be registered in their new abode unless their new settlement was of more than ten years. They were to be forcibly taken to their place of service. A note of particular interest stated: "the surveyor shall keep in mind that those single men who have in their possessions peasant farms [*çiftlik* or *bashtina*] are classified as married *reaya*." Thus, the land unit was considered the decisive factor in determining the tax liability. A *çiftlik* owner was always treated as a household as far as impositions, tax or services were concerned.

Considering how important registration was for the people and the government, the sultan warned the surveyor to proceed with extreme care and caution and not to deviate from impartiality nor to take bribes. The surveyor was given the power to make full investigations on all matters concerning taxation, possession of land, legality of immunities, tax exemptions, etc. Thus, as he was responsible for implementation of the established Ottoman principles concerning land tenure and personal status, and was in constant consultation with the central government, the surveyor had the power to investigate and decide every particular case during the survey. His decision as recorded in the register had the strength of law. He drew up a list of controversial issues and requested the sultan's decision as the ultimate authority.

The surveyor also was asked to investigate and record ancient customs on the rates of market dues or other local impositions, and also measurements, the time of their collection, etc.; but the rates and collection methods of basic Ottoman rural taxes – *çift*-tax, tithes, dues on vineyards, vegetable gardens, orchards, mills, beehives, fees for marriage and building plots or fines – were already described in the general sultanic law codes.[7] The surveyor drew up a draft regulation, *kanunname*, for the sub-province, with provisions on all the taxes as well as rules on matters of frequent dispute between the peasant *reaya* and the *sipahi*s and imperial agents, or among the military. In fact, the decisions of the kadi regarding disputes drew upon the regulation as a guide or legal text. These regulations thus ensured the smooth functioning of the whole Ottoman agrarian–fiscal system.

The register as well as the draft regulation of a sub-province was ultimately submitted to the sultan, that is, to his central bureaus to be examined and to receive final approval. From that moment, the register determined the status of individuals, their tax obligation, place of residence, and so on. Once registered, there was re-inspection at regular intervals. It is obvious that the central administration had to know the changes which occurred over time: on the sources of revenue, the beneficiaries, the status of land and the *reaya*, or immunities, old or newly established. Over a period of time the peasantry grew in numbers; a new generation of taxable peasants came into existence at the same time as new lands were opened for cultivation and new settlements were established. All of these changes necessitated a new survey updating the status and tax liabilities of the *reaya*. As noted in the instructions, "by the passing of years the figures and names change and the number of the population increases or decreases" and "the established rules and customs change or deteriorate," so that a new survey became imperative to prevent injustices, mistakes and losses for the treasury.

In the intervening period between the two surveys, the extra revenues from the peasant youth who became taxable or from the reclaimed or recultivated lands were collected by the *timar*-holder for his benefit or by state agents. Therefore, it was recommended that a new survey be conducted at ten, fifteen, or twenty-year intervals for purposes of inspection or to record the impact of an event – new conquests, rebellions or large-scale population movements. Surveys which were completed around 1430–32 might be connected with the capture of Salonica following the important conquests in the Balkans; those made around 1455 with the conquest of İstanbul, and those made around 1528 with the invasion of Hungary. Sometimes a new survey was ordered immediately as a result of the shortcomings and complaints about the survey in progress, and was completed upon the appointment of a new surveyor. As the number of peasants and the size of arable land changed over time, the actual income of the *timar*-holders from the peasants' taxes also changed. If there was a considerable drop in the actual income of the *timar*-holders, the military service could be impaired; so a re-adjustment through a new survey became necessary.

In a new survey, the extra farms with peasant households and their estimated tax revenue were registered separately under the heading "additional increases" (*ziyade, ifraz*). Obviously, the comprehensive tabulations of such increases may indicate either that there were omissions in the prior survey or a real increase or both. When an increase is unexpectedly high, this surely may indicate a real improvement in economic conditions.

A general survey of the entire empire was to be carried out at the time of the succession of each sultan to the throne, since, upon the death of a sultan, all deeds and titles became legally null and void until the new sultan confirmed them. Sometimes a survey was entrusted to one who guaranteed that he would find a considerable surplus. During the period of decline when the sources of revenue suffered in certain regions, the government either selected such persons as surveyors or stopped making new surveys. The old registers continued to be used as assessment documents despite the discrepancies and injustices such a decision entailed.

An Ottoman survey is not a cadastre in the modern sense. But the Ottoman system of registration of land and population, comparable to the English doomsday book, was functional and practical and made a systematic cadastral registration unnecessary, which was in any case an impossible task under medieval conditions. In addition to being a long and costly process, the cadastre was not practical under conditions of extensive grain cultivation. Just by counting households with complete or half *çiftliks*, the administration knew the extent of both the land and the population and the potential tax revenues. Precise measurements were made on valuable lands such as vineyards or when a serious dispute arose. Only then, under the local kadi's supervision, were exact measurements made using a standard rope, and a final document was issued with all the details noted.

In the sixteenth century, a separate survey register was prepared for each sub-province (*sancak*), although the kadi's jurisdiction, the *kada*, was the main registration area. In earlier times, the Ottomans adhered to the preconquest administrative boundaries, which usually were decided by physical and economic factors. In short, the survey books, including about 2,000 volumes preserved in the Ottoman archives in İstanbul and Ankara, record not only the adult male population or households, but also landholdings, the type and amount of products, taxes and dues.[8]

The Ottoman survey system was intended to serve as a base and as a device to implement the *çift-hane* system. Data in the survey books should be interpreted within the requirements of the system. Attempts by modern historians to use them to obtain exact statistics on population and production appear to be too ambitious. However, by knowing the methods employed in the survey and the exact definition of the terms and measures used, quite a reliable picture can be obtained of the vast regions subjected to Ottoman registration. In fact, there exist Ottoman survey books on Hungary, Slovakia and Kaminiec-Podolski (Poland) in the north, the Balkans, Anatolia and the eastern Mediterranean islands which made up the core lands, Syria, Palestine and Iraq in the south, and on Georgia and Tabriz in the east. This huge collection constitutes our only detailed source on the social and economic structure of the regions under the Ottoman rule. Repeated periodically for each region, the surveys enable us to follow demographic and economic changes. We must, however, remember that the collection offers complete material only for the sixteenth century when the Ottoman *çift-hane* system was in its most developed stage, and surveying and bookkeeping methods reached their perfection. It is no wonder that the Ottoman Empire's centralist golden age coincides with this development. Surveys of most provinces indicate that they experienced a large-scale growth in sources of revenue, a strong settlement movement with the extension of cultivated lands, a decline in the number of deserted villages and farms, reclamation of marginal lands, growth of villages and towns in population and income.

OTTOMAN LAND CATEGORIES: A RECAPITULATION

The classification of landholding from the legal–fiscal and administrative–military point of view can be summarized as follows:

A. *Legal classification*

1 *Miri* lands, whose eminent domain belongs to the state: this type of land is not subject to sale, mortgage or donation by its possessor and inheritance rights are restricted. However, the possession rights can be subject to transfer, by the possessor under the supervision and permit of a state agent or trustee of a *vakf*. *Miri* lands are classified as:

 a. *Tapulu*, that is, possessed under a specific *tapu* contract and land law. A *tapu* contract is a kind of perpetual lease made directly with the peasant, who acquires the possession and usufruct of the land and automatically leaves these rights to his male descendants upon his death. *Tapu* also makes the peasant subject to certain obligations to fulfill specific services to the state or *sipahi*. The *tapu* is the basis of what we call the *çift-hane* or Ottoman agrarian–fiscal system and involves the great majority of the arable land in the core regions.

 b. *Mukataalu* lands, those possessed under a simple lease contract by anyone, not necessarily a peasant. They are not subject to the obligations of *tapulu* land; namely, the possessor is not obliged to carry out the cultivation himself or fulfill personal services. He can lease the land to a third party. His sole obligation is to deliver to the state or its agent the cash or tithes agreed upon in the initial contract. In the last analysis, the position of the contractor of such lands can be compared to that of a tax-farmer. *Miri* lands of this type include those arable lands not possessed and cultivated under the *tapu* by dependent peasants. They are mostly abandoned lands which the treasury tries to turn into a source of revenue. *Mukataalu* land becomes *tapulu* when it is given to peasants under *tapu*. Those who actually rent such lands under *mukataa* are village communities, urbanites and members of the military class. Accumulating cash through salaried income, the latter became particularly aggressive during the second half of the sixteenth century and many of them, profiting from the loopholes in the legal system, were able to turn such lands into hereditary private estates. This became the main device for the "powerful" to appropriate *miri* lands. The *mukataalu* lands which, for the most part, are separately registered in the survey books as *çiftlik* or *mezraa*, made up as much as 50 percent of the arable lands in some regions.

2 Freehold lands, *mülk*, fall into four main categories:
   a. *Mülk* through sultanic grants (*temlik*) of freehold rights on *miri* land.
   b. *Mülk* acquired through reclamation of waste land.
   c. *Mülk* through a sale contract made in accordance with Islamic Law.
   d. *Mülk* lands in the hands of the pre-conquest elite, confirmed by the Ottoman sultan.

In principle, no sales were valid for arable land without a sultanic grant in the conquered regions, but once sold by collusion or as a result of neglect it became hereditary freehold property under the supremacy of Islamic Law. Mostly vineyards and orchards, or arable lands concealed as such, were subject to the sales establishing freehold property rights.

3 Pious endowment, *vakf* (plural *evkaf*). The greater part of freehold lands transformed into *vakf* often served personal and family interests. *Vakf* lands, though always under state supervision, were held independently and administered under a charter by a trustee who was in most cases a progeny of the founder.

4 *Mevat*, wastelands. They consisted of lands which never had been under cultivation, such as virgin forests, swamps or deserts. Some lands included in this category were arable lands abandoned for a

long time and covered with shrubs. Anyone improving such lands for cultivation acquired full ownership rights. In practice, these two categories are confused and deserted arable lands often were categorized as "dead" land.

B. *Administrative–military classification: the* timar *system*

The bulk of the state-owned lands in the core provinces were divided into prebendal "territories" with fixed limits and rights. The *timar* registers classified prebendal territorial divisions within the larger territorial divisions of *sancak*s and *kada*s. Like the peasant *çiftlik*s, the fixed *timar* or *ziamet* territories (*kılıç*) and their fixed revenues (*hasıl*) could not be partitioned. The newly created *timar*s subsequent to the previous survey were given a territorial status as a unit only in a new survey. This military–administrative division of land must be considered as a system parallel to the legal and economic classification, although all are juxtaposed in practice. The administrative–military classification of land comprises the following principal types:

1 Imperial demesne (*hass-i humayun*), the revenues of which are reserved for the central state treasury (not for the sultan's private use as sometimes stated).

2 *Hass* for dignitaries which were prebends for viziers and begs. These were units conventionally registered with over 100,000 *akça* in income.

3 *Ziamet*s, prebends assigned to the lesser commanders (*subaşı* or *zaim*) of the *timariot* army in the provinces. Conventionally, these units varied between 20,000 and 100,000 *akça*.

4 *Timar*s or *dirlik*s, prebends assigned to the *sipahi*s or the provincial cavalry. Typically, these units went up to 20,000 *akça*. The average *timar* was around 1,000 *akça* in the fifteenth century and double that figure in the sixteenth century. In fact, a distinction should be made between the poor *sipahi*s who barely sustained themselves and those who had a relatively high income. The minimum subsistence level defined by the kadis was 500–750 *akça* during the fifteenth century,[9] while the *timar*s of many *sipahi*s were below 1,000 *akça*.

5 *Mevkuf*, detained *timar*. The income of *timar*s which became vacant was collected by government agents called *mevkufçu* for the treasury, until they were re-assigned to *sipahi*s.

6 Non-military appanages called *arpalık, paşmaklık, özengilik* etc. When granted as appanages or pensions to palace favorites or retired members of the elite, the *hass* and *timar*s were considered by the

bureaucrats as a deviation and interference with law and regulation. It is claimed that *timar*s were originally intended to provide prebends to the active military–administrative personnel; hence, these appanages were set up separate from the military fiefs.

NOTES

1 İnalcık (1969b), pp. 1–23; on *tahrir* see İnalcık (1954b), pp. xviii–xxiii.
2 Cited by Hill (1948), III, p. 842 note 2; Ottoman sources estimate 80,000, see İnalcık (1969b), p. 20.
3 For instructions to the surveyor, see İnalcık (1969b), p. 7.
4 *Ibid.*, p. 9.
5 İnalcık (1973c), p. 138.
6 Celālzāde (1981), p. 159 a-b.
7 İnalcık (1975b) and (1975c).
8 For a tentative list of the surveys, see Lowry (1980), pp. 46, 54–55; many registers have already been published in facsimile or translation, see *TA*.
9 On the minimum subsistence level, see İnalcık (1982b), pp. 126–27.

6

ㅎ

THE *ÇİFT-HANE* SYSTEM: THE ORGANIZATION OF OTTOMAN RURAL SOCIETY

THE PEASANT FAMILY FARM (*ÇİFT-HANE*) IN HISTORICAL PERSPECTIVE AND THEORY

It is no coincidence that the agrarian, economic and fiscal policies under-taken in areas which came successively under Roman, Byzantine and Ottoman rule share striking similarities. Since the late Roman Empire, the family farm unit, cultivated and managed by "free" peasant house-holds, was the dominant form of agrarian production in these empires. In the semi-arid belt of dry-farming, agricultural production was devoted mainly to wheat and barley. Agrarian organization was based on the peasant family's labor (*caput, oike, hane*) and the yoked pair of oxen (*jugum, zeugarion* or *çift*), which together determined the size and pro-duction capacity of the farm land. The late Roman *colonus*, the Byzantine *paroikos* and the Ottoman *raiyyet* (plural *reaya*) all defined this type of peasant. As the theoretician of peasant economy, A.V. Chayanov,[1] argued, in this geographic zone the traditional peasant family farm was the most economically efficient system of production and, irrespective of political changes, it remained for thousands of years the "basic cell" of rural society. In fact, it constituted "one of the organizational forms of private economic undertakings."

As a basic mode of production, Chayanov argues, the system had its own logic which was totally independent of the forms under the capitalist regime. Here, the peasant's motivation is not maximization of interest or surplus, but the whole production process is determined by "the equilib-rium between drudgery and marginal utility." In this type of production the family as a whole, without hired hands, supplies labor, and this labor is adaptable under various situations. It is "an economic structure serving exclusively to meet the needs of the laboring families." Thus, labor-consumer balance is "the basic economic equilibrium between drudgery of labor and demand satisfaction. Therefore, family labor and capital are organized into *a specific unit*, a distinct production machine which represents an independent mode of production."

Chayanov stresses that the unity of family labor as the basic factor was of central importance in the whole production system. Here family, or more exactly peasant household, was considered as one single unit and its annual income "as a single labor income." The "full male worker" in the family was taken as the standard measure and female and child labor are expressed in its terms (in the Ottoman survey books peasant taxes are based on male adults). In the areas where the patriarchal family survived, the household often included married sons as part of family labor. However, Chayanov adds, the biological nuclear family was always essential.

On the other hand, it was the family make-up that determined variations in the volume of capital, notably the size of land and, let us add, animal power. Family composition, whether young, mature or aged, defined consumer-demand equilibrium, and consequently the labor and production process. The family adjusted the intensity of its work to existing conditions, basically to the consumer-demand equilibrium. The self-exploitation of the family was intensified in conditions of limited availability of land. However, where possible the peasant expanded his land by purchase or renting, or by encroaching upon communal land in the village. Thus, the system worked better in thinly populated lands where land was relatively more available.

"Since," Chayanov says, "this production is carried on within the limits of the family farm, its special features have decisive influence on the degree of its labor and capital intensity and on its labor organization and some influence on the assortment of produce grown on the farm." However, the peasant labor farm was "naturally limited by the relationships between family consumer demands and its work." It was established at a level and in accord with the production conditions in which the farm family found itself. Also, it should be emphasized that in the system, family labor, land and animal power were articulated into one organic unit of production. From this observation, it becomes clear why wheat and barley, so vital for peasant subsistence, always constituted the predominant produce. Shifting to more labor-intensive labor crops is a way out when land becomes scarce or other external pressures become effective. However, the shift means "a smaller labor payment than do more extensive crops."[2]

Chayanov believes his theory applies well to all traditional, agrarian systems including those of Russia and the Ottoman Empire. "This production machine," he observes, signifies an *independent mode of production*, which is to be found under various regimes, Western feudalism, Russian servage and even in a capitalist system of national economy. Such an ingenious "machine" is actually the outgrowth of a long experiment in human history.[3]

I believe Chayanov's theory, based on empirical data on the traditional Russian peasant economy, furnishes a comprehensive framework for understanding the basic agrarian structure in the core lands of the Ottoman Empire. However, it is necessary to add that the most important pre-requisite for the continuity of such a system appears to have been centralist state control over land possession and family labor.[4] An imperial bureaucracy had systematically to struggle to eliminate encroachments of local lords, while concomitantly striving to prevent its own provincial agents from transforming themselves into provincial gentry. In this system, the peasant was both dependent and free: "dependent" in the sense that his mobility and use of land were regulated strictly by the state to ensure that he surrendered to the government whatever amount of revenue had been decided in the state registers, and "free" in the sense that he could independently organize the production of the family farm and no one could use his labor arbitrarily.

Another basic element overlooked by Chayanov in the family labor farm system is animal power, the team of plow oxen, *zeugarion* or *çift* which recur so persistently in the Byzantine and Ottoman surveys. The system can no more be explained without reference to it than modern capitalistic agriculture can be explained without agricultural machines.

THE OTTOMAN *ÇİFT-HANE* SYSTEM

Just as the Ottomans considered the craft guild system as the fundamental institution of the city, so they regarded the family labor farm system as the foundation of agricultural production and rural society in their empire. Maintenance of these two institutions formed, so to speak, the constitutional underpinnings of the traditional imperial system until the nineteenth century, when the Tanzimat reformers discarded them in favor of Western-inspired liberal policies. Since the Ottomans considered this dual system the backbone of their estate society, the state strove to maintain it through the vigilance of a central bureaucracy equipped with a highly developed system of controls, in the form of survey registers and periodic inspection. In fact, the fundamental instrument which the imperial bureaucracy used in regulating the system was the survey and registration of the peasant family-land units (*çift-hane*s) – a task which the Ottoman government in the classical period considered of the utmost importance (see above, pp. 132–38).

Thanks to incomparably rich and systematic surveys it is possible for us to give a detailed description of Ottoman rural society based on the *çift-hane* system. In principle, surveys consisted of the registration of all taxable adult male peasants who represented a *çift-hane* unit or its fractions. The regular unit was a married peasant (*hane*) holding a certain unit of land, a *çiftlik*, a farm workable by a pair of oxen.

Thus, the *çift-hane* unit basically was a combination of three elements: fields forming a certain unit workable by a team of oxen and used to grow grain, the family household which provided labor, and a team of oxen as traction power. The first of these elements, the *çiftlik*, had to be large enough both to feed a family and to yield enough surplus to cover protection money (tax) as well as reproduction costs. Actually, as will be explained later, these three elements were considered as forming an indissoluble agrarian and *fiscal* unit.

It was mainly because of the state's concern to keep the *çift-hane* units intact that the Ottoman sultans declared all arable lands in the empire – more exactly those regions of dry-farming in Asia Minor and the Balkans – to be *miri*, that is, under state ownership. *Dominium eminens* on land empowered the government strictly to control the land and maintain the *çift-hane*, which constituted the basis for the state's agrarian–fiscal organization. The peasant, for his part, enjoyed the status of perpetual tenancy under this land regime. The peasant's lease on the land gave him hereditary rights of possession through the direct male line. The law stipulated that the farm unit never was to be divided. The state strictly forbade its agents – usually *sipahi*s – from occupying and cultivating land reserved for peasant households.

Thus, corresponding to the Roman *iugum-caput* and the Byzantine *stasis* or *zugokefalai*, as a production unit, the Ottoman *çift-hane* formed at once a fiscal unit consisting of a peasant family farm with two oxen and a defined amount of land.[5] Let us now examine each of the components of the *çift-hane* unit separately.

The size of the çiftlik

It has been argued that in pre-capitalist agricultural systems based on the family labor force, its ability to realize and sustain the highest possible

Table I:33. A peasant's *(raiyyet)* average *çiftlik* land in *dönüm*s (one
dönüm = 920 sq. meters)

Sub-province	First quality	Middle quality	Poor quality	*Barkan*
Hüdavendigar (1489)	70–80	100	130–150	p. 23
Aydın (1528)	60	80	130–150	p. 8
Konya (1528)	60	80	100–120	p. 47
Erzurum (1540)	80	100	130	p. 66
Syrmia (c. 1580)	70–80	100–110	120–130	p. 308
		80–90		
Morea (1711)	80	100–120	150	p. 327
Diyarbekir (1540)	80	100	150	p. 131

Source: Barkan (1943), index: *çiftlik*.

income from land was the economic principle which determined optimal
farm size. Since the size of this labor unit could not be increased or
decreased at will, Chayanov points out,[6] other factors of production had
to be put "in an optimal relationship to this fixed element." "Peasant
farms," he continues[7]

> are structured to conform to the optimal degree of self-exploitation of the
> family labor force and in a technically optimal system of production factors
> as regards their size and relationship of the parts. Any excess of production
> means available to labor or of land above the technically optimal level will
> put an excessive burden on the undertaking. It will not lead to an increased
> volume of activity, since further intensity of labor beyond the level estab-
> lished for its self-exploitation is unacceptable to the family. As the capital
> intensification of the farm grows and its relative labor intensification falls
> the productivity of the capital expenditure continually declines.

Thus, as the family labor farm reaches optimal size, any incentive to
expand the farm further disappears.

Because of this structure, traditional peasant society consisted mostly
of households in possession of two oxen and a certain optimal amount
of farm land. As will be seen, the Ottomans in their regulations set this
amount at between 5 and 15 hectares, according to the fertility of the
soil (see Table I:33). This whole unit, composed of separate independent
fields *(tarlas)* was called *raiyyet çiftlik*. *Çift*, originally referring only to
a *pair* (of oxen) stood also for the land workable by a pair of oxen, or
the Turkish construct *çiftlik* (land for a *çift*) was also used. The *raiyyet
çift* or *çiftlik* denoted primarily fields used for grain cultivation.

The law said,[8] "the consensus on the size of a *çiftlik* is that a *çiftlik*
should be of the size sufficient for the fields actually cultivated and those
left as fallow. The peasant farmers call it a *çiftlik*." The definition of the
size of a peasant *çiftlik* differed in the regulations for various parts of the
empire[9] (Table I:33).

Ideally, arable land was to be organized into *raiyyet çiftliks*, and both their integration into big landed properties and their partition into smaller holdings were to be prevented. In fact, however, both the Byzantines and the Ottomans accepted half of the *zeugarion* or of a *çift* under the name *voidion* or *nim-çift* respectively as the smallest land unit for a family. When a family possessed less land than this, officials classified the peasant as poor, *fakir* or *yoksul* in Turkish, or as *pezos* or *aktemones* in Greek. Although there were peasant families which possessed more than one *çiftlik*, these were regarded as exceptional cases. Normal sized *raiyyet çiftliks* typically made up the state-owned lands throughout Asia Minor and the Balkans and the administration strove to put all arable lands under this type of land tenure.

Indivisibility of the çiftlik unit

Economic, demographic, and political pressures as well as the fact that other forms of land tenure survived and developed affected contemporaneously the size of the *çiftlik*. The state nevertheless went to great lengths to ensure that the *çiftlik* would remain indivisible and sufficiently large for the upkeep of a peasant family. The law reads:[10] "It is by no means permissible for *çiftliks* and *bashtinas* [*çiftliks* in Slavic provinces] to be divided up and parcelled out." In actuality, although contrary to law, there were loopholes for breaking up and distributing a registered *çiftlik*. In such a case, if a peasant came forward, offering to return the divided *çiftlik* to its original form and willing to pay all of its taxes, the authorities would give the broken-up land to his possession. Another measure to ensure the unity and continuity of a *çiftlik* or family possession was this: should a deceased *raiyyet* leave behind a minor son unable to manage by himself the cultivation of his land, it temporarily was taken away from him until he reached maturity. A widow, however, could retain possession of a *çiftlik* for herself or her minor son if, through the use of hired hands, she could manage its cultivation and pay the tithe and other taxes. Widows in this system were recognized as taxable persons (*bive*) and recorded as such in the registers.

In his discussion of the principle of the unity and indivisibility of the *çift*, Abussu'ud[11] set forth the fiscal argument that it was almost impossible for the government or the *timar*-holder to collect the *çift*-tax from a divided *çift*.

The varying composition of the peasant family itself in part accounts for the variations. The existence of half *çifts* is one indication of it.

Whereas *çift* households (families possessing a *çiftlik* and normally also a pair of oxen) certainly were "mature" families, *half-çift* households (families possessing less than a *çiftlik* and presumably only a single ox) evidently were "young" families.

The fiscal basis of the çift-hane *system*: çift-*tax*

The whole Ottoman agrarian–fiscal system is actually epitomized in a peasant family tax which was called *çift*-tax (*çift-resmi*) in the Ottoman tax system.[12] In the Ottoman law on peasantry, "personal" taxes were based on the person's labor capacity. A peasant with a family paid the highest rate, while those who had limited work capacity, such as single men or widows, were subjected to the minimum rate, and those who could not do any productive work, such as the elderly, disabled, single women and children, were altogether exempted.

This was actually a tax system assessing peasants' labor and land in combination, i.e., *çift-hane*. It also typified the organization of rural society as a whole. The classification and statutory organization of the rural population on the basis of personal labor tax, an outgrowth of an age-old bureaucratic experience, was a translation in bureaucratic terms of the actual complex socio-economic structure of the peasant population in the countryside.

The fiscal system of the *çift*-tax is actually the key to understanding social stratification in Ottoman rural society. It classifies peasants capable of paying the *çift*-tax, the half *çift*-tax, the married peasant (*bennak*) tax, and the poor or unmarried peasant (*mücerred, caba* or *kara*) tax. The *tütün-resmi* (hearth tax), the *dönüm*-tax, and other minor taxes also fall within the system. Broadly speaking, in this tax system the amount of land, together with the labor capacity, determined tax status. The registration of peasants in an imperial survey book, based on his tax status, established his obligations until the next survey. The laws required a peasant family in possession of a full *çift* or *çiftlik* to pay the equivalent of one gold piece, or 22 *akça* in silver coins, and those in possession of half a *çift*, 12 *akça*. If less than one-half *çift* of land was involved, then the laborer's marital status, that is, the potential labor force which he represented, determined tax rates. A family in possession of less than half a *çift* was called *bennak* and had to pay 9 *akça*, and an unmarried peasant, or a widow, in possession of land, only 6 *akça*. The assumption was that, irrespective of the quantity of land in his possession, a married man would control a larger amount of labor than would a bachelor. As soon as an individual came into possession of enough land to create a *çift* or half a *çift*, he had to pay correspondingly higher taxes, either 22 or 12 *akça*. It appears that originally this tax was calculated as 10 percent of the economic value which a peasant family was expected to create in a year. So the family unit with a *çiftlik* constituted a work team which would pay, in addition to tithes, a *çift-resmi* as peasant family tax. Unmarried sons who did not serve their father and who made their livings separately were subject to the *6 akça kara* tax which corresponded to an adult male's work.

A synonym for *çift-resmi, kulluk akçası*, more precisely discloses its nature and origin. *"Kulluk"* refers to the status of being a dependent, or a subject, or services owed as such. In this light, the cash payment, or *çift-resmi*, becomes the equivalent of the peasant's obligations to the landlord for *kulluk* or *labor services*. Fifteenth-century Ottoman law codes[13] record the 22, 12, 9, and 6 *akça* taxes as cash equivalents of certain labor services or *kulluks* owed to the lord. These equivalents were 3 *akça* for three days' personal service, 7 *akça* for providing a wagon-load of hay, 7 *akça* for half a wagon-load of straw, 3 *akça* for a wagon-load of firewood, and 2 *akça* for service with a wagon. As the law code of Mehmed the Conqueror states,[14] "if money is to be taken for these seven services then twenty-two *akças* will be taken."

Although this law code demands only 3 *akça* for personal labor service, the landless unmarried peasant had to pay 6 *akça*. The same code resolves this seeming discrepancy. It explains that, in order to earn money, landless peasants usually worked as agricultural workers or owned animals or carts which they used to carry goods for people, or occupied themselves with crafts. This personal labor was the only service which a landless peasant could perform. Only those with land and capital equipment could undertake the other services.

In their tax registers, the Byzantines classified dependent peasant families in the same way.[15] A *zeugarate*, someone possessing a pair of oxen or a definite amount of land, corresponds to the Ottoman *çift* and paid one gold *nomisma* as a land and hearth tax; a *voidate*, someone possessing one ox or half of the land of a *zeugarate*, corresponds to the Ottoman half-*çift*; and *aktemones*, someone possessing no land or, more accurately, a plot of land less than one-half a *çift*, corresponds to the Ottoman *bennak*; and finally, a *pezos*, or the poor peasant, corresponds to the Ottoman *caba* or *kara*.

The state evidently was unable to use the feudal labor services existing within the empire and consequently converted them into a lump sum cash tax to create important revenue for the treasury. Replacing labor services, the tax was fixed once and for all to be paid in two installments at the convenience of the peasant. At the same time, the state abolished most of the personal services which the local lord or *sipahi* could easily abuse. The Ottoman conversion of labor services into cash payments was revolutionary in nature and obviously beneficial to the peasantry.[16]

Labor services had existed since pre-Ottoman times and served an important function in Byzantium and successor states. As part of their services, peasants then helped maintain the military, they cultivated land set aside for the sustenance of the families of soldiers and lords, cut the hay for their horses, and supplied their firewood and straw. In order for the cavalrymen to survive and perform their services in royal campaigns or to protect the peasantry and agriculture against marauders, these basic labor impositions were deemed necessary. Since the peasantry resented these services and did their best to avoid them, the Ottoman bureaucrats sought to convert them, under the *çift-tax* system, into lump sums whenever economic-monetary conditions made it possible. From a practical point of view, the cash payment to the *sipahi* alleviated the load on the state treasury, since in the *timar* system the *çift*-tax was always paid in cash to the *timar*-holder to enable him to meet his expenses during imperial campaigns in distant lands. On the other hand, the *çift-resmi* and its components made up a complete tax system comprising and shaping the entire agrarian society. The state considered peasant labor taxable and varied its rate according to the combinations of labor and land, or marital status whenever labor became the main component; then labor capacity alone was considered taxable. The state considered a landless peasant still productive and able to earn a livelihood. In rural areas, such persons commonly worked as agricultural laborers, as carriers with carts, as blacksmiths, or as weavers of coarse fabrics. When the state permanently assigned to a specific group certain services – such as the guardianship of a mountain pass or work in mines or salt-works – it reduced substantially the rate of the personal tax and exempted them from emergency services for the state. The regulations state explicitly that the reason for such reductions or exemptions was the special labor service.

In general, in the ancient and medieval world, the peasant represented not only a producer of soil products, but also a potential labor force capable of providing services and creating other kinds of economic value. It is interesting to note that in the Roman Empire, too, the rates of personal tax varied according to labor capacity. In A.D. 386 one *caput*, or peasant family, was fiscally computed as two and one-half men or four women.[17] Another interesting case is the personal tax imposed upon the labor of a manumitted slave farmer in the Ottoman Empire. A manumitted sharecropper-slave (*ortakçı kul*) had to pay between 45 and 60 *akça*, even if he was no longer engaged in agriculture. This amount equalled one gold piece – between 10 and 14 percent of the estimated subsistence earnings of the labor force of an adult male – in the late fifteenth-century Ottoman Empire. Many taxable subjects who lay outside the regular peasant populations paid 50 *akça* in personal taxes. These were the so-called *ellicis*, "those who paid fifty *akça*s," or *florici*, "those who paid one gold piece."[18]

In the Mediterranean basin and in Western Europe, from ancient times and through subsequent periods, the personal tax assessed on the labor force of an adult married male had been set at the rate of one gold piece. It existed under the Islamic caliphate as the *cizye* or *haraç*, under the Byzantines as one gold *nomisma* tax, and under the Ottomans, in an assessment of 22 or 25 *akça*, as *çift*-tax or *ispence* respectively.[19]

In this system of taxation, the gold piece usually was divided into twenty-four units and the authorities charged the peasant population, classified according to land and labor capacities (a married man with two oxen and land, married without land, or single), at rates based on this duodecimal system. (The Ottomans used a 22 rather than a 24 *akça* system, I believe, because in the 1330s one *mithkal* of gold was worth 22 *akça*.) As Svoronos[20] has shown in his edition of the cadastre of Thebes, the Byzantine agrarian tax system followed the same duodecimal breakdown – twenty-four, twelve, nine, and six. Since the establishment of elaborate land cadastres or personal income lists was impractical, this system obviously constituted a convenient bureaucratic device for assessing with some fairness rates of personal taxes on the basis of work capacity.

Finally, I would like to touch upon the long controversy over the nature of *iugatio-capitatio* and *zeugaratikion* in pre-Ottoman empires. F. Lot and V. Déléage in their studies of the land–head tax (*iugatio-capitatio*)[21] in the late Roman Empire, and Marc Bloch in his analysis of the socio-economic nature of the medieval *mansus*, showed that the existence of the family farm unit as the basic cell of rural society continued after the decline of the Western Roman Empire. Always aware of the enigmatic nature of this peculiar head–land tax, Ostrogorsky defined the *iugum*, which corresponds to the Ottoman *çift*, as "a piece of land that can feed a *caput*, and the *caput* stands for the human labor expended on a *iugum*."[22] Actually, the tax imposed upon the peasant family was always related to "the occupation of a definite unit of land."

The problem of *iugatio-capitatio* in the late Roman Empire has provoked the propounding of various theories. Most recently A. H. M. Jones, in a paper on *iugatio-capitatio*, has agreed that there is "a system of assessing land tax and other levies on *iuga*, fiscal unit of land, and *capita*, poll tax, which are combined in some way, and this is still a problem to be investigated. The laws, census records and lists of estates give only fragmentary evidence, and it is not possible to make a full description of the system." Nevertheless, Jones asserts that one point at least is clear, that in a number of laws "*iuga* or *iugatio* and *capita* or *capitatio* are *coupled together as the units of assessment* for various taxes and levies." "A tax," he points out, "might be levied on both *units combined* (as was usually the case) or on one only." On the nature of *iuga* he agrees that "there is no question: they were units of land" whereas *capitatio* covered human beings or *coloni* and animals at the same time. In a listing of estates in western Anatolia we find *zugokefalai* in which, Jones points out, farms and *coloni* are combined as an "assessment unit."[23]

It is my belief that a complete description of the Ottoman *çift-hane* system – made possible through the utilization of the Ottoman survey registers – helps clarify the nature of *iugatio-capitatio* in the late Roman and Byzantine systems. A person's productive force was the basis of tax assessment. He paid more or less according to his personal status – whether or not he controlled the labor of a wife and children, whether or not he possessed a piece of land and the requisite animal power. But the family farm unit was the economic and fiscal basis of the entire system. Despite changes in the political super-structure, the peasant family farm remained at the core of the rural economic and fiscal order throughout medieval times. The Ottoman Empire inherited and maintained this system.

NOTES

1 Chayanov (1966), pp. 41–42, 116; there are, however, questions whether or not Chayanov's theory is valid for peasant societies outside Russia.

2 Ottoman Law allows for a reduction in the rate of tithes for crops such as flax which demand more intensive labor than grain.

3 The diffusionist theory believes that the family farm unit emerged for the first time in Sumer, spreading therefrom to the rest of the world: see Duby (1962).

4 State ownership of arable land combined with a class of independent peasantry is a dominant feature of the agrarian system in most traditional empires,

including the Byzantine Empire; recent studies on Byzantine rural society emphasize this point, see Udal'cova and Chvostoka (1981); Kaplan (1981); cf. Jones (1978), pp. 154–57.

5 See Ostrogorsky (1954), pp. 296, 303; Lefort (1974), pp. 315–54; Laiou-Thomadakis (1977), pp. 69, 147, 153, 161–63, 173 note 46. In the Byzantine *practica* the fiscal unit is defined on the basis of either the number of oxen or, less frequently, the size of land, but actually these two were the components of the unit *zugokefalai*, see Déléage (1945), p. 194, who defines the unit as "l'unité-joug" or "l'unité-tête," cf. Mommsen (1869), p. 431 and Jones (1957), pp. 88–91; *iugum-caput* corresponds exactly to the Ottoman *çift-hane*; and it is interesting to note that the land measure *mudd* is borrowed from the Byzantine *modios*, see Schilbach (1970), pp. 67–70.

6 Chayanov (1966), p. 90.

7 *Ibid.*, p. 92.

8 Barkan (1943), p. 47, article 17.

9 The minimum size of the Byzantine *stasis* is 40 *modioi* or 3.6 hectares and the maximum is 215 *modioi* or 19.3 hectares, cf. Laiou-Thomadakis (1977), pp. 147, 153, 161–63; for the late Roman Empire, see Lot (1928), p. 121.

10 İnalcık (1965c), pp. 32–33.

11 *Ibid.*

12 For details, see İnalcık (1959a), pp. 576–81.

13 See, for Mehmed the Conquerer's law code, Kraelitz (1922), pp. 13–48 and İnalcık (1959a), pp. 577–83, cf. Kosminsky (1955), pp. 12–34.

14 Barkan (1943), p. 390; İnalcık (1959a), p. 581.

15 Still basic for the Byzantine agrarian–fiscal system is Ostrogorsky (1954); also see Svoronos (1959); Lefort (1974); Laiou-Thomadakis (1977), pp. 161–63, and İnalcık (1958b), pp. 237–42.

16 It must however be pointed out that Ottoman extraordinary levies, or *avarız-ı divaniyye*, actually replaced feudal levies and most of the labor services so that there was in the end no real relief for the peasantry, especially when the imperial government had recourse to emergency levies too frequently; enlightened Ottoman bureaucrats warned the sultan not to misuse this privilege.

17 Lot (1928).

18 See İnalcık (1965d), pp. 914–15.

19 *Ibid.*

20 Svoronos (1959).

21 Lot (1928) and Déléage (1945).

22 Postan *et al.* (1963), p. 205.

23 Jones (1957).

7

·ิ

SETTLEMENTS

THE RURAL LANDSCAPE AND THE FIELD SYSTEM

The state's determining role in promoting and maintaining a particular agrarian system under the state ownership of land (*miri*) and *çift-hane* system, and its consequences for the whole rural landscape, cannot be minimized.

We have seen that only the grain fields were subject to state ownership, a point stressed in the regulations on several occasions. "The *miri* lands are those cultivated lands that lie around the villages." For example, conversion of such fields into pastures, vineyards or orchards was prohibited because they could then be disposed of as freehold property; they could be sold, donated or given as surety and partitioned among the heirs. Conversion of a field to pasture or orchard was interpreted as the abandonment of its cultivation, and no state-owned land could be left uncultivated for three consecutive years. Vineyards, orchards and vegetable gardens in the vicinity of towns and villages were freehold property. Although they made up a vital part of the urban economy, they were distinguished from fields at large under state ownership.

Orchards and gardens were more widespread in the villages near large agglomerations than in remote areas; consequently, freehold farms privately owned by urbanites or rented were more numerous in such villages. Such lands usually were irrigated lands, and private irrigation made a considerable difference in landholding rights.[1]

There is strong evidence to support the view that the ability of the Ottoman state to establish and maintain its specific land regime through the *tapu* system in a region determined the settlement and field pattern of that area. On the other hand, changing relations between the state and provincial title-holders to land, for instance the *vakfs* and the *ayan* regime of the eighteenth century, led to considerable alterations in the social fabric and the emergence of new patterns. Obviously, the rural landscape varied in the Ottoman Empire from one region to another and from one period to another.

It is not a coincidence that the rural landscape and social structure, in the core lands where the *çift-hane* and *tapu* system prevailed, differed fundamentally from the peripheral provinces – Egypt, parts of Syria and Iraq, all annexed to the Ottoman Empire in the sixteenth century. Of course, physical conditions, irrigation cultivation, and the Islamization of these lands long before the Ottoman conquest account for the difference, which actually made the application of the *tapu* system impractical. By contrast, the Ottoman regime was successfully applied in Hungary, Cyprus, and Georgia. It is important to note that in the parts of Syria and Iraq where grain cultivation with dry-farming prevailed, the Ottomans were able to introduce their *tapu* and *timar* system. Discussing the point at the level of microeconomy, the average peasant farm size in the village parish (the village including fields) in Anatolia under traditional agriculture was limited to an average area of 100 *dönüms*.

Human geographers[2] have examined the interrelations of social structures and settlement patterns in rural areas by focusing primarily on the "settlement situation." They have studied the cases where the settlement was carried out by a group of nomads, migrant peasants, by squatters from nearby villages, or by state initiative. Hütteroth believes[3] that the decisive factor in land distribution and the ground plan of the fields depended on the "settlement situation." But, in the earlier periods, we know, a settlement of nomads or slave farmers ultimately led to independent family farms under the *tapu* system.[4] It is suggested[5] that as far as the ground plan of the fields is concerned, the field pattern depended first on topography; on the flat land we find regular strips and in hilly land irregular square fields. As for the ethnic–social conditions, Hütteroth observes[6] in nineteenth-century Syria, for instance, Bedouin settlement involved the *mushaa* system – the division of state-owned lands into regular compounds of field strips, with periodic re-divisions to give fair allotments to settlers. A similar situation emerged in eastern Anatolia when tribal chieftains turned into big landowners. In the inner Anatolian steppe, the patterns in settlement and the field system were due to the successive settlements by indigenous peasants, Turcoman and Kurdish nomads and immigrants from the Balkans, Caucasia and the northern Black Sea (Fig. I.2). By contrast, in Balkan and west Anatolian villages, communal ownership existed only on village commons – pastureland, harvest plots and forest, not on arable lands. It should be recalled that during the classical age, every peasant family with an indivisible *çiftlik* or half *çiftlik* ideally had permanent possession rights and independence in organizing exploitation of the land. As a result, ground plans must have had basically a permanent character, and were not subject to divisions. In Syria and Palestine, too, the same pattern must have been the norm in the traditional village.[7] Since the Ottoman archives do not yield ground plans of fields we can only speculate that the new settlements of Turkish nomads in western Anatolia and the Balkans must have begun with a square field system but over time these, too, were divided into strips. Such was the evolution in the settlement of inner Anatolia during the nineteenth century.[8]

Hütteroth suggests that a particular ground plan of fields reflects the settlement history and social structure of a village (see Fig. 1:2). He gives examples of villages of various origins with differing field patterns.[9] In the first phase of village formation, he says, square fields prevailed, followed by a strip field pattern by successive divisions of square fields jointly possessed and tilled. In fact, the head of the family farm in the Ottoman *çift-hane* system sometimes decided the actual partitioning of land when his sons married and continued to live in the father's household. Also under the *tapu* system, the family farm had to be possessed and cultivated jointly by the sons after the death of the father. But Ottoman law also speaks of the land being partitioned among the sons for tax purposes. Thus, the partitioning must have led to the strip (open) field system.

In the strip field system, the fields lying quite far from the village are not fenced but bounded only by a low hedge for delimitation and against grazing animals. In general, strip-cultivation is identified as more advanced than the square field system. But the fact that the square field with stone hedges is found mostly in the mountains (in Syria for instance) indicates that a specific type of land use – horticulture, olive groves or orchards, and gardening – may also be a determinant in the square field system, at least in certain territories. In any case, the patriarchal-patrimonial character of landholding in general with a dominant father, state or big landowner as well as the characteristic agricultural pattern – dry-farming with grain cultivation on the flat lands – must have been the basic determinants of the traditional field system in the Ottoman core lands.

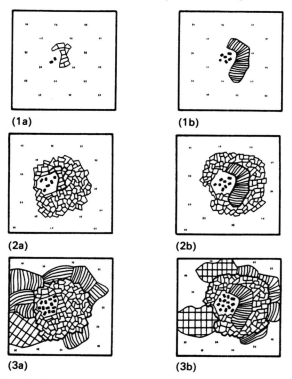

(1a)   (1b)

(2a)   (2b)

(3a)   (3b)

Fig. I:2. The development of field patterns. 1a: Settlement of joint families or similar small groups – nucleus of square fields; 1b: At the same time settlement of equally privileged groups (refugees, nomads) – nucleus of a strip field; 2: Further development, if legal, economic and other situations are favorable; individual additions of new fields according to influence and necessity – widening of the square field pattern; 3a: Distribution of remaining land on a cooperative basis – peripheral strip fields; 3b: Official division of remaining land according to schematic principles – checkerboard fields.
Source: Hütteroth (1974), p. 44.

THE RURAL LANDSCAPE AND THE SETTLEMENT OF NOMADS

As far as the Ottoman rural landscape is concerned, agricultural expansion, or shrinkage, settlement of nomads, their causes and conditions must be examined in detail.

Extension of arable land became possible mainly through the introduction of more efficient techniques, stimulus of the market, surplus labor by immigration or natural growth, and more efficient public security and state protection for small farmers against marauders as well as the rapacity of its own agents. Also, mass flight to inaccessible places such as mountains, islands or forests because of epidemics, brigandage, plunder and tax abuses gave a specific pattern to the settlement under the Ottomans. Peasants frequently chose to have their main settlement sites on the hillsides and maintained a *mezraa* down on the flatland as a satellite exploitation. This holds true for many areas in Anatolia and the Balkans.[10] The period 1470–1570 witnessed a general expansion of arable land and settlement of marginal lands on the highlands as well as on the lowlands.

In Asia Minor, the Balkans, Syria and Palestine, regional development after the Ottoman conquest shows a gradual replacement of the preconquest "feudal" landowners by the *sipahi*s with the typical Ottoman *timar* regime and adjustment to the *çift-hane* system. Ottoman surveys provided a mechanism to achieve the change. Peace and better protection of the peasant under the new regime generally secured a substantial increase in cultivated arable land, in population, and urban development.[11] The subsequent long-term crisis at the turn of the sixteenth century apparently derived from the imbalance between the rapid population growth and food resources.[12]

A parallel development is the settlement of nomads either forcibly by the state and/or spontaneously under the pressure of economic factors. No doubt, nomadic settlement led to a further extension of cultivated land, although in some regions it resulted in serious crises which expressed themselves in insurrection or flight, generally into Azerbaijan, which attracted Turcomans with its lush pasturelands and favorable political atmosphere.

Under Süleyman I, the Yörük nomads in Sivas province, for example, formed many communities, mostly by settling deserted villages. Along with these settlements we find a great number of summer and winter pasturelands, each assigned to a particular nomadic group (see Table I:34).

The table shows that in nomadic settlements the strikingly high percentage of small or temporary settlements, *mezraa*s, is observed. The Yörüks of the region included the historically well-known tribes of Zülkadriye, Bayındır, Avşar and Harbendel. Here, the nomadic groups that exclusively engaged in stock raising were clearly distinguished from those which did some cultivating at the same time. On the other hand, several Yörük groups became sedentary while keeping their nomad-clan status. To understand better the process of a nomadic settlement, we shall take the history of the Yörük settlement of Sakal-Tutan, a village 35 km from the city of Kayseri.[13]

Table I:34. The settlement pattern of the Yeni-İl *kada*
in the province of Sivas

Village	*mezraa*	*yaylak* and *yurt*	Groups (*cema'at*)
75	125	75	90

Source: *Munsha'at*, British Library, Or. MS 9503, fol. 5–12.

At the beginning of the sixteenth century, the plain of Köstere where Sakal-Tutan village emerged was the grazing ground for numerous clans of nomadic Yörüks. But the survey of 1583 indicates an extensive settlement with 35 villages, and its economy was transformed from sheep breeding to grain cultivation. It is interesting to note that the area was originally under the control of a local lord of the pre-Ottoman Zülkadirid principality, in which nomadic Turcomans predominated. The Yörüks of the Köstere plain belonged to the Danishmendlü tribal confederation. Settled by different small clans, the villages were noticeably of small size at the early stage, but in the period 1550–83 their population recorded an increase of 50 percent. Talas and Tomarza, older villages situated in the better watered land to the north of Erciyas mountain and inhabited earlier, in majority by Christians, experienced "a phenomenal population growth" in the same period.[14]

Down to the twentieth century, the Yörük villages remained backward in their general culture, being less exposed to the influence of Kayseri city than the older, non-Muslim villages. Situated in the favored riverine valleys, the latter were engaged in horticulture and irrigated cultivation, and they marketed their produce in Kayseri.

We observe in Bursa province the same economic, social and cultural contrast between the Turkish-Yörük villages, depending predominantly on grain agriculture inland, and the older Greek villages of the Marmara coasts engaged in wine and olive oil production for the İstanbul market.[15]

At least two-thirds of today's villages and nine-tenths of the cultivated parts of inner Anatolia were established only in the period after 1860.[16] Until then, no noteworthy new settlement had occurred in the greater part of the country. Settlement became possible, Hütteroth believes, mainly as a result of better security against nomads, and better protection of possession rights through the state-sponsored title deed. However, I believe the persistence of nomadism in the central steppe area, down to 1860, might be due to specific economic conditions. For example, the Cihanbeyli tribal confederation that raised stock dominated in the northern part of the inner Anatolian steppe because stock raising was then the most profitable and rational exploitation of this marginal land. The chief of the tribal confederation annually was supplying, under a government contract, 300,000 sheep to İstanbul. Similarly, persistence of stock raising and seasonal transhumance with the dominant tribal social organization in eastern Anatolia must have been due to the fact that this region supplied livestock to all the big cities, including İstanbul, Aleppo, Damascus and Jerusalem.[17]

As in earlier centuries, the temporary or small settlements in the central steppe area constituted the initial phase of village formation. At the beginning, the tribal chief (*agha*), the patriarch and leader in the community, played a dominant role in the formation of the village, deciding all matters concerning the land and cultivation, thus replacing the state agent (*timariot sipahi*), convent sheikh or governor's steward. The nucleus in a *mezraa* type settlement was always "a joint family," or *çift-hane* household.

One interesting set of settlements was on the Çukurova (Cilicia) flood plain, concentrating on the large Yüregir marshes which stretch to the sea between the Seyhan and the Ceyhan rivers. Here too, the landscape changed little down to the nineteenth century in its basic settlement pattern.

According to the register of 1572, here most of the arable land was used as *mezraa* and cultivated by nomadic groups. Sixty percent of the cultivable lands were converted into regular agricultural exploitations under the *çift-hane* system, while the rest still was cultivated on a temporary basis by nomadic groups. The first group can be considered seminomadic with fixed holdings while the second group also held *mezraa*s but mostly used it for grazing and a winter camp and paid a lump sum for its use. In the spring they left their *mezraa* with the herds for the mountain summer pastures, in a short circuit, which took 10 to 15 days to walk.[18] In general, settlement was very sparse in the plain compared to the hilly country in the north. In 70 percent of the settled places or *mezraa*s the population did not exceed twenty households. Village formation occurred almost exclusively in the district east of the Ceyhan river, whereas in the west there were only nomadic groups and their *mezraa*s. Essentially, the regular transhumance of the large nomadic population between the summer pastures in the Taurus Mountains to the north and the Yüregir plain accounted for this situation there.[19] In the Yüregir plain, nomadic as well as public revenues showed a noticeable growth between 1547 and 1572 in common with the general demographic and economic growth. The annual cotton production (amounting to

3,520 *kantar* or 200 tons) was worth 1,267,200 *akça* and grain cultivation equaled that of cotton, whereas tithes from wheat and barley were c. 10,000 *kile* or 205 tons.[20] With the addition of those from the "rented" *mezraas*, public revenues from soil products in the Yüregir plain amounted altogether to about 720,000 *akça*. If we include revenues from other taxes, the total comes to one million *akça* or 16,660 gold ducats – quite modest for this relatively large region. This is a good example of how in the Ottoman Empire large tracts of land under nomadic control were not extensively exploited. But we must remember that the greater part of the plain consisted of swamps until the mid-nineteenth century.

Interestingly, nomadic production in the *mezraas*, amounting to one-fourth of total production, on average, appears to have been market-oriented. This consisted of cotton and rice, a characteristic we also find in western Anatolian settlements of nomadic origin. In the Çukurova plain, the state also exploited the nomadic work force in rice cultivation. These nomads claimed a monopoly on rice growing in the region. To the east in the Kınık district, rice cultivation was organized under quite a complicated system, apparently inherited from Mamluk times.[21] Here there were twenty-four rice plantations, all state owned (seven more were in the Yüregir plain). Although village settlement here was quite advanced, the greater part of the rice production, c. 60 percent, was carried out by nomadic groups. Production on the state plantations was worth 772,000 *akça* and by contrast only 165,000 *akça* on privately owned cultivation. It is to be remembered that since the 1470s, to keep prices low for the urban population and for the army, Mehmed the Conqueror had put all lands and water canals suitable for rice cultivation under direct state control and supervision in his empire.[22]

TEMPORARY OR DESERTED SETTLEMENTS: *MEZRAA* AND VACANT *ÇIFTLIKS*

Special attention should be given to *mezraa* in the process of settlement in the Ottoman Empire. In the survey registers, *mezraa* or *ekinlik* designate a periodic settlement or a deserted village.[23] According to regulations, to register a land as *mezraa* it was required that it be checked to see whether the place had a village site in ruins, its own water supply, and a cemetery. We often find the following note on *mezraas*: "previously it was a village, now its population is scattered and the fields abandoned." Unlike the village (*köy, karye*), *mezraa* did not have a *kethüda* or imam representing the village community.

Every *mezraa* is, however, referred to by a specific typonym which often reveals its origin or first possessor. In the province of Karaman, for example, many *mezraa* names are coupled with *hisar*, referring probably to abandoned Byzantine castles, or with *ağıl*, sheepfold, or having reference to a nomadic group which used the site as pastureland. A great number of village names in Anatolia bearing *viran* or *ören* (meaning, abandoned or in ruin) must originally have been *mezraa*s which over time were transformed into full villages. When we speak of a *mezraa* as an abandoned village we mean, basically, not just the site of the village itself, but also its fields.

On the other hand, human geographers place *mezraa*s among the periodic settlements or small rural settlements on the way to becoming villages.[24] The fact that a small group of permanent settlers with their houses may be found there does not change its basic *mezraa* character. Settlement of marginal lands as a result of rural overpopulation is considered the underlying reason for the spread of these types of *mezraa*. In fact, the term *mezraa* was used for arable lands which were cultivable or actually cultivated by nearby villagers, wandering peasants or nomads. Summer and winter pasturelands could also be the scene of settlement and agricultural activities and could be transformed into *mezraa*s or villages. Like *mezraa*, *kom*, *oba* and *divan* are mentioned as types of small rural or periodic settlements. *Kom* is to be found in eastern Anatolia; it differs from a *mezraa* in being a kind of ranch for animal breeding, usually owned by an absentee landlord. It encompasses sheepfolds and shepherd huts. *Oba* is the grazing area of a nomadic household and should be studied rather within the *yayla* pastureland structure.[25] When settled by a nomad household which shifts to agriculture as its main occupation, the *oba* assumes the character of a *mezraa*. The process is attested from early Ottoman times. At present, all *oba*s are of this developed type. A *divan* was apparently the name for a tribal superstructure over the *oba*,[26] which disappeared as settlement progressed. Some isolated *çiftlik*s, settled by one or a few families devoted to agriculture and livestock breeding, are considered, like the *mezraa*, as a kind of settlement liable to develop into a village. In Palestine, Transjordan, and Syria,[27] *mezraa*s were "small agricultural areas, dispersed amongst the hills, lying within the village area but apart from the main fields belonging to the village, as is still the case today."

According to the regulations and survey registers, the size of a *mezraa* varied widely.[28] It could consist of only one or two *çiftlik*s or have the size of a village, judging from its estimated revenue.[29]

In western Anatolia and the Balkans, the Ottomans inherited the Byzantine rural landscape with its sub-villages and periodic settlements. Under the Byzantines, the *mezraa*-type lands as dependents of a village were known as *agridia* and *proasteia*, the former designating partly settled and the latter unsettled satellite land. As was the case under the Ottomans, when the village rented such land collectively, it paid the rent collectively. But this special case cannot be used as an argument for the theory that in general village land was subject to collective ownership.[30] From the standpoint of land use, a *mezraa* is basically a field for grain production as opposed to pasture, vineyard, orchard, etc. Viticulture, horticulture, olive growing and livestock breeding were only preponderant on the hillsides while fields for grain production were located in the *mezraa* on the flatland. The Syrian and Palestinian villages with hillside vineyards, orchards, and olive groves and lowland or valley *mezraas* also provide instances of this pattern. This village/*mezraa* pattern develops into an upper village and a lower village when the satellite *mezraa* on the lowland is fully settled. Village names preceded with *zir-*, *bala-*, *yukarı-* and *aşağı-*, or in the Balkans *dolni-/dolne-/dolnje-* and *gorni-/gorne-/gornje-* reflect this process.

The fact that most of the *mezraas* were registered as dependent on a village shows that the Ottoman administration generally recognized the *mezraa* as an indivisible part of village economy, a kind of reserve land. Such *mezraas* secured an extra source of income for the villagers and provided land for the surplus population. Often villagers cultivated this land without the government's knowledge, arguing that it had always belonged to them. As a result, the rule was made that no abandoned land could be exploited without the sultan's prior approval.[31] Because the benefits of such exploitation were vital for the village economy, villagers vigorously contended against *timar*-holders or government agents who chose to rent *mezraas* to outsiders or to distribute them under the *tapu* system. In opposition to outsiders, including members of the military elite, who were interested in renting *mezraas* to turn into estate *çiftliks*, villagers often rented them collectively.

Under the renting system, abandoned or unregistered lands such as *mezraa* or *çiftlik* were offered to any bidder, military or townsfolk, Muslim or Christian, or even foreigner, anyone who would guarantee to the treasury a steady revenue. In 1545 in Bosnia, for instance, Venetians were able to rent *mezraas*.[32] Otherwise, in principle, the government's policy was ultimately to convert all such lands into villages or peasant *çiftliks*. Once registered in the survey with an estimated rent, a *mezraa* could be subject to various types of assignments by the sultan – it could be granted as freehold property, a *vakf* or a *timar*. In the survey registers, a *mezraa* often was assigned as part of a *timar* or a *vakf*, since it could be cultivated and produce revenue. When it was included in *timar* revenue, its cultivation became the *timar*-holder's concern. He could rent it and obtain a lump sum for its rent or he could let "outsiders," nomads or wandering unregistered peasants, use it in return for the payment of tithes and incumbent dues.

The next question to determine is how *mezraa*s emerged and under what conditions their numbers changed. Peasant populations abandoned their villages, temporarily or permanently, for various reasons. Natural and economic conditions conducive to mass flight included exhaustion of the land, desertification, and epidemics. Social and political conditions were no less important. On the İstanbul–Belgrade highway, peasants abandoned their villages to set up new ones on inaccessible sites. First and foremost, peasants left their villages en masse to avoid attack by passing troops, brigand bands or caravans. A particularly important cause of flight was to avoid registration for taxes and tax collection. The peasant's most effective means of getting a tax reduced or abolished was the threat to abandon the tract. Assuming the character of a mass protest, this flight from the land became in effect a peasant strike. Since peasants did not *own* the land and as there were always other lands available, flight from their tract was frequently resorted to. The growing number of villages in the forests was largely due to this phenomenon. On the other hand, the big landowners, and particularly *vakf* lands, promised better conditions to attract the registered peasants of the lands under *tapu*.

In the Ottoman Empire, a shift of rural population was a continuous process which produced thousands of deserted villages and farms in the countryside. But there also occurred mass migrations due to famines or insecurity over a large area. Famines were so destructive that peasants migrated to the neighboring regions or towns for a livelihood and even sold themselves and their children as slaves.[33] Peasant migration as a result of famines or insecurity totally upset the empire's settlement pattern fixed in the land and population surveys and destroyed the state's tax basis and military structure. During the famine of 1583–84 the Bedouin of the Syrian steppe fell upon the cultivated lands between Damascus and Tripoli with their 4–50,000 camels and destroyed all of the fields. The most destructive of such peasant migrations occurred during the Celali depredations in Anatolia, called "the great flight," during the period

1593–1610.[34] In this case the exodus was not caused by natural factors, but rather by attacks of unemployed mercenary troops, the *sekban* and *sarıca* companies, upon defenseless settlements in the countryside.[35] Celali depredations were followed by the devastation of cultivated lands by the herds of Turcoman pastoralist nomads, known as Boz-Ulus, in eastern Anatolia and in the northern Syrian steppes, who migrated to central and western Anatolian provinces from 1613 on.

The changing number of *mezraas* can be taken as an indication of demographic and economic decline or development in a particular region, and the relative number of villages and *mezraas* can be determined for most of the provinces through the survey books.[36] In 1597, in some districts of Palestine,[37] the number of *mezraas* was two or three times greater than the number of villages (in the *sancak* of Safad there were 610 *mezraas* as against 282 villages), whereas in the *sancak* of Aleppo both the villages and the *mezraas* numbered each about one thousand.[38] By 1800, apparently about half the Anatolian population depended on the various types of periodic settlements.

In the formation of *mezraas*, conditions other than peasant flight also have to be considered. Sometimes the peasants used nearby marginal land or pasturelands for cultivation, or reclamations were made on wasteland in the forests or swamps.

When the central bureaucracy's control of the provinces weakened during protracted wars, struggles for succession to the throne, or uprisings, the military's appropriation of abandoned lands became more widespread. For example, in certain districts of Konya province, which had become the scene of protracted rebellions, a number of settlements were abandoned by its peasant population. To encourage their re-settlement, they were granted to the members of the military class or sheikhs as freehold or *timar*.[39] In this example, an extensive amount of uninhabited land, *çiftliks* and *mezraas*, was given as *hass* to the Ottoman crown prince sent there as governor. The prince-governor exploited them on the basis of sharecropping by attracting *reaya* or nomads from the surrounding areas.

At other times, because of a labor shortage, the military converted their *mezraas* into livestock ranches. During the Celali disorders, the Rescript of Justice abolished such *çiftliks*, saying,[40]

> those who set up *çiftliks* on the lands of the villages whose peasant populations fled because of the exactions since 1600 shall demolish the houses and stables and take away their servants, draft oxen, sheep and cattle and leave the site completely [for the peasants].

Such ranches were mainly owned by members of the sultan's standing army, Janissary and *sipahi*s. Once the military established such a ranch, pressure or intimidation caused further abandonment of land by peasants in the surrounding villages.

When *mezraa* owners were able to attract *reaya*, they usually had recourse to sharecropping (*ortakçılık*). They furnished land and often also seed, oxen, and domiciles to the sharecroppers. In the sub-province of Novigrad, for example, those who obtained *mezraa*s under the renting system were the petty commanders of the provincial army, such as *alay-begi*s or garrison commanders.[41]

Such shifts in land use, however, may also have resulted from economic factors, since animal breeding sometimes proved to be more profitable than grain production. In Anatolia, large areas of arable land abandoned by villagers were converted into ranches, partly because of the generally high price of meat and partly because the military found it difficult to obtain sufficient labor for cultivation.

RECONSTRUCTION (*ŞENLENDİRME*) AND METHODS OF COLONIZATION

It is a universal phenomenon, both in the West and the Middle East, that when peasants had to desert their lands, the military took over the land and turned the newcomers into their sharecroppers, *colon*s, or serfs. The Islamic caliphate, Iran, and the Ottoman Empire were not strangers to this type of agrarian transformation.

The Ottomans in their policy toward unused and waste lands seem to have emulated the Byzantines, who gave *pronoia*-holders and monasteries similar opportunities to reclaim such lands. The big landowners either partitioned the land and rented the parts to their own *paroikoi* or unregistered outsiders, or they took complete ownership of the land by obtaining an imperial diploma and thereby turning it into an estate. Obviously, aside from a small reserve which his *paroikoi* was obliged to cultivate for him, the *pronoia*-holder controlled directly only those unused lands which were not in the possession of the *paroikoi*.

In the Ottoman Empire there were cases where state slaves or serfs cultivated abandoned land for the ruler's treasury, which often furnished them with land, seed and oxen, and closely supervised the production. The most spectacular example was that of Mehmed the Conqueror in 1453. Seeing that the Greek peasants of the 164 villages around his new capital city of İstanbul had fled or were enslaved during the siege, he

brought war prisoners and settled them in these villages as his sharecropper slaves, as well as Turcoman nomads.[42] In reconstruction, the state
often employed, as in certain areas of newly conquered Hungary, the
renting system, coupled with such attractive conditions as temporary
exemption from taxation. In contrast, the direct organization and supervision of production using servile labor must have been preferred in the
settlement of the İstanbul villages because of the urgent situation. Once
the area was restored to its original prosperity, the slave sharecropping
system was relaxed, giving way to the basic agrarian system of the empire,
çift-hane based on free peasant families, *reaya*, on land divided into peasant farms under *tapu*.

As seen earlier, a grant of land as freehold to the high echelons of the
military was another method in reconstruction. The following example
will illustrate this. The village called Baş-Çiftlik in the district of Niksar
with its two *mezraas*, being on the highway, was abandoned and stayed
uninhabited for about forty years. Then it was granted by the sultan's
diploma as a freehold estate to Sinan Beg for his services in an imperial
campaign. It was exempted from taxation, including extraordinary levies.
Enjoying such favorable conditions, it grew into a village with the settlement of local peasants and unregistered immigrant peasants from other
areas. Sinan Beg built a mosque and a dervish convent in the village and
reclaimed some land around the granted land. Finally, during the new
survey under Süleyman I, the whole estate was registered as a village
with two *mezraas* and the reclaimed *çiftliks*. Sinan Beg retained one share
of the land out of fifteen as freehold for himself, and the rest was made
a *vakf* for the dervish lodge he built in the village.[43]

Without the laborers who would cultivate and make the improvements,
however, the entire enterprise of reclamation or reconstruction would
have been futile. Such laborers might have been drawn from the slaves
whom the Ottoman elite employed extensively during the first period of
conquests, or from "outsiders" who were mostly uprooted and impoverished peasants or impoverished pastoral nomads, or from peasants
already registered on *timars* who offered themselves as sharecroppers or
day laborers for pay. The last group thus would be responsible both for
giving tithes to the owner for the reclaimed land, and for paying personal
taxes to their *timar*-holder to whom they were assigned in the registers.
While the Ottoman government encouraged such reclamations of land,
it also warned the new landowners not to force registered peasants to
work such lands. The state's attitude meant that the usual practice was
to invite and settle "outsiders" on such lands.

The grant of land to dervishes is a method widely used from the beginning of the Ottoman state.[44] In general, the dervishes were given *mezraas*, or rather, a piece of land of the *çiftlik* size to bring back to cultivation, and in return the state expected them to perform a public service by giving shelter and food to travellers in their hostel. Since villages tended to locate away from highways, the government used this institution to promote settlement on abandoned lands along the highways.

In Serbia, abandoned villages were brought back to cultivation by the settlement of nomadic Vlachs[45] in the same way that nomads or wandering peasants were encouraged to settle *mezraas* in Anatolia.

A particularly interesting example of the government's efforts to convert *mezraas* in use by neighboring villages into new settlements is Syrmia's reconstruction after the conquest.[46] In this region, the vast stretches of abandoned arable land were first liberally recognized as *mezraas* pertaining to nearby villages. But later on, when security was re-established and peasants who had emigrated began to return, these *mezraas*, as well as *çiftliks* which were much larger than the standard peasant *çiftliks*, were surveyed and distributed to immigrant peasant families. The native villagers then attempted to prevent the newcomers from settling. The newcomers were mostly wandering peasants who had abandoned their homes during the Hungarian–Ottoman wars of 1521–26. The distribution of the large *mezraas* under the renting system, followed by the application of the *tapu* system, was the most effective policy pursued by the central government to expand the tax base in the provinces or in newly conquered and ruined countrysides.

Under the impact of the İstanbul market, a specific settlement process occurred in the Kilia–Akkerman region between 1484 and 1540.[47] In addition to the economic boom which the region enjoyed when the south–north trade route shifted from Caffa to Kilia–Akkerman and the lower Danubian ports (see below, pp. 285–99), İstanbul's growing demand for foodstuffs and raw materials triggered an unprecedented expansion of agriculture and cattle raising in the virgin fertile lands of the Bucak (lower Bessarabia). Two economic factors should be underlined for this spectacular development. First, there was the low cost of sea transportation of bulky necessities, transport costs being the most important determinant for interregional trade in the Ottoman Empire. Secondly, the great demand of the İstanbul market led to an unusual cash accumulation. The case has a particular interest since it shows how a market economy could rise within an oriental empire and make a tremendous impact on the development of agriculture and colonization in an undeveloped area. Although the region's development had its own unique characteristics, it had common features with other developing areas under the traditional Ottoman methods of agricultural expansion and settlement. These included reclamation and settlement and the use of renting by contract in opening new arable lands. Since the demand for sheep, cattle and horses for the capital and army grew, settlements showed a spectacular expansion in the countryside of Akkerman, Bender and Kilia in the period 1538–70. Then a large amount of abandoned or reclaimed land around these towns came into use as big farms or ranches (*çiftliks*, *mezraa*s or *kışlak*s). Over time many of these would develop into prosperous villages (see Table I:35).

Originally meaning the winter camp and pastureland of nomads, the term *kışlak* in this area assumed a special connotation. The local military or townspeople, engaged in large-scale livestock exports by sea to İstanbul, used abandoned land to create livestock ranches called *kışlak*s, sometimes synonymously called *mezraa* or *çiftlik*. Those transhumant people using a *kışlak* may also have engaged in limited cultivation.

Such *çiftlik*s, being held under a renting contract (*mukataa*), changed hands over time, so there was nothing unusual in a *çiftlik* held by a military person later falling into the hands of a tailor or a peasant.[48] The renter of a *mukataalu* land paid a lump sum to the treasury and exploited the land in the way he thought the most profitable for himself. If he invited people of peasant *reaya* status to cultivate it, he took tithes. But the specific peasant taxes were to be paid by the *reaya* to the treasury or its agent because "the *reaya* belong to the sultan," or to the *timar*-holder. If the sultan granted land with full ownership (*temlik*) then these taxes too belonged to the beneficiary.

In the same region *çiftlik*s and *kışlak*s, each comprising originally quite an extensive area, were divided over time into normal-sized Ottoman peasant *çiftlik*s. There were 82 *çiftlik*s in the survey of 1542, by 1570 they numbered 186.

In short, various methods were employed by the state, members of the military class, or peasants to develop sub-village or periodic settlements. Concerned to maintain and develop the tax base in the countryside, the state led in the settlement and exploitation of such lands. And by incentives such as lower tax liability or complete tax exemption, the state encouraged individuals or groups to rent and exploit abandoned lands. The *mukataa* renting system specifically applied to this category of lands since it had more favorable provisions than the *tapu* system and offered a basic advantage for those who rented such lands.

Table 1:35. Village formation in Kilia and Akkerman

Area	1542		1570	
	Village	*çiftlik*	Village	*çiftlik*
Kilia	2	—	4	29
Akkerman	13	—	34	157
Total	15	82	38	186

Source: Veinstein (1985).

Ottoman survey registers also show that, besides belonging to villages, a great number of "vacant" *çiftlik*s and *mezraa*s were registered as "dependent" on towns within the boundaries of the urban *kada* district.[49] This situation reflects the economic dependence of the towns on such agricultural reserve land, without which the towns could not have survived. Given the high transportation costs of the time, towns had to rely on this *Lebensraum* for an important part of the foodstuffs, fuel and raw materials such as cotton, wood, fruits, vegetables and hides, for their populations. The social and economic dynamics of such villages and sub-village settlements appear to be extremely vivid and complex compared to that of "independent" rural settlements. As a result, *mezraa*s around towns bear quite special characteristics. In describing the city of Bursa, Evliya[50] speaks of "the great number of its *mezraa*s and abundance of provisions." Many villages near towns were transformed into *mezraa*s or *çiftlik*s also because the village population, attracted by better opportunities in town, migrated there. Once deserted, the village land was acquired under *mukataa* by well-to-do town residents and turned into a kind of estate-*çiftlik*. In the survey registers we find that most renters of such *çiftlik*s and *mezraa*s were military or well-to-do townsmen. While *mezraa*s at large were exploited mainly for grain production, great numbers of vineyards, orchards and gardens around every important town provided fruit and vegetables.

SİPAHİ AND VILLAGERS

A village community on the whole was isolated and defenseless in the open country and was exposed to attack and plunder from all kinds of marauders. This precarious situation made effective protection for the peasantry a fundamental requirement of rural society. Like western feudal lords, the *sipahi* lived in the village as a visible instrument of imperial protection. Whenever an attack occurred, the *sipahi* was to alert the district local commander, *subaşı/zaim*, who would summon all the *sipahi*s in the area. During the campaigns some *sipahi*s were left behind in the villages as a protection. In about 1634, Henry Blount[51] incisively observed that the *timariot*s had the responsibility "to awe the provinces wherein they lived and cause them to be well cultivated." Also, the provincial commanders of higher ranks, *sancak beg*s in particular, had the duty to make periodic tours of their jurisdictional areas and to identify vagabonds or wrongdoers. At the turn of the seventeenth century, the central government lost effective control of its provinces in Anatolia, and commanders made exactions on defenseless villagers to sustain their retainers, while the towns had relatively better protection. In the justice rescripts[52] the basic duty of the governors is formulated in these terms:

> The real purpose in appointing *beglerbegi* and *sancakbegi*s to each province and in assigning them *hass* prebends is not just to make tours of the country and to collect money and goods, and thus cause the ruin of the land, but to guard and protect and make the country prosper by following God's command to act as one is ordered in the divine words and to refrain from what is prohibited in order to prevent anyone from committing injustices and oppression against the peasants contrary to the stipulations of the Islamic and sultanic law and to take into custody through proper means those who disturb public security.

The *timariot*s formed a vital part of the *çift-hane* system, acting to ensure the survival of the village communities. As a rule, the *reaya* were prohibited from owning or using weapons.

As reflected in sultanic regulations, peasants had many complaints about their relationship with the *sipahi* and with government agents who visited their villages. To protect peasants the rules regarding the collection of taxes were particularly detailed and restricting. According to one law, peasants could not harvest their fields, put grain in a barn or pick fruit until the *sipahi* was present. To prevent the product from perishing the law makers introduced new regulations. If the *timar*-holder did not appear in time to determine, together with the peasant, his share of the tithes on the harvest, the village head, or *kethüda* and imam were authorized by law to do the job. Also, the *sipahi*s disregarded the law that exempted fruit and vegetables and beehives for family consumption, as well as all crops harvested by hand, from tithes. Again, *sipahi*s did not respect the law which prohibited collection of dues on lands reclaimed by peasants from the forest and waste land which were not entered into the official survey books. Among the *sipahi*s' exactions, double taxation was the largest and most common. Double taxation was possible as a result of the alternatives the law maker considered, revival of an abolished custom, or confusion in the text of the law. After a peasant delivered one cartload of wood and one cartload of hay as part of his obligatory service, the *sipahi* still required payment of the cash equivalent of these services. Since the central government sought to be solicitous to complaints about illegal exactions and injustices[53] peasants often sought the local kadi's intervention or that of the Porte. Bribery, of course, existed at every level. But as long as the central bureaucracy was efficient and the bribery did not cost too much, the complaint system functioned. In the seventeenth century, a special bureau and registers were created at the capital for such individual or communal petitions of grievance.[54]

An imperial order of 1549 indicates that Janissaries were actively engaged in agriculture in the villages. Although there was no special treatment or exemption for the military as far as taxation was concerned, the law recognized certain personal immunities for the servants of the sultan. They were, for instance, exempt from the yoke-tax, a typical levy on the dependent peasant *reaya*. Also, the law prohibited *sipahis* from forcing Janissaries to perform labor services, such as carrying the *sipahi* shares to the market place or to his barn. The military also was exempt from paying market dues or marriage tax owed by the ordinary *reaya*.

THE VILLAGE AS A COMMUNITY AND VILLAGE TYPES

Since village types varied from one geographic region to another and were influenced by various ethnic and cultural traditions, it is meaningless to talk about the Ottoman, even Anatolian or Rumelian village. The point here is whether or not the Ottoman regime imposed certain common characteristics or uniformities resulting from a common imperial land-holding system, taxation and local administration. Such an inquiry makes sense when we remember that the Anatolian and Rumelian provinces, the core lands of the empire, were subjected to a general law code along with the universal *timar* regime. To constitute a village it was not enough to have peasant families assembled and living in a certain area, since there were other types of rural settlement which were not considered villages. One determinant factor was registration for a certain length of time in the imperial Ottoman registers. Official registration defined a village as a communal and territorial unit with fixed boundaries of arable land and pastures and total tax liability (*hasıl*). The number of peasant families or the amount of arable land were not apparently decisive factors. Thus, the continuity of a settlement with an agricultural base was the decisive factor; so the surveyor inquired as to whether the settlement had a cemetery, a water source, pastures and fixed boundaries verifiable by the testimony of trustworthy local witnesses. The tomb of a saint was often accepted as proof of the continuous existence of a village. The administration attempted to restore deserted villages to their original state. In other words, tradition and the imperial concern for maintaining the tax base were the guiding principles in establishing villages.

Under the *çift-hane* system, the peasant family was a legally autonomous unit, in terms of the possession and exploitation of land. Villages under the Ottomans generally constituted agglomerations of independent peasant households. It was an exception to find villages in possession of common arable land and practicing periodic parcelling and redistribution. Nomads who carried out transitory agriculture on *mezraas* or settled permanently on such land were the exception. But even such exploitations were over time transformed into typical "Ottoman" villages under the *tapu* system with independent *çift-hane* units. Thus, it can safely be said that the classical Ottoman regime tended to extend a specific type of village throughout the core lands of the empire. Since, in the *tapu* system, a peasant maintained a certain status with specific obligations and tax liabilities which were totally different from those of an urbanite (*şehirli*), a clear definition of each group was needed. It is specified that a peasant is a man who is the son of a peasant registered as such in the official survey and actually living in the village.

The village community acquired its communal character through its common interests in such areas as the village meadows, threshing floor, water sources and, in particular, pastures. The village acted collectively when there was a need to protect the village territory and its fields against outsiders, particularly against pastoralists. Peasants did not have too many livestock, so cooperation became a necessity in the pasturing of animals. Since this was one of the basic concerns of peasant households, they jointly hired a shepherd who gathered animals each morning in the village square and took them to the outlying common pastureland. A pasture's protection was a common responsibility which led not infrequently to "battles for pastureland" among the neighboring villages. To protect the communal rights and interests, the leaders of the village, *sipahi* and the village *kethüda* or imam, sought the local kadi's legal sanction. If a solution could not be reached locally, the village had the right to complain directly to the sultan by submitting a joint petition or by sending a delegation. Thus, in defining a settlement as a village, the presence of these two agents was considered necessary. The *sipahi* represented the sultan's authority and interests, the *kethüda* or imam, chosen from among the villagers or invited from outside, was paid jointly by the villagers and represented the village community.[55]

Specific social, economic and administrative conditions gave rise to various types of villages under the Ottoman regime. Aside from the ordinary type of village, those which developed from a dervish group around a convent preserved the initial character of the village with a saint's tomb, visited by outsiders and with tax immunities. Villages centrally located or situated near a thermal spring or fountain were apt to become the bazaar for neighboring villages. A great number of villages throughout the core lands were distinguished by certain permanent services assigned by the state, such as safeguarding a mountain pass (*derbendci*), or bridge (*köprücü*), working in state mines (*küreci*) or rice exploitation (*çeltükci*); or supplying bows and arrows (*okçular*) or butter (*yağcı*). Today, the toponymy of villages throughout Anatolia and the Balkans reflect this Ottoman background.

It was of vital importance to delimit a village. Those who were attributed the revenues of a village as part of a prebend, freehold or *vakf* land, had to know exactly the area granted. Disputes often arose among the prebend-holders themselves or between them and neighboring villages or government agents. Each prebend-holder was to collect the revenues from the land and the peasants personally assigned to him in the register. The boundaries were determined by the local kadi or one of his deputies who went to the place and made inquiries of trustworthy people on the spot and produced a document delimiting the village boundaries according to the locally known signs – trees, rocks, streams, etc. On the basis of the kadi's document, the sultan conferred a delimitation document, *sınırname* (*sınır* is a loan word from Greek). In fact, the boundaries of villages must go back long before Ottoman times. What was customarily established from olden times was taken as proof of communal rights. Villagers' conservatism was espoused by the imperial bureaucracy. So it was the state which mainly was responsible for the continuity of the rural landscape and topography. The state was concerned because the protection of tax resources depended on the identification of village units.

The village inhabitants might change drastically but the village, its fields and its name remained. There were few villages which disappeared altogether from the survey registers. The deserted villages were registered as *mezraas* mostly under the same name and the state took measures to restore them to their initial conditions. Thus, it was possible to identify each village, each *mezraa*, each *çiftlik*, and each pasture through the registers; and it was possible to identify even each field (*tarla*) with its local name. Each unit in the village had a specific name, mostly after the name of its registered first possessor; thus the unit was identifiable to the officials making assignments in İstanbul and to the local taxpayer. Identification by name of a land unit eliminated the need for the administration to perform a detailed cadastral survey.

It not infrequently appears that there were no precise boundaries between the villages and because of this members of the elite sometimes included in their estates large tracts of land traditionally belonging to neighboring villages. Kadi court documents provide evidence of frequent disputes between village communities and the elite over boundaries. The central government supposedly remained impartial in such confrontations, but influential landlords, such as the pashas, viziers, sultan's daughters or sons-in-law were favored and took advantage of their position to enlarge their domains. Also, disputes occurred frequently over lands commonly exploited by two villages. In such cases the law maker usually recognized its common possession (*mushaa*). Then the *timar*-holders collected taxes not on a territorial basis but on the registerment of the peasant. Wherever the peasant cultivated he paid taxes to his own registered *sipahi*. Where the land between two villages was a large wasteland such as a mountain or forest neither could claim it. In such a case the boundary of each village extended to the land that opened onto the wasteland.

To sum up, all of the arable lands in the empire were divided as traditional village parishes and each represented a territorial, communal and fiscal unit. Each village in turn was divided into *çiftlik* units or its fractions, depending on the available peasant families or work force. To survive as an economic unit each village needed arable land sufficient to sustain the community, pastureland for draft animals and livestock, a meadow usually not too far away from the village, a harvest floor, a fountain and a cemetery. Thus, in a village where there was a stream to supply water power, we also find a flour mill. *Çiftliks* and its fractions were further divided into fields measured in *dönüms* (each *dönüm* was about 920 sq. meters). Grain fields generally were bounded by a ditch, shrubs or stones.

Since fields predominantly were reserved for grain or other relatively cheap produce, no elaborate enclosures were necessary. As explained above, the open-field system predominated in the Ottoman rural land-scape as today it does in the Middle East. To protect crops from roaming animals or nomadic herds was an important village concern. Each village maintained collectively a watchman, *kır-bekçisi* or *deştiban*. Gardens and orchards often were enclosed by stone walls that were to be respected. The spiritual mentor of Mehmed II, Sheikh Ak-Shemseddin, became furious when he learned that a shepherd had let the herd get into "his pasture protected by a wall." The *sipahi* collected a special fine from those not taking care of animals which harmed the crops of others.

NOTES

1 İnalcık (1983a), pp. 878–83.
2 Hütteroth (1974), pp. 19–47.
3 *Ibid.*, pp. 40–41.
4 Barkan (1939–40), pp. 165–80.
5 Hütteroth (1974), pp. 20–21.
6 *Ibid.*
7 Venzke (1981).
8 Hütteroth (1974), pp. 27–35; Hütteroth and Abdulfattah (1977).
9 Hütteroth (1974), Table 2b.
10 Tanoğlu (1954), pp. 27–28.
11 Cohen and Lewis (1978), pp. 19–41; McGowan (1969), pp. lix–lxxii; İnalcık (1969b).
12 For a Malthusian approach to Ottoman demography, see Cook (1972).
13 Jennings (1978), pp. 89–98.
14 *Ibid.*, p. 95.
15 İnalcık (1991a), pp. 161–76.
16 Hütteroth (1974), p. 21.
17 Greenwood (1988); Cohen (1989), pp. 11–61.
18 Soysal (1976), p. 17.
19 *Ibid.*, p. 26.
20 In Soysal's (1976) calculation, 250 tons.
21 İnalcık (1982b), pp. 86–88, 103–6.
22 *Ibid.*, p. 78.
23 See qv. "mazra'a", *EI²*; Adanır (1988).
24 Tanoğlu (1954), p. 1; Hütteroth (1968), pp. 24–52; Tunçdilek (1960), pp. 17–55; Hütteroth and Abdulfattah (1977), pp. 29–32.
25 Tunçdilek (1960), p. 44.
26 *Ibid.*, pp. 47–54; Barkan (1943), pp. 28–32.
27 Hütteroth and Abdulfattah (1977), pp. 29–32.
28 Barkan (1988), p. 156 no. 12.
29 *Ibid.*, p. 114.
30 Lemerle (1958), pp. 59–60, rightly rejects the communal ownership of land in Byzantium; Gorecki (1984), pp. 77–107.

31 See Mehmed the Conqueror's law code in Barkan (1943), p. 390, article 16.
32 Gökbilgin (1964), p. 208.
33 Güçer (1964), pp. 10–11; İnalcık (1965a), p. 130.
34 Akdağ (1963), pp. 250–57.
35 *Ibid.*, pp. 250–58; Güçer (1964), pp. 19–29; cf. İnalcık (1980a), pp. 281–303, in particular 294.
36 Tanoğlu (1954), map.
37 Hütteroth and Abdulfattah (1977), pp. 23, 24, maps 3, 10, 13.
38 Venzke (1981), p. 40.
39 BBA, TTD, Konya 40, dated 906 H/1500–1.
40 İnalcık (1965b), p. 127.
41 Bayerle (1973), p. 70.
42 Barkan (1939–40), pp. 27–74, of the 164 villages 45 were settled by Akçakoyunlu Turcomans and 119 by war prisoners.
43 Barkan (1942b), p. 307; for a large-scale reclamation project, see İnalcık (1985b), pp. viii, 108–11.
44 Barkan (1942), pp. 279–304.
45 Zirojević (1987).
46 McGowan (1983), xxiii–xxv; Barkan (1943), p. 230.
47 Veinstein (1985), pp. 177–210.
48 *Ibid.*, pp. 197–99, but it is not appropriate to characterize these lands as "military," since they were simply *mukataalı* lands that anybody could lease.
49 Faroqhi (1984), pp. 191–266.
50 Evliya Çelebi (1896–1938), II, p. 12.
51 Blount (1636), p. 583.
52 İnalcık (1965b), p. 124.
53 İnalcık (1989).
54 Majer (1984), pp. 17–21; İnalcık (1988b).
55 Faroqhi (1980), pp. 87–99.

D TRADE

8

٠̇

İSTANBUL AND THE IMPERIAL
ECONOMY

FEEDING A GIANT CITY

İstanbul was the great transit center of the south–north trade artery between the Black Sea and Danubian ports, and the principal cities of the eastern Mediterranean, Arabia and India. The İstanbul-based merchants imported manufactured goods of European origin, principally woolen cloth, and also the so-called oriental goods, in particular, pepper, and other spices and dyes. Caffa, Kilia and Akkerman were the chief transit centers for this north–south trade, with Akkerman superseding Caffa, particularly after the Ottoman conquest of İstanbul. İstanbul merchants and industries supplied the Black Sea and northern area with woolen cloth, ready-to-wear clothing and Bursa silk textiles, which were also in great demand in Poland, Sweden and Muscovy. But much more important than international commerce was the regional trade between the northern and southern Black Sea areas. A major concern of the imperial government was to ensure an uninterrupted flow of the principal food-stuffs for the huge population of İstanbul. Intermittent wheat and flour shortages among the masses caused serious problems for the government.

Providing bread to the urban masses on a daily basis, and at a reasonable price, became such a vital governmental task that one of the most important duties of the grand vizier was to go personally every week to the bazaar and inspect grain supplies, bakeries, and the price and quality of bread. In times of severe shortage, the sultan would visit the bazaar in disguise and inflict the severest punishments on those merchants found guilty of cheating the public. Anyone creating public discontent was considered as undermining the sultan's rule; hence, the sultan had to prove to the public that their daily bread was his personal concern. In times of shortage, the government strictly regulated prices by periodically recalculating and adjusting prices and distributing free grain to the poor through the hospices. To remedy delays in the flow of supplies, the government also organized milling operations. Even seed was given to the growers at a loan discount of up to 50 percent off the market price.

İstanbul's daily grain consumption in the early eighteenth century has been estimated at about 200 tons.[1] The principal grain-growing regions for İstanbul included the following: the plains of Thrace from the port of Tekirdağ; the Danubian basin, shipped from Brăila, Isaccea, and Costanţa, Bulgarian grain from Burgaz; the steppe region from the Dobruja to the Don river, shipped from Kilia, Akkerman, Azov and Caffa; the plain of Thessaly from Volos; western Anatolia from Foçalar and İzmir; and Egyptian grain and beans exported from Damietta and Alexandria. All of these regions were thus easily accessible by sea to the

Table I:36. Provisions arriving in İstanbul by sea (according to a register of market dues [*ihtisab*] dated *Zülkade* 1092/1681, preserved at the Municipal Library, İstanbul, Cevdet Collection, B. 2).

Ships coming from	Provisions	Type of ship
Egypt	Spices, rice, flax, henna, sugar, ammonium nitrate	Big ships (*kalyon*) and *miri* boats; small boats (*firkata* and *şayka*)
İzmir, Kuşadası, Edremid, Foçalar, Karabarun, İstanköy	Dried fruits (raisins, figs, etc.)	*Miri* boats
Marmara Sea region	Olives, grapes, apples, pears, plums, cherries, apricots, etc. in baskets	*Miri* boats (*kayık*)
Southern Black Sea ports	Apples, chestnuts	*Miri* boats
Aegean ports	Citrus fruit	Boats called *iskaponya* and boats of Chios
Giresun and other southern Black Sea ports	*Nardenk*, hazelnuts	*Miri* boats
Erdek, Aydıncık, etc.	Dried olives	*Miri* boats
Gallipoli, Burgos, Bosphorus, Kazdağı	Molasses, pickles in jars	*Miri* boats
Lemnos, Mytilene, etc.	Uncured cheese	*Miri* boats
Kilia	Dried beef meat of Kilia	In sacks of 7 & 3 *kantar* by ship
Tripoli (Syria) and İzmir	Soap	In sacks of 3 & 1.5 *kantar*
İstanköy and vicinity	Lemon juice	Boats called *mayestra* or *darbuna*
Edremid and vicinity	Olive oil, fruit	*Miri* boats
Mytilene	Olive oil	In boats of 1,000, 600 or 300 kantar
Black Sea ports	Sesame	*Şayka, mayestra, darbuna*
	Flax seed	*Mayestra, darbuna şayka* and Bartin *kayık*
Galatz	Rock salt	*Şayka, mayestra* and *darbuna*

Table 1:36. (*cont.*)

Ships coming from	Provisions	Type of ship
Mediterranean and Black Sea ports (mostly Tekirdağ, Volos, Caffa, Akkerman)	Barley, millet	
Mainly Bandırma, Burgos, Bigados, Silivri, Çekmece	Straw	
Mainly Karabiga, Şehirköy	Broadbeans, resined wood	
Anadolu-Hisar and Rumeli-Hisar, İzmit, Midye, Terkos, etc.	Charcoal	
Ahtabolu, Bartın, İnebolu, Midye	Logs	
Akçay, Sakarya, Ereğli	Lumber	
Hora, Mirefte	Bricks	
Enez, Şar	Big and small jugs	
İliyota	Vinegar	
Crete, Kalyomoz	Harub (carob)	
via Varna (from Samakov)	Iron	
Santor island, Foça	Burrstone	
Kavak on the Bosphorus	Stones for building	
Kazdağı, Mytilene	Acorns of *valonia* oak, resined wood, pitch, olives	
Kazdaği, Edremid	Olive oil, pinetree bark	
Eyüp, Üsküdar	Yogurt, cream	
Mytilene	*Kaşkaval* cheese	
Tekirdağ and Çorlu, Wallachia and the Black Sea	*Tekerlek* cheese	
Wallachia and Rumeli	*Tulum* cheese	
İzmit, Darıca, Yalova	Jewish *kaşar* cheese	
Talanda, Ağrıboz, Anadolu	*Kızıl-tekerlek* cheese	
Black Sea	Tallow for candle making	

imperial capital. Since Mamluk times, Egypt had supplied the Hejaz with large quantities of grain.[2]

It was from the Black Sea region that İstanbul received the largest part of its provisions and raw materials including grain, meat, hides and lumber. Fertility of the land and large surpluses, low prices and water transportation were the determining factors for this dependency. In order to deliver grain supplies on time and in sufficient amounts the government took strict measures.[3]

Without a doubt, shipping constituted the most serious problem in İstanbul's provisioning. The Greek shipping businesses centered at Yeniköy on the Bosphorus were mainly responsible for the transport of bulky goods from the Black Sea to İstanbul. Big vessels departing from İstanbul kept regular schedules but small ships at specific ports-of-call around the Black Sea plied the sea lanes between İstanbul and the ports on the western and southern Black Sea coasts, the Marmara Sea or the Aegean islands and their ports (see Table I: 36). The most favorable season for navigation on the Black Sea was limited to the six-week period between 15 August and 30 September. During the winter months navigation almost stopped. These conditions required an efficient system for organizing shipping and storage.

All types of boats or ships of varying size moved between İstanbul and the Black Sea ports. According to a ship-tax register, dated 1483, 2,019 ships and 2,265 boats visited the port of İstanbul in one year.

An official report of 1520[4] indicated that 70 or 80 ships from the ports of İstanbul, Trabzon, Samsun and Sinop crossed the Black Sea regularly and carried cotton goods, silks, mohair, figs, lemons, etc. to Brăila, where they then loaded grain coming from the Danubian ports of Nicopolis and Vidin. The transport of wheat from the Danubian provinces by water, through the Danube and the Black Sea to İstanbul, was the cheapest and only sensible way. Concerned with the low price of this basic commodity, the government also required that customs dues be imposed only once on the producer. Also, in order to protect the local producer, the government agents took measures to keep local prices at reasonable levels. Extremely low prices adversely affected the tax revenues and income of the provincial *sipahis*. The government made careful investigations through the local kadis and fixed grain prices separately for each *sancak*.[5]

In the early seventeenth century, the government commissioned 118 ships belonging to a consortium of fifty-six shipowners to make 658 individual grain transport voyages to deliver to İstanbul about 17,000 tons of grain and flour from the ports of Isaccea, Azov and Burgaz in the Black Sea region. This cost the government about 5.5 million *akça*.[6] Freight rates were quite high. For example, grain shipments from Isaccea on the lower Danube to İstanbul were assessed at the rate of 8 *akça* per *kile* (25.65 kg), about 15 percent of the intrinsic value of the goods shipped.

The availability of wheat supplies, so vitally important for provisioning the imperial capital and armies on campaign, was strongly influenced by Italy's demand for grain and the higher prices Italian cities were willing to pay.

GRAIN SUPPLIES AND EUROPE

In short, Venice and İstanbul competed for the grain supplies of the Levant. It is suggested[7] that the drop in Italy's wheat imports from the

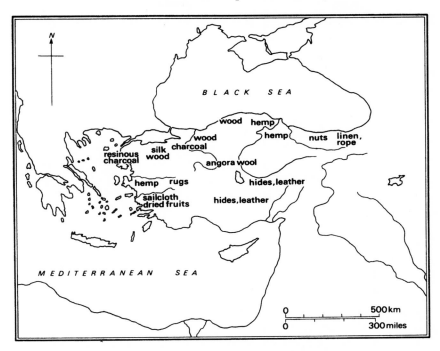

10 Anatolian goods marketed in İstanbul. *Source*: McCarthy (1982), p. xxx.

Ottoman dominions during the period 1564–1600 can be taken as an indication of population pressure in the Ottoman Empire. But the yearly fluctuations in grain trade were dependent on such factors as wars, government policies, and climate. The question remains whether or not the changes observed were really long-term ones determined by population growth or short-term ones caused by other variables.

Mustafa Akdağ suggested, [8] on the basis of the growing frequency of reports on shortages in the major cities, that it was not before the middle of the sixteenth century that a long-term shortage in grain seems to have appeared in Turkey. And later on the government, increasingly concerned with the difficulty of supplying the big cities, made every effort to stop contraband wheat trade. It is interesting to read in Ottoman reports of widespread contraband trade carried on in the coastal areas: the profiteers, offering 20 percent more than the officially set prices, amassed in their storehouses large quantities of wheat to sell to European ship owners. Thus *timar*-holders, governors, Janissaries and even members of the ulema were actively involved in this profitable trade. According to Akdağ,[9] however, the real cause of long-term shortage in Anatolia was not the contraband trade stimulated by higher European prices, but the spread of the *çiftlik* system which produced a decrease of cultivated land in favor of animal breeding. The grain trade in the second half of the sixteenth century, according to the Venetian documentation of Aymard,[10] can be summarized as follows:

1548–53	Bad harvests and shortages in Italy; exceptional abundance and low prices in Turkey; 300–400,000 *staia* (240–320,000 hectoliters) were exported from Turkey in 1552
1553–60	Poor crops persist in Italy (excluding 1553); the Ottoman government imposes export prohibitions because of shortages and warfare
1565–67	Ottoman prohibitions
1570–72	Ottoman–Venetian War prohibitions
1574–75	Shortage and famine in Anatolia and İstanbul
1582–88	Fluctuations in the imports from the Levant
1588	Shortage in İstanbul
1589	Great shortages in the Levant
1590	Great shortage in Italy; wheat imports from Baltic countries
1591–93	Re-opening of wheat markets in the Levant
1594	Ottoman prohibition; Italy's massive imports from northern countries
1595–1629	The Levant competes with Baltic countries in supplying Italy's wheat needs

Whether by permit or smuggling, the Aegean area and Albania provided the main source for Venetian wheat purchases. The crop shortages and rising prices in western Anatolia in 1564–65, mentioned by the Venetian sources, led to active traffic in wheat from Macedonia and Thrace to the Aegean coasts of Asia Minor. Akdağ,[11] in a sweeping generalization, concluded that there was an almost permanent shortage of grain and high prices in western Anatolia and the Marmara basin in the sixteenth century because Western nations made massive purchases there. As to the shortages and rising prices in İstanbul in the 1580s, these are attributed in the Venetian sources to a diversion of surplus grain to the army fighting in Iran between 1578 and 1590.

Prior to 1549, the republic relied upon Italian wheat-producing areas, and then after 1593 massive wheat imports from the Baltic countries changed the pattern without, however, eliminating the imports from the Levant. In fact, in the years 1600–1 and 1628–29, because of favorably low price levels, Levantine wheat supplies replaced those from Baltic countries. Within this broad picture variations in wheat imports from the Levant do not seem to suggest a progressive decline which might be attributed to a constant factor, such as long-term population pressure. The boom of 1549–53, taken as the beginning of a new era in the east–west trade, may simply have been the outcome of an unusual disparity of prices between the two areas resulting from exceptionally good harvests in the Levant and great shortages in Italy. In any case, because of the high transport costs, imports from the Levant were economically feasible only when prices in the Levant sank below half the Italian prices. In fact, price seems to be the most comprehensive single indicator of the east–west trade.

The major challenge always was to supply the İstanbul grain market and to keep prices low. One might recall that ultimately Ottoman state ownership of arable land and the *çift-hane* system were designed to ensure a steady supply of grain to the market. Thus, the provisions of İstanbul and the army could not be left to traders and to the free interplay of market forces, since famine and the ensuing suffering often brought the populace and the troops to the brink of revolt.

But eventually, the state had to resort to more flexible methods, since trade monopolies and price fixing often produced opposite results. Deliveries fell behind if peasants were forced to sell at low government prices. These realities forced the government to resort to more liberal and economically sound methods of making purchases at market prices. Such liberal methods were applied particularly in sensitive ethnic areas and borderlands where it was important to gain peasants' support. During the critical war period between 1593 and 1606 in Hungary, wheat, barley and meat provisions for the army were procured either from the local market or by sending supplies by river boats from the depots in Belgrade and the southern Hungarian fortresses.[12]

Burgaz, Varna, Kilia and Akkerman on the Black Sea, and Vidin, Nicopolis, Rusçuk and Silistre on the Danube were the principal ports for channeling the surplus wheat of their respective hinterlands. While on the Aegean it was difficult to prevent contraband trade in wheat, the government exercised more control over production in the Marmara and Black Sea regions by checking all traffic through the straits. In times of shortage or famine, special agents of the government resorted to forced purchases in the production areas or principal outlets. Annually the voyvodes of Wallachia and Moldavia had to provide, at fixed prices, a predetermined amount of grain for the İstanbul market.[13]

A Venetian *bailo* observed[14] that purchases at fixed prices was believed to be one of the main reasons for the drop in wheat production in the Ottoman Empire. Peasants had no incentive to produce for low prices more than what was required for their own subsistence. This unwise policy appears to have made İstanbul more than ever dependent for its food supplies on the Danubian principalities. The revolt of the Wallachian Voyvode Michael the Brave (1593–1601), who stopped the requisite supplies, caused the prices of wheat and meat to soar in İstanbul.[15] Egypt, another important source of wheat for İstanbul, sent huge amounts of wheat to the Ottoman capital.

We saw earlier that İstanbul's growing demand for grain and meat transformed the steppe between Dnieper and Varna into a vast region of commercial agriculture and livestock breeding. By digging wells and using underground water, Tatars and Turcoman Yörüks settled the Dobruja steppe, which was previously a no-man's-land. Most new villages in the sixteenth century were named after the local well-digger. Varna, a port outlet of the steppe region in the north, densely populated by Yörüks, was an active commercial center for livestock, wool, hides, and leather products. Similar changes, from animal husbandry to grain growing, occurred in the steppelands bordering Kilia and Akkerman. In the Danubian delta, Brăila developed as the main transit port between the Danubian lands and the Black Sea. By 1520 the port was visited by some eighty ships from Trabzon, Sinop, Samsun, İstanbul, and from Europe.[16] Ships arriving from the Danubian ports from as far away as Vidin brought grain, textiles and iron products, which were sold in the local marketplace or were directly transferred to sea-going vessels.

The southern coastal villages of the Marmara Sea present another interesting example of the structural impact of the İstanbul market on regional agriculture. Perched on the slopes of the coastal range of the southern Marmara Sea, the Greek villages of Kurşunlu, Seki, Mudanya, Bigados, Stos, and Koçi, principally producing wine, olives and fruit, were totally dependent on the İstanbul market. They maintained quite a high standard of living compared to the inland villages, which depended on wheat and barley production.[17] To maintain the prosperity of the Greek villages, the Ottoman government gave to them the status of a sultanic endowment, which perpetuated their ethnic, economic and social character into the twentieth century.

The demand for milk and milk products, such as yogurt and fresh cream, gave rise to a great number of dairy herds in the countryside surrounding İstanbul. Members of the ruling elite, interested in the potential profits, owned many such dairies and farms, particularly in the Eyüp and Üsküdar areas. An important sector of regional trade for the empire derived from providing İstanbul with aged cheese. Wallachia, Rumeli and certain Black Sea ports exported significant amounts of *teker-lek* and *tulum* cheese to İstanbul, while the islands of Lemnos and Myti-lene were mentioned as exporters of uncured cheese and Jewish *kaşar* (kosher) which came from the nearby mainland towns of İzmit, Darıca and Yalova. Cheese appears as an important trade item in all of the customs' daybooks.

Bulky, cheap and perishable goods such as fresh fruit as well as olives, molasses and pickles came from the fertile plains and valleys surrounding the Marmara Sea. Consequently, horticulture, which was tied to the huge market of İstanbul, flourished in these regions. Other fruits such as apples, citrus fruits, chestnuts and hazelnuts came from more distant areas. Raisins and figs came from western Anatolia, hazelnuts from Trab-zon and Giresun, and chestnuts from Bursa and the southern Black Sea coast. The island of Istanköy (Cos) in the Aegean was an important producer of citrus fruit. Olives and olive oil, a basic foodstuff for the masses, were imported principally from Edremid and Mytilene, the near-est supply areas. Olives and olive oil also came from the rich groves of the valley near Athens.

NOTES

1 Murphey (1988), pp. 230–34.
2 Annually 48,000 tons in Murphey (1988), p. 222; the figure given by Faroqhi (1990), pp. 118–22, is much lower.
3 Murphey (1988), p. 222.
4 Beldiceanu-Steinherr (1964b).
5 Güçer (1952), pp. 58–60.
6 Murphey (1988), pp. 226–28.
7 İnalcık (1978a), pp. 80–83, cf. Cook (1972).
8 Akdağ (1949), XVI, pp. 390–95.
9 *Ibid.*
10 See İnalcık (1978a), pp. 80–83.
11 Akdağ (1949), XV, p. 513.
12 Finkel (1988), pp. 138, 147–49, 155–59, 175–77.
13 In the 1550s, for instance, the two principalities shipped nearly 5,000 tons of barley to İstanbul for the imperial stables, Bulgaru (1969), p. 666.
14 Bailo Giovanni Moro (1587–90) cited by Bulgaru (1969), p. 667.
15 *Ibid.*, p. 671.
16 Cvetkova (1971), p. 323.
17 İnalcık (1993).

9

∴

INTERNATIONAL TRADE: GENERAL
CONDITIONS

CAPITULATIONS AND FOREIGN MERCHANT
COMMUNITIES

The stipulations of Islamic Law were supreme and governing in Ottoman relations with Europe, and no study can be intelligible without them.[1] That is why the grant of capitulations or supplements thereof had always to be approved by the Sheyhülislam. Having said this, one must admit that the Ottomans adopted practices from such non-religious areas of government operations as customs regulations and commercial taxation; thus Byzantine and Italian practices were incorporated into the Ottoman imperial laws.[2]

Prior to 1800, international trade between the Ottoman Empire and Europe was conditioned not only by transport costs but also by the frequent conflicts between the two religiously and culturally competitive worlds, constant frontier warfare, and corsair activities. Nevertheless imperative economic interdependency compelled both sides to maintain close trade relations even during wartime. The imam-sultan granted the necessary guarantees for residence, travel and trade in the Ottoman territories under the Islamic principle of amnesty (*aman*), only to those non-Muslims from the Abode of War who gave the pledge of "friendship and sincere good will." Consequently, those nations or individuals considered hostile to Muslims were denied such formal guarantees. Such people could be enslaved by any Muslim in Ottoman territory. Trade with Austria, for example, did not fully flourish until the eighteenth century, mainly because the sultans did not grant the Habsburgs the same trade freedom which the "friendly" nations such as the French or English enjoyed. It will be seen that the favor and political decision of the Porte was generally responsible for the prosperity or crisis of a particular nation's Levantine trade. On the other hand, even Western nations lacking capitulations until the second half of the sixteenth century had been quite active in the Levant trade thanks to the privilege of traveling and doing business either under the flag of a nation having capitulations or through the go-between role of the Genoese, Venetians and Ragusans.

The basic principle of a capitulation is always an "amnesty" formally granted by the head of the Islamic community in return for the pledge of friendship on the part of the non-Muslims. The Ottomans often were inclined to interpret such pledges as a kind of allegiance. Capitulations belonged to the category of documents known as *ahdnames*. An *ahdname* is given unilaterally but recognizes, under oath, a privilege which binds the giver before God.

On the basis of the "friendship" pledge, Ottomans expected, though not expressly stated in the document, reciprocal privileges for their own subjects. Ottoman non-Muslim subjects, Jews, Armenians, Greeks and Slavs particularly, profited from Ottoman protection abroad and created, already in the fifteenth century, thriving merchant colonies in Venice, Ancona, and Lwow. On the other hand, citizens of the city state of Dubrovnik spectacularly expanded commercial and maritime activities in the sixteenth century thanks to its being under Ottoman suzerainty (see below, pp. 256–70). Ottoman colonies abroad also included Muslim Turks and even Iranians. In the second half of the sixteenth century, the Muslim colony in Venice became large enough to have its own *fondaco dei Turci* in 1592. Muslim merchants, however, were suspiciously watched, even harassed in the city.

In conferring capitulations the Ottomans primarily anticipated securing political advantages from the applicant state, the opportunity of acquiring an ally within Christendom. Venice often was, for example, neutralized by such commercial privileges and prevented from putting its powerful navy at the service of the crusading Popes.[3] The Western nations – France, England and the Dutch – obtained their capitulations when the Porte believed they were "fighting against idolatry" and common enemies, the Habsburgs and the Pope.

The Ottomans also benefited from trade relations with Europe, obtaining scarce and strategic goods such as tin, lead and steel, gunpowder, chemicals, and, in particular, silver and gold coins, as well as luxury goods consumed by the elite, in particular fine woolen cloths, jewelry, crystal and mirrors, and watches.

The fiscal benefits derived from trade was considered one of its most important aspects. Customs dues provided a substantial amount of much needed cash revenue for the imperial treasury. This factor explains the scrupulous concern of the sultan to abide by the provisions of capitulations. A capitulation guarantee had preeminence over the laws of the empire and, upon drawing up a capitulation, the sultan sent orders to local authorities to abide strictly by its provisions. As the European powers in the eighteenth century won military supremacy over the Ottomans, the Europeans began to interpret the capitulations as binding bilateral treaties. Prior to this development, the sultan had full discretion to decide unilaterally when the grantee had broken his "pledge of friendship" and when, in consequence, the capitulation became void. Since a capitulation was granted by each individual sultan personally, it had to be renewed by his successor, giving the ruler a chance for a revision. On the other hand, at each renewal the European nations sought to add new provisions, mostly to secure a formal sanction to a long-exercised practice, or to extend the scope of the original document. As noted earlier, each new provision was carefully checked by the administration and had to be approved by the religio-legal authorities. A threat to boycott Ottoman ports, and consequently reduce customs revenues, alarmed the Ottomans, and of course gifts and bribes also helped to convince the Porte to allow such supplementary clauses.

FOREIGN MERCHANT COMMUNITIES

The Ottoman government considered the foreign merchant communities as *millet*s or *taife*s, autonomous groups or assemblies organized under a deputy or consul. Consuls received diplomas from the sultan which confirmed the privileges of these assemblies and promised to enforce the decisions of the consuls with the cooperation of the Ottoman authorities. Such a situation originated from the basic Ottoman notion of capitulations. From the beginning, Ottomans were aware of the Byzantine experience with the Genoese and Venetians; they did not permit European merchant communities to establish themselves as independent colonies and never recognized territorial rights. Even the resident ambassadors at the Porte were regarded simply as representatives of their respective *millet*s. But by 1600, with the advent of the French and English and as a result of the Porte's growing economic and political dependence on westerners, the European notion of extra-territoriality became prevalent – so that consuls and foreign communities began to be regarded as being under the direct authority of the ambassadors representing their respective governments. In the later capitulations, a consul gained full diplomatic immunities as the deputy of the ambassador. A consul was to supervise the affairs of the merchant community in the area under his jurisdiction. He was supposed to register imported goods and to collect the appropriate fees for the ambassador and himself. No ship of his nation could leave port without his permit. He resolved disputes and settled suits between members of his nation according to his home country's laws and customs. However, criminal cases and suits between *taife* members and a Muslim had to be heard in the Ottoman courts. Many new articles were added to the capitulations to ensure that the foreigners received just treatment in court. A case could not be heard unless the dragoman was present – a provision already introduced in the Venetian capitulations of 1521.

Apart from İstanbul, the most numerous foreign *millet*s were resident at İzmir. From the end of the sixteenth century chiefly the English, then the French and the Dutch established communities, but there were only a few Venetians. In Sidon, the French; in Aleppo, the French and later on other nationalities; in Cairo, the French, the Venetians and for a time the English were the largest *millet*s.

The collective responsibility of the *millet* for crimes or debts of individuals was recognized in the capitulations from the earliest times. In case of pirate attacks or the failure to pay a public debt arising from a tax-farm held by a *millet* member, the Ottoman government imposed a collective fine on the nation. Foreigners complained, mostly about the so-called *avania*s (from Arabic *'awān*, "anything extorted"), the fees or gifts expected by local authorities, in particular governors or customs officers, from foreign merchants. European consular reports frequently mention *avania*s.[4] Not infrequently, it became an arbitrary and heavy burden on merchants which threatened to disrupt the normal course of trade. In the end, consuls began collection of a special tax, *cottimo*, from their merchants to pay for the *avania*s. Over time this fee became a regular impost. To stop *avania*s European nations insisted on introducing additional articles to the capitulations.

Under the capitulations non-Muslim foreigners were granted permission to go around and trade freely throughout Ottoman territories. But in practice the members of foreign nations were permitted residency only in certain ports and within these ports in specified quarters or caravanserais. In İzmir, Aleppo and Galata they enjoyed considerable freedom of movement.

Since travel in general was hazardous for individuals, even for Ottoman subjects, a blanket permit for foreigners was actually impractical. Every foreign merchant or visitor had to obtain from the sultan or local kadi a special authorization for safe conduct. According to Islamic Law, an individual Muslim had the right to enslave a non-Muslim foreigner who did not qualify for capitulation guarantees. So foreigners were even permitted to wear Muslim dress and to carry arms during travel. In general, residences of foreigners were non-violable; but upon suspicion of harboring fugitive criminals or slaves or smuggled goods, Ottoman officials made searches. Foreigners residing on the waterfront in İzmir occasionally were caught smuggling goods out their back doors into vessels.

Numerous articles were introduced into the original capitulations to safeguard the property of foreign merchants. If a merchant died in Ottoman territory or if his heir(s) were resident elsewhere, his estate was taken into trust by the local kadi and passed by him to the consul or to the partners or friends of the deceased. The kadi usually appointed an executor to take care of the affairs of the deceased.

Islamic maritime law developed through the capitulations, particularly under the Ottomans. The sultan granted freedom of navigation to nations bearing capitulations. Safeguards even against Ottoman corsairs were given. Officials had to provide anchorage in Ottoman harbors and to permit capitulation-holders the right to take on supplies and water at any point along the Ottoman coasts. In some capitulations, a special article was added to block the state's impressment of foreign ships and crews. Also, foreigners were pledged assistance and protection if driven ashore. Actually such safeguards were badly needed, as the dire situations outlined in some reports indicate.

Ottomans claimed sovereignty over the Aegean Sea, the Black Sea, the Red Sea, the Straits (Bosphorus and the Dardanelles) and the Strait of Otranto. The sultan's fleet had to make periodic tours in these waters to deter Christian corsairs. Coastal waters within the range of cannon were declared under direct Ottoman sovereignty.

Frequent inspections by Ottoman authorities enforced regulations on goods prohibited from export to hostile countries. If ships were discovered taking banned items to hostile countries, the sea patrol not only confiscated the goods but also seized the ship and enslaved the crew and passengers.

HISTORY OF THE CAPITULATIONS

In the fourteenth century, the newly established Turcoman principalities in western Anatolia, namely from south to north Menteşe, Aydın,

Saruhan, Karesi and Ottoman (Osmanlı) were imbued with *gaza* spirit or *cihad* and declared themselves to be *gazi* states, Islamic Holy War being their principle of legitimacy in the face of Mongols controlling Asia Minor. In Anatolia now even Mongol governors, Timurtash and later Eretna, professed support for Islamic Holy War in order to accommodate themselves among a population stirred with unprecedented *cihad* enthusiasm. Without this powerful factor no explanation can be found for the profound changes in Asia Minor. However, once established as small Islamic sultanates coming under growing influence of the Muslim ulema from the hinterland, a new trend in favor of commercial interests began to influence state policy. The benefits were evident: now the wealthy ruling elite needed the luxuries of Europe and trade brought in substantial amounts of cash revenue through the customs, and a Muslim class of merchants arose who, as tax-farmers or otherwise, were able to influence state policies. Even the settled Turcoman population who were engaged in growing grain and cotton for Western customers were supporting peaceful relations with the "infidels." There arose conflict between those representing constant Holy War on the frontier and becoming prosperous with booty, or *gaza malı* (acquisitions from the Holy War), and those townsmen, merchants and agriculturists whose prosperity depended on peaceful trade relations with the "infidels." This situation was highlighted in the commercial agreements which these emirates made with the Venetians and Genoese in the years 1331–75.[5] The conflict between the *gazis* on the frontier and the center is dramatized in the dissension between the two sons of the Aydın ruler Mehmed Bey, Ghazi Umur who was conducting with his powerful fleet extensive *gaza* activities in the Aegean from İzmir, and Hızır Beg in Ayasoluk (Altoluogo of the Latins), which was the principal trade center of western Anatolia in this period.[6] A similar conflict is quite manifest in the Ottoman emirate, too. Under Sultan Orhan, his son, Süleyman Pasha, leader of the *gazis* on the frontier, came to differ several times on the policy to be pursued against Byzantium.

In the history of the Ottoman capitulations, two principal periods can be determined.

1. The first period extends from the first capitulation granted to the Genoese in 1352 to 1517, when the Italians, chiefly Genoese and Venetians, had monopolized Ottoman trade with Europe. First, Ottoman capitulations were granted to the Genoese primarily on political grounds. At that time, Genoa was at war with Venice (1350–55), and an alliance between the Ottomans and the Genoese against Venice and its allies –

Byzantium and the Catalans – was concluded. Only the text of the renewal of the 1387 capitulation has survived.

Down to the fall of Pera in 1453, the Ottomans continuously supported the Genoese and secured the cooperation of Genoese colonies in the Levant despite the intermittent anti-Ottoman policies of the Genoese mother city. In return, the Ottomans obtained immense economic profits and naval assistance.

It is interesting to note that in the same period, toward 1352, when under attack by the Ottomans, the czar of Bulgaria sought Venetian support. Bulgaria was one of the countries from which Venice obtained vitally important wheat supplies. Venice secured trade privileges from Bulgaria quite similar to those current in the Turkish capitulations of 1352 (3 percent customs duty).[7]

After the Genoese capitulations of 1352, the Venetians obtained their own capitulations under Murad I, some time between 1384 and 1387. Venetian capitulations were renewed with new concessions, particularly regarding wheat exports, by Süleyman Çelebi in 1403. Later, renewals were granted by Musa (1411), Mehmed I (1419), Murad II (1430) and Mehmed II in 1446 and 1454. Warring with Venice over control of the Balkan coasts and the islands in the Aegean, Mehmed the Conqueror favored the Florentines with the same capitulations as those granted to the Venetians. Also Bayezid II, when he declared war against Venice, extended capitulations to the king of Naples in 1498.

2. Upon the conquest of Egypt, in 1517, Selim I renewed Mamluk capitulations which the Mamluks had extended to the French and the Catalans. Thus, for the first time the French had gained privileges to trade in the Ottoman dominions, though they were not as extensive as the Italian capitulations. Under Süleyman I (1520–66), Ottoman concern to find allies in Western Europe against the Habsburgs as well as economic advantages led the Ottomans to extend full capitulation privileges to France (1569). Later on England (1580) and the Netherlands (1612), obtained capitulations.

The most comprehensive capitulations granted to Venice in 1540 were extended to France in 1569 when the Ottoman government decided to declare war against Venice for the conquest of Cyprus. The so-called French capitulations or "treaty" of 1536 was drafted but never ratified by the sultan. The French commerce in the Levant developed fully in the Ottoman dominions only after the capitulations of 1569, when France replaced Venice in the dominant trading position in the Levant. A special article, dated 1581, permitted other European nations, including the

English, Portuguese, Spaniards, Sicilians, and Anconans, to sail and trade under the French flag. When the Porte realized that the Protestant nations, the English and the Dutch, had fought against Philip II of Spain and were thus natural allies of the empire and also economically useful, the Ottoman government favored them with capitulations.

CUSTOMS ZONES, ORGANIZATION AND RATES

The Roman and Byzantine Empires organized into large customs zones the frontier and coastal regions, and the provinces in the interior which formed economic units on the main trade routes. As a rule an important port, a frontier post on a trade route or an administrative center was chosen as the center of a customs zone.[8] Although as a result of the economic and administrative changes customs zones in the Byzantine Empire underwent rearrangements, the main zones seem to have survived down to the Ottoman period. The Constantinople–Hellespont customs zone, for example, came into existence, at the latest, in the second half of the fifth century; Hieron (Ottoman Yoros) on the Bosphorus and Abydos on the Dardanelles were two posts of control on the northern and southern tips of the zone. At the beginning of the seventh century, the Hellespont was included in the customs zone of Asia, that is, western Anatolia. Byzantium never gave up its control over the vital trade route of the straits between the Crimea and the Hellespont.

The Ottomans maintained these customs zones as economic–fiscal units under the *mukataa* or tax-farm system. As a rule the administrative center was at the same time the center of the customs zone. However, because a *mukataa* can be farmed out by a tax-farmer into smaller units, some local ports had their own customs houses. Thus, a mosaic of customs zones in the empire emerged. Customs dues were to be paid in each zone, and each had its own separate regulations and rates. To give an example, İstanbul's customs zone under the Ottomans included the ports or landings all the way from Varna on the Black Sea down to Kilidülbahr or Ece-ovası on the Gallipoli peninsula. On the Asiatic side, it covered the coasts from Yoros at the mouth of the Black Sea down to the southern end of the province of Aydın, on the Aegean coast. In 1482, the Sinop–Samsun customs zone was placed under the İstanbul customs regulations, although certain higher rates of customs were continued in the Black Sea. As for the customs zones in the interior, centers were established on the main caravan routes. Caravans had to follow officially assigned routes so that they would pass through the customs center, possibly a commercial center or just a village or caravanserai. For example, caravans coming from Tabriz to Bursa had to pay their first customs at the city of Tokat and the second at Bursa. It was prohibited to take loads to places other than these centers. In Bursa, the caravanserai, called *Ipek Hanı*, was reserved for the caravans from Iran where their silk bales were weighed and the scales-tax was paid. Then, bales were handed over to brokers who sought purchasers at a fair price for both sides. Iranian merchants were permitted to leave the caravanserai only after they had obtained a document to show that they had paid all the incumbent taxes. The document protected the merchant against further claims. By 1473 Mehmed the Conqueror's order for a second tax on raw silk at Tokat caused deep discontent among Iranians, and was used against him as a device of political propaganda. In the seventeenth century, when İzmir became the chief outlet for Anatolian and Iranian trade with Europe, the government could not prevent caravans deviating from Bursa to other locations. Finally a third customs charge for raw silk was placed on merchants at the İzmir port. Caravans from Mecca had to pay customs dues for their loads of spices and textiles in Han-Yunus at the crossroads of the pilgrimage caravans from Palestine and Egypt, or at the village of Kisve near Damascus on the pilgrimage road from Damascus to Mecca. There were four customs zones in the Black Sea, including that of İstanbul from Varna to Sinop on the southwest coasts, that of Sinop extending to Trabzon, that of Kefe (Caffa) on the northeast extending to Circassia, and Akkerman on the northwest. The Akkerman (Moncastro) customs zone included Cankerman (Özü), Kilia and Bender (after 1538). The Danubian ports in the *sancak* of Silistre, Brăila, Tulča, Sakçi, Mačin, Harsova and Kara-Harmanlık were related to the Akkerman zone since they were transit centers between the Danubian lands and the Black Sea in this region. Ships from all over the Black Sea could come all the way to these ports and customs agents were present at the ports of Brăila, Tulča, Sakci, and Mačin. Principal goods subject to customs dues included imports of wine, textiles and spices, and exports of livestock, horses, meat, fish and flour as well as slaves.

The best studied customs zone of Caffa[9] gives a clear idea about the great port of Caffa (Kefe) and the ports of Azak, Kerch, Taman, and Copa, each having its own customs regulations. Basic customs dues were common to all of these ports and were collected by the principal customs administration located at Caffa. The regulations of the dependent ports determined only the local dues. Standard customs duty in the zone was different from İstanbul: it was 4.2 percent *ad valorem* for Muslims and non-Muslims alike.

In one customs zone duty was paid only once. No duty was payable if the same item was transported to other points in the same zone. The İstanbul customs zone, as the transit center between Europe and the Ottoman Empire, was considered the central zone. Its regulations were extended to the Antalya customs zone in 1477 and to that of Sinop in 1482. In the İstanbul customs zone, those ships sailing between İstanbul and the Black Sea coasts were checked at Yenice-Hisar, also known as Anadolu-Hisarı, and at Yoros at the tip of the Bosphorus on the Black Sea, while those vessels active between the Mediterranean and İstanbul were inspected at Kilidülbahr, opposite Çanakkale in the Dardanelles. Traffic between Rumeli and Anatolia was checked at Lapseki (Lampasque) and Gelibolu. Trade between Anatolia and the island of Chios, which became then the emporium of trade between Europe and Anatolia, was monitored at the ports of Çeşme and the two Foçalar (Phocaea). Caravans between İstanbul and Bursa, the emporium of imports from Arabia, India and Iran, was subjected to customs duties at Bursa itself or at Mudanya on the Marmara Sea in the Bursa customs zone.

Merchants had to take their goods first to one of these centers, and only then could they move inland. Those who brought their wares by sea had to pay import dues, but no dues were required on goods transported over land. Mehmed II changed this rule and imposed customs dues at the same rate on all goods, whether coming by sea or by land. Muslim merchants trading between Arabia and Bursa and importing goods of high value, such as precious textiles, spices and sugar, complained bitterly about this innovation. Mehmed's successor Bayezid II, who reversed his father's harsh policies in various fields, also abolished this innovation. Once again only goods arriving by sea were subjected to customs dues, as previously. Goods arriving by land were to pay dues if they were imported by foreign non-Muslims, but not by Muslims and tribute-paying non-Muslims. In other words, the Ottoman government considered all goods coming or going by sea as import or export items. This interpretation must have derived from the Christian European mastery of the Mediterranean Sea and the papal order to blockade Islamic lands in 1291. However, goods exported to Syria and other Islamic lands by sea were still subject only to the minimum 2 percent rate. Export to Europe was discouraged and subjected to the highest rate because Muslims believed that economic prosperity and political stability depended on a well supplied internal market, and that "enemies of Islam" should not be favored by an easy export policy. However, they were permitted to bring in goods which were in high demand in the Levant, such as fine woolen cloth, metals and, in particular, bullion from the west. The Ottoman government periodically issued lists of goods the export of which was prohibited.

The Roman and Byzantine Empires placed commerce, circulation and sale of merchandise under state control.[10] The export of certain goods of economic or strategic importance, such as wheat, wine, olive oil, iron, arms or silk was prohibited. Smuggling brought arrest of the merchant and the confiscation of his goods. Duties were placed on imports as well as on exports. In addition, there were a host of dues imposed upon circulation and sale. The original customs duty, *portorium*, was one-fortieth or 2.5 percent of the value of the goods. Originating in the first half of the fourth century, the *octava* was a composite tax consisting of 2.5 percent customs duty and *dekate*, a tax originally granting a license for the sale of real estate or slaves. Called *kommerkion* (Ottoman *gümrük*) toward the end of the eighth century, the new composite tax was generalized as a standard customs duty of 12.5 percent. However, the one-fortieth, the *quadragesima*, continued as a customs duty in such lands as Asia, Bithynia, Paphlagonia and Pontus. Payment of the *kommerkion* guaranteed the payee import tax immunity and a license to sell his goods. Goods were also brought to and taxed in special places, called *apothiki* (in the Ottoman Empire *kapan* or *kabban*). Customs agents stamped the goods after they were weighed and taxes paid. A certificate called *poliza* was delivered to the merchant. Government agents collected customs duties but, from the ninth century on, the farming out of customs operations became widespread. Bursa and Ankara were important customs centers from Roman times. Revenue from customs dues constituted a substantial part of the state budget. Taxation on the basis of measure, paid half and half by the buyer and seller, called *pratikion* or *metriatikon* was included in a separate category of commercial taxes which was known under the Ottomans as *bac* and *tamga* dues. *Siliquaticum*, a 2 percent sales tax paid half and half by the buyer and seller may be the origin of *tota* tax in Caffa under the Genoese and Ottomans.

Roman–Byzantine customs principles and organization were basically followed under the Ottomans. They were apparently borrowed by the Umayyads and continued under the subsequent Islamic empires.

Taxation on commercial commodities is interpreted in Islamic Law as part of *zakat* or obligatory property tax and its rate is determined as one-fortieth of the merchandise for Muslims, one-tenth for the people from the "Abode of War," and 5 percent for non-Muslim subjects. For Muslims, however, religious intention for this type of *zakat* is necessary.

The rates of one-fortieth and one-tenth correspond to 2.5 and 10 percent of the Roman system and survived only as 2 and 5 percent rates under the Ottomans in the fifteenth century.

Some Muslim legists were of the opinion that even if religious intention for *zakat* was expressed, commercial taxes cannot be accepted for Islamic *zakat*. In reality, pre-Islamic practices and rules were followed in regard to commercial taxes. Muslim legists favored a low rate in the tariff if it was advantageous to the community to encourage the import of certain goods. Ottomans seem to have directly followed Byzantine practices.

Since Roman times the 2.5 or 2 percent customs duty appears to have been established as the basic regular tax in Mediterranean lands. Higher rates of 10 or 12.5 percent applied to precious goods did not replace the 2 percent everywhere. While the 12.5 percent rate was in force in Syria and Egypt on precious goods, the 2 percent rate was the norm in the commercial treaties of 1220 between the Anatolian Seljukid sultanate and Venice, of 1403 between the Menteşe principality and Venice, of 1439 between Byzantium and Florence, and of 1454 between Venice and the Ottoman state. The Byzantine government imposed the rates of 3 percent for the Catalans and 4 percent for Provence, while it maintained 2 percent for the Venetians and Genoese. Then the latter two nations obtained full exemption from the Byzantine government. Later on, until the reign of Mehmed II, the Ottomans adhered to the 2 percent rate, although they never granted any nation full exemption.

Under the Ottomans, customs duty was a tax on imports and exports, not on a commercial transaction itself, and could be adjusted according to existing conditions. Thus, to a certain degree customs policy reflected the state's commercial policy. Capitulations, granted to certain Christian states, were principal instruments which regulated trade with European countries. In fact, customs rates varied according to the kind of commodity, legal status of the importer or exporter, and the customs zone (see Table I:37).

Customs dues were computed *ad valorem*, that is, on the value of the commodity as estimated by the government agent or the tax-farmer. Apparently, the evaluation of the imported goods at the customs house was made on the basis of the prices at the local market, as suggested in a note by the Venetian consul in Aleppo dated 1596.[11] Because of the frequent conflicts on estimated values, European nations would later impose a tariff system.

As noted above, the rates of dues differed from one customs zone to another. Foreign merchants had to pay for the cloth they imported into

Table I:37. Customs duty rates, 1470–1586

| | Date | (% ad valorem) | | |
		Muslims	Non-Muslim subjects	Non-Muslim foreigners
İstanbul and Galata	?	4	4	–
		flour: 2	flour: 3	–
Grains at Istanbul	?	4	4	–
		flour: 2	flour: 3	–
İstanbul	?	4	4	5
İstanbul and Galata	?	4	4	4 or 5
The Gelibolu market	?	4	4	5
İstanbul, Galata and Gelibolu	1476	4	4	5
Samsun and Sinop	1482	1	2	4
Caffa	1487	4.2	4.2	4.2
Akkerman	1505	2	4	5
Aydın	1528	2	4	5
Bursa (mohair)	1546	-	3	3
Bursa, imports	1546	2	4	5
Harsova	1569	3	4	5
Akkerman	1569	2.2	4	5
Feth-i-Islam	1586	3	4	5

Bursa at the rate of 3 percent; in İstanbul, 5 percent; and 4.2 percent at Caffa. Also, different kinds of goods paid different rates. While imported luxury textiles paid normal rates, necessary provisions such as wheat and flour paid half or three-quarters of regular rates. In Cairo, under the Ottomans, who were obviously continuing the Mamluk practices, customs on all kinds of spices was 10 percent and was levied in kind, as in Aden. Spices stored at the state storehouse had preemptive right for sale – unless the sultan's spices were sold, no spices were cleared from customs. Since this practice clashed with the principle of freedom of trade, in 1586 foreigners objected to it and quoted the capitulations, saying that "all men were at liberty to buy where they could." Although an embargo or "monapolya," a preemption on the sale at the market of goods belonging to the sultan or members of the military class for a certain period of time, was a general rule in the Ottoman Empire, the capitulations superseded native laws. In principle, foreigners' freedom of trade was guaranteed by the capitulations and secured a free market at price formation. Local authorities not infrequently ignored the principle, claiming that what was in the best interest of the imperial treasury was followed and usually a compromise was reached.

Goods destined for the consumption of military units or shipments belonging to the state were exempt from customs and other dues. Such shipments came under the category of "state shipments" (*irsalat*, or *irsaliyye*).

Since Ottoman customs taxation was based on the *ad valorem* principle, law makers abolished the practice of taking a percentage of the wares in lieu of customs dues. However, on certain goods in the Arab provinces, for example, at Damascus and Basra, the former practice survived for a long time. Also, for certain types of goods customs dues were not taken on the basis of estimated value but per measure. Duty on wine, for example, was taken per cask, and per bale on paper or glass, which arrived in bales. Customs dues on imported woolen cloth were levied by bolt (*pastav*). This practice should not be confused with regular market dues (*bac* or *tamga*), which were always taken per load or bale. The latter dues consisted usually of small amounts and the regulations specified in each case the nature of the tax. Also, for market dues, a tariff was drawn up specifying the amount of duty for each item. An important rule was that an imported item paid customs dues whether or not it was sold, while a tariff (*bac*) had to be paid every time the same item was subject of a commercial transaction.

Regulations made it clear under what circumstances wares on a ship were to be considered imported goods and subject to taxation. If a ship lowered its anchor into the sea, the cargo was subject to taxation. Apparently in theory, only while at anchor could items be unloaded. The transfer of goods from one ship to another was also considered importation and entailed taxation. If wares changed hands between merchants at the port and the second merchant took them away, he also paid a duty for export. In order to prevent smuggling, the loading of certain goods, particularly grain, was subject to the permission of the responsible customs official. No ship could load wares and leave a port without a permit. For the protection of the merchant but also for the government controller, it was mandatory to receive documents from the tax-farmer or the government agent which indicated wares imported, with their exact amount, and whether the goods were on the way from one port to another in the same customs zone, or loadings were made for export.

The customs system was designed to ensure collection of duties on all goods imported or taken from one customs region to another. However, smuggling was a general practice, perhaps excused by the perpetrator because duties on trade and the circulation of goods were considered injustices unapproved by Islamic Law. Since customs revenues were, as a rule, farmed out to private interests, there was a constant struggle between the tax-farmer and taxpayer. For his part the tax-farmer believed that strict control and even overtaxing served the state's interests as well as his. Imperial regulations concerning customs were issued to prevent smuggling and cheating in most cases upon the complaints of a tax-farmer. The sultan empowered these agents with absolute authority in applying imperial orders, and sent one of his *kuls* to support the tax-farmer. The *kul* could, if necessary, use force in collaboration with the local authorities. Penalties included exposing the culprit to the public in the streets of the town, pulling him along with a string in his nose, and the confiscation of the smuggled goods for the treasury. By trusting customs tax-farms to private persons, the government not only ensured a better method of tax collection by thus converting public interest into private interest, but also it spared the ruler from being a direct target of public blame. It was of prime importance for an Eastern ruler to keep his image of a "just" ruler. One of the first public acts of a newly enthroned ruler in Islamic countries was to declare that he abolished taxes on trade, considered illegal and oppressive, despite the fact that the government soon re-introduced old practices or the system went on as if no such declaration had been made.

Common forms of fraud included transporting goods on routes other than the customary ones, using the city gates or other points of transshipment outside the officially designated ones, or unloading wares at landings on the seashore outside the ports where customs houses were established. No merchant could load, unload or leave a port, a caravanserai or a public station without the permit of a tax-farmer, a broker or man in charge of the place. Cheating was particularly widespread on valuable goods such as silk. Documents revealed a special trick to avoid publicly disapproved new taxes on silk at Tokat. Native merchants went out of the city to meet the silk caravans from Iran, bought their loads and took them straight to Bursa, thus paying tax only once. This trick was possible for the native merchants because they were free to take their wares anywhere in the country without paying tax from one customs zone to another. In order to prevent this practice, the government made it mandatory for all merchants to produce documents certifying that they had paid the tax twice for the silk in their possession. Another trick concerning imported silk was to soak the load so that it weighed heavier at the time it was handed over to the broker for sale. To insure that merchants and buyers were not cheated and that a fair price was established, precious goods, such as silk, cloth, arms or slaves had to be sold only through officially appointed brokers in the bazaar. All goods subject to the payment of customs duty paid also a brokerage tax.

Brokers in a particular bazaar were organized under the head broker, who was responsible to the government. The broker had to have the completed sale registered in the book of the tax-farmer or the government agent within twenty-four hours. This provided another means of checking that all incumbent taxes were paid. Brokerage also provided an extra revenue for the government. The broker received a fee for his service from both the seller and the buyer. At Caffa, for example, it was 30 *akça* per slave.

If a merchant sold his wares without the services of a broker, he still had to pay a brokerage fee for himself and for the buyer. Because of his function of guaranteeing a fair sale and of checking on the actual conditions of sale for purposes of taxation, a broker was appointed by a special diploma of the sultan and conducted his functions under the supervision of a head broker called *simsar*. His appointment was made with the consent of the pertinent tax-farmer. He had to find a guarantor whose name was registered in the official book kept by the government agent. A broker could not be involved in commercial transactions in his own interest, be a merchant at the same time, or become a partner with a merchant. He was in charge of selling in a particular bazaar so that he could not sell in another bazaar. A measurer would help a broker in measuring precious cloths sold at the bazaar, and an additional tax was paid for his services.

The head of the brokers was also appointed by the sultan's diploma and he himself was under the supervision of the city steward. Both had to be present at sales involving large sums, as was the case with sales of silk loads coming from Iran and bound for Bursa. The head broker was responsible for the brokers under his authority. Their appointments and dismissals were made through him. While brokers were walking around in the bazaar, the head broker had to sit in a certain location all the time. He was not allowed to change the location as he pleased, so that merchants could find a responsible person any time they had business or problems connected with the sale of their goods. Representing the interests of the townspeople, the town steward supervised dealings to prevent tricks, in particular those causing unjustified price hikes on raw materials needed by the guilds. We find a steward present at the kadi's court whenever there was an important dealing concerning the government or townsfolk.

In the bazaar the broker, as a rule, put goods up for auction and tried to reach a fair price for the item. Cases are mentioned, however, in which a broker attempted to conspire against fair prices with the auctioneers.

The porters serving the brokers were also subject to strict discipline under the brokerage regulations. They were not permitted to carry goods from one place to another without the permit of the tax-farmer and the government agent.

MARKET DUES

Market dues (*bac*) were taken on goods brought to the town market to be sold wholesale. No dues were paid on sales made in villages although they were taken at fairs held in the countryside. Imported goods, for which customs dues had already been paid, did not require the payment of any other dues.[12] Grain bought by the sack for home consumption was not considered wholesale and did not attract market dues, nor did any retail sales. Market dues were paid by load, pack, weight or according to value. Cheap bulky goods, such as wood, hay and fish paid by the cart; foodstuffs and cheap cloth paid by horse pack, as well as by weight; and wine paid by the cask. Expensive goods such as spices, iron, tin, lead and copper were weighed on the public scales (*kantar*) and dues were taken on the basis of weight.

For foodstuffs such as butter, honey, and dried fruits, which were sold in containers by weight, the seller paid market dues by the load. But if they were brought in great quantity and taken to the public scales at the town hall (*kapan*), the importer paid a scales fee – 2 *akça* per *kantar*. Market dues for fresh fruit and vegetables were paid by horse pack or cartload, and, for livestock, by the head (see Table I:38).

In accordance with the general trend of incorporating the dues or fees which were taken by local authorities into the public treasury, the transit dues and customs duties taken at Smederevo port on the Danube about 1500 were added to the public revenues and taken exclusively for the treasury. In principle, commercial dues were paid by the importer and the seller of the merchandise, although in certain special cases both the seller and buyer paid dues at equal or different rates. Market dues were paid on the sale of cattle at equal rates, 2 *akça* for cattle at Smederevo. When cattle was weighed on the public scales and sold, both the seller and the buyer paid the scales due.

As for the rates of market dues, they were set at a modest level, apparently estimated on the basis of the Islamic property tax *zakat*, one-fortieth of the value of the goods. Since, in general, transit and market dues were strongly criticized by the public as a nuisance and as being contrary to Islamic Law, the government compared these rates to the

Table 1:38. Goods sold at Nicopolis town market and dues (*bac*) paid in the sixteenth century

	Unit	Dues in *akça*	
Salt	4-wheel cart	4	Salt sent for the soldiery pays no dues
	2-wheel cart	2	
	horseload	1 to 2	
Horse	per head	2	by both buyer and seller
Wine	per cask	4	on imported and exported wine
Cattle	per head	1	by both buyer and seller
Slave	per head	4	by both buyer and seller
Grain	per cart	4	
	per horseload	1 to 2	
Cloths of Bursa	per pack	2	
Carpets, cotton goods & rope	per pack	no dues, only customs dues	when they pass in transit for Wallachia and Hungary
Shovels of iron	per cart or horseload	1	when in transit to Wallachia no dues but customs duty
Shovels of wood	per cart or horseload	one half	
Felt cloak	per cart or horseload	4	
Mats	per cart	4	
	per horse	2	
Lumber	per cart	1 piece	
Logs	per cart	1	
Hay	per cart	one bunch	
Sheep for slaughter	per each four	1	
Cattle for slaughter	per head	1	
Swine	per head	1	
Sheep for sale	per two	1	
Grain for sale	per *kile*	one handful	
Fresh fruit	per cart	2	
Onions, garlic	per cart	4	
	per horseload	2	
Butter, tallow, honey	per cart	4	
	per horseload	2	
Hides of cattle, sheep or goat	per cart	4	either imported or exported from town
Cheese	per cart	4	
Vinegar	per *tulum*	1	
Felt of Edirne	per pack	1	
Wool	per cart	4	
	per cart	4	
	per horseload	2	
Timber	per cart	2	loaded and exported from the town
Flax and cotton	per cart	4	
	per horseload	2	
Grain loaded in boats	per cart	4	grain loaded at the mouth of Osma
Salt loaded in boats	per cart	4	salt loaded at Somoya but no dues on salt sent by the supervisor of salt works

Source: BN, MS: Paris no 85.

Islamic *zakat* paid by traders. The rate of one-fortieth was made clear on the sale of foodstuffs, leather and felt goods in the regulations of Smederovo. This rate does not seem to have been applied for other goods. Two *akça* per horseload of cloth or tin was a very small fraction of the actual value of the goods, while one *akça* for a horseload of grain is about one-thirtieth of its value (one horsepack was about 150 kg and 25 kg of wheat cost about 4 or 5 *akça* in the early sixteenth century).

The sale of real property such as houses, flour mills and vineyards was not subject to market dues, though local authorities claimed it.

On certain goods which were badly needed for the consumption of the military and administrative personnel, the dues were accepted in kind. At Smederovo, one piece of wood was taken from each donkey load, and one piece of lumber from each cartload of lumber.

MONEY AND CREDIT

Since precious metals were in limited supply in the market-place and gold and silver coins were not readily available, most of the transactions were made through credit or bartering, particularly before the massive flooding of western silver into the Ottoman Empire in the 1580s (see below, Appendix). Bartering was also widely practiced in rural areas among the peasants, who paid in wheat for most of the goods and services they needed, such as the services of a village imam, field watchman and shepherds. It was also widespread among the big merchants, both local and foreign.[13] Pearls imported from Bahrain were particularly welcomed in payment by Iranian silk merchants because they were high priced and small in weight and convenient to carry and conceal from customs agents.

Credit extended for goods sold were usually on a six-month or one-year basis to allow the purchaser to sell the goods and obtain the cash to make the payments. Sureties were always provided and carefully recorded in the kadi's court register. In 1485, for instance, a money-changer of Bursa, Musliheddin, sold to the merchant Muzaffer of Tabriz rubies and pearls worth 64,500 *akça* on credit for six months with another merchant from Tabriz acting as surety.[14] A concealed interest was added to the payment on credit as if it were a loan.[15] If the sum was not paid at the end of the term, the debt was renewed with interest.[16] Under Mehmed II, when all of the Ottoman silver coinage in circulation was ordered to be changed with newly minted ones, the total stock of silver coins thus obtained amounted to 218 million *akça*.[17] Although quite a substantial portion of the coins in circulation was not exchanged with the mint, for one reason or another, this figure nevertheless shows the limited amount of total silver stock in the market. Although copper coins were issued on a large scale[18] and met the everyday bazaar needs of the commoner, they were never used in transactions between merchants.

Since comprehensive price lists have not been collected and published, questions such as differentials in price structure between the main trade zones in the Ottoman Empire, and between European countries and the Ottoman Empire, cannot be answered. Without such materials no conclusions can be reached on such topics as Ottoman–European trade patterns, shifts in production, changes in living conditions, state tax policies and changes in economic conditions in general. The pioneering works of Ö.L. Barkan and L. Berov[19] in this area can be expanded through a systematic use of the immense materials available in the Ottoman archives. Since Barkan considered only foodstuffs there are discrepancies in his calculation of price changes from those of Berov.

In examining changes in price structure as a basic factor in the East–West balance of trade, Berov suggests that, in the fifteenth and the first half of the sixteenth century, because of the prohibitive land transport costs, market prices of the basic foodstuffs and raw materials – wheat, meat, wool, hides and wax – doubled in İstanbul in comparison with those in the Balkans. İstanbul was the principal Ottoman market for these goods competing with Europe. Berov concludes that in this period "prices of wheat and most other important articles calculated in terms of weight of silver were comparatively close to the level of prices of these articles in the main countries trading with Turkey such as Italy, France, England and the Netherlands." So, during that period the foreign trade of the empire with Europe, Berov suggests, decreased as a whole. However, a closer look at his charts reveals that Ottoman prices correspond in general to the lowest European prices although they show sharper fluctuations as, for example, in the 1570s and between 1610 and 1620. The general trend in wheat prices in the period 1550–1640 is a steady increase. But still Ottoman wheat prices proved to be substantially below those in Italy so that after 1560, especially in the 1580s, Turkey's exports experienced a "substantial increase." For the same reasons olive oil and rice exports became profitable. However, exports were profitable only when the price differential between Turkey and Italy was about 1 to 2. In this calculation transport expenses, duties and insurance or losses at the hands of pirates were to be added. These factors are of importance for the export of bulky goods. According to Berov, average freight for transport by land per 10 kg of goods over a distance of 100 km vacillated between 5 and 47 grams of silver, but in most cases it was between 100 and 120 grams. Transport expenses alone from İstanbul to Italy reached approximately 10–15 grams of silver per kg and duties amounted to 7 to 29 grams. During the second half of the sixteenth and the first years of the seventeenth century, Berov concludes,[20] the trade balance of the Ottoman Empire with Europe "gradually ceased to be as active as it was in the beginning. . . . At the beginning of the seventeenth century prices in Turkey reached a record level . . . and approached those in Europe. . . . Consequently, conditions for Turkish exports changed in a negative direction, particularly in terms of wool, hides, wax, and silk."

On the other hand it has been suggested that low population density and the relatively abundant land and cheap labor in the Ottoman Empire, along with the rise of the capitalist economy in the West, had created a specific structural pattern of trade based on the exchange of textiles and metals with foodstuffs and raw materials between East and West.[21] In other words, the price differential between the two regions, determined by varying land rents and labor costs, was responsible for a kind of division of labor between East and West. Europe, however, had to compete with İstanbul for imports from the bread basket of the empire in the north-western Black Sea steppe, Thrace, western Anatolia and the plain of Thessaly as well as Egypt, which were all linked to the crowded Ottoman capital by sea. The imperial bureaucracy, vitally concerned with provisioning İstanbul and the army, was engaged in a continual struggle against Europe's high prices, which attracted speculators, mostly from the military class in control of large estates and *vakf*s. Prohibitions proved to be ineffective in the face of extensive smuggling activities, particularly in the Aegean islands.

A kind of letter of credit was a *havale*.[22] *Havale* was an assignation of a fund from a distant source of revenue by a written order. It was used in both state and private finances to avoid the dangers and delays inherent in the transport of cash. A real letter of credit, in Arabic *suftaca* or *sakk*, was known and used in the first centuries of Islam. Orthodox Muslim legists did not legalize it because of possible elements of speculation and unjustified profits. However, the transfer of credits through a document issued by a kadi, and thereby used to make payments and clear debts between people living in distant places, was possible and the Ottomans practiced it. Sahillioğlu identified this kadi letter as a letter of credit,[23] giving examples from the Bursa court records.

Although such a practice was not frequently applied, payments through proxy between merchants living in distant places were a routine practice.[24] From the mid-seventeenth century, the use of letters of credit, in Turkish *poliçe* from Italian *polizza*, became quite widespread among merchants and in government payments.

GREEKS AND JEWS

Ottoman Jews and Greeks were particularly active in tax-farming in the fifteenth and sixteenth century. In fact, tax-farming became the major means of capital formation in the empire.[25] The tax-farmers' main capital sources included *commenda* (*mudaraba*) in trade enterprises, in particular, profits from transporting İstanbul's provisions. Many starting from scratch as scribes at a customs house or at the mines ended up as big businessmen.[26] These "capitalists," accumulating huge sums, became indispensable for the state finances and the palace, and, thereby, played a major role not only in the empire's finances but also in politics.

In Giacomo Badoer's *Book of accounts* (1436–40), Greeks form the second largest ethnic group after Venetians in Constantinople's commercial life.[27] However, Greek merchants were overshadowed by Italian predominance except in retail trade and shipping, which was of secondary importance.[28] But Greek merchants were engaged in international trade and banking, too. For example, just before 1453, a Greek shipowner, conducting business with the Venetians and Jews, had acquired a very prosperous position with a large fortune. His capital was estimated at 30,000 ducats.[29]

The most important change which occurred with the Ottoman conquest was that Italian predominance was terminated in favor of the native Ottoman non-Muslim subjects, Armenians, Jews and Greeks in particular. After the Ottoman conquest, Greeks replaced Italians in large-scale trade in Caffa and Pera/Galata,[30] while in the pre-Ottoman period the Genoese as a rule excluded natives from overseas big business.[31] Moreover, already in the fifteenth century Ottoman Greek and Jewish merchants began to settle in such major Italian commercial centers as Ancona and Venice.

Galata was the center of activities for Greek businessmen under the Ottomans as was the case under the Palaeologi. The city had become a Greek town population-wise even before the Ottoman conquest.[32] Many rich Greek financiers, among them Yani Palaeologus, continued to live a rich bourgeois life in Galata after the conquest while many rich Genoese families had left the city during and after the Ottoman occupation. Greeks were favored by Mehmed the Conqueror, and they played a particularly active role in Ottoman finances and politics during his reign. He made Greek converts viziers, as in the case of Rum Mehmed, Hass Murad and Mesih, the last two being of the Palaeologian family.[33]

It appears that after 1453 many Greeks continued their business and careers as tax-farmers, as large-scale merchants and in shipping; the last field became particularly prosperous thanks to the provisioning needs of the growing Ottoman capital. In the period immediately after the conquest of Constantinople, we find many Greeks active in tax-farming for the government. Members of the old Byzantine aristocracy, the Palaeologi, Cantacuzeni, Chalcocondyli and Rhali, were prominent tax-farmers under Mehmed the Conqueror and his successors. During the fifteenth and sixteenth centuries, the western Anatolian ports, with İstanbul as their center, made up one large customs zone, and it often came under the sway of Greek tax-farmers, who were competing with Muslim Turks and Jews for its control. A list of the Ottoman treasury accounts[34] demonstrates how the customs zone of İstanbul changed hands during the period from October 1476 to December 1477.

1. The estimated customs revenue for three years was 9.5 million *akça* from October 1476. Ya'kub, newly converted Muslim, Palologoz of Kassandros, Lefteri son of Galyanos of Trabzon, Andriya son of Halkokondil and Manul Palologoz, offered an increase of 1,500,000 *akça* on October 16, 1476.

2. Hoca Satı, Çiriş İlyas, Şahin, freed slave of Yusuf Simsar (chief broker) and Hoca Bahaeddin, together offered an increase of two million just five months later.

3. The Greek group then offered an additional increase of 833,334 for each year on condition that the tax-farm should be farmed out to them for a period of four years. This bid was made on May 6, 1477.

4. Seydi Küçük of Edirne, Altan (a Jew) and Nikoroz Efrenci (an Italian) offered an additional increase of one million four months later.

5. The Greek group made a new bid one month later and then the group of Seydi, Altana and Nikoroz made a bid of 20 million *akça* altogether for four years on October 12, 1477.

In 1481, the mints of Gelibolu and Edirne were farmed out for 18 million *akça* or c. 360,000 ducats to a consortium which included Andronikus Cantacuzenos. Apparently, just before that date, he had converted to Islam and had taken the name of Mustafa.

During the same period another Byzantine aristocratic family was active in Serbia, farming out the rich silver and gold mines in that province. In 1474 Yani Cantacuzenus, his brother Yorgi, Nicola Dandjovil and Lika farmed out, in partnership, the silver and gold mines in upper Serbia for a total sum of 14 million *akça* for six years. In the previous year the enterpreneurs were Yani Cantacuzenus of Novobrdo, Yorgi

Ivrana and Toma Cantacuzenus who were from Seres, and Palaeologus of İstanbul, all acting as partners. Later in 1476 they were replaced by a new group of partners, including Yani and Yorgi Cantacuzenus, Vuk and Knez Yuvan and Andriya. The latter three were evidently Slavs. On the other hand, the important mines of Kratova in the province of Küstendil were farmed out by Yani Palaeologus of Galata in partnership with Istipa Blasica, Istepan Lesh, and Dimitri son of Konstantin in 1473 for a total sum of 1,600,000 *akça*. There were less prominent Greeks in Ottoman service even before 1453 who started their careers as Ottoman scribes at customs houses or mines.[35]

In competition with Muslim or Jewish tax-farmers, Greek businessmen were also active as tax-farmers of the important monopolies of salt production and distribution in the Balkans on the Aegean or Black Sea coasts in this period. These monopolies were, as a rule, farmed out together with the revenues of fisheries in the neighborhood. Demetrius Palaeologus, the last despot of the Morea, was involved in this business. According to an Ottoman register of tax-farms, "Kir Demetrius Tekfur" possessed the poll-tax and other state revenues of Aenos on the basis of a *timar*. But from July 11, 1469 onwards, a partnership of three Jewish tax-farmers, Eleazar son of Yakub of Salonica, Avraham son of Eleazar of Nicopolis and Musa son of İsmail of Vidin undertook it. The total sum of these revenues was estimated as 555,000 *akça* for three years. Six years later, Yuvan Dhapovik and Knez Yuvan of Novobrdo attempted to outbid Yorgi Ivrana and Toma Cantacuzenus without success.

Ethnic, personal or factional connections as well as secret practices appear to have played a part in managing big tax-farms. Apparently, Greeks or converts with influence at the sultan's court favored Greek bidders. Complaints against favoritism for Greek or Jewish tax-farmers during the Conqueror's reign are voiced in contemporary Muslim sources. Perhaps it is not just a coincidence that members of the Palaeologi family obtained the tax-farm of the İstanbul customs zone exactly in the 1470s when two pashas, Hass Murad and Mesih of the same family were the most influential people with the sultan.

In the second half of the sixteenth century the spectacular fortune of Michael Cantacuzenus is worth mentioning. Like many other Greek tax-farmers before him, Michael made his fortune first at the salt works of Anchialos and in the İstanbul customs. Like other tax-farmers, he was engaged also in commerce. The sultan appointed him as his "imperial" agent to buy furs in Russia. Thanks to his wealth and connections with the Ottoman palace, Michael became the most distinguished and revered archont in the Greek Orthodox community. He played a major role in the election and dismissal of patriarchs and the voyvodes of Rumanian vassal principalities. But finally, falling into debt with the Ottoman treasury, allegedly 30 million *akça*,[36] he was executed by order of the sultan in 1578. Upon his death, in his palace at Anchialos his legendary riches, including one hundred servants, forty pages and a harem, were all confiscated.

In the second half of the sixteenth century, Jewish bankers and tax-farmers gained a predominant place in Ottoman finances and long-distance trade.[37]

In the mid-sixteenth century, victims of the Inquisition in Catholic countries, the Marrano Jews decided to immigrate to the Ottoman Empire. Controlling the spice trade in Europe, the Marrano banking house of Mendès moved to and settled in İstanbul. In 1552, under the protection of Sultan Süleyman the Magnificent, the head of the family, Dõna Gracia Mendès, arrived in İstanbul. Her relative and partner, Don Joseph Nasi, became the most prominent member of the family. Initially his spectacular rise was due to his financial services to Prince Selim, who had made him one of his intimates as a *müteferrika* (distinguished attendant) in his provincial palace. When, in 1566, Selim acceded to the Ottoman throne he appointed Don Joseph "the duke of Naxos" (Nakşa Dükası), which comprised the Cyclades Archipelago, a group of islands producing rare wines for export. This appointment must be related to his being the tax-farmer of wine exports to the northern Black Sea countries, and to Poland in particular. The tax-farm from the dukedom was fixed in the amount of 6,000 gold pieces. Joseph's control of this trade was a loss for Venice. Previously, the duke of Naxos had been a Venetian who did not give up his claim and harassed Don Joseph afterwards.[38] Customs dues on wine exported from the Aegean and from Venetian Crete to Poland entailed Joseph's actual monopoly of the wine trade, since under the Ottoman tax-farm system the government controlled the traffic to enable the tax-farmer to prevent smuggling, and to realize the maximum amount of revenue. His annual revenue from the monopoly on the export of Cretan wine was estimated at 15,000 ducats a year. Around 1575 it is reported that one thousand casks of wine were exported from Crete alone.[39]

Don Joseph's influence on Ottoman policy against Venice in Cyprus, which was another center of wine production, comes to us in the form of a tale.[40] Believed to be an expert in European affairs, Don Joseph became one of the most trusted counselors to the sultan at this time, and evidently he was one of the supporters of Vizier Lala Mustafa's plan to conquer Cyprus, in opposition to grand vizier Sokollu Mehmed, who was against the plan and wanted to continue the war in the north against Muscovy.[41] The plan to colonize the conquered island with Jewish settlers is also worth noting in this context.[42] The conquest of Cyprus leading to the Christian Holy League in the Mediterranean resulted in the Ottoman disaster at Lepanto in 1571. However, Don Joseph continued to keep the sultan's favor. Upon his death in 1579, Joseph's estate was confiscated by the government. Here it should be remembered that, although Islamic Law strictly forbids confiscation of private property from either Muslims or non-Muslims, the property of the tax-farmer or any government-related fortunes were always suspect as to their origin and were therefore subject to confiscation. Speculative possibilities in making fortunes through the sultan's favor and serving the interests of the ruling elite, as well as the precarious nature of such fortunes, clearly demonstrates the conditions and the nature of capital formation in the Ottoman patrimonial system.

Later, in 1588, Alvaro Mendès, like Joseph Nasi, an arch-enemy of Phillip II of Spain, came to settle in İstanbul bringing with him reportedly 850,000 gold ducats, and received the same favors once enjoyed by Don Joseph.[43] The Jewish woman Esther Kyra, a favorite of the ladies in the palace and a liaison between them and Jewish interests outside, became involved in tax-farming and trade undertakings and amassed a large fortune during her long connection with the Seraglio.[44] In the end, deprived of large profits as collectors of the non-Muslim poll-tax, the *sipahis* at the Porte rebelled and murdered her and her sons, who had obtained control of large tax-farms. Her fortune at the time of her death was reported to have amounted to 50 million *akça*.

It is suggested that the Marrano Jews introduced into the Ottoman Empire the techniques of European capitalism, banking and even the mercantilist concept of state economy.[45] Also, perhaps under the guidance of Jews from Europe, Ottoman financial officials became aware of the working of the Gresham Law in the market and made monetary reforms accordingly in 1589.[46]

Large-scale banking operations formed part of the activities of the House of Mendès in the Ottoman capital in this period. International trade and banking operations were inseparable and the family's operations were carried on through a network of agents in the principal centers of Europe. Thus, the Mendès family controlled a large portion of international commerce, which consisted of the exchange largely of

European woolens for wheat, pepper and raw wool.[47] Also, investments by merchants in the treasury's tax-farms seem to have been quite high. In 1555 when Pope Paul IV confiscated the possessions of Jews in the papal territory, the sultan protested, saying that many Jews of Salonica and İstanbul had gone bankrupt and were unable to meet their payment obligations to the treasury to the sum of 400,000 gold ducats. Under the management of Dōna Gracia (d. 1568 or 1569), a Jewish bank (called *dolab* in Turkish, hence *dolabi* later meant speculator, fraudulent person) appears to have involved Ottoman finances and capital investments within European markets. Gracia's son-in-law, Don Joseph, became a big creditor for European kings. His large loans to the king of Poland procured for him various commercial concessions. Under the sultan's protection, he obtained a monopoly on the export of beeswax from Poland.[48] Also, when, in 1555, the French King Henri II was pressed for money, Don Joseph floated a loan in France in which the interest increased from 12 to 16 percent. Little wonder that many Turks invested money in the loan through Don Joseph.

Judging from the conditions of Jewry in general under the Ottomans during the sixteenth century, Salo Baron[49] concludes that "the rise and splendor of Ottoman Jewry" is unparalleled in that century:

> the Sephardic and Romaniot [Jewish] communities now lived almost exclusively under Ottoman rule and its system of legislation was character- ized by great stability and basic protection of human rights. . . . With the great freedom of movement guaranteed by legal and administrative enactments, communication between the various Jewish communities became very intensive. . . . Making use of the vast opportunities offered it by Turkey's Golden Age the regrouped Mediterranean Jewry, too, now enjoyed a new efflorescence. It, too, may have legitimately classified the sixteenth century as another Golden Age of its own.

Along with its liberal policy of encouraging Western nations to import their goods under capitulatory guarantees into the empire – a policy considered to be contributing to the economic well-being of the empire as a whole – the Ottoman government also actively protected its own subjects in international trade. Thus "the victory of the Ottoman Empire symbolized, in the sphere of economics," in Stoianovich's words,[50] "a victory of Greeks, Turks, renegade Christians, Armenians, Ragusans, and Jews over the two-century-old commercial hegemony of Venice and Genoa." While the old school of Levantine trade, represented by Wilhelm Heyd,[51] declared that the "barbaric" Ottomans had no interest in promoting commerce and were concerned exclusively with outright military conquests, they were held responsible for the ruin of the Levant trade. But new research examining events within a broader context and freed from eurocentrism has modified this view fundamentally. In the first place, the native ethnic groups had been kept apart by the Genoese and Venetian masters as employees and dependents and not permitted to participate in overseas commerce. These groups now cooperated with the Ottomans and to a great extent replaced Italians in both the regional trade and in the international traffic between the Ottoman ports and Muscovy, Poland, Transylvania, Hungary and Italy, venturing as far as Lyons and Antwerp; in 1582 the duke of Brabant authorized four "mercatores graeci ex provinciae [Galatiae]" to bring Ottoman wares to Antwerp, and provide themselves with goods for export to Turkey.[52] Under Ottoman protection, Dubrovnik achieved a spectacular expansion and challenged Venetians in Mediterranean traffic. Even the Levantine Genoese adopted Ottoman "citizenship" as *dhimmi* in Pera and Chios and thus became part of the Ottoman imperial system, enjoying continued prosperity until the Ottomans changed their policy and took Chios under their direct control in 1566.[53] Four years later the Ottoman decision to end Venetian domination on Cyprus seems to have been part of this new strategy, in which Jewish interests associated with Ottoman finances apparently played an important role. On the other hand, between 1450 and 1600, Turkish or Muslim merchants played a major role in the interregional trade and in some sectors became numerically superior to the non-Muslim subjects.

Also, although the actors changed in the Levant trade and even a decline appears to have been true from the Genoese and Venetian standpoint, the Levant trade as a whole seems to have made a substantial growth in international as well as in regional trade. It is especially noteworthy that trade in bulky goods produced in the Ottoman lands – such as grain, cotton, wool, hides, fish, wine, olive oil, dairy products and textiles – recorded spectacular increases while the traditional *grand commerce* in spices, drugs, raw silk and precious stones resumed its importance in the Levant in the period 1520–1600. As will be seen below, the Iranian raw silk exports in particular responded to the expanding silk industries in Europe and rapidly growing demand for silk created a boom that competed with the spice trade in value and importance. Thanks to Ottoman protection, Florence could prosper in the Levant trade, particularly in the exchange of its fine cloths with raw silk in the period 1460–1560. Venice, enjoying long periods of peace (1481–97, 1503–37, 1540–70) with extensive commercial privileges under the capitulations, realized one of the most prosperous periods in its Levantine trade and its economy as a whole.[54]

NOTES

1 On capitulations in general, see İnalcık (1971).
2 Anhegger and İnalcık (1956), nos. 30, 33, 34, 35, 36, 45, 53, 56, 59.
3 Setton (1976–84), II, pp. 44–46, 146–49, 155, 396–98, 425–29, 438–43.
4 Masson (1896), pp. 1–4.
5 See Zachariadou (1983), pp. 123–73; the earliest of these trade agreements was made between the Duca di Candia Marino Morosini and the emir of Menteşe Orhan in April 1331, then between the duke and the emir of Aydın in 1337 and 1353, the duke and the emir of Menteşe in 1337, 1358 and 1375. Similar agreements were concluded between the Hospitallers and the emir of Aydın in 1348, and the Genovese and the Ottomans in 1352.
6 İnalcık (1985a), pp. 179–217.
7 Heyd (1936), II, pp. 530–31; Sakâzov (1929), pp. 158–62.
8 Antoniadis-Bibicou (1963), pp. 211–14.
9 İnalcık (1992b).
10 Antoniadis-Bibicou (1963).
11 Steensgaard (1972), p. 172.
12 BN, MS Paris no. 85:183b.
13 İnalcık (1991a), pp. 63–65.
14 İnalcık (1981), document nos. 109, 151, 153.
15 *Ibid.*, document no. 109.
16 Sahillioğlu (1975), p. 109.
17 İnalcık (1951), pp. 651–55.
18 İnalcık (1981), document no. 5.
19 Barkan (1979), pp. 1–380; Berov (1974), pp. 168–88.
20 Berov (1974), p. 178.
21 Barkan (1975), pp. 3–28.
22 İnalcık (1969e), pp. 283–85.
23 Sahillioğlu (1975), pp. 124–36.
24 For examples, see İnalcık (1981), document nos. 131, 133, 142, 155, 156.
25 İnalcık (1969d), pp. 121–24.
26 İnalcık (1988b) pp. 524–27.
27 Laiou-Thomadakis (1982), p. 111.
28 *Ibid.*, pp. 112–15.
29 Thiriet (1958–61), III, no. 3009.
30 Argenti (1958), pp. 477–527.
31 Balard (1978), I, pp. 269–89, 334–54; II, pp. 502–3; Laiou-Thomadakis (1982), pp. 100–12.
32 İnalcık (1991a), pp. 41–42, 55–57.
33 Babinger (1952), pp. 197–210.
34 İnalcık (1967), pp. 154–47.
35 İnalcık (1988a), pp. 520–25.

36 Iorga (1971), pp. 11–13, 118–25, 192–95.
37 Ravid (1978), pp. 25–49.
38 Safvet (1332 H), pp. 1446–47; Safvet (1328 H), p. 991.
39 *Ibid.*
40 Hammer (1815), III, pp. 563–64.
41 İnalcık (1947), pp. 47–106.
42 Baron (1983), pp. xviii, 102–3, 117.
43 *Ibid.*, pp. 141–44.
44 *Ibid.*, pp. 141–44.
45 İnalcık (1969d), p. 122 note 54.
46 İnalcık (1978a), p. 95, for Muslim awareness of it, now see Kafadar (1991), pp. 381–400.
47 İnalcık (1969d), p. 122.
48 Safvet (1328 H), p. 991.
49 Baron (1983), pp. 120–21.
50 Stoianovich (1960).
51 Heyd (1936), II, pp. 257–60, 350.
52 A. Goris cited by Stoianovich (1970), p. 238.
53 Argenti (1958), xcii–cxxx.
54 Luzzatto (1954); Braudel (1972), I, pp. 562–69; Lane (1973), pp. 284–335.

10

⌢

BURSA AND THE SILK TRADE

THE TRADE TO 1550

The motto "commerce is the wheel of the economy" should be modified to "fashion is the wheel of the economy." In fact, it is fashion that develops or destroys an industry and trade. The popularity of silk cloth in Europe, particularly following the establishment of the crusader states in Syria,[1] appears to have been one of the decisive factors in the thirteenth-century commercial revolution. Along with the highly developed native woolen industries, silk became the principal source of international exchange and wealth for Western countries from the thirteenth to the eighteenth centuries. Raw silk and silk fabrics were a substantial part of the commerce. The spread of the use of expensive silk cloth among the ruling elite in the West gave rise to a flourishing industry of luxury silks, first at Lucca in Tuscany, which became the capital of this industry in Europe as early as the 1250s.[2] For two or three centuries, Luccese merchants sold their luxury products in Rome, Bruges, London or at the international fair of Champagne. Learning the superior techniques of Luccese silk weavers, Bologna, Genoa, Florence and Venice rose as competitors in the fourteenth century. Incidentally, as happened in the East, so also in Italy, where the transfer of silk weaving techniques led to the alluring and settling of expert workers from Lucca. Italian industries greatly expanded their production and met the growing demand when China began to send its abundant and cheap raw silk supplies to the West after 1257.[3] Chinese supplies were arriving, as R. Lopez put it,[4] in "unlimited amounts." The principal export from China to Europe was now raw silk. But it disappears from Genoese notarial records before the end of the thirteenth century[5] and was totally replaced by Iranian raw silk. When Chinese silk stopped arriving massively as a result of disorders in the Mongol Empire, Genoa became increasingly dependent on Iranian silk, which their merchants bought directly at Tabriz or Azov.[6] Although expensive and of better quality, Iranian raw silk was imported to Italy by the Genoese as early as the middle of the thirteenth century.[7] Beginning in 1300, most of the raw silk consumed by the Italian silk industry came from the Caspian provinces of Iran. Around 1400 travellers' sources[8] described Gilan, Shamakhi and Karabagh as the most important silk-growing areas in northern Iran. However, as early as the first half of the tenth century, Istahri made reference to Lahican (in Gilan) as a center of raw silk production.[9]

The impact of the expansion in the use of silk cloth and of silk industries in Europe cannot be underestimated. It formed the structural basis for the development of the Ottoman and Iranian economies. Both empires drew an important part of their public revenues and silver stocks from the silk trade with Europe. The silk industries in the Ottoman Empire, principally in Amasya, Bursa, İstanbul, Mardin, and Diyarbekir, depended on imported raw silk from Iran. The growing demand in Europe for raw silk seems to have been responsible for the expansion of silk production in the provinces of northern Iran at the expense of rice agriculture, principally in Mazandaran, Gilan and Shirvan.

Bursa became a world market between East and West not only for raw silk but also for other Asian goods as a result of the revolutionary changes in the network of world trade routes in the fourteenth century.[10] By this time, under the Mongols, Tabriz had assumed a central role in world trade. The city became the great emporium for Asian trade, overshadowing Baghdad and other Near Eastern outlets of world trade. The trade route from Tabriz followed the Erzincan–Sivas "imperial" route to Konya or to Ayas (Lajazzo) on the bay of İskenderun, which had become the main outlet for Asian products under the Mongols.[11] From Konya, caravan routes reached, via Denizli, the ports of Ephesus or Antalya. The spectacular evidence of this boom is the series of monumental caravanserais built during the period on the caravan routes in Seljukid Anatolia.[12] Western merchants obtained Asian products, silks and spices, from these ports.[13] Through this network of international trade routes which experienced unprecedented development under the *Pax Mongolica*, Asia Minor became a vehicle for world trade and experienced great prosperity. Italian merchants settled in Tabriz could exchange their woolen cloth there with Iranian silk and Indian spices arriving via Hormuz and Baghdad.

By about 1350, although the center of world trade once again shifted south to the Red Sea, to Egypt and Syria under the Mamluks,[14] Asian goods, particularly raw silk, still followed the old route from Tabriz (or

11 Trade routes of the empire

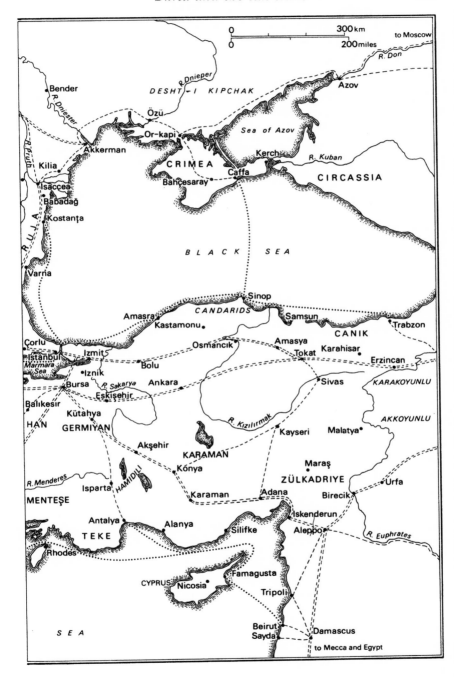

0 300 km
0 200 miles

to Moscow

R. Don

Bender

R. Dniester

Dnieper

DESHT – I KIPCHAK

Özü

Azov

Or-kapi

Sea of Azov

Akkerman

Kerch

R. Kuban

Kilia

R. Pruth

CRIMEA

Caffa

CIRCASSIA

Isaccea

Bahçesaray

Babadağ

Kostanţa

R. ?

BLACK   SEA

Varna

Sinop

Amasra

CANDARIDS

Samsun

Trabzon

Kastamonu

CANIK

Çorlu

Osmancık

Amasya

Karahisar

Erzincan

İstanbul

İzmit

Tokat

Marmara Sea

İznik

Bolu

Ankara

Sivas

KARAKOYUNLU

Bursa

R. Sakarya

Eskişehir

Balıkesir

R. Kızılırmak

AKKOYUNLU

HAN

Kütahya

Kayseri

Malatya

GERMİYAN

Akşehir

KARAMAN

Maraş

R. Menderes

Kónya

ZÜLKADRİYE

Urfa

Isparta

HAMİDİLİ

Karaman

Adana

Birecik

MENTEŞE

Antalya

Alanya

Silifke

İskenderun

TEKE

Aleppo

R. Euphrates

Rhodes

Famagusta

CYPRUS

Nicosia

Tripoli

SEA

Beirut

Damascus

Sayda

to Mecca and Egypt

rather Sultaniye, which replaced Tabriz under Olcaytu) to the Anatolian ports of Ephesus, Antalya and Trabzon. After the massacre and expulsion of Italians from Tabriz (1340–41) and the siege of Genoese Caffa by the khan of the Golden Horde, Djanibek, in 1343, the Genoese had to rely on the Trabzon–Pera or Constantinople route for silk supplies from Iran, hence the commercial revival of Pera–Constantinople. This new situation, which made Pera the main Genoese entrepôt, must also have paved the way for Bursa's future as a market for Iranian raw silk. The Genoese obtained their first trade privileges, the so-called capitulations, from the Ottoman sultan Orhan in 1352.

On the other hand, the Caspian Sea–Astrakhan–Tana silk route assumed a new significance when the Italians were expelled from Tabriz.[15] The Genoese received Iranian raw silk at Tana or Caffa which was vitally important for their expanding silk industries and trade, and they transported it by sea to Genoa. Incidentally, supplied by this source, Caffa had, like Genoa, an important silk industry exporting its famous products as late as the fifteenth century. The silk of Shirvan, Gilan and Mazandaran was taken directly to Astrakhan by sea and then either went to Saray on the Volga or by caravan to Tana. Demand for Iranian silk became particularly acute when the price of Chinese silk went up or it ceased to be imported because of the collapse of the *Pax Mongolica* across Asia in the mid-fourteenth century.

In 1395, Timur's deliberate destruction of the trade centers of Astrakhan, Saray and Azov seems to have been aimed at bringing back to Tabriz the raw silk supplies of Shirvan (Shamakhi) and Gilan (Lahican and Rasht), which were then moving directly by sea to Astrakhan.[16] The Tabriz silk trade as well as substantial customs revenue on silk must have been lost from this diversion. Before Timur, in 1341, the revenue in Tabriz from the raw silk customs dues (*tamga*) reached 300,000 dinars, which was the highest among all *tamga* revenues.[17] Timur's efforts to protect Tabriz as the center of the trade of raw silk and silk cloth ultimately favored the earlier Tabriz–Asia Minor route. Before long Asia Minor came under Timur's control. His destruction of the main stations of the silk trade in the north and the ensuing long struggle for the throne among the descendants of Batu Khan in the Golden Horde, each of whom rallied the rival tribes around him, made the Eastern European steppe a dangerous region for caravans. Barbaro,[18] who visited the area in 1436, asserts that by this date spices and silk supplies had already left the northern route for Syria. Although there is evidence that caravans followed the Astrakhan–Tana route as late as 1520,[19] it evidently lost its importance after Timur's blow. Besides, by then Bursa had become one of the major world markets for raw silk and the Genoese of Pera, favored by the Ottomans, could find as much silk as they wanted at this market. It should be added that, along with Constantinople and Pera, the rise of Bursa as a world market in the second half of the fourteenth century became the economic foundation of Ottoman power.

Bursa's rise as an international market must be dated back to the middle of the fourteenth century. The granting of trade privileges to the Genoese in 1352, and the Ottoman annexation of Ankara in 1354, were important steps in this direction. Also it is interesting to note that in the second half of the fourteenth century the Ottomans concentrated their efforts on taking control of the principal centers of the silk route to the east, namely Ankara (1354, 1362), Osmancık (1392), Amasya (1392) and Erzincan (1401). This daring push on the way to Tabriz brought the ambitious Ottoman sultan Bayezid I in conflict with Timur at the battle of Ankara in 1402. What is clear is that the Ottomans were always concerned with keeping the silk route open or maintaining it under their control. Under Selim I, they occupied Tabriz for the first time (1514). The local dynasty of Gilan, one of the richest silk-producing provinces of Iran, always sought Ottoman protection until its independence was eliminated by Shah Abbas I in 1592.

There is no doubt that toward 1400 Bursa was reputed to be one of the great centers for silk commerce and industry. At that time Johannes Schiltberger[20] observed: "[the silk] of which good stuffs are made at Tamash [Damascus] and at Kaffa [Caffa] and also at Wursa (Bursa) . . . the silk is also taken to Venice and to Lickka (Lucca) where good velvet is worked." On his return from Samarkand in 1405, Clavijo used the Tabriz–Bursa silk caravan route. By the end of the fourteenth century, the old silk routes of Caffa–İstanbul, Trabzon–İstanbul and Sivas–İstanbul had lost their former importance.

Western Anatolian ports also appear to have profited, like Bursa, from the Iranian silk trade as early as the mid-fourteenth century. Raw silk, obviously of Iranian origin, was also exported from Ephesus (Altoluogo) and Milet (Palatia–Balat)[21] and must have followed the old caravan route Tabriz–Konya–Denizli. In about 1341 Rudolf von Suchen observed[22] that silk as well as cotton and wheat were exported from Ephesus. By annexing Ephesus and other western Anatolian ports in 1390, Bayezid I brought under his control all important outlets of Iranian trade via Asia Minor.

Now under Ottoman protection, silk caravans could travel safely as far as Bursa from which Italian merchants, stationed in Pera, could purchase the precious commodity. As Bursa court records from the second half of the fifteenth century demonstrate,[23] Iranian merchants, mostly Muslims from Azerbaijan, exchanged in Bursa their silk loads for Western goods imported by Italians. During the period when the Mongol route was disturbed, Bursa rose as an international market not only for Iranian raw silk, but also for spices and other Asian products. In the silk trade the only other market competing with Bursa was Aleppo, where the Iranian caravans using the southern route Bitlis-Diyarbekir-Mardin brought their silk loads to Aleppo (Table 1:39).

Since Iranian raw silk merchants were obtaining cash and making their purchases at Bursa, the Ottoman capital became an entrepôt for all kinds of exports to Iran. In addition to the Western woolen cloth, they bought in Bursa pearls from the Gulf, sugar from Cyprus and Egypt and even spices from India.

Bursa's role in the silk trade explains the enduring close cooperation between the Genoese and the Ottomans in the period 1352–1453. Ottomans also granted the Genoese the very profitable monopoly of the alum trade from Anatolian mines. According to the Genoese capitulations renewed on June 8, 1387,[24] Murad I exempted the Genoese from customs dues for the goods imported and exported from Pera and instead required a market duty at the rate of 8 percent on the value of goods. This meant that the Ottoman sultan was not considering Genoese Pera a foreign land. An Ottoman agent was settled in Pera who was responsible for the revenue from the market duty.

Later, in 1432, Bertrandon de La Brocquière[25] observed that "Turks visit Pera very frequently" ("grant hantise") and because of trade they have an agent in Constantinople. In order to go to Pera, La Brocquière waited in Bursa to meet "the merchants who were to come and take spices to Pera which they would purchase from the caravan [which arrived from Damascus]." Traffic between Bursa and Pera was under Ottoman control, so La Brocquière could pass to Pera in the company of Genoese merchants who had capitulatory immunities. To pass over to Pera from Üsküdar, he boarded a ship belonging to Greeks. Pera's dependence on the Ottomans became so strong that in 1423 or 1424 the Peran Genoese proposed to Murad II that he put his emblems on a tower to be built on the walls and asked him to provide materials and a monetary contribution.[26]

In 1453 Constantinople was conquered and the sultan tried to take Pera unharmed under an agreement with its Genoese, Greek, Armenian and Jewish population. Although many Genoese fled in panic at seeing the fate of the population of Constantinople, some stayed in the city and

Table I:39. The population of Bursa

Date	Households	Source
1485	5,000	Households for the *avarız* tax, see İnalcık (1960b), p. 45
1520–30	6,351	Barkan (1975), pp. 27–28, estimates 34,930 individuals
1571–80	12,852	Barkan (*ibid.*) estimates 70,686 individuals

Note: To estimate the number of individuals Barkan adopts a coefficient of five for a household and adds 10 percent for those not subject to tax and therefore not included in the original figure.

agreed to become Ottoman subjects, as did members of other religious communities. Genoa's citizens who stayed in Pera under the capitulatory privileges continued, according to the notary records, with their normal commercial activities "as if nothing had changed."[27] In the following period we find the Genoese among the most active silk traders at the Bursa market. A caravan route from Bursa to Çeşme on the extremity of the Aerithrea peninsula linked the Bursa market with Chios. It is reported that already in 1456 a sizable silk cargo was shipped from Chios to Genoa.[28] But the shorter route of Bursa–Mudanya–Pera was the principal channel for the export of Iranian raw silk. This was a riposte of the Muslim world to the papal declaration of a blockade of the Muslim lands in the eastern Mediterranean since 1291. The Latins tried to hold on to their Levantine strongholds – Caffa, Trabzon, Chios and the other eastern Aegean islands as well as Cyprus (Acre, the last stronghold remaining in Western control, had fallen in 1291). Under the circumstances the Italians retreated and placed their main business headquarters in Constantinople–Pera, which became the main center of their activities and enjoyed a period of renewed trade boom. On the other hand, the rise of the Turcoman principalities in western Anatolia and the emergence of the Ottoman state, the nearest to Byzantium and Genoese Pera and the most powerful and promising power in the region, are intelligible under the new conditions in the Levant. Stimulated by great demand and the high prices offered by Florentine, Genoese and Jewish merchants, the Bursa silk market made record imports of raw silk during the period 1487–1512 (Table I:40).

La Brocquière and Maringhi (below, pp. 234–35) provide testimony that the trade pattern between Pera and Bursa and its clientele did not change from 1432 to 1500. On the other hand, as the tributary of the

Table I:40. Total revenue from the scales (mizan) tax on raw silk at
Bursa (for a three-year period, in million akça)

Year	Total revenue	
1487	6.00	
1508	5.45	
1512	7.35	Gallipoli scales-tax revenue included
1513	7.30	
1521	2.10	1514–20 blockade
1523	3.00	
1531	3.10	
1540	2.90	
1542	3.80	
1557	4.20	
1558	4.10	
1577	2.38	Iranian War, 1578
1598	4.55	Iranian War
1606	5.20	Iranian War
1638	3.12	Iranian War

sultan since 1415, the Genoese of Chios too had a lively trade at Bursa.
Merchants from Chios brought to Bursa large quantities of mastic to
exchange for raw silk. Bursa became a market for mastic, where Eastern
and Western merchants purchased this precious commodity, and this
explains why the Genoese of Chios had a policy independent from Genoa
toward the Ottomans.

Although, as a result of Mehmed's prohibition, greatly reduced from
their previously flourishing trade in the export of slaves from the Black
Sea, the Genoese trade in the Levant flourished particularly in raw silk
(Table I:41). By 1500 Maringhi mentions only Genoese and Jews as com-
petitors with the Florentines for Iranian raw silk at the Bursa market.
The Genoese of Caffa continued to be active partners of the old Genoese
Chios–Pera–Caffa traffic system until Caffa was conquered and the Gen-
oese population was deported to İstanbul in 1475.[29]

In the fifteenth and sixteenth centuries the overwhelming majority of
Iranian silk merchants coming to Bursa were Muslims, Iranians or Azeris
mostly from Tabriz, Shamakhi, Saad-çukuru, Gilan, and Shirvan, but also
from Yazd, Shiraz, Kazvin, Kazerun, Isfahan, Kashan and Sebzavar. Some
of them settled in Bursa: for instance, a Hoca İmadeddin, who authorized
a certain Alagöz to collect his credits from the merchants in Bosnia. Bursa
became, like Tabriz, a headquarters for Iranian merchants and money-
changers who acted as agents for their partners in Iran. In Bursa they conducted business transactions directly with Italians or sent their own agents

Table I:41. Genoese imports from the
Ottoman Empire, 1519 (in gold ducats)

Raw silk	369,991
Wool	106,194
Cotton	67,377

Source: Compiled from Gioffré (1960), pp. 233–34.

to the Balkans and Italy. A typical Iranian wholesale merchant was Hoca Abdürrahim of Shamakhi who brought to Bursa, in 1467, 4,400 *lidre* or 1,408kg of raw silk worth 220,000 *akça* or 5,000 gold ducats.[30] Turkish silk merchants also exported the raw silk they bought in Bursa from Iranians directly to Italy, sometimes employing their freed slaves as agents.

In the fifteenth and the first half of the sixteenth century, Muslim Iranians dominated the silk trade together with the Ottomans and Italians. Iranians are referred to as *Azemi* (from the Ottoman *Acem* for Iranians and Azeris) in Italian documents. During the period Armenian merchants are mentioned less in the Bursa court records.[31] From the time of Shah Abbas onward, however, they replaced the Muslims and dominated Iranian trade as far as Venice and Leghorn.

The growing silk industries of Italy were dependent upon the supply of Iranian raw silk, imported from the Bursa market in the fifteenth century. We have a vivid picture of this market in 1500 from the business reports of a Florentine merchant by the name of Giovanni di Francesco Maringhi (see below, pp. 234–36).

As we have noted, around 1500, trade in Iranian silk at the Bursa market flourished (see Table I:40). The foreign merchants impatiently awaited the arrival of the silk caravans in Bursa and were in keen competition to buy as much silk as possible. In the first half of the year 1501, the Florentines bought 60 bales, a purchase twice as much as the Genoese and Jewish purchases combined.[32] In August when there was no silk to buy, the price went up to 69 *akça* per *lidre*. So prices fluctuated seasonally between 62 and 69 *akça* according to available supplies in the market, with silk prices in Florence following those of Bursa. The peak season was in the spring. Approximately six silk caravans arrived in Bursa annually, each carrying an average 200 *fardello* of raw silk, or an annual total of 96 metric tons (at *c*.79.821 kg/*fardello*). Bursa home industries, with one thousand looms at this time,[33] consumed quite an important part of it. On average, 36 tons was needed annually. In 1617 Shah Abbas offered to the English 2–3,000 bales for export; the total annual production was estimated at 20–22,000 bales. Three-quarters or half of the Iranian raw silk imports were re-exported to Italy. Aside from the consumption of the Bursa silk industry, raw silk was exported to the Balkans, and central and northern Europe in the 1500s, as witnessed by the customs registers of Caffa, Akkerman and the Danubian ports.[34] The best quality raw silks sold at the Bursa market in this period were *astarabadi (stravai)*, *lahican (leggi)* and *sari*.

It is no exaggeration to say that the silk trade, like the spice trade, constituted one of the most important economic issues affecting world politics from 1250. The states involved in the silk trade, namely Iran, the Ottoman Empire and the Italian city-states, were keenly conscious of its vital importance to their economies and finances. The struggle for control of the silk route between Tabriz and Bursa persisted between the Ottomans and the rulers of Iran in the fifteenth and sixteenth centuries. In 1472, Uzun Hasan deliberately destroyed Tokat where Mehmed II had established a new customs house in order to prevent smuggling. However, under Bayezid II, who kept peace in the east, silk imports reached record levels (see Table I:40). Determined to destroy Shah Ismail, Selim I resorted to an unusual measure. He placed an embargo on all silk imports from Iran and prohibited trade in raw silk in the Ottoman territories.[35] The definitive embargo was declared in the spring of 1514 when the campaign against the shah started. In order to stop all Iranian silk exports to Europe, the sultan extended the embargo to include Arab lands under the Mamluks. He declared that any Turk, Iranian or Arab found with Iranian silk in his possession was subject to cargo seizure.[36] Despite dispatching an ambassador to explain the decision, this measure became an additional cause of friction with Egypt. Selim's embargo seems to have been an unusually radical move. In the Middle East tradition, conflict between rulers should not concern or cause harm to the taxpaying common people. The latter, whose only concern should be earning their livelihood, must be protected in all circumstances. Interference in the everyday life of his subjects or their source of livelihood was something a just ruler should carefully avoid in order to maintain his reputation. Consequently, the idea of an embargo was an unacceptable innovation for the society at large. The prohibition was evidently a temporary measure during the period of hostility. Since it was illegal to confiscate any traders' merchandise for political reasons, seized goods were carefully recorded with a declaration that they would be returned when normal conditions resumed. Nevertheless, this unusual and drastic measure had such an impact on public opinion that Ottoman historians take pains to explain that the actual purpose of the sultan was not confiscation, but merely to deprive the enemy of its source of revenue.[37] To justify this action, it was also argued that merchants were taking weapons to Iran. Iranians caught in Ottoman territory were deported to Rumeli and placed under custody and their silk loads were seized. In 1518, the sale of raw silk was altogether banned in Ottoman territory. Ottoman subjects, acting against orders, were forced to deliver to the treasury the equivalent money of the amount of silk sold.[38] Besides the harsh measures against the silk merchants, the embargo had disastrous economic consequences, not only for Iranians, but also for the Ottomans and Italians. There must have been extensive unemployment and bankruptcies in the Bursa silk industry as a result of the embargo. When, later in 1586, the Ottoman Empire and Iran were at war, again only half of the Iranian merchants arrived, causing raw silk prices to soar on the Bursa market and three-quarters of the silk weaving looms in Bursa to shut down. Big weavers, owning as many as 60, 40 or 30 looms, went bankrupt and many of them disappeared apparently because of their debts.[39] During the period of the embargo, 1514–18, raw silk coming from Georgia via Sokhum was exempt from restrictions.[40] There was some production in the Ottoman territories, including Morea, Prizren, Albania in the Balkans and Bursa, Bilecik and Amasya in Anatolia. In normal times, the high quality and relatively cheap raw silk of Iran was available in abundance at the Bursa market, which discouraged the development of native production.

Selim's embargo, which deprived the Italian silk industry of its main source of raw material, created panic in Italy. The enterprising Genoese planned to revive the old trade traffic of the Astarabad–Caspian Sea–Astrakhan route.[41] The Astrakhan–Moscow route was already active by 1476 when Contarini[42] visited Astrakhan, through which Moscow was receiving silk cloth from Yazd. Later, the English tried to establish such a trade route for Indian and Iranian goods. (see below, pp. 364–72).

It was evident that the embargo imposed by the forceful Sultan Selim was causing great losses for all concerned by disrupting a long-established pattern of international trade. When Süleyman I (1520–66) succeeded his father, not only did he restore the silk trade with Iran, but he also released the detained merchants and returned their silk if it had been preserved under a trust, and if not, they were compensated. But from this point on, direct control of the silk-producing provinces in Azerbaijan must have been an Ottoman target. During Süleyman's Iranian campaigns in the years 1533–36, 1548–50, and 1553–55, Azerbaijan was invaded and Tabriz occupied twice (1534, 1548). Since Selim I's time, local dynasties in Daghestan, Shirvan and Gilan sought Ottoman protection. But it was during the war of 1578–90 that Azerbaijan as far as Shirvan was occupied and annexed by the Ottoman Empire. Thus, principal silk-producing areas came under direct Ottoman control until Shah Abbas undertook a counter-offensive and expelled the Ottomans from Azerbaijan in 1603–05. In any case, in the 1540s, Bursa was the chief emporium for the Iranian merchants who purchased mainly western woolens and tin there. Around 1600, Iran's need was estimated at 2,000 bales of cloth and 40–50 tons of tin.[43] Interestingly, Iranians bought Indian spices at Bursa, too. In one instance, the Iranian merchant, Alaeddin, spent 32,000 akça or 640 ducats there to buy sugar imported from Cyprus and pepper from India.[44]

THE FLORENTINES IN PERA AND BURSA

Florentine merchants had a privileged position in Byzantium for selling their woolen cloth. As it was in great demand in the luxury trade throughout Asia, it secured a good profit for the city. However, until the final acquisition of Pisa in 1421, Florence, in her trade with the Levant, depended on the Genoese and Venetians who used to buy and re-export Florentine cloth to the East. In 1423 the Venetian Doge Tommaso Mocenigo could still boast that

> the Florentines were sending annually 15,000 pieces of cloth which Venice channelled into Barbary, Egypt, Syria, Cyprus, Romania [Balkans], Crete, Morea and Styria. They deliver, in addition, many other commodities the value of which reaches 70,000 ducats a month or 840,000 ducats a year. They buy, in exchange from Venice, wool of France and Catalonia, cloths dyed of cochineal, carded wool, silk, silver and gold threads and precious stones.[45]

The presence of Florentine merchants in Bursa is documented as early as 1432.[46]

In the period 1463–1500, the Florentine colony of Pera had become very influential and prosperous, thanks to the policy of Mehmed II.[47] When the Venetians and the Genoese challenged Mehmed II's plans to expand into Morea, Albania, Bosnia and the Black Sea, he showed special favor toward the Florentines, in order to lessen his dependency on their rivals, the Venetians, in the vital trade relations of his empire with the West. The Ottomans also were aware that fine woolen cloth, the principal export item from the West, was originally made or finished by the *arte di lana* of Florence, and exported to the Ottoman markets through Venice.

The Levant trade experienced a real boom in this period. Benedetto Dei, a Florentine agent settled in Galata, became the most trusted advisor to the sultan in the years 1460–72. In fact, Mehmed II's interest in encouraging Florence in the Levantine trade dated back to the days of his conquest of Constantinople. Already by 1455, the sultan was extending favors to the Florentines in his territories. Indicative of the growth of trade after 1454, the number of Florentine ships visiting İstanbul increased from one to a convoy of three ships annually in the period 1454–61.

Considering the huge benefits they obtained, Florentines gladly paid the annual expense of 5,000 gold pieces to maintain their agents in Galata. In 1461, the sultan found a pretext to expel the Venetians from government-owned houses and settled Florentines instead. The following year, when Mehmed conquered Mytilene, the three Florentine ships then anchored in the Golden Horn joined in the victory celebration to please the sultan. Again in 1463, on the occasion of the sultan's victory in Bosnia, the Florentines of Pera decorated their houses and streets and the sultan himself honored them by visiting and dining at the mansion of the banker, Carlo Martelli. Finally, the consul Mainardo Ubaldini, head of the Florentine colony of Pera, and the Florentine agents and merchants of Pera, were actively involved in Mehmed II's decision to declare war against Venice in 1463.

While at war with the sultan, the republic of Venice dispatched a special ambassador to Florence asking that ships not be sent to İstanbul during that particular year. The reaction of Florence is of interest. A great amount of cloth, they said, was already prepared for the Ottoman market, and the ships to be sent actually could protect the large number of Florentines residing there. In fact, political and economic circumstances created a natural alliance between the sultan and Florence against Venice. The pressure which Venice and the Pope placed on Florence was countered by Mehmed II, who demonstrated an unusual friendship toward the Florentines in Galata.

When in 1467, under pressure from public opinion in Italy, Florence decided to evacuate Pera and all the heads of the commercial houses set sail for home with their wealth on Anconian ships, the Venetians intercepted them and looted everything. Florentine traffic with Galata remained halted until 1472. Although Florentines were now able to continue traffic with Pera via Genoa, in 1467 and 1469 the outbreak of a terrible plague in the Ottoman territories, including İstanbul and Pera, caused another setback to Florentine trade in the Levant. The epidemic began in mid-summer of 1467, and, according to Kritovoulos,[48] an eye-witness, there were more than 600 deaths a day in the Ottoman capital. Despite these setbacks, there were fifty Florentine commercial agents in the Ottoman Empire located in Edirne, İstanbul, Gallipoli and Pera.

The first formal capitulation was granted to the Florentines by Mehmed II, the text of which has not been discovered. Without such an instrument, the Florentine colony could not have remained in Pera. Despite the restitution of peace with Venice in 1479, Bayezid II (1481–1512) was no less concerned with encouraging friendship with the Florentines and their continued presence in his capital; perhaps all the more so because of Cem Sultan, pretender to the Ottoman throne, who had been in Europe since 1482. In 1483, through his ambassador to Florence, the new sultan promised to purchase, annually, and exempt from tax, 5,000 *pastav* (one *pastav* or *fardello* was about 50 *arşun* or 34 m) of woolen cloth for the palace.[49] In 1507, Florentine merchants at Galata numbered sixty or seventy, with an annual turnover reaching 5–600,000 gold ducats.

The capitulations granted by Bayezid II and Selim I to the Florentines were renewed by Süleyman I in October 1527.[50] A comparison with the capitulations granted to Venice in 1482 shows that the Florentines were granted the same guarantees for freedom of trade and travel, and the same provisions concerning security for the persons and properties of the merchants and customs rates.

In the instructions to the Florentine envoy in 1488, complaints were voiced about the difficulties caused by local Ottoman authorities at Avlona when the Florentines took the Lecce–Avlona sea route, as well as the reimposition of the same dues twice or three times on the way from Avlona to Edirne. Florentine merchants took the sea route from Ancona or Ragusa to İstanbul usually on Anconian or Ragusan ships. But in order to avoid corsairs or Venetians, they preferred the sea and overland routes of Ancona–Ragusa–Sarajevo–Novibazar–Edirne–Pera, or Lecce (in Pulia)–Avlona–Edirne–Pera. These overland routes, also used by Ragusans and Muslim merchants, became the main trade routes crossing the Balkan peninsula from the Adriatic to Edirne. Finally, a special provision (article 20) tells us what difficulties and hazards the Florentine merchants were exposed to while crossing the Balkans overland.

The security of merchants passing from Avlona to the Italian coast also was of vital importance for the Florentine merchants, so a special provision guaranteed the security of their property against piracy at sea committed by the Venetians and the Genoese. By implication the same guarantee was applicable to the acts of the Ottoman privateers (*levend*s) at Avlona. The Florentines felt it necessary to enter in their capitulations special provisions concerning double taxation, the hiring of native non-Muslims as aides, and the validity of documents issued in the different zones of jurisdiction, because local authorities often annoyed them in such situations. It was indeed a special favor on the part of the Ottoman government to agree to add such specific provisions in the document. There were Florentine consuls and merchants in İstanbul, Pera, Bursa, Edirne, Gallipoli, Sofia and Rhodes.

In a challenge to Venetian supremacy, Benedetto Dei claimed, Florence's business in the Ottoman Empire was expanding and had great prospects for the future.[51] While the volume of Florentine woolen cloth exports to Turkey was far larger than Florentine silk goods, the latter textiles, including precious velvets and brocades, supplied, on a large scale, the fairs of France, England and the Netherlands (Antwerp).[52] The "Golden Age" of Florence in the Levant was rapidly disappearing in the age of Selim I, although both this sultan and his successor Süleyman I renewed the capitulations. Foreign competition and the discovery of the New World, which "turned men's attention from the Levant," may be the main causes of Florentine decline. Lower prices paid for foreign woolens and the availability of cheaper stocks of silver and gold originally coming from the New World must be particularly emphasized in the process.[53] Venice itself then produced relatively limited amounts – never beyond 3,000 pieces of woolen cloth.[54] But in 1569 the Venetian annual output of fine cloth was over 26,000 pieces. During the sixteenth century Venice's woolen output became "one of the pillars of the city's economy."[55]

However, Florentine trade experienced a boom at the turn of the sixteenth century. The Ottoman–Venetian War of 1499–1503 excluded Venetians from the Ottoman markets and, as prices were high, this stimulated Florentine business in Ottoman Turkey. Florentines were happy to see that, because of the war, the sultan became more favorable to them than ever.[56] After the Ottoman–Venetian peace was signed in 1503, the aggressive trading policy of Venice appears to have been the real cause for Florentine commercial decline in the Levant in the first decades of the century. It was not a coincidence that the upsurge in the output of Venetian woolen industries occurred from the second decade of the sixteenth century[57] and the Florentines were replaced by the Venetians in the Levant markets. As noted above, Sultan Süleyman encouraged trade by renewing the trade privileges with Florence in 1527. In the period 1530–70 the empire's unprecedented accumulation of wealth and growing demand for luxury fabrics from the West probably is partly responsible for the revival of the Florentine woolen industries. According to the Venetian ambassador, writing in 1529, Florence annually used to produce over 4,000 pieces of fine "San Martino" cloth (made of fine English wool) and 18–20,000 *garbi* cloths made of Spanish wool.[58] The latter made up the bulk of exports to the Ottoman market. The Florentine woolen industry made a remarkable recovery, producing 33,312 pieces of cloth in 1572, when Venice was again engaged in a ruinous war against the Ottomans for Cyprus. Much of the Florentine output went to the Levant.[59]

The Ottoman–Venetian War of 1537–40 obviously affected the cloth output of Venice and the war for Cyprus, 1570–73, is the beginning of the decline in the Venetian woolen industries. We shall see that after 1569 France and England would be favored by the sultans, and then would replace Venice and Florence in the fine woolen cloth exports to the Ottoman Empire.

A Florentine agent in Pera: Giovanni di Francesco Maringhi, 1497–1506

The letters of the Florentine merchant and agent, Giovanni di Francesco Maringhi, in the period 1501–2, to the Florentine firms he represented and to his agents in Ottoman trade centers, uniquely portray the activities and conditions of Italian business in the Ottoman Empire. Maringhi was a Florentine resident agent at Pera from 1497 to 1506. He represented the Florentine firms of Venturi, Medici, Galilei and Michelozzi and appears to have been a partner rather than an employee.[60] In March 1502, for example, he made an agreement with Leonardo Venturi of Florence as an associate for three years. According to the contract, he would draw three-fifths of the profit and Venturi two-fifths. They would share the living expenses of "apprentices" on the same basis. Venturi & Co. had to invest at least 7,000 ducats and dispatch all the *panni* (bolts of woolen cloth) they finished to Maringhi for sale or barter in Turkey. An alternative to such agreements to procure *panni* was to buy up with ready money in Florence.[61]

Maringhi's business headquarters was in Pera, and he had salaried agents in Bursa, Gallipoli, Edirne and Sofia who bought and sold for him.[62] One of his agents, named Risalti, who knew Turkish, made regular trips between Florence, Pera and Bursa and back to carry goods and information. His travel expenses overland amounted to 700 *akça* per load of silk. Some of his agents made agreements with firms similar to

Maringhi's so that it was not easy to keep them in the service.[63] Maringhi himself made visits to these market cities.

Maringhi sold cloth at Galata to the wholesale drapers. He had to sell at least 200 *panni* a year to cover his annual expenses in Pera, that amounted to 180–200,000 ducats. *Panni* bought by indigenous merchants, mostly Jews of İstanbul or the Genoese of Pera,[64] were dispatched or taken to other market towns in the empire. For instance, Antonio da Lagnasco, a well-known Peran Genoese draper, used to buy on credit and take *panni* to Caffa, paying his debts when he sold the cloth.[65]

Maringhi's main business was the exchange of Iranian silk for Florentine *panni* on the Bursa market, as was true for the whole Ottoman–Florentine trade in general.[66] However, as a typical Renaissance merchant, he was involved in trade in every commodity, including Ankara camelots, silk cloth and furs, as well as pepper, wax, Chinese rhubarb, musk, scamona, coarse woolens, and flax of Alexandria, among other items.[67] His planned joint business venture with three other Florentine partners in Moncastro (Akkerman) is of particular interest.[68] In March 1502, Maringhi planned to invest 200 or 300 ducats in a partnership that intended to send an agent to Moncastro to get hold of 4–5,000 pieces of leather or hides. This would be repeated each year.

As the political atmosphere was always of prime importance for trade in the Levant, Maringhi kept in close contact with the Ottoman government through the Florentine *emino* in İstanbul.[69]

Maringhi died on February 22, 1506, with properties worth at least 97,000 ducats in value and "goods from various merchants to the value of 127,000 ducats."[70] His career can be taken as an example of other Florentines who were active in the Ottoman Empire, for example, members of the Medici family, Francesco, Giovanni and Raffaello, who were trading at Pera, Bursa and Edirne.[71] Francesco at Pera in 1470 already represented Medici & Co. and visited Bursa and Edirne. Other Medicis in the empire were engaged in various economic activities from banking to the manufacture of soap and cloth dyeing.[72]

Records kept at the Bursa kadi's court give a closer picture of the actual transactions and disputes of the Italian merchants and agents in the city. In 1478 a Florentine agent by the name of Piero bartered Western cloth valued at 207,920 *akça* or 4,000 ducats, to four Muslim merchants for raw silk and cloth.[73] The breakdown of Western cloth bartered is shown in Table I:42.

In October 1478, when Piero died in Bursa, the kadi appointed a Genoese as executor for his estate to collect his credits from his debtors.[74]

Table I:42. Varieties of Western cloth imported to Bursa

	Quantity	Value (in *akça*)
	113 bolts	135,600
Florentine woolen cloth	6 bolts	9,000
	19 bolts	23,000
Bergamese woolen cloth	18 bolts	10,000
Frengi (Italian) velvet	57.5 *arşun*	11,400
Frengi satin	82.5 *arşun*	7,420
	32.5 *arşun*	6,500
Velvet with gold	25 *arşun*	5,000

Note: One *arşun* equaled 68 cm and one gold ducat equaled about 45 *akça* in 1479.
Source: İnalcik (1960e).

It turned out that the famous Damascene spice merchant, Abdurrahman, held a debt of 86,000 *akça* owed by the late Florentine agent. The Syrian merchant first put claims for Piero's advance to four Italians, Zano, Berto (or Breto), Andrea and Bartolomi and the estate of the deceased. Then the Greek executor Michael intervened and Abdurrahman reached an agreement for the debt, which was formally entered into the court records.[75] Bartolomi, a resident of Pera, owed to Piero 67,200 *akça* from the sale of 1,101.5 *lidre* of raw silk.

Like Maringhi, Piero bought and sold raw silk on credit from Iranian merchants and spices from Arab merchants of Damascus. Thus Arab, Iranian, Genoese and Florentine merchants were involved in direct transactions. Levantine Italians or Greeks, familiar with local conditions, also were involved. On the other hand, the kadi of Bursa arranged and guaranteed all legal matters. In other words, the Bursa international market was a complex net of relations in which the Ottoman kadi played an important role in its smooth functioning.

Commodities exchanged

Silk   In Florence, the *arte di seta* existed as early as 1193 and "by the fifteenth century it ranked with the *arte di lana* in importance and in wealth."[76] In 1473 silk manufacturers had agencies in the Ottoman Empire as well as in France, England, and the Netherlands; there were 270 shops belonging to the wool merchants' guild and 83 to the silk merchants'. In the 1470s Benedetto Dei, Florentine agent at Pera, boasted that in these places are sold "more Florentine wares of all kinds, especially silken cloth and gold and silver brocades than [from] Venice, Genoa and Lucca put together."[77]

Table I:43. Prices of silk purchased by Florentines in Bursa, 1501

Date	Kind of silk	Price in *akça* per Bursa *lidre*
May	Seta leggi	59–60
May	Seta leggi	59
May	Stravai (?)	64
June	Stravai	65
1 July	Leggi, stravai	65–69
14 July	Sari	69–70
August		66

Note: One Bursa *lidre* equaled 320.7 gr.
Source: Richards (1932), pp. 67–70, 111–12.

The silk trade between Bursa and Florence was the most profitable business of all. Around 1509 a profit of 70 to 80 gold ducats per bale of raw silk was realized in Florence despite the fact that transport costs were unusually high – 900 *akça* or 18 ducats a bale.[78] According to the account book of Guanti,[79] between 1484 and 1488 the total weight of raw silk sold in Florence under his name amounted to 4,795 pounds (one Bursa pound or *lidre* equaled 320.7 gr), costing 6,022 "large" florins, with expenses amounting to 1,172. (One "large" florin equaled about 48 *akça*.) The net profit came to 977 florins (Table I:43).

Woolen cloth of Florence Exchange of woolen cloth for raw silk in Bursa was the basis of Florentine prosperity. In the period 1400–1630, Bursa was the international market for raw silk from Iran and also the emporium of Western fine woolen cloth for the whole of Asia. Already toward the mid-fourteenth century the customs regulations of Tabriz[80] speak of "European manufactures such as cloths and *scarlat*," which demonstrates the importance of the trade of Western cloth in Iran. As noted earlier, in the second half of the fourteenth century, traffic between Italy and Tabriz shifted from the Trabzon–Constantinople route to the direct caravan route between Tabriz and Bursa. Thus, the Ottoman capital became the major international market for the European cloth trade. Western cloth bales arriving at Byzantine Constantinople and Genoese Pera from Italy were now transported to Bursa. Besides the re-export to Iran, a significant part of the imports, of course, was purchased by the local merchants for shipment all over the Ottoman Empire. It can safely be said that the prosperity of the silk and woolen industries in Florence depended on the import and re-export of Iranian silk acquired at the Bursa market. Greater purchases of silk encouraged increased production of woolens because of the high profit realized in bartering them for silk. Maringhi observed that it was a better business to barter silk with woolen cloth than to sell directly to drapers in Bursa. In one instance, 91 pieces of *calisse*, an inexpensive kind of cloth of Spanish manufacture, were bartered for one and a half bales of silk.[81] Bartering silk bales with woolen cloth was a well-established practice in Florence, too.[82] Thus, the Florentine agent always stressed the great demand for and good profits in the trade of woolen cloth, urging firms to send more and more. He said,[83] for instance, that 260 *panni* sent by Venturi & Co. in the course of three years could have been consumed in one year and urged the firms to supply him annually with at least 500 to 600 bolts of cloth. Woolen cloths made in Turkey could not compete in quality with those of Florence, but every shipment sold quickly and prices were rising constantly.

In addition to their own high-quality *panni*, Florentine firms re-exported, after finishing, a great quantity of woolen cloth from France, Spain (*calisse*), and England (*panni inglese*). In one instance in 1501, 4,000 pieces of *calisse* were imported for re-export to the Ottoman Empire.[84] Foreign *panni* were handled separately from *panni fiorentini*.

Because of the high ratio of gold to silver at the Bursa market and the difficulty of bringing gold from Florence via Ragusa, bartering was always preferred.[85] However, Florentine woolen cloth sometimes did not arrive in sufficient quantities, so that the Florentines had to import cash from Florence;[86] Maringhi regularly dispatched cash in gold pieces and *akça* to his agent in Bursa.

For *calisse* and *panni*, there was always a ready market in Turkey. By 1500, Florentine firms exported 4–5,000 pieces (136–170,000 meters) of first-quality *panni*, called San Martino, designed for palace and elite consumption, and a much larger amount of poor-quality cheaper cloths called *panni de Garbo*. In the 1490s a better quality of the latter, called *sopramani*, was manufactured for the Ottoman market; one *panno* of poor-quality cloth sold for 20 large florins in Bursa.[87]

In this period the trade in Florentine *panni* brought a net profit of 11.9 percent, but when profit from the sale of *astarabadi* silk sent from Bursa was added the profit realistically amounted to 20 percent,[88] an average rate under medieval conditions when the interest rate in general was 15 percent. Transport costs amounted to 31 percent of the production costs for *panni* and 19 percent of the purchase value for raw silk. Customs dues were 4 percent on the transit from Chios to the Ottoman mainland, 2.5 percent for Avlona and 3 percent at the Bursa customs house. All in all there was no big difference in customs payments between

Table I:44. Cloth merchants and bankers in İstanbul, Pera and Bursa, mentioned in Maringhi's letters, 1501–2

	Cloth merchants	Money-changers and bankers
In Istanbul and Pera		
Italians	19	13
Jews	19	2
Greeks	—	1
In Bursa		
Italians	6	8
Jews	2	—
Greeks	—	1

Source: Richards (1932).

Table I:45. Prices of woolen cloth imported from Florence according to Maringhi, 1501–2

	Price per *panno* (in *akça*)
panni, high quality	1,366–1,600
calisse	640–70

Note: 1 *panno* equals 50 *arşun* or 34 m.
Source: Richards (1932).

the Leghorn–Chios–Bursa and Lecce–Avlona–Bursa routes (see Tables I:44 and 45).

Pepper Bursa was an important transit center for spices from India and Arabia in the fifteenth century. The city imported a great quantity from Aleppo and Damascus, mostly by Syrian Arab merchants.[89] From Bursa, pepper was re-exported to the Balkans and to the northern and east-central countries beyond the Danube and the Black Sea. The Florentine agent Maringhi experimented with pepper exports from Bursa to Florence,[90] but his shipment did not sell well. The price of pepper was then 24 ducats per load in Florence, which Maringhi believed high enough to make a good profit. But soon it became evident that it was not a good investment and Maringhi asked for the return of the balance from the three sacks of pepper. "There is," he observed, "no bargain to be expected from the spices"[91] (see Table I:46).

Other goods Besides raw silk, typical Ottoman exports included rhubarb, wax, musk, mohair, pepper, Bursa silk cloth, drugs, and occasionally fish-roe, wool, cotton, fine cotton cloth, rugs, hides and furs.

Table I:46. Prices of pepper and rhubarb at Bursa or
Pera, 1501–2

	Price (ducats)	Measure
Pepper	25–27	per sack
Rhubarb	14	per pound (320.7 gr)

Source: Richards (1932).

Rhubarb brought high profits in Florence. Bursa silk brocades were greatly admired there, but exports were in very limited amounts. Conversely, Florentine silk cloth, as a luxury item, sold well in Bursa but again apparently in small quantities.[92]

The mohair of Ankara was an expensive luxury textile in great demand in Italy, where it was much in vogue among the elite. Bursa was the principal market for the famous Ankara mohair.[93] In March 1502, Maringhi bartered Florentine *panni* for three bolts of mohair and remained in debt for an extra 200 or 250 ducats.[94] He sent his agent, Viatti Erminia, to buy mohair for him in Ankara. One bolt (*tavola*) contained 50 pieces of mohair and each piece sold in Florence at from 4.75 to 5 gold ducats. Florentines re-exported part of their mohair imports to Lyons in France.

Business practices

Maringhi's letters shed light on the Italian business strategies and practices in Turkey. He regularly informed cloth makers in Florence not only about profits to be gained from bartering and the available raw silk supplies but also about the size, quality and color of the *panni* that was popular on the Ottoman market. He sometimes even sent samples.[95] Such practices would be followed later on by mercantilist–capitalist Western economies to promote market expansion. In 1501, for instance, Maringhi informed the firms that red and dark blue cloth would make a good profit. He urged them to maintain their high quality to keep up the reputation of Florentine cloth in the Bursa market. However, as happened with Ottoman silken manufacturers, less expensive cloths sold well and created a wider market at Bursa. Later on their competitors, the English in particular, would take advantage of this trend and beat out the expensive, high-quality cloth of Florence and Venice. Turkish and Greek merchants ventured to Florence "to buy big loads of *panni*,"[96] since the profits were so attractive.

In Bursa most transactions were on credit and at the end of a certain period accounts were balanced.[97] This was practiced not only among Florentine merchants but also between Florentines and Ottomans. The Florentine agents in the empire often sent silk or mohair loads to liquidate debts owed to the Florentine firms. Maringhi's agent in Bursa sold a Jewish draper 8 *panni* of Florentine cloth to be paid for in four monthly payments.[98] Maringhi's estate showed that he had credits with Turks, Jews and Italians. Jewish drapers predominated among indigenous merchants buying *panni* on credit at Pera or Bursa. Sales on credit for short periods of two to four months were common. The creditor had to wait until the debtor was able to sell the *panni* he had purchased. When unable to pay as agreed, the debtor was able to make new arrangements. Florentines frequently had to deal with the kadis or customs agents. In one of his letters to Nicolo Michelozzi in Florence,[99] Maringhi wrote that he hid one box of musk inside a sack of pepper to avoid duty. In any event, he managed to make friends with the *emino*, who helped him make arrangements to retrieve the debt for *panni* which he had sold to a Peran Genoese merchant on credit.[100]

The Venetian ducat was the standard gold coin in Ottoman foreign trade. The fact that it replaced Florentine florins (*fiorini d'oro*) from the beginning of the fifteenth century[101] can be interpreted as an indication of Venetian supremacy in the Ottoman trade. In May 1501, the ratio of gold to silver was about 19 percent higher in Bursa than in Genoa. So cash dispatches from Florence were in gold ducats, and when cash was short bankers at Pera purchased loans at interest with the rate at 15 percent per year.[102] For payments in gold long credit periods were allowed. Sales in gold were always considered more profitable.

Trade routes

The sea traffic between Florence and Ottoman commercial centers, usually on Genoese ships, moved between Pisa or Leghorn and Chios, whence cargoes were taken to the Anatolian port of Çeşme, and by caravan reached Bursa and İstanbul. The long sea route was not secure because of Venetian control of the sea and of piracy, against which Florentines were powerless. This situation illustrates once more that, in the late Middle Ages, control of the overseas markets depended fundamentally on naval supremacy. It will be seen that later, Venice too would lose the Levant market to the English and Dutch mainly because these

Western nations established their naval supremacy in the Mediterranean in the 1590s.

By contrast, thanks to Ottoman protection, the land route starting at Dubrovnik or the Albanian port of Avlona and Scutari offered more security. From 1492, the Ottoman government, anxious to promote economic activity in Avlona, settled Sephardic Jews expelled from Spain. This important port, seat of a *sancak-beg*, and the Adriatic base of the Ottoman navy, was the terminus of the southern highway crossing the Balkan peninsula over Salonica to Edirne, İstanbul and Bursa. The northern terminus, Dubrovnik, profited from Ottoman protection as a tribute-paying city-state. Most of the traffic between Florence and Pera or Bursa was carried out via Dubrovnik.[103] Florentine cargoes left the Italian ports of Pesaro, Fano or Ancona to reach Dubrovnik and then took the land route. Even during this short passage on the Adriatic Sea, Florence sought capitulatory guarantees of Ottoman protection against Venice and piracy. Incidentally, such requests were always interpreted by the Ottomans as leading to a protectorate. The cargoes left or reached Dubrovnik by horse and mule caravans following the route Bosnasaray–Novibazar–Skopje–Plovdiv–Edirne. Edirne was the distribution center in the Balkans where merchants of Pera maintained their agents. Traffic from Edirne to Bursa took the Gallipoli–Lapseki route. The whole land passage required about six weeks. (A messenger, moving much faster, made the journey between Galata and Dubrovnik in ten days.)[104] In one instance, the İstanbul–Florence transport costs for one and a half bales (about 375 *lidre* or 120 kg) of raw silk was c. 900 *akça* or 18 gold ducats.[105] Florentine diplomats made special efforts in Rome to keep open the Florence–Ancona land route, while traffic across the Adriatic and the Balkans was the responsibility of the Ottoman government.

An interesting episode indicates the Ottoman concern for security on the land route. A shipment of silk of about 150 ducats in value (one load of *seta leggi*) was stolen in Novibazar. The sultan sent an officer and asked the villagers to find either the load or the thieves. Finally twenty villagers agreed to pay 15,000 *akça* as compensation. Fees and bribes amounted to about 2,000 *akça*.[106]

The Ottomans always showed a keen interest in Apulia and the port of Ancona. They always remembered their short occupation of Otranto in 1480, and Süleyman I's so-called Corfu campaign originally was intended to be an invasion of Italy.[107] In 1487, Boccolino Guzzoni's plot to bring Ottoman forces to Italy to help seize the marches of Ancona caused alarm throughout Italy.[108]

Later, in an effort to replace Venice as the center of spice distribution in southern Europe, the grand duke of Tuscany approached both the Ottomans and the Portuguese,[109] and finally made Leghorn a free port in 1593.

Ancona Pre-Ottoman Bosnia already had established an active trade with Italy through Dubrovnik as well as through the ports of Split, Zadar, Šibenik, and Tragir on the Dalmatian coast. In the second half of the fourteenth century, merchants had settled in Ancona from Kotor, Zadar, Zagreb, Medrusa and Dubrovnik, maintaining trade relations with the mainland.[110] Emerging as the main transit center for the Florence–Ottoman trade, the seaport of Ancona, beyond Venetian control, emerged as one of the first areas in Europe with a merchant colony from Ottoman territories.

In 1514, the Ottoman government obtained special commercial privileges for its subjects in Ancona, both Muslims and non-Muslims, and the "palatio della farina" of the city was turned into a *fondaco* for numerous "mercanti turchi et altri Maumetani."[111] Toward the mid-sixteenth century, there were about 200 Greek trading houses in Ancona and many Ottoman Jewish firms. Not only grain exports for growing urban centers in Italy, but also oriental luxuries followed the Ancona route. Through the Adriatic ports, such wares reached the central Italian fairs of Lanzan and Recanti to such an extent that Venice became worried over its own Levantine trade. Now "the Ottoman merchants, Greek, Turkish and *Azemini* [Iranians] were present doing business directly in these fairs."[112] In the middle of the sixteenth century, rumors about Ancona's inclination to seek Ottoman protection caused serious anxiety in Rome and Venice. In 1555, when Pope Paul IV began to arrest and burn Marrano Jews and confiscate their possessions, the Ottoman government intervened vigorously on their behalf, because many Jews of Salonica and İstanbul, whose capital was invested at Ancona, had gone bankrupt. Actually some of these Jews were agents of Ottoman merchants. The Jewish banking family of Mendès then attempted to get the Jews in the Ottoman Empire to declare a boycott against the city of Ancona.[113]

THE TRADE FROM 1550 TO 1630

Silk industries were introduced in Western countries quite late: in France under Francis I (1515–47) and in England under Elizabeth I (1558–1603). A mercantilistic concern to prevent the huge amount of gold involved (in France 4 million gold pieces were paid for Italian and Eastern silks) from leaving the realm was the stimulus for their rapid development. Lyons was said to have had 7,000 looms by 1600.[114] In England large quantities of raw silk imports began in the 1590s, and by the 1620s silk had become its largest import.[115] In 1617 the English silk industries required an estimated 300–600 bales of raw silk annually, while the shah proposed to send 2–3,000 bales. By 1628 the annual demand by the Dutch had reached 1,200 bales.[116] The English and the Dutch re-exported their surplus imports to other European countries, thus replacing Venice and Genoa in this market. By the mid-seventeenth century, silk became "the most important among a number of imported goods."[117] The new expanding silk markets obtained their supplies of raw silk through the Ottoman Empire from Iran. In other words, the Iranian and Ottoman economies now found, in the expanding silk market of the West, a new source of prosperity. "At the beginning of the seventeenth century silk was for Asian trade," Steensgaard noted,[118] "what gold and silver had been for the *conquistadores* . . . and the Persian raw silk, after all, was the second biggest European import from Asia." As the Dutch ambassador in İstanbul reported in 1615,[119] trade in silk had increased considerably "on account of the passion for display that is daily becoming greater in Christendom." In the 1620s, total European imports of Persian silk are estimated at about one million lb per annum.[120]

By 1600, Aleppo was the most important silk-exporting market in the Levant, where Venice alone purchased half of the Iranian and Syrian raw silk, amounting to about 140 tons with a value of 1.5 million ducats per annum.[121] The second half was bought by other European nations (see Table I:47). From Venetian consular reports it is possible to follow fluctuations in the Iranian silk trade in the years 1578–1627 at this market.[122] While the traffic slackened during the Ottoman–Iranian War of 1578–90, the following period of peace from 1590–1602 witnessed a boom in this market, reaching its highest level from 1599 to 1602, just before the resumption of the Ottoman–Iranian war in 1603. The Aleppo customs experienced a record annual revenue of 300,000 gold ducats during this period, the greater part of the annual total revenue surplus of 460,000 sent from Syria to the Porte.[123] Despite war, customs revenues still amounted to 200,000 gold ducats in 1604. It is to be noted that Venetians actually paid for raw silk at Aleppo by the sales of substantial amounts of woolen and silk cloths which they imported. In the 1590s they imported annually 200,000 *braccio* (ell) of silk cloth alone (Table I:48).

Table I:47. Estimate of the annual import of Persian silk to Europe in
the 1630s (in bales)

Marseilles	3,000	(previously only 100–200)
Venice	1,500	but only 300 in 1623 and 600 in 1629
England	600	but only 295 in 1623
Netherlands	500	
Genoa, Lucca, Messina and Florence	400	
Total	6,000	

Source: Steensgaard (1972), pp. 159–64.

Table I:48. European imports at Aleppo, 1605

	Imports (1,000 gold ducats)	Ships coming to Alexandretta
Venice	1,500	4–5, mostly woolen and silk cloth
France	800	20, mostly silver coin
England	300	2–3, chiefly kerseys
Netherlands	150	

Source: Texeira, in Steensgaard (1972), p. 180.

The rise of İzmir/Smyrna in the seventeenth century [124] was to a great extent due to the fact that, in competition with Bursa and Aleppo, the city became the principal market of Iranian silk for the Europeans. What actually happened was that İzmir assumed the commercial role that Ephesus, Chios, Çeşme and the two Foças had played in the region prior to 1590. Initially Western nations used Chios as a transit center for Asian trade before obtaining from the sultan direct trade privileges under the capitulations; the newcomers, the English and Dutch, overshadowed other nations in İzmir. Its port prolonged the cheaper seaway into the Anatolian continent and offered a safer refuge against the corsairs and the vagaries of the Aegean Sea. Leghorn, converted to a free port for the Atlantic mercantile nations in 1593, shared İzmir's role as a market for Iranian silk. Employed by Shah Abbas as part of his policy of selling Iranian silk directly to Europe, the Armenians of Iran became very active first in İzmir and then in Leghorn in making the latter city the chief silk market in Europe in the seventeenth century.[125] Five or six Iranian caravans each year followed the Tabriz–Erivan–Kars–Erzurum–Tokat–Ankara–Afyon–İzmir route. By 1670, out of the 22,000 bales of silk produced in Iran, 3,000 arrived in İzmir for export.[126] By 1671, the

French considered Aleppo in fourth place among the Levantine centers of trade, following İzmir, Alexandria and Sayda (Sidon).[127] By 1621, İzmir was "the greatest emporium of all kinds of merchandise in transit between Europe and Asia."[128]

Shah Abbas' attempts to divert the silk route from Ottoman lands

The embargo policy imposed in 1514 by Selim I, designed to destroy Iran economically and financially, was attempted by Shah Abbas I (1587–1629) for Iran in the period 1603–29. Abbas' plan was to divert the silk route from Ottoman territory to the Indian Ocean. He found that the English and Dutch, who had established their supremacy in the Indian Ocean by that time, were eager to cooperate in eliminating the Ottomans as an intermediary because of the extra taxes which were paid at the Ottoman ports.[129] Ottoman–Iranian rivalry took on the nature of an economic war leading to a mutual blockade. As the Iranians prohibited silk exports, the Ottomans took measures to prevent the shipping of gold and silver to Iran, which intensified the monetary crisis in Persia. Shah Abbas tried to find a solution to this problem by selling a large quantity of silk to the northerners at Bandar-Abbas. Let us see how this interesting struggle, which threatened to isolate the Ottoman Empire from the rest of the world, unfolded.

In the summer of 1599 the shah sent a man from his personal entourage, named Hüseyn Ali Bey, together with Sir Anthony Sherley, to the major European capitals. This delegation was charged with working out an alliance with the Christian sovereigns against the Ottoman Empire, and gaining assurances that the trade route would be redirected, outside Ottoman dominions. The German emperor, who was at war with the Ottomans, received the delegation warmly and gave a favorable reply. Besides promising to continue to strive toward the goal of organizing a league against the Turks among Christian governments, he announced that he would attempt to ensure that the Christians would not engage in trade with the Turks. The Iranian delegation went on to Spain and from there to England.

The shah was unable to come to an agreement with the Spanish on this subject because the Spanish had designs on Bahrain, and the situation in Hormuz was causing the Persians additional anxiety.

In 1603 war broke out again between the Ottomans and the Iranians. Shah Abbas again sent representatives to Europe. In 1610, along with another delegation sent to Europe, he shipped 200 bales of silk to Lisbon as proof that the sea route was more economical. According to information from the Venetian ambassador in Madrid, one of the main objectives of the Iranians was to deny the sultan the large amount of revenue he derived from customs duties on Iranian silk. The envoys' proposal also carried a political–military stipulation that Spain attack the Ottoman Empire. These initiatives alarmed the Venetians, as it was thought that they would wreak havoc on the Venetian market. In 1611 Robert Sherley (the brother of Anthony Sherley), a member of the Persian delegation to England, wanted ships to be sent to Persia for silk and to deliver arms to be used against the Turks. However, negotiations yielded no results.[130] Meanwhile, envoys from İstanbul arrived in London and the king of England refused Sherley an audience. In that same year, substantial quantities of English steel and swords were sent to Turkey. But, on the other hand, the English, following the Dutch, severely crippled the Indian trade of the Ottomans through the Gulf and the Red Sea. By 1613, the raids of English and Dutch corsairs in the Red Sea had reached such serious proportions that the Ottoman Imperial Council felt it necessary to take strong action against them, and sent five galleys of lumber to Egypt for construction of a fleet in the Red Sea. Shortly thereafter, the English government seriously took up the matter of attempting to seek a new route for the Persian silk. In 1617 the English ambassador to India, Thomas Roe, by order of the king of England, sent an agent to Persia to enter into negotiations for diverting the silk trade from Turkey. It was hoped that this would lead to the establishment of a less expensive and more secure silk route than through the Ottoman ports. The English thought that, as a result, even if they were obliged at some point to abandon their Levant trade, they would be able to procure the cotton and gallnuts they needed most through other European merchants. Because the Spanish and Portuguese took measures to block trade between Persia and England, the English preferred the Moscow route to the Indian Ocean as a new silk route. They envisaged shipping cloth and tin to Persia by this route, in exchange for silk. The English calculated that silk purchases from the shah would amount to three or four million gold pieces for England alone. The English, considering the difficulty of coming up with that much cash inside the kingdom and naturally reluctant to ship it abroad, offered payment in kind. Shah Abbas offered a credit system. Finally, in 1618 he agreed to accept a payment of one-third currency and two-thirds goods. These details show once again Iran's dependence on precious metals coming through the Ottoman territories. It appears that the Ottoman government, too, felt the impact of the

Persian embargo: the grand vizier told the Venetian *bailo* that his country's silk demands could be met by domestic production alone, if necessary. The loss incurred by the Ottoman treasury when the silk and spice route was severed in 1622 is estimated to have been at least 300,000 gold pieces annually in customs duties. The Venetian *bailo* in İstanbul sent a message to the Ottoman government warning that the traffic in silk and other goods along the Syrian silk route might completely cease. The grand vizier noting, in particular, the length of the sea route, did not seem to have shared this concern. In fact, by this time, peace had been signed with Persia (the Peace of Serav in 1618), and great quantities of silk and other goods had begun to arrive at the Aleppo market via the Baghdad route.

It is interesting to note that in the Serav peace treaty the Ottomans, who had lost all their conquests in the Caucasus, accepted an annual delivery of two hundred bales of silk as a tribute from Iran. As soon as peace was concluded, the Venetians announced the good news that a caravan from Baghdad had brought one thousand bales of Iranian raw silk and one thousand boxes of indigo.[131] Nonetheless, some Persian silk was still reaching England via northern Persia and Bandar-Abbas.

At this time the shortsighted policy of the Ottomans in Aleppo of trying to collect new taxes on silk only served to intensify the resolve of those working to establish an alternative silk route. The Venetian representative in London reported in 1622 that three ships had arrived from India, loaded with substantial quantities of Persian silk. Shortly after this a new Ottoman–Persian war erupted. During these years, Anglo-Persian friendship developed considerably, and in 1622 the Persians, with the assistance of English ships, conquered Hormuz from the Portuguese. In 1624 Baghdad, which was at that time an important transit center for Indian commerce in the Near East, fell to the Iranians. A new Iranian diplomatic delegation visited Spain, France, Holland and England (eighty bales of silk were sent along to the last nation). Their purpose was to sign an alliance and commercial agreement in London. In 1626, in response to the shah, Charles I sent a delegation to Persia. The shah promised to deliver 8,000 bales of silk per year to England from Persian ports. Having taken Baghdad, he was holding out the possibility of capturing Aleppo from the Ottomans and transporting the silk via this shorter route. However, the difficulty in finding gold and silver, particularly sought after by the Iranians for the purchase of that much extra silk, the length of the southern route, the hostility of the Portuguese and Spanish, and finally the uncertainty concerning the future of the Levant

Company, left the English in a state of indecision regarding the shah's proposals. The English, and after them the Dutch, were assuming the position formerly held by the Spanish and the Portuguese in the Indian Ocean. Not only were they cooperating with the shah in the Persian Gulf, but, at the same time, they were attacking the pilgrim and commercial traffic leaving India for the Red Sea. This resulted in a decrease in tax revenue in Cairo, which angered the Ottoman government. In 1627, a party of Arabs approached the Ottoman Imperial Council with complaints that the English and Iranians were plundering their ships in the Persian Gulf. The shah's newly established port of Bandar-Abbas (Gombroon) began to expand rapidly as a result of English and Dutch commerce. In 1633, the Venetian ambassador to England reported that English trade in Bandar had greatly increased and that silk brought from there was being shipped to many destinations in Europe.

Now the Portuguese–Spanish, who had lost their supremacy in the Indian Ocean to the British, found themselves in an unusual venture with their old enemies, the Ottomans. They offered to transport spices, silk and other Indian goods via the Gulf and the Red Sea. Recognizing the possibility that this might open the way to an Ottoman–Spanish rapprochement, the English ambassador sent an urgent note to the Ottomans saying that the plan was unfeasible and deceptive, and reminded them of the danger of reopening the Red Sea to the Spanish.

Nevertheless, for the reasons mentioned above, Iranian trade did not completely disappear from Ottoman ports. The long, debilitating struggle between Turkey and Iran, the economic aspects to which we alluded above, was brought to a long-term conclusion. Upon the death of Shah Abbas (1629), his successor abandoned his silk policy. Abbas was compelled to follow a monopoly policy in the silk trade in Iran itself in order to divert raw silk to Bandar-Abbas. Before him the silk, which was gathered by countless private individuals, was shipped to Ottoman markets. According to the Venetian ambassador, the new shah's decision to leave the operation of the silk trade completely to his subjects was very popular at home.

The Ottoman Empire, while able to partially salvage the Iranian silk trade, had almost completely lost the Indian spice traffic by 1630. Baghdad, Aleppo and Cairo were no longer the transit centers for east–west international trade. Venice, which owed its wealth and power to this trade, acknowledged its commercial loss in 1628. The report of the five *Savii*, dated March 31, 1628, put it this way: "In the past the Levant trade was the basic foundation of this [Venice's] market, and this market furnished

Table I:49. Raw silk prices at Bursa, 1467–1646

Year	Composite index of a *lidre* of silk in *akça*	Year	Composite index of a *lidre* of silk in *akça*
1467	50	1578	99
1478	67–68	1580	84
1488	70	1581	136
1494	82	1582	151
1501	60–70	1584	250
1513	77	1588	182
1519	93	1597	224
1521	62	1603	351
1548	59	1607	233
1557	83	1617	174
1566	94	1622	338
1569	68	1630	99
1570	41	1634	240
1571	74	1637	394
1572	81	1639	250
1573	67	1646	199

Source: Bursa court records; Çizakça (1980).

spices to all of Germany, but now the English and Flemish are providing [them]."

Silk prices at Bursa, 1467–1646

Obviously, the price of raw silk at the Bursa market was determined primarily by the volume of supplies from Iran. The Ottoman–Iranian war periods of 1578–90, 1603–12, 1615–18 and 1624–39 created a shortage of supplies and sharp price fluctuations (Tables I:49 and 50).

The unusual shifts in 1603, 1622 and 1637 must have resulted from hostilities on the eastern front. Venetian reports from Aleppo [132] indicated a shortage of supplies because of the war situation. In sum, three periods can be identified, 1470–1580 with an average price of 70 *akça* per *lidre*, that of 1580–97 with 200 *akça* and that of 1597–1639 with 320 *akça* (Table I:51). But the real increase in adjusted prices in view of the inflation in silver *akça* against gold should be interpreted as resulting both from the rapidly growing Western demand and a decrease in imports from Iran.

Taxes

The state treasury received large amounts of revenue from taxation on the raw silk trade. According to a law dated 1570,[133] for every 30 *lidre*

Table I:50. (a) Prices of various kinds of raw silk, 1482–83
(in *akça*)

Bursa market		Kilia market	
Astarabadi	56	Crimson	90–100
Tilani	49	Heft-renk	80
Gilan	44	Black	70–80
		White	70

(b) Prices of raw silk at Bursa during the embargo, 1519 (in *akça*)

Tilani	93–100
Kenar (inferior quality)	49–77
Tisaki	57
Albania	72–80
Tripoli	80

Source: Bursa Court Records.

Table I:51. Average prices and price increases in raw silk, 1557–1639
(per *lidre* in *akça*)

Period	Average price	One gold piece	Real increase in adjusted prices (%)
1557–80	77	60	
1580–1608	201	120	60
1608–39	320	120–250	116–200

Note: One *lidre* equals 100 *dirhem* or 320.7 gr.
Source: based on Çizakça (1980).

or about 9.6 kg of raw silk there was a tax of 104 *akça* shared equally by the seller and buyer. It was computed at the rate of 1.5 or 2 *akça* per *lidre*.[134] In addition, a brokerage tax was levied at the rate of one gold piece (60 *akça*) per load, and also 6 *guruş* (240 *akça*) as *yasakiyye* for one load of raw silk (one load is then accepted as equal to 550 *lidre*).[135] This was altogether about 2,200 *akça*. By 1589 a new tax called *kassabiye*, levied at the rate of one *akça* for every hundred *akça*-worth of raw silk, was added. Since a load of raw silk sold for an average of 38,500 *akça*, the taxation altogether corresponded to about 6.7 percent of the total value by 1589. Before the raw silk arrived at the Ottoman customs, various taxes were levied in the Iranian territory under the Akkoyunlus in the late fifteenth century, amounting to 234 *akça*. A customs duty had to be paid by non-Muslim foreigners. Ottoman subjects, Muslim and non-Muslim, did not pay duty. Around 1500 the rate for non-Muslim foreigners (Italians) was 5 percent *ad valorem*. But because the exemption was misused by the Ottoman Jews and Christian subjects for the exports of foreigners, the sultan ordered them to pay customs duty in 1521.[136]

NOTES

1 Heyd (1936), I, pp. 170–80.
2 Roover (1950), p. 2907.
3 Lopez (1952b), pp. 346–54.
4 Lopez (1952a), p. 76; cf. Bautier (1970), pp. 289–91.
5 Lopez (1952a), p. 74; Bautier (1970), p. 291.
6 Bautier (1970), p. 291.
7 Lopez (1952a), p. 73.
8 Clavijo (1943), p. 112.
9 İstahri (1969), pp. 202–4.
10 Bautier (1970), pp. 280–92.
11 Heyd (1936), II, pp. 74–92; Bautier (1970), pp. 280–86.
12 Erdmann (1961).
13 Pegolotti (1936), index: *Turchia, Loluogo, Setalia, Laiazo, Palattia*; Turan (1958); Cahen (1951), pp. 317–25; Heyd (1936), I, pp. 534–54.
14 Bautier (1970), p. 285; Ashtor (1983), pp. 3–102.
15 Bautier (1970), p. 287.
16 Heyd (1936), II, pp. 189, 377.
17 Māzandarāni (1952), pp. 58–59.
18 Barbaro (1873), p. 31; Tafur (1926), p. 134.
19 İnalcık (1979–80), p. 464.
20 Schiltberger (1879), p. 34.
21 İnalcık (1969a), p. 212; Zachariadou (1983), p. 169 note 717.
22 Foss (1979), pp. 146–47.
23 İnalcık (1981a), document nos. 18, 21, 22, 27, 35, 36, 53, 103, 109, 113, 114, 131, 164, 172; İnalcık (1988b), no. 100.
24 Heyd (1936), p. 259.
25 La Brocquière (1892), pp. 86–87, 102.
26 Heyd (1936), II, pp. 278–85.
27 İnalcık (1991a), pp. 57–60.
28 Heers (1961), p. 54.
29 Balard (1978), II, pp. 533–98, 852–62.
30 İnalcık (1960a), p. 53.
31 Dalsar (1960), p. 274; İnalcık (1960a), document no. 32.
32 Richards (1932), p. 118.
33 İnalcık (1967), p. 216.
34 İnalcık (1979a), pp. 74–110.
35 Sadeddin (1863), II, p. 276.
36 Feridun (1858), I, p. 425.
37 Sadeddin (1863), II, p. 275.
38 Dalsar (1960), pp. 200–13.
39 *Ibid.*, document no. 273.

40 *Ibid.*, document no. 83.
41 Heyd (1936), II, p. 507.
42 Contarini (1873), p. 151.
43 Steensgaard (1972), p. 368.
44 Dalsar (1960), p. 272.
45 Heyd (1936), II, p. 296; around 1420 Venice used to purchase yearly as many as 48,000 pieces of cloth, largely to export to the Levant, Luzzatto cited by Sella (1968), p. 111.
46 La Brocquière (1892), p. 82.
47 İnalcık (1991a), pp. 60–66.
48 Kritovoulos (1954), pp. 219–21.
49 İnalcık (1991a), p. 62.
50 *Ibid.*, pp. 63–66.
51 Richards (1932), p. 215.
52 *Ibid.*, pp. 46, 154, in August 1501 cholera broke out and the plague caused 25,000 deaths, gravely affecting the Florentine business in Turkey.
53 For the economic decline of Florence see Luzzatto (1954), p. 101.
54 Sella (1968), p. 111.
55 *Ibid.*, pp. 109, 112, 115.
56 Richards (1932), p. 147.
57 Sella (1968), p. 112.
58 *Ibid.*, p. 114.
59 *Ibid.*, p. 115.
60 Richards (1932), p. 147.
61 *Ibid.*, p. 182.
62 *Ibid.*, pp. 99, 143.
63 *Ibid.*, p. 171.
64 *Ibid.*, p. 155.
65 *Ibid.*, pp. 152–53.
66 Hoshino (1984), p. 984.
67 For Maringhi's inventory, see Richards (1932), pp. 185–201.
68 *Ibid.*, p. 172.
69 Richards (1932), p. 167.
70 *Ibid.*, p. 184.
71 *Ibid.*, p. 55.
72 *Ibid.*, pp. 227–28.
73 İnalcık (1960e), document no. 1.
74 *Ibid.*, document no. 29.
75 *Ibid.*, document nos. 37, 41.
76 Richards (1932), p. 44.
77 *Ibid.*, p. 45.
78 Richards (1932), pp. 102, 104, 112, 169, 262.
79 Hoshino (1984).
80 Māzandarāni (1952), pp. 99b, 133b.
81 Richards (1932), p. 81.
82 *Ibid.*, p. 110.
83 *Ibid.*, pp. 85, 120.
84 *Ibid.*, p. 146.

85 *Ibid.*, pp. 67, 158, 163.
86 *Ibid.*, pp. 105, 130, 140, 158, 263.
87 Hoshino (1984), pp. 48, 52.
88 *Ibid.*, p. 51.
89 İnalcık (1960b), pp. 131–39.
90 Richards (1932), pp. 82, 108.
91 *Ibid.*, p. 117.
92 *Ibid.*, p. 168.
93 *Ibid.*, p. 127; İnalcık (1953a), pp. 51–57.
94 Richards (1932), pp. 131, 161.
95 *Ibid.*, pp. 68, 83, 71, 75, 77.
96 *Ibid.*, p. 226.
97 *Ibid.*, pp. 61, 78, 104, 138.
98 *Ibid.*, pp. 99, 168.
99 *Ibid.*, p. 135.
100 *Ibid.*, pp. 138, 153.
101 Hoshino (1984), p. 47.
102 Richards (1932), pp. 24, 70, 150–51.
103 Hoshino (1984), p. 46.
104 Richards (1932), pp. 56, 97.
105 *Ibid.*, p. 104.
106 *Ibid.*, p. 163.
107 İnalcık (1973a), p. 36.
108 İnalcık (1989), p. 337.
109 Braudel (1972), I, p. 557.
110 Stoianovich (1960), p. 236.
111 Documents cited by Stoianovich (1960), p. 237.
112 Sanuto (1893), pp. 406–7; Ashtor (1983), pp. 213–53.
113 İnalcık (1969d), pp. 121–26.
114 Boulnois (1963), p. 218.
115 A. Millar cited by Davis (1970), p. 196.
116 Steensgaard (1972), p. 375.
117 Davis (1970), p. 196.
118 Steensgaard (1972), p. 367.
119 Cited by Steensgaard (1972), p. 191.
120 Steensgaard (1972), p. 162. However, he concluded that it could be half the estimate; actually estimates vary between 4,000 and 7,500 bales a year. One bale weighed, Steensgaard states, 280 lb or 90 kg; a horseload consisted of two bales weighing 550 lb, or 165 kg, cf. Dalsar (1960), p. 289; İnalcık (1984), pp. 132–35.
121 Consul Emo's estimate in Steensgaard (1972), p. 160.
122 Steensgaard (1972), pp. 175–83.
123 *Ibid.*, p. 178.
124 Goffman (1982), pp. 50–76.
125 McGowan (1981), p. 21.
126 Masson (1896), I, p. 421.
127 McGowan (1981), p. 281.
128 Tavernier cited by Steensgaard (1972), p. 186, cf. Goffman (1982), pp. 51–66.

129 Transport costs by camel amounted to 40 *guruş*, or about 26 gold ducats; when various dues paid en route are added, the costs rose to 122 *guruş*; the customs duty at İzmir was 46 *guruş*; one *guruş*, equaled two-thirds of one gold ducat, cf. Steensgaard (1972), p. 34.

130 Steensgaard (1972), pp. 323–33.

131 *CSP*: Venice XII, document no. 352.

132 Steensgaard (1972), pp. 161, 175–84.

133 Dalsar (1960), p. 271 document no. 201.

134 Anhegger and İnalcık (1956), nos. 31, 32.

135 Dalsar (1960), p. 289.

136 *Ibid.*, p. 271 document no. 202.

11

☾

DUBROVNIK AND THE BALKANS

DUBROVNIK

The Balkans became the backbone of the Ottoman Empire not only politically in the wake of Timur's blow in 1402, but also as the main source of supply for foodstuffs and raw materials to the Ottoman capitals of Edirne and İstanbul in the fifteenth and sixteenth centuries. In the northern Balkans the Danubian ports of Smederevo, Vidin, Nicopolis, Silistre, Rusçuk and Kilia were linked to Edirne and İstanbul and grew into important transit centers in the trade of Moldavia, Poland, Transylvania and Hungary. In the western Balkans, Dubrovnik (Ragusa), Avlona (Vlorë), Ston (Stagno), and Nova (Hercegnovi) experienced unprecedented growth. Also, in the hinterlands, the towns along the caravan routes between Edirne and the Danubian and Adriatic ports developed into prosperous centers of trade[1] (Table I:52). In this picture of general development, Dubrovnik played a crucial role as a transit point for Balkan trade with Italy in the period 1400–1600.

From the thirteenth century, Italy, in the midst of a full economic expansion, depended on silver from the Bosnian and Serbian mines, imported via Dubrovnik. There was a Ragusan colony in Ancona and a Florentine colony in Dubrovnik as early as 1290. Thus, the tiny mercantile republic owed its initial development to its role as the main outlet for the silver trade, which then proved to be important for the European economy as a whole.[2] In addition, a caravan route started from Dubrovnik and crossed the Balkans already at the turn of the fourteenth century. Ragusan merchant colonies also settled in the major Balkan cities exporting leather, fats, wool, cheese, fish, honey, beeswax, furs, and slaves and importing from Italy woolen cloth and other textiles. Inexpensive *panni de Londra* are mentioned as early as 1441 in Dubrovnik,[3]

Table 1:52. Population of the principal cities in Anatolia and the Balkans, 1520–30 (households)

	Muslims	Christians	Jews	Total
İstanbul	9,517	5,162	1,647	16,326 (in 1478)
Bursa	6,165	69	117	6,351
Andrianople (Edirne)	3,338	522	201	4,061
Angora	2,399	277	28	2,704
Athens	11	2,286		2,297
Tokat	818	701		1,519
Konya	1,092	22		1,114
Sivas	261	750		1,011
Sarajevo	1,024	-		1,024
Monastır	640	171	34	845
Skopje	630	200	12	842
Sofia	471	238		709
Salonica	1,229	989	2,645	4,863
Seres	671	357	65	1,093
Triccala	301	343	181	825
Larissa	693	75		768
Nicopolis	468	775		1,243

Note: Non-taxable population is not included.
Source: Barkan (1957), p. 35.

while Ragusan merchants were active in the Levant trade importing pepper.[4] It was as a result of this intense commercial activity with Italy that Italian gold and silver coins, ducats and *grossi* replaced the Byzantine *perperi* in Dubrovnik and the rest of the Balkans in this period.

It was first in the western Anatolian ports belonging to the Turcoman Aydın principality that Dubrovnik came in contact with the Turks. Big Ragusan ships by the mid-fourteenth century visited these ports to carry bulky goods, such as grain. Their relations with the Ottoman Turks apparently started as soon as the Ottomans began to invade the eastern Balkans where Ragusans were already active under the trade privileges granted by the Bulgarian Czars.

Under the Ottomans, the Ragusan trade pattern did not change essentially as far as the export of foodstuffs and raw materials to the then highly industrialized Italy was concerned. The important change, however, came about when the Ottomans implemented a strict prohibition of silver export to Italy.

Dubrovnik is integrated into the Ottoman economy

Dubrovnik's recognition of Ottoman suzerainty is typical of the experience of other Balkan states. In the period 1386–91, powerful Ottoman frontier begs conquered and settled upper Macedonia with Üsküp (Skopje) as their base and in northern Albania at Croia (Krüye), which were Dubrovnik's immediate areas of activity.[5] In its conflicts with Serbian and Bosnian rulers or with the Venetians, Dubrovnik found support from the Ottoman frontier begs. The city's government sent envoys to Kavala (Kephalia) Şahin, the Ottoman beg in Albania, when he attacked Bosnia in 1386. Later, Paşayiğit of Üsküp made an agreement with them and encouraged trade through reduced customs rates. Albanian wheat and trade interests in Macedonia were of vital importance to the republic. In 1413–21, a period of prosperity began for Dubrovnik when the Ottomans favored Ragusan merchants in the trade of Western products and Serbian silver.[6]

Dubrovnik's export of silver became one of the most important issues between Italy, Hungary and the Ottomans from the 1380s. First, Murad I forced the Serbian Prince Lazare to deliver a certain amount of silver as an annual tribute in 1386.[7] In the first half of the fifteenth century, Srebreniča's annual silver production reached 5 tons and Novobrdo's 9 tons.[8] In 1436 the Ottoman sultan had prevented the Serbs from exporting the silver produced at Trepča to Ragusa, requiring them to bring it to his own mint instead.[9] Mehmed the Conqueror's first campaign after the conquest of Constantinople aimed at establishing his full control over the silver-producing areas in upper Serbia, and the principal mining area at Novobrdo in particular.

In the period of the consolidation of Ottoman rule in Albania and Epirus following the conquest of Salonica from the Venetians in 1430, Dubrovnik became increasingly dependent for its trade, as well as in regional politics, on the Ottomans. In 1433 in its conflict with the Bosnian king over the Konavli valley, Dubrovnik asked for Ottoman support, which became the occasion for the city's official recognition of the sultan's suzerainty. The Ragusan embassy then promised to pay a yearly tribute of 500 ducats to the sultan, and a charter was granted by Murad II permitting Ragusan merchants freedom of trade all over his dominions and guarantees of peace and protection for their city. Thus, through this document, an existing relationship was extended and formalized. Starting from the 1440s, Ragusan merchants served the Ottoman government as tax-farmers of customs and mines not only in Bosnia and other adjacent lands but also in Bulgaria.[10] The capital which they accumulated through trade thus found a means of investment in Ottoman mining industries and finance. Summarizing the economic consequences of the unification of the Balkan lands under the Ottoman Empire, Constantin Jireček says:

"The commerce of Ragusa took an unequivocal upswing . . . [and] due to the Turkish conquest, the many existing borders and customs of the numerous small states were eliminated. In the region a powerful and unified empire with low tariffs was formed." Now the routes, Jireček notes,[11] were safer and Ragusan merchants extended their activities as far as the Black Sea.

As realistic businessmen, Dubrovnik merchants remained loyal to the Ottomans in order to guarantee their trade in the Balkans and to have protection against their ambitious neighbors, the Bosnian rulers. In 1441, with the renewal of the Ottoman charter, freedom of trade was guaranteed with various immunities.

Since 1358 Dubrovnik had been under Hungarian suzerainty, and the Hungarian kings wanted the Ragusans always to remember this, even when the state of affairs forced the republic to recognize, at the same time, Ottoman overlordship. Caught in a difficult position between Hungary, which was pressing with the Papacy for the republic to join their crusading activities, and Mehmed the Conqueror, who threatened to arrest Ragusan merchants in his empire and attack the city, Dubrovnik finally decided to renew its allegiance to the sultan in 1458. In return for paying a token amount of 1,500 ducats as yearly tribute, it obtained a sworn charter which included all previously granted privileges and immunities. Interestingly enough, the Ragusans then asked the sultan to send orders to his vassal states of Bosnia and Serbia allowing Ragusan merchants to enjoy free passage and trade in their territories.

This submission was the beginning of a new era for the merchant republic, which had become fully integrated into the economy of the empire.[12] Before long the Conqueror annexed Serbia (1459) and Bosnia (1463) to his empire. Then, in 1467, following territorial extensions, the sultan asked for an increase in the Ragusan tribute to 5,000 ducats (Dubrovnik was paying before the Ottomans a tribute of 2,500 *perperi* or about 1,250 ducats to the king of Bosnia). The Ragusans were earning 25,000 ducats annually from the export to Bosnia and Herzegovina of their salt. The higher tribute "was amply compensated by the commercial benefits" to Dubrovnik.[13] In fact, Dubrovnik was in a privileged position under Ottoman protection, and paid a reduced rate of customs duty. Also under Ottoman protection, Venice, the uncompromising enemy of the city, was neutralized.

Although, according to the Islamic Hanafite school of law, Ragusans were not supposed to be the sultan's *reaya*, or subjects under the direct rule of the sultan, they were still called and treated as such.[14] Dubrovnik's autonomy was guaranteed and respected through a specific type of charter given by the sultan under oath.[15] It maintained its own government without any interference; it appointed consuls in Ottoman territory and foreign countries, received envoys and established diplomatic relations with them, and minted its own coinage (dinars or *grossi*). The sultan guaranteed full protection for Dubrovnik as an integral part of the empire against enemies from outside and his own officials' abuses. Foreign countries recognized the sultan's sovereignty and the protection of the republic.

Since the republic enjoyed full autonomy, no Muslim officer was allowed to enter the city. However, two Ottoman officers had residences there and represented the Ottoman governors of Bosnia and Herzegovina in levying the specific dues.[16]

As far as customs dues were concerned, Ottoman policy was in general favorable towards Ragusa to encourage its trade, particularly in its imports of woolen cloth. According to the general regulations, non-Muslim Ottoman subjects were to pay more than Muslims and less than foreign non-Muslims. But occasionally the Ottomans asked the Ragusans to pay them a higher rate of 5 percent, as was applied to foreigners, on the assumption that Ragusans imported goods belonging to foreigners. From time to time the sultan had to issue orders to protect Ragusan merchants from various extra dues that the local authorities attempted to extract.[17] In 1472, against the extortions of the local authorities, the sultan issued a general order to the judges in Rumeli saying that, as tribute-paying subjects, the Ragusans should be protected as other non-Muslim Ottoman subjects. Violations against the order were to be punished by capital punishment. Then, the sultan's increase in the customs due to 5 percent, and his attempt to control all of the imports and exports of the republic at the new nearby customs station of Ledeniće, led to a crisis.[18] Upon the promise of payment of an additional 2,500 ducats the sultan gave up the customs at Ledeniće (Table I:53).

Although during the period 1440–70 Dubrovnik lost its highly lucrative trade to the West in silver exports from Bosnian and Serbian mines, the city compensated its loss by extending its trade throughout the Balkans under Ottoman protection and gained a monopoly in the export of such bulky goods as hides, leather, wool and wax to Italy. For Dubrovnik, "the tribute the city paid for these advantages proved a most profitable investment."[19]

The special privileges and low-rate customs dues for the Ragusans resulted in the growth of Ragusan trade and gave them almost a monopoly in the face of their Italian competitors in the Balkan trade.[20]

Table I:53. Ragusan tribute

Year	Tribute (in ducats)	Customs duty (percent *ad valorem*)
1458	1,500	2
1468	5,000	—
1471	9,000	—
1472	10,000	—
1476	10,000	5
1478	12,500	4
1480	15,000	2
1481	12,500	2
1510	12,500	2
1525	12,500	5 at İstanbul 3 at Bursa and Edirne 2 in Rumeli

Source: Bojić (1952), pp. 188–205, 222.

In 1510 they benefited from the lowest customs rate of 2 percent, while Muslims still had to pay 3 and foreigners 5 percent. However, in İstanbul and at Aegean ports, Ragusans could not compete with Venetians for the simple reason that the latter reached these ports by sea and transportation costs for bulky goods were much lower than for the caravan route.

Under Mehmed II, problems arising from Ottoman infringement upon the outlying territory of the republic or upon the salt trade caused long disputes with the Ottoman authorities. Bayezid II, being more favorable to Dubrovnik, returned some territories occupied under his predecessor.[21] Because of the Ottoman monopoly on salt, which was applied everywhere as an important source of revenue, the Porte tried to impose restrictions upon the sale of Dubrovnik's salt to protect the production of Nova. Since the salt trade was also an important source of revenue for Dubrovnik, the dispute dragged on for a long time until an agreement was reached in 1485. Perhaps the most effective means which the Ragusans could use against the abuses of the local officials, or for obtaining favors from the sultan, was the threat of abandoning trade in the Ottoman lands. Such a move would have directly affected Ottoman finances.

The sultan's charter was not always respected by Ottoman privateers (*levend*) who were based in Nova and Avlona and attacked Ragusan ships from time to time. The sultan sent orders to return the men and property which they captured, which was obviously an unsatisfactory solution. In the upper Adriatic, the Uskoks were the Christian counterpart of the Ottoman privateers. Uskok attacks seriously threatened traffic on the Adriatic, particularly in the seventeenth century.[22]

Table I:54. Annual customs revenue for the port of Dubrovnik (in gold ducats)

Year	Revenue	
1535–37	17,000	
1538–41	52,000	Ottoman–Venetian War
1552–55	19,700	
1560–69	26,000	
1570–72	106,000	Ottoman–Venetian War
1576–80	28,000	
1591–1600	23,000	

Source: Krekić (1972).

The development of Balkan trade in the sixteenth century

There is a consensus that it was in the sixteenth century that the Balkans witnessed an unprecedented economic development and this was also the period of the greatest economic activity for Dubrovnik (Table I:54).

Since Dubrovnik was used as a neutral transit center during the Ottoman–Venetian Wars, the great increases in the periods 1538–41 and 1570–72 should be considered unusual: an average revenue of 23,000 gold ducats should be taken as normal. On the basis of such customs revenues, Tadić calculated[23] that the total volume of annual imports and exports through Dubrovnik amounted to between 400,000 and 500,000 gold ducats, of which a quarter was imports from the Ottoman lands. But in 1571, the year of the Ottoman invasion of Cyprus, imports from the west soared to 2,500,000 gold ducats, and exports from Ottoman dominions came to about 230,000 gold ducats. The actual figures must be higher since the merchants invested part of their profits in Italian banks to avoid paying duty in Dubrovnik: at the turn of the century the money thus invested amounted to 700,000 ducats.

Dubrovnik continued to be a vital link for traffic between the Ottoman dominions and Italy. Ragusan merchants, like many Ottoman merchants, avoided Venice and concentrated their activities at Ancona, which became a rival of Venice in the Ottoman cloth trade with Europe. Anconian and Florentine merchants chose the caravan route beginning at Dubrovnik for their travel to Edirne and İstanbul. The bulk of imports by the Balkans consisted largely of woolen cloth, which Ragusan merchants bought at Venice and Ancona (Table I:55).

Out of this total, 870 pieces went to İstanbul, 587 to Adrianople, and 213 to Rhodes. Kersey, the cheapest variety of imported woolen cloth, was distributed in far greater amounts in Balkan towns and villages,

Table I:55. Varieties of woolen cloth
imported by Dubrovnik for Ottoman
dominions, 1531

Variety of cloth	Pieces
Kersey	26,404
Londra	643
Carcassoni	297
Sopramani	2,272
Largi of Florence	21
Ragusan	975
Scarlatti	87
Veronesi	78
Bresciani	16
Paduani	19
Cloth of Perpignan	4
Others	301
Total	31,117

Source: Archives of Dubrovnik, cited by Tadić
(1961), p. 249 note 1.

in particular in Serbia and Bulgaria, while the most expensive varieties, *sopramani*, *largi* of Florence and *scarlatti*, were destined for major Ottoman cities. It must be added that Jews, Greeks, and Bosnian and Turkish Muslims became quite active in the woolen cloth trade in the sixteenth century. Jews who settled in Dubrovnik at this time took over the greater part of the woolen cloth transit trade there before they moved to Split and Venice in the late sixteenth century. As a result of the growing importance of this cloth trade in the Balkans, Dubrovnik itself had doubled its own cloth industries since 1420.[24] The city's transit trade in woolen cloth, nevertheless, declined when "new" ports on the Adriatic coast began to attract Bosnian and Jewish merchants. The trade activity of these new Ottoman and Venetian ports increased then, especially after the opening of Split in 1590.

In order to compensate for its loss in transit trade, the republic increased its carrying trade. By developing its merchant fleet from the mid-sixteenth century, Dubrovnik became one of the leading merchant marine powers in the world by 1580. The tonnage of the Ragusan merchant marine went up from 20,000 *carri* in 1530 to 35,000 in the 1560s (one *carro* equals 20 hectoliters of wheat), with a total value of 700,000 gold ducats.[25] We learn that by 1580, "Dubrovnik had the third largest fleet of big ocean-going vessels" in the world.[26]

Next to salt, the most important export items from the Balkans which passed through Dubrovnik were animal skins, either raw or processed.

Buffalo and ox hides came from Serbia. Sheepskins and wool were exported by Ragusan merchants in great quantities from an area in the eastern Balkans stretching from Thrace to Dobruja, a region settled by the Yörüks, Turcoman pastoralists from Anatolia. Varna and Tekirdağ (Rodosto) were the principal ports for the export of these goods.[27] In the interior, raw skins were sent to towns like Filibe, Sofia, Silistre and Rusçuk, where they were treated and stored for export. Leather industries flourished in Edirne and in Bulgarian towns, and fine colored cordovan was a speciality item included in exports to Italy. Ragusan merchants purchased the wheat of western Anatolia at the ports of Foça, İzmir, Ephesus and Palatia and carried this not only to their home port of Dubrovnik but also to İstanbul. Volos and Patras were other ports from which Ragusan ships regularly loaded wheat.[28]

When the Ottomans supported Venice's rivals, Dubrovnik and Ancona, and actively protected Ottoman subjects – Bosnians and Jews – the Republic of Saint Mark failed to maintain its full control in the Adriatic. It appears that with their naval base at Avlona, the Ottomans challenged Venetian naval and commercial supremacy on that sea in the sixteenth century.

Being an integral part of the Ottoman imperial system on the one hand and having close relations with Italy, Spain and England on the other, Dubrovnik played a vital role as middleman between the empire and Europe. In addition to its critical economic role for the Balkans, the republic of Dubrovnik became, like Galata, a window on Europe for the Ottoman Empire. It was the principal center of intelligence for the Ottomans on European political developments and on anti-Ottoman plans. It was also through Dubrovnik that some vital Western technologies were transferred to the Ottomans. Gun making, the most important of all in this respect, was introduced into the Balkans through Dubrovnik first in the 1390s, and the technology was subsequently borrowed by the Ottomans as early as the last decade of the fourteenth century.[29] Moreover, on several occasions during the sixteenth century, Ragusan shipbuilding experts were called to the Ottoman dockyards in Avlona and Gallipoli.[30] Ragusans were known as "the best and perhaps the most ingenious" specialists in ship building. Finally, all the novel business practices then found in Italy, such as the *collegantia* type of company, bills of exchange and the various banking procedures, were adopted by Ragusan merchants.[31] We do not know whether such practices were adopted by Ottoman subjects. Ottomans had allowed business disputes between Ragusan merchants to be settled by the Ragusan authorities, but cases involving an Ottoman subject and a Ragusan had to be referred to an Ottoman kadi. Particularly important cases were referred to the imperial council in İstanbul.

THE RISE OF BOSNIA

Albania and Bosnia-Herzegovina in particular benefited, like Dubrovnik, from the growing traffic between Italy and the western Balkans during the sixteenth century. The Albanian port city of Avlona rose to importance as a naval base and a transit center in the period. Albania supplied Dubrovnik with wheat and salt; salt imported from Albania was then exported to Bosnia and Serbia. The spectacular rise of Sarajevo is the most important development in the region in the sixteenth century as a whole.

It was in 1429, under the pressure of the frontier beg, İshak, that the Bosnian king Tvrtko II recognized Ottoman suzerainty, and Turks soon settled the plain of Hodidjed or Saray-Ovası. A small town in 1462, Sarajevo grew to become the capital of the Ottoman sub-province of Bosnia when the kingdom of Bosnia was conquered in 1463. From a military outpost on the frontier, Sarajevo's importance increased in the period 1520–40, when Ottoman control expanded towards the Adriatic. With further conquests toward the Adriatic Sea, the Ottomans finally created the *beglerbegilik* of Bosnia which included Bosnia and Herzegovina, as well as parts of Slavonia and Dalmatia (1580); then Banjaluka, a city closer to the Venetian Dalmatia, was made the capital city of the new province.

By this time Sarajevo had become the main commercial center of all the western Balkans with a population estimated at 40,000. Its transit trade flourished, since it was the principal terminus of the busy caravan route linking Bursa, İstanbul and Edirne with the Adriatic ports. The burgeoning trade along this route through the Balkans had also led to the rise of Foça and Novibazar as important trading links between the emporium of Sarajevo and the East. Merchants from Belgrade, Sofia, Üsküb and other centers in the hinterland now frequented Sarajevo.[32] This commercial expansion gave rise in the city to a native burgher class of various religions. The construction of the two *bedestan*s to warehouse luxury goods from the East is the most significant sign of Sarajevo's economic importance.[33] Since 1500 the merchants of Bosnia, mostly from Sarajevo, Goražda and Olovo, competed successfully with the Ragusans not only in the trade of oriental goods, but also in the export trade from the Balkans. The efforts of the Ottoman frontier begs in the fifteenth century and the Ottoman policy of favoring Ottoman subjects, without a doubt played a major role in this spectacular development. Prior to Ottoman rule, Bosnian merchants were systematically barred by Dubrovnik from participating in the transit trade;[34] but the Ottoman government actively protected Bosnian and Turkish merchants in the Adriatic trade, and they further ventured to settle in Ancona and Venice. Already, the Grand Vizier Rüstem (1544–53) intervened on behalf of Muslim merchants in Venice.[35] They had finally succeeded in having their own magnificent *fondaco dei Turchi* in Venice by 1621.[36]

Following the conclusion of peace in 1573, Ottoman–Venetian trade through the Dalmatian ports experienced significant growth, and Bosnian Muslim merchants were particularly active in this trade. In the previous period, commerce in the Dalmatian ports, including Zadar (Zara), Šibenik (Sbenico) and Split (Spalato), was insignificant; trade was limited to some export to Venice of local products, principally figs, hides, fish, wines and horses.[37] But during the last two decades of the century, traffic in these ports witnessed brisk development. In 1590, with Ottoman cooperation, Venice made Split a major transit port for its trade with Ottoman lands.[38] Its connection with this port further enhanced Sarajevo's commercial importance and proved to be a blow to Dubrovnik's Balkan trade.

The example of the Bosnian merchant Hoca Tahsin illustrates the importance of business in which Bosnian merchants were engaged at this time.[39] In 1591 Tahsin went to *Frengistan* (Venice or Ancona) with a huge amount of capital, 2 million *akça* (or 16,000 gold ducats), to buy woolen cloth. On his way back he died at Dubrovnik, leaving behind 138 bolts of woolen cloth, including expensive *scarlatti*.

Bosnian merchants appeared as competitors of the Ragusans in the internal Balkan trade also. By the end of the sixteenth century, they had replaced the Ragusans in Serbia in such trade centers as Belgrade, Prokuplje and Novibazar.[40] In the mid-seventeenth century Sarajevo almost completely replaced Dubrovnik in the export of skins and wax.

JEWS IN THE ADRIATIC SEA

Under the protection of the Ottoman government, Jews promoted their trade in Venice throughout the sixteenth century.[41] Ottoman-protected Sephardic Jews settled in the Adriatic ports during this period, 1492–1520, and emerged as the most active partners and rivals of Dubrovnik in the Adriatic trade. Avlona was one of the important port cities where

Jews, expelled from Spain in 1492, from Portugal in 1497 and from Italy in 1510–11, were settled by the Ottoman government. Earlier the Jewish population of the city had been deported, along with Jews from other Balkan towns, to İstanbul by Mehmet II in 1454 and 1455. Under Bayezid II the Sephardic Jews from Spain were welcomed into the Ottoman territories and settled by the government in the towns and ports such as Salonica and Avlona with the purpose of enhancing further the economic prosperity of the place. They constituted one-third of the population of Avlona, with 527 households by 1520.[42] Jewish immigrants included not only Sephardic Jews expelled from the Iberian peninsula but also Jews settled in southern Italy, making the port of Avlona the third city of the empire after Salonica and İstanbul, in terms of Jewish residents. Among the three communities of the city of Avlona, the Jews appear to have had a dominant position over Christians and had a "great freedom of action" as the court records demonstrate.[43]

Since the time of Mehmet II, the Ottoman government had taken measures to make this port a naval base to challenge Venetian supremacy on the Adriatic Sea, and used it also in its plans to invade Apulia.[44] As was true with other frontier towns, such as Skopje, Sofia, Smederevo and Sarajevo, Avlona developed from a military base into a major commercial city. The Jews of Avlona were principally engaged in long-distance trade. They dominated the city's trade with Venice as attested by Venetian insurance documents. In the register of insurance covering the years 1592–1609, there were sixteen Jews of Avlona resident in Venice.[45] Being the principal trade partners of the merchants of Avlona, Dubrovnik and Venice maintained their consuls at Avlona. Ancona and Apulia were also important trade zones for the merchants of this port. In the sea traffic, ships belonging to Muslims and non-Muslims of Avlona were employed, as attested again in the court records.

By the 1580s, the port competed with Dubrovnik and had established traffic with İstanbul, Bursa and the Danubian basin, as well as close connections with Dubrovnik, Venice, Ancona and Florence. The principal exports from the port included wheat and skins and hides, destined for Dubrovnik and Venice. Also exported to Venice and Galata was pitch, which gave rise to an important export trade through Avlona, as pitch was an indispensable material in ship building. The pitch was produced in the surrounding areas and stored in a public storehouse. Its trade was controlled by state monopoly.[46] Jewish merchants bought silk cocoons for export, which were bred in large quantities in the villages around Avlona.[47] As in other Ottoman commercial centers, in Avlona also there were many Jews who specialized in the textile trade.[48] They too held a dominant position in credit operations: among their debtors were merchants, shopkeepers, villagers, mostly Ottoman Christian and Jewish subjects, and an occasional Muslim.

Avlona's role in the Adriatic trade declined in favor of new ports closer to Venice. Many Jews moved to Dubrovnik during the Ottoman–Venetian war of 1570–73, when woolen cloth imports from Venice shifted to this neutral port. Meanwhile, the Ottomans deported and settled a great number of Sephardic Jews in Nova (Hercegnovi) when it was reconquered in 1570.[49] Many Ottoman Jews, chiefly those engaged in the cloth trade, settled in Venice or moved to Split (Spalato) in the last decades of the sixteenth century. The massive Jewish emigrations from Avlona to northern Adriatic ports appears to have started in the 1530s and became precipitous after 1573; 212 Jews were found in the Ottoman tax registers of 1583, but only 50 in the same registers in 1597.[50]

On the heels of the Ottoman–Venetian peace of 1573, an enterprising Jewish merchant, Daniel Rodriguez, proposed developing Split into a free port by improving its facilities and abolishing or reducing customs dues.[51] Venice was hesitant; then Ottoman Jews approached Dubrovnik and obtained a privileged tariff for a time. In the end, with the support of Ottoman Jews residing in Venice and the active involvement of the pasha of Bosnia, the Venetian Senate finally decided to go ahead with Rodriguez's plan. On June 20, 1590, it was decided that Split would become a free port, that customs dues on the imports from Ottoman dominions through Split to Venice would be reduced by half, and that dues on the export of soap, rice and some other goods would be totally abolished. Ottoman Jews who arrived in Venice would not be subject to any resident tax and could settle in the old Jewish quarter. Rodriguez's plan can be seen as part of the Jewish attempt to organize an international trading complex under Ottoman auspices.[52] Venetian–Ottoman trade based mainly on the export of wax, moroccos, timber, silk, mohair and hides from the Ottoman lands rapidly flourished. From 1590 onward Split, superseding Dubrovnik and Avlona in Ottoman trade with Venice, assumed "a very important role" in the overall Venetian commerce.[53]

At the turn of the seventeenth century a more serious challenge to Venetian control of the Adriatic appeared when the superior English, Dutch and French ships forced their way into the sea to trade at Fiume and Trieste, then under the Habsburgs. The French were already competing in the purchase of wheat at Cattaro and in Albania, thus threatening the wheat supplies of Venice.

After receiving full capitulation rights, from the 1580s English kerseys were imported directly by English merchants. In 1621 the Venetian senate forbade the purchase of Western cloth by Ragusans at Venice.[54]

NOTES

1 On the development of the Balkan cities, see Todorov (1983); Kiel (1985), pp. 273–349; Mehlan (1938).
2 Krekić (1972), p. 251.
3 Jireček (1899), p. 147.
4 Krekić (1961).
5 Bojić (1952), pp. 1–61.
6 *Ibid.*, p. 29.
7 Neschri (1951), p. 58.
8 Krekić (1972), p. 251.
9 Jireček (1879), p. 58.
10 Bojić (1952), pp. 315–23.
11 Jireček (1899), p. 159, cf. Bojić (1952), pp. 231–32.
12 The sustaining of parity already in the period 1391–1410 between the Ottoman silver coin *akça* and the Ragusan *gross* can be interpreted as another indication of economic dependence.

The value of one Venetian gold ducat in terms of Ottoman and Ragusan silver coins

Years	Ottoman *akça*	Ragusan *gross*
1351–60		24–26
1391–1400	30	30 (1388)
1411–20	30–36	35–36 (1431)
1431–40	36–42	39–40 (1444)
1461–70	39–41	42–43 (1460)

Source: Krekić (1972), p. 253.

13 Heyd (1936), II, p. 294; Krekić (1972), pp. 24, 62, 169.
14 Biegman (1967), pp. 33–36.
15 İnalcık (1991a), pp. 17–31, the text in *TV*, XII.
16 Evliya Çelebi (1896–1938), VI, pp. 448–49.
17 Bojić (1952), pp. 265–71.
18 *Ibid.*, p. 200.
19 Carter (1972), p. 196.
20 *Ibid.*, pp. 223–46.
21 *Ibid.*, pp. 206–17, 247–71.
22 For the Uskok depredations in the first half of the sixteenth century, see Gökbilgin (1964), pp. 1–2, 6–7, document no. 83; on the Uskoks in the second half of the same century see Tenenti (1967), Ch. 1.
23 Tadić (1961), p. 252.
24 Krekić (1972), p. 56.

25 Tadić (1958), pp. 14–17.
26 Mirković cited by Carter (1972), p. 392.
27 Carter (1972), pp. 361–62.
28 *Ibid.*, p. 371.
29 Petrović (1975), p. 169.
30 Tadić (1958), p. 13.
31 Krekić (1972), p. 51.
32 Tadić (1961), p. 257.
33 İnalcık (1980d), p. 9.
34 Carter (1972), p. 356.
35 Gökblgin (1964), I, p. 2 document no. 33; in 1546, a Turkish merchant of Bursa by the name of Ağabey oversaw the shipment to Venice of spices worth 4,200 gold ducats, *ibid.*, p. 137 document nos. 1–7; likewise, in 1586 another Turkish merchant by the name of Seyyit Ahmet was in charge of a shipment to Venice of 36 bales of mohair, see Turan (1968), p. 256; for Muslim merchants doing business at Rialto see *ibid.*, pp. 251–62, also Kafadar (1986), pp. 198–218.
36 Turan (1968), p. 258, originally this palace belonged to the duke of Ferrara; prior to its being converted to the *fondaco*, Muslim–Turkish merchants had a house of their own at Rialto in about 1550.
37 Tadić (1961), pp. 242–45.
38 *Ibid.*, pp. 255–74.
39 Document published in facsimile by Carter (1972), Fig. 83.
40 Carter (1972), p. 361.
41 Ravid (1978).
42 Veinstein (1987), p. 820 note 28.
43 *Ibid.*, p. 791.
44 İnalcık (1989), pp. 330–31.
45 Tenenti cited by Veinstein (1987), note 83.
46 İnalcık (1954b), p. 126.
47 Veinstein (1987), p. 796.
48 *Ibid.*, p. 797.
49 Carter (1972), p. 377.
50 Veinstein (1987), pp. 786–87.
51 Tadić and Raci (1971).
52 Ravid (1978).
53 Tadić and Raci (1971), p. 262; since the Ottoman–Venetian treaty of 1419, Ottoman subjects including Muslims, Jews and Christians enjoyed freedom of trade in Venice, see Turan (1968), p. 249; the Ottoman government showed concern about their protection, see Gökbilgin (1971), *Bl*, v–viii document nos. 119, 120.
54 Carter (1972), p. 377.

12

THE BLACK SEA AND EASTERN EUROPE

THE GENOESE COLONIES AND THE OTTOMANS

In the existing literature, the history of the Italian mercantile republics in the Levant is interpreted by Western scholarship exclusively from the viewpoint of Italian interests and is based solely on the evidence available in the archives of the Italian city-states.[1] Everything affecting these states adversely is viewed in a negative light and little attention is paid to the conditions in the Levant and the motivations of the Ottomans. In the following pages, for the sake of a balanced view, we shall focus on the other side of the story.

From antiquity the Black Sea region and the Aegean had formed a closely knit economic entity. With its coastal outlets in Moldavia and the Crimea, the sparsely inhabited northern Black Sea land produced and exported huge quantities of grain, meat, fish and other animal products. Conversely, the densely populated southern Black Sea and the Aegean depended on these foodstuffs for its survival. In exchange, the latter exported wine, olive oil and dried fruit and also to the steppe chiefs and rulers, luxury goods such as textiles, jewelry and drugs. The Byzantine political and economic control of the Black Sea–Aegean entity had collapsed by 1204. During the thirteenth century, while Venice became supreme in the western Aegean and İstanbul, its rival, Genoa, conquered the eastern Aegean – Mytilene, Chios, the two Foças – and built a colonial empire in the Black Sea. They made Pera (Galata) its hub, facing the imperial city across the Golden Horn. Later on in rebuilding the unity of the Black Sea and Aegean regions under his rule, Mehmed II doubtless received tacit acquiescence from the Greeks, Armenians, Bulgars and Tatars. When the sultan destroyed the Latin colonies or compromised with them to buy time, many felt that he had restored the old Byzantine imperial tradition for the benefit of the indigenous peoples. The Genoese were confronted everywhere with the problem of sovereignty: in the Crimea by the Genghis Khanids, in Pera and Chios by the Byzantine emperor, and in Trabzon by the Comneni. Initially, the Genoese requested from the local ruler a small area outside or some distance from the main city to use exclusively for commercial purposes. For security they preferred islands such as Chios, Licostomo or peninsulas such as Amastris. In the beginning, these would be small unfortified settlements, mainly of the Genoese factors. Over time, proving their usefulness to the local ruler in securing necessary imports and growing customs revenues, they obtained authorization to fortify the settlement.

The Genoese trade centers attracted indigenous people as well as the Armenians and Jews who played the role of middlemen. Their settlement expanded into new districts around the original Genoese *contrada* quarters. The Genoese found, time and again, opportunities to surround the expanded city with new walls. In many cases, the new Genoese entities thrived to such an extent that they superseded the main city as a commercial center. We have, for example, the Genoese of Pera superseding the Greeks of Constantinople and the success of Caffa over the Tatar Muslim city of Salgat.[2]

The Byzantine Empire, which lost all of its overseas territories to the Italian city-states, became economically dependent on them and had to give them full exemption from tariffs and a free run in the region in return for grain supplies for Constantinople.[3] Not only were the profits from the spectacular commercial expansion of the trans-continental trade in the thirteenth century monopolized by the Latins, but also the food-stuffs and the raw materials, notably wheat, salt, hides, wool, salted fish and meat were taken from the Black Sea to the hungry communes of Italy.

Indigenous peoples were now either exploited as serfs, *parikoz*, in the countryside by their Catholic Latin feudal masters or were made dependent on Italian merchants for the supplies of foodstuffs in the cities. This led to hatred of the Latins and was the cause of rebellions, such as the terrible insurrections of Cretan Greeks against the Venetians. The Italian colonial states exploited even the desperate struggle of the Greeks against the invaders in Asia Minor and the Balkans to strengthen their own political and economic control. When the Greek populace in Byzantium suffered from a shortage of wheat, they accused, often with justification, the Latin merchants of grain speculation and of diversion from İstanbul of Black Sea supplies. In general, it was the upper-class Byzantines and businessmen that cooperated with the Latins while common people, led by the Orthodox clergy, sought relief in other ways. Many wealthy Greeks, who were to serve the Ottomans after the conquest as tax-farmers or palace merchants, lived not in Constantinople itself but rather in prosperous Pera from Genoese times.[4]

The general policy of the Ottomans toward the Genoese colonies was the same from the beginning: to abolish sovereignty rights over the territories which originally belonged to the pre-Ottoman states, to pull down fortifications and to deal with the colonies according to Islamic rules regarding non-Muslim subjects or foreigners under capitulatory amnesty. This policy is evident when the Venetians failed, under Murad I, to obtain an area in Ottoman Scutari, just opposite Genoese Pera, to settle a colony.[5] Ottomans were careful not to repeat the mistake of the earlier weaker governments, and did not allow Italian maritime states to gain territorial sovereignty or erect fortifications in the areas where they were permitted to settle trade colonies.

Mehmed II required complete control of the resources of the Black Sea region for the reconstruction and development of his new capital city, which he had taken over in ruins in 1453. Under the Ottomans, the spectacular growth of the imperial capital of İstanbul became possible only owing to the cheaply supplied wheat, meat, and salt of the northern Black Sea. Without these inexpensive supplies, İstanbul could not have been the most populous city of Europe in the sixteenth century. When the construction of the fortress on the Bosphorus was completed in August 1452, Sultan Mehmed II named it Strait-cutter. Its main purpose was to intercept Black Sea provisions destined for Constantinople which he planned to besiege the following spring. He then declared that every ship passing the fortress had to stop for inspection. On November 25, 1452, a Venetian vessel carrying grain to Constantinople disregarded the order and was sunk by a volley from the castle.[6] After the conquest of Constantinople, the straits were put under strict control to establish complete Ottoman domination of traffic between the Mediterranean and the Black Sea. Every ship leaving İstanbul or coming from the Black Sea had to stop at the castles on the Bosphorus to be inspected for smuggled wares and runaway slaves by the commander of the fortress. Ships were not permitted to proceed without his license. Mehmed the Conqueror, inspired by the idea of reviving the Eastern Roman Empire under his scepter, was determined to restore the imperial political and economic control of the Aegean and the Black Sea; thus he preferred the titles "the sultan of the two lands" (Asia Minor and the Balkans) and "the khakan of the two seas" (the Aegean and the Black Sea).

Facing the imperial city, Genoese Pera, on the other side of the Golden Horn, had overshadowed the Byzantine Constantinople in trade and prosperity. Pera surrendered to the Conqueror on June 1, 1453, and recovered its prosperity after a few years of decline resulting from the flight of the Genoese merchants. Many of these merchants soon returned under the guarantees of the capitulations, and many of the Genoese residents of Pera accepted Ottoman citizenship, as most of the Greek, Armenian and Jewish Perans had done already.[7] Abolishing its autonomous status under the Byzantine state, the sultan nevertheless took measures to enhance its economy and make it the principal port for İstanbul's commerce with Europe. As the Genoese notarial records of Pera from 1453 to 1490 demonstrate,[8] the Genoese continued their commercial activities as if nothing had changed. What had changed was that the Ottomans now had complete political control of the place and integrated it into their own imperial economy. Before the end of the century Pera became more prosperous and populated than ever with the establishment of new Muslim quarters and market-places.[9] In a survey made in 1477 the population composition of Pera was as follows:

Households

Muslims	535
Greek Orthodox	592
Europeans	332
Armenians	62
Total	1,521

In its further growth, Pera benefited considerably from the fact that the naval base and shipyard at Kasımpaşa, a district adjoining Pera, had developed into the principal ship-building and naval center of the empire in the sixteenth century.[10] With its cosmopolitan population and lifestyle, Pera became the major port-city for European trade with the empire. Ottomans built various new storehouses and a *bedestan* or covered market halls to store and trade in precious goods. Over time, European embassies and merchants settling there reinforced the cosmopolitan and European character of the city. Thus, Galata became one of the major places not only for commercial but also for intercultural influence between the continent and the Ottoman Empire. Expanding on the hillside into the Beyoğlu district, Ottoman Galata attained a Muslim majority in its population toward the end of the sixteenth century.

The importation of large quantities of silk, cotton, and hemp manufactures from Anatolia to the northern Black Sea ports of Caffa, Akkerman and Kilia, and the export to İstanbul from the same locations of animal and agricultural stuffs, constitutes an important aspect of the north–south trade in the fifteenth and sixteenth centuries. This large market for Anatolian manufactures undoubtedly became one of the basic factors in the development of textile industries in Anatolia. From Tokat, Çorum, Merzifon, Kastamonu, Borlu, and Konya came cotton cloth; from Bursa, silk; from Tosya and Ankara, mohair; and from Trabzon, hemp. In other words, Asia Minor had become an "industrialized" region in the empire before the Western and Russian manufactures competed with Turkish and Indian textiles in the late eighteenth and nineteenth centuries. Until then Anatolian cotton textiles, prints of Tokat, *bogası* of Tokat, Amasya and Kastamonu and great quantities of coarse cotton fabrics supplied the vast market in the Crimea and the steppe area, from the northern and western Caucasus to Dobruja in the Balkans. Low prices and traditional taste among the Muslim population of the region guaranteed the market for the Anatolian industries. While coarse cotton cloth such as *kirbas*, *bez*, and *astar*, imported in bulk, were used for a variety of domestic costumes and furniture, caftans and dresses were made of fine *bogası*.

The Crimean khanate and the Genoese

In the wake of his conquest of Constantinople and Pera, and in establishing control over the waterways between the Mediterranean and the Black Sea, Mehmed II demanded that all of the Genoese colonies in the Black Sea area recognize his suzerain authority. On condition that a tribute was paid to the sultan, they were left free to continue their regional and interregional trade. Caffa was the center of this commercial network. The port city was first established by the Genoese around 1266 as a small settlement dependent on the great Golden Horde city of Salgat or the city of Krim, but later it became the main emporium for Black Sea trade. The great khans of the Golden Horde always considered Caffa territorially a part of their empire. In fact, a high Tatar official, the *tudun*, represented the khan in Caffa and collected certain taxes in the name of his master. He also exercised jurisdiction over the large Tatar city population and the surrounding countryside where they were dominant.

This remunerative post was held by the beg of the Crimean Shirin clan, who was the head of the tribal aristocracy and the most powerful man in the khanate. The Genoese exploited the ever-present conflict between the khan and the Shirin Beg, who tried to keep the khan under his influence and control. During the khanship of Hacı Giray Khan (1433?–66),[11] disputes over the tribute and Genoese interference in the khanate's internal affairs produced grave conflicts. Hacı Giray sought cooperation with the Ottoman sultan against the Genoese. To regain the economic independence of the khanate, Hacı Giray attempted to make İnkerman the center of trade with the Ottoman Empire and Kerch the center for the Caucasus. Moreover, he wanted to create a merchant navy and end the Genoese role of middleman in regional trade. The Genoese admitted that these measures had begun to affect Caffa's prosperity. At his death, the struggle for power among the sons of Hacı Giray and the Genoese resulted in the Ottoman occupation of the Genoese Crimean possessions in 1475.[12] Eminek, the head of the Shirin clan, played a key role in cooperating with the sultan, who seized this opportunity to capture Caffa; then, by appointing Mengli Giray Khan with the support of Eminek, the sultan succeeded in making the khanate a vassal of his empire.

CAFFA-KIEV-MUSCOVY

Desertion of the "Tatar route" is believed to date from Timur's invasion in 1395 when he deliberately destroyed the Golden Horde cities of Saray on the Volga river and Azov on the mouth of the Don. However, despite this blow and the subsequent internecine struggle on the Kipchak steppe, the oriental caravan trade, coupled with pilgrimages, kept the route from Khwarezm or Azerbaijan to the lower Volga and to Azov active until the 1520s.[13] There are hints that in the fifteenth century oriental goods still reached Novgorod, Sweden and Denmark through Kiev. Malowist believes[14] that Kiev had lost its importance as an international emporium for oriental goods by this time mainly because of unsettled conditions on the steppe following Timur's invasion.

Before the "Moldavian route" from Akkerman to Lwow was firmly established, Lwow traditionally received so-called "oriental goods" – costly silk cloths and spices – through the so-called "Tatar or Mongol route," from Caffa or Azov through the Ukrainian steppe, the Dogan (or Tavan) pass on the Dnieper, Kiev and Kaminiec.[15] In the fifteenth century, large caravans, usually numbering one thousand people, spent over two weeks on the dangerous route from Kiev to Caffa.[16] Merchants from Moscow joined this route at Kiev. In the second half of the fifteenth century, the Ottomans still received northern goods through this route, including furs, walrus tusks, and quicksilver as enumerated in the Ottoman customs regulations.[17] To Muscovy in particular and also to other lands the Ottomans exported silk cloth through this route.

In the fifteenth century, some incidents mentioned in contemporaneous sources constitute our only source on the traffic along the route of Caffa–Kiev–Muscovy. In the 1470s, a serious conflict broke out between the Genoese of Caffa and Prince Ivan III of Muscovy.[18] The Caffa merchants, including eight Italians and two Greeks, were robbed on their return trip from Muscovy. When Muscovy denied any responsibility for the robbery, the Genoese authorities confiscated, for indemnification, the goods in the storehouses of the Muscovite merchants at Caffa and sold them. The dispute was still unresolved when the Ottomans occupied Caffa in 1475. The Caffa–Muscovy trade apparently experienced similar incidents and also complaints were heard of malpractices by Ottoman customs agents.[19] Incidentally, the Italian architects who were invited to Moscow to build the famous onion-domed cathedral of St. Basil also used the Caffa route.

As the fifteenth century progressed, Lwow became the center of the "Rus"/Ruthenian trade and the emporium of oriental goods for the Baltic countries. In King Casimir's trade privileges, dated 1472, which were granted to the merchants of Lwow, imports included such oriental goods as pepper, ginger, cloves, brocades, satins, *dimi* cloth and rice.[20] In fact, it was the Genoese Caffan merchants who brought them either from Alexandria or from closer and more convenient Ottoman trade centers such as Bursa, İstanbul and Pera. It was Caffan merchants, Italians, Armenians, Jews and Tatars, who took these goods to Lwow and over time many settled there. In Poland, the king's charter gave the trade monopoly in oriental goods to the citizens of Lwow, thus prohibiting merchants coming from the east to trade in the country. Apparently, the Caffan merchants were engaged in smuggling. The merchants importing spices and silk cloth from Ottoman dominions bought in Lwow the woolen cloth made in Poland, Silesia and Bohemia as well as furs and beeswax. Lwow was the emporium for oriental goods from where they were taken by Europeans to Flanders and the Baltic countries. Even the Swedish elite then wore exquisite Bursa brocades.[21]

Thus, prior to the fifteenth century, Caffan merchants monopolized the south–north trade between Caffa and Lwow because, as Malowist points out,[22] the merchants of Lwow had not accumulated enough capital to venture so far afield. But later, when the Akkerman–Lwow route supplanted the Caffa–Lwow route, the merchants of Lwow became more active in oriental trade. The Ottoman sultans granted the Poles privileges of free trade in the Ottoman dominions as early as Mehmed I; Bursa court records from the late fifteenth century contain evidence of their presence in that city. Muslim merchants, Turks, Tatars and Syrians appear in the thriving market of Lwow particularly after 1454, when the Moldavian ports of Akkerman and Kilia were granted trade privileges by Mehmed II and the Moldavian route for oriental goods became the main avenue of trade between the south and the north (see below, pp. 291–93).

In sum, in the fifteenth century, the general trend even before the fall of Caffa in 1475 was that the Genoese were losing their control of the oriental trade in the northern countries and were being replaced by Ottoman subjects, mostly Armenians, Greeks, Jews and Moldavians, and the old Tatar route of Caffa or Azov–Kiev–Lwow was overshadowed by the Moldavian route between Akkerman and Lwow. As for the southern section of the south–north trade over the routes Bursa–İstanbul–Caffa or Akkerman by sea and overland by Edirne–Kilia–Akkerman, Muslim merchants – mostly Anatolian and Rumelian Turks – outnumbered the others. Although the Genoese of Pera, mostly subjects of the sultan, as well as those from Chios continued to use these routes, their activities were now drastically reduced.

Traffic was active between Caffa and "Rus," which in Ottoman documents apparently stands for Ruthenia and/or for Muscovy. The important political and economic interests between the Ottoman Empire and the grand duchy of Muscovy led to a rapprochement between Ivan III and Bayezid II, beginning in 1492. The Ottoman sultan acting as the suzerain of the Crimean khan Mengli Giray supported him against attacks from the khans of the Golden Horde, which was in an alliance with Poland–Lithuania. Mengli Giray maintained cooperation with Muscovy against their common enemies and worked towards the establishment of friendly relations between İstanbul and Moscow. Because it was desirable to import precious brocades from Bursa as well as other exotic goods, the Russian ruler tried to elicit commercial privileges from the sultan and sent, through the good offices of the khan, an ambassador to İstanbul in 1495.

Apparently since Mehmed II's time merchants from Muscovy were engaged in trade in the Ottoman territories;[23] and settled in the Ottoman ports of Azov and Caffa. Already in 1492 in the wake of an attempt by the Golden Horde to invade the Crimea, Ivan III's envoys contacted Ottoman officials in Azov and Caffa to establish friendly relations with the sultan; and they received an encouraging answer.[24] Not enjoying the protection of a capitulation, these merchants met with difficulties and finally had to abandon the ports. In his letter of August 31, 1492, Ivan III repeated his desire to establish friendly relations and asked for immunity for Russian merchants and envoys. Giving guarantees for the properties left by deceased Russian merchants on Ottoman territory, which was one of the main points made by the grand duke in his letter,[25] the sultan encouraged him to send an ambassador to the Porte. The duke of Lithuania and the khan of the Golden Horde did not permit the Ottoman ambassador to pass through the territories under their control, thereby demonstrating their disapproval of the Ottoman–Muscovite rapprochement. Eventually, in 1495, the grand duke sent his ambassador Pleshcheyev to the sultan, as usual with the Crimean khan's mediation. The Muscovite ruler gave strict instructions to his ambassador to avoid any behavior which might be interpreted as his master's allegiance to the sultan. However, ignorant of Ottoman protocol, Pleshcheyev followed too strictly his master's instructions in İstanbul. His aloofness was interpreted as an insult to the sultan and caused the Porte to decide not to reciprocate the Muscovite embassy, leaving relations with Muscovy to the care of the Ottoman authorities in the Crimea. In 1499, a ship loaded with commercial goods took Russian merchants and the ambassador Golokhvastov to İstanbul. At this juncture Polish–Ottoman relations deteriorated. From John Albert's invasion of Moldavia in 1497 hostilities broke out between Poland and the Ottoman Empire and the large forces under Bali Beg invaded Poland in 1498. Mengli Giray urged the sultan to support the Crimean–Muscovite bloc against Poland–Lithuania. This time the Russian ambassador obtained what his master anxiously desired. The sultan, considering Muscovy a friendly country, granted to Russian merchants, in an imperial letter, guarantees of free trade in the Ottoman territories. This can be considered as the first capitulation granted to Russia. Ivan III then badly needed Crimean–Ottoman cooperation against Poland. In the following years, Russian–Ottoman trade appears to have grown. The grand duke's revenue from this trade reached the substantial sum of twenty thousand roubles in 1501,[26] although Russian merchants continued to complain about unjust treatment and even conspiracy on the part of the Ottoman officials in Caffa.

After 1512, when the Crimean–Muscovite cooperation ended and Crimean raids against Russia began, Russian commercial relations with the Crimea and Caffa must have suffered. However, Selim I favorably received Ivan's ambassador to İstanbul and sent his own ambassador to

Muscovy with guarantees of friendship. For Muscovy and İstanbul, Poland–Lithuania was always a common enemy and Selim I needed peace in the west in order to carry out his plans in the east. The Ottomans eventually took a hostile attitude towards Muscovy when Sahib Giray Khan (1532–51) convinced Süleyman I of Muscovy's plans against Kazan and Astrakhan.[27]

Caffa

Caffa continued to be an important transit center between the south and the north for regional trade in the Black Sea into the sixteenth century. According to an Ottoman survey made in 1520,[28] there were about 2,783 Muslim and Christian households in the city (see Table 1:56). The civil population had a Christian, mostly Armenian, majority which formed about 60 percent of the total population. Ottoman military and religious groups made up about 7 percent of the population. If we accept the coefficient of five persons per household, the entire population of the city of Caffa was about 19,000 or an average of 48 persons per quarter.

A customs register of Caffa covering the period 1487–90[29] is a precious document informing us of the busy traffic of the port of Caffa under the

Table 1:56. *The population of Caffa, c. 1520*

Communities	Subject to taxation	Exempt from taxation
Muslim households	760	
Muslim unmarried men	169	
Christian households	2,013	
Christian unmarried men	103	
Christian households dependent on widows	391	
Professors at theological seminaries		3
Kadis		3
Other religious men		114
Tax collectors		4
People dependent on the Crimean khan		14
Sea captains		1
Seamen		67
Garrison		39
Others		9
Total	3,436	254

Note: There were 39 quarters in the city.
Source: Ottoman survey of c. 1520: see Veinstein (1980).

Table 1:57. Exports via Caffa from the northern regions to İstanbul,
c. 1470

Origin	Merchandise
Crimea, the steppe area to the north of the Black Sea	Wheat, flour, honey, clarified butter, cheese, tallow, fish, caviar, hides and skins, leather, salt, slaves, horse harnesses, bows and arrows
Azov, Circassia	Sturgeon, cod, caviar, honey and slaves
Georgia	Raw silk
"Rus" (Ruthenia and/or Muscovy)	Woolen cloth, iron tools (knives, shovels, axes), walrus tusks, quicksilver, flax, precious furs and slaves

Source: Anhegger and İnalcık (1956).

Ottomans. From Caffa came foodstuffs and raw materials to the Ottoman capital city from a vast area stretching from the Crimea and the steppe area between Dnieper and Astrakhan as well as from Muscovy, Kazan, Circassia and Georgia. Caffa was also a transit center for a large variety of manufactured and natural goods imported from İstanbul, Asia Minor, the Aegean and Europe. The large quantities of basic foodstuffs such as wheat, animal products, salted fish, honey, beeswax, hides and skins, as well as slaves, constituted the bulk of the exports from the north. Meanwhile, cotton and hemp textiles came from Asia Minor, silks from Bursa, woolen cloth from Europe, alum and copper from northern Anatolia and raisins, figs, and olive oil from the Aegean. Also, spices from India, and sugar and dyes arrived at Caffa and were re-exported to the lands north of the Black Sea (Tables 1:57 and 1:58).

Wheat was grown by Tatars in the Crimea and in the steppe area to the north of the peninsula and was exported from Caffa by sea, providing an important part of İstanbul's wheat supplies (there were 150 shiploads by the mid-eighteenth century). The large İstanbul consumer market encouraged the pastoral nomads of the steppe to become engaged in cultivation along with animal husbandry. Members of the Crimean tribal nobility turned part of their steppe pasturelands into cultivated land and settled on them slaves captured in raids in Poland, Russia and Circassia as a part of the agricultural labor force. In the period 1596–1610, when Celali bands ruined the agriculture in Anatolia, the southern coasts of the Black Sea depended on Crimean wheat production. Kerch at the Strait of Azov competed as another major transit center with Caffa for the exports of wheat, hides, fats, hemp, honey, salt, and slaves to the Ottoman ports on the southern Black Sea coast. Kerch exported also its own production of large sturgeon to these ports in exchange for wine

Table 1:58. Goods arriving at Caffa, 1487–90

Merchandise	Coming from
Cotton goods	
Muslin	Iran
Cotton yarn	İstanbul, Ankara
Coarse cotton cloth	Northern and central Anatolian towns (in large quantities)
Quilts	Ankara
Coverlets	Bergama, Bursa, İstanbul, Konya
Mattress sheets	Kastamonu
Handkerchiefs	
Linings	Sinop
Turbans	Konya, Ankara, Bursa, İstanbul
Aprons	Bursa, İstanbul, Yazd
Tents	Merzifon
Silks and satins	
Caftans of brocade	
Variety of brocades	Amasya, Aleppo, Yazd, Bursa
Variety of velvets	Amasya, Kastamonu, İstanbul
Satin	Amasya
Variety of taffetas	Bursa
Silk aprons	
Linen	
Coarse cloth of flax	Uşak, Ankara, Kerç
Cloth of flax	Canik, Denizli
Russian tents	
Woolen cloth	İstanbul
Hides and skins	
Cow hides ⎫	
Horse hides ⎬	the steppe area
Buffalo hides ⎭	
Sheep skins	
Marten skins	Niğde
Fox skins	Kastamonu, Ankara
Sheep skins	Shamakhi
A variety of leather (Morocco)	Shamakhi
Soft leather	Kastamonu, Sinop
Animal products	
Fish	Azov (in large quantities)
Caviar	Azov
Cheese	Taman
Clarified butter	Taman, Azov, Canik
Honey	Trabzon, İstanbul, Karaman
Metals	
Iron	Sinop
Copper	Sinop, Küre
Caldrons	Küre
Tin	İstanbul (originally England)
Eflak knives	İstanbul (originally Styria)
Swords	Konya, Beyşehir
Salt	Crimean Khanate (in large quantities)
Spices and dyes	
Red dye	Merzifon, Ankara, Bursa
Pepper	İstanbul
Indigo	
Incense	

Table 1:58. (*cont.*)

Merchandise	Coming from
Sugar	Ankara (originally Egypt and Cyprus)
Nutgalls	Merzifon, Kastamonu
Opium	Beyşehir
Grain	
Millet	Taman
Wheat	Azov, Taman (in large quantities)
Flour	Bartın, Bayburt
Other	
Wine	Trabzon, southern Crimea
Walnuts	Bursa
Wood and lumber	Kerpe, Hurzuf
Raisins	Tokat
Mats	Küre

Source: İnalcık (1992b).

and textiles and other southern products. A regular passage service by transport ships was available at the strait.

In the fifteenth and sixteenth centuries, one of the principal imports to the Ottoman south from the Russian Empire was precious furs.[30] Trade in precious furs was a monopoly under the Muscovite government so the Ottoman sultans sent merchants attached to the imperial palace with substantial amounts of gold to Muscovy and asked the czar for favorable treatment. In 1551 one of these imperial merchants went with 10,000 gold pieces to Moscow. In Moscow, merchants from the Middle East were also permitted to purchase slaves, but in a limited number. Goods from Western Europe, including tin and textiles, were also available in Moscow. Judging from the value of the wares seized by Nogays or Cossacks on the steppe, which varied between 40,000 to 70,000 gold pieces, the Ottoman caravans from Caffa or Azov to Moscow must have been quite large.

The slave trade

Taxes on slaves and customs duties at the Crimean ports constituted the most important source of revenue for the Ottoman treasury, amounting to 1,310,000 *akça* or c. 21,000 gold ducats in 1520.[31] In the years 1577–78 the revenues from the slave tax for fourteen months were estimated at 29 percent of the total revenue of the Ottoman possessions in the Crimea. The slave tax alone increased from 620,000 in 1520 to 650,000 in 1529. Customs duties at Caffa were 4.2 percent *ad valorem* on imports and exports by sea. The slave tax was apparently higher and was calculated at the rate of 256 *akça* or about 4 gold ducats per head. In larger Ottoman cities the market price of one average slave fluctuated between 25 and 50 gold pieces in the second half of the fifteenth century.[32]

Slaves in Islamic countries, in Ottoman society in particular, were indispensable. They were employed not only in domestic service but also in military and economic areas. In earlier centuries slaves were extensively used as agricultural labor on the reclaimed lands of the military elite. Settled as peasant families, endowed slaves retained their servile status for centuries. In other cases they mostly became integrated into the large mass of the *reaya*, the free peasantry. Even the urban craftsmen employed slave labor, organized under the Islamic system of limited service contracts.[33] Under this system the slave was allowed to work independently and to retain his earnings so that he would be capable of ransoming himself after a period determined in the contract. This institution as well as Islam's encouragement of manumission as a meritorious, charitable act resulted in a constant erosion of the slave population in Ottoman society. The manufacture of heavy brocades was a labor-intensive specialized type of work; hence, such industries in Bursa as well as in Italy relied heavily on slave labor. Venetians and Genoese regularly bought slaves in the Levant for the slave markets in Italy and in Arab countries and also for agricultural labor in their Levantine colonies. It was a blow to the Genoese Black Sea trade when Mehmed II established strict control over the export of slaves in 1453.

Clearly, not only the state but also various segments of the economy in the Ottoman Empire depended on slavery. This demand gave rise to a very lively slave market in such urban centers as İstanbul and Bursa, and served as a strong incentive for the raiding and enslavement activities of the Ottoman frontier forces during the first three centuries: captives always brought a good price in the main slave markets. But after the mid-sixteenth century the Ottomans met up with stiff resistance on the western borderlands at a time when there was a growing demand for slaves on the Ottoman market. Thus, the Crimean Tatars became the principal suppliers of slaves and were involved in extensive slave raids into Poland, Russia and Circassia. In fact the slave trade became the main source of support for the Crimean economy. An unsuccessful Crimean raid entailed an economic crisis in the land. Enslavement raids into Russia and Poland intensified in the period 1514–1654. On the basis of the tax revenue figures of 1578, 17,502 slaves were imported into Caffa in that

year alone.[34] The price of an average slave varied from 20 to 40 gold
ducats during that period. This corresponded to the maintenance
expenses of a poor adult for a period of two or three years.[35] Calculations
based on Russian sources[36] provide the figure of 100,000 captives in the
years 1607–17 and 26,840 in the period 1632–45. From Circassia alone
there were reportedly 50,000 captives taken in Sahib Giray Khan's campaign in 1539.[37] It can safely be said that the annual slave population
imported only from these two sources, Poland–Muscovy and Circassia,
amounted to over 10,000 in the period 1500–1650.

The other important provenance of slaves was Egypt. According to a
customs register from the port of Antalya dated 1559,[38] of the large
variety of imports from Egypt via Antalya by sea, black slaves, both male
and female, constituted the bulk of the traffic. Many ships carried slaves
exclusively. The slave merchant Seydi Ali, for instance, brought eighteen
black slaves from Egypt in one expedition. Black slaves imported via
Antalya went to Anatolian cities, in particular to Konya and Bursa. From
Antalya, white slaves were shipped to Syria and Egypt, though in much
smaller number than black slaves.

The Ottoman state, like all pre-industrial societies, relied on human
energy for all kinds of enterprises, and these, in turn, depended on a
regular and sustained flow of slaves. Slave labor provided manpower not
only for an imperial army and navy but also for colossal construction
works[39] and transportation. However, even in these areas, except for the
extended households of the elite, servile labor declined over time for
various reasons. From the seventeenth century onward, the centralized
power of the sultan grew weaker and the wars, consequently, were not
as successful as before. At the same time the tracking of fugitive slaves
became difficult, causing slave prices to soar dramatically.[40]

THE BURSA-İSTANBUL-AKKERMAN-LWOW ROUTE

The earliest evidence of commercial traffic between Lwow and Akkerman
via Moldavia dates from the fourteenth century.[41] The Genoese were
interested in establishing trade relations with the lower part of the Moldavian principality in 1386. (This area was then ruled by a Christian
Tatar prince, Dimitri.)[42] The merchants of Lwow obtained commercial
privileges there in 1409, and the Genoese opened their first factory at
Akkerman two years later. Oriental goods, pepper, silk and silk cloth,
as well as Greek wine, now were imported at Akkerman via the Crimea
by the Genoese of Pera. Already in this period, the "Rus," as well as

Poles, Germans, Armenians, Jews and Tatars, were quite active on the "Moldavian route," but the Armenians, who obtained the privilege of trade for all Ruthenia in 1402, were predominent in this trade and throughout the fifteenth century kept this position.[43] The leader of the caravan on the route Akkerman–Lwow was always an Armenian.

Ottoman interest in taking control of the south–north trade dates back to the turn of the fifteenth century when the lower Danubian ports and Akkerman emerged as the main outlets of this trade. The Ottomans under Mehmed I attempted to capture Kilia and Akkerman in 1420.[44] They had acquired a key position in the lower Danube by capturing Giurgiu (Yergögü) on the left bank of the Danube in 1419. In the same period Hungarians, realizing its great importance, also tried to get control of the lower Danube. Interestingly enough, in 1428 Ulugh Muhammad, khan of the Golden Horde, proposed to Murad II that they should act in concert to eliminate "the Vlach infidels" occupying the land between their territories.[45] Crimean khans would continue this policy of cooperation in later periods.

Thus, during the fifteenth century, Kilia, the gateway of the traffic between the Black Sea and east-central Europe via the Danube and Transylvania, became one of the most important issues of contention between Hungary and the Ottomans. As long as the Ottomans could maintain their suzerainty over Wallachia they could control Kilia.

In 1428, the Moldavians occupied Kilia, profiting from the Ottoman campaign against the Wallachian Voyvode Dan II, thus blocking Hungarian access to the Black Sea. When John Hunyadi, in 1448, forced Moldavia to return Kilia to his vassal, the Wallachian voyvode, and installed a Hungarian garrison, the Ottomans renewed their attack on the city. Interestingly, this time an Ottoman fleet participated in the operations. At this time, attracted by growing commercial and fiscal interests, Hungary, the Ottoman state and Poland, as well as the local rulers and the Genoese, were all involved in a complex network of relations.

Wallachia and Moldavia, as buffer states, pursued a carefully calculated policy among the great powers. Since the early fifteenth century, Moldavian voyvodes also came into conflict with the Genoese over their monopoly of trade. In the fifteenth century, Akkerman served as one of the Genoese centers of trade in the Black Sea alongside Caffa and Azov. To break the Genoese monopoly of overseas trade, the voyvodes gave commercial privileges to the Venetians. The Senate decided to send the Black Sea *muda* (convoy) to visit Akkerman. But commerce there did not prove practical and the plan was abandoned.

The Moldavian voyvode favored the Armenians and the Vlachs. Finally, in 1455, the Voyvode Petru, taking advantage of the Ottoman occupation of Pera, seized the Genoese fortress of Lerici on the mouth of the Dnieper. In general, this active policy of favoring native merchants was largely responsible for the rise of the "Moldavian route" and the development of the regional trade in the Black Sea at the expense of the Genoese colonies.[46]

Legal documents from the city of Lwow show that Bursa was the chief emporium from which oriental goods flowed along the so-called Moldavian route.[47] Genoese merchants from Pera and Caffa, merchants from Akkerman and Suceava, the capital of Moldavia, and even from Lwow took oriental goods directly from Bursa. Although the Armenians and the Genoese of Pera appear to have kept a dominant position in this traffic, Vlachs and merchants of Lwow also visited Pera and Bursa to purchase these goods. In 1449, for instance, a merchant of Lwow by the name of Johannes Simicfal visited Bursa and bought pepper worth 4,000 gold ducats. He represented Petru Manu, a Moldavian merchant of Suceava who had given him goods to be sold at Akkerman.[48] Obviously bulky native products were sold at Akkerman for shipment to İstanbul or Chios, and the cash was used to buy oriental goods on the Bursa market. This example appears to illustrate the usual pattern of this trade.

On the other hand, Muslim merchants from Bursa and Syria traded in Lwow. A certain "Bubekr of Damasco" and his companion "Haczachmeth" (Hacı Ahmed) were mentioned as doing business in Lwow in connection with the Genoese Barnabas of Galata. So, it is no surprise that the trade privilege of King Ladislas, dated July 6, 1444, included Muslims (*Bessermeni, Saraceni, Pagani*) among the merchants allowed to make wholesale transactions at Lwow. Besides Muslims, Greeks, Armenians, Tatars, Jews and Italians are mentioned in the same document. It appears that the Genoese of Pera were in the forefront of merchants who bought pepper, silk and silk cloth in Bursa, and Pera had become the main emporium of such goods for merchants coming from Caffa, Lwow, Akkerman and Kilia. The Bursa court records of the 1480s,[49] mentioning a number of "Frenk" (Italian) merchants doing business in Bursa, confirm the situation. Of course, there were Genoese merchants who took oriental goods further, to the northern Black Sea ports, but as early as the mid-fifteenth century they appear to have been losing ground to the "natives."[50] Now, it was mostly the Armenians and the Germans of Lwow who took oriental goods from Pera to Akkerman and Lwow.

Armenian settlers in the Crimea and in the mercantile centers of Moldavia, Wallachia and Poland appear to have played a central role in this period. As immigrants from eastern Anatolia and the Crimea, these Armenians spoke Turkish and many of them bore Turkish names, and felt at home under the Ottomans. We encounter them frequently as merchants in the court records of Bursa, Galata and Caffa. Serving Moldavian princes as merchants, advisors and mercenaries, they played a key role in the establishment of the Moldavian route during the fifteenth century.

At any rate, this was the beginning of the policy to eliminate Italian control of the Black Sea, one that gained full momentum with the Ottoman dominance of the region in the second half of the fifteenth century. The Ottoman customs registers of the period 1480–1500[51] show complete domination by the "native" merchants: Muslim Turks, Armenians, Greeks and Jews, now all Ottoman subjects. It must be noted, however, that the Genoese retained their lead in the long-distance trade of the region in exporting wheat, salted fish, caviar, beeswax, hides and slaves.

One may distinguish three categories of goods in this trade in the Lwow documents of 1441–48.[52] The bulk of the trade consisted of the natural products of the Akkerman–Kilia–Moldavia area: wheat, fish, caviar, cattle, hides and beeswax. The second category included the "oriental goods," which were chiefly pepper, silk cloth of Bursa, Aegean wine, cotton and carpets. Bursa's precious brocades particularly were appreciated by the princes and the elite as luxury fabrics. The Moldavian tribute to the king of Poland included this precious cloth.

The third category of goods consisted of fine woolen cloth from Flanders, England, Florence, Silesia (Gorlitz) and Poland, and articles made of metal from Central Europe and southern Germany. These constituted the main imports highly valued by the Ottomans.

While the imports to Lwow from Bursa passed mainly through the hands of the Armenians, the exports of Western origin were controlled by the Lwow merchants. It is interesting to add that transactions frequently were made on credit, and barter exchange was also mentioned.

The intensification of commercial relations between the Ottoman lands and Moldavia, Wallachia and Poland was marked by the growing use of Ottoman coins, the *akça* as well as "Turkish gold pieces" together with Venetian and Hungarian gold coins. The earliest reference to Ottoman gold coins in Moldavia (*ducatin, turchis*)[53] – evidently Ottoman imitations of Venetian gold ducats – occurs in 1431. In Lwow, Ottoman gold coins had quite a large circulation.

In 1455, the Moldavian voyvode made a monetary reform designed to adjust the Moldavian coin to the Ottoman *akça*. The Wallachian voyvode attempted a similar reform in 1452, abandoning the Hungarian system.[54] In both cases, the real objective was to make the currency acceptable in Ottoman markets. After the capture of Constantinople and Pera, the traffic from the south had come under full Ottoman control.

Import and export trade between the south and the north was absolutely dependent on this traffic through Kilia and Akkerman, and the economic survival of Moldavia depended on coming to terms with the sultan. For his part, the sultan must have seen the importance of this traffic for Bursa and the feeding and prosperity of his new capital, İstanbul. An agreement for tribute was signed by Petru Aron, evidently following the Ottoman naval attack on Akkerman in 1454.[55] The privilege that Mehmed II granted to the merchants of Akkerman in 1456 actually was the necessary link in Ottoman–Polish trade. It stated: "Merchants of Akkerman in his [Petru's] territory may come in ships and trade by making transactions and purchases in Edirne, Bursa and İstanbul; [I vow] that my men, begs, subashis, sipahis or others will not cause any harm to their persons and wares."[56]

Under Stephen the Great (1457–1504), it appears that economic–fiscal considerations were mostly responsible for the changing relations between Moldavia, the Ottomans and Poland. Stephen's immediate economic interests with the Ottoman Empire and Poland dictated conciliatory relations with both suzerains during the period 1460–70. This policy secured the growth of trade with the Ottoman Empire.[57] His recognition of full freedom of transit trade for the merchants of Lwow in 1460 actually completed both Mehmed II's grant of freedom of trade to Petru Aron and the Polish–Ottoman trade agreement of 1460. Stephen earned from this traffic a good annual income from customs revenues. On the frontier, Wallachian or Turkish merchants were to pay "two Turkish gold pieces" per cart for valuable loads of pepper and woolens.

In 1465, Voyvode Stephen, seizing Kilia and combining it with his hold on Akkerman, came into full control of the traffic between east-central Europe and the Black Sea on the one hand and that between the Ottoman south and Poland on the other. Apparently, the Wallachian crisis of 1458–62, which involved Moldavia, Hungary and the Ottoman Empire, had an economic basis. The Wallachian-Brašov route (see below, pp. 295–99) competed with the Moldavian route, and Kilia, then a Wallachian port, played a key part in this trade.

Wallachian merchants had almost a monopoly of the international trade on the Danube between east-central Europe and the Ottoman Empire and attempted to divert traffic from the Lwow–Akkerman route to their own territory. In his trade privilege of 1439, Vlad Dracul had promised free circulation not only in Wallachia but also in the "Turkish territories." Then the Wallachian voyvode, Vlad the Impaler (1448, 1456–62, 1466), wanted a larger share of the benefits of the trade and he sought to protect the interests of Wallachian merchants. Supported by the Hungarians, he rebelled against his suzerain, the sultan, defeating an Ottoman force in 1458. Later, in 1461–62, when the sultan was away on the Trabzon campaign, he seized Giurgiu, the Ottoman bridgehead on the left bank of the Danube, and plundered and burned a number of Ottoman ports on the river. But the delicate position of Wallachia between Hungary and the Ottoman Empire, that manifested itself in a double vassaldom from 1394, was resolved in favor of the Ottomans by Mehmed II's campaign of 1462.

In the summer of 1462, Mehmed II took revenge by burning down Břaila, the principal port of Wallachian–Hungarian trade, and using the Ottoman navy and Moldavian forces to attack Kilia, which was defended by a Hungarian garrison. The sultan placed Radu III (1462–74) on the Wallachian throne, and he proved to be a loyal vassal of the Ottomans. Thus, the sultan strengthened the Ottoman position and commercial interests on the lower Danubian basin against Hungarian penetration and rivalry. As noted earlier, three years later, the Moldavian voyvode seized Kilia to establish his full control of this trade. Apparently, the Ottomans accepted the new situation, since Stephen appeared to be a faithful vassal and guaranteed the commercial interests of Ottoman subjects. An intermediary role between the continental spice–silk route through Bursa and the Ottoman Danubian ports on the one side and the Hungarian Brašov-Nagyvarad route on the other had made double dependency on the Ottomans and Hungary a necessity for Wallachia.

From 1473 the good relations of the Moldavian voyvode with the sultan deteriorated,[58] because now Mehmet II wanted to establish his full control over the outlets of the south–north trade including Akkerman, Caffa in the east, Kilia and the Danubian ports in the west. He conquered Caffa and other Genoese colonies in the northern Black Sea in 1475.

Following the Ottoman conquest of Kilia and Akkerman in 1484, a state of open war existed between the Ottomans on the one hand and Moldavia and Poland on the other. Stephen of Moldavia, who had become a Polish vassal, resisted Ottoman pressure. But he finally realized that his survival depended on coming to terms with the Ottomans and renewing his vassalage to the sultan. Despite temporary peace agreements, Poland never lost interest in controlling Moldavia and the Black Sea coast from the Dniester to the Dnieper, an area which Lithuania had claimed since Grand Duke Vitold had temporarily occupied it at the turn of the fifteenth century. The ambitious plans of King John-Albert (1492–1501) of Poland to control the Moldavian route and the ports of Kilia and Akkerman led Stephen to cooperate more closely with the Ottomans. John-Albert suffered a crushing defeat in Moldavia in 1497. The next year, Stephen joined forces with the Ottoman frontier troops under the *sancak beg* of Silistre, Bali Beg, in a devastating raid into Polish territory.

Later on, under Süleyman I, among the conditions of Ottoman peace and friendship with Poland, as listed in the correspondence, was always the security of trade routes for the Ottoman merchants between Akkerman and Lwow. One of the Polish complaints was that the merchants from the Ottoman Empire, mostly Armenians and Greeks, avoided the usual itinerary and customs stations and traveled through uninhabited areas. There was a constant concern for security on the Moldavian route throughout the sixteenth century.

Actually, the struggle involved not only the Akkerman–Lwow route but also a larger area including the steppe region between the Dobruja and the Crimean Khanate. There, the Cossacks on Poland's frontier zone and the Tatars of the Akkerman–Dobruja steppe were engaged in a fierce struggle for the control of the steppe region. This would bring the Ottoman and Polish states into a long series of conflicts in the sixteenth and seventeenth centuries.

KİLİA AND AKKERMAN

By 1484, the Ottomans had established full control of the three most important ports of the northern Black Sea, namely Caffa, Akkerman and Kilia, which flourished as emporiums for trade between Eastern Europe and their rapidly growing capital on the Bosphorus. Earlier we witnessed the important role of Caffa for Eastern Europe. For trade from the ports of Akkerman and Kilia under the Ottomans, the Ottoman customs registers for the years 1495–1504 constitute a major source.[59]

According to this source, ships made a circuit visiting successively İstanbul, Sinop, Caffa, Akkerman and Kilia and back to İstanbul. In this period sea captains trafficking between Caffa, Akkerman, Kilia on the northern Black Sea and Trabzon, Sinop, Samsun and İstanbul on the southern coasts were mostly Greeks and Turks, all Ottoman subjects (for example Greek Kosta of Trabzon, Papas of Trabzon, Yani Chermo of Misivri, Türk Ali of Gallipoli, and Menteşe of Samsun). Genoese merchants from Galata or Chios were visiting in these ports but almost no Genoese captain is recorded for this period (Lucian Frenk, apparently a Genoese merchant, for example, purchased 15 casks of fish at Kilia in 1496).

Ships from İstanbul brought to Kilia Aegean products, such as raisins, figs, hazelnuts, walnuts, cotton, rice and wine. On their return they took from Kilia sturgeon and codfish pickled in brine, and caviar, which were the principal exports to İstanbul and to Italian colonies in the Aegean and Italy. Livestock merchants settled in Akkerman were mostly Turkish butchers or merchants. They regularly sent by sea large numbers of sheep and cattle to İstanbul. Hides for the Genoese of Chios made up the bulk of the exports from Caffa, Akkerman and Kilia until the island was occupied by the Ottomans in 1566. Between March 16 and June 12, 1496, from Kilia alone these merchants exported over 3,200 cow hides, with a value of about 85,000 akça. Also large quantities of morina or codfish, salt and tallow were exported from Moldavia by way of Akkerman and Kilia. Kilia also became one of the main transit ports for slaves captured in the north. The guards from the fortresses of Özü and Akkerman were heavily engaged in the slave trade.

A report by the tax-farmer of the port of Kilia, dated 1505, indicates the importance of wine exports from the Aegean to Poland and Muscovy.

> The fish caught and exported from the port of Kilia [he stated] were, for the most part, sold to the ships bringing wine from the lands under Venetian control. They brought wine but it was not sold at Kilia. After paying the customs duties, they passed on in transit to Poland and Muscovy. In those countries the wine was exchanged for native products which once again were taxed at the time of their passage through Kilia. Thus, a substantial revenue for the Ottoman fisc was realized from this traffic. But now, since the wine ships no longer come to this port, the revenue from customs and the sale of the fish, which was estimated at three hundred thousand akça a year, is lost.

Evidently, in the light of this report, the Ottomans permitted the Venetians to bring to Kilia wine from Crete until the last decade of the sixteenth century. Wine came to Kilia also from Ottoman lands through the Danubian ports of Vidin and Silistre, or the eastern Bulgarian ports of Varna and Misivri, as well as from Trabzon. Quality wine of Monemvasia, as it was in great demand in Galata, Samsun and Sinop, could be found at Kilia. No noticeable change can be detected in the pattern of trade between the south and the north through Kilia in the period 1470 to 1570. In the entire period, basic exports from the steppe area in the north included grain, meat, fish, hides and skins, horses and slaves and imports such as dried fruit, wine and cotton goods arrived then from Asia Minor and the Aegean.

The customs registers of Akkerman give documentary evidence of the central importance of the port for the international trade between the south and the north by the first decade of the sixteenth century (Table I:59). According to the records of 1507–8, a great number of Moldavian merchants visited Akkerman while non-Muslim Ottomans, as well as Muslim Tatars and Turks, formed the majority of traders there. The busy traffic between Akkerman and Özü was carried on with smaller vessels, but large ships were engaged in the traffic with İstanbul, Trabzon and other Black Sea ports. In the period September 8, 1507 to February 3, 1508, the customs revenue for five months amounted to 23,785 *akça*, market dues to 498, port taxes to 6,803 and dues paid for wine to 3,050. Starting in October traffic slowed considerably, as indicated by the monthly tax revenues. In January only 75 *akça* was paid at customs.

SHEPHERDS AND COSSACKS

As seen earlier, threatened by the alliance of the Golden Horde and the Polish–Lithuanian commonwealth, the Crimean Khanate under Mengli Giray pursued a policy of complete cooperation with the Ottomans and placed Polish lands under constant pressure with continual raids while, at the same time, seeking to strengthen the Crimean hold on the steppe between the Dnieper and Dniester.

Also, as a result of large-scale sheep and cattle exports to İstanbul and taxation involved in this activity, the use of pastures in Moldavia and the steppe north of Akkerman and the mouth of the Dnieper became a critical issue between the Ottoman government and Moldavia and Poland. With the growing demand for sheep and cattle for İstanbul, more and more people became engaged in the business. This demand caused merchants of Kilia and Akkerman to take territories in Moldavia and the steppe between the Lower Dniester and the Lower Dnieper to use as pasturelands for their herds. The people involved in sheep and cattle breeding and trade were Tatars and Turks from Kilia, Akkerman, Özü and Dobruja. In 1539, in his letter to the Polish king, Sultan Süleyman admitted that "Each year, herds of sheep coming from Kilia and Akkerman cross over the river Dniester and go into your [Polish] country. Along

Table I:59. Customs duties and other dues at Akkerman according to the regulation of 1484[60]

	Citizens of Akkerman, percent ad valorem (in Ottoman akça)	People from outside Akkerman ad valorem
Cloth	2 percent customs dues	5.5 buyer and seller
Merchandise in transit from "Rus" to the Black Sea and back		10 akça per 300 akça value "Rus" merchants or others in transit from "Rus" to the sea or back do not unload their merchandise at Akkerman. They pay the 3.33% transit tax but when merchandise is unloaded regular duty is to be paid.
Grain leaving port by ship	1 market due for each keylçe	
Sheep either from inside or outside the fortress is sold	1 by seller for each two; 1 by buyer for each four sheep	
Cattle sold by outsiders	5	Shared by seller and buyer equally
Cattle sold between inhabitants	2	Shared by seller and buyer equally
Horses	12	Shared by seller and buyer equally
Cloth (low cost) from "Rus" sold at bazaar	7.5 for each 100 zira	5 paid by seller and 2.5 by buyer
Mares	6	Shared by seller and buyer equally
All goods not mentioned here taxed as before the conquest		

Source: Topkapı Library, MS Revan no. 1935, 123a–124a and 1936, 131a–134a, text in facsimile, MS Bibliothèque Nationale, Paris; N. Beldiceanu (1973), pp. 410–12, 417–18.

with them, Tatars and adventurers from Dobruja, Akkerman and Kilia, pretending to be the owners of these herds, move into Polish lands and oppress your subjects."[61]

In the period following the campaign of 1538, Ottomans established control in southern Moldavia (Bucak), now organized as the sancak of Akkerman, thus beginning the closer control by the Ottomans over Moldavia, Wallachia and the Akkerman steppe. They also organized

systematic exploitation of their resources. The period 1538–41 is charac-
terized by the imposition of a series of political, economic and military
obligations on the two principalities. In 1544, they were both required
to provide İstanbul annually with 100,000 sheep. The herds were to be
driven by their owners or other men and sold at a fixed price determined
periodically by a commission led by the kadi of Akkerman. The Porte
considered this a profitable trade for the owners of herds, but the voyvodes had the responsibility to ensure that the exact number arrived on
schedule in İstanbul, which was suffering from a chronic shortage of
meat supplies. Upon the objection of the voyvode of Wallachia, the
number was reduced to 50,000 for the following year. This quota was in
addition to the purchase of sheep by private individuals who came to
Ottoman Kilia and Akkerman to make purchases, a practice dating back
to the fifteenth century. In times of shortage or when the army and
navy needed provisioning, the Porte sent commands to the voyvodes to
procure sheep, cattle, grain, flour, honey and tallow. Such demands from
the voyvodes may be considered within the general Ottoman system of
extraordinary levies, *avarız*.

By the mid-sixteenth century, Cossack raids into Ottoman territory
on the western side of the Dniester river, to capture sheep, cattle and
shepherds, became routine as more and more herds belonging to the
Nogay Tatars, the Kazaks of Akkerman and the Tatars of Dobruja were
crossing the border and grazing along the Dnieper river. In 1564, a temporary agreement was reached between the Polish and Ottoman governments to avoid conflicts.[62] Since the Tatars were under the Crimean
khan's authority, the sultan in 1564 sent an imperial order to the khan
to remove them through persuasion. On the other hand, shepherds from
the Akkerman area were to be controlled and the number of sheep and
cattle were to be registered on the frontier so that the pasture tax could
be collected. But none of these measures helped reduce tension in the
area. The fundamental issue was whether the rich soil of the Ukrainian
steppe would be a pastureland exploited by Tatar herds to feed the Ottoman capital city or a settlement zone for the Slavic or Moldavian peasants.

THE BURSA–BRAŞOV ROUTE

Since the publication of Wilhelm Heyd's work on the Levantine trade,[63]
historians have believed that the Ottoman conquest of Constantinople
was a deadly blow to the traffic in oriental goods between the Levant
and east-central Europe via the Black Sea, or the Danube–Wallachia.

More recently R. Lopez and M. Malowist accepted this theory.[64] However, it is shown that during the period 1400–1520, despite political rivalry and frequent confrontations, the Ottoman territories established quite active commercial relations with east-central Europe and southern Germany.[65] Through their outposts on the Danube – principally Brăila, Silistre, Rusçuk, and Nicopolis, Vidin and Smederevo – and beyond the Danube through the vassal principality of Wallachia, quite an active trade developed, based mainly on the exchange of woolen cloth and metals from Europe and silk and cotton cloth and spices from the Ottoman lands. This trade route, the main transit center of which was Brašov on the Wallachian–Transylvanian border, competed successfully with the Venice–east-central Europe traffic for the Levantine trade (see Table I:60). This new trade route coincided with the rise of Bursa and Edirne in the last decades of the fourteenth century as international emporiums of "oriental goods" – silk and cotton textiles and spices. We have seen that the Genoese of Pera and Caffa then were purchasing "oriental goods" in Bursa, a closer and more secure market than Trabzon and Tabriz. Then, Ottoman expansion from the fourteenth century on made it possible for Ottoman subjects to bring these goods directly by caravan from Edirne to the Danubian ports.

Hungarian historian Z. Pach has recently examined this question, asking whether or not the Danube route constituted a major channel for oriental goods, whether it indeed followed the Danube or the Saxon towns of Transylvania, and what impact in general the Ottoman conquest had on this trade route.[66] Focusing on sources of the fifteenth century, mostly grants of privileges of commerce to the merchants of Brašov, Pach demonstrated that this city was the main transit center for traffic in oriental goods from the Black Sea and the Danube. Brăila was the main port on the Danube for the Black Sea trade before Kilia replaced it in importance. However, a commercial privilege granted by the Bulgarian Czar Stratsimir (1371–93) at Vidin to the merchants of Brašov, suggests that a land route also existed to the south. The Danubian ports visited by Saxon and Wallachian merchants were Drustor (Silistre), Giurgiu and Nicopolis.

In fact, by securing the cooperation of the Genoese, through a Danubian–Black Sea route, the Hungarian kings, Louis of Anjou (1342–82) and Sigismond of Luxembourg (1387–1437) already had endeavored to receive oriental goods – mainly silk, silk cloth, a kind of fine cotton textile called *bogası*, and spices – directly and more cheaply from Pera.

Table I:60. Development of the foreign trade of the city of Brašov,
1484–1600 (the value of goods passing through customs in florins)

Year	Total	Export and transit goods	Import of natural goods from Wallachia and Moldavia	Transit of oriental goods
1484–85	65,000	—	—	—
1501	80,000	—	—	—
1502	85,000	—	—	—
1503	167,000	60,000	22,000	85,000
1504	140,000	—	—	—
1505	95,000	—	—	—
1507–8	70,000	—	—	—
1515	100,000	—	—	—
1516	75,000	—	—	—
1517	60,000	—	—	—
1529–30	33,000	10,000	15,000	8,000
1532–38	100,000	—	—	—
1542	80,000	23,000	16,000	41,000
1543	82,000	26,000	22,000	31,000
1545	65,000	19,000	29,000	17,000
1546 (incompl.)	74,000	24,000	32,000	18,000
1547	67,000	21,000	26,000	20,000
1548 (incompl.)	56,000	2,300	30,000	23,700
1549	76,000	22,000	31,000	23,000
1550	70,000	19,000	31,000	20,000
1551 (incompl.)	48,000	15,000	33,000	—
1552–53	80,000	—	—	—
1554	82,000	23,000	27,000	32,000
1555–96	80,000	—	—	—
1600	60,000	—	—	—

Source: Manolescu (1960), p. 219.

Thus, Hungarians were able to deprive the Venetians, their rivals in Dalmatia, of the benefits of the Levantine trade in their region. It is clear, therefore, that the long struggle between the Hungarians and the Ottomans for control of the Lower Danube basin (Wallachia and northern Bulgaria) in the period 1366–1428 had a significant economic and commercial dimension.

At the turn of the fifteenth century, the goods in transit to the south from the north still included Western fine woolen cloth of southern Germany and Silesia and iron tools, particularly knives of Styria. Already in the Transylvanian Charter of 1412, among the articles brought by Muslims (*Saracenos*) were pepper and fine spices as well as "bombasio" (*bogası*), saffron, cotton and mohair. *Bogası* and saffron were typical Anatolian export products. Interestingly, Turkish carpets appear to have been a valuable import item in Brašov, since the wealthy burghers of that mercantile city appear to have invested a great deal in these precious objects of art from the Orient, and, later on, donated them to the cathedral in their city. Today, the Brašov collection of early Turkish carpets is one of the richest in the world.[67]

The fine woolen cloth imported from the West to Brašov (valued at 613,045 akça in 1503) and re-exported through Wallachia to the Ottoman lands included that manufactured in the Low Countries (Bruges, Maastricht, Mecheln), Germany (Aachen, Breslau, Freiberg, Cologne, Nürnberg, Werden, Speyer, Zwickau, Linde, Lauenberg), Italy (Verona, Bergamo) and Czech towns (Jihlava, Kutna-Hora, Zhorolec), Poland (Lwow) and Transylvania.[68] Of these imports, 43.9 percent went to Wallachia, 7.7 percent to Moldavia and 48.4 percent to Transylvania. A special item, knives of Styria, Graz and Nürnberg, which became an object of spectacular trade between the Ottoman Empire and Austria, is of particular interest. The imports through Brašov were already mentioned in a charter given by Voyvode Mirčea to the merchants of that city in 1413.[69] According to the customs register of Brašov, [70] 2,400,000 knives valued at 1,457,820 akça were imported in 1503 and the greater part were re-exported to the Ottoman lands. Famous as "Wallachian knives" (eflak-bıçağı), because the Ottoman merchants bought them from Wallachians, they were inexpensive and very popular throughout the empire. In 1480, a merchant from Bursa, engaged in commerce between Bursa and Egypt, had 11,400 of them in his stock.[71] The merchants of Brašov participated in commercial traffic beyond the Danube to Ottoman territory, as attested as early as 1413.[72]

In 1429, when peace with the Ottomans was reestablished, the Wallachian Voyvode Dan II (1420–31) informed the Brašov merchants that they could resume their commercial activities "as far as the sea," that is, the Black Sea. The voyvode of Wallachia twice collected a customs duty of 3 percent – once on the passage of merchandise taken to the other side of the Danube and the other when merchants brought back other goods.

In the privilege granted by the same voyvode in 1431, the ports of call for commercial exchange are identified as Silistre, Giurgiu and Nicopolis. To this list Brăila should be added as the chief port for oriental goods during this period. On the other hand, Ottoman merchants visited the fairs and other places in Wallachia and "were almost as numerous as the Wallachian [merchants] there." The Wallachian voyvode in 1476 informed Brašov merchants of the arrival of "a Turkish merchant with a great quantity of fine merchandise."[73] But in general, oriental goods were exchanged with imports via Brašov by the Wallachian and Moldavian merchants at ports on the Danube and the Black Sea. While Brašov's role as a transit center developed, certain export industries also developed in the city, such as those for woolen cloth, dresses, vehicle frames, horse equipment, furniture and hardware. The fact that goods at the Brašov customs were valued in Ottoman *akça* already at the turn of the fifteenth century is illustrative of its close economic dependency on the Ottoman market to the south. Larger sums were computed in Hungarian florins, which equaled 50 *akça* throughout the first half of the sixteenth century.[74] The Ottoman *akça* had a higher circulation value there as compared to the home market.

The gradual increase of Wallachian merchants among the merchants of Brašov in the trade of oriental goods must be related to the growing dependence of Wallachia on the Ottoman sultan and the impact of the Ottoman conquest on the Black Sea basin.

By 1503, oriental goods at Brašov customs included (aside from pepper and other spices) cotton, copper and raisins, which were all Anatolian products. Ottoman Muslim merchants at the Danubian ports of Wallachia were called in the documents "Sarracenos," a common name for Muslims. Evidently, these Sarracenos were mostly Turkish merchants who, following the Ottoman annexation of Danubian Bulgaria in 1393, extended their activities to the shores of the river. In the late fourteenth century, no Muslim merchant is mentioned in the lists. One century later, Ottoman customs registers mention them in Brăila, Hirsova, Rusçuk, Silistre, Nicopolis and Vidin with the same commodities.[75]

The import merchants at Sibiu (Nagyszeben) may all have been Wallachians, while at Brašov those who imported 80 percent of the spices were Wallachians, Transylvanians and Moldavians. It can be concluded that spices imported into Hungary must have come first in caravans via Bursa and Edirne to the western Danubian ports and were bought there by Wallachians, while Transylvanians and Moldavians joined them, buying the shipments at the eastern ports. The Moldavian share in this trade, however, is quite insignificant.

The Bursa–Hungary pepper route

Wallachian transit trade appears to have realized big profits from the exchange of the woolen cloth of Central Europe for oriental goods,

pepper in particular. It appears that after, as well as before, the Portuguese arrival in India, the Ottoman Empire was quite well supplied with
spices, so that the needs of the internal market were met and the surplus
was re-exported to the northern Black Sea and the Danubian regions.
Actually there were two spice routes to east-central Europe, Venice–
Pozsony and Bursa–Brašov.[76] Pepper imports via Venice–Pozsony to
Hungary in the fiscal year 1457–58 equaled only 166 quintals or 98 metric
quintals, with a value estimated at the custom house of 2,833 florins (in
another estimate 5,004 florins), while yearly imports from the East, i.e.,
Ottoman territories, were much larger, amounting to about 463 metric
quintals (at Brašov one quintal equaled about 56 kg). Imports from the
East were large and far exceeded local demand in supplying the markets
of Transylvania and Hungary. According to the Sibiu customs register
of 1500, two Vlach merchants from Curtea de Argeş came to that city
six times and bought altogether about 105 quintals of pepper and paid
4,120.5 florins for it. Pach estimated the then annual import at 825 quintals of pepper with a value of 36,000 gold florins in these two transit
centers combined.[77] This was, Pach added, an enormous amount when
compared to the imports to Pozsony via Venice in 1457–58. However,
the price of the imports through Venice proved to be only 30 gold florins
a quintal but those arriving in Transylvanian cities cost 43.6 florins per
quintal.[78] Actually, pepper fell about 50 percent on the Venetian wholesale market between the 1420s and the 1440s and until the end of the
century remained at 40 to 50 ducats per cargo (120 kg), which was well
below the prices common during the first decades of the century.[79] Surplus pepper imported from the East to Transylvania was re-exported to
the fair of Nagyvarad. Changing hands there, carts loaded with high-
valued oriental goods proceeded to the cities further west in Hungary,
where Saxon merchants of Brašov and Kassa (Kaschau) monopolized this
long-distance trade. Also, by 1500, merchants of Kassa exchanged cloth
with wine imported by the merchants of Brašov. The cloth purchases
involved big investments. In one case, the transaction amounted to 8,709
florins.[80]

The bulk of spice imports consisted of pepper, ginger and incense,
followed far behind by cloves. Expensive spices such as saffron,
cinnamon and nutmeg were imported in negligible amounts (see Table
I:61).

As indicated above, from the end of the fourteenth century and perhaps
even earlier the principal emporium of oriental goods was Bursa, and
spices arrived at the Danubian ports from there. It is a well-established

Table I:61. Pepper prices around 1500 (in florins/ducats)

	1480–1500	1500–05	1515–25
Egypt	19 (1496)	—	—
Bursa	19–24	—	—
Pera	—	27 (1501)	—
Adrianople (Edirne)	—	18–19 (official price 1502)	
Giurgiu	—	—	36 (1525)
Kilia	—	40–48 (1504)	—
Akkerman	—	20–36 (1504)	36 (1515)
Brašov	—	40–55 (1503)	—
Nagyszeben	40–44 (1500)	—	—
Nagyvarad	—	45 (1502)	
Venice	19–23	—	—
Florence	24	—	—
Pozsony	30 (1457–58)	—	—

Note: Prices are adjusted as follows: 1 Ottoman *kantar* = 56 kg; 1 Vienna and Buda *kantar* = 56–59 kg; 1 Egyptian *kantar* = 185 kg; 1 Venetian *cargo* = 120 kg; 1 Hungarian florin = 50 *akça*
Sources: Lane (1973), pp. 288–89; İnalcık (1960b), pp. 131–40; Pach (1980), pp. 12–15.

fact that by 1500 the spice trade was big business in Bursa and was controlled by Turkish and Jewish merchants on the one side and the importing Arabs of Aleppo and Damascus on the other.[81]

The Middle Eastern nations were the beneficiary and chief agents of the international spice commerce. The change brought about by Ottoman expansion in the period 1400–1500 meant that the Genoese lost control of this trade to Ottoman subjects, as well as the slave trade which was the other source of their fortune. The prices of Bursa and Adrianople were almost doubled at Transylvanian customs. Profits made through the Venice–Pozsony route appear to be less than the eastern route. One should keep in mind, however, that various factors, including transportation costs, different measurements, volume and place of origin make all our comparisons tentative. In this connection a comparison should be made between the privileged trader system of Central and Eastern European states, where trade monopolies in oriental goods were reserved to certain cities and groups of merchants, in contrast to more liberal Ottoman policies.

In Brašov, beginning with the end of the fourteenth century, the total annual value of exports and transit goods peaked in 1503 and 1504, and fluctuated between 70,000 and 80,000 florins in the first half of the sixteenth century (see Table I:60). The fall in exports derived from the development of substitute industries in Wallachia and Moldavia. Wars between the Habsburgs and the Ottomans sometimes even blocked transit goods moving from Central Europe toward the Ottoman Empire.

The sudden decline in the market in the years 1529 and 1530 was due to the attacks on Austria by the Ottomans and their Wallachian and Moldavian vassals. The imports of oriental goods were unusually high in 1503, amounting in value to 85,000 gold pieces. This high traffic may have been due to the Ottoman–Venetian War. During war years, Central Europe received the bulk of its supplies of oriental goods through Brašov instead of Venice, whereupon this trade sharply fell below normal levels. But during the Ottoman–Habsburg War of 1529–30, the average volume of trade at Brašov remained at around 33,000 florins a year. Exports from Brašov and transit goods from Europe to the Romanian and Ottoman territories averaged 10,000 florins, in the same period. It should be noted that direct export or transit trade from Brašov to the Ottoman cities appears to have been limited, since most of these goods were taken by the Moldavian and Wallachian merchants to be re-exported to Ottoman lands. Wallachian merchants included Armenians, Greeks and Jews along with Vlachs.[82] As in the case of the Ottoman Empire, big merchants, whose average investment was about 1,450 florins at the beginning of the sixteenth century, were almost exclusively engaged in the wholesale trade of oriental and Western goods. Their clients were merchants of small investment, retailers or members of the ruling class or wealthy burghers who were interested in fine Western woolen cloth or the silk cloth of Bursa.

In the first half of the sixteenth century, Brašov lost its former significance both as international emporium and as a trade center within Romanian lands. In the period of economic decline the average investment of a great merchant in an enterprise drastically fell from about 1,450 florins to 641 florins, while there was a concomitant shrinkage in the import and export trade in luxury goods.[83]

Competition among the "Levantine merchants," Greeks, Jews, Armenians and Turks, was sharp during the second half of the sixteenth century. "With the support of the Turks," read the Ottoman government, "these Levantine merchants specialized in the commerce in oriental goods, and being free from all kinds of corporate regulations, violated the rights of transit and storage of the merchants of Brašov, and, finally, they extended their trading all over Transylvania." The efforts of Brašov merchants and the measures taken by the municipalities to protect the trade monopoly all failed. By the end of the sixteenth century, Greeks in Brašov, along with Transylvanian merchants, Vlachs, Armenians and Turks, Arabs, Italians and Poles, were trading as well. Voyvodes of Wallachia and Moldavia supported their subjects in breaking the Brašov's trade monopoly.[84] Its annual fair, held since 1364, gave foreign merchants the opportunity to exchange their merchandise freely. In 1554, about one thousand merchants visited Brašov, mostly from Wallachia, Moldavia and Transylvania.

In the second half of the sixteenth century, the century-old trade pattern with Poland did not change much. Poland imported wine, hides, cattle, fish and salt from the south, which were destined for the fairs of Hotin, Jaroslav, Lwow, and Krakau, and Poland exported woolen cloth, now mainly of English manufacture but also from the Netherlands, the Rheinland and Italy. Part of this export was met by the textile industries which had been organized by the Italians in Sibiu during the sixteenth century.[85] Thus, besides Western transit goods, the native industries of Transylvania, Poland and Habsburg Hungary and its hereditary lands provided manufactures for the Ottoman market. Western merchants also used the Lwow–Moldavia–İstanbul route in the last decades of the sixteenth and first decades of the seventeenth century (see below, pp. 364–72).

East-central European commerce gave rise to quite a complex network of trade routes in the areas surrounding the Ottoman-controlled lands in upper Hungary, Slovakia, Silesia and Poland. "During the Turkish domination in the Karpathian basin, the trade relations of Transylvania with Silesia and the neighboring German lands were stronger than those with Austria and upper Germany."[86]

During the sixteenth century the Ottoman government intervened to protect Serbian merchants in Austria.[87] The treaty concluded at Zsitva-Török in 1606 granted for the first time a formal recognition of the freedom of trade between Austria and the Ottoman Empire and guaranteed the security of the merchants.[88] The freedom of commerce was granted to the merchants of the Holy Roman Empire and all the countries under the Habsburgs including Austria, Hungary, Flanders and Spain. Merchants coming to Ottoman territory were required to carry the emperor's patent and to pay customs duty at the rate of 3 percent *ad valorem* on imported and exported goods alike. In addition, they paid a 2 percent fee to the emperor's agent or consul. Once the customs duty was paid, no additional duties could be exacted in any other place. The emperor's agent or consul was required to attend to any problems arising among the merchants in accordance with Austrian law. Legal cases involving a sum of more than 4,000 *akça* were brought before the sultan's *divan*. And when a merchant died, the emperor's agent or consul took his properties into custody and Ottoman agents were not to interfere.

Thus, the treaty of 1606 provided the basic capitulation privileges for merchants from the territories under Habsburg control. In 1617, Sultan Ahmed I granted full capitulations and in 1666, following the peace treaty of Vasvar (1664), the emperor attributed great importance to the renewal of the capitulations. Now, the Austrian government, eager to emulate Western mercantile economies, attempted to play a more active role in the Levant trade and to set up the first Austrian Levant company.

During the two decades following the Habsburg capitulations of 1666, the expansion of trade with the Ottoman south triggered the settlement of Serbian, Armenian and Greek communities in commercial centers such as Eperjes, Buda, Pozsony (Pressburg), Vienna, Prag, Breslau and Leipzig, which grew into real merchant colonies in the eighteenth century.[89]

HUNGARY: THE NEW FRONTIER

A stronghold on the Danube built under the Serbian ruler George Branković (1427–59), Smederevo became the most important Ottoman center for military operations and trade following the annexation of the despotate in 1459. The *sancak* of Smederevo, which corresponded to the old Serbian despotate, faced Hungary, and until the conquest of Belgrade in 1521 its governor held a special place among the other begs of Rumeli.

In addition to his regular income, the commander of Smederevo collected dues for himself from the traffic of goods and boats operating between Hungary and the Ottoman lands. The Hungarian kingdom, then including Transylvania, Slovakia, Slavonia, Croatia and the Banat, exported mainly woolen cloth, metals, cattle and horses to the Ottoman Empire. Smederevo was the main port of entry.

There, commercial dues consisted of three categories: customs dues, market dues, and transit dues.[90] Customs duty on goods imported from Hungary amounted to 8 percent *ad valorem*, 5 percent going to the commander, and 3 percent to the treasury.

After their crushing victory at Mohács (1526), the Ottomans appear to have intended to maintain Hungary as a vassal state beyond the Danube, under Janos Zapolya (1526–41), in the same manner as they had Wallachia or Moldavia. But circumstances – the minority of King Zapolya's successor and Habsburg claims on the Hungarian heritage – compelled the Ottomans to take the central plains under their direct control and organize them as a frontier province (*beglerbegilik*) in the period 1541–66. In addition to the central Hungarian plains, the new province included Sirem (Szerem) between the Drava and Sava rivers as well as the *sancak* of Smederevo on the right bank of the Danube.

Under Ottoman rule, Buda's position changed from capital of a powerful central European kingdom to a frontier city of a Middle Eastern empire. From 1526 on, Transylvania (Erdel) became a tributary country, thereby enjoying the protection of the Ottoman state. As such, it appears to have continued its role as an intermediary in trade between the Ottoman Empire and east-central Europe.[91]

Ottoman rule brought to Hungarian society a radical disruption, because the Ottomans abolished the royal Hungarian administrative and legal system and applied Ottoman laws.[92] Hungarians had to go to Ottoman courts for their legal affairs except for those situations directly under religious law. Since the Ottomans had to construct a large network of fortified places and maintain numerous garrisons, the government was obliged to supplement local revenues with large sums from the central imperial treasury. On the other hand, there occurred striking increases, in some cases as much as fourfold, in revenue collection in Hungary between 1552 and 1580. These monies allowed the government to pay the garrisons from surpluses in local revenue.[93]

As frontier territory, the Hungarian lands became the scene of almost constant warfare between the Ottoman and Habsburg empires for 150 years and large areas near the frontier reverted, it is argued, to pasturelands or swamps. Booty became an important source of livelihood. Under the circumstances both Ottoman and Austrian governments agreed that small-scale raiding should not be considered a cause for breaking the peace.

In frontier fortresses, in addition to the regular salaried soldiery, there was a large group of volunteers who lived exclusively on booty. These volunteers were unemployed youths, mostly landless peasants, who came to the frontier areas to make their livelihood by joining the raids, and they expected to obtain a salaried appointment as regular guards whenever there was a vacancy through dismissal or death.[94]

In the course of the sixteenth century, the Muslim Ottomans apparently established only small communities, which were mostly settled in towns. Nowhere in Hungary was the Ottomanization and Islamization process as complete as in western Anatolia or the eastern Balkans. The extent to which a Hungarian town came under Ottoman influence was determined by the size of the military–administrative personnel settled there. Only in the large administrative centers, such as Buda, Pest, Segedin (Szeged), and Istolni-Belgrade, did community life come under the direct influence of Ottoman culture. While the Turkish military and administrative personnel settled in the fortresses, the *varoş*, the outside quarters, preserved its autonomous communal life and even the pre-Ottoman Hungarian municipal institutions survived.[95] However, the responsibilities and authority of a Hungarian *biro* or quarter headman were very different from those of his pre-Ottoman peer, some of them even enjoying an Ottoman *timar*.[96] In general, because of the Bosniak origin of most Ottoman soldiers in Hungary, the Bosniak version of Ottoman–Islamic culture was more visible than in other areas.

Strategic conditions were responsible for economic-urban developments in certain provincial centers, such as Istolni-Belgrade and Solnok, while on the Danube the ports of Estergon, Vác and Kuvin grew in importance. Old Hungarian fairs continued to be held in Buda, as before. Buda, Varadin, Kopan, Simintorna, Istolni-Belgrade, Sombor, Sytila, and Varat were strongly Ottomanized towns whose physical structure changed with the construction of mosques, religious colleges and schools, hospices for the traveller and the destitute, bathhouses for men and women, dervish convents, public water fountains and kiosks and mansions for dignitaries and notables which contained private baths. For security reasons the Christian-Hungarian population in many fortified cities was transferred to *varoş*. The *varoş* also included poor Muslim districts protected by outer walls. In some fortified cities the Christian population was exempted from extraordinary tax levies in return for repairing the defenses. Such a policy must also have been thought to ensure the loyalty of the native Christian population.

In the countryside each Hungarian village was put under a Hungarian *biro*, elected from among themselves and representing the village community. The *biro* collected taxes in the village and delivered them to the Ottoman authorities and was responsible for making arrangements for the implementation of government orders. As for the *timar*-holding Muslim *sipahi*s, they lived mostly in the fortified cities as guards or in a nearby town. In the countryside, the Ottoman impact on peasant life became profound mainly because the Ottoman government, abolishing the privileges of the Hungarian nobility through the application of the *çift-hane* and the *timar* system, established its own system of landholding and taxation.

In Hungary, as in other frontier areas, members of the soldiery, the Janissaries or *azeb*s from the fortress garrisons who had an entrepreneurial spirit were active in trade, specializing in goods which their fellow soldiers could not find in local markets. Some of them over time became merchants with large investments in luxury goods. Even dignitaries in high positions, including pashas, invested their extra income in inter-regional commerce.[97] But the law-maker stipulated that military men engaged in trade could not evade paying customs duties on their transactions.

In order to meet the needs and demands of the soldiery, new crafts were introduced, particularly in the clothing, metalwork, and leather industries. Later, the French would invite Hungarian experts to convey to them the secrets of fine Turkish leather goods.[98]

As time went by, cultural interaction between the rulers and the ruled became pronounced, particularly in towns, conversions to Islam increased, and Turkish crafts and arts were imitated. All these in turn entailed closer and more intensive economic relations between Hungary and the Ottoman Balkans and Anatolia. Ottoman frontier culture (*serhadlı*) in language, lifestyle and clothing with a strong Bosnian flavor was transplanted into Hungary. Bosnian soldiery and settlement were particularly strong in the southern Hungarian towns and there Serbo-Croatian became the prevalent language.[99]

The slave trade flourished in this frontier province. In Evliya we have a vivid description, after a raid into enemy territory in 1666, of how the booty and slaves were sold in Kanija, the principal stronghold at the Ottoman–Austrian frontier.[100] The raiding party entered the city which was in a jubilant mood and each soldier was offered hospitality by the townsfolk in their houses, while the slaves were placed in dungeons. The next morning the slaves and the booty were taken for sale to the main bazaar. The slaves, their clothing, swords and posses-sions were sold in an auction which lasted five days. Slaves were sold for between 200 and 1,000 gold coins. Ten of the fifty slaves were surrendered to the pasha in payment for the imperial one-fifth share (*pencik*). After everything was sold, the booty money amounted to 18,160 gold coins. The raiders' losses as well as the fees of the two guides were paid out of this sum and 40 *guruş* for the poor, 10 *guruş* for the two gate-keepers of the fortress and other expenses for the sheep sacrificed for the dead soldiers, and the care of the wounded. Afterwards, everybody came together in the mosque of Sultan Mehmed III and the shares were distributed among 1,490 raiders (*gazi*). Evliya obtained four extra shares, two for his two faithful servants and two for his services as scribe in drawing up the roll call of the raiders and the distribution. The mosque employees were not forgotten and received five gold pieces. Evliya recited the verse of *fath* and the ceremony ended with the loud prayers of all fighters for Islam, for the Prophet, the martyrs, the dead raiders and the saints.

In general, trade was difficult and dangerous in Hungary, not only because of robbers (*haydut*) infesting the countryside but also because of the raids of Hungarian bands from Habsburg territory. Unsafe conditions on the highways and the high cost of travel and transportation made trade sluggish, and bartering seems to have been more widely practiced in Hungary than in the hinterland.

The main military highway, the Osk–Tolna–Cankurtaran route, also was used by trade caravans. River traffic, however, was safer.

The Danube was used particularly for the transport of bulky goods, such as grain, and other agricultural products coming from the south. The largest ships held 1,200–1,400 *kile*, or 30–34 tons, and smaller boats, half this amount. Traffic on the iced-over Danube stopped during the winter months. Toward 1567, under the governor Sokollu Mustafa Pasha, a bridge was constructed between Buda and Pest.

It appears that a great part of the imports from the south were consumed by the Ottoman soldiery and staff who settled in Hungarian cities and towns. Their lifestyle, diet and dress habits apparently determined the nature of the imports and trade patterns in Ottoman Hungary.[101] It is important to note also that Ottomans were responsible for the introduction of certain staples, such as rice, and certain types of grapes into Hungary. In order to meet the growing need for rice, which was costly to transport, the Ottomans brought cultivators specialized in rice growing, and rice cultivation spread in the countryside.

Textile imports were mostly from the Ottoman Balkans and Anatolia. As in other northern provinces, woolens of Yanbolu, Tirnovo and Salonica were also popular in Hungary and were evidently in demand by the Muslim population of the fortresses and garrisons.

By 1545, there were regular trade relations between Ottoman Hungary and Vienna and the Hungarian lands under Habsburg rule. In this trade, items of international commerce included spices, knives of German steel, and, in particular, European woolen cloth. Pepper imports from the Ottoman Empire were of negligible quantity: 409 and 707 bales in 1571 and 1573 respectively, but by 1580 even these quantities had fallen sharply. Cotton goods, brought into Hungary from the south in quite sizable amounts, must have been consumed locally, not re-exported further to the west (Table I:62).

It appears that the export of oriental goods, including silk and cotton goods and carpets, was not substantial in the Hungarian transit trade to

Table I:62. Total textile imports at the ports of Buda and Pest

	1571	1573	1580
Woolens			
Çuha (woolen cloth)	35 *denk*	51 *denk*	over 32 *denk*
Felt (*aba*)	12 *denk*	13 *denk*	31 (?) *denk*
Kebe (cloaks)	over 89 *denk*	over 10 *denk*	over 2 *denk*
Aba (cloaks)	24 *denk*	50 *denk*	—
Kebe of Yanbolu	over 25 *denk*	4 *denk*	—
Kebe of Tirnovo	3 (?)	—	—
Mohair	—	—	1 *denk*
Carpets (*halı, kilim*)	over 3 *denk*	900 pieces	44 *deste*
Cotton goods			
Cotton	43 *denk*	11 *denk*	3 *denk*
Kırbas	over 56 *denk*	over 22 *denk*	1 *denk*
cotton thread	23 *denk*	—	—
Bogası	17 *denk*	83 *denk*	over 32 *denk*
Muslin (*dülbend*)	—	15 (?)	—
Flax	45 *denk*	54 *denk*	over 59 *denk*
Bürümcük	—	—	4 *top*

Source: Fekete and Káldy-Nagy (1962); Barkan (1943).

Habsburg territories. Evidently the bulk of the imports into Buda and Pest met the needs of Ottoman military personnel and small Muslim settlements.

Vác was the main transit center for Hungary's trade with Austria. The carts leaving Vác with rock salt or empty in early spring, returned laden with wares from the West — in particular woolen cloth from Breslau, Nürnberg, Languedoc and other Western cloth manufacturing centers (see Table I:63). Transylvanian salt, an important item of export to Austria, was transported by boats on the rivers Maroş and Tisza to the port at Tibel, where it was stored.[102]

Large-scale imports from Austria consisted, in addition to woolen cloth, of a special cap called *astarhal* worn by Hungarians, or knives which were taken further into the Balkans and Anatolia. The *Londra* and *Londrina* cloth mentioned in the registers was rather an imitation of English woolen cloth made in Languedoc. Popular *ıskarlat* and *karziya* (*karazsia*) types also were imported through Vác.

Livestock breeding and export was important to the Hungarian economy long before the Ottomans appeared.[103] In the sixteenth century, about 50–60 percent of Hungarian commerce with Western countries consisted of livestock, 30 percent in textiles.

It has been argued that the Ottoman occupation of Hungary, by causing a sharp decline in cattle exports to Germany and Italy, was responsible for a substantial increase in meat prices and thus hurt the general

Table I:63. Textile imports from Habsburg territories and taxation at Estergon and Buda (in *akça*)

Woolen cloth	Imports 1571	Imports 1573	Imports 1580	Customs duties
One bale of *iskarlat* (100 *çehle*)	—	—	—	200
One bale of *iskarlat* (80 *çehle*)	—	—	—	100
Grane	—	—	—	12 per *dhira'*
Dimi	—	—	—	25 per *pastav*
Linç (Linz?), Desplum	—	—	—	500 per *denk*
Portugal	—	—	—	250 per *denk*
Linen of Linç (Linz?)	—	—	—	150 per *koçi*
Londura	—	—	—	50 per *pastav*
Braslavi (of Breslau)	1,309 *pastav*	713 *pastav*	2 *denk*	150 per *denk*
Karziya	112 *pastav*	313 *pastav*	—	
Igler (of Iglau?)	915 *pastav*	128 *pastav*	—	
Norinbergi (Nürnberg)	217 *pastav*	25 *pastav*	—	
Kisniče	609 *pastav*	10 *pastav*	165(?)	
Asterhal *süveg* (a kind of cap worn by Hungarians)	119,325 pieces	78,000 pieces	3,350 *fuçi*	25 per 100

Note: 100 *çehle*=50 *endaze* (*dhira'*) =39 meters; 1 *denk* = half a horseload; 1 *pastav* = one bale.
Source: Fekete and Káldy-Nagy (1962); Barkan (1943).

economy of those countries.[104] But recent studies have shown that this hypothesis stemmed from a misinterpretation of the sources.[105] In fact, cattle exports continued under the Ottomans, as before, as one of the main sources of Hungary's revenue. According to the Ottoman customs records of Vác,[106] just over 100,000 head of cattle were exported to Austria between June 1560 and April 1562, and from this the Ottoman fisc obtained 1,177,377 *akça*, or about 20,000 gold pieces, as customs duties. In 1580, 75,000 oxen were exported to Vienna and, in 1584, 9,000 head of cattle were sent to Zara for the Italian market. An estimated 80,000 oxen were exported yearly to Vienna and Germany. Incidentally, the exported oxen were not just for meat consumption but also for plowing.

It has also been argued that, as a result of the tax collectors' oppression, the peasant population abandoned their lands, which were then converted into pasture.[107] But the argument can be reversed: it actually was the European offer of higher prices for cattle exports that caused the expansion of animal husbandry at the expense of agriculture. We now know that the generalization claiming that whole villages were abandoned and agricultural economy was ruined under Ottoman rule is misleading. At least in certain areas, village lands were abandoned by peasants who settled in other areas and established new villages. Desertion of villages

Table I:64. Total imports of metal goods at the ports of Buda and Pest, and taxation

| Metal goods | Year | | | |
	1571	1573	1580	
Knives (*bıçak*)	436,750 pieces and 36 *fuçi*	274,250 pieces and 113 *fuçi*	1,500 pieces and 159 *fuçi*	Customs duty of 1,000 pieces 25 *akça*; if low quality, 12 *akça*
Swords	300 pieces	6 *denk*		
Horseshoes	76 *denk*	146 *denk*	22 *denk*	

Source: Fekete and Káldy-Nagy (1962); Barkan (1943), p. 303.

in fact was a general phenomenon under medieval conditions of agriculture and landholding, as witnessed in the Byzantine and Ottoman empires.

Imports from Austria also included knives, copper and tin. In particular, cheap Austrian knives, very popular in the Ottoman lands constituted, along with woolen cloth and *süveg* caps, the principal imports from the West (see Table I:64). In the "great city" of Sopron, Evliya[108] found a large number (3,000?) of shops engaged in the production of knives and other iron implements as well as a large group of manufacturers making woolen cloth and paper products destined for the Ottoman market.

NOTES

1 This is easily visible in Heyd's classic work (1936); now see Ashtor (1983), but the latter concentrates on Egypt and Syria for the period 1300–1500.
2 On the Genoese colonies in the Levant now see Balard (1978), especially I, pp. 177–309.
3 Stein (1924), pp. 1–62; Laiou (1972), pp. 260–80.
4 İnalcık (1991a), pp. 41, 103.
5 Thiriet (1958), I nos. 423, 461.
6 Barbaro (1873), p. 10.
7 İnalcık (1991a), pp. 17–31; Balard (1978), I, pp. 256, 269–354; II, pp. 701–883.
8 Pistarino (1980), pp. 66–67.
9 İnalcık (1991a), pp. 44–57.
10 Mantran (1962), index: Galata.
11 İnalcık (1965e), pp. 43–45.
12 İnalcık (1944), pp. 185–229.
13 İnalcık (1981b), p. 464.

14 Malowist (1947), p. 80.
15 *Ibid.*, p. 308.
16 *Ibid.*, p. 77.
17 Anhegger and İnalcık (1956), no. 36.
18 Malowist (1947), pp. 297–98.
19 İnalcık (1991b).
20 In 1339, the Genoese authorities of Caffa prohibited the following precious goods to be loaded on ships other than armed light galleys of 1,000 *kantars*: woolen cloth, silk, cloth of hemp, furs, saffron, amber, coral, costly woolen cloth of France, Lombardia and Ultra-Montana and such imports from the Levant as mohair, *bogası* (a fine cotton cloth), brocades which originated in Turkey, as well as gumlac, indigo and incense: see Balard (1978), II, pp. 567–71.
21 Wace cited by Öz (1946), p. 4.
22 Malowist (1947), p. 70.
23 İnalcık (1988b), document no. 16.
24 Malinovskiy (1793), pp. 210–212.
25 *Ibid.*, pp. 223–24.
26 *Ibid.*, p. 149.
27 İnalcık (1981b), pp. 445–66; İnalcık (1986b), pp. 184–89.
28 Berindei and Veinstein (1981), pp. 251–328; Veinstein (1980), pp. 228–49.
29 İnalcık (1991b).
30 Bennigsen and Lemercier-Quelquejay (1970), pp. 363–90.
31 İnalcık (1996), p. 143.
32 İnalcık (1979b), pp. 30–35, 43–44.
33 On the system called *mukataba* contract, *ibid.*, pp. 27–28.
34 *Ibid.*, pp. 35–41.
35 *Ibid.*, p. 44.
36 *Ibid.*, p. 40.
37 İnalcık (1979–80), p. 643.
38 BBA, MD 102, dated 967 H /1559–60.
39 See Barkan (1972), I; this is a basic source for Ottoman labor history.
40 İnalcık (1979b), pp. 43, 45, 52 note 67.
41 Berindei (1986), p. 50; Panaitescu (1933), pp. 172–93.
42 Papacostea (1981), p. 17.
43 Berindei (1986), p. 51.
44 *Ibid.*, p. 53.
45 Kurat (1940), p. 14.
46 Berindei (1986), p. 59.
47 *Ibid.*, pp. 55–59.
48 *Ibid.*, p. 58.
49 İnalcık (1988b), document nos. 1, 37, 41, 61b, 74, 82, 91; İnalcık (1981a), document nos. 73, 80, 97, 106, 123, 132, 140.
50 By 1386, in Caffa the Genoese had to leave the handling of local traffic in the Black Sea trade to the indigenous captains – Greeks, Armenians and Tatars, while they themselves kept the monopoly on overseas grand commerce, see Balard (1978), II, p. 572.

51 İnalcık (1996), index: Greeks, Armenians, Tatars.
52 Berindei (1986), pp. 55–56.
53 Beldiceanu-Steinherr and Beldiceanu (1964), pp. 39–42; Berindei (1986), p. 62.
54 Berindei (1986), p. 50.
55 *Ibid.*, p. 62.
56 Kraelitz (1921), document no. 1, pp. 44–45.
57 Berindei (1986), pp. 64–71; Papacostea (1981), pp. 28–39.
58 Papacostea (1981), pp. 39–54.
59 İnalcık (1979a), pp. 91–92.
60 According to Beldiceanu (1973), p. 174 note 1, "Rus" here stands for "la Russie Rouge" and merchant of "Rus" for "les marchands de Lemberg [Lwow]." Beldiceanu's translation, pp. 173–76, contains several errors due to misreading or misinterpretation. *Kepçe* is obviously a copy mistake for *keylçe*; one Akkerman *keylçe* equals 84.5 kg. The passage "if he unloads his wares" (p. 147) is correctly rendered in the other versions: "if he does not unload his wares" (p. 411); also in Topkapı MS Revan no. 1935, 123b, and no. 1936, 133a. *Bez* is an inexpensive kind of cloth, usually of cotton, linen or hemp, while expensive silk and woolen cloth is called *kumaş*, pl. *akmişe*.
61 Veinstein in Lemercier-Quelquejay *et al.* (1986), p. 134.
62 BBA, *Mühimme Defteri*: V, p. 28.
63 Heyd (1936); the first edition of the work, titled *Geschichte des Levanthandels*, appeared in 1879.
64 Pach (1968), pp. 57–58; Pach (1975), p. 454.
65 Manolescu (1965), pp. 151–52.
66 Pach (1976) and (1980), cf. Manolescu (1960), p. 451.
67 See Schmutzler (1933).
68 Manolescu (1960) and (1965).
69 Berindei (1986), p. 54.
70 Manolescu (1960), p. 55.
71 İnalcık (1960b).
72 Manolescu (1960), p. 209. The Ottoman quintal of 44 *okka* became the standard measure used by the merchants of Braşov.
73 Manolescu (1960), p. 209; Pach (1973), p. 452, calls them "Arabs."
74 One Hungarian florin was valued officially at 58 *akça* in İstanbul around 1500, Manolescu (1960), p. 179.
75 İnalcık (1993) p. 267; Cvetkova (1971), pp. 345–54.
76 Pach (1973), pp. 454–55; Pach (1980), pp. 5–35.
77 Pach (1973), p. 455.
78 In 1438 the price went down as low as 17 gold florins a quintal.
79 Lane (1973), p. 288.
80 Pach (1980), p. 32 note 141.
81 İnalcık (1960b), pp. 131–43.
82 See Table 2 in Manolescu (1960), p. 220.
83 *Ibid.*, pp. 217–18.
84 *Ibid.*, p. 210.
85 *Ibid.*, pp. 212–14.

86 Kellenbenz (1971), pp. 46–47.
87 Stoianovich (1960), p. 238; Panova (1983).
88 In the treaty of 1615 (Muahedat III, 75), the article concerning freedom of trade stated: "Merchants from our territories and the other side shall come and go freely for trading. They shall carry special certificates issued by the authorities or agents and must produce them at the frontier. The Ottoman commander or agent of the place shall stamp the document with his seal but no fee will be required for it. When the merchants want to go somewhere they shall be provided escorts, escorts strong enough to take them through dangerous places. No one shall trouble the merchants once they have paid the incumbent taxes and dues nor will they be prevented from going to the places they want to go." Still, the conditions were complex enough to discourage a brisk trade.
89 Stoianovich (1960), p. 234; Panova (1983).
90 In the so-called law code of Süleyman I, this law was actually codified c. 1500, see İnalcık (1969c), pp. 117–20. The rates of customs duties and market dues at Smederevo are entered in this general law code under a separate heading.
91 Deményi (1968), pp. 761–77; Goldenberg (1963), pp. 255–88.
92 Fekete (1949), p. 679.
93 Fekete and Káldy-Nagy (1962), p. 661.
94 İnalcık (1965f), pp. 1120–21; Evliya Çelebi (1896–1938), VII, p. 163.
95 Fekete (1949), pp. 694–96.
96 *Ibid.*, p. 696.
97 Fekete and Káldy-Nagy (1962), p. 707.
98 Fekete (1949), p. 701.
99 Evliya Çelebi (1896–1938), VII, pp. 52, 79.
100 *Ibid.*, pp. 27, 37–39.
101 See Fekete and Káldy-Nagy (1962), pp. 722–26, goods imported included wheat, rice, olive oil, walnuts, salted fish, wine, pepper and coffee. In 1580, 705 casks of wine were imported. Pepper imports sharply declined from 707 *denk* (bales) in 1573 to 81 in 1580. In 1571, out of 63 ships arriving at the customs at Buda, 29 were from Belgrade, 28 from Smederevo, 17 from Petervarad, 14 from Esseg. The first reference to coffee imports was in 1579.
102 Evliya Çelebi (1896–1938), VII p. 362.
103 Vaas (1971), pp. 1–39.
104 Abel cited by Slicher van Bath (1963), p. 204.
105 Káldy-Nagy (1970), pp. 243–45.
106 *Ibid.*
107 *Ibid.*, p. 247.
108 Evliya Çelebi (1896–1938), VII, p. 11.

13

◦̇

THE INDIA TRADE

SHIFTS IN SPICE TRADE ROUTES BEFORE 1500

As seen earlier, under the *Pax Mongolica* in the period 1260–1345 the major trade routes from Asia to the Mediterranean, with the caravans of spice and silk from India, China and Iran, shifted north to the Black Sea ports – Tana (Azov), Soldajo and later to Caffa or, via Sultaniya or Tabriz to the Anatolian ports of Trabzon, Samsun, Ayas (Layas), Antalya and Ephesus. The shift was highlighted by the fierce struggle between the Arab Middle East under the Mamluks and the Mongols in Iran who took control of Iraq and the Gulf, and attempted to establish a monopoly on the trading of Indian spices, precious stones, Bahrain pearls, and Chinese porcelain, silk, musk and rhubarb. Tabriz became the crossroads of international trade routes, over-shadowing Cairo and Baghdad, as the most important international trade center between East and West. In Tabriz as well as in the Anatolian ports mentioned above, Genoese and Venetian merchant communities settled and carried on an active trade of domestic products as well as Asian goods, in particular spices and silk. Western merchants could now load at Tana bales of Indian spices, arriving there via India – Urgenc, Astrakhan or Saray, in exchange for European woolen cloth[1] (see Table I:65).

Our sources do not yield enough information to illustrate the situation in the second half of the fourteenth century. But it is known that in the wake of the outbreak of anti-Latin popular uprisings and the hostile attitude of the Mongol rulers in Tabriz, Almaligh and the Golden Horde in the years 1338–43, the Latin merchants, renewing trade privileges with the Egyptian Mamluks, returned to Alexandria and Beirut for Asian goods (Catalans in 1341, Genoese and Venetians in 1345). Most recently Bautier[2] has argued that the Ottoman Sultan Bayezid I's policy of driving

Table I:65. Prices of spices and European woolen cloth, mid-fourteenth century

Woolen cloth	Price per bale of cloth (in florins)	Spice	Price of 1 bale of pepper (c. 91 kg) (in florins)
Brussels	400–500	Pepper	75–85
Chalons or Louviers	150–250	Girofle	170
Beauvais	110–60	Ginger	35–45
Cadis de Perpignan	90	*Cannelle*	40
Languedoc coarse woolen cloth	50–60	Sugar (box)	30
		Saffron	370
		Indigo	65
Raw silk	300–400		

Source: Heers (1955), pp. 157–209, summarized by Bautier (1970), p. 300.

the Venetians out of their strongholds on the coasts of the Balkan penin-sula and then Timur's invasion of Anatolia and his anti-Latin policy (capture of İzmir, 1402), caused an eclipse of Asian trade through Asia Minor, and the Tabriz–Trabzon route was cut off.

But actually, during this period, Ottomans and Venetians, though politically clashing, maintained regular trade relations, since Venice vitally needed local products and, in particular, wheat from the region. After Timur's departure from Anatolia, Venetian traffic made a rapid recovery following the favorable treaty concluded in 1403 between Venice and Byzantium on the one hand and Venice and Ottoman Sultan Süleyman on the other.[3]

The Venetian convoy (*muda*) of 1404 could again load in Trabzon quite a rich cargo: 20 tons of pepper, 20 tons of indigo, 7 tons of *cannelle*, 4 tons of ginger and also a cargo of raw silk (31 tons) and pearls from the Gulf. On its way to Venice, the *muda* also picked up from the depots of Modon 42 tons of pepper which had arrived from Beirut and Alexandria.[4] The Genoese ships, in contrast, loaded in Trabzon mostly Anatolian products, alum, beeswax, cheese and leather. Their pepper cargo consisted of only one ton. It should, however, be noted that now the spices available in the Black Sea ports were insignificant when com-pared to the massive Venetian purchases in Alexandria and Beirut. Spices, arriving via Tur–Cairo to Alexandria or via Jidda–Mecca–Damascus to Beirut and bought by the Latins amounted to an average 600 or 700 tons annually during the period. Venice dominated the spice trade there with its share of 500 tons.[5] In other words, the southern route of Asian trade had fully recovered by this time while the northern routes terminating at Trabzon, Tana and Caffa lost their former significance.[6] It was the shift of the spice trade again to the south that prepared the way for Ottoman Bursa to become a new market for Indian–Arabian goods as well as Iranian silk.

As discussed earlier, in the fifteenth century, or perhaps even earlier, Bursa became the emporium of Iranian and Indian goods for İstanbul and for a greater part of Southern and Eastern Europe. Historians of the spice trade have completely ignored the fact that the Latin merchants of Pera were able to exploit this new spice market in Bursa.

Shipments of Indian spices to Jidda were undertaken by merchants who joined the pilgrimage caravan at Mecca, which brought them to Damascus. A group from the great Mecca caravan of 3,000 camels as witnessed by La Brocquière arrived in Bursa after a journey of about fifty days via Aleppo, Konya, Akşehir and Kütahya. In Akşehir he came across twenty-five Arabs in a caravanserai.[7]

In Bursa spices brought by the Damascus caravan were delivered to Genoese merchants from Pera.[8] Later in 1470 Benedetto Dei,[9] a Florentine agent in Pera, could claim that his countrymen could get sufficient amounts of spices in Bursa in exchange for woolen cloth. The duties from the imported pepper, gumlac and saffron in Bursa were 100,000 *akça* (or 2,000 gold ducats) in 1487. They rose to 135,000 *akça* subsequently.[10]

In the fifteenth century, the sea route of Alexandria–Antalya was also used for the import of Indian goods to Ottoman Turkey. After the sack of Antalya by the Venetians in 1472, the quantity of spices available at this Ottoman port made a strong impression on its pillagers.[11] At that time, Bursa merchants were active on this route. One striking example is a partnership of two merchants, Hayreddin and his freed slave, Hacı Koçi. They invested the huge sum of 545,500 *akça* or 11,000 gold ducats in the export of lumber, wood, iron, leather, furs and pitch by sea, and such valuable goods as Bursa cloth and saffron by land to Egypt. They imported from Egypt spices and Syrian soap. The Antalya customs regulation of 1477 confirms that cloth, raw silk, mohair, iron tools, wood and lumber were the principal export items and that spices, sugar and indigo were the principal import items. A detailed journal of customs dated 1560 from the same port[12] shows that spices and dyes were still imported to Antalya but in rather small quantities compared with the large amounts of rice, linen and sugar imports. From Tripoli in Syria soap, cotton and olive oil were shipped in quite large quantities to Antalya. But wood and lumber exported from Antalya, Alaiye and Finike

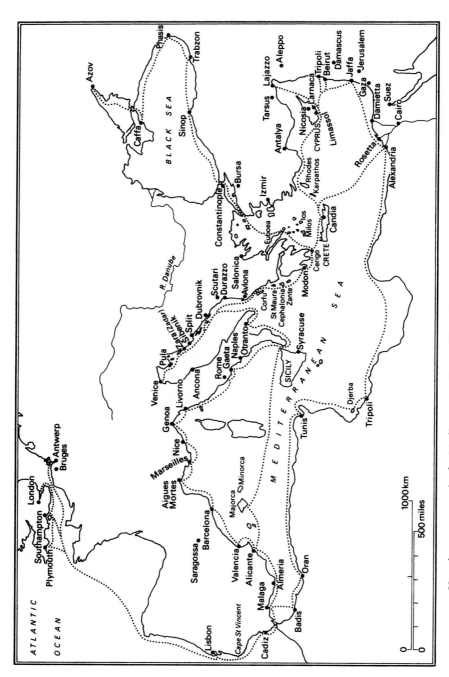

12 Venetian sea routes in the Mediterranean in the fifteenth century. *Source:* Sottas (1938), p. 106

overshadowed all other traffic with Egypt. The wood export, going back to the earlier centuries, was derived from the permanent dependence of Arab lands devoid of forests on forest products of the Anatolian Taurus range.[13] The Ottoman state made this lucrative traffic a state monopoly which brought an annual revenue of 3,000 gold ducats in 1477. For the Turcoman tribes on the mountain range from Maraş to Teke the production of lumber and charcoal formed one of the principal economic activities. The group of tribes engaged in this activity were known as *ağaç-eri* (woodmen) or *tahtacı* (lumbermen). In any case, Antalya lost its importance in the international trade of Indian spices in the sixteenth century when in 1522 the Ottomans conquered Rhodes and established a safe, direct sea route between İstanbul and the Egyptian ports of Alexandria and Damietta. But the main avenue of precious Indian goods was always the caravan route of Damascus–Bursa, and Bursa remained the emporium of these goods for Turkey and an important part for South-eastern and Eastern Europe.

THE PORTUGUESE IN THE INDIAN OCEAN AND THE OTTOMAN STRUGGLE FOR CONTROL OF THE RED SEA

After Vasco da Gama's arrival in India the first spice cargo arrived in Lisbon in 1501. In order to take complete control of the traffic in the Indian Ocean, Portuguese naval operations proceeded at a bewildering speed. The beneficiaries of the world spice trade, Egypt and Venice, reacted immediately in the face of the collapse of their centuries-old monopoly of this trade. Already in 1502, Venice sent an ambassador to Cairo and warned the Mamluk sultan of the disastrous consequences of the Portuguese success.[14] The sultan requested that the Malabar rulers close their markets to the Portuguese. The rulers of Calicut and Gujerat sided with the Muslims against the Portuguese. These two territories were the traditional centers for the Muslim spice merchants in India. Soon after, in the winter of 1503, the Portuguese penetrated the Red Sea, which alarmed Cairo.[15] The Mamluk sultan, however, began to take serious measures against the Portuguese only when he suffered a substantial fall in customs revenues.[16] The Mamluk fleet under the command of the emir Hüseyn, a Turcoman with about 1,500 Rumi (Turkish) mercenaries, surprised the Portuguese at Chaul near Cochin in 1508, but were routed when the Portuguese counter-attacked in 1509.[17] On this occasion, the rulers of Calicut and Gujerat cooperated again with the Mamluks. The defeat resulted not only in securing Portuguese control of the Indian

Ocean, but also laid the groundwork for the fall of the Mamluks, since now the Islamic world, including the Mamluk sultans themselves, realized that the only power capable of carrying on the crucial struggle was the Ottoman state.[18] Mecca and Medina were now threatened by a Portuguese invasion.

In 1510, the Mamluk sultan, Kansu al-Gawri, asked Bayezid II to send materials and experts to build a fleet at Suez. The Ottomans sent thirty shiploads of lumber, cannons, and other materials. But the convoy was intercepted and destroyed by the Hospitallers of Rhodes, apparently at Portuguese request.[19] The Ottomans, without accepting compensation, moved in new convoys of arms, powder, materials and experts to Egypt in the following years. An Ottoman captain Mehmed at Suez reported:[20] "I am sent here by our [Ottoman] sultan to prepare the necessary materials to build ships intended to eliminate those Frenks [Portuguese] who appeared on the side of India . . . Before me the sultan's captains, Hamid and Hasan, have been sent [for the same purpose]." Portuguese intelligence informed Lisbon of these preparations.[21]

The Portuguese squadrons, cruising along the coast of Malabar, were trying to cut off the traffic by sinking, burning, and capturing the Indian and Muslim ships destined for the Red Sea. Apart from a complete blockade, they needed, in addition to their naval base on the island of Sokotra, to control the Bab al-Mandab strait and Aden, which had been the terminus for Indian spice ships. In fact, during all this time Mecca had been receiving shipments of spices from India.[22] In 1513, the Portuguese seizure and fortification of the island of Kamaran as a base in the Red Sea created a critical situation for the Mamluks. The struggle now involved not only the Mamluks and the Ottomans but also their rivals, the Safavids. Because of the Portuguese successes, new alignments were taking shape in the whole area. The shah of Iran established friendly relations with the Portuguese, who sent him firearms, and rumors spread that the shah planned to attack Aleppo in 1515.[23]

While the Mamluk sultan tried to attach Yemen and Aden to Egypt, Albuquerque, the Portuguese admiral and governor, made an unsuccessful attack in 1513 to seize Aden.

Sending fleets into the Red Sea from 1503, and almost every year after 1513, the Portuguese were determined to establish their control by setting up strongholds at strategic points along the coasts for the purpose of blockading Indian trade. The immediate goal was to destroy the fleet which the Mamluks and later the Ottomans were maintaining at their Suez naval base. Unless destroyed, this fleet remained a constant threat

to the Portuguese domination of the Indian Ocean. Control of the Red
Sea was the most efficient way to stop Indian trade with Egypt and
Syria, since Arab and Indian merchant ships could easily slip through
the Portuguese cruising squadrons on the high seas. In the end, by con-
quering Yemen and Suakin, and taking control of Aden, Shihr and the
Abyssinian coast below the Bab al-Mandab, the Ottomans foiled a major
strategic plan of the Portuguese to intercept Indian trade with the Middle
East.

Actually, Ottoman soldiery and seamen had been in the forefront of
the struggle against the Portuguese since 1509 or 1510.[24] Apparently the
Ottoman government permitted volunteers, mostly mercenaries and free-
booters of Turcoman origin, to go and serve the Mamluk sultan. Some
of these Anatolian adventurer-soldiers, equipped with muskets and
known as Rumis among the Arabs and Indians, played a prominent role
in Yemen and elsewhere from this time on. These Ottoman soldiers,
deserting their leaders, spread from Yemen to the Gulf and India,
entering the services of the local rulers. Having the skill of making and
using firearms, they were much in demand as efficient professional soldiers to be used against the Portuguese. In 1513 Alfonso de Albuquerque
wrote to the king that unless the Rumis were eliminated there would be
no security for the Portuguese in the region. Later, in 1538, when the
Ottoman army was fighting against the Portuguese at Diu, some of the
Ottoman soldiers entered the service of Mahmud, sultan of Gujerat, who
promised a salary ten times higher than they received under the Ottoman
sultan. By 1525 Babur, the founder of the Mughal Empire in India, had
retained in his service two Ottoman gun founders, whom he treated with
special favor. In short, Ottomans, being familiar with European warfare,
were welcome everywhere from Central Asia to India and Sumatra.

The new Mamluk fleet, nineteen ships altogether, was built with the
aid of the Ottoman sultan. They left Suez under the Ottoman captain
Selman on September 30, 1515. The fighting men on board numbered
3,000, 1,300 of whom consisted of Turkish soldiery – Janissaries, levends
and Turcoman mercenaries from Anatolia.

Selman planned to attack and drive away the Portuguese from the
Indian Ocean, but unexpected complications delayed him in realizing the
plan. First, the construction of a fortress on the island of Kamaran took
too long, and the Mamluk commander failed in taking Yemen and Aden
(September 17, 1516), which showed a staunch resistance to the combined
fleet. Indian rulers awaited in vain the arrival of the Mamluk fleet. In the
meantime Selman received the news that the Ottoman army had routed

Mamluk forces at Marj Dabık and that the Egyptian sultan had fallen in the battle (August 24, 1516). Now the struggle against the Portuguese would be taken up directly by the Ottoman sultan.

In the wake of the Ottoman occupation of Egypt, Captain Selman and his Rumi soldiers entered the direct service of the Ottoman sultan. Back with the fleet at Jidda, Selman was an ardent advocate of a naval expedition against the Portuguese.

Upon the conquest of the Mamluk sultanate in 1516–17, Selim I assumed the task of protecting Islam and its vital interests, which were being jeopardized by the Portuguese in Arabia and the Indian Ocean. His assumption of the title of "Servitor of Mecca and Medina," previously borne by the Mamluk sultan and implying primacy among Muslim rulers, carried with it the duty to keep open the pilgrimage and trade routes for all Muslims in the world. Now that the Portuguese were attacking pilgrim and merchant ships on the Indian Ocean and even threatening to occupy and bring sacrilege to the sacred cities of Islam, the Ottoman sultan had to take action without delay. The prosperity of the newly conquered lands, and the protection of substantial customs revenues from the Indian trade depended on the security of the traffic with India. Also, to accomplish what the Mamluk sultan had been unable to do would help consolidate the Ottomans' position in the Arab world. Hard-pressed by the Portuguese in his homeland, the sharif of Mecca, Abu'l Barakat (1497–1525), hastened to recognize Ottoman suzerainty (February 1517) and to put to death the Mamluk governor.[25] Two days after this execution, a powerful Portuguese fleet under the command of Soares entered the port of Jidda. Failing to capture the city, he retreated under the guns of Selman. Anticipating the Portuguese occupation of Mecca, the sharif had made preparations to flee to the hills.[26] Now that the heart of the Islamic world was saved, Selim I took measures to fight the enemy on the Indian Ocean, while Venice was closely watching Ottoman initiatives.[27] The sultan appointed a governor to Hejaz who resided at Jidda (September 1517). He represented the sultan's authority in the region, keeping the sharif under supervision. In future this situation would lead to frequent conflicts between the Ottoman governor and the sharif. One of the main issues would be the customs revenue of Jidda from the Indian trade, which was estimated at 90,000 gold pieces annually. The sultan ordered that the receipts would be shared equally between the Ottoman treasury and that of the sharif, but the latter claimed all of it. Upon instructions from the sultan, the Ottoman governor of Jidda, Kasim Shirvani, opened without delay negotiations with the sultan of Gujerat for common action against the Portuguese.[28] Always through his governor in Jidda, Selim I informed the Gujerati ruler, Muzaffer Shah, that he had conquered all of the Arab countries including Yemen and Suakin, and had decided to drive the Portuguese out of India. To this end, he had ordered the construction of a powerful fleet at Suez in addition to the Mamluk fleet waiting at Jidda. The Gujerati sultan responded in a most favorable fashion, while his governor in Diu called the Ottoman sultan a pillar of all Islam and all Muslims in the world. This correspondence leaves no doubt that Selim had taken up the Portuguese problem immediately after his victory at Ridaniyya (January 1517).[29]

At the same time, Ottoman mercenaries and Mamluk forces at Yemen, previously sent there by the Mamluk sultan, recognized the Ottoman sultan, thus bringing Yemen under Ottoman sovereignty. However, the rebellion of Ahmed Pasha in Egypt in 1524 made Ottoman control of Egypt and Arabia critical. The situation required the Grand Vizier İbrahim to visit Egypt in 1525 to restore Ottoman sovereignty and order in the newly conquered lands. Upon his order, the Ottoman fleet left Suez for Yemen and Aden to establish control against the Portuguese. In his report to İbrahim Pasha from Yemen, dated June 2, 1525,[30] Selman Reis tells us that because of the arrival of the Ottoman fleet (altogether eighteen ships with 299 cannons) the Portuguese were discouraged and retreated, and that, with this fleet, it was possible to seize all the Portuguese forts and fortresses on the coasts of the Indian Ocean. Selman's report of 1525 is the key to understanding the Ottoman evaluation and subsequent strategy and operations in the broad defense line from Abyssinia to Hadramawt.

Selman wanted first to guarantee Ottoman control on the Red Sea by taking the principal ports facing the Bab al-Mandab strait. These ports, he noted, brought in large revenues from trade with India. He mentioned, in particular, that annually fifty or sixty ships arrived at the port of Aden bringing in customs revenues of 200,000 gold pieces; Suakin, on the African coast of the Red Sea, had also become prosperous, since Indian merchants had left Jidda for that port because of the heavy customs exactions in Jidda. The Ottoman admiral was well-informed of the strategic and economic issues which arose as a result of Portuguese operations in the region. He noted, in particular, the consequences of the Portuguese monopoly of the spice trade, saying that all kinds of spices coming from the islands of south Asia were now under Portuguese control and "all these spices go directly to Portugal. Before they seized these places, the customs duties from the spice trade amounted to a large percent of the revenue of Egypt."

In the first place, he recommended thwarting Portuguese plans to control the traffic on the Red Sea. The key importance of the island of Dahlak, where the Portuguese had plans to build a fort, was emphasized. If the Portuguese were to establish a naval base on the island, he said, "No ships can go out of the Bab al-Mandab because ships coming from India and going there have definitely to stop and pass through this gate."

On a broader strategic plan he saw the necessity of establishing Ottoman control of Yemen, Aden and Abyssinia. He also proposed the conquest of the fertile inland country between Suakin and the Nile and the important city of Atbara, a center for the gold and ivory trade from Sudan and Abyssinia. Reference was also made to the Holy War activities of Muslims in the area, who might cooperate with the Ottomans.

Selman stressed also that the African coast in the Indian Ocean controlling the Bab al-Mandab, with the ports of Zeila and Berbera should be taken under Ottoman control. He noted that Muslims in the area were forced to give tribute to the Christian Abyssinian ruler. Already by 1525 the Ottomans were supporting Muslims in the region north and east of Abyssinia in order to establish their control in the area, but meanwhile the Portuguese were welcomed by Christian Abyssinians.

In the second stage of operations in his plan, Selman dealt with the elimination of the Portuguese from the Indian Ocean. The information the admiral was able to obtain convinced him that this was not a difficult task, since he said that the Portuguese were scattered in forts guarded by small garrisons at great distances from each other, and altogether their forces consisted of only 2,000 men. He added that the native population on the Malabar coast was hostile to the Portuguese.

One particular point should be noted in Selman's plan. He always placed a special emphasis on the revenues to be derived for the sultan's treasury from the proposed conquests. Speaking of the conquest of Yemen, he noted that it was a vast and rich land which presently was without a master and was exploited only by a few Arab chieftains. Its conquest, he asserted, would be easy and would make five good-sized Ottoman *sancaks*. On the other hand, thanks to the Indian trade and exports of red dye to India, Yemen could provide immense revenues in gold to the Ottoman treasury. He also noted the rich customs revenues from the Indian trade at Aden, Suakin and Egypt. The fact that he was exclusively interested in revenue for the sultan's treasury must have been the typical Ottoman attitude – a basic difference between the patrimonial mentality of the Ottomans and the new mercantilistic policy of the West.

OTTOMANS IN ADEN AND INDIA

After Selman's death, his nephew Mustafa, who succeeded him in controlling Yemen, challenged the Portuguese in Aden (1530–31), and he went to the defence of Diu in Gujerat which was besieged by a powerful Portuguese fleet under the viceroy Nuño da Cunha. Artillery brought in by Mustafa proved to be the decisive factor in the retreat of the Portuguese (February 1531). Thus, already at this time, the cooperation of Muslim Gujerat with the Ottoman forces provided a check to Portuguese expansion.[31] However, before long the Portuguese made an agreement with Bahadur Shah, sultan of Gujerat, who recently had been defeated by the Mughal emperor Humayun. But the Portuguese, deceiving Bahadur, had built a strong fortress facing the city of Diu. Now once again threatened by the Portuguese, Bahadur Shah turned to the Ottomans. It was these developments which resulted in İstanbul deciding to undertake the famous sea expedition under Süleyman Pasha, governor of Egypt, in 1538. Since 1517 the Ottomans had believed that, with Gujerat's cooperation, it would be possible to shift the struggle against the Portuguese from the Red Sea to India itself.

Süleyman, an influential eunuch and former head of the sultan's palace, was appointed governor of Egypt in 1525. He implemented the centralist policy of the Porte in Egypt and its dependencies. Like the Mamluk sultans before him, he was also responsible for the Red Sea, Hejaz, Nubia and Yemen, and the Ottoman policy on the Indian Ocean. He insisted that a powerful fleet should be constructed at Suez, but the imperial court of İstanbul did not give priority to it until 1530. It appears that by that time the Portuguese control of the Red Sea traffic had become tighter than ever. Venetians could not find supplies of spices in Egypt in that year. In 1530, the Portuguese attempted to take Diu which, along with Surat, formed one of the main supply centers for Egypt's trade with India. The Portuguese took Gogala, a stronghold near Diu also called Bender-i Türk. The Ottoman government now gave priority to the struggle against the Portuguese and sent Süleyman the necessary funds. A strong fleet of about 80 vessels, including 17 galleys and 2 galleons,[32] was built at Suez and the digging of a canal between the Nile river and Suez was started (1531–32). But the capture of Coron in the Morea by

Emperor Charles V in 1532 and Süleyman's campaign against Iran in the period 1533–35 forced the Ottoman government to delay again the Indian expedition.

In 1536, when Bahadur Shah asked for help, the Ottoman imperial *divan* believed it was the right time to make the naval expedition. The objective was "to expel the Portuguese from the Indian Ocean." Well informed through spies in İstanbul, the Portuguese killed Bahadur (February 1537) before the Ottoman fleet arrived. Despite the efforts of the pro-Ottoman forces under the leadership of Captain Hoca Sefer, a man whom Selman had left at Gujerat, the situation had completely changed by the time the Ottoman army arrived at Diu in early September. On his way to Diu, Süleyman Pasha established Ottoman sovereignty over Aden. After inviting the sultan of Aden, Sheikh Amir b. Dawud, along with his main councillors aboard ship, the pasha seized them and hanged them all while his Janissaries occupied the city. Süleyman Pasha was aware of the ruler of Aden's alliance with the Portuguese and the task was to capture this unusually strong place[33] without a siege, which might cause the failure of the expedition to Diu. In his report, Süleyman added that Aden was the key to the control of Yemen and its conquest gave the Ottomans control of an immense territory stretching up to Mecca. Leaving Aden on August 19, 1538, the Ottoman fleet had arrived at Diu on September 4, 1538.

The city of Diu, though battered by powerful Ottoman siege artillery of 130 cannons, resisted stoutly; Süleyman finally lifted the siege when he learned of the approach of a strong Portuguese fleet. It is believed that the new sultan of Gujerat, suspecting Süleyman's intention of establishing Ottoman domination, did not give the support needed for Ottoman success.[34] Portuguese sources confirm the duplicity of the ruler of Gujerat.[35] By now the Portuguese had learned to exploit local rivalries in order to use the native rulers for their own purposes. On his way back to Suez, Süleyman arrived at Shihr, an important port on the south Arabian coast whose ruler had accepted Ottoman suzerainty.[36] He then went to Zabid, where he forced the local rulers to accept Ottoman suzerainty and reorganized Yemen and Aden as an Ottoman province or *beglerbegilik*. Fortified with a strong Ottoman garrison, Zabid became the center of the province of Yemen.[37] In the last analysis, Süleyman Pasha's naval expedition completed Captain Selman's work by consolidating Ottoman sovereignty and direct rule in the areas under Portuguese threat in Arabia and the Red Sea. His announcement of a second expedition must have caused concern among the Portuguese, since the campaign of 1538 had posed a serious threat to Portuguese domination in India. But after this costly and unsuccessful initiative against the Portuguese, no Ottoman initiative in India would be taken in the following years.

The Portuguese authorities in India and Lisbon, however, were alarmed by the news that the Ottomans were preparing a new expedition. In 1540, the Portuguese retaliated by sending a fleet into the Red Sea, massacred the garrison in Suakin, destroyed Kusayr and attempted to take Suez.[38]

Just before Süleyman Pasha's expedition of 1538, the Portuguese had made a peace overture. The conditions each side put forth at that time are interesting as they indicate each power's principal interests. While the sultan insisted on 5,000 *kantar* (250 tons) of pepper in return for 5,000 *mudd* (c. 2,500 tons) of wheat, the Portuguese demanded the dismantling of the Ottoman navy at Suez and free access to the Red Sea.[39] In 1541, negotiations continued in the wake of the Portuguese attack of 1540. The sultan asked the Portuguese not to send any ships into the Red Sea to the ports of Zabid, Jidda and Suakin, but was ready to receive their merchant ships in Aden. The Portuguese were obviously aware that the sultan had to concentrate his forces in the Mediterranean against Charles V and the Venetians. However, Süleyman Pasha, now a vizier in the imperial council, was favored by the sultan. In the following years, the activities of Ottoman galleys in the Indian Ocean increased. Renewed Portuguese initiatives for peace might have been interpreted as a sign of their concern in the face of Ottoman power, which reached its peak with the annexation of Hungary in 1541. In addition, since the creation of the Ottoman province of Basra in 1546 and the construction of a new naval base there, the Portuguese must have been concerned more than ever for the future of Hormuz and their empire in the Indian Ocean.

OTTOMAN-GUJERAT-ATJEH COOPERATION

To explain the arrival of large quantities of spices in the Mediterranean ports, or the so-called revival of the spice trade in the Mediterranean, in the period following the Ottoman naval defeat in the Gulf in 1554, emphasis is placed on the general deterioration of the administration and control of the Portuguese Empire in the Indian Ocean.[40] However, interest has recently been shifted to the continuing Ottoman attempts to gain advantage of the energetic struggle of the sultanate of Atjeh in Sumatra.[41]

The first coalition against the Portuguese between Gujerat, Atjeh and the Ottomans apparently came into existence in connection with

Süleyman Pasha's plans against the Portuguese. Prior to the 1538 expedition, the first Atjehnese pepper shipments to the Red Sea had arrived around 1530, and there is a reference to a treaty which gave the Ottomans a "customs house" and a factory at the port of Pasai, at the heart of the pepper-growing region in Sumatra.[42] According to Portuguese sources, the sultan of Atjeh, Alaeddin, received an Ottoman contingent of 300 men, evidently equipped with firearms. The Ottoman soldiery played a major role to help him in extending his domain, and enabled him to attack the Portuguese in the Malacca Straits (September 1537).[43]

With the ambition of becoming the major supplier of pepper, Alaeddin extended pepper plantations in Sumatra and continued to send large pepper shipments to the Red Sea. In his attack against the Portuguese at Malacca later, in 1547, a detachment of Turks was again mentioned among his troops. The peak of the "Muslim counter-crusade," as Reid put it,[44] against the Portuguese came about later, in the 1560s.

Ottoman archival evidence demonstrates that there was indeed an alliance between these two powerful Muslim states, and an attempt at full cooperation in the period 1560–80. Thanks to their big carracks, which were equipped with powerful artillery, the Portuguese dominated the Indian Ocean. But they were repulsed on the Red Sea and in the Gulf by the Ottomans and at Sumatra by the rising seaborne empire of Atjeh. The other Muslim state of Gujerat must be mentioned as the vital link between the Atjehnese and the Ottomans in trade and diplomacy. Determined to eliminate Portuguese control and their monopoly, these three Muslim states in cooperation must be taken into account in explaining the Portuguese failure to establish complete control of the traffic between the Ottoman dominions and the East. This cooperation found a strong expression in the Islamic ideology of Holy War. In supporting Islamic states in the Indian Ocean, the Ottoman sultan Süleyman declared that he was the protector of all Muslims in the world and of the pilgrimage routes.[45]

The Ottoman–Atjehnese diplomatic exchanges shed light on developments in the period 1560–80. In a letter dated January 1566,[46] the sultan of Atjeh informed the Ottoman sultan that he himself as well as the Muslims of the Maldive Islands and the Muslim rulers of India recognized him as their suzerain and protector; and to this end they mentioned his name in the Friday prayers (*hutbe*). If the Ottoman sultan would send his fleet into the Indian Ocean, the Atjehnese sultan said, they could join him in a coalition against the Portuguese. While he underlined the Ottoman caliph's duty of Holy War and the opening of the pilgrimage routes to Muslims, he also added that innumerable riches could be gained in jewels, gold and silver in the area currently exploited by the "infidels." But the sultan of Atjeh pointed out the recent worsening conditions of their traffic in the Red Sea since the Portuguese took control of all the passages to the Maldive Islands in 1563. He added that previously, under the Muslim ruler of the islands, the traffic was safe. Indian and Atjehnese ships were mostly able to slip through the Portuguese cruisers in the Indian Ocean in order to reach Aden and the Red Sea.[47]

In the Atjehnese sultan's letter, special reference is made to the sinking of a big Atjehnese ship laden with spices. In fact, in 1561 a large ship bound for the Red Sea carried for the Ottoman sultan a rich cargo of jewels and gold worth 200,000 cruzados. Portuguese sources[48] confirm that the Portuguese were intercepting Atjehnese ships at the Maldive passages or off the coast of the Hadramawt. Later, they planned to blockade Atjehnese ports in order to ruin their maritime trade and ultimately to conquer their land. These worsening conditions resulted in the sultan of Atjeh's decision to send an ambassador to İstanbul and to request immediate Ottoman aid. The Ottoman sultan responded by dispatching an envoy with eight gunners to Atjeh. The sultan of Atjeh had asked in particular for experts and architects to build fortresses and warships as well as cannon. The non-Muslim rulers of Ceylon and Calicut, he said, fighting against the Portuguese, were ready to cooperate if an Ottoman fleet arrived. The Ottoman government showed a keen interest in the situation. A fleet of fifteen galleys and two *barças* was prepared at Suez to sail under the captain of the Ottoman fleet at Alexandria, Kurdoğlu Hızır, in 1567. A group of eight gun-makers were among the soldiers on the ships. In return for their military aid, the Ottomans asked the Atjehnese to send cargoes of spices to be loaded on the *barças*. In September 1567 imperial orders were issued to the *beglerbegis* of Egypt and Yemen to permit the merchants of the Atjehnese sultan to buy and export strategic goods, including copper, weapons and horses. In addition to the carpenters, blacksmiths, shield makers, designers and other artisans were assigned by the Ottoman sultan. The Atjehnese were allowed to hire Ottoman soldiers in Egypt who would like to go to the Indies of their own free will. But when news arrived in the winter of disorders in Yemen, the departure of the fleet was postponed. "Only two ships carrying 500 Turks, including gun-founders, gunners and engineers, together with a number of heavy bronze guns and other war material, reached Atjeh in 1567." Turkish experts cast cannons for the sultan of Atjeh for his major naval campaign in order to expel the Portuguese from Malacca in 1568. This expedition and the subsequent attacks on Malacca in the 1570s failed.[49] Apparently the news of Sultan Alaeddin's reverses had reached the Ottoman capital.

In this period, the Ottoman government, headed by the great statesman Sokollu Mehmed, was interested in global issues and in making a reality of Süleyman's claim to be the protector of all Muslims in the world. In addition to the decision to send a fleet against the Portuguese in the Indian Ocean in 1568–69, an expedition was prepared and executed to expel the Muscovites from Kazan and Astrakhan in order to reopen the Khwarezm–Crimea route for the merchants and Muslim pilgrims of Central Asia.[50] The rulers of the Central Asian Khanates sent ambassadors and requested aid against the Muscovites and Iranians. At this time the Ottomans ambitiously planned to use their main fleet in the Indian Ocean and the Caspian Sea. In 1568, in order to use the Mediterranean fleet against the Portuguese, they conceived the scheme of digging a waterway between the Mediterranean Sea and the Red Sea. One year later they started to dig a canal between the rivers Don and Volga to expel the Muscovites from Kazan and Astrakhan and descend on the Caspian to encircle Iran. Thus, the Indian Ocean and the Volga basin began to be given serious attention in the new Ottoman world politics, while the struggle of vital importance in Central Europe against the Holy Roman Empire and in the Mediterranean against Spain and Venice continued. When Selim II came to the throne in 1566, Sokollu's rivals had their chance to challenge him, saying that he was exhausting the state's resources in useless adventures.[51] In 1570, the invasion of Cyprus planned by his rival Mustafa, tutor of the sultan, indicated a radical change in Ottoman world politics. Now the Volga and the Indian Ocean began to be considered too far for the empire to take an interest there.

It was at this time when Spain, Venice and the Papacy joined forces in a Holy League and inflicted a disastrous defeat on the Ottomans at Lepanto in 1571. Selim II's promise to the sultan of Atjeh was never fulfilled, and, following the death of the Atjehnese Sultan Husayn (1571–79), his country was torn apart by civil war.

Thus, Ottoman efforts against the Portuguese in the Indian Ocean, encouraged this time by the rise of Atjehnese power and alliance, ended in a complete failure militarily. The spice trade, however, continued to flourish, since by the end of the century the Portuguese had given up their efforts to cut off the traffic between Atjeh and the Red Sea. Then, with the arrival of the Dutch in the Indian Ocean and as a result of Ottoman involvement in the long struggle in Iran and Central Europe

(1578–1606), conditions of world politics and commerce radically changed.

Diplomatic exchanges, to be sure, continued between the Atjehnese and the Ottomans. In a letter written c. 1574, Selim II took pains to explain the delay in the departure of the Ottoman fleet because of the rebellion in Yemen, the Cyprus campaign and the struggle for Tunis. He emphatically confirmed his decision about sending aid.[52] In the 1580s, Ottoman support of Atjeh still haunted the Portuguese. In 1585 a Portuguese report asserted that the Atjehnese were receiving large bronze cannons from the Turks, and vast quantities of spices, gold and jewels had arrived in the Red Sea from Atjeh.[53]

As a last episode in the Ottoman and Portuguese rivalry in the Indian Ocean, the naval expeditions of Mir Ali Bey in 1585 and 1586 to East Africa should be told here. Declaring that he was the vanguard of a large Turkish fleet, Mir Ali, exploiting the anti-Portuguese feelings of the native rulers, succeeded in establishing Ottoman suzerainty on the East African coast from Mogadishu down to Mombasa. The ruler of Mombasa declared himself a vassal of the Ottoman sultan. The Portuguese admitted that the Ottomans now had the upper hand on the African coast facing India and had the capacity to cut their communications with Portugal. Although a Portuguese counter-attack by their fleet based in India in the following year re-established Portuguese control in East Africa, Mir Ali came back with a squadron of five ships in 1588 and found a Portuguese fleet waiting to attack his small force; however, he was not eliminated by the Portuguese, but rather by an African tribe, the Zimba. He saved his own life by taking refuge on board a Portuguese ship.

OTTOMANS IN THE YEMEN

During the sixteenth century, the Ottomans were unable to pursue a forward policy in the Indian Ocean primarily because of recurrent rebellions and the loss of control in Yemen.

The governor of Egypt, with the naval base at Suez under his command, was given the main responsibility to organize the struggle against the Portuguese and to maintain trade with India. But the defence of the entrance to the Red Sea and the new far-flung Ottoman acquisitions along the Arabian coast on the Indian Ocean called for a strong and unified command in the region. It was precisely to this end that Yemen and Aden were merged to create a powerful *beglerbegilik* in 1539. Although Hejaz under the Ottomans had gained a favorable position in the age-old competition with Aden and Yemen to attract the Indian spice ships and become the center of distribution, Aden, after the conquest in 1538, kept its position as the emporium of Indian spices for Arab merchants. Starting with Süleyman Pasha's organizing of the *beglerbegilik* of Yemen in 1539, the Ottomans attempted to introduce their own imperial centralist regime by establishing tight control over the autonomous local dynasties. The *beglerbegi*, a servant of the Ottoman sultan from İstanbul, was given, as in Egypt and Baghdad, vast authority to organize the country as a typical Ottoman province. By constructing new fortresses at strategic points or taking control of older ones from the hands of the local dynasties, the Ottoman governors simply followed the normal Ottoman methods of establishing the sultan's centralist rule. One example was the conquest of the Habb fortress in 1562 near the Zaydi domain. But constructing and keeping these places garrisoned required considerable financial resources. Also, governors often ignored the delicate balances of power in these feudal societies as they implemented standard Ottoman methods of control.

As was the case in most of the Arab lands under the Ottomans, Ottoman methods of centralization, with the gradual undermining of the local dynasties' feudal position, met with strong resistance in the newly created province of Yemen. Yemeni society was extremely compartmentalized into Zaydis, İsmailis, tribal chiefs and ulema families. In the beginning, the Ottomans made compromises with each of these groups to establish control over the province. In spite of this policy, they planned eventually to abolish feudal privileges; over time the indigenous families were to be either totally assimilated by the Ottoman ruling elite or replaced by the sultan's *kuls*, the loyal servants trained in the sultan's palace. But as the local communal leaders of Yemen were all Muslims they could not be eliminated as they might have been in a conquered Christian land. In particular, the Yemenite communal organizations, including sects and tribes, were too strong to undergo such a transformation.

Taxation to meet the expenses of this type of centralist government was often coupled with the autocratic methods of the Ottoman governor. This situation caused widespread discontent not only among feudal dynasties but also among the populace and the tribal population, who soon made common cause with their old masters against the Ottomans. Moreover, the initial tax exemptions granted to the semi-autonomous communities were abolished.[54]

Not properly informed about this remote province, the Ottoman central government expected that, enriched by the Indian trade as was Egypt,

Yemen–Aden should meet all its administrative and military expenses and even send surplus revenue to the sultan. So the province was given financial autonomy with the responsibility of making its own budget. The *beglerbegi*'s salary, amounting to over one million *akça*, had to be raised from local sources. Such a big salary for a *beglerbegi* was intended to enable him to organize strong military retainers who would be powerful enough to stand against local lords and enemies on the frontier. As was true in the sharifate of Mecca, here too the indigenous ruling families now had to share the sources of revenue with the Ottoman government or its agents. To aggravate matters further, Yemen apparently was suffering from a chronic shortage of silver and could not meet the huge salaries of the newly established Ottoman commanders and soldiery. Hence the abrupt debasement of the *osmani akça* and speculation in silver became another significant factor in the spread of discontent among the masses.[55]

It might be for the same reason that governors' salaries were paid in part in spices, which they converted to cash by selling the spices in Jidda and Mecca. They enjoyed exemption from customs dues. The state obtained spices either by levying customs in kind or making purchases at fixed low prices at the port of arrival in Yemen or Aden. Even ordinary soldiers began to exchange their military equipment for spices in the hope of making big profits.[56] The monetary instability caused widespread discontent among the merchants, soldiery and the populace at large. Considering all these conditions, it is not difficult to see why rebellion, especially in the highlands, where feudal lords and tribes were supreme, became endemic. The most powerful of these local leaders, the Zaydi İmam al-Mutahhar, autonomous in the southern highlands, had recognized the Ottoman sultan's suzerainty in 1552. Thereafter, during the period 1552–60, the province was effectively put under Ottoman rule under the governor-general Özdemir Pasha, who garrisoned the main cities, built new fortresses and rendered secure the main routes. But his successor Mahmud Pasha (1560–65), disregarding the delicate balance of power in Yemen, hastened to advance a program of centralization. He apparently used his authority unscrupulously and tactlessly, alienating all the dynasties and special groups, causing them to forget the rivalries among themselves and to band together against the Ottomans.

It is interesting to note that al-Mutahhar's rebellion followed the increase of the "token" annual tribute from one *kise* (40,000 *akça*) to eight *kise*. The rebellion started with the murder of the Ottoman tax collector by the populace in al-Mutahhar's territory. Despite the fact that

Ottoman troops, equipped with muskets and cannon, had an advantage over the rebels, the Yemenites in general prevailed against Ottoman rule. The highland tribes in 1566 furnished the bulk of Mutahhar's forces in his fight against the Ottoman troops.

Centralization involved not only administrative and fiscal measures but also kadiships in the cities and towns of Yemen, which must have caused the alienation of the local ulema class. Native kadis joined al-Mutahhar in his uprising, and encouraged by this support, he declared his independence as the ruler of Yemen when the news of Sultan Süleyman's death reached Yemen in 1567. The Ottoman garrison at Aden, a strategically as well as commercially very important post, also surrendered. The native Arab dynast Sultan Badr, who acted nominally as an Ottoman governor in Shihr, also loosened his ties with the Ottomans, and, like his predecessors, collaborated with the Portuguese when the Ottomans began to have difficulties in Yemen. The Ottoman government received reports that Badr's equivocal attitude was creating difficulties for the Ottoman merchants en route to India.[57]

In 1565 Yemen split into two provinces: one with Sa'dah as its capital and the other with Ta'izz. This split proved to have disastrous consequences for Ottoman control of Yemen as it created two rival authorities. Al-Mutahhar shrewdly exploited the new situation, and his forces attempted to drive out all of the Ottoman troops from the country. The newly appointed Ottoman *beglerbegi* Hasan repulsed with difficulty a Zaydi attack against the important strategic center of Zabid. From there, the Ottomans in 1567 started to restore their control in Yemen. In 1569 massive regular Ottoman forces under Sinan Pasha arrived, and in the years 1569–70 Sinan completely restored Ottoman rule in Yemen and Aden.[58] If, in the following year, the Ottomans had not had a shattering blow to their naval power at Lepanto, they might have continued their aggressive policy in the Indian Ocean and the reconquered Yemen might have assumed an important strategic role. But, under the new conditions, naval forces based at the port of Mocha did not have a chance to expand. In 1564, there were only two Ottoman warships stationed there, and Suez remained the main base for any campaign on the Indian Ocean.

The revolts and disorders in Yemen have always been considered as one of the principal causes of the decline and shortage of spice supplies in the Ottoman ports of Egypt and Syria. A later report, dated 1627–32, tells us that, because of a revolt, no spices arrived in Egypt, hence they had to be imported from Europe.[59]

According to the balance sheet in the Ottoman archives of the Yemen province, dated 1600,[60] it was only under normal conditions that a surplus was available to be sent to İstanbul. In the fiscal year 1599–1600, the local revenue amounted to 16 million *para* or 390,000 gold pieces, with a deficit of 5 million *para* (one *para* equals 1.5 *akça*, or 41 *para* one Ottoman gold piece in 1600). During the long governorship of Sinan Pasha (1574–1602), the province was divided into three districts: Zabid, Ta'izz and San'a. The *beglerbegi*'s seat was then San'a.

By the end of the sixteenth century Yemen came under the close control of the government of Egypt. In order to establish Ottoman control, *sancak begi*s had to come with their troops from Egypt to join the other *sancak begi*s of Yemen. Interestingly enough, nine of the *sancak begi*s in Yemen belonged to native feudal families, including three members of al-Mutahhar's family, who had assisted the Ottoman army in previous military operations. In other words, Ottoman masters always wisely shared tax revenue levied from the people with the native lords. The deficit of the provincial budget was met with a subvention from the treasury of Egypt.

In order to keep Yemen under control, the Ottomans maintained 38 fortresses in the country. The garrisons were paid about two million *para* annually in 1600. Most of the soldiery in the fortresses appear to have been transferred from Cairo. In such important fortresses as Ta'izz, Sa'dah and Zabid, Janissary companies were present. There was a sea captain also stationed at Mocha who had under his command soldiers from Suez.

As will be evident from Table 1:66, about one-third of the province's revenue came from customs duties and other dues levied at the ports. Mocha was clearly the main commercial center by 1600. Aden, bringing about 700,000 *para*, was the next most important port, while Hudaydah, Luhayyah and Jizan were used apparently for local traffic. The madder, or red dye root of Yemen, was indispensable for the dyeing industry of Gujerat and constituted one of the principal items of Yemenite export to India.

THE PORTUGUESE-OTTOMAN STRUGGLE IN THE GULF

The Ottomans were apparently interested in the Gulf area by the 1520s. Invading Hormuz, the gateway to the Gulf, in 1509, the Portuguese had an aggressive plan to take the entire region under their control, including

Table I:66. Revenue from the ports of
Yemen, 1600

Port	Revenue in *para*
Aden	702,363
Mocha	3,596,352
Salif-Kamaran	44,280
Hudaydah	229,600
Jizan	106,600
Shihr and Hadramawt	25,800
Luhayyah island of Feresan	147,980
Hud	19,926
Total	4,872,901

Note: 1 *para*=1.5 *akça* or 41 *para*=1 gold piece
Source: Sahillioğlu (1985), p. 303.

Bahrain, Al-Hasa and Basra. Safavid control of lower Iraq being nominal at this time, the Portuguese exploited the disputes among native Arab lords in the area and attempted to establish control of Basra in 1529.[61] It appears that by 1534 the Ottomans were well aware of Portuguese plans and the threat to the Gulf and to Basra.

Before Süleyman I's campaign of 1534 into Iraq, the Arabs of the region tried to resist the Portuguese and their firearms, and appealed to the Ottoman sultan for aid. The anti-Portuguese party at Hormuz, for example, called on Süleyman repeatedly in 1526, 1528 and 1529. By that time, the Rumis, Turkish mercenaries equipped with firearms, appeared in the service of local Arab rulers, including those of Bahrain and lower Iraq.

The Ottoman advance toward the Gulf took twenty years, the first stage of which was the conquest of Baghdad from the Safavids in 1534. The lord of Basra and other Arab sheikhs of lower Iraq immediately recognized Ottoman sovereignty.[62] Later, as was the case in Yemen and Aden, local Arab rulers were reluctant to give up their rule as the Ottomans tried to establish direct control of the region. They found the Portuguese to be useful in balancing power in the region to protect their trading revenue. In 1545 the Porte conceived of an ambitious plan against the Portuguese. The governor-general of Baghdad, Ayas Pasha, was ordered to conquer Basra and Hormuz and open the route to India.[63] Since Basra was much nearer to the Portuguese headquarters in India, the news caused alarm in Lisbon. By that time, the Ottomans had signed an armistice with the Habsburgs (1545) in Central Europe and had decided to concentrate their energies towards the east and the south.

Ottoman action in the Indian Ocean through the Red Sea was also intensified in the same period.

Occupied by Ottoman forces under Ayas on December 26, 1546, Basra was made the seat of an Ottoman governor-general with extensive powers in 1547. By 1550 Al-Katif was made a base as the seat of a *sancak begi*.[64] In the same year, the Portuguese promptly reacted by demolishing the fortress of Al-Katif and threatening Basra. The important naval base constructed soon after the conquest of Basra was a constant worry to the Portuguese. In 1552 the creation of the *beglerbegilik* of Al-Hasa, along with Al-Katif, provided a further Ottoman advance and a threat to the Portuguese.[65] In 1552, by sending the Suez fleet under Piri Reis (25 ships with 800 soldiers) and attempting to capture Hormuz,[66] the Ottoman government made a final effort to banish the Portuguese from the Gulf. It ended in complete failure, and naval operations the following year demonstrated Portuguese naval superiority. In 1556 the Portuguese attempted to capture Basra, without success. Then Bahrain became the main focus of the Portuguese–Ottoman conflict in the Gulf. The Portuguese had indirect control of Bahrain and their fleet was ready to protect it against the Ottomans, while the latter used their new base at Al-Hasa with the intention of annexing this strategically and economically important island to the province of Al-Hasa. As well as being a thoroughfare for the vital trade of Basra with India, Bahrain was also the center of an important pearl industry.[67]

The creation of the *beglerbegilik* of Al-Hasa in 1552 was primarily designed to protect Basra's trade with India, since the Portuguese were making raids on the coasts and shipping in the Gulf. Following the disastrous outcome of the *beglerbegi* of Al-Hasa's attempt to invade Bahrain in 1558, the Portuguese squadron based in Hormuz controlled all traffic in the Gulf. They raided Al-Katif in 1552, 1559 and 1573. During the raid of 1573, which came after the crushing Ottoman defeat at Lepanto, the Portuguese captured twelve galleys and two galleons together with a number of Muslim merchants.[68]

In 1567 it was reported[69] that an Ottoman fleet of forty galleys sailed to Sumatra, and the year after the Ottomans made further naval preparations to capture Bahrain. But in that year the rebellion in Yemen curbed all such plans. Braudel[70] suggests that, beginning in 1570, the pendulum swung in favor of the Portuguese in the Indian Ocean. Now the Ottomans had to concentrate all their forces on the Mediterranean front in their crucial struggle against the Holy League.

Later on, the Ottomans made new preparations at Al-Hasa to take Bahrain, but in general they remained defensive, especially when in 1578 a new war against Iran started. For the Ottoman defensive attitude in the Gulf, financial difficulties in particular should be remembered. In 1558, 200,000 gold pieces had to be transferred from Egypt to Basra just to construct a fleet.[71] Local resources were strained to maintain garrisons placed at the newly built fortresses and to meet the *beglerbegi*'s huge salary of 900,000 *akça*. In addition to financial difficulties, the Arab chieftains, and in particular those of the paramount tribe of Bani Khalid, rebelled, making Ottoman rule quite unstable in the province.

Some scholars argue that the Persian Gulf traffic with India gained importance at the expense of the Red Sea traffic under Ottoman control.[72] First, the Portuguese appear to have contributed to the expansion of Indian trade via the Gulf. Being in control of Hormuz since 1509 and the entrance to the Gulf, they encouraged, for political and economic reasons, the traffic between Indian ports and Iraq, which was then under Safavid control. Starting in 1514, the Portuguese supplied the Safavids with Indian goods and firearms to be used against the Ottomans. Godinho[73] places emphasis on the price factor by indicating that higher prices offered in the Levant attracted the Portuguese spice trade into the Gulf. In fact, since the Portuguese in Hormuz controlled the Indian trade with Iran and the Ottoman Empire, it was in their interest to use this route at the expense of the Red Sea, which was under Ottoman control. For the Asian trade, Hormuz played a similar role to that of Lisbon for Europe.[74] In 1551, Hormuz was described as an international emporium of Asian trade for "the merchants from Arabia, Mesopotamia, Venice, Mecca, small and great Tataria and Iran."[75] In return for a huge tribute (60,000 Egyptian gold) paid to the Portuguese, Muslims of Hormuz were permitted to traffic in the whole Indian Ocean, with the exception of the Red Sea. On the other hand, it is argued that by the mid-sixteenth century Portuguese difficulties, particularly the insufficient supply of bullion to buy spices and also the involvement of Portuguese officers in smuggling at Hormuz, further contributed to the expansion of Indian trade in the Gulf. It appears that as a result of the growing importance of the Gulf traffic at the expense of the Red Sea, a busy caravan route from Basra channelled Indian goods, chiefly spices, indigo and fine cottons to Aleppo, which experienced an unprecedented commercial expansion during the second half of the sixteenth century. An Indian merchant colony settled in Aleppo. The Basra–Aleppo caravan route appears to have always been a major supply channel of Indian goods for Ottoman lands. Even in an early Portuguese report dated 1510,[76] a shortage of spices in the Ottoman lands was noted when a caravan of 2,000 camels

on this route was attacked and plundered. Indian goods made their way
to Aleppo and then to Bursa, as confirmed by late fifteenth-century Bursa
court documents.

Following the Ottoman failure at Hormuz in the 1550s, a *modus viv-
endi* appears to have been reached between the Ottomans and the Portuguese in the region, as witnessed by a marked expansion in the trade
with India through the Gulf. Hormuz under the Portuguese experienced
an unprecedented commercial expansion exactly at this time, doubling
the tax revenue from the Indian trade.[77] The prosperity continued until
the fall of Hormuz in 1622. By then, 20 to 30 ships were arriving at
Hormuz from India every year.[78] Another explanation for Portuguese
leniency must be that they imported a great quantity of horses from the
Arabian desert through Basra. On the other hand, sea traffic between
Gujerat and the Gulf was always shorter and safer for ships sailing along
the Iranian coastline.

The Basra–Baghdad–Ana–Hit–Aleppo caravan route appears to have
seen considerable activity already in the first half of the sixteenth century,
while a direct route via Al-Kusayr, Karbela, Kubays and Kusur-al-Ihvan
also crossed the desert to reach Aleppo. This route was preferred when
Iranians threatened Baghdad. At times when the desert route became
dangerous because of Bedouin attacks, a safer route was followed up the
river on rafts to Birecik (Al-Bira) or Mosul. Normally, Bedouins played
a central role also on this route. The organization of the caravans and
security in the desert totally depended on the tribal chieftains of the
Syrian desert.[79] It took three days for a caravan to go from Birecik to
Aleppo. Caravans going in the opposite direction loaded the cargoes on
barges on the Euphrates at Birecik. At Falluja, one or two days away
from Baghdad, the cargoes were again loaded on caravans.[80] In 1583 John
Eldred observed that ships from Hormuz arrived at Basra every month,
"laden with all sorts of Indian merchandise such as spices, drugs, indigo
and Calicut cloth." Eldred journeyed to Aleppo, joining a caravan of
4,000 camels, "laden with spices and other rich merchandises."[81] We have
a detailed description of such a caravan in an Ottoman archival document
dated 1610.[82] Out of 120 merchants in the caravan ten were definitely
Muslim Indians with cargoes of indigo dye, Indian cloth and perfumes.
Merchants from Baghdad and Iran formed the majority, carrying indigo
and Lahore fabrics. "Franks" (Italians) were five in number, including
their consul, and had a great variety of goods. Obviously, Western merchants ventured to join the caravans between Aleppo and Basra in order
to maximize their profit. In 1583 there is mention[83] of four Venetian

merchants who carried twenty bales of cloves, long pepper, cinnamon, musk and ostrich feathers from Basra to Aleppo. The Venetian shift from the Damascus market to Aleppo in the mid-sixteenth century[84] must be related to the growing importance of the Persian Gulf–Aleppo caravan route, not only for Iranian silk but also for Indian spices. The Aleppo market, however, showed instability when the Ottomans were at war with Iran (1548–55), or with the Portuguese in the Gulf (1560–63). It is suggested[85] that the establishment of Ottoman control over the Syrian desert made possible the development of the Gulf–Aleppo traffic and Aleppo's emergence as an emporium for Iranian silk as well as for the Indian spices and textiles for Europeans. This was also due to the direct and more complete integration of the region into the south–north trade route developing during that period. Ottoman subjects, Armenians and Turks, as well as Venetians were present in Hormuz, the bustling center of the Indian–Gulf trade under Portuguese control. Interestingly enough, many Portuguese renegades joined the Ottomans and provided valuable knowledge.[86]

THE REVIVAL OF THE SPICE TRADE VIA THE MIDDLE EAST

Spices were not only needed for culinary use but were also essential ingredients of a great variety of medicines. The spice dealers in the bazaar were among the most respectable of the shopkeepers. In addition to pepper, the most frequently cited spices in the Ottoman archival documents are ginger, cloves, cinnamon, rosemary, coconut, gum benzoin and incense.[87] Next to the spices, cotton goods and dyes, in particular indigo, appear to have been the most important items of import. The use of spices became widespread in Europe first among the members of the feudal class, particularly after the establishment of the crusader states in the Middle East. As prosperous cities arose, the use of oriental spices spread in the West. Since spices were high in value and weighed little, the spice trade became the most important branch of the long-distance trade between East and West.

European imports of spices included, in addition to those coming from South Asia through the Indian Ocean, the indigenous products of the Middle East. Perhaps the most important one of the latter category was alum, extensively used as a dye fixer in dyeing textiles. Until 1462, when alum beds were discovered at Tolfa in Italy, European textile industries depended on the import of alum from Turkey[88] (Table I:67).

Table I:67. Alum production in western
Anatolia, 1547

Area of production	Amount in *kantar*
Kütahya	1,331
Saruhan	950
Teke (Hamid)	1,520
Gedos (Gediz)	1,200
Alaiye and Manavgat	230
Total	5,231

Source: Faroqhi (1979b).

The Genoese held the monopoly of alum export from Turkey in the fifteenth century. In 1547, the Venetians had the monopoly for 1.5 million *akça* or 25,000 gold ducats for three years. Şebin-Karahisar in eastern Anatolia was also an important production center. A great quantity of its prime quality alum had been exported to Europe since the Middle Ages.

Picking up where the studies of H.O. Lybyer, F. Lane, R. Lopez and F. Braudel left off, recent studies have brought forth more evidence against the theory of the complete diversion of the spice trade from the Ottoman-controlled Middle East to the Atlantic in the wake of the discovery of the Cape route to the Indian Ocean.

V.M. Godinho[89] argued that the spice trade through the Mediterranean had suffered setbacks even prior to the Portuguese discoveries. The wars between the Mamluks and the Ottomans (1485–91), and the Ottomans and Venetians (1499–1503) as well as internal disorders in Cairo, G.-V. Magalhães points out, had disastrous effects on the spice and silk trade. Consequently the public debt in Venice went from 1,600,000 in 1495 to 2,800,000 million ducats in 1508.

However, after 1501 the impact of the Portuguese discovery of the Cape route accounts for the long-term decline. Venice lost its northern markets. The spices purchased by Venetians at Alexandria and Beirut fell from 6,850 *colli*[90] in 1496 to 1,720 in 1502 (see Table I:68). In the years 1504–15, there were almost no Venetian purchases in Alexandria and only 3,234 *colli* in Beirut. The first news of the Portuguese embargo and the attack on Muslim ships engaged in the spice trade at Calicut caused the pepper price to rise from 75 to 95 ducats per *collo* in Venice.[91]

In 1502 pepper was sold at 19 ducats per Ottoman *kantar* (see Weights and Measures) in Edirne and Bursa, and 24 ducats in Florence. In 1501, when Vasco da Gama was already back with spices in Lisbon, the price

Table 1:68. Estimates of the spices coming to Europe via Lisbon, Beirut
and Alexandria, 1497–1513 (in lb)

	Lisbon	Beirut	Alexandria
1497	—	2,858,037	3,668,810
1498	—	3,249,000	3,344,304
1499	—	—	—
1500	—	3,465,600	2,886,225
1501	224,000	?	?
1502	173,000	c. 1,000,000	
1503	3,336,000	c. 1,000,000	
1504	1,344,000	c. 1,000,000	
1505	2,576,000	c. 1,000,000	
1506	1,904,000	?	
1507	2,800,000	?	
1508	?	c. 1,141,800	
1509	4,480,000	—	
1510	?	1,038,000	
1511	?	—	
1512	?	1,494,840	
1513	4,256,000	314,000	

Source: Romano *et al.* (1970), p. 112.

of pepper rose in Edirne from 19 ducats to 29, and to about 33 in Venice.
Apparently the price per *kantar* stabilized at 36 ducats in the northern
Black Sea ports.

Germany, England, and Flanders now drew their supplies from
Lisbon. Venetian imports to England consisted mainly of Aegean wine,
which was exchanged for English wool and tin for the Levant. Portuguese
pepper shipments, which reached a capacity of 20–30,000 quintals, now
easily provided European markets. Then, a group of Venetian statesmen
supported the idea of taking spices from Lisbon, and the first Venetian
ship appeared there in 1521. But others feared the Ottoman reaction as
the Venetians abandoned the Levant ports.[92]

Venice, the indispensable link

While the Ottomans sustained a long struggle to ensure the flow of
Indian spices to Egypt and Syria, Venice was the indispensable link for
export to Europe in order to obtain bullion and other precious articles
from the West. Despite higher price of spices in the Levant in relation
to Lisbon, there were vital economic links that kept Venice tied to the
Levant market. First, Venice exported woolen and silk products on a
massive scale in exchange for spices and raw silk in the Ottoman market.[93]

Bartering helped to maximize profits in this trade. A Venetian colony as large as 4,000 families was involved in this trade. Consequently Venice took a hostile attitude toward the new trade route, banning spice imports from Lisbon or imposing a high tariff. On the other hand, Venice supplied with oriental goods a vast area of Europe including Italy, Germany and Central Europe. All this constituted a complex traditional economic pattern that Venice was reluctant to alter to compete with the new Atlantic system under Portuguese monopoly. This situation helped to provide economic coherence to the eastern and western Mediterranean during the sixteenth century until it began to break down through Western interference at the turn of the century.

The reason that half of the South Asian spice supplies passed through Ottoman dominions in the sixteenth century was because Eastern Europe, Ottoman Asia and the Balkans constituted a vast market, and the Portuguese themselves came to terms with the Ottomans in order to engage in contraband or even official trade through Hormuz. Geographic and economic considerations, transport costs in particular, resulted in the establishment of a separate zone for spice on a line east of Vienna and Italy. Even French Provence came into the purview of this eastern zone, since Marseilles obtained large supplies of spices from Alexandria and Tripoli in order to compete with Venice. Other competitors in the zone were Dubrovnik for the German trade and the western Balkans, and Bursa and Lwow, linked up via Moldavia to Eastern Europe.

During the years 1501–12, quite large supplies of spices must have reached the Levant. During this period, the Genoese, French and Ragusans took advantage of the break-up of Venice's monopoly of the spice trade.[94] In addition, there is evidence that in these years a sizable portion of the spices arriving in Egypt and Syria took the south–north overland route. The spice supplies reaching Bursa and İstanbul were exported overland to the Balkans, toward the Adriatic Sea and to east-central Europe and Lwow.

Venice, though shocked and alarmed, did not go so far as to openly oppose the Ottoman takeover of Egypt and Syria in 1517. Now the ports of Beirut, Tripoli and Alexandria, from which Venice obtained its spice shipments, were under Ottoman control. In 1527, pepper imported in large quantities reached the level of the fifteenth century although other, more valuable spices, retained their high prices, three times higher than in the fifteenth century.[95] The Levantine trade of Venice fully recovered toward the mid-sixteenth century, and there was remarkable progress in

Table I:69. *The price of pepper in Cairo, 1496–1531 (in gold ducats per* collo*)*

Year	collo
1496	66–68
1497	74–75
1501	90–102
1505	192
1520	90
1524	98
1525	90
1530	90
1531	130

Note: 1 *collo*=3 Egyptian *kantar* or 133 kg[96]
Source: Godinho (1953).

the last three decades of the century when Aleppo and Tripoli acquired large supplies of spices coming via the Persian Gulf (Table I:69). "Political reunification," Magalhães points out,[97] "of the Middle East under Turkish power has a lot to do with that development although the formation of this colossus entailed harsh blows to the Venetian prosperity when connections with Alexandria and Beirut were so fundamentally responsible for its trade before the Turkish take over of these two ports."

Venice was well aware of the central role the Ottomans could play in reviving the India–Red Sea route. After the conclusion of peace with the Ottoman Empire in 1503, Venice recognized the fact that it was the Ottomans who were the only power capable of maintaining the route against the Portuguese.[98] The peace treaty of 1503 renewed, at the same time, all the capitulatory guarantees for Venetian trade. Under the circumstances the Venetian Senate decided to pursue a more subtle, even submissive, policy toward the Ottomans.

MORE EVIDENCE FOR THE REVIVAL OF THE SPICE TRADE

Throughout the sixteenth century the spice trade was still the most important branch of international trade. Along with precious textiles, raw silk and precious stones, spice was big business in terms of capital investment and large profit margins. The "capitalist spirit," Hermann Kellenbenz pointed out,[99] "found in the commerce of pepper one of its most important fields of activities." To a great extent this is also true for the Islamic world. According to the Bursa court records of 1480–1550, the wealthiest merchants were those involved in the spice trade, and, next to silk, the largest capital investments were made in the spice trade.[100] In 1500, for example, an Aleppan merchant, Hacı Abu Bakr, imported to Bursa a large supply of ginger with a value of 200,000 *akça* (4,000 gold coins), just when Vasco da Gama was loading his ships with the same product in India.

Since navigation was hazardous for big ships in the northern Red Sea, Jidda was the terminus of the ships from India. Every year in May or November small sailing vessels or large galleys left Jidda for Tur (Tor) from where the caravans took precious cargoes to Cairo. The Ottoman historian Ali speaks of twenty ships from India arriving at Jidda every year.[101] The figure is confirmed by Portuguese sources that give the number of ships as sixteen to eighteen prior to 1570.[102] As against 90,000 in the early sixteenth century, annual customs revenues in Mecca were estimated at 150,000 gold ducats in 1587.[103] Customs duties taken from goods arriving by sea at the port of Jidda were shared half and half by the Ottoman treasury and the sharif of Mecca. The spice trade through Cairo and Syria was the main avenue by means of which the Ottomans drained gold and silver specie from Europe. An important part of the spice cargoes arriving at Jidda took the land route Mecca–Damascus–Aleppo and from thence to Bursa. At Damascus customs fees of seven gold pieces were collected on each camelload of about 250 kg of spices and cloth coming from Mecca. If these were sold to the "Frankish party," nineteen gold pieces were assessed, of which nine were to be paid by the Franks.[104]

Venetian ships transported to the Levant copper bars and woolen cloth, silk cloth, kerseys, caps, coral, amber, various trinkets, paper and coins. When returning, the ships brought back spices, including pepper, ginger, cinnamon, nutmeg, cloves, frankincense and gum arabic, as well as sugar, sandalwood and other more exotic goods.

Also from Dubrovnik and Avlona, both under Ottoman control, shipments of spices found their way not to Venice but to the international fairs of central Italy, Lanzan and Recanati. Toward 1524 Greek, Turkish and Iranian (*Azemini*) merchants were present at these fairs. What is surprising is that in those fairs we also find English merchants exchanging their woolen cloth with oriental merchandise.[105]

We have seen earlier that, as a result of the Ottoman–Atjehnese alliance against the Portuguese, large shipments of pepper had been arriving via the Red Sea since the 1430s. However, the Portuguese, well informed through their spies in Cairo, date "the marked revival of the Red Sea spice trade" and their concern about it from 1545.[106] The period 1554–67 witnessed an expansion in the Atjeh–Red Sea spice trade, which must have been due to the renewal of Atjehnese–Ottoman cooperation. The sultan of Atjeh sent to the Red Sea unusually large cargoes of spices in order to encourage the Ottomans to send a fleet into the Indian Ocean and to pay back the sultan for military aid. When in 1569 vast quantities of pepper arrived in the Ottoman ports, the price of pepper dropped in Flanders.[107] Now more and more Ottoman ships appeared in the Indian Ocean as far away as Sumatra. The Portuguese failed to intercept the Atjehnese ships, which were reinforced with guns and Turkish soldiers. When they attacked them, they had to put up a fierce battle to overcome them. Many Atjehnese ships succeeded in reaching their destination of Al-Mukha (Mocha), Jidda, Suez or Tur in the Red Sea. In 1565 a Venetian source reported the arrival in Jidda of five Sumatran ships and twenty ships from various ports in India. The following year five ships from Atjeh brought a total of some 24,000 *kantar*s of pepper. Thus, the trade route of Atjeh–Red Sea or Atjeh–Gujerat–Basra became the most important commercial artery of Asian trade from the middle of the sixteenth century.

The volume of Ottoman–Atjehnese commerce must have been quite significant. By 1585, the annual income of the Atjehnese ruler from trade with the Red Sea was calculated at three or four million gold ducats a year. The merchandise exported included 30–40,000 quintals of pepper, ginger, benzoin and cinnamon as well as gold, camphor, sandalwood, sulphur and silk.[108] Now it was Gujerati ships which carried Atjehnese goods to the Red Sea. In the 1590s Atjehnese pepper arriving in the Red Sea was "much more than the Portuguese were taking around the Cape of Good Hope to Lisbon."[109]

An interesting episode connected with this development is the migration of Turks as mercenaries and merchants into the South Asian world. Along with the Ottoman government's attempt to replace the Portuguese in the Indian Ocean and the spread of Ottoman soldiers as mercenaries (Rumis), the active traffic gave rise also to Turkish merchant colonies in the area from Gujerat to Atjeh. Common Islamic law and facilities provided by kadi courts in all Islamic lands, or Islamic internationalism, appears to have been no less a factor in the close commercial relations of these countries; it in turn contributed to the spread of Islam in South Asia. Quite a large group of Rumi merchants, 400 in number, had settled in Diu (Gujerat).[110] By 1600, there was a Muslim Indian colony in Aleppo. In the sixteenth century in Calicut, the center of the spice trade in Malabar, there was a community of Turks with its own head merchant along with other foreign Muslim traders.[111] Muslim merchants of Malabar, upon their eviction by the Portuguese from India, took sanctuary in Sumatra and deflected part of the pepper and other valuable spices from the island via Aden to Cairo and Damascus.

In 1596, from the Javanese town of Bantam, "many Turkish and Arab merchants" set sail on board a Dutch ship to return home to İstanbul.[112] It was reported that the chief agent of the Ottoman sultan had his headquarters on the island of Atjeh with a capital of one million in gold coins to buy valuable spices. Ottomans had obtained a trading post at Pasai in Sumatra as early as about 1540.

TWO EMPORIA OF THE SPICE TRADE: TRIPOLI AND BASRA

Tripoli became the principal outlet of the spice trade from Damascus, while Alexandria had the same function for spice exports from Cairo. By 1583 Tripoli was mentioned as the port most frequented by Christian merchants.[113] One important reason why European trade shifted to Tripoli in the second half of the sixteenth century was that initially the ship tax for foreign ships was lower there.[114] Then a new regulation was issued in 1571: European ships anchoring at the port of Tripoli were to pay 614 *akça* for big vessels, 200 for middle-sized, and 25 for small-sized vessels at the time of departure. Interestingly enough, this regulation was arranged unanimously, after a long correspondence, by Ottoman customs agents and European merchants together and then approved and made law by the sultan. By 1571 the ports of Latakia, Cebele, Banyas and Antartus were dependencies of the port of Tripoli, comprising a customs zone on this part of the Syrian coast. Tripoli became one of the main ports for the import of European textiles, woolens or silks, minerals, tin and steel, and the export of spices, Lebanese raw silk and cotton. As mentioned in the Ottoman regulations of the mid-sixteenth century, ships visiting Tripoli were from Venice, France, Chios or Cyprus. Before the Ottoman conquest in 1570, Cyprus was the principal transit center for European merchants who did not have capitulation guarantees for trade within the Ottoman dominions (see Tables I:70 and I:71).

Goods from Iran and Syria arriving at the Tripoli market by caravan were subject to the scales tax. The scales tax corresponded to the marketplace due and was light compared with customs duties. Many Europeans,

Table I:70. Customs dues on Western goods imported at the port of Tripoli, 1571 (in akça)

	Customs duty percent and *ad valorem*	Pen-fee (*resm-i kalem*)	Scales-tax (*kantar*)
Woolen cloth	2	1 per bolt	
Satin (*atlas*)	2	6 per 100 *arşun*	
Brocade	2	8 per 100 *arşun*	
Velvet, plain or with gold thread and other varieties	2	8 per 100 arsun	
Tunis coral	3	1 per *kantar*	1 per *kantar*
Amber	3	1 per *kantar*	1 per *kantar*
Copper	3	1 per *kantar*	1 per *kantar*
Iron	3	1 per *kantar*	1 per *kantar*
Lead	3	1 per *kantar*	1 per *kantar*
Chemicals	3	1 per *kantar*	1 per *kantar*
Paper	7		1 *akça* or 7 pieces
Knives	7		1 *akça* or 7 pieces
Crystal objects	7		1 *akça* or 7 pieces
Steel	4 per *batman*	10 per *kantar*	10 per *kantar*

Source: Barkan (1943), pp. 211–16.

however, are said to have finished their transactions in Damascus or Aleppo.

Two percent customs duty had to be paid for all goods loaded on ships at Tripoli destined for Ottoman and other Muslim countries. Since abundant supplies of olive oil and potash were available in Syria, Tripoli and other Syrian towns had a very active soap industry and exported large quantities of soap to İstanbul and other parts of the Ottoman Empire. Two gold pieces for each box of soap were paid as customs duty. While there were four state-owned soap factories in Tripoli before 1571, they shut down apparently as a result of competition from private soap factories. In the Tripoli regulation, special reference is made to the corals of Tunisia. In fact, when the merchants of Marseilles obtained the rights to coral fishing off Tunis, they took most of the coral to Tripoli and Alexandria in exchange for spices. Spices from Tripoli competed with those imported from Lisbon to the French market.[115] Some of these French imports found their way as far afield as Rouen and England.[116] Even at Antwerp, which was the European emporium of spices under Spanish control, Levant spices arriving regularly competed with those coming from Lisbon. When the English were granted capitulation privileges in 1580, they imported large quantities of oriental goods, mainly from Tripoli. The Ottomans permitted them to buy cotton and cotton

Table I:71. Customs dues on exports to Europe from Tripoli, 1571 (in *akça*)

	Customs duty percent and *ad valorem*	Pen-fee	Scales (*kapan*)	
Spices, including pepper, cinnamon, clover, ginger, indigo, coconut	10 + 11		1	Shared by seller and buyer
Iranian raw silk	110 per *kantar*	2	1	
Syrian raw silk	110 per *kantar*	4+4	1	by seller and buyer
Rhubarb	110 per *kantar*		1	
Cotton	4+4	1	1	
Cotton yarn	5+5	1	1	by seller and buyer
Mohair	66 per load			Each load (*denk*) contains 50 pieces
Taffeta	66 per load			Each load (*denk*) contains 50 pieces
Cowhides	3			
Leather	44 per load of 75 pieces	2		
Henna	110 per each 100 batman		1	
Gallnuts	3		1	1 *kantar* of gallnuts, value: 700 *akça*
Beeswax	3	1	1	
Carpets	11 per load			

Note: 1 *kantar* = c. 56 kg
Source: Barkan (1943).

yarn in Tripoli, which were as a rule among the goods prohibited for export.[117] In May of 1609 an English ship from Syria had a cargo worth about 150,000 crowns in silk, indigo, gallnuts and cotton goods.[118]

According to a Venetian report of 1593, Tripoli enjoyed a kind of autonomy and European merchants had to pay extra protection money to the local Arab emir, Fahreddin Ma'n, then acting as the Ottoman tax-farmer and governor. This is mentioned as the principal cause of the shift of European trade, at least partly, from Tripoli to Sidon and İskenderun (Alexandretta) in the last decade of the sixteenth century.[119]

For a reliable source for the Gulf traffic and regional economy of the Ottomans we have the two Ottoman customs and market dues regulations of Basra, dated 1551 and 1575,[120] which evidently originated from previous regulations going back to Safavid or even earlier times. Transit goods of Indian and Iranian origin as well as regional products are listed in these documents (see Table I:72).

Table I:72. Imports from India to Basra, 1551, 1575

Spices	Dyes	Textiles	Other
Pepper and other spices (chiefly cinnamon, nutmeg, ginger)	Indigo	Fine muslins for *bayrami* cloth	Steel
	Gumlac		Iron
Cotton		Other cotton fabrics	

Source: Mantran (1967), pp. 224–77; Steensgaard (1972), pp. 354–58.

At Niksar, the landing for ships from India and Hormuz, the annual customs revenue amounted to 1,394,799 *akça* in 1551, with a decrease of 244,216 to 1,150,583 in 1575. The customs revenue from goods coming from Baghdad, Daurak (Iran) and Djezayir (lower Iraq) on small ships was 527,269 in 1551 and increased to 749,338 in 1575. Those Indian imports, in particular indigo, which could not be sold at Basra, were re-exported to Baghdad or to other Ottoman trade centers, and a second customs due had to be paid. It should also be kept in mind that the total customs revenue on Indian imports at Basra does not represent the complete revenue from this trade, since a number of merchant ships proceeded to Baghdad without paying customs dues at Basra. However, even in the seventeenth century, the Ottoman government included Basra among the richest cities of the empire.

On their way to Basra, ships from India and Hormuz stopped at Al-Katif, leaving some of their cargoes there, including cotton and cotton goods. An anchorage due had to be paid there. Imports of raw cotton and indigo dye from India gave rise to an important cotton industry in Basra, Al-Katif and Bahrain. The tax on cotton, amounting to 135,232 *akça* in 1575, indicates the significance of and the quantity of Indian cotton imports to Basra.

At Hormuz the Portuguese levied a 6 percent customs duty on the spices taken by Arab merchants to Basra, which produced a total revenue of 25,000 cruzados per annum. In other words, spices imported annually to Basra through Hormuz had a value of 400,000 cruzados.[121]

Basra was by far the most important emporium in the Gulf for Portuguese imports destined for the Ottoman and Iranian markets. It was quite normal for Portuguese authorities in the Gulf to cooperate with the Ottomans. Mostly it was Arab merchants, or Turks either in disguise as Iranians or condoned by the Portuguese authorities, who took the bulk of the imports from Hormuz to Basra and Baghdad. The *capitaõ* of

Hormuz owed his large annual income to the trade with Basra. The *Estado da India*'s annual revenue in Hormuz was the highest compared to that of the other Portuguese port cities.[122] The Dutch agent Visnich reported that 54 ships arrived at Hormuz with a variety of cotton cloth, including calicoes and precious linens, and brought various kinds of spices, drugs and dyes. The annual Portuguese customs revenue was estimated to be between 250 and 500 thousand cruzados.[123] The Ottoman regulations reveal that there were indeed official arrangements between themselves and the Portuguese authorities at Hormuz. A Portuguese "faytor" (*feitor*, factor) represented the "kaptan" (*capitão*) of Hormuz at Basra, who himself visited Basra every three years. Purchases made for him, principally horses and textiles, were not subject to taxation. His exports of horses enjoyed the same exemption at Bahrain. In fact, the most important export to India was Arab horses, while silver, mostly coming from Ottoman-controlled centers, overshadowed all exports. The amount of silver annually taken by the Portuguese from the Gulf as a whole is estimated at two million cruzados in the 1590s.[124]

In this period Basra appears to have been also the principal center of trade for Iran, not only for the exchange of native products but also for Indian goods. By capturing Hormuz (1622) and shifting trade to Bandar-Abbas, Shah Abbas would bring a total change in this pattern of trade (Table 1:73).

Iranians in general came to the landing called Sif in Basra, which was the popular local port with depots for grain and vegetables. Caravans from Luristan and Shiraz as well as from the landings of Daurak, Bandar and Abu-Shihr arrived regularly at Sif. There seems to have been quite an active traffic between these ports and Basra by sea and on the Karun river, passing through Huwayza, Dizbul, Shushter and Wasit.

Many Iranian merchants visited the island of Hormuz. As mentioned above in relation to the caravan of 1610, Iranian merchants used the Basra route to import Indian goods.

The great variety of goods – silk and cotton textiles as well as foodstuffs and raw materials – imported to Basra denotes the significance of Iranian trade for the region. Perhaps some of the valuable silks from Iran were re-exported to India.

Almost all ships from Djezayir/Jaza'ir and Baghdad brought native products but big caravans from Baghdad, Damascus and Aleppo carried goods of international traffic. We have mentioned the importance of the export of horses which came from Al-Hasa and Baghdad. In addition to red dye, henna, dates, gallnuts and buffalo hides made up the bulk of

Table I:73. Imports from Iran to Basra, 1551, 1575

Cotton goods	Silk	Other
Blue cloth of Isfahan	Yazdi black	Sheep
White cloth of Isfahan	Yazdi *mahazim*	Grain, flour
Coarse white cloth of Daurak	Caftans of Shushter	Carpets
Malla, head covers for women	Cummerbunds of Shushter	Wool
	Aprons (*futa*)	Wool yarn Flax, rosewater Sheep and cattle Dried fruits (hazelnuts, walnuts, figs raisins, pistachio) Bowls of Shiraz

Source: Ottoman customs regulations of Basra.

exports. Along with the export of horses, fabrics or cloaks of camel wool, and goods passing in transit, such as Syrian soap and the red-dye of Yemen, the Arabian peninsula appears to have had an important share in Basra's international and regional trade. Arab felt was famous and the object of an active trade at Basra. *Mashlah*, a large cloak of camel wool, and smaller cloaks called *busht* were apparently in great demand.

In the caravan transportation through the deserts separating Basra from Syria and the Hejaz, Bedouins of the Arabian desert played a major role. Interestingly enough, some goods of Indian origin, such as indigo and cloth, came to Basra, via Najd and Al-Hasa, from Mecca. The Djezayir, islands of lower Iraq, provided goods for local consumption such as rice, dates, fish and mats. Other important ports in lower Iraq included Zakiyya, where ships from India arrived and sheep from Iran passed in transit; and Kurnah, which merchant ships trafficking between Basra and Baghdad visited. Here, they charged a passage toll of 80 *akça* per ship.

Goods of local production, namely fine muslins from Bahrain and coarse cotton textiles woven in Basra and Al-Katif, indicate that there existed quite an active handicraft production for local consumption as well as export in this area in the sixteenth century. Substantial increases in tax revenues between 1551 and 1575 give the impression of a growing prosperity for these local industries. Part of the imported indigo dye was used locally for textile manufacture. The revenue of the large dye-house of Basra amounted to 262,001 *akça* in 1551. Apparently, imported Indian raw cotton spun and turned into cotton yarn in the region came to Basra to be dyed.

Because of extraordinary defense expenditures, the government did not expect to receive a surplus revenue from Basra. On the contrary, it had to send an appropriation to support the local budget. After driving the Ottomans out of the silk-producing provinces in Azerbaijan in the last decade of the century, Shah Abbas planned to reconquer Iraq and to deprive the Ottoman Empire of this economic lifeline. Furthermore, by capturing Aleppo, as the Ilkhanids of Iran had attempted in the thirteenth century, he planned to take direct control of the entire Indian trade with Europe. To this end he had already established his control over Hormuz (1622) and Kandehar (1623), emporium of the Indian caravan trade in Asia. He captured Baghdad in January of 1624 and his governor-general of Shiraz attempted to take Basra at the same time. Isolated from the Ottoman bases in the north in the wake of the fall of Baghdad, and facing the actual independence of the local lord Afrasiyab in lower Iraq, the pasha of Basra made an alliance with the Portuguese for the safety and economic future of the city. In the meantime, following the Iranian occupation of Hormuz, the Portuguese succeeded in replacing Hormuz with Muscat as the center of their trade with Basra. Portuguese ships began to arrive in Basra after 1623, which illustrated a renewed prosperity in the following years. Indian goods brought to Basra by the Portuguese were now conveyed to Aleppo through a direct route across the desert, entirely avoiding Baghdad. In reaction to this, the Iranians gave commercial privileges to the English at Bandar-Abbas and at Kung to the Portuguese (1630) and tried to bring this trade under their monopoly. Both places rapidly developed, with Bandar-Abbas becoming one of the great port cities of Asia during this period. The Portuguese, however, showed greater interest in the old route to Basra which led directly to the Syrian ports. The Ottomans after a long struggle finally succeeded in reconquering Baghdad in 1638. This marked the end of an epoch with the definitive hegemony of the English and Dutch over the Indian Ocean as well as the Gulf. Now, Iranians in the Gulf as well as Ottomans in Basra continued to receive Indian goods, mostly cotton goods and indigo, through the English and Dutch East India Companies.

In the new epoch, the Ottoman and Iranian position in the world economy was dwarfed by the tremendous expansion of the Atlantic economy and the substitution of Western staples by colonial production—sugar, tobacco, coffee and cotton. In the new era, the cotton trade began to overshadow that of silk as a result of the new widespread fashion in the West, as in the Ottoman Empire, for cotton fabrics; cotton industries expanded in the West. Because of these developments, the old pattern of the Indian–Levant trade as the principal artery for world exchange underwent a complete structural change during the period 1620–60. The Ottoman Empire, like Venice, its principal partner, was the chief loser.

During the sixteenth century, the Ottoman Empire struggled to protect its middleman role in the world trade of spices and silk between India, Indonesia and Iran, on the one hand, and Europe on the other. We have seen that the transit trade of Iran's silk became increasingly important in world trade as silk industries developed in the West. Fernand Braudel, who for the first time helped us understand the Ottoman role in the world trade, concentrates on spices, wheat and bullion, leaving out another vital commodity in international trade, namely cotton and cotton goods. This oversight may be justified for sixteenth-century Europe. But imports of Indian textiles had a very important place in the Middle East traffic with India, perhaps more important than spices in terms of the drain of bullion from the region in the sixteenth century, and apparently even earlier.[125] In the early sixteenth century, when the Portuguese attempted to blockade the Red Sea, Egypt complained in particular of the scarcity of Indian textiles. Mention was made of fine Indian muslins from which turbans were made. By the same date, Cambay's cotton fabrics were exported all over the world, including Iran, Syria, North Africa and Turkey.[126] In the same century, the production and export of Indian cotton fabrics to the Middle East and Europe reached unprecedented levels.[127] Cheap Indian calicoes were in great demand by the masses, while the very expensive fine turban muslins were an indispensable luxury item for the elite. In 1623, the Dutch agent Visnich mentions eight ships arriving from India at Hormuz loaded with white and colored fabrics, three with calicoes and coarse *baftas*.[128]

By 1670, an English East India Company officer confessed that through the India–Basra route merchants from the Middle East "carried off five times as many calicoes as the English and the Dutch."[129] The import of Indian textiles through the Red Sea route appears to have been no less important throughout the sixteenth and seventeenth century. Cairo was, like Basra, an entrepôt for Indian fabrics.

In 1647, in the important centers of Ottoman cotton industries, native dealers took their complaints to the imperial council against the Armenians of Iran who brought and sold Eastern cotton fabrics.[130] Armenians were particularly active in the Indian textile trade during this period. An invasion of Indian fabrics was so alarming that even an official annalist of the empire, Naima,[131] complained of the drain of bullion from the empire, saying, "so much cash treasury goes for Indian merchandise that . . . the world's wealth accumulates in India." The East India Companies of the English and Dutch were engaged now in the massive trade of cotton goods in their imports to Basra and Gombroon. Soon Ottoman weavers began to produce imitations of Indian fabrics in such industrial centers as Bursa and Aleppo. When, following the Middle East Indian cottons, fine muslins as well as cheap and attractive calicoes invaded Western European markets, riots broke out among the wool and flax industries against the import and use of cottons. In panic the French and English governments introduced restrictions on the import of Indian fabrics. In fact, in Europe too, this trade overshadowed the spice trade in the period 1650–1750.

Germans and the spice trade

Already during the sixteenth century, individual German merchants were establishing direct trade relations with Ottoman lands.[132] Although Venice prohibited German merchants in the *fondaco dei Tedeschi* from cooperating with the Venetians in maritime ventures, there were exceptions. An early example is a merchant of Augsburg, Jacob Rehlinger, who had established trade relations with İstanbul in luxury goods in 1530. During the Venetian–Ottoman War of 1537–40, the firms of Augsburg attempted to get spices for the German market from Dubrovnik, where shipments from Alexandria had shifted from Venice. In 1559, the Fuggers sent one of their agents to Alexandria and bought spices worth 10,000 cruzados. The cargo loaded on a Ragusan ship arrived at Dubrovnik, and from there it sailed on to Fiume, which belonged to the emperor. The following year, the agent came to Alexandria with a larger sum. The possibility of a German shift to the Levant route alarmed Portugal.[133] Along with the Fuggers, the German firm of Ulstetter also had agents in Cairo and Alexandria.

Especially during times when Venice was at war with the Ottomans, the Germans either attempted to get supplies of oriental goods from the Levant through Venice's rivals – Genoa, Trieste, Marseilles and Dubrovnik – or to penetrate the Levantine markets directly. It was possible for non-Muslims from the Abode of War without capitulatory guarantees to trade under the protection of those nations with capitulations. During the war of 1570–73, when Ottoman–French trade relations showed an unprecedented expansion, the German businessman, Melchior Manlich, established a headquarters in Marseilles.[134] His seven ships trafficked with Alexandria, İstanbul, Famagusta and Tripoli. Most interestingly, he also planned to use the Danubian route for trade with the Ottoman lands.

Manlich exported from Germany minerals, tin and lead, in particular quicksilver and small metal goods, *Nürnberger Kram*, which were in great demand in the Levant. But the traffic which his ships were conducting with Tripoli of Syria, Alexandria, Chios and İstanbul, and Cadiz, Rouen and the English ports indicate that he was involved in the classic pattern of Levantine trade, based on the exchange of woolen cloth with spices and silk. In 1572 one of the company's ships was bringing from the Levant a cargo of pepper worth 50,000 *gulden*. And records show that German traders going from Tripoli to Aleppo sold at this great Levantine market woolen cloth and bought spices and drugs, silk, cotton, colored cotton cloth, carpets, precious stones and pearls. The people they traded with at Aleppo included merchants from Iran, Anatolia, Egypt and India. Special mention should be made of raw cotton, indispensable for the flourishing industries of fustian cloth, a mixture of flax and cotton, in Augsburg.

In the beginning, Manlich's enterprise proved to be quite successful with a net return of 30 percent, and other merchants of Augsburg invested money in the enterprise. But in 1574 Manlich went bankrupt with a debt of 700,000 *gulden*. The loss of his two ships and the return of the Venetians to the Levant market following the peace concluded with the Ottomans in 1573 were cited as the principal reasons for bankruptcy.

Other merchants from Augsburg were also active in the Levant trade through Marseilles. It is interesting to add that while the merchants of Augsburg continued their business dealings in the Levant from their headquarters in Venice and Marseilles, the Portuguese were threatened by other European intruders too, coming from France, Germany, Italy and the Flemish lands, who mostly reached India via the Aleppo–Hormuz route. The Gulf road was particularly attractive for its pearls. It should be remembered that big business always involved trade in spices, drugs, jewels and pearls.

Besides these Germans from Augsburg and Nürnberg trying to participate in the Levant–India trade, Hanseatic ships coming to the Italian ports with their grain cargo might have ventured as far as Ottoman dominions to get oriental goods around 1600.

Before Lisbon began to get spices and drugs from South Asia, Venice was the principal intermediary conveying these precious commodities from the Levant to Germany. But the year 1569, when the Ottomans decided to attack Venetian Cyprus, was the real turning point.

In 1570, in his grand project for a spice trade monopoly for Europe, Konrad Rott of Augsburg estimated the total European demand for spices at 28,000 quintals, which was distributed among various regions as follows.[135]

Portugal	1,500
Spain	3,000
France	2,500
England, Scotland and Ireland	3,000
Italy	6,000
Germany, Poland, Baltic countries, Bohemia, Austria, Silesia and Hungary	12,000
Total	28,000

When Melchior Manlich's attempt proved to be a failure, German commercial houses became involved more than ever in cooperating with Lisbon. The big companies of Augsburg, the Welsers and the Fuggers, chose Spanish–Portuguese cooperation – thus shifting from the Mediterranean to the Atlantic – for large-scale pepper imports to Europe. Their representative, Ferdinand Cron, settling in Goa in 1587, established a prosperous business there at a time when the Dutch arrived to challenge the Portuguese monopoly.[136]

The Welsers and Fuggers, who had lent large sums to Philip II, participated in the contracts made by the Spanish king for the import and distribution of 30,000 quintals of pepper in Europe in 1586 and 1591. In 1586 the annual amount was estimated at 30,000 quintals in the contract made by Philip II with G.B. Rovelasca.[137] While countries supplied by Venice or the Levant were always the largest markets, now the pepper shipments arrived principally at the ports of Hamburg, Lübeck and Amsterdam from Lisbon. What is surprising is that a portion of the pepper arriving in the northern ports found its way to Leghorn and Venice to compete with supplies from the Levant.[138]

Bought for 5⅔ cruzados per quintal in India, pepper cost 16 cruzados (or gold ducats) at the Casa da India at Lisbon about 1586. Having a monopoly in the spice trade, the king added his share so that it was sold to the European merchants at 37 cruzados and in times of shortage as high as 60 cruzados.[139] After 1600 a new period began with the powerful intervention of the English and Dutch into the spice trade. After the defeat of the Spanish armada in 1588, English privateers intensified their attacks against Spanish–Portuguese ships and spice shipments to Lisbon sharply declined. The Dutch and the English soon began to compete against the Portuguese in supplying spices taken directly from India. Lisbon tried to fight back against the intruders by offering more favorable conditions in the payment of its pepper to the ports of Hansa. In Lisbon, the pepper price then dropped from the average of 36 cruzados to 20 per quintal.

In the short period between 1591 and 1600, Portugal, in cooperation with the German Hansa, under the control of the Spanish king since 1580, made a final effort to protect its monopoly on Indian trade against the Dutch and English.

On the other hand, the competition from the Levant in supplying the European markets through Venice, Dubrovnik, Marseilles and Messina continued to be quite serious. As evidence from the years 1591–92 demonstrates,[140] supplies of pepper from the Levant substantially influenced prices in Venice and Central Europe. The Fuggers had special agents in Venice in order to get regular information about the market conditions there and on spice supplies arriving in the Ottoman ports.[141] The Fuggers planned to raise the price on the news from Venice that the Ottoman fleet was cruising to intercept shipments from the Levant. But in February of 1593 news came of the arrival of 30,000 quintals of pepper through the Red Sea, exactly the same amount expected through the Atlantic route to Lisbon. Then the Spanish king had difficulty in finding good customers for the pepper arriving in the Casa da India. Because of its rivalry with the Habsburgs in the Mediterranean and Central Europe, the Ottoman Empire encouraged and cooperated with the English and Dutch in the first stage of their struggle in the Levant which resulted in the collapse of the Venetian monopoly of the spice trade.

Steensgaard[142] argues that the East India Companies of Western nations brought in a structural change in this trade against the traditional "peddling trade" and they were responsible for the eclipse of the Levant as a competitor in Asian trade in the first decades of the seventeenth century. There is consensus that the final blow to the Levant spice trade came about 1625 when the Dutch and English firmly established their domination in the Indian Ocean and also established a strict monopoly over the Atlantic route. Due to the Dutch East India Company's monopoly, the scarcity of spice supplies in Alexandria was referred to in Venetian reports there in the 1610s. It should be remembered that a substantial part of the pepper and other precious spices came to the Indian ports from Indonesia to be trafficked to the Red Sea and the Gulf. Now this source had come completely under Dutch control. It should be added that the Ottomans lost control once more of Yemen following the revolt in the 1620s.

But, when we speak of the decline of Ottoman transit trade, there is always a risk in making generalizations on the basis of reports coming from one individual source for one specific period and one specific commodity. While spices ceased to come through the Red Sea as a result of the Dutch monopoly, the customs revenue from the growing trade in silk and in Mocha coffee appears to have substantially compensated for the loss and, while Iranian silk supplies from Iran decreased in Aleppo, they increased in İzmir. On the other hand, although the spice trade was abandoned in the Levant, Indian trade in cotton goods and dyes always flourished.

In the face of better quality and cheaper products coming from Dutch and English industries, the Ottoman economy completely lost its competitiveness in terms of price and quality in such commodities as woolen cloth (including mohair industries), steel production, and mining, particularly in silver production. Also, cheaper production of sugar from the plantations in the Canaries and Brazil eliminated the Ottoman sugar refineries in Cyprus and Egypt. As a result of the Ottoman open-door policy under the capitulatory regime, no systematic policy was introduced to protect and improve native industries. Ottoman economic decline experienced also by other Mediterranean economies, namely Italian and Spanish, was a fact already by 1630. In the Ottoman case it appears to be chiefly the result of the obsoleteness of a medieval traditionalist system in the face of a modern capitalist system.[143] The Ottoman economy also became a market for so-called colonial goods in the subsequent era. One of the first colonial goods imported by English merchants into Turkey was tobacco, around 1600. It soon became a widely consumed commodity in Turkey. In the seventeenth century, the rapidly growing commerce in colonial goods dwarfed the Levant trade.[144]

NOTES

1 Bautier (1970), pp. 287–88.
2 *Ibid.*, pp. 295–301.
3 Zachariadou (1983), p. 154.
4 Bautier (1970), p. 295.
5 *Ibid.*, pp. 297.
6 Ashtor (1983), pp. 64–199.

7 La Brocquière (1892), p. 76.
8 *Ibid.*, pp. 80, 82, 86.
9 Babinger (1951).
10 İnalcık (1960b), p. 146.
11 Heyd (1936), II, p. 355.
12 İnalcık (1960b), p. 146.
13 *Ibid.*, pp. 147.
14 Heyd (1936), II, p. 515; Romano *et al.* (1970), pp. 109–32.
15 Labib (1965), p. 445.
16 Godinho (1969), p. 736.
17 *Ibid.*, pp. 445–48, 737, 740.
18 İnalcık (1957a), pp. 503–4.
19 Godinho (1969), p. 74; Bacqué-Grammont and Kroell (1988), p. 3.
20 İnalcık (1957a), pp. 503–4.
21 Godinho (1969), pp. 741–42.
22 *Ibid.*, pp. 742–47.
23 Labib (1965), p. 455.
24 Bacqué-Grammont and Kroell (1988), pp. 2–5.
25 *Ibid.*, p. 32.
26 Selman's letter in Bacqué-Grammont and Kroell (1988), pp. 32, 33.
27 Sanuto cited by Stripling (1942), p. 79.
28 Bacqué-Grammont and Kroell (1988).
29 Bacqué-Grammont and Kroell (*ibid.*) believe that the Ottoman sultan had no such plan.
30 Lesure (1976), pp. 137–60.
31 Mughal (1974), pp. 102–10.
32 It cost about one million *akça*, see Özbaran (1977), pp. 95–97.
33 Süleyman's letter published by Kurtoğlu (1940), pp. 67–69.
34 Mughal (1974), pp. 156–66.
35 Melzig (1943), p. 68.
36 Serjeant (1963).
37 Yavuz (1984), pp. 39–73.
38 Özbaran (1977), pp. 102–3.
39 *Ibid.*, p. 106; Melzig (1943), p. 79.
40 Godinho (1969); Lach (1965), I, pp. 129–30.
41 Meilink-Roelofsz (1962); Boxer (1969a); Özbaran (1972).
42 Reid (1969), pp. 401–2.
43 *Ibid.*
44 *Ibid.*, p. 403.
45 İnalcık (1947), pp. 47–106.
46 Şah (1967), pp. 381–88.
47 Boxer (1969b), pp. 414–20.
48 *Ibid.*, p. 423.
49 Danvers (1894), I, p. 557; Boxer (1969a).
50 İnalcık (1947), pp. 70–84; Allen (1963), pp. 19–23.
51 İnalcık (1947), pp. 71, 72, 84.
52 Şah (1967), pp. 380–81.

53 Boxer (1969b), p. 420.
54 Blackburn (1979), p. 133.
55 Sahillioğlu (1985).
56 Blackburn (1979), pp. 131–32, 137; Yavuz (1984), pp. 47–73.
57 Blackburn (1979), p. 165.
58 Yavuz (1984), pp. 78–125.
59 Steensgaard (1972), p. 185.
60 Sahillioğlu (1985), p. 288.
61 Barros cited by Özbaran (1977), pp. 113–14.
62 For Rashid's letter, see *ibid.*, p. 115 note 11.
63 For the letter, see *ibid.*, p. 116.
64 Özbaran (1977), p. 118; Özbaran (1971), pp. 25, 58.
65 Mandaville (1970), p. 488.
66 Özbaran (1972), pp. 60–62.
67 The pearl trade had a significant place in the Ottoman economy. The elite preferred investment in pearls because of the facility it offered in hoarding and moving large sums. For the same reason Iranian importers of raw silk invested their cash at Bursa in pearls, since they were not permitted to take silver and gold outside the Ottoman dominions.
68 Mandaville (1970), p. 490; Özbaran (1972), p. 69.
69 Braudel (1972), I, pp. 554–56.
70 *Ibid.*, p. 554.
71 Mandaville (1970), p. 493.
72 Godinho (1969), pp. 750–57; Lane (1940), p. 584.
73 *Ibid.*, (1969), p. 299.
74 Aubin (1975), II, pp. 77–179.
75 A. de Silva cited by Özbaran (1977), p. 134.
76 Duarte Catanho to the king, see Melzig (1943), pp. 77–78.
77 Godinho (1969), pp. 762–72; Aubin (1975), pp. 167–75.
78 Steensgaard (1972), p. 198.
79 *Ibid.*, pp. 37–39.
80 Newberry's report of 1580 cited by Steensgaard (1972), pp. 37–39.
81 Hakluyt (1847–1940), I, pp. 176–77.
82 Sahillioğlu (1968), pp. 63–70.
83 Purchas cited by Steensgaard (1972), pp. 26–27.
84 Lane (1940), p. 584.
85 Stripling (1942), pp. 81–82; Steensgaard (1972), p. 62.
86 Braudel (1972), I, pp. 564–65.
87 For a complete list of spices, see Godinho (1969), pp. 577–96.
88 Faroqhi (1979b); Heyd (1936), II, pp. 565–71.
89 Godinho (1953), pp. 283–86.
90 *Ibid.*, pp. 284–87.
91 *Ibid.*, p. 292; Ashtor (1973), pp. 31–48.
92 Godinho (1953), I, pp. 554–59.
93 Braudel (1973), I, pp. 558–60; Sella (1968), pp. 88–105.
94 Godinho (1969), p. 29.
95 Godinho (1953), p. 295.

362 I The Ottoman state: Economy and society, 1300–1600

96 It is difficult to arrive at exact figures on pepper imports since the measures vary widely. A Venetian *collo* in the pepper trade was accepted as about three *kantar*s corresponding to 1,120 English lb, but actually it varied between 968 and 1,222 English lb, see Lane (1940), p. 583 note 8. A regular Ottoman *kantar* equaled 56.4 kg. In Tripoli or Syria a load of pepper varied between 260 and 522 lb, see Braudel (1973), i, p. 563. One quintal equaled 100 lb in Lisbon, Hanseatic ports and England but the Lisbon lb was heavier. Pepper was sold in bags, *colli*, in the northern ports.

97 *Ibid.*, p. 298.

98 Brummett (1987), pp. 17–18; Romano et al. (1970), p. 129.

99 Kellenbenz (1956), p. 27.

100 İnalcık (1960b), p. 133–35.

101 İnalcık (1951), p. 664.

102 Braudel (1972), I, p. 555.

103 *Ibid.*, p. 564.

104 Barkan (1943), p. 221.

105 Sanuto (1879–1903), XXXVI, pp. 406–7.

106 Boxer (1969b), p. 417.

107 *Ibid.*, p. 421.

108 *Ibid.*, pp. 423–27.

109 *Ibid.*, p. 427.

110 Varthema (1863), pp. 37–38.

111 Pearson cited by Kafadar (1986a), p. 194.

112 Van Leur (1955), pp. 195, 162. "There came such a multitude of Javanese, and other nations as Turks, Chinese, Bengali, Arabs, Gujerati." It is to be noted that Turks are mentioned separately from other Muslim nations, Arabs and Gujerati. Our source, writing in 1596, says: "Many Turks and Arab merchants came on board [the Dutch ships]." One of them was "Kojah [Hoca] Rayoan" from İstanbul who had visited Venice.

113 Hakluyt (1847–1940), II, p. 268 cited by Braudel (1973), I, p. 564.

114 Barkan (1943), p. 211.

115 Masson (1928), pp. 123–25.

116 Braudel (1972), I, pp. 547–48.

117 Kütükoğlu (1974), p. 17 note 48.

118 *CSP: Venice* XII, document no. 497.

119 Steensgaard (1970), p. 177; on the struggle between the local and Arab chieftains and the Ottoman administration for tax-farms, particularly on silk and cotton, see İnalcık (1992).

120 Mantran (1967), pp. 224–44.

121 Steensgaard (1972), p. 199.

122 *Ibid.*, p. 88.

123 *Ibid.*, p. 198.

124 *Ibid.*, p. 199.

125 İnalcık (1980b); Goitein (1966), pp. 329–50.

126 Varthema (1863), p. 151.

127 Chaudhuri (1978).

128 Steensgaard (1972), p. 197.

129 Chaudhuri (1978), p. 246.
130 Çağatay (1942), document nos. 44, 61.
131 Naima (1281 H/1864), IV, p. 293.
132 Kellenbenz (1990), pp. 611–12.
133 Lane (1940), pp. 587–88.
134 Kellenbenz (1990), pp. 611–22.
135 Kellenbenz (1956), p. 7.
136 Kellenbenz (1963).
137 Kellenbenz (1956), p. 2.
138 In 1592, 426 bags against a total of 6,279 bags, one bag containing 2.3 quintals.
139 Kellenbenz (1956), p. 20.
140 *Ibid.*, pp. 4–5, 21.
141 *Ibid.*, p. 13.
142 Steensgaard (1972), pp. 22–153.
143 Chirot (1989), particularly Adanır (1988), pp. 131–76; İslamoğlu-İnan (1987), pp. 1–24.
144 McGowan (1981), pp. 1–44.

14

â

NORTHERNERS IN THE MEDITERRANEAN

THE ENGLISH

As described above, from at least the early fifteenth century Flanders and English woolen cloth arrived in the Levant not only through the Mediterranean but also overland from Antwerp to Lwow and then to the Ottoman dominions. Until 1580, the Genoese and Venetians were the principal middlemen for Levantine products arriving in England. Every year five or six large ships took currants and wine from Cephalonia, Zante and Crete to the north and returned with wool for the Italian woolen industries, and kerseys, tin and lead for the Levant.[1] Sporadic references, however, show that English merchants established a direct connection with the Levant as early as 1446.[2] As Hakluyt tells us,[3] English ships were visiting Tripoli and Beirut and obtaining Turkish and Iranian wares in Chios from the early sixteenth century. In 1518, Henry VIII appointed a resident Italian as the English consul on the island of Chios. In the period 1534–35 one ship took home a cargo of silks, camelot, rhubarb, Turkish carpets, and cotton as well as spices, Greek wines and olive oil.[4] A report[5] on the "Turkey trade," dated 1578 or possibly earlier, said that the English should sell their goods themselves for the highest profit "before they fell into the hands of strangers" and "they should take goods from Turkey to England and other parts of Europe that will enrich England."

Obviously by the mid-sixteenth century, when mercantilism began to dominate the economy of the national monarchies of the West,[6] England sought to share in the profits of the East–West trade in which its own woolen cloth played such a significant role. This new spirit and outlook can be observed in the Hakluyt adventures of English seamen, merchants and the queen herself, who turned England

364

from an underdeveloped country to an industrial one,[7] ready to expand in world markets.

In the period 1552–70, we are told of an eclipse of English shipping in this trade. It was maintained that the English then preferred the Antwerp market, which was easily accessible and abundantly supplied with oriental goods.[8] However, even after 1552 English merchants in trade with the Levant had not completely ceased their activity. There is evidence[9] that English merchants were importing spices from the Levant in Venetian and French ships in the years 1560–80 and that Italian merchants continued with business in London in the goods they imported from the Levant. Their imports included spices, dyes, silk, alum and cotton. Italians bought and exported chiefly English kerseys. In the 1560s and 1570s, Armenian merchants from Iran were purchasing English cloth, mainly kerseys, in Tripoli of Syria and Aleppo. After an eclipse of twenty years, English ships reappeared in full strength in the Mediterranean in 1573.[10] This change came about because of Venetian inability to carry on the former traffic between England and the Levant during the Ottoman–Venetian War of 1570–73 and hence they employed the ships of the neutral English.

The English sought capitulations, which had become a necessity in order to continue trade with Ottoman Turkey after the establishment of direct Ottoman rule over Chios in 1566. Until then Chios had served as the main transit center for English imports and exports. In the seventeenth century, the English, having gained a capitulation, made İzmir on the mainland their principal trade center in the Levant, replacing Chios. Thus, İzmir assumed the role of the most accessible outlet for trade with Asia Minor and Iran. By the 1570s, both the Mediterranean and the Antwerp–Lwow routes came under the control of Philip II of Spain, the champion of a Catholic crusade against northern Protestantism and Ottoman Islam. In fact, Lepanto (1571) and the fall of Antwerp (1572) were turning points ushering in a new age in the history of relations between the northern countries and the Ottoman Empire. Antwerp, the emporium of oriental goods and the transit center for English cloth exports to Europe and Asia, was ruined as a result of Spanish repression against the rebels in the Low Countries in 1576. A few years earlier, France fell under reactionary Catholic leadership as a result of the massacre on St. Bartholomew's Day in 1572. Then, Philip II became the master of all Portuguese colonies by annexing Portugal in 1580. Under these circumstances, a resurgence of English merchants in the Levant took place under totally new political circumstances.

English–Ottoman rapprochement, 1571–80

It was no mere coincidence that the Ottoman sultan was interested in extending capitulations to Western countries in 1569 exactly when he was preparing the invasion of Cyprus, then held by Venice. France was the first Western nation to obtain the same comprehensive capitulations as the Venetians.[11] Ottoman interest in approaching the West became a vital policy following the disaster of Lepanto in 1571, when the Venetian–Spanish–papal coalition became a threat to the very existence of the Ottoman Empire. Also, in order to obtain vital materials such as English tin, steel and lead as well as to give a fatal blow to the Venetian economy, the Porte was anxious to establish direct trade relations with the northerners. Incidentally, it should be remembered that the Ottoman government was kept well informed of major political developments in the West through the French, the Ragusans and Marrano Jews. The Ottomans also must have been aware that the mortal struggle of the Spanish navy against the English and the Dutch prevented it from being a major threat to the Ottomans in the Mediterranean. This situation created a *de facto* cooperation between Ottomans and northerners. When the latter reentered the Mediterranean in the 1580s, English pirates were allowed to use Ottoman ports in North Africa, Albania and Morea as bases and markets for the spoils they were taking from Catholic states. Some English privateers even joined the Algerian–Turkish corsairs and guided them in their activities in the Atlantic.[12]

Venetian galleys in the Mediterranean became an easy target of the English *bretoni*, which were heavily armed with bronze and iron guns. The Ottomans also appreciated the naval superiority and potential of the newcomers against Venice and her allies. The invasion of the sea by northern ships from the Atlantic marked a turning point in the history of the Mediterranean, with an impact on every dimension of the economic life of the region. In the first phase of the rapprochement, both the English and the Ottoman governments seem primarily to have been interested in political–military advantages against the Spanish hegemony. The course of events makes it clear why England sought the sultan's favor in the 1570s. The ruin of Antwerp and the Spanish annexation of Portugal and its colonial empire blocked England from world shipping lanes, which would bring about economic collapse since England could not export its woolen cloth, the basis of its industries and commerce. Also, England herself was under the threat of a Spanish invasion. Under these circumstances, Elizabeth I (1558–1603) was left no choice but to turn to the only great power capable of checking Philip II's plans of world domination, the Ottoman Empire, as Italian states in the fifteenth and then Francis I in the first half of the sixteenth century had done. Before the defeat of the Spanish armada in 1588, "the only course open to her was an alliance with the Turk," and the political motive "was present from the start in the reopening of connections with Turkey."[13] In the 1580s Spain was anxiously following the negotiations between Elizabeth and the sultan.

Already in a 1572 letter to the king of France, Selim II offered the assistance of the Ottoman fleet against Spain and suggested a concerted attack by France, England and the princes of the Low Countries. In 1575 the sultan gave safe conduct to William Harborne, the first English ambassador to the Ottoman state.[14] Contemporary official correspondence testifies that in the period 1579–88 Elizabeth I always hoped that the sultan would send a powerful armada against Philip II of Spain to foil his plans against England, and the sultan reiterated his intention to this end.[15] In İstanbul a group of statesmen urged the sultan to end the ruinous war against Iran and to prepare an armada against Spain.[16] Since the 1550s the Ottomans regarded all Protestant nations in the West as natural allies under the general term "Lutherans" (Elizabeth was called "the Lutheran queen"), fighting against the Pope and the "idolaters." In fact, the Ottoman threat caused Philip II to leave part of his naval forces in the Mediterranean in order to protect the Spanish coasts. The sultan promised the queen that he would send a fleet of 300 ships against Spain. But then, in İstanbul, the party supporting the war against the Habsburgs in Central Europe got the upper hand and the naval campaign against Spain was abandoned.[17]

English capitulations and the growth of trade

The safe conduct that Süleyman I at Aleppo gave to the Englishman, Anthony Jenkinson, in 1553, permitted him to visit "the Ottoman ports to load and unload goods wherever he wished and trade throughout the empire."[18] But this privilege was given to his person under the protection of a capitulatory Western nation. Such individual safe conducts, which were quite a widespread practice, cannot be interpreted as a blanket capitulation.

The English traded under the French banner for protection until they obtained their first capitulation.[19] Actually, the English move for rapprochement began as a trade "venture" of three London merchants with the full support of the queen's government in 1579, and which found a ready response in the Ottoman capital.[20] The first ambassador, William Harborne, supported by the queen's government, was a merchant, organizing this "venture" in cooperation with Edward Osborne and Richard Staper, the founders of the Levant Company. Harborne brought to İstanbul quite a sizable amount of merchandise, consisting of tin, lead, and English cloth, and immediately engaged in business activities.[21] In his letter to the queen, dated March 1579, the sultan granted all English merchants a permit to trade in Ottoman territory under his protection as "the French, Venetians, and Poles have come and traded in safety and security."[22] Upon Harborne's petition to the grand vizier, the sultan at the same time granted a personal safe conduct for trade to William Harborne and his associates.[23] But actually the first capitulations were granted to the English nation only when the queen formally promised her "faithful friendship and gratitude" and asked for it in her letter to the sultan dated October 25, 1579.[24] All this was in conformity with the Islamic–Ottoman procedure of issuing a capitulation. The arduous negotiations were complicated by intrigues by the French, who wanted to keep the English under the French banner in their trade in the Levant; and by Venice, which did not want to lose its profitable role of middleman in the English–Ottoman trade. In the end, the Ottoman sultan granted full capitulatory privileges to the English nation in May 1580.[25] They are essentially modeled on the French capitulations of 1569 and gave the English in the Ottoman Empire "legal status equal with the French." With a reduced customs duty of 3 percent instead of 5 percent paid by other nations, the English became the most favored nation in the empire. The French would obtain the low rate of 3 percent only with the renewal of capitulations in 1673.[26] However, according to Ottoman regulations, different rates were applied depending on the port in question (see above, pp. 195–204) so that, from the beginning, disputes arose between local Ottoman agents and the English. In September 1581, the Turkey company was founded by queen's charter and under the capitulation guarantees English merchants enthusiastically began their trade venture in Turkey. In January 1592, the groups of merchants trading under the names of Venice Company and Turkey Company were united in the Levant Company under a new charter.[27] The Levant Company now monopolized English trade in the eastern Mediterranean, including Ottoman and Venetian possessions. English consulates were set up in Aleppo (1580), Alexandria (Egypt) (1583), Patras (1589), and İzmir

(1611). At other important commercial centers, such as Athens, Salonica and Acre, English merchants were under the protection of French consuls.

It is interesting to note that in 1579 Harborne employed the two traditional routes to import his wares through which English goods used to reach the Levant markets, namely the northern route via Germany, Poland and Moldavia and the Mediterranean route terminating in Chios. Harborne himself travelled via Hamburg to Lwow, where he obtained from the Polish king, Stephen Bathory, a proclamation promising protection to the English merchants. The document stated that[28] "the English merchants used to trade" in Poland. Since Bathory had made peace with the Porte in 1577 and had Ottoman support against his enemies, the English apparently hoped to channel their wares overland through this route because Spain might hinder them in the Mediterranean. Harborne joined the Turkish caravan at Lwow in the company of the Ottoman agents who had concluded the peace treaty with the king. The usual caravan route went through Kamenets (Kaminiec)–Khotin–Stefaneşti–Iasi–Tecuci and over into Wallachia to the Danube, then through Silistre–Provadiya–Kırkkilise to İstanbul. Harborne exchanged his wares in İstanbul for angora camelot and the like. Later, in March 1579, a ship loaded with cloth arrived for him at Chios. On his return the ship was to take home a cargo of Malmsey wine valued at 3,000 ducats at Crete, paid in cash.[29] This was to become an established pattern of English trade in the Levant: the exchange of woolen cloth, tin, and lead for raw silk and the subsequent purchase of wine and currants at the Greek islands under Venetian rule.

Rising English mercantilism dreamed of reaching the Orient, the El Dorado believed the source of all wealth in the East. What was actually of prime importance for England was to market the products of its expanding woolen cloth industries. The Ottoman Empire itself was an important market and through Galata and Bursa a significant part of the imported cloth was channeled to Iran and other Asian countries. As soon as they had their first capitulation in 1580, English merchants appeared in the Aegean with their cargoes of cloth, lead and tin to exchange with Levantine products, currants and wine in particular. Crucial improvements and developments in the English woolen cloth industries coincided with the establishment of direct English trade with the Ottoman market. Prior to the capitulations of 1580, the chief English exports to the Levant were kerseys, lead and tin. "The lead and tin supplied much of the Turkish war needs."[30] *Karziya* (kersey) or *"Londra"* cloths referred to in

Table I:74. English export of
kerseys and broadcloths to
the Levant (in *pastav*)

Year	Kerseys	Broadcloths
1598	18,031	750
1606	10,349	2,776
1621	7,500	2,300

Note: One bolt called *pastav* had usually 50 *zira* or 34 m. Meanwhile the
Ottoman customs registers of Hungary attest to the consumption of *ingi-
liz* and *karziya* woolen cloth even in
this distant province of the empire.

fifteenth-century Ottoman sources[31] consisted of cheap coarse woolen
cloth, the so-called shortcloth. In addition to the immigration of Flemish
skilled artisans, the direct import of Eastern dyestuffs from the Levant
after the grant of capitulations in 1580 is recognized as one of the crucial
factors in releasing English woolen industries from their dependence on
Flemings and Italian middlemen for the dyeing and finishing of their
white cloth.[32] Then, by making dyed broadcloth instead of kerseys,
English industries took the place of Venice in the woolen cloth trade in
the Levant. In 1598, the Levant Company first exported 750 broadcloths
together with 18,031 kerseys;[33] over time broadcloths totally replaced
kerseys in the chief Levantine markets of İstanbul, İzmir and Aleppo.
The yearly average broadcloth export to the Levant was estimated at
3,000 (see Table I:74).

English cloth sold for less because of Britain's cheaper native wool and
low wages; and the English managed to keep their cloth prices stable
while their competitors suffered from steadily rising prices.[34] English
exports also included key strategic goods such as powder, arms, tin and
steel,[35] which were badly needed by the Ottomans. Next to woolen
imports, English tin was a strategic metal for making bronze guns and
for tinning the copper utensils commonly used in Turkey. As a Protestant
country, England did not obey the Pope's ban on the export of tin and
lead to the Ottoman Empire.

Imports from the Levant included chiefly goods which can be classified
in four categories according to their origins: (1) Anatolian goods, namely
cotton, cotton yarn, carpets, gallnuts; (2) Iranian goods, mainly raw silk;
(3) products of the Greek islands mostly under Venetian control, namely

Table I:75. English imports from the Levant, 1588 (in lb)

Raisins (of Damascus)	10,850	
Oil	6 (barrels)	
Nutmeg	49,705	
Indigo	54,120	
Galls	104,500	
Pepper	8,380	
Aniseed	10,000	
Cinnamon	2,196	
Bark of cinnamon	10,100	
Cloves	580	
Ginger	550	
Salamoniac	856	
Mastic	600	
Various spices	c.7,500	
Pistachio	200	
Raw silk	9,133	
Cotton	66,500	For weaving fustians, making quilts and candle-wicks
Cotton yarn	15,840	
Flax	700	
Cotton cloth	11,590	(pieces)
Turkish carpets	13	
Sponges	1 bag	
China	1 box	
Mirrors	1 box	

Source: Willan (1955).

currants, wine, and olive oil; (4) Indian or Indonesian products, mainly spices, drugs and dyes. It is interesting to note that already in the 1570s English imports to the Ottoman Empire included items of American origin, such as dye wood.[36]

As typical examples, Table I:75 gives a list of imports in five ships returning home from the Levant in 1588.[37] The total value of the goods was officially estimated at c. 16,600 gold ducats.

The first Ottoman merchants arrived in London in 1580 to make purchases for the sultan: they were an Armenian by the name of Garabet, Nikole, apparently a Greek, and Ahmed.[38]

Between the first English capitulations of 1580 and the founding of the East India Company in 1600, the Levant Company became the most important and only successful English overseas venture. A Venetian report tells us that the annual turnover of the London merchants in the Levant by 1604 was at least 250,000 crowns a year.[39] The company claimed to have extended its sphere of activity to India through the Levant in order to fulfill the ultimate English goal of reaching India, after

Table I:76. English silk imports from the
Levant (in lb)

1560	1621	1669
11,904	117,740	357,434

Francis Drake's arrival in the Mollucas in 1580 and John Newberry's voyage through Ottoman lands to the Persian Gulf in 1581 and India in 1583.

On the other hand, in 1589, a group of London merchants were attempting to reach India directly by sea through the Cape of Good Hope and the expedition reached the East Indies in 1592. This proved to be another turning point for the Levant trade.

In conclusion, in the period of 1580–1600, thanks to the Ottoman capitulations, the Levant was the principal trade region for the English.[40] It can safely be said that English mercantilism–capitalism owed much of its initial development to the Levant market. High-quality and cheap raw silk of Iran was now abundantly available in Aleppo and İzmir, thus giving an impetus to English silk manufacturing which became one of the thriving industries in the late seventeenth century. This was a replication of what had happened to Italy and France previously in the fifteenth and sixteenth centuries. In this period, the English competed with Venice in the transit trade, supplying Italian silk industries through Leghorn. Silk thereafter became the basis of Ottoman–English trade despite periodic crises when the silk caravans from Iran did not arrive. The English interest in imported Persian silk grew considerably later on (Table I:76). In order to buy it cheaper, they tried to establish direct traffic through Trabzon with Iran. The news alarmed Venice, the principal purchaser of Iranian silk in Syria, a fear that Armenian and Georgian silk merchants shared.[41] Aware of the intrigues of the Sherley brothers with the shah, the Ottoman government forbade the English project.[42]

THE DUTCH

As earlier explained, the Ottomans were in trade relations through Genoese Chios and Polish Lwow with the Low Countries already by the fifteenth century.

In the beginnings of Ottoman–Dutch relations Joseph Nasi, also known as Don Juan Miquez, played a decisive role. He was active in the

Antwerp banking house of Mendès before he came to settle in İstanbul, where he was employed by Süleyman I and Selim II. In 1569 the prince of Orange, William I, sent a secret envoy to Nasi seeking Ottoman support in the Dutch revolt against Philip II.⁴³ Nasi had become the chief advisor on Western affairs to the Ottoman government, hence his great influence with the sultan. French resident ambassadors in İstanbul also informed the Porte about the Dutch revolt and their need for support. There was even talk of a Dutch alliance with the Ottomans.⁴⁴ In a letter to the "Lutherans" in Flanders and other Spanish provinces, the sultan promised to send troops to their aid at a time to be determined by them.⁴⁵ Although there apparently could be no real desire for actual cooperation with the "infidel" Turks, the Dutch, like the Italians and French before them, came to employ, under desperate conditions, the threat of the sultan's power against Spain. But it is certain that, hoping to find natural allies to fight the Habsburgs in the newly rising nations in the West, the Ottomans had a definite policy to encourage them, and the granting of capitulations was part of this policy.

The presence of the Dutch in the Levant trade existed as early as the 1570s. Taking advantage of the individual grant of "amnesty" provision in Islamic Law, Antwerp merchants joined the Galata foreign merchant community in that period. The first voyage of a Dutch merchant ship from Holland to the Levant occurred in 1589. The Dutch first participated in the Levant trade under the protection of the French, who had the right to take non-capitulatory nations under their protection to trade in Ottoman territories. Also, the English, who had their capitulations in 1580, and apparently also the Marranos, who had a strong base in the Ottoman capital, helped the Dutch in entering the Levant trade. The Dutch, following the French and English, appear to have concentrated their efforts initially on the Aleppo market, which was an emporium for Indian spices and Iranian silk. Dutch merchants even then had a local representative of their own known as a "consul." Later, they chose to trade in the Ottoman dominions under the English flag. Because of the problems created by Anglo-French competition, and with the rapid growth of Dutch trade in the Levant, the Dutch government decided to take steps which led to the establishment of their own capitulations. Somewhat unenthusiastic at first and concerned not to appear as if they were betraying the common cause of the crusade still lingering in Western Christendom,⁴⁶ the Dutch authorities later followed a more realistic course in establishing friendly relations with the Porte as hostility against the common enemy Spain rose in the period 1604–9. From the beginning, the Ottoman grand admiral, Halil Pasha, who was responsible for the naval interests of the empire in the Mediterranean, played a decisive role in establishing friendly relations between the Dutch Republic and the Ottoman Empire. Indeed, against the Catholic frontier in the Mediterranean, the Ottomans took the initiative in establishing an agreement with this Protestant country, which had a powerful navy.[47] On the other hand, Dutch merchants in the Levant wanted a resident ambassador of their own in İstanbul and a chief consul in Syria. Finally, the Dutch government sent an extraordinary ambassador, Cornelius Haga, to İstanbul in 1612. Since a truce was signed with Spain in 1609, Holland's main interest was now commercial.[48] In İstanbul, Haga met with the opposition of the French, Venetian and English resident ambassadors. But, in the end, the Ottoman state, impressed by Dutch naval power, favored the grant of capitulations. In his audience with the sultan, Haga stressed the forty years of Dutch struggle against Spain and the resolution not to submit to the Pope's authority and "idolatry."[49] Ottoman–Dutch negotiations spread the rumor that the Dutch alliance would provide the Ottomans with a modern fleet or war materials from the West. Ottomans already were getting iron guns and superior quality powder from England.[50]

It is also interesting to note that in a secret report that the rival nations submitted to the sultan[51] against the Dutch, the Dutch as a political and military power were minimized and the claim was made that Dutch exports of spices, cloth and olive oil could damage the Ottoman economy. Their woolen cloth, they said, was inferior in quality and "would result in a loss to the Salonica and Edirne cloth industries." Also, it was claimed that the Dutch were taking gold and silver out of the empire and that Dutch pirates created insecurity for Ottoman traffic in the Mediterranean.

By such claims one may see to what particular economic matters the Ottomans were then sensitive. In his efforts to speak for the Dutch, Halil Pasha found in the Jews from Antwerp and in the Morisco Arab colony of Galata, both enemies of Catholic Spain, active supporters. The Dutch Republic was finally granted capitulations on July 6, 1612, modelled on those given to the French and English.

This was not a "treaty" but, as with other capitulations, it was an "amnesty" (*aman*) granted for the Dutch to trade in Ottoman territories. Reciprocity and political advantages for the Ottomans are implied in the introductory section by the explicit expression declaring that the Dutch would abide by a relationship of "sincere friendship and loyalty" toward the sultan.[52] On the other hand, the sultan solemnly promised (articles 6 and 55) that capitulatory guarantees were above the law. Those Ottoman subjects who resisted their application or violated them were declared rebels against the sultan and punishable as such.

The instrument granted the Dutch all capitulatory privileges and guarantees; all rights included in the French and English capitulations applied to the Dutch. Although Western historians in general are not comfortable about the Western political–military cooperation with the Muslim empire, such points are quite explicit in the Dutch–Ottoman relations. In a special provision (article 51), Dutch ships fighting against the ships of the non-capitulatory nations were allowed to use Ottoman ports and to replenish their supplies. Article 21 made it clear that corsair ships from Algiers remained entitled, as formerly, to provide themselves with munitions and materials in Dutch ports.[53]

On the other hand, guarantees against corsair acts show how concerned Western nations had become about increased privateering in this period. The sultan vowed that any Dutch, enslaved by the corsairs of Algiers, would be freed and their property returned in its entirety. If hostility arose between them because of the non-compliance of the corsairs, this situation would not invalidate the present capitulatory guarantees (article 17). The Dutch capitulations provided the most extensive privileges and guarantees and enabled Dutch merchants to develop their trade in the Levant. The Dutch were granted a 3 percent rate of customs duty instead of the 5 percent paid by the Venetians and French. Dutch merchants, like the French, were permitted the favor to export from Ottoman lands non-strategic goods such as cotton, cotton yarn, leather and beeswax (article 3). As for the most important trade items, reference is made to silk from Aleppo and other places, and to Dutch imports of lead, tin, iron and steel (articles 43 and 46).

The Porte's regulations on precious metals, as formulated in the capitulations granted to the English (1583) and the Dutch (1612), stipulated that no duty was to be levied on coined gold and silver. These coins were not to be converted to Ottoman coins in the local mints (article 1) and orders were sent to the provincial authorities to this effect. Such measures served Ottoman finances and economy in general, since exactly at this time the empire was suffering from a dearth of precious metals.[54] But, on the other hand, it will be seen that this policy would finally result in a financial and economic upheaval in the empire with the invasion of the Ottoman market by counterfeit coins imported chiefly by the Dutch. The Dutch were permitted to bring in and take out goods by sea to the Black Sea ports, including Trabzon and Caffa, and by land to Azov and

Muscovy, and Dutch ships coming from Damietta and Alexandria could carry goods to İstanbul or other places belonging to the Muslims. These clauses were evidently favored by the Ottomans in order to profit from Dutch shipping and contribute to the feeding of İstanbul from the two most important areas, Egypt and the northern Black Sea.

CORSAIRS

In the years 1580–90, Tenenti points out,[55] the struggle in the Mediterranean for hegemony degenerated into sheer sea robbery with its profound social and economic consequences. Whether it was fought for religious ideology, national economic interests, or simple theft, the end result was the ruin of the old Mediterranean naval powers of Venice, Spain and the Ottoman Empire. It had been demonstrated that piracy was not a monopoly of the Muslim sea *gazi*s, but rather a universal Mediterranean phenomenon. Spanish, French, Dutch, Italian and English seamen and even merchants were all involved in corsair activities in the Mediterranean during the sixteenth and early seventeenth centuries. Having lost their naval power, the Ottomans proved to be ineffective in the struggle against this Western piracy. English pirates intensified their activities along all the main routes from the Levant to Venice. The route Alexandria/Beirut–Crete yielded particularly rich spoils (in 1605 the capture of the ship *Videla* with a cargo of spices yielded 150,000 crowns).[56] In the 1590s, the question of how to cope with this situation became a major concern for the Ottoman and Venetian governments.

The advent of the invincible English *bretoni* upset the whole naval balance of power in the Mediterranean. Now the rival Mediterranean states attempted to use the new master of the sea for their own advantage. English cooperation with the enemies of the empire created concern in İstanbul for the safety of their sea traffic, particularly between İstanbul and Egypt. In one instance, the grand duke of Tuscany, using ships made in England, had captured an Ottoman ship carrying the sultan's "Egyptian treasure." This situation resulted in the sultan's sending an envoy to England to voice complaints in 1607. Interestingly enough, the envoy Çavuş Mustafa also asked the king to permit the export of powder and arms to Turkey.[57] At this time, the Ottoman nightmare was the cooperation of Venetian and English naval forces in the Mediterranean. It was feared that there might be a crusade under the Pope and Spanish king, who had English ships under the command of Anthony Sherley, a friend and ally of Shah Abbas. The esteem of the English was growing in İstanbul and was no doubt responsible for the grant of further commercial privileges. Venice was alarmed over the news that England was going to reinforce the projected "Turkish armada" with a large fleet of galleons.

Generally speaking, the northerners' piracy in the Mediterranean ruined Venetian trade in the Levant: "They attacked every ship that they met on their voyages."[58] In 1603 there were twenty English pirate vessels at Tunis. The year 1604 was a turning point, when English piracy was actually organized in Ottoman North Africa. The pirate fleet of the famous Englishman, John Ward, included many Turks in its crew. The local authorities at the Ottoman bases of Avlona and Patras shared in the spoils. In fact, these ports owed their economic prosperity as much to the regular traffic as to the sale of spoils from piracy.

By 1620, Venetian shipping in the Levant was totally eclipsed by that of Western nations. By that time, in "the great traffic in corn from Ottoman Greece to Italy, English ships replaced the Venetians. Generally speaking, in the development of the English carrying trade the Levant appears to have given the first impetus."[59] Dutch and English ships being large and strong and capable of defending themselves with powerful gunnery were preferred and employed in Ottoman navigation between Egypt and İstanbul.[60] The English had settled in Leghorn, a free port since 1593, which was to become the chief transit center for their Levant traffic in the seventeenth century. While in shipping and the cloth trade the English predominated in the northern ports of the empire, namely in İstanbul, İzmir and Aleppo, the French retained their primacy in southern Syria and Egypt.

While the English and Dutch ruined Venetian shipping in the Levant, they, at the same time, obtained privileges from the sultan to settle their consuls and factors in the Levant in place of the Venetians. An interesting development was the export of currants from Greece. The Ottoman Patras and the Morea owed their prosperity to the English–Venetian rivalry. Because of restrictions on leaving the Venetian island of Zante, the great exporter of currants, the English went to settle in Ottoman Patras and increased their purchase of Morean currants. In 1602 Patras, with its consul, became an entrepôt for English trade in Greece. This development alarmed Venice, because the English currant trade with Zante supplied an annual sum of 30–40,000 ducats to Venice;[61] and now the English began to buy olive oil, which had previously come through Venice, directly from the Ottoman ports of Modon and Coron.

NOTES

1 Willan (1955); Braudel (1972), I, pp. 612–15.
2 Wood (1935).
3 Wood (1935), pp. 3–4; Skilliter (1977), pp. 5–6.
4 Hakluyt cited by Braudel (1972), I, p. 614; Skilliter (1977), p. 5.
5 Skilliter (1977), p. 28.
6 Dobb (1963), pp. 147–220.
7 Dobb (1963), pp. 123–76; Cipolla (1977), p. 276.
8 Willan (1955), p. 403.
9 *Ibid.*
10 *Ibid.*, pp. 400–5; Braudel (1972), I, pp. 621–24.
11 For the so-called first capitulations in 1536, see p. 194.
12 Lewis (1973), pp. 140–44.
13 Braudel (1972), I, p. 625.
14 Skilliter (1977), p. 27.
15 Zinkeisen (1840–63), III, pp. 569–78; Kurat (1953), pp. 306–15.
16 Kurat (1953), pp. 314–15.
17 Another reason was the difficulty in finding the necessary funds.
18 Skilliter (1977), p. 7.
19 *Ibid.*, pp. 9–22.
20 *Ibid.*, p. 37.
21 *Ibid.*, document no. 5.
22 The letter was published for the first time by Uzunçarşılı (1949), p. 615, then reproduced by Skilliter (1977), document no. vi.
23 Uzunçarşılı (1949), pp. 615–16, in Skilliter (1977), document no. vii.
24 Skilliter (1977), document no. 10.
25 For the full text, see Skilliter (1977), document no. xiv and its analysis, pp. 98–103.
26 Kütükoğlu (1974), p. 51.
27 Wood (1935), pp. 19–23; Willan (1955), pp. 406–8.
28 Skilliter (1977), p. 41.
29 *Ibid.*, p. 66.
30 Davis (1961), p. 119.
31 Hamilton and Beldiceanu (1968), pp. 330–46.
32 Davis (1961), p. 119.
33 Willan (1955).
34 Davis (1961), pp. 123–24.
35 *CSP*: Venice XII, document no. 860, dated 1610.
36 Skilliter (1977), p. 22.
37 Willan (1955), pp. 408–9.
38 Uzunçarşılı (1949), p. 575.
39 Tenenti (1967), p. 79.
40 Davis (1961), pp. 135–36.
41 *CSP*: Venice XII, document nos. 886 and 908.
42 *Ibid.*, document no. 140.
43 Groot (1978), p. 84 note 17, p. 289.
44 *Ibid.*, p. 8.

45 Feridun (1858), pp. 542–44; Groot (1978), p. 84.
46 *Ibid.*, pp. 91–92.
47 *Ibid.*, pp. 94–103.
48 *Ibid.*, p. 99.
49 *Ibid.*, p. 114.
50 İnalcık (1975a), pp. 215–16.
51 Groot (1978), p. 109.
52 *Ibid.*, p. 40; cf. İnalcık (1971), pp. 1179–80.
53 *Ibid.*, p. 304 note 46.
54 İnalcık (1951), pp. 651–61.
55 Tenenti (1967), pp. 82, 150–51.
56 *Ibid.*, p. 76.
57 *CSP*: Venice XII, document nos. 2, 45, 53, 65, 71, 73, 82, 93, 122, 129.
58 Tenenti (1967).
59 Davis (1961), p. 132.
60 *Ibid.*, p. 130.
61 *CSP*: Venice XII, document no. 464.

BIBLIOGRAPHY

Abel, W. (1973). *Crises agraires en Europe (XIIIe–XXe siècle)*, Paris.

Abou El-Haj, Rifa'at Ali (1991). *Formation of the modern state. The Ottoman Empire, sixteenth to eighteenth centuries*, Albany.

Abū Yūsuf, Y. (1302 H/1884–85). *Kitāb al-Kharadj*, Bulak. Turkish trans. by Ali Özek, *Kitabü'l-Haraç*, İstanbul.

Adanır, F. (1988). "Mezra'a: Zu einem Problem der Siedlungs- und Agrargeschichte Südosteuropas im ausgehenden Mittelalter und in der frühen Neuzeit", in R. Melork *et al.*, eds., *Festschrift für Karl Otmar Freiherr von Aretin zum 65. Geburtstag*, Stuttgart.

Afetinan, A. (1975). *Life and works of Piri Reis*, Ankara.

(1976). *Aperçu général sur l'histoire économique de l'empire Turco-Ottoman*, Ankara.

Ahmad, K. (1980), ed. *Studies in Islamic economics, a selection of papers presented to the First International Conference on Islamic Economics, Makka*, Jeddah.

Ahmad al-'Alī, S. (1986). *Hitat al-Basra wa Mintakatihā*, Baghdad.

Aşıkî, Ahmed (1947). *Tevarîh-i Âli Osman*, ed. by N.C. Adsız, İstanbul.

Akdağ, M. (1949). "Osmanlı İmparatorluğunun Kuruluş ve İnkişafı Devrinde Türkiye'nin İktisadî Vaziyeti," *B*, XV, 497–571; XVI, 319–418.

(1963). *Celâlî İsyanları (1550–1603)*, Ankara.

(1971). *Türkiye'nin İktisadi ve İçtimaî Tarihi*, I–II, Ankara.

Akgündüz, A. (1988). *İslâm Hukukunda ve Osmanlı Tatbikatında Vakıf Müessesesi*, Ankara.

Alberi, E. (1839–63). *Le relazioni degli ambasciatori Veneti al senato, durante il secolo decimosesto*, Florence.

Alessandri, V. d' (1873). "Narrative of the most noble Vincentio d'Alessandri," trans. by C. Grey, *A narrative of Italian travels in Persia*, London.

Alexander, J. C. (1985). *Toward a history of post-Byzantine Greece: the Ottoman Kanunnames for the Greek lands circa 1500–circa 1600*, Athens.

Alexandrescu-Dersca, M.-M. (1957). "Contribution à l'étude de l'approvisionnement en blé de Constantinople au XVIIIe siècle," *Studia et Acta Orientalia*, I, 13–37.

'Alī, 'Ayni. (1862). *Kawānin-i Āl-i 'Osmān der Khulāsa-i Madāmın-ı Defter-i Diwān*, İstanbul.

Allen, C.H. (1981). "The Indian merchant community of Masqat," *BSOAS*, 44, 39–53.

Allen, W.E.D. (1963). *Problems of Turkish power in the sixteenth century*, London.

Angelov, D. (1956). "Certains aspects de la conquête des peuples balkaniques par les turcs," *BS*, XVII, 220–75.

Angiolello, J.-M. (1909). *Historia Turchesca (1300–1514)*, rev. by Donado da Lezze and ed. by I. Ursu, Bucharest.

Anhegger, R. (1943–45). *Beiträge zur Geschichte des Bergbaus im Osmanischen Reich*, I–III, İstanbul.

Anhegger, R. and İnalcık, H. (1956). *Ḳānūnnāme-i Sulṭān-ı ber Mūceb-i ʿÖrf-Sulṭānī*, Ankara.

Antoniadis-Bibicou, H. (1963). *Recherches sur les douanes à Byzance*, Paris.

The Anonymous (1922). *Die Altosmanischen anonymen Chroniken*, ed. by F. Giese, Breslau.

The Anonymous Chronicle BN: *Tevarikh-i Al-i Osman*, Bibliothèque Nationale, No. 1047.

Arbel, B. (1988). "Venetian trade in fifteenth-century Acre: the letters of Francesco Bevilaqua (1471–1472)," in B.Z. Kedar and A.L. Udovitch, eds., *The medieval Levant: studies in memory of Eliyahu Ashtor (1914–1984)*, pp. 227–88.

Argenti, P.P. (1941). *Cius Vincta or the occupation of Chios by the Turks (1566) and their administration of the island (1566–1912)*, Cambridge.

(1958). *The occupation of Chios by the Genoese and their administration of the island, 1346–1566*, III: *Notarial deeds*, Cambridge.

Arıkan, Z. (1991). "Osmanlı İmparatorluğunda İhracı Yasak Mallar (Memnu Meta)," *Prof. Dr. Bekir Kütükoğlu'na Armağan*, İstanbul.

Asdrachas, C. (1970). "Producteurs directs et marché," *BS*, VI, 36–69.

Ashtor, E. (1973). "La découverte de la voie maritime aux Indes et le prix des épices," *HEMM*, 31–48.

(1974). "The Venetian supremacy in Levantine trade: monopoly or precolonialism?" *JEEH*, XVII (2), 227–57.

(1975a). "Profits from trade with the Levant in the fifteenth century," *BSOAS*, XXXVII (2), 250–75.

(1975b). "The volume of Levantine trade in the later Middle Ages (1370–1498)," *JEEH*, XVII(3), 573–612.

(1976a). "Les lainages dans l'Orient médieval, emploi, production, commerce," in M. Spallanzani, ed., *Produzione, commercio e consumo dei panni di lana (nei secoli XII–XVIII)*, Florence.

(1976b). *A social and economic history of the Near East in the Middle Ages*, London.

(1976c). "Il commercio levantino di Ancona nel basso medioevo," *Rivista storica italiana*, 88, 213–53.

(1981). "The economic decline of the Middle East during the late Middle Ages: an outline," *AAS*, XV, 253–86.

(1983). *Levant trade in the Late Middle Ages*, Princeton.

(1988). "Catalan cloth on the late Medieval Mediterranean markets," *JEEH*, XXXII(2), 227–57.

Ashtor, E. and Cevidalli, G. (1983). "Levantine alkali ashes and European industries," *JEEH*, XII, 475–522.

Aşık Paşazade (1947–49). *Tevarih-i Al-i Osman*, ed. by Ali, İstanbul; ed. by F. Giese, Leipzig, 1929; ed. by Ç.N. Atsız, İstanbul, 1947–49.

Aslanapa, O. and Y. Durul (1972). *Türk Halı Sanatı*, İstanbul.

Aspetti (1984). "Aspetti della vita economica medievale," papers presented to the Convegno di Studi, Florence.

Aubin J. (1975). "Hormuz," *Mare Luso-Indicum*, II.

Aymard, M. (1966). *Venise, Raguse et le commerce du blé pendant la seconde moitié du XVIe siècle*, Paris.

Ayni, A. (1280 H/1863–64). *Kavanin-i Al-i Osman*, İstanbul.

Aziz Efendi (1985). *Kanunname-i Sultani*, ed. and trans. by R. Murphey, Cambridge, Mass.

Babinger, F. (1951). "Maometto II il conquistatore e l'Italia," *Rivista Storica Italiana*, 63, 4.

(1952). "Eine Verfügung des palaeölogen Châss Murad-Pasha von mitte Regeb 876 h. – Dez./Jan. 1471/2," *DII*, 197–210.

(1957). *Die Aufzeichnungen des Genuesen Iacopo de Promontorio-de Campis über den Osmanenstaat um 1475*, Munich.

(1958). "Vier Bauvorschläge Leonardo da Vincis an Sultan Bayezid II (1502–1503)," *Nachr. der Akademie der Wissens. in Göttingen, Phil-His. KL.*, no. 1.

(1962–76). *Aufsätze und Abhandlungen zur Geschichte südosteuropas und der Levante*, I–III, Munich.

(1963) "Lorenzo il Magnifico e las corte Ottomana," *Archivio Storico Italiano*, 121, 305–61.

(1978). *Mehmed the Conqueror and his time*, Princeton.

Bacqué-Grammont, J.-L. (1975). "Études turco-safavides, I: Selim Ier," *Turcica*, VI.

(1976). "Notes sur une saisie de soies d'Iran en 1518," *Turcica* VIII (2), 237–53.

(1985). "Soutien logistique et présence ottomane en mediterranée en 1517," *ROMM*, XXXIX, 7–34.

Bacqué-Grammont, J.-L. and E. van Donzel (1987). *Comité International d'Études pre-Ottomanes et Ottomanes, VIth Symposium, Cambridge, 1984*, İstanbul, Paris and London.

Bacqué-Grammont, J.-L. and P. Dumont (1983), eds. *Économie et sociétés dans l'Empire Ottoman*, Paris.

Bacqué-Grammont, J.-L. and A. Kroell (1988). *Mamlouks, Ottomans et Portugais en Mer Rouge*, Cairo.

Badoer, G. (1956). *Il libro dei conti di Giacomo Badoer*, ed. by U. Dorini and T. Bertele, Rome.

Baeck, L. (1989). "The economic thought of classical Islam," in *Perspectives on the History of Economic Thought*, V: ed. by W. J. Barber, Louvain.

Bakhit, M.A. (1982). *The Ottoman province of Damascus in the sixteenth century*, Beirut.

Balard, M. (1978). *La Romanie génoise*, I–II, Paris.

Balta, E. (1989). *L'Eubée à la fin du XVe siècle; économie et population, les registres de l'année 1474*, Athens.

Barbaro, G. (1873). *Travels*, trans. by W. Thomas, London.

Barbosa, D. (1921). *The book of Duarte Barbosa, an account of the countries bordering on the Indian Ocean and their inhabitants*, ed. by M.L. Dames, II, in Hakluyt, vol. 49, ser. 2.

Barkan, Ö.L. (1937) "Osmanlı İmparatorluğunda Çiftçi Sınıflarının Hukuki Statüsü," *Ü*, nos. 49–59.

(1939). "Malikâne-Dîvâni Sistemi," *THIM*, II, 119–84.

(1939–40). "Les formes de l'organisation du travail agricole dans l'empire Ottoman au XVe siècle," *IFM*, I, 14–44; II, 165–80.

(1939–41). "XV. ve XVI. Asırlarda Osmanlı İmparatorluğu'nda Toprak İşçiliğinin Organizasyon Şekilleri, I: Kulluklar ve Ortakçı kullar," *IFM*, I (1) and (II), 29–74; 448–56.

(1942a) "Vakıflar ve Temlikler," *VD*, II, 278–386.

(1942b) "Kanunname-i İhtisab-ı İstanbul," *TV*, I(5), 326–40; "Kanunname-i İhtisab-ı Bursa," II(7), 15–40.

(1943). *XV. ve XVI. Asırlarda Osmanlı İmparatorluğu'nda Zirai Ekonominin Hukuki ve Mali Esasları*, İstanbul.

(1944). "Avarız," *IA*, II, 13–19.

(1946–50). "Deportations comme méthode de peuplement et de colonisation dans l'empire Ottoman," *IFM*, XI, 524–69; XIII, 56–79; XV, 209–329.

(1953–54). "Osmanlı İmparatorluğu Bütçelerine dair Notlar," *IFM*, XV, 239–329.

(1955). "Quelques observations sur l'organisation économique et sociale des villes Ottomanes," *Recueil Société Jean Bodin*, VII, 289–311.

(1955–56). "Osmanlı Bütçeleri," *IFM*, XVII, 193–347.

(1957). "Essai sur les données statistiques des registres de recensement dans l'empire Ottoman au XVe et XVIe siècles," *JESHO*, I.

(1961). "Le declin de Venise dans ses rapports avec la décadence économique de l'empire Ottoman," in *Aspetti di cause della decadenza economica veneziana nel secolo XVI*, Venice, pp. 275–79.

(1964). "894 (1488/1489) Yılı Cizye Tahsilâtına Ait Muhasebe Bilançoları," *BL*, I, 1–117.

(1968). "Edirne Askeri Kassamına Ait Tereke Defterleri (1545–1659)," *Bl*, III, 1–479.

(1970). "Research on the Ottoman fiscal surveys," in Cook, ed., 1970, 163–71.

(1972). *Süleymaniye Camii ve Imareti İnşaatı*, Ankara.

(1973). "Les mouvements des prix en Turquie entre 1490 et 1655," *HEMM*, I, 65–79.

(1975). "The price revolution of the sixteenth century. A turning point in the history of the Near East," *IJMES*, VI (1), 3–28.

(1979). "İstanbul Saraylarına ait Muhasebe Defterleri," *Bl*, IX, 1.

(1988). *Hüdavendigâr Livâsı Tahrir Defteri*, I, Ö.L. Barkan and E. Meriçli, eds., Ankara.

Barkan, Ö.L. and E.H. Ayverdi (1970). *Istanbul Vakıfları Tahrir Defteri, 943 (1546) Tarihli*, İstanbul.

Barnes, J.R. (1986). *An introduction to religious foundations in the Ottoman Empire*, Leiden.

Baron, S.W. (1983). *A social and religious history of the Jews*, XVIII: *The Ottoman Empire, Persia, Ethiopia, India, and China*, New York.

Barozzi, M. and G. Berchet. (1871–72). *Le relazioni degli stati europei lette al*

Senato dagli ambasciatori veneziani nel secolo decimosettimo, ser. Va, Tur-chia, I–II, Venice.

Bautier, R.-H. (1970). "Les relations économiques des occidentaux avec les pays d'Orient au Moyen Âge, points de vue et documents," in M. Mollat, ed., *Sociétés et compagnies de commerce en Orient et dans l'Ocean Indien*, Paris.

Bayerle, G. (1973). *Ottoman tributes in Hungary*, The Hague and Paris.

Beldiceanu, N. (1964a). *Réglements miniers, 1390–1512*, Paris and The Hague.

(1964b). "La conquête des cités marchandes de Kilia et de Cetatea Alba par Bayezid II," *SF*, XXIII, 36–115.

(1967), ed. *Code de lois contumières de Mehmed II*, Wiesbaden.

(1973). *Recherche sur la ville ottomane au XVe siècle, étude et actes*, Paris.

Beldiceanu, N., J.-L. Bacqué-Grammont and M. Cazacu (1982). "Recherches sur les Ottomans et la Modavie ponto-danubienne entre 1484 et 1520," *BSOAS*, XLV(1) 48–66.

Beldiceanu-Steinherr, I. (1976). "Fiscalité et formes de possession de la terre arable dans l'Anatolie pré-ottomane," *JESHO*, XIX, 233–322.

(1987). "A propos des tribus Atçeken (XVe-XVIe siècles)," *JESHO*, XXX (2), 121–95.

Beldiceanu-Steinherr, I. and N. Beldiceanu (1964). "Acte du règne de Selim I concernant quelques échelles danubiennes de Valachie, de Bulgarie et de Dobrudja," *SF*, XXIII.

Belin, A. (1864). *Essai sur l'histoire économique de la Turquie*, Paris.

Belon, P. (1553). *Les observations de plusieurs singularités et choses mémorables trouveés en Grece, Asie, Judeé, Egypte, Arabie et autres pays estranges*, Paris.

Benedict, P. E. Tümertekin and F. Mansur (1974). *Turkey, geographic and social perspectives*, Leiden.

Bennigsen, A. and C. Lemercier-Quelquejay (1970). "Les marchands de la cour ottomane et le commerce des fourrures moscovitées dans la seconde moitié du XVIe siècle," *CMRS*, XI (3), 363–90.

Berindei, M. (1986). "L'Empire Ottoman et la 'route Moldave' avant la conqûete de Chilia et de Cetatea Alba (1484)," *RRJTS*, X.

(1989). "Les Venitiens en Mer Noire, XVIe–XVIIe siècles," *CMRS*, XXX (3–4), 208–23.

Berindei, M. and G. Veinstein (1975). "Réglements de Süleyman Ier concernant le liva de Kefe," *CMRS*, XV, 57–104.

(1976). "La Tana-Azaq, de la présence italienne à l'emprise Ottoman (fin XIIIe – milieu XVIe siècle)," *Turcica*, VIII, 2.

(1981). "Réglements fiscaux et fiscalité de la province de Bender-Ackerman, 1570. Les possessions Ottomanes entre Bas-Danube et Bas-Dniepr," *CMRS*, XXII, 251–328.

Berov, L. (1974). "Changes in price conditions in trade between Turkey and Europe in the 16th–19th centuries," *EB*, X (2–3), 168–78.

Biegman, N.H. (1967). *The Turco-Ragusan relationship, 1575–1595*, The Hague and Paris.

Blackburn, J.R. (1979). "The collapse of Ottoman authority in Yemen 968/1560–976/1568," *WI*, XIX (1–4), 119–76.

(1980). "The Ottoman penetration of Yemen," *AO*, VI, 55–93.

Blaskovics, J. (1979). "Osmanlılar Hakimiyeti Devrinde Slovakya'daki Vergi Sistemi Hakkında," *TD*, XXXII, 187–210.

Blount, H. (1636). *A voyage into the Levant*, 2nd ed., London.

Bojanić-Lukač, D. (1976). "De la nature et l'origine de l'*ispendje*," *WZKM*, LXVIII, 9–30.

Bojić, I. (1952). *Dubrovnik i Turska u XIV i XV veku*, Belgrade.

Bolay, H. *et al.* (1987). *Türk Tarihinde ve Kültüründe Tokat*, Symposium July, 2–6, 1986, Ankara.

Bombaci, A. (1965). *Histoire de la litterature turque*, Paris.

Bono, S. (1964). *I cosari barbareschi*, Turin.

Bosworth, C.E. *et al.* (1988). *The Islamic world: essays in honor of Bernard Lewis*, Princeton.

Boulnois, L. (1963). *La route de la soie*, Paris.

Boxer, C.R. (1969a). *The Portuguese seaborne empire*, London.

(1969b). "A note on Portuguese reactions to the revival of the Red Sea spice trade and the rise of Atjeh, 1540–1600," *JSAH*, X, 415–28.

Braude, B. (1979). "International competition and domestic cloth in the Ottoman Empire, 1500–1650." *R*, II (3), 437–51.

Braudel, F. (1972 and 1973). *The Mediterranean and the Mediterranean World in the Age of Philip II*, trans. by S. Reynolds, I–II, New York.

Braudel, F. and R. Romano. (1951). *Navires et marchandises à l'entrée du port de Livourne, 1547–1611*, Paris.

Brocquière, B. de la (1892). *Le voyage d'Outremer*, ed. by Ch. Schefer, Paris.

Brummet, P. (1987). "Venice and the Ottoman expansion 1503–1517," Ph.D. dissertation, University of Chicago.

(1989). "Foreign policy, naval strategy, and the defence of the Ottoman Empire in the sixteenth century," *IHR*, XI (4), 613–27.

Bulgaru, A.-D. (1969). "Quelques données sur le ravitaillement de Constantinople au XVIe siècle," *Congrès International d'Etudes du Sud-Est Européen*, III, 661–72.

(1987). "Une relation vénitienne sur l'empire Ottoman à l'époque de Süleyman le Magnifique," *CIEPO*, VI. *Symposium*, 136–45.

Burr, M. "The code of Stephan Dušan," *SR*, XXVIII, 198–216; trans., XXIX, 517–39.

Busbecq, O.G. de. (1968). *The Turkish letters of Ogier Ghiselin de Busbecq, Imperial Ambassador at Constantinople, 1554–1562*, trans. by E.S. Foster, Oxford.

Çağatay, N. (1942). "Osmanlı Imparatorluğunda Maden Hukuku ve İktisadiyat Hakkında Vesikalar," *TV*, II, No. 10.

Cahen, C. (1951). "Le commerce anatolien au début du XIIIe siècle," *Mélanges du Moyen Âge*, Paris.

(1953). "L'évolution de l'iqtāʿ du IXe au XIIIe siècle," *Annales, ESC*, VIII.

(1988). *La Turquie pre-Ottomane*, İstanbul and Paris. Expanded French ed. of *Pre-Ottoman Turkey*, trans. by J. Jones-Williams, London (1968).

Capidan, Th. (1942). "Darstellung der ethnologische Lage am Balkan mit besonderer Berücksichtigung der makedorumänen," *SF*, VII, 497–545.

Carruthers, D. (1929). *The Desert Road to India*. London.

Carter, F.W. (1972). *Dubrovnik (Ragusa): a classic city-state*, London and New York.

Celālzāde, M. (1981). *Geschichte sultan Süleymān kanūnīs von 1520 bis 1551*, ed. by P. Kappert, Wiesbaden.

Cessi, R. (1968). *Storia della Republica di Venezia*, Milan.

Cezar, Mustafa. (1965). *Osmanlı Tarihinde Levendler*, İstanbul.

Charrière, E. (1848–60). *Négociations de la France dans le Levant ou correspondances, memoires et actes diplomatiques des ambassadeurs de France à Constantinople et des ambassadeurs, envoyés ou residents*, I–IV, Paris.

Chaudhuri, K.N. (1978). *The trading world of Asia and the English East India Company, 1600–1760*, Cambridge.

Chayanov, A.V. (1966). *The theory of peasant economy*, ed. by D. Thorner and R.E.F. Smith, Homewood; a new edition by T. Shanin, Madison, 1986.

Chesneau, J. (1887). *Le voyage de Monsieur d'Aramon*, ed. by M. Ch. Schefer, Paris.

Cin, H. (1969). *Miri Arazi ve Bu Arazinin Mülk Haline Dönüşü*, Ankara.

Cipolla, C.M. (1970), ed. *The economic decline of empires*, London.

(1977), ed. *The Fontana economic history of Europe*, II: *The sixteenth and seventeenth centuries*, Hassocks and New York.

Chirot, D. (1989). *The origins of backwardness in Eastern Europe, economies and politics from the Middle Ages until the early twentieth century*, Berkeley.

Čirković, S. and Kovačević-Kojić (1982–83). "L'économie naturelle et la production marchande aux XIIIe–XVe siècles dans les régions actuelles de la Yougoslavie," *Balcanica*, XIII–XIV, 45–56.

Clavijo, R.G. de (1943). *Embajada a Tamorlani*, ed. by F.L. Estrada, Madrid.

Cohen, A. (1976). *Ottoman documents on the Jewish community of Jerusalem in the sixteenth century*, Jerusalem.

(1989). *Economic life in Ottoman Jerusalem*, Cambridge.

Cohen, A. and B. Lewis (1978). *Population and revenue in the towns of Palestine in the sixteenth century*, Princeton.

Coleman, D.C. (1969a), ed. *Revisions in mercantilism*, London.

(1969b). "El. Heckscher and the idea of mercantilism," in Coleman (1969a), pp. 92–117.

Contarini, A. (1873). *Travels in Tana and Persia*, ed. by Lord Stanley of Alderley, London.

Cook, M.A. (1970), ed. *Studies in the economic history of the Middle East*, London.

(1972). *Population pressure in rural Anatolia, 1450–1600*, London.

Cozzi, G. and M. Knapton (1986). *La Repubblica di Venezia nell'età moderna, dalla guerra di Chioggia al 1517*, Turin.

Cvetkova, B. (1964). "Recherches sur le système d'affermage (*iltizam*) dans l'Empire Ottoman au cours du XVIe–XVIIIe siècles par rapport aux contrées bulgares," *RO*, XXVII(2), 111–32.

(1971). *Vie économique de villes et ports balkaniques aux XVe et XVIe siècles*, Paris.

Cvijić, J. (1918). *La peninsule balkanique. Géographie humaine*, Paris.

Çizakça, M. (1980). "Price history and the Bursa silk industry: a study in Ottoman industrial decline, 1550–1650," *JEH*, XL, 3.

(1983). "A short history of the Bursa silk industry (1500–1900)," *JESHO*, XXIII(1–2).

(1985). "Incorporation of the Middle East into the European world-economy," *R*, VIII, 3.

Dalsar, F. (1960). *Bursa'da İpekçilik*, İstanbul.

Dalton, G. (1968), ed. *Primitive, archaic and modern economics: essays of Karl Polanyi*, Boston.

Dames, L. (1921). "The Portuguese and Turks in the Indian Ocean in the sixteenth century," *JRAS*, I.

Dan, M. and S. Goldenberg, (1967). "Le commerce Balkan-Levantin de la Transylvanie au cours du XVIe siècle et au début du XVIIe siècle," *RESEE*, 87–117.

Danvers, F.C. (1894). *The Portuguese in India*, London.

David, G. (1974). "Some aspects of 16th century depopulation in the Sanjaq of Simontornya," *AAH*, XIII (1).

Davis, R. (1961). "England and the Mediterranean, 1570–1670," in F.J. Fisher, ed., *Essays in the economic and social history of Tudor and Stuart England*, Cambridge, pp. 119–24.

(1970). "English imports from the Middle East, 1580–1780," in Cook, ed. (1970).

Delaborde, H.F. (1888). *L'Expedition de Charles VIII en Italie*, Paris.

Déléage, A. (1945). *La capitation du Bas-Empire*, Mâcon.

Deményi, L.A. (1968) "Le commerce de la Transylvanie avec les régions du sud du Danube effectué par la douan de Turnu Roşu en 1685," *Revue Roumaine d'Histoire*, VII (5), 761–77.

Depping, G.B. (1830). *Histoire du commerce entre le Levant et l'Europe depuis les croisades*, I–II, Paris.

Dernschwam, H. (1923). *Hans Dernschwam's Tagebuch Einer Reise Konstantinopel und Kleinasien (1553–1555)*, ed. by F. Babinger, Leipzig. Turkish trans. by Y. Önen, *İstanbul ve Anadolu'ya Seyahat Günlüğü*, İstanbul, 1987.

Dilger, K. (1967). *Untersuchungen zur Geschichte des Osmanischen Hofzeremoniells*, Munich.

Divitçioğlu, S. (1969). "Modèle économique de la société Ottomane," *La Pensée*, 144, 41–60.

Djurdjev, B. *et al.* (1957). *Ḳānūni Ḳānūnnāme*, Sarajevo.

Dobb, M. (1963). *Studies in the development of capitalism*, London.

Duby, G. (1962). *L'économie rurale et la vie des campagnes dans l'Occident médieval*, I–II, Paris.

Du Fresne-Canaye, P. (1897). *Le voyage du Levant de Philippe Du Fresne-Canaye (1573)*, ed. by M.H. Hauser, Paris.

Dumont, P. and J.-L. Bacqué-Grammont, (1983), eds. *Contributions à l'histoire économique et sociale de l'empire Ottoman*, Louvain.

Duncan, T.B. (1975). "Niels Steensgaard and the Europe–Asia trade of the early seventeenth century," *JMH*, 47, 512–18.

Earle, P. (1969). "The commercial development of Ancona, 1479–1551," *EcHR*, XXII.

Eldred, J. (1904). *The voyage of M. John Eldred to Trypolis in Syria by sea, and from thence by land and river to Babylon and Balsara, 1563*, in Hakluyt, extra ser. VI, Glasgow.

Erder, L. (1975). "The measurement of preindustrial population changes: the Ottoman Empire from the 15th to the 17th century," *MES.*

Erder, L. and S. Faroqhi, (1979). "Population rise and fall in Anatolia, 1550–1620," *MES*, XV, 322–45.

Erdmann, K. (1961). *Das Anatolische Karavansaray*, I–II, Berlin.

Ergin, O.N. (1922). *Mecelle-i Umūr-i Belediyye*, I, İstanbul.

Evliya Çelebi (1896–1938). *Seyāhatnāme*, I–X, İstanbul.

Faroqhi, S. (1979a). "Sixteenth century periodic markets in various Anatolian sancaks," *JESHO*, XXII (1), 32–80.

(1979b). "Alum production and alum trade in the Ottoman Empire (about 1560–1830)," *WZKM*, LXXI.

(1980). "The development of the Anatolian urban network during the sixteenth century," *JESHO*, XXIII (3), 265–303.

(1984). *Towns and townsmen of Ottoman Anatolia, Trade, crafts and food production in an urban setting*, Cambridge.

(1986a). "Coffee and spices: official Ottoman reactions to Egyptian trade in the later sixteenth century," *WZKM*, LXXVI, 87–93.

(1986b). *Peasants, dervishes and traders in the Ottoman Empire*, London.

(1986c). "The Venetian presence in the Ottoman Empire," *JEEH*, 15(2), 345–84.

(1987). *Men of modest substance, house owners and house property in seventeenth-century Ankara and Kayseri*, Cambridge.

(1990) *Herrscher über Mecca. Die Geschichte der Pilgerfahrt*, Munich and Zurich.

(1991). "The Anatolian town and its place within the administrative structure of the Ottoman state," *BF*, XVI, 209–44.

Fekete, L. (1949). "Osmanen und Ungarn, 1366–1699," *B*, XIII, 663–743.

Fekete, L. and G. Káldy-Nagy, (1962). *Rechnungsbücher türkischer Finanzstellen in Buda (Offen), 1550–1580, Türkischer Text*, Budapest.

Feridun, A. (1858). *Munsha'āt-ı al-Salātin*, I–II, İstanbul.

Filipović, N. (1953–54). "Bosna-Hersek'te Timar Sistemi," *IFM*, XV.

Finkel, C. (1987). *The administration of warfare: the Ottoman military campaigns in Hungary, 1593–1606*, Vienna.

(1991). "The costs of Ottoman warfare and defence," *BF*, XVI, 91–104.

Fisher, S. (1935). *Foreign relations of Turkey*, Urbana.

Flachat, J.-C. (1766). *Observations sur le commerce et les arts d'une partie de l'Europe, de l'Asie, de l'Afrique et des Indes orientales*, I–II, Lyons.

Fleischer, C. (1986). *Bureaucrat and intellectual in the Ottoman Empire: the historian Muṣṭafā Ālī (1541–1600)*. Princeton.

Forand, P.G. (1971). "The status of the land and inhabitants of the Sawād during the first two centuries of Islam," *JESHO*, XIV (1).

Foss, Clive (1979). *Ephesus after antiquity: a late antique, Byzantine and Turkish city*, Cambridge.

Foster, W. (1933). *England's quest for eastern trade*, London.

Frances, E. (1933). "La féodalitée byzantine et la conquête turque," *Studia et Acta Orientalia*, IV, 69–90.

Futūhāt-ı Fīrūz Shāhī. (1954). *Futūhāt-ı Fīrūz Shāhi*, ed. by Shaykh Abdur Rashid, Āligharh.

Gabriel, A. (1958). *Une capitale turque: Brousse*, I–II, Paris.

Gerber, H. (1988). *Economy and society in an Ottoman city: Bursa 1600–700*, Jerusalem.

Giese, F. (1922), ed. *Die altosmanischen anonymen Chroniken*, I, Breslau.

Gioffré, D. (1960). *Gênes et les foires de change*. Paris.

Glaman, K. (1958). *Dutch-Asiatic trade 1620–1740*, Copenhagen.

Glykatzi-Ahrweiler, H. (1958). "La politique agraire des empereurs de Nicée," *Byzantion*, XXVIII, 51–66.

Godinho, V. Magalhães (1953). "Le répli venitien et égyptien et la route du cap,'" in *Evantail de l'histoire vivante, Hommage à Lucien Febvre*, Paris, 283–300.

(1969). *L'économie de l'empire portugais aux XVe et XVIe siècles*, Paris

Goffart, W. (1974). *Caput and Colonate*, Toronto.

Goffman, D. (1982). "The Jews of Safad and the maktu system in the sixteenth century: a study of two documents from the Ottoman archives," *JOS*, III, 81–90.

Goitein, S.D. (1966). *Studies in Islamic history and institutions*, Leiden.

Gökbilgin, T. (1952). *XV.–XVI. Asırlarda Edirne ve Paşa Livası: Vakıflar-Mülkler-Mukataalar*, İstanbul.

(1957). *Rumeli' de Yürükler, Tatarlar ve Evlâd-i Fâtihân*, İstanbul.

(1964, 1968–71) "Venedik Devlet Arşivindeki Vesikalar Külliyatında Kanunî Süleyman Devri Belgeleri," *Bl*, I(2), 119–220; V–VIII (9–12), 1–151.

Goldenberg, S. (1963). "Notizie del commercio italiano in Transylvania nel secolo XVI," *ASI*, 255–88.

Goodrich, T.D. (1990). *The Ottoman Turks and the New World: a study of Tarih-i Hind-i Garbi and sixteenth century Ottoman Americana*, Wiesbaden.

Gordlevski, V. (1941). *Gosudarstvo Selçukidov Malov Azii*, Moscow and Leningrad, Turkish trans. by A. Inan, *Anadolu Selçuklu Devleti*, İstanbul.

Görecki, D.M. (1981). "Land tenure in Byzantine property: *iara in re aliena*," *Greek, Roman and Byzantine Studies*, XXII (2), 191–210.

(1984). "The Slavic theory in Russian pre-revolutionary historiography of the Byzantine farmer community," *Byzantion*, LVI, 77–107.

Göyünç, N. (1979). " 'Hane' Deyimi Hakkında," *TD*, XXXII, 331–48.

Greenwood, A. (1988). "İstanbul's meat provisioning: a study of the *celepkeşan* system," Ph.D. dissertation, University of Chicago.

Gregorovius, F. (1891). *Geschichte der Stadt Rom in Mittelalter*. Berlin.

Griswold, W.J. (1981). "Djalālī," *EI²*, 238–39.

(1983). *The Great Anatolian Rebellion, 1591–611*, Berlin.

Groot, A.H. de (1978). *The Ottoman Empire and the Dutch Republic. A history of the earliest diplomatic relations, 1610–1630*, Leiden.

(1981). "The organization of Western European trade in the Levant, 1500–1800," in L. Blussé and F. Gaastra, eds., *Companies and trade*, Leiden.

Güçer, L. (1950). "Le commerce interieur des céréales dans l'empire ottoman pendant la seconde moitié du XVIe siècle," *IFM*, XI, 397–416.

(1951–52). "Osmanlı İmparatorluğu Dahilinde Hububat Ticaretinin Tâbi Olduğu Kayıtlar," *IFM*, XIII, 76–98.

(1962–63). "XV.–XVII. Asırlarda Osmanlı İmparatorluğunda Tuz İnhisarı ve Tuzlaların İşletme Nizamı," *İFM*, XXIII, 397–416.

(1964). *XVI.–XVII. Asırlarda Osmanlı İmparatorluğunda Hububat Meselesi,* İstanbul.

Güran, T. (1985). "The state role in the grain supply of İstanbul: the grain administration, 1793–1839," *IJTS*, III.

Gyóni, M. (1951). "La transhumance des Valaques balkaniques au moyen âge," *BS*, XII, 29–42.

Hakluyt, R. (1847–1940). Hakluyt Society, works issued by: 1st series, 100 vols., London 1847–1939. 2nd series, 85 vols., London 1899–1940. Extra series, 12 vols., Glasgow, 1903–5.

Halaçoğlu, Y. (1979). "Tapu-Tahrir Defterlerine Göre XVI. Yüzyılın ilk Yarısında Sis (Kozan) Sancağı," *TD*, XXXII, 819–92.

Halasi-Kun, T. (1980). "The Rumanians of *Districtus Valahalis Tverd,*" *AO*, VI.

Hammer, J. von, (1815). *Das Osmanischen Reichs. Staatsverfassung und Staatsverwaltung,* I–II, Vienna.

(1827–35). *Geschichte des Osmanischen reiches,* Pest; repr., Graz, 1963.

Hamilton J. and N. Beldiceanu. (1968). "Recherches autour de 'qars', nom d'une étoffe de poil," *BSOAS*, XXXI (2), 330–46.

Handžić, A. (1976). "Rudnici u Bosni u Drugov Polivini XV Stoljeca," *Prilozi za Orientalni Filologiju,* XXVI, 7–42.

Haque, Z. (1977). *Landlord and peasant in early Islam,* Islamabad.

Hartmann, M. (1918). "Das Privileg Selims I für die Venezianer von 1517." *Orientalist. Studien F. Hommel,* II, 201–22.

Hasluck, F.W. (1929). *Christianity and Islam under the Sultans,* I–II, Oxford.

Hattox, R. (1985). *Coffee and coffeehouses, the origins of a social beverage in the medieval Near East,* Seattle and London.

Heckenast, G. (1977). *Aus der Geschichte der Ostmitteleuropäische Bauernbewegungen im 16–17. Jahrhundert,* Budapest.

Heckscher, E.F. (1935). *Mercantilism,* trans. by M. Shapiro, I–II, London.

Heers, J. (1954). "Les Génois et le commerce de l'alun à la fin du Moyen Age," *RHES*, XXXII, 31–53.

(1955). "Il commercio nel Mediterraneo al fine del sec. XIV e nei primi anni del XV," *ASI*, CXIII (2), 157–209.

(1959). *Le livre de comptes de Giovanni Piccamiglio, homme d'affaires génois, 1456–1459,* Paris.

(1961). *Gênes au XVe siècle, activité économique et problèmes sociaux,* Paris.

(1971). "La mode et les marchés des draps de laine," *Annales, ESC,* XXVI, 1093–117.

Heimpel, H. (1930). "Zur Handelspolitik Sigismunds," *VSWG*, XXIII, 145–56.

Hess, A.C. (1968). "The Moriscos: an Ottoman fifth column in sixteenth-century Spain." *AHR*, LXXIV (1), 1–25.

(1970). "The evolution of the Ottoman seaborne empire in the age of the Oceanic discoveries, 1453–1525," *AHR*, LXXV (7), 1892–919.

(1978). *The forgotten frontier: a history of the sixteenth century Ibero-African frontier,* Chicago.

Heyd, W. (1866–68). *Le colonie commerciali degli Italiani in Oriente*, I–II, Venice.

(1936). *Histoire du commerce du Levant*, I–II, trans. by F. Raynaud, Leipzig.

Heyd, U. (1960). *Ottoman documents on Palestine, 1552–1615*, Oxford.

(1973). *Studies in old Ottoman criminal law*, Oxford.

Hill, G.A. (1948). *A history of Cyprus*, 3 vols., Cambridge.

Hinz, W. (1950). "Das Steuerwesen Ostanatoliens im 15. und 16. Jhd.," *ZDMG*, XXV, 177–201.

(1955). *Islamische Masse und Gewichte*, Leiden.

Hopwood, K. (1991). "Nomads or bandits? The pastoralist/sedentary interface in Anatolia," *BF*, XVI, 179–94.

Hoshino, H. (1984). "Il commercio fiorentino nell'impero ottomano: cesti e profitti negli anni 1484–1488," *Aspetti*, Pisa.

Hoszowski, St. (1954). *Les prix à Lwow (XVIe–XVIIe siècles)*, trans. from Polish, Paris.

Hovári, J. (1984). "Customs register of Tulča (Tulcea), 1515–17," *AAH*, XXXVIII, 115–41.

(1989). "The Transylvanian salt in the Ottoman Semendire (Smederevo) 1514–16," *Economy, Society, Historiography*, dedicated to Zsigmond Pal Pach, Budapest, 41–61.

Howard, D.A. (1987). "The Ottoman timar system, 1563–1656," Ph.D. thesis, Indiana University.

Howe, S.E. (1949). *In quest of spices*, London.

Hurmuzaki, E. de (1887–1922). *Documente privitore la istoria Romậnilor*, I–XIX, Bucharest.

Hütteroth, W.-D. (1968). *Landliche Siedlungen im südlichen Inneranatolien in den letzten vierhundert Jahren*, Göttingen.

(1974). "The influence on social structure of land division and settlement in Inner Anatolia," in Benedict, Tümertekin and Mansur, eds., 19–47.

(1982). *Türkei*, Darmstadt.

Hütteroth, W.-D. and K. Abdulfattah. (1977). *Historical geography of Palestine, Transjordan and southern Syria in the late 16th century*, Erlangen.

Ibn Battuta (1962). *The travels of Ibn Battuta, A.D. 1325–54*, ed. by H.A.R. Gibb, Cambridge.

Ilescu, O. (1971). "Le montant du tribut payé par Byzance à l'empire ottoman en 1379 et 1424," *RESEE*, IX.

Imber, C.H. (1972). "The costs of naval warfare. The account of Hayreddin Barbarossa's Herceg Novi campaign in 1539," *AO*, IV, 203–16.

(1980). "The navy of Süleyman the Magnificent," *AO*, VI, 211–82.

İnalcık, H. (1944). "Kırım Hanlığının Osmanlı Tâbiliğine Girmesi ve Ahidname Meselesi," *B*, VIII, 185–229.

(1947). "The origins of the Ottoman-Russian rivalry and the Don–Volga canal, 1569," *Les Annales de l'Université d'Ankara*, I, 47–106.

(1950). "Hacı Giray I," *İA*, V, 25–27.

(1951). "Türkiye'nin İktisadi Vaziyeti Üzerine Bir Tetkik Münasebetile," *B*, XV, 629–90.

(1952). "Timariotes chrétiens en Albanie au XVe siècle d'après un registre de timars Ottoman," *Mitteilungen des Österreichischen Staatsarchivs*, IV, 118–38.

(1953a), "Stefan Duşan'dan Osmanlı İmparatorluğuna," *Fuat Köprülü Armağanı*, İstanbul, pp. 207–48.

(1953b). "15. Asır Türkiye İktisadî ve İçtimaî Tarihi Kaynakları," *IFM*, XV, 51–57.

(1954a). *Fâtih Devri Üzerinde Tetkikler ve Vesikalar*, I, Ankara.

(1954b). *Hicrî 835 Tarihli Sûret-i Defter-i Sancak-ı Arvanid*, Ankara.

(1954c). "Ottoman methods of conquest," *Studia Islamica*, II.

(1957a). "Review: David Ayalon, *Gunpowder and firearms in the Mamluk Kingdom*," *B*, XXI, 501–12.

(1957b). "Mehmed II," *İA*, VII, 506–35.

(1958a). "Arnawutluk," *EI²*, I, 650–58.

(1958b). "The problem of the relationship between Byzantine and Otttoman taxation," *Akten XI. Internationalen Byzantinisten Kongresses*, Munich.

(1959a). "Osmanlılarda Raiyyet Rüsûmu," *B*, XXIII, 576–610.

(1959b). "Bāyazid I," *EI²* I, 1117–19.

(1960a). "Bursa," *IA*, I, 1333–36.

(1960b). "Bursa and the commerce of the Levant," *JESHO*, III, 131–47.

(1960c). "'Örf," *IA*, IX(2), p. 480.

(1960d). "Çiftlik," *EI²*, II, 32–33.

(1960e) "Bursa XV. Asir Sanayi ve Ticaret Tarihine dair Vesikalar," *B*, XXIV, fasc. 93, 45–102.

(1963a). "Djizya," *EI²*, II, 563–66.

(1963b). "Dobrudja," *EI²*, II, 613.

(1965a). "Ghulām," *EI²*, II, 1085–91.

(1965b). "Adâletnâmeler," *BL*, II, 49–145.

(1965c). "Çiftlik," *EI²*, II, 32–33.

(1965d). "Filori," *EI²*, II, 914–15.

(1965e). "Hadjdjı Giray," *EI²*, III, 43–45.

(1965f). "Gönüllü," *EI²*, II, 1120–21.

(1965g). "Gelibolu," *EI²*, II, 983–87.

(1967). "Notes on N. Beldiceanu's translation of the Ḳānūnnāme, fonds turc ancien 39. Bibliothèque Nationale, Paris," *Der Islam*, LXIII, 139–57.

(1969a). "Ḥarīr," *EI²*, III, 211–18.

(1969b). "Ottoman policy and administration in Cyprus after the conquest," in H. İnalcık, *The Ottoman Empire: conquest, organization and economy*, London.

(1969c). "Suleiman the Lawgiver and Ottoman Law," *AO*, I, 105–38.

(1969d). "Capital formation in the Ottoman Empire," *JEH*, XXIX(1), 97–140.

(1969e). "Ḥawāla," *EI²*, III, 283–85.

(1969f). "L'Empire Ottoman," in Actes du Premier Congrès International des Études Balkaniques et Sud-Est Européennes, III, 75–104, Sofia; repr. *Studies in Ottoman social and economic history*, London, 1985.

(1970a). "The Ottoman economic mind and aspects of the Ottoman economy," in Cook, ed., pp. 207–18.

(1970b). "The foundations of the Ottoman economico-social system in cities," in *La ville balkanique*, Sofia, 17–24.

(1970c). "Islam in the Ottoman Empire," *Cultura Turcica*, V–VII, 19–29.

(1971). "Imtiyāzāt," *EI²*, III, 1179–89.

(1972). "The Ottoman decline and its effects upon the reaya," in H. Birnbaum and S. Vryonis, eds., *Aspects of the Balkans, continuity and change*, The Hague, pp. 338–54.

(1973a). *The Ottoman Empire: The classical age, 1300–1600*, London.

(1973b). "İstanbul," *EI²*, IV, 224–48.

(1973c). "İskender," *EI²*, IV, 138–40.

(1974). "Lepanto in the Ottoman documents," in *Il Mediterraneo nella seconda metà del '500 alla Luce di Lepanto*, Florence, pp. 185–92.

(1975a). "The socio-political effects of the diffusion of fire-arms in the Middle East," in V.J. Parry and M.E. Yapp, eds., *War, technology and society in the Middle East*, London, pp. 195–217.

(1975b). "Ḳānūn," *EI²*, IV, 556–62.

(1975c). "Ḳānūnnāme," *EI²*, IV, 562–66.

(1977a). "An outline of Ottoman–Venetian relations'," in Beck, Manoussacas and Pertusi, eds., *Venezia centro di mediazione tra Oriente e Occidente*, Florence, pp. 83–90.

(1977b). "Centralization and decentralization in Ottoman administration," in Naff and Owen, eds., pp. 27–52.

(1978a). "The impact of the Annales School on Ottoman studies and new findings," *R*, I(3/4), 69–96.

(1978b). *The Ottoman Empire: conquest, organization and economy*, London.

(1979a). "The question of the closing of the Black Sea under the Ottomans," *Arkheion Pontu*, XXXV, 74–110.

(1979b). "Servile labor in the Ottoman Empire," in A. Archer *et al.*, eds., *The mutual effects of the Islamic and Judeo-Christian worlds*, New York, pp. 25–52.

(1980a). "Military and fiscal transformation in the Ottoman Empire, 1600–1700," *AO*, VI, 283–337.

(1980b). "Osmanlı Pamuklu Pazarı, Hindistan ve İngiltere: Pazar Rekabetinde Emek Maliyetinin Rolü," *TITA*, II, 1–65.

(1980c). "Social and economic history of Turkey," in O. Okyar and H. İnalcık, eds., *Papers, First International Congress on the Social and Economic History of Turkey*. Ankara.

(1980d). "The hub of the city: the Bedestan of İstanbul," *IJTS*, I, 1–17.

(1981a). "Osmanlı İdare, Sosyal ve Ekonomik Tarihiyle İlgili Belgeler," *Bl*, X, 1–91.

(1981b). "The Khan and the tribal aristocracy: the Crimean Khanate under Sahib Giray I," *HUS*, X, 445–66.

(1982a). "Kuṭn," *EI²*, V, 557–66.

(1982b). "Rice cultivation and the çeltükci-re'āyā system in the Ottoman Empire," *Turcica*, XIV, 59–141.

(1982c). "Ottoman archival materials on millets," in B. Braude and B. Lewis, eds., *Christians and Jews in the Ottoman Empire*, New York, pp. 437–49.

(1983a). "Ma'," *EI²*, V, 878–83.

(1983b). "Marchés et marchands Ottomans," *Bulletin du Mauss*, VIII, 13–37.

(1983c). "Introduction to Ottoman metrology," *Turcica*, XV, 311–48.

(1983d). "Arab camel drivers in western Anatolia in the fifteenth century," *Revue d'Histoire Maghrebine*, X, 247–70.

(1984). "Yük (*himl*) in Ottoman silk trade, mining and agriculture," *Turcica*, XVI, 131–56.

(1985a). "The rise of the Turcoman maritime principalities in Anatolia, Byzantium, and Crusades," *BF*, IX, 179–217.

(1985b). "The emergence of big farms, *çiftliks*: state, landlords and tenants," in *idem* (1985c).

(1985c). *Studies in Ottoman social and economic history*, London.

(1986a). "The Yürüks, their origins, expansion and economic role," in R. Pinner and W. Denny, eds., *Oriental carpet and textile studies*, London, pp. 39–65.

(1986b). "Power relationships between Russia, the Crimea and the Ottoman Empire as reflected in titulature," in *Passé turco-tatar, present soviétique, Etudes offertes à Alexandre Bennigsen*, Paris.

(1988a). "Jews in Ottoman economy and finances, 1450–1500," in C.E. Bosworth *et al.*, eds., *The Islamic world*, Princeton, 513–50.

(1988b). "Osmanlı İdare, Sosyal ve Ekonomik Tarihiyle İlgili Belgeler," *Bl*, XIII, 1–41.

(1989). "The Ottoman Turks and the Crusades, 1329–1522," in K. Setton (gen. ed.), *A history of the Crusades*, VI, H. Hazard and N.P. Zacour eds., Madison.

(1990). "Matbakh," *EI²*, 809–13.

(1991a). "Ottoman Galata, 1453–1553," in E. Eldem, ed., *Première rencontre internationale sur l'empire Ottoman et la Turquie moderne*, İstanbul.

(1991b). "Tax collection, embezzlement and bribery in Ottoman finances," *TSAB*, XV (2), 327–46.

(1992a). *The Middle East and the Balkans under the Ottoman Empire: essays on economy and society*, Bloomington.

(1996). *Sources and documents on the Ottoman Black Sea*, Cambridge, Mass.

İnalcık, H. and R. Murphey (1978), eds. *The history of Mehmed the Conqueror*, Chicago and Minnesota.

Iorga, N. (1899–1915). *Notes et extraits pour servir à l'histoire des Croisades au XVe siècle*, I–II, Paris; III–V, Bucharest.

(1937). *Histoire des états balkaniques*, Bucharest.

(1971). *Byzance après Byzance: continuation de la vie byzantine*, Bucharest.

İslamoğlu, H. and S. Faroqhi. (1979). "Crop patterns and agricultural production trends in sixteenth-century Anatolia," *R*, II (3), 401–36.

İslamoğlu, H. and Ç. Keyder. (1977). "Agenda for Ottoman history," *R*, I (1), 37–55.

İslamoğlu-İnan, H. (1987), ed. *The Ottoman Empire and the world-economy*, Cambridge.

(1988). "Les paysans, le marché et l'état en Anatolie au XVIe siècle," *Annales, ESC*, V, 1025–43.

Issawi, C. (1958). "Comment on Professor Barkan's estimate of the population of the Ottoman Empire," *JESHO*, I, 329–31.

(1980). *The economic history of Turkey, 1800–1914*, Chicago.

(1981). "The area and population of the Arab empire: an essay in speculation," in *Arab World's Legacy*, Princeton.

(1982). *An economic history of the Middle East and North Africa*, New York.

İstahrī, A.A. (1969). *Masālik wa Mamālik*, ed. by Iradj Afshar, Tehran.

Jacoby, D. (1971). *La féodalité en Grèce médiévale*, Paris.

Jennings, R.C. (1976). "Urban population in Anatolia in the sixteenth century: a study of Kayseri, Karaman, Amasya, Trabzon and Erzurum," *IJMES*, VII, 21–57.

(1978). "Sakaltutan four centuries ago," *IJMES*, I (1), 89–98.

Jireček, C. (1879). *Die Handelsstrassen und Bergwerke von Serbien und Bosnien während des Mittelalters*, Prague.

(1899). *Die Bedeutung Ragusas in der Handelgeschichte des Mittelalters*, Vienna.

Jones, A.H.M. (1957). "Capitatio and Iugatio," *The Journal of Roman Studies*, XLVII, 88–91.

(1958). "The Roman colonate," *PP*, XIII.

(1964). *The later Roman Empire*, II, Oxford.

(1978). *The decline of the ancient world*, London.

Jorga, N. (1908–13). *Geschichte des Osmanischen Reiches*, I–V, Gotha.

Kafadar, C. (1986a). "When coins turned into drops of dew and bankers became robbers of shadows: the boundaries of Ottoman economic imagination at the end of the sixteenth century," Ph.D. dissertation, McGill University.

(1986b). "A death in Venice (1575): Anatolian Muslim merchants trading in the Serenissima," *JJS*, X, 198–218.

(1991). "Les troubles monétaires de la fin du XVIe siècle et la prise de conscience ottomane du déclin," *Annales, ESC*, March.

Kahane, R. and A. Tietze. (1958). *The lingua franca in the Levant. Turkish nautical terms of Italian and Greek origin*, Urbana.

Kahle, P. (1927). *Piri Reis, und seine Bahriye*, Berlin and Leipzig.

(1933). *Die Verschollene Colombus Karte von 1498 in einer Türkishschen Weltkarte von 1513*, Berlin and Leipzig.

Káldy-Nagy, G. (1960). "Bevölkerungsstatistischer Quellenwert der Ğizye-Defter und der Tahrir-Defter," *AOr*, II, 259–67.

(1970). "Statistische Angaben über den Warenverkehr des türkischen Eroberungsgebiets in Ungarn mit dem Westen in den Jahren 1560–64," *Annales, Sectio Historica*, XI, Budapest.

(1977). "The first centuries of the Ottoman military organization," *AOr*, XXXI (2), 147–83.

Kaplan, M. (1981). "Remarques sur la place de l'exploitation paysanne dans l'économie rurale Byzantine," *XVI. Internationaler Byzantinisten Kongress, Akten I/2, Jahrbuch der österreichischen Byzantinistik*, 32(2), Vienna.

Karpat, K. (1985). *Ottoman population: demographic and social characteristics*, Madison.

Kellenbenz, H. (1956). "Le commerce du poivre des Fugger et le marché international du poivre," *Annales, ESC*, XI (1), 1–28.

(1963). "Le front hispano-portugais contre l'expansion hollandaise dans l'Inde," *Centro de Estudos Historicos Ultra-marinos, Studia*, Lisbon.

(1967). "Handelsverbindungen zwischen Mitteleuropa und İstanbul über Venedig in der ersten Hälfte des 16. Jahrhunderts," *Studi Veneziani*, IX, 193–99.

(1971). "Südosteuropa im Rahmen der Europäischen Gesamtwirtschaft," in O. Pickl, ed., *Die wirtschaftlichen Auswirkungen der Türkenkriege*, Graz.

(1990). "From Melchior Manlich to Ferdinand Cron: German Levantine and Oriental trade relations," *JEEH*, XIX (3), 611–22.

Kerr, R. (1811). *A general history and collection of voyages and travels*, II, Edinburgh.

Keyder, Ç. and F. Tabak. (1991), eds. *Landholding and commercial agriculture in the Middle East*, Albany.

Khalidi, T. (1984), ed. *Land tenure and social transformation in the Middle East*, Beirut.

Kınalızade, A. (1248 H/1832–33). *Akhlāk-i 'Alā'ī*, I–III, Bulak.

Kiel, M. (1985). *Art and society of Bulgaria in the Turkish period*, Assen and Maastricht.

(1989). "Urban development in Bulgaria in the Turkish period: the place of Turkish architecture in the process," *IJTS*, IV (2), 79–158.

(1990). "Remarks on the administration of the poll tax (*cizye*) in the Ottoman Balkans," *EB*, XXVI (4), 70–93.

Kissling, H.J. (1950). "Das Menākibnāme Scheich Bedr ed-dīns des Sohnes des Richters von Samavna," *ZDMG*, C, 112–76.

(1975). "Shâh Ismâ'īl I er, la nouvelle route des Indes et les ottomans," *Turcica*, VI, 89–102.

Klaveren, van J. (1960). "Fiskalismus, Merkantilismus, Korruption. Drei Aspekte der Finanz- und Wirtschaftspolitik," *VSWG*, 47.

Koçi Bey (1939). *Koçi Bey Risalesi*, ed. A.K. Aksüt, İstanbul.

Köprülü, M. Fuad. (1935). *Les origines de l'empire Ottoman*, Paris.

Kortepeter, C.M. (1966). "Ottoman imperial policy and the economy of the Black Sea region in the 16th century," *JAOS*, LXXXVI, 86–113.

(1972). *Ottoman imperialism during the Reformation, 1578–1608*, New York.

(1983). "Habsburg and Ottoman in Hungary in the 16th and 17th centuries," *Habsburg-Osmanische Beziehungen, CIEPO colloque, Vienna, 26–30 Sept.*, Vienna.

Kosminsky, E. (1955). "The evolution of feudal rent in England from the XIth to the XVth centuries," *PP*, VII–X, 12–34.

Kostis, K. (1990). "Structures sociales et retard économique: Salonique et l'économie de la laine XVIe–XVIIIe siècles," *EB*, I, 100–14; II, 41–52.

Kovačević, D. (1960). "Les mines d'or et d'argent en Serbie et Bosnie," *Annales, ESC*, XV, 248–58.

Kraelitz, Fr. (1921). *Osmanische Urkunden in türkische Sprache aus der zweiten hälfte der 15. Jahrhundert*, Vienna.

(1922), ed. "Kānūnnāme Sultan Mehmeds des Eroberers," *MOG*, I, 13–48.

Krahl, R. (1986). "Export porcelain fit for the Chinese Emperor. Early Chinese blue-white in the Topkapı Saray Museum," *JRAS*, 68–94.

Kreiser, K. (1986). "Icâreteyn: Zur 'Doppelten Miete' im osmanischen Stiftungswesens," *JTS*, X, 219–26.

Krekić, B. (1961). *Dubrovnik (Raguse) et le Levant au Moyen Âge*, The Hague.

(1972). *Dubrovnik in the 14th and 15th centuries: a city between East and West*, Norman.

Kritovoulos, M. (1954). *History of Mehmed the Conqueror*, trans. by C. T. Riggs. Princeton.

Kun, T.H. (1964). "Sixteenth century Turkish settlements in southern Hungary." *B*, XXVIII, 1–72.

Kunt, M. (1983). *The Sultan's servants. The transformation of Ottoman provincial government, 1550–1650*, New York.

Kuran, T. (1989). "On the notion of economic justice in contemporary Islāmic thought," *IJMES*, XXI, 171–91.

Kurat, A.N. (1940). *Topkapı Sarayı Müzesinde Altınordu Kırım ve Türkistan Hanlarına ait Yarlık ve Bitikler*, İstanbul.

(1953) "Hoca Sadeddin Efendinin Türk-İngiliz Münasebetlerinin Tesisi ve Gelişmesindeki Rolü," *Fuad Köprülü Armağanı*, İstanbul, pp. 305–15.

Kurtoğlu, F. (1940). "Hadim Süleyman Paşa'nın Mektupları," *B*, IV, 55–87.

Kütükoğlu, M. (1974). *Osmanlı-İngiliz İktisadî Münasebetleri (1553–1610)*, Ankara.

(1983). *Osmanlılarda Narh Müessesesi ve 1640 Tarihli Narh Defteri*, İstanbul.

(1991). "Lütfi Paşa Asafnâmesi," in *Prof. Kütükoğlu'na Armağan*, İstanbul, 49–100.

Labib, S. (1965). *Handelsgeschichte Ägyptens im Spätmittelalter*, Wiesbaden.

La Brocquière, B. de (1892). *Le voyage d'Outremer*, ed. by C. Schefer, Paris.

Lach, D.F. (1965). *Asia in the making of Europe*, I (ii), Chicago and London.

Laiou, A.E. (1972). *Constantinople and Latins, the foreign policy of Andronicus II, 1282–1328*, Cambridge, Mass.

Laiou-Thomadakis, A.E. (1977). *Peasant society in the late Byzantine Empire*, Princeton.

(1982). "The Greek merchant of the Palaeologan period: a collective portrait," *Praktikates Akademias Athenon*, LVI, 96–132.

Lane, F. (1933). "Venetian shipping during the commercial revolution," *AHR*, XXXVIII (2), 219–39.

(1940). "The Mediterranean spice trade, further evidence of its revival in the sixteenth century," *AHR*, XLV (3), 581–90.

(1944). *Andrea Barbarigo, merchant of Venice, 1418–1449*, Baltimore.

(1973). *Venice, a maritime republic*, Baltimore and London.

(1977). "Double entry bookkeeping and resident merchants," *JEEH*, VI (1), 177–91.

Lefort, J. (1974). "Fiscalité médiévale et informatique," *RH*, 512, 315–54.

Lemercier-Quelquejay, Ch. *et al.* (1986). *Turco-Tatar past, Soviet present. Etudes offertes à Alexandre Bennigsen*, Paris.

Lemerle, P. (1957). *L'Emirat d'Aydın, Byzance et l'Occident, recherches sur la geste d'Umur Pacha*, Paris.

(1958). "Esquisse pour une histoire agraire de Byzance," *RH*, CCXIX (1), 219.

Lesure, M. (1976). "Un document ottoman de 1525 sur l'Inde portugaise et les pays de la Mer Rouge," *Mare Luso-indicum*, III.

Lewis, B. (1952). *Notes and documents from the Turkish archives*, Jerusalem.

(1958). "Some reflections on the decline of the Ottoman Empire," *SI*, IX 111–27.

(1962). *The emergence of modern Turkey*, 2nd ed., London.

(1973). "Corsairs in Iceland," *ROMM*, XV–XVI, 140–44.

(1980). "Acre in the sixteenth century according to the Ottoman tapu registers," in *Memorial Ömer Lûtfi Barkan*, Paris.

Lezze, D. da. (1909). *Historia Turchesca*, ed. by I. Ursu, Bucharest.

Lindner, R.P. (1983). *Nomads and Ottomans in medieval Anatolia*, Bloomington.

Lokkegaard, F. (1950). *Islamic taxation in the classic period*. Copenhagen.

Lombard, D. and J. Aubin (1988), eds. *Marchands et hommes d'affairs asiatiques dans l'Océan Indien et la Mer de Chine, 13e-20e siècles*, Paris.

Lopez, R.S. (1952a). "China silk in Europe in the Yuan period," *JAOS*, 72–76.

(1952b). "Nuove luci sugli Italiani in Estremo Oriente prima di Colombos," *Studi Colombiani nel v centenario della Naseita*, III, 337–98.

Lopez, R.S. and I.W. Raymond. (1962). *Medieval trade in the Mediterranean world*, New York.

Lopez, R.S., H. Miskimin and A. Udovitch (1970). "England to Egypt, 1350–1500: long-term trends and long-distance trade," in Cook, ed.

Lot, F. (1928). *L'impôt foncier et la capitation personnelle sous le Bas-Empire et à l'époque franque*, Paris.

Lowry, H.W. (1980). "The Ottoman Liva Kanunnames contained in the Defter-i Hakani," *JOS*, II, 43–74.

(1980–81). "Portrait of a city: the population and topography of Ottoman Selanik (Thessaloniki) in the year 1478," *Diptyka*, Athens.

(1981). *Trabzon Şehrinin Islâmlaşma ve Türkleşmesi, 1461–1583*, İstanbul.

(1991). "The fate of Byzantine monastic properties under the Ottomans: examples from Mount Athos, Limnos and Trabzon," *BF*, XVI, 275–312.

Lütfi Pasha. (1910). *Asafname*, ed. by Tschudi, Leipzig; ed. by Ali Emiri, İstanbul, 1909.

Luzzatto, G. (1954). *Storia economica*, Padua.

Lybyer, A.H. (1919). *The government of the Ottoman Empire in the time of Suleiman the Magnificent*, Cambridge.

Mahmud, E.S.M. (1990). *XVI. Asırda Mısır Eyâleti*, İstanbul.

Majer, H.G. (1982). "Ein osmanishes Budget aus der Zeit Mehmeds des Eroberers," *Islam*, LIX (1), 40–63.

(1984). *Das osmanische "Registerbuch der Beschwerden" (Şikâyet Defteri) vom Jahre 1675*, I, Vienna.

Mal, J. (1924). *Uskočke seobe i slovenske pokrajine*, Ljubljana.

Malinovskiy, A.F. (1793). *Relations between the Khans of Crimea and Kazan with the Russian Grand Dukes and Tsars, 1462–1733*, Moscow (in Russian).

Malowist, M. (1937). "The Baltic and the Black Sea in Medieval Trade," *Baltic and Scandinavian Countries*, III.

(1947). *Kaffa, kolonia genuenska na Krymie i problem wschodni w latach 1453–75*, Warschaw.

(1973). "Le commerce du Levant avec l'Europe au XVIe siècle, quelques problèmes," *HEMM*, 349–57.

Mandaville, J.C. (1970). "The Ottoman province of Al-Hasā in the sixteenth and seventeenth centuries," *JAOS*, XC (3), 486–513.

(1979). "Usurious piety: the cash–waqf controversy in the Ottoman Empire," *IJMES*, X, 289–308.

Manolescu, R. (1960). "Le role commercial de la ville de Brašov dans le sud-est de l'Europe du XVIe siecle," *Nouvelles Etudes d'Histoire*, II, Bucharest.

(1965). *Comeţtul Tării Romineşti şi Moldovei cu Braşovul (Secolele XIV–XVI)*, Bucharest.

Mantran, R. (1962). *İstanbul dans la seconde moitié du XVIIe siècle*, Paris.

(1967). "Règlements fiscaux ottomans: la province de Bassora," *JESHO*, X, 224–44.

Mantran, R. and J. Sauvaget. (1951). *Réglements fiscaux ottomans, les provinces syriennes*, Beirut.

Mas-Latrie, J.L. (1886). *Traités de paix et de commerce*. I–II, Paris.

Masson, P. (1896). *Histoire du commerce français dans le Levant au XVIIe siècle*, I, Paris.

(1928). *Les compagnies du corail*, Paris.

Masters, B. (1988). *The origins of Western economic dominance in the Middle East, mercantilism and the Islamic economy in Aleppo 1600–1750*, New York and London.

Matuz, J. (1974). *Das Kanzleiwesen Sultan Süleymāns des Prächtigen*, Wiesbaden.

Maxim, M. (1972). "Recherches sur les circonstances de la majoration du kharadj de la Moldavie entre les années 1538–74," *AISEE Bulletin* X (2), 233–61.

(1974). "Circonstances de la majoration du kharadj payé par la Valachie à l'empire Ottoman durant la période 1540–75," *AIESEE, Bulletin* XII (2), 367–81.

(1988). "Ottoman documents concerning the Wallachian salt in the ports on the lower Danube in the second half of the sixteenth century," *RESEE*, XXV, 113–22.

Māzandarānī, A. (1952). *Die Resālä-ye Falakiyyä*, Wiesbaden.

McCarthy J. (1982). *The Arab World, Turkey and the Balkan provinces, 1878–1914*, Boston.

McGowan, B. (1969). "Food supply and taxation on the middle Danube (1568–79)," *AO*, I, 139–96.

(1982). *Economic life in Ottoman Europe*, Cambridge and Paris.

(1983). *Sirem Sancağı Mufassal Defteri*, Ankara.

McNeill, W.H. (1964). *Europe's steppe frontier, 1500–1800*, Chicago and London.

(1974). *Venice, the hinge of Europe, 1081–1797*, Chicago.

(1982). *The pursuit of power, technology, armed force, and society since A.D. 1000*, Chicago.

Mehlan, A. (1938). "Die grossen Balkanmessen zur Türkenzeit," *VSWG*, XXI (1), 10–49.

(1939). "Die Handelsstrassen des Balkans während der Türkenzeit," *SF*, IV.

Meilink-Roelofsz, M.A.P. (1962). *Asian trade and European influence in the Indonesian archipelago between 1500 and about 1630*, The Hague.

(1974). "The earliest relations between Persia and the Netherlands," *Persica*, VI, 1–50.

Mélanges en honneur de Fernand Braudel: histoire économique du monde méditerranéen, 1450–1650, I–II, Paris, 1987.

Melzig, H. (1943). *Büyük Türk Hindistan Kapılarında*, İstanbul.

Memorial Barkan (1980). *Mémorial Ömer Lûtfi Barkan*, Paris.

Milkova, F.G. (1965). "Razvitie i character na osmanskoto pozemleno zakonoda-telstvo ot 1839 do 1878 g.," *Istoričeski pregled*, XXI (5), 31–55.

(1966). "Sur la teneur et le caractère de la propriété d'État des terres miriyé dans l'empire ottoman du XVe au XIX s.," *EB*, V.

(1970). *Pozemlenata sobstvenost v bulgarskite zemi prez XIX veki.*, Sofia.

Modarressi, H.T. (1983). *Kharāj in Islamic Law*, London.

Mommsen, T. (1869). "Syrisches Provinzialmass und Römischer Reichskataster," *Hermes*, III, 429–38.

Morimoto, K. (1981). *The fiscal administration of Egypt in the early Islamic period*, Dohosha.

Morony, M.G. (1981). "Land holding in seventh century Iraq: late Sasanian and Early Islamic patterns," in Udovitch, ed., pp. 135–75.

Muahedat (1300 H/1882–83). *Muahedat Mecmuası*, III, İstanbul.

Mughal, Y.M. (1974). *Kanunî Devri Osmanlıların Hint Okyanusu Politikası . . ., 1517–38*, İstanbul.

Munsha'at 9503: British Library, Turkish Manuscripts, Or MS 9503.

Murphey, R. (1980). "Silver production in Rumelia according to an official Otto-man report circa 1600," *SF*, XXXIX, 75–104.

(1984). "Some features of nomadism in the Ottoman Empire," *JTS*, VIII: T. Halasi-Kun Festschrift, 189–97.

(1987). *Regional structure in the Ottoman economy: a sultanic memorandum of 1636 A.D. concerning the sources and uses of the tax-farm revenues of Anatolia and the coastal and northern portions of Syria*, Wiesbaden.

(1988). "Provisioning İstanbul: the state and subsistence in the early modern Middle East," *Food and Foodways*, II, 217–63.

Mutafčieva, V.P. (1981). *Le Vakıf: un aspect de la structure socio-économique de l'empire ottoman (XVe–XVIIe s.)*, Sofia.

(1988). *Agrarian relations in the Ottoman Empire in the 15th and 16th centur-ies*, New York.

Naff, T. and R. Owen (1977), eds. *Studies in eighteenth century Islamic history*, Carbondale, Ill.

Nagata, Y. (1979). "16. Yüzyılda Manisa Köyleri," *TD*, XXXII, 731–58.

Naima, M. (1281 H/1864). *Ravdat al-Husayn . . .*, İstanbul.

Neschrī, M. (1951). *Ğihannümā, Die altosmanische Chronik des Mevlānā Mehemmed Neschrī*, I, ed. by F. Taeschner, Leipzig.

(1987). *Kitābı Cihannümâ, Neşrī Tarihi*, ed., F.R. Unat and M.A. Köymen, Ankara.

Netta, C. (1920). *Handelsbeziehungen zwischen Leipzig und Ost- und Südost-europa bis zum verfall der Warenmessen*, Zürich.

Newberry, J. (1904). *Two voyages of Master John Newberry, one into the Holy Land: the other to Balsara, Ormus, Persia, and back throw Turkie*, ed. Purchas, VIII, Glasgow.

Nicol, D.M. (1968). "The Byzantine family of Cantacuzenus," *DO*, XI.

Nistor, J. (1911). *Die auswärtigen Handelsbeziehungen der Moldau in 14., 15. und 16 Jh.* Gotha.

Nizām al-Mulk. (1893). *Siasset Namèh*, trans. by Schefer, Paris.

(1962). *Siyar al-Mulūk also known as Siyāsat-nāma*, ed. by H. Drake, Tehran.

Oğuz, B. (1980). *Türkiye Halkının Kültür Kökenleri: Tarım, Hayvancılık, Meteoroloji*, II (2), İstanbul.

Ohsson, I.M. d'. (1788–1824). *Tableau général de l'empire Ottoman*, Paris.

Okić, M.T. (1960). "Les Kristians (Bogomiles Parfaits) de Bosnie, d'après des documents turcs inédits," *BS*, XIX, 108–33.

Okyar, O. and Ü. Nalbantoğlu, eds. (1975). *Türkiye iktisat Tarihi Semineri, June 8–10, 1973*, Ankara.

Orhonlu, C. (1967). *Osmanlı İmparatorluğunda Derbend Teşkilâtı*, İstanbul.

(1970a). "Hint Kaptanlığı ve Pîrî Reis," *B*, CXXXII, 235–54.

(1970b). *Telhîsler (1597–1607)*, İstanbul.

(1974). *Osmanlı İmparatorluğunun Güney Siyaseti: Habeş Eyaleti*, İstanbul.

Oruç, B.A. (1925). *Die Frühosmanischen Jahrbücher des Urudsch*, ed. by F. Babinger, Hanover.

Osmanlı Arşivi Bülteni, I, İstanbul, 1990.

Ostrogorsky, G. (1954). *Pour l'histoire de la féodalité byzantine*, Brussels.

(1969). *Die ländliche Steuergemeinde des byzantinschen Reiches im X. Jahrhundert*, Amsterdam.

Öz, T. (1946). *Turkish textiles and velvets*, Ankara.

Özbaran, S. (1971). "Basra Beylerbeyliğinin Kuruluşu," *TD*, XXV, 53–72.

(1972). "The Ottoman Turks and the Portuguese in the Persian Gulf, 1534–1581," *JAH*, VI (1), 45–87.

(1977). "Osmanlı İmparatorluğu ve Hindistan Yolu," *TD*, XXXI, 66–146.

Özdemir, H. (1988). *1463–1640 Yılları Bursa Şehri Tereke Defterleri*, İstanbul.

Özergin, M.K. (1965). "Anadolu'da Selçuk Kervansarayları," *TD*, XX, 141–70.

Pach, Z.P. (1966). "The development of feudal rent in Hungary in the fifteenth century," *EHR*, 2nd. series, XIX (1).

(1968). "Favourable and unfavourable conditions for capitalist growth: the shift of international trade routes in the 15th and 16th centuries," in *IV. International Conference of Economic History*, Bloomington.

(1973). "La route du poivre vers Hongrie médiévale," *HEMM*, 449–58.

(1975). "Levantine trade and Hungary in the Middle Ages," *Études Historiques Hongroises*, I, à l'occasion du XIVe Congrès Internationale des Sciences Historiques.

(1976). "Le commerce du Levant et la Hongrie au Moyen Age," *Annales, ESC*, VI, 1176–94.

(1980). "The Transylvanian route of Levantine trade at the turn of the 15th and 16th centuries," *Studia Historical* (Budapest), 138, 5–36.

Pakalın, M.Z. (1946–54). *Osmanlı Tarih Deyimleri ve Terimleri Sözlüğü*, I–III, İstanbul.

Panaitescu, P.P. (1933). "La route commerciale de Pologne à la Mer Noire au Moyen Âge," *RIR*, III, 172–93.

(1938). "Mircea der Alte und die ungarische Lehnsherrlichkeit," *Académie Roumaine, Mem. Sect. 1st.*, III, XX(3), Bucharest.

Panova, S. (1983). "Zum Handel der Länder Südosteuropas mit dem übrigen Europa im 17. und 18. Jahr.," in G. Heiss and G. Klingenstein, eds., *Das Osmanische Reich und Europa, 1683 bis 1789, Konflict, Entspannung und Austausch*, Vienna.

(1989). "Die Anwendung des Handelsrechtes der jüdischen Kaufleute im Osmanischen Reich im 16. und 17. Jahrhundert," *Österreichische Osthefte*, XXXI, 44–60.

Papacostea, Š. (1978). "Die politischen Voraussetzungen für die wirtschaftliche Vorherrschaft des Osmanischen Reiches im Schwarzmeergebiet (1453–84)," *Münchner Zeitschrift für Balkankunde*, I.

(1981). *Stephen the Great, Prince of Moldavia, 1457–1504*, Bucharest.

Parker, G. (1988). *The military revolution*, Cambridge.

Parry, V.J. and M.E. Yapp. (1975), eds. *War, technology and society in the Middle East*, London.

Pegolotti, F.B. (1936). *La pratica della mercatura*, ed. by A. Evans, Cambridge, Mass.

Perjes, G. (1989). *The fall of the medieval kingdom of Hungary, 1526–41*, trans. by D. Fenyõ, New York.

Petrović, D. (1975). "Fire-arms in the Balkans on the eve of and after the Ottoman conquests of the fourteenth and fifteenth centuries," in Parry and Yapp, pp. 164–94.

Peyssonel, Ch. (1787). *Traité du commerce dans la Mer Noire*, I–II, Paris.

Pinner, R. and W.B. Denny, (1986). *Oriental carpet and textile studies*, II: *Carpets of the Mediterranean countries, 1400–1600*, London.

Piri, M. (1935). *Kitâb-ı Bahriyye*, İstanbul.

Pistarino, G. (1980). "The Genoese in Pera-Turkish Galata," *MHR*, 63–85.

Pitcher, D.E. (1972). *An historical geography of the Ottoman Empire*, Leiden.

Planhol, X. de. (1958). *De la plaine pamphylienne aux lacs pisidiens, nomadisme et vie paysanne*, Paris.

(1959). "Geography, politics and nomadism in Anatolia," *International Social Science Journal*, XI.

Plumidis, G. (1974). "Considerazione sulla populazione greca a Venezia nella seconda meta del'500," *Studi Veneziana*, XVI, 219–26.

Polanyi, K., C.M. Arsenberg and W.H. Pearson (1957), eds. *Trade and markets in the early empires*, Glencoe.

Postan, M.M. (1966). *The Cambridge economic history of Europe*, I, Cambridge.

Postan, M.M., E.E. Rich and E. Miller (1963), eds. *The Cambridge economic history of Europe*, III, Cambridge.

Preto, P. (1975). *Venezia e i Turchi*, Florence.

Pullan, B. (1968), ed. *Crisis and change in the Venetian economy in the sixteenth and seventeenth centuries*, London.

Purchas, S. (1905–7). *Hakluytus Posthumus or Purchas. his pilgrims contayning a history of the world in sea voyages and lande travells*, I–XX, Glasgow.

Raby, J. (1986). "The porcelain trade routes," in Raby and Yücel, eds.

Raby, J. and Ünsal Yücel (1986), *Chinese ceramics in the Topkapı Saray Museum, Istanbul. A complete catalogue*: I, *Historical introductions, Yuan and Ming Dynasty celadon wares*, Regina Krahl with Nurdan Erbahar, ed. John Ayers, London.

Raci, P. (1970). "La Scala di Spalato e la politica Veneziana in Adriatico," *Quaderni storici*, V, 13.

Rambert, G. (1951), ed. *Histoire du commerce de Marseille*, III, ed. by R. Collier and J. Billioud, Paris.

Rapp, R.T. (1975). "The unmaking of the Mediterranean trade hegemony: international trade rivalry and the commercial revolution," *JEH*, XXXV(3), 499–525.

Ráu, V. (1970). "Les portugais et la route terrestre des Indes à la Méditerranée aux XVᵉ et XVIᵉ siècles," *MOI*, I, 91–98.

Ravid, B. (1978). *Economics and toleration in seventeenth century Venice*, Jerusalem.

Raymond, A. (1979). "La conqûete ottomane et le développement des grandes villes arabes," *ROMM*, XXVII, 115–34.

(1984). *The great Arab cities in the 16th–18th centuries. An introduction*, New York.

(1988). "Le commerce des épices au Caire, du XVIᵉ au XVIIIᵉ siècle," *Herbes, drogues et épices en Méditerranée*, Paris.

Refik, A. (1930). *Anadolu'da Türk Aşîretleri*, İstanbul.

(1930–31). *İstanbul Hayatı*, I–II, İstanbul.

Rehman, F. (1974). "Islam and problems of economic justice," *Pakistan Economist*.

Reid, A. (1969). "Sixteenth-century Turkish influence in western Indonesia," *JSAH*, X (3), 395–414.

Ricaut, P. and R. Knolles (1687–1700). *The Turkish history from the original of that nation to the growth of the Ottoman Empire*, I–III, London.

Rich, E.E. and C.H. Wilson, (1967), eds. *The Cambridge economic history of Europe*, IV, Cambridge.

Richards, D.S. (1970), ed, *Islam and the trade of Asia*, London.

Richards, G.R.B. (1932). *Florentine merchants in the age of the Medicis*, Cambridge, Mass.

Richards, J.F. (1983), ed. *Precious metals in the later medieval and early modern Worlds*, Durham, N.C.

Riedlmayer, A. (1981). "Ottoman-Safavid relations and the Anatolian trade routes: 1603–18," *TSAB*, V, 7–10.

Rivkin, E. (1965). "Marrano-Jewish entrepreneurship and the Ottoman mercantilist probe in the sixteenth century," Paper presented at the Third International Congress on Economic History, Munich, August.

Rogers, M. (1990–91). "To and from: aspects of Mediterranean trade and consumption in the 15th and 16th centuries," *ROMM*, 55.

Röhrborn, K. (1973). *Untersuchungen zur osmanischen Verwaltungsgeschichte*, Berlin.

Romano, C., A. Tenenti and U. Tucci (1970). "Venise et la route de Cap: 1499–1517," *MOI*, 109–32.

Roover, F.E. (1950). "The beginnings and the commercial aspects of the Lucchese silk industry," *CIBA*, LXXX, 2907–30.

Roth, C. (1949). *The House of Nasi: the dukes of Naxos*, Philadelphia.

Sadeddin, (1863). *Tācüttevārīkh*, I–II, İstanbul.

Safvet. (1328H/1910). "Yusuf Nasi," *TOEM*, XVI, 982–93.

(1912). "Bir Osmanlı Filosunun Sumatra Seferi," *TOEM*, X, 606–9.

(1332H/1913–14). "Nakşa (Naxos) Dûkalığı, Kiklad Adaları," *TOEM*, XXIII, 1444–57.

Şah, R. (1967). "Açi Padişahı Sultan Alâeddin'in Kanunî Sultan Süleyman'a Mektubu," *TAD*, V, 373–410.

404 / *The Ottoman state: Economy and society, 1300–1600*

Sahillioğlu, H. (1967). "Osmanlı İdaresinde Kıbrıs' 'in' İlk Yılı Bütçesi," *Bl*, IV (7–8), 1–34.
    (1968). "Bir Tüccar Kervanı" *BTTD*, IX, 63–70.
    (1970). "*Sıvış* Year Crises in the Ottoman Empire," in Cook, ed.
    (1973–74). "Yeniçeri Çukası ve II. Bayezid'in Son Yıllarında Yeniçeri Çukası Muhasebesi," *GDAD*, 2–3, İstanbul.
    (1974). *Mīzāniyāt al-Shām fi'l-karn al-Sādis 'Ashr, Al-Dār al-Muttahida li'l-Nashr*, Beirut.
    (1975). "İç ve Dış Ödemelerde Aracı olarak 'Kitabü'l-Kadı' ve 'Süfteceler,' " in Okyar and Nalbantoğlu, eds., pp. 103–44.
    (1983a). "1524–25 Osmanlı Bütçesi," in *Lûtfi Barkan'a Armağan*, pp. 415–52.
    (1983b). "The role of international monetary and metal movements in Ottoman history, 1300–1750," in Richards, ed.
    (1985). "Yemen'in 1599–1600 Yılı Bütçesi," in *Yusuf Hikmet Bayur Armağanı*, Ankara.
Sakazov, I. (1929). *Bulgarische Wirtschaftsgeschichte*, Berlin.
Sanders, J.T. (1949). *Balkan village*, Lexington, Ky.
Sanjian, A. (1965). *The Armenian communities in Syria under Ottoman domination*, Cambridge, Mass.
Sansovino, F. (1582). *Historia universale dell' origine e impero di Turchi*, Venice.
Sanuto, M. (1879–1903). *I diarii*, I–LVIII, Venice.
Schilbach, E. (1970). *Byzantinische Metrologie*, Munich.
Schiltberger, H. (1879). *Bondage and travels*, trans. by Telfer, London.
Schmucker, W. (1972). *Untersuchungen zu einigen bodenrechtlichen Konsequenzen der islamischen Eroberungsbewegung*, Bonn.
Schmutzler, E. (1933). *Altorientalische Teppiche in Siebenburgen*, Leipzig.
Scott, J.C. (1985). *Weapons of the weak, everyday forms of peasant resistance*, New Haven.
Seeck, O. (1903). "Colonatus," *Paulys Real-Encyclopedie der Classischen Altertums Wissenschaft*, by G. Wissowa, IV.
Selânikî, Mustafa. (1989). *Tarih-i Selânikî*, I–II, ed. by M. İpşirli, İstanbul.
Sella, D. (1968). "The rise and fall of the Venetian woolen industry," in Pullan, ed., pp. 88–105.
Serjeant, R.B. (1963). *The Portuguese off the South Arabian coast, Hadrami Chronicles*, Oxford.
Setton, K. (1976–84). *The Papacy and the Levant (1204–1571)*, I–IV, Philadelphia.
Shaw, S. (1962). *The financial and administrative organization and development of Ottoman Egypt, 1517–1798*, Princeton.
    (1968). *The budget of Ottoman Egypt, 1005–06/1596–97*, The Hague.
Sherley, T. (1936). *Discourse of the Turkes*, ed. by D. Ross, *Camden Miscellany*, XVI.
Shmuelevitz, A. (1984). *The Jews of the Ottoman Empire in the late fifteenth and the sixteenth centuries*, Leiden.
Sidi Ali Reis (1899). *Travels and adventures of the Turkish Admiral Sidi Ali Reis*, trans. and ed. by A. Vambery, London.
Silberschmidt, M. (1923). *Das Orientalische Problem zur Zeit der Entstehung des türkischen Reiches, 1381–1400*, Leipzig.

Singer, A. (1990). "Tapu Tahrir Defterleri and Kadı Sicilleri: A happy marriage of sources," *Tārih*, I.

Skilliter, S.A. (1977). *William Harborne and the trade with Turkey, 1578–82, a documentary study of the first Anglo-Ottoman relations*, London and Oxford.

Slicher van Bath, B.H. (1963). *The agrarian history of Western Europe*, A.D. 500–1850, London.

Smith, A. (1937). *An inquiry into the nature and causes of the wealth of nations*, ed. by I. Cannau, New York.

Sottas, J. (1938). *Les Messageries maritime de Venise aux XIVe et XVe siècles*, Paris.

Souza, F.Y. (1695). *Portuguese Asia*, I, London.

Soysal, M. (1976). *Die Siedlungs- und Landschaftsentwicklung der Çukurova*, Erlangen.

Spremić, M. (1971). "I tributi veneziani nel Levante nel XV secolo," *Studi Medievali*, V, 221–51.

Stahl, H.P. (1974). *Ethnologie de l'Europe du sud-est*, Paris and The Hague.

Steensgaard, N. (1972). *Carracks, caravans and companies*, Copenhagen.

Stein, E. (1924). "Untersuchungen zur spätbyzantinischen Verfassungsgeschichte," *MOG*, II, 88–105.

Stoianovich, T. (1960). "The conquering Balkan Orthodox merchant," *JEH*, XX, 234–313.

(1970). "Model and mirror of the pre-modern 'Balkan city'," *SB*, III.

Streuver, S. (1971), ed. *Prehistoric agriculture*, New York.

Stripling, G.W.F. (1942). *The Ottoman Turks and the Arabs*, Urbana.

Stromer, W. von (1974). "Die Schwarzmeer-und Levante-Politik Sigismunds von Luxemburg," *Miscellanea Charles Verlinden*, Rome, 601–11.

Subtelny, M.E. (1988). "Socioeconomic bases of cultural patronage under the later Timurids," *IJMES*, XX, 479–505.

Sümer, F. (1949–50). "XVI. Asırda Türk Aşiretlerine Umumî bir Bakış," *IFM*, XI, 509–23.

(1957). "Azerbaycan'ın Türkleşmesi Tarihine Umumî bir Bakış," *B*, fasc. 83, 429–47.

(1967). *Oğuzlar (Türkmenler): Tarihleri, Boy Teşkilâtı-Destanları*, Ankara.

Svoronos, N. (1959). "Recherche sur le cadastre byzantin et la fiscalité au XI et XII siècles: le cadastre de Thebes," *Bulletin de Correspondance Hellenique*.

Şahin, İ. et al. (1989). "Turkish settlements in Rumelia (Bulgaria) in the 15th and 16th centuries: town and village population," *IJTS*, IV (2), 23–40.

Şakiroğlu, M.H. (1982). "1521 Tarihli Osmanlı-Venedik Andlaşmasının Asli Metni," *TAD*, XII, 387–404.

Tabakoğlu, A. (1985). *Gerileme Dönemine Girerken Osmanlı Maliyesi*, İstanbul.

(1986). *Türk Iktisat Tarihi*, İstanbul.

Tadić, G. and R. Raci (1971). *La scala di Spalato e il commercio veneziano nei Balcani fra cinque seicento*, Venice.

Tadić, J. (1958). "Le port du Raguse et sa flotte au XVIe siècle," in M. Mollat, ed. *Travaux du Deuxième Colloque Internationale d'Histoire Maritime*, Paris.

(1961). "Le commerce en Dalmatie et à Raguse et la décadence économique de

Venise au XVIII siècle," in *Aspetti e cause della decadenza economica veneziana nel XVII s.: Atti*, Venice, pp. 238–74.

Taeschner, F. (1923). "Die geographische Literatur der Osmanen," *ZDMG*, LXXVII 31–80.

(1924–26). *Das anatolische Wegenetz nach osmanischen Quellen*, I–II, Leipzig.

(1929). "Beiträge zur Geschichte der Achis in Anatolien (14.-15. Jht.)," *Islamica*, IV(1), 1–47.

(1933). "Die Islamische Futuwwabünde," *ZDMG*, XII, 6–49.

(1960). "Akhī," *EI²*, I, 321–23.

Tafur, P. (1926). *Travels and Adventures, 1435–1439*, trans. by M. Letts, New York and London.

Tanoğlu, A. (1954). "İskân Coğrafyası," *TM*, XI, 1–32.

Tavernier, J.-B. (1970). *Voyages en Perse*, ed. by V. Monteil, Geneva.

Temimi, A. (1986). *La vie économique des provinces arabes et leurs sources documentaires à l'époque ottomane*, Zaghouan.

Tenenti, A. (1959). *Naufrages, corsaires et assurances maritimes à Venise 1591–1609*, Paris.

(1967). *Piracy and the decline of Venice, 1580–1615*, Berkeley.

Teixeira, P. (1902). *The travels of Pedro Teixeira*, in Hakluyt, IX, London.

Thiriet, F. (1957). "Les lettres commerciales des Bembo et le commerce vénitien dans l'empire ottoman à la fin du XV siècle." *Studi in onore di Armando Sapori*, Milan.

(1958–61). *Registres des délibérations du Senat de Venise concernant la Romanie*, I–III, Paris.

Thomaz, L.F.F.R. (1988). "Malaka et ses communautés marchandes au tournant du 16 siècle," in *Marchands et hommes d'affaires asiatiques dans l'océan et la Mer de Chine, 13e–20e siècles*, Paris, pp. 31–48.

Tietze, A. (1979–82). *Mustafa Ali's counsel for Sultans of 1581*, I: text; II: translation, Vienna.

(1983). "Mit dem Leben gewachsen: zur osmanischen Geschichtsschreibung in den letzen fünfzig Jahren," *Wiener Beiträge zur Geschichte der Neuzeit*, X, Vienna.

(1985), ed. *Habsburgisch-Osmanische Beziehungen*, Vienna.

Todorov, N. (1970). "Les études balkaniques en Bulgarie," *EB*, V, 649–72.

(1983). *The Balkan town, 1400–1900*, Seattle.

Tolmacheva, M.A. (1990). "The Cossacks at sea: pirate tactics in the frontier environment," *EUQ*, XXIV, 483–512.

Topping, P.W. (1949). *Feudal institutions as revealed in the assizes of Romania, the law-code of Frankish Greece*, Philadelphia.

Tucci, U. (1957). *Lettres d'un marchand vénitien: Andrea Berengo (1553–1556)*, Paris.

(1981). *Mercanti, navi, monete nel cinquecento veneziano*, Bologna.

Tunçdilek, N. (1960). "Sakarya Vadisinin İktisadî Tarihi Hakkında," *IFM*, XVII.

(1970). "Eine Übersicht über die Geschichte der Siedlungsgeographie im Gebiet von Eskişehir," *CED*, V.

Turan, O. (1958). *Türkiye Selçukluları Hakkında Resmî Vesikalar*, Ankara.

(1959). "L'Islamisation dans la Turquie du Moyen Âge." *SI*, X.

Turan, Ş. (1961). *Kanunî'nin Oğlu Şehzâde Bayezid Vak'ası*, Ankara.

(1966). "Sakızın Türk Hakimiyeti Altına Düşmesi," TAD, *IV*, 173–99.

(1968). "Venedik'te Türk Ticaret Merkezi (Fondaco de Turchi)," B, XXXII, 247–83.

Turnau, I. (1988). "The organization of the European textile industry from the thirteenth to the eighteenth century," *JEEH*, XVII (3), 583–602.

Udal'cova, Z.V. and K.V. Chvostova. (1981). "Les structures sociales et économiques dans la Basse-Byzance," *XVI. Internationaler Byzantinistenkongress, Akten*, II (2), Vienna.

Udovitch, A.L. (1962). "At the origin of the western *Commenda:* Islam, Israel, Byzantium?" *Speculum*, XXXVII.

(1970). *Partnership and profit in medieval Islam*, Princeton.

(1981), ed. *The Islamic Middle East, 700–1900: Studies in economic and social history*, Princeton.

Ülgener, S. (1965). *Tarihte Darlık Buhranları ve Iktisadî Muvazenesizlik*, İstanbul.

Uluçay, Ç. (1942). *Manisa' da Ziraat, Ticaret ve Esnaf Teşkilâtı*, İstanbul.

(1954–55). "Yavuz Sultan Selim Nasıl Padişah Oldu?" *TD*, VII, 117–42; VIII, 185–200.

Unat, F. and M. Köymen, (1987). *Cihannüma, Neşrî Tarihi*, I–II, Ankara.

Uzunçarşılı, I.H. (1943–44). *Kapıkulu Ocakları*, I–II, Ankara.

(1945). *Osmanlı Devletinin Saray Teşkilâtı*, Ankara.

(1947–59). *Osmanlı Tarihi*, I–IV, Ankara.

(1948). *Osmanlı Devletinin Merkez ve Bahriye Teşkilâtı*, Ankara.

(1949). "Türk-Ingiliz Münasebetlerine dair Vesikalar," B, XIII, 573–648.

(1963). *Ilmiye Teşkilâtı*, Ankara.

Vaas, E. (1971). "Türkische Beiträge zur Handelsgeschichte der Stadt Vać (Waitzen) aus dem 16. Jahrh.," *AOr*, XXIV (1), 1–39.

Vakalopoulos, A.E. (1963). "La retraite des populations grecques vers des régions éloignées montagneuses pendant la domination turque," *BSt*, IV, 265–76.

(1970–76). *Origins of the Greek nation*, I–II, New Brunswick.

Validi, A.Z. (1931). "Moğollar Devrinde Anadolu'nun İktisadî Vaziyeti," *THIM*, II.

Van Leur, J.C. (1955). *Indonesian trade and society, essays in Asian social and economic history*, The Hague.

Varthema, L. (1863). *The travels of Ludovico di Varthema in Egypt, Syria, Arabia, A.D. 1503 to 1508*, trans. by J.W. Jones and ed. by G.P. Badger, in Hakluyt, vol. 32, London.

Vasić, M. (1964). "Die Martolosen im osmanischen Reich," *Zeitschrift für Balkanologie*, II, 172–189.

Vaughan, D.M. (1954). *Europe and the Turk: a pattern of alliances*, Liverpool.

Veinstein, G. (1980). "La population du sud de la Crimée au début de la domination ottomane," in *Mémorial Ömer Lûtfi Barkan*, Paris, 227–249.

(1985). "Les çiftliks de colonisation dans les steppes du nord de la Mer Noire," *İFM*, XLI, 177–210.

(1987). "Une communauté ottomane: les Juifs d'Avlonya (Valona) dans la deuxième moitié du XVIe siècle." in G. Cozzi, ed., *Gli Ebrei di Venezia*, Milan.

(1989). "Prelude au problème cosaque," *CMRS*, XXX (3–4), 329–62.

Venezia e il Levante (1973). *Venezia e il Levante fino al secolo XV, Atti del Convegno internationale di storia della civiltà veneziana, 1968*, Florence.

Venzke, M. (1981). "The sixteenth century Ottoman sandjak of Aleppo: a study of provincial taxation," Ph.D. dissertation, Columbia University.

(1986). "Aleppo's Mālikāne-Dīvānī system" *JAOS*, 106 (3), 451–469.

Villain-Gandossi, C. (1983). *La Mediterranée aux XII–XVIe siècles*, London.

Viner, J. (1969). "Power versus plenty as objectives of foreign policy in the seventeenth and eighteenth centuries," in Coleman (1969a), pp 61–91.

Vryonis, S. (1971). *The decline of medieval Hellenism in Asia Minor and the process of Islamization from the eleventh through the fifteenth century*, Berkeley, Los Angeles and London.

(1975). "Nomadization and Islamization in Asia Minor," *DO*, XXIX.

(1976). "Laonicus Chalcocondyles and the Ottoman budget," *IJMES*, VII, 423–32.

(1981). *Byzantina kai metabyzantina*, II: *Studies on Byzantium, Seljuks and Ottomans, reprinted studies*, Malibu.

Vucinich, W.S. (1951). "Postwar Yugoslav historiography," *JMH*, XXIII, 41–57.

Wake, C.H.H. (1979). "The changing pattern of Europe's pepper and spice imports, ca. 1400–1700," *JEEH*, VIII, 361–403.

Wallerstein, I. (1974–80). *The modern world system*, I–III, New York.

Warburg, R. and G. Gilbar, (1984), eds. *Studies in Islamic society, contributions in memory of Gabriel Baer*, Haifa.

Werner, E. (1985). *Die Geburt einer Grossmacht–Die Osmanen (1300–1481)*, Weimar.

Willan, T.S. (1955). "Some aspects of English trade with the Levant in the sixteenth century," *EHR*, LXX.

Wirth, E. (1974). "Zum Problem des Bazars (Sūq, alçarşı)," *Der Islam*, LI (2), 203–60; LII (1).

(1990). "Alep et les courants commerciaux entre l'Europe et l'Asie du XII au XVI siècles," *RMMM* (55–56), 44–56.

Wittek, P. (1934). *Das Fürstentum Mentesche. Studie zur Geschichte westkleinasiens im 13.–15. Jahrhundert*, İstanbul.

Wolf, E. (1966). *Peasants*, Englewood Cliffs.

Wood, A.C. (1935). *History of the Levant Company*, repr., London.

Wright, L.W. (1935). *Ottoman statecraft: the book of counsel for Vezirs and Governors of Sarı Mehmed Pasha, the Defterdar*, Princeton.

Yahya b. Ādam. (1958). *Kitāb al-Kharādj*, ed. by Ben Shemesh, Leiden.

Yalçın, A. (1979). *Türkiye Iktisat Tarihi*, Ankara.

Yavuz, H. (1984). *Yemen'de Osmanlı Hakimiyeti*, İstanbul.

Yediyıldız, B. (1985). *Institution du Vaqf au XVIII siècle en Turquie, étude socio-historique*, Ankara.

Yetkin, Ş. (1972). *Historical Turkish carpets*, İstanbul.

Yücel, Y. (1988). *Osmanlı Devlet Teşkilâtına Dair Kaynaklar: Kitâb-i Mustetâb, Kitâbu Mesâlihi'l-Muslimîn ve Menâfi'i'l-Mu'minin, Hirzü'l-Mulûk*, Ankara.

Zachariadou, E.A. (1983). *Trade and Crusade, Venetian Crete and the Emirates of Mentesche and Aydın (1300–1415)*, Venice.

Zakythinos, D.A. (1948). *Crise monétaire et crise économique à Byzance du XIIIe au XVe siècle*, Athens.

Zinkeisen, J.W. (1840–63). *Geschichte des osmanischen Reiches in Europa*, I–VII, Hamburg and Gotha.

Zirojević, O. 1987: "Zur historischen Topographie der Heerstrasse nach Konstantinopel zur Zeit osmanischen Herrschaft," *EB*, II.

WEIGHTS AND MEASURES

These apply primarily to the period 1300–1600

ardabb, see *irdabb*
arşun of mason or architect = 0.758 m.
  for textiles, see *endaze*
  of *charshu* (bazaar) = 8 *rub⁾* = 16 *gireh* = 0.680 m. or 68.579 cm.

balla, balya (silk, Genoa) = 300 *libbra* = 90 kg.
bar (Albania) = 120 *okka* = 153.936 kg.
bardak = a cup (of butter, oil) = 10 *men* = 8.3 kg.
baril = a cask up to 20 *medre* (see below)
  (for wine, Genoa) = 78 kg.
barre = 6 *kile* (İstanbul) = 153.953 kg.
batman (standard) = 72 *lidre* = 7,200 *dirhem* = 23.094 kg.
  (Asia Minor, 19th cent.) = 7.694 kg.
  (Adana, 19th cent.) = 4.848 kg.
  (for silk, Mosul) = 800 *dirhem* = 2.566 kg.
  (Mosul, 19th cent.) = 9.236 kg.
  (Urfa, 19th cent.) = 2.309 kg.
  (Bursa, 15th cent.) = 15–16 *okka* = 19.245–20.528 kg.
  (Erzincan) 12 *nügi* = 1920 *dirhem* = 6.158 kg.
botte (large cask, Genoa) = 500 *libbra* = c.159 kg.
brasse (Epirus, for wood) = 1,862 *okka* = 2,388.946 kg.

camel-load = 200–300 kg.
caratello (Genoa) = 2 or 2.5 *baril* = c. 300 *liter*
carro (wheat) = 20 hectoliters
cartoutso (Preveza) = 150 *dirhem* = 481 g.
collo = 2.5 *kantar* = 141.122 kg.; see also *çuval*
çap (Van) = 36–45 *okka* = 46–57 kg.
  (Malatya) = 12 standard *kile* = 307.680 kg.

çaryek (iron) = 0.25 *männ* = 750 g.
  (for silk) = 0.25 *lidre*
  (Bursa, 1500) = 22.5 lidre = 8.661 kg.
çaryek = 0.25 *arşun* = 17 cm.
çeki (standard) = 4 *kantar* = 225.798 kg.
  (for wood) = 195 *okka* = 250 kg.
  (Ayvalık, 19th cent. = 100 *okka* = 128.29 kg.
  (Salonica, 19th cent.) = 135–40 *okka* = 173–79 kg.
  (İzmir, 19th cent.) = 180 *okka* = 230.896 kg.
  (for mohair, 19th cent.) = 4.564 kg.
  (for opium, 19th cent.) = 763 g.
  (for gold and silver) = 100 *dirhem* = 320 g., cf. *lidre*
  (Crimea, 18th cent.) = 150 *dirhem* = 480 g.
çetvirnik = 0.25 *kabal*
çift = a pair (of shoes, oxen, etc.)
çiftlik (of *raiyyet*) = a farm for one peasant household, varying between 60 and
  150 *dönüm*
  (Bursa) = a plot of land of 12 *mudluk*
  = a plot of land for 2,3 or 4 *mudd* of seed
çile, a bundle, hank or skein; one bundle of ten in a *pastav*
çit = a big basket (of fruits)
çubuk, see *dönüm*
çuval = 2 *kantar* = 112.898 kg.
  (of hazelnuts) = 2.5 *kile* = 74 cu. decimeter
  (of rice) = 18 *kile* = 46.184 kg.

dang, see *dirhem*
denk or *deng* = 50 *top* = 20 *çile* = 2 *pastav*; a horseload
deste = a bunch of 10 or 12
dirhem (Ottoman standard) = 16 *kirat* = 64 *dang* = 3.207 g.
  (Byzantine and early Islam) = 3.125 g.
  (Sharia or canonical) = 3.125 g.
  (in the Cairo copper measure) = 3.0898 g.
  (Dimishki) = 3.086 g.
  (Tabriz, in coinage down to 1700) = 3.072 g.
dizi = a string (of figs)
donkeyload = 60–80 kg.
dönüm (standard) = 4 *evlek* = 10 *nishan* = 100 *çubuk* = 1,600 sq. *arşun* =
  919.30 sq.m.
  (Republican period) = 1000 sq.m.

endaze = 0.650 m.
erlik, literally land for one man's work, term used in particular to measure vineyard, ricefield or garden; or a plot of land for cultivation of rice seed of 50
  okka or 2.5 *dönüm* of surface
evlek or *evleg* = division of a field for one day's work with oxen
  (grain) = 10 *kile* = 12.829 kg.

for measuring vineyard or garden = 0.25 of a *dönüm* (c. 400 sq. *arşun* or 254.8 sq.m.

fardello (silk, Genoa) = 252 *libbra* = 79.821 kg.; see also *yük*
farsah = 7,500 *arşun* = 5,685 m.
fuçı (standard, Akkerman, 1500) = 2 *sihaf* = 8 *kantar* = 226.596 kg.
  (caviar, Akkerman, 1500) = 52 *medre* = 225.798 kg.
  (wine, honey, etc.) = 40 *medre* = 89.810 kg.
  = 2 *karatil* = 4 *baril*

gaz or *gez* = 68.58 cm.
gaz-i shāhī = 95 cm.
girār or *garār* = 50 *okka* = 64.150 kg.
girbāl, see *kalbūr*.

harār, see *girār*
himl, see *yük*
horseload = *150–200 kg.*
hiyaşa (large) = 24 *kabal*
  (small) = 12 *kabal*

irdabb (grain, Egypt) = its size varied between 90 and 198 liters
'idl (silk, Bursa, 15th cent.) = 176 *lidre* = 68 kg.

kabal (grain, Serbia) = 65.664 kg.
  (grain, Serbia) = 140 or 144 *okka* = 180–185 kg.
  (minerals, Serbia) = 19 *okka*, 135 *dirhem* = 24.894 kg.
kabran (rice) = 10 *kile* = 128.294 kg.
kadeh = 0.25 of the standard *kile*.
kalbur or *galbur* = one-sixteenth of a *kile* = 1.604 kg.
kantar (Ottoman standard) = 100 *lodra* = 17,600 *dirhem* = 44 *okka* = 56.449 kg.
  (Arab lands) = 100 *ratl* = 45 kg.
  (Anatolia, 19th cent.) = 180 *okka* = 230.922 kg.
  (Syria, 19th cent.) = 200 *okka* = 242.400 kg.
  (Mardin, 19th cent.) = 240 *okka* = 307.896 kg.
  (Aleppo, 19th cent.) = 250 *okka* = 320.725 kg.
  (Genoa) = 100 *rottolo* = 47.600 kg.
kapa = one-sixty-fourth of a *kabal*
kara (dates, Basra) = 2,000 *okka* = 2,565.9 kg.
karataş (Erzurum) = 1 *okka* 100 *dirhem* = 1.603 kg.
karatil = a cask between 20 and 40 *medre*
  = 18 Genoese *libbra*
karta (Albania) = 80 *okka* = 102.640 kg.
kentiarion (Greek), see *kantar*
keylçe, see *kile*
kıbıl, see *kabal*

kırba = a leather sack (of implements)
kile = 4 *shinik* = 8 *kutu* = 50 *kadeh* or *kāse* = 5,000 *habbe*
   (standard) = 36 *liter* = 37 cu. decimeter
   (standard) = 20 *okka* = 25.659 kg.
   (İstanbul, 1500) = 18 *okka*, 350 *dirhem* = 24.215 kg.
   (Nicopolis) = 100 *okka* = 128.294 kg.
   (Sofia) = 50 *okka* = 64.122 kg.
   (Zištovi, Tirnovo) = 80 *okka* = 102.535 kg.
   (Hezargrad) = 60 *okka* = 76.976 kg.
   (İzladi) = 20 *okka* = 25.659 kg.
   (Yenibazar) = 44 *okka* = 56.449 kg.
   (Saraybosna before 1565) = 20 *okka* = 25.659 kg.
   (Saraybosna in 1565) = 22 *okka* = 28.224 kg.
   (İşkodra/Škodër in 1536) = 36 *okka* = 46.285kg.
   (İşkodra, in 1520) = 80 *okka* = 102.535 kg.
   (İpek) = 40 *okka* = 51.267 kg.
   (Mohac, 16th cent.) = 24 *okka* = 30.768 kg.
   (Pečuy 16th cent.) = 32 *okka* = 41.054 kg.
   (Hungary, July 1579) = 30 *okka* = 38.488 kg.
   (Balıkesir) = 16 *okka* = 20.527 kg.
   (Mardin, Adana) = 16 *okka* = 20.527 kg.
   (Bursa) = 12 *okka* = 15.395 kg.
   (Isparta) = 14 *okka* = 17.961 kg.
   (Edirne, rice) = 9 *okka* = 11.546 kg.
   (of rice) = 10 *okka* = 12.828 kg.
   (Crimea) = 4 standard *kile* = 85–90 *okka* = 109–15 kg.
   (Akkerman, 1500) = 40 *okka* = 51.317 kg.
   (Konya, Karaman) = 24 *okka* = 30.790 kg.
   (Ankara) = 24 *okka* = 30.790 kg.
   (Malatya, 1528) = 10 *okka* = 12.829 kg.
   (Diyarbekir, 1518) = 10 *okka* = 12.828 kg.
   (İzvornik) = 132 *okka*
   (Sarajevo) = 50, 64, 66 *okka*
   (Kilis, Bosnia) = 66 *okka* = 84,678 kg.
   (Depelen) = 38.484 kg.
kırat (canonical) = 0.2232 g.
   (Ottoman, standard) = 4 *dang* = 0.2004 g.
krina = 2 *kabal*
kutu = one-eighth of a standard *kile* = 4.62 decimeter

libbra sottile (Genoa) = 316.750 g.
   (Venice) = 301.230 g.
libbra grossa (Genoa) = 348.450 g.
   (Venice) = 357.749 g.
lidre (Seljukid and Ottoman, standard) = 100 *dirhem* = 320.7 g.
   (for silk) = 120 *dirhem* = 384.840 g.
   (silver, Serbia) = 115 *dirhem* = 368.805 g.

litra (Byzantine *argiriki litra*) = 333.333 g.
  (Byzantine *logariki litra*) = 322.320 or 319 g.
  (Epirus) = 427 g.
lodra = 176 *dirhem* = 0.564 kg.
lukna (grain, Smederovo) = 140 or 144 *okka* = 186.320 or 191.851 kg.
  (Braničevo) = 72 *okka* = 93.360 kg.
  (Serbia) = 4 Edirne *kile* = 92.372 kg.
luknića (Serbia) = 0.5 *lukna*
lukno, see *lukna*

māna (Pahlavi), see *männ*
männ (standard, Iran and Asia Minor) = 260 *dirhem* = 833 g.
  (heavy) = 12 *okka* = 15.388 kg.
  (light) = 6 *okka* = 7.694 kg.
  (Tabriz) = c. 3 kg.
  (Diyarbekir) = 580 *dirhem* = 1.860 kg.
  (Harput) = 1800 *dirhem* = 5.773 kg.
  (Egypt) = 812.5 g.
  (Syria) = 819 g.
  (Seljukid) = 977 g.
männ-i shāhī = 2 *männ* = c. 6 kg.
medre (caviar, Akkerman 1500) = 4.349 kg.
  (copper) = 5750 *dirhem* = 18.442 kg.
  (wine) = 8 or 9 *okka* = 10 or 11.5 kg.
  (wine, Euboea) = 40 *kuze* = 55 *okka* = 70.561 kg.
  (Serbia) = 10 *pinte* = 4 *okka* = 5.131 kg.
metrāta (wine, Genoa) = 2 *baril* = 156 kg.
miskäl (medieval Islam) = 4.233 g.
  (Ottoman, standard) = 1.5 *dirhem* = 24 *kirat* = 4.81 g.
mīzāne (from It. *mezzane*) = 0.5 *karatil*
moggio (wheat, Venice) = 4 *staio* = 333.2 *liter*
modios (Byzantine, Gallipoli) = 583.170 *liter*
moz (Albania) = 160 *okka* = 205.280 kg.
mudd (standard) = 20 *kile* = 1000 *kāse* = 100.000 *habbe* = 513.160 kg.
mudluk = a piece of land for one *mudd* of seed, or one-sixth, one-ninth or
  one-twelfth of a *çiftlik* according to the fertility of soil
muzur (salt, Salonica, 1478) = 45 *okka* = 57,726 kg.
  (rice, Silistre) = 150 *okka* = 192.420 kg.
  (Albania, 1583) = 32 *okka* = 41.049 kg.
  (salt, Anchialos) = 90 *okka* = 115.452 kg.

nügi = one-twelfth of a *batman* (silk)
  (standard) = 72 *miskal* = 346.392 g.
  (Mardin, Ergani, 1516) = 200 *dirhem* = 641.4 g.
  (silk, Erzincan, 1576) = 160 *dirhem* = 513.120 g.

okka (standard) = 4 *ratl rūmī* = 400 *dirhem* = 1.282945 kg.

(heavy, Mesopotamia) = 3.210 kg.
(Egypt, Jedda, 19th cent.) = 1.050 kg.
(Albania) = 1.412 kg.
onghion (Epirus) = 11 *dirhem* = 35.277 g.
onki (Serbia) = 6 *miskāl* = 28.863 g.

pad-män (Pahlavi), see *batman*
pastav (standard) = 10 *kile* = 50 *arşun* = 32.500 m.
  (Akkerman, 1500) = 21 *arşun* = 13,650 m.
polovaç = 0.5 *kabal*
poluknice (grain, Serbia) = 12 *okka* = 15.393 kg.

quintal (standard) = 80 *okka* = 102.616 kg.
  (goods from Europe) = 78 *okka* = 100.066 kg.
  (goods from England) = 39 *okka* = 50.033 kg.

ratl (standard) = 12 *Ūķiya* = 333.6 g.
  (İstanbul, 18th cent.) = 876 *dirhem* = 2.809 kg.
  (Jedda 19th cent.) = 113 *dirhem* = 360 g.
  (Mesopotamia, 19th cent.) = 1 *okka* = 1.283g.
  (Syria, 19th cent.) = 2 or 2.5 *okka* = 2.564 or 3.205 kg.
  (Sivas) = 1440 *dirhem* = 4.618 kg.
  (Ahlat and Nisibin, 11th cent.) = 300 *dirhem* = 962.1 g.
  (standard, *lidre/litra* in Arab lands) = 12 *ükiya* = 337.55 g.
  (Andalusia) = 453.3 g.
  (spices, North Africa, 11–12 cent.) = 140 *dirhem* = 437.5 g.
  (silk, Aleppo, 17th cent.) = 700 *dirhem* = 2.217 kg.
  (Syria) = 600 *dirhem* = 1.850 kg.
ratl folfoli (spices, Egypt) = 144 *dirhem* = 450 g.
ratl kebir (Egypt) = 160 *dirhem* = 500 g.
ratl rūmī (Anatolia) = 100 *dirhem* = 320.7 g.
ratl zāhiri (Syria) = 480 *dirhem* = 1.500 kg.
rottolo or *rotolo* (It.), see *ratl*
rub' = one-eighth of an *arşun* of *charshu* = 0.085 m.

sanduk or *sandık* = a wooden container of various sizes, 220 *okka* for figs, 60
  okka for opium
  a container of 88 *okka* at Akkerman, 1500
sapo or *sapi* (salt, clarified butter, Crimea) = 16 *keylçe* = 410.416 kg.
shihta or *shihsa* (minerals, Serbia) = 120 *verkçe* = 1313.280 kg.
shinik = 0.5 *kile*, also 0.25 *kile*
sihaf = a large bowl (of cheese)
  (Akkerman, 1500) = 4 *kantar* = 225.796 kg.
  = 0.5 *kantar* = 22 *okka* = 28.224 kg.
sikla (Epirus, wine) = 50 or 60 *okka*
som (silver, Golden Horde) = 5 oz.
somar = 12 İstanbul *kile* = 307.966 kg.
some (Iran, 15th cent.) = 155.615 kg.

staio (grain, Venice) = 83.3 *liter*
ster (Morea) = 110.802 kg.

tagār (heavy) = 1560 *okka* = 2000 kg.
  (Mosul) = 200 *okka* = 256 kg.
  (Crimea) = 150 *okka* = 192.420 kg.
  (Epirus) = 20 *okka* = 25 kg.
  (Iran) = 100 *männ* = 83.4 kg.
ṭāḳ = piece (fabric, turban)
tay (bale, bundle) = 700 pieces (of coarse cotton cloth)
tenbelīd = half a horseload = 300 *lidre* = 96.210 kg.
ton (Caffa, 1490) = 50–55 *arşun* = 32.50 to 35.75 m.
top = 20 *arşun* = 13 m.
  = 50 *arşun* = 32.5 m.
  (silk taffeta) = 100 *arşun* = 65 m.
  (silk *vale*) = 120 *arşun* = 78 m.
  (velvet) = 15 *arşun* = 9.75 m.
  (cotton cloth) = 13 *arşun* = 8.45 m.
tulum (Akkerman) = 1 or 1.5 *kantar*
turra see *çile*

ūḳiya = 27.8 g.
  (Arab Caliphate) = 72 *misḳāl* = 346.392 g.
  (Seljukid) = 100 *dirhem* = 320.7 g.
  (Syria, 19th cent.) = 66.5 *dirhem* = 213 g.
  (Maghreb, 19th cent.) = 10 *dirhem* = 32 g.; see also *raṭl* and *ünge*
ünge (silver, from Greek *ungia* or Latin *uncia*) = 6 *misḳāl* = 9 *dirhem* = 28.863 g.

varil see *baril* and *fuçı*
vakiyya see *okka*
verkçe see *shihta*
vezne (standard) = 120 *dirhem* = 384.84 g.
  = 30 *lidre* = 3600 *dirhem* = 11.545 kg.
  = 72 *lidre* = 23.09 kg. = 7,200 *dirhem*
  (Baghdad) = 78 *okka* = 100.066 kg.
  (Mosul) = 10 *okka* = 12.282 kg.
vezniye see *vezne*
vukiyye see *okka*

yük (silk, Bursa) = 405 *lidre* = 155.86 kg.
  (silk, Erzincan) = 10 *batman* = 61.574 kg.
  (mining, Serbia) = 4 *kile* = 102.636 kg.
  (silk, Mardin) = 8 *bogça* = 3 batman = 126.4 *okka* = 162.179 kg.
  = 1 *kabal* (cf. *lukna*)
  (minerals, Serbia) = 4 *kabal* = 99.576 kg.
  (Albania) = 120 *okka* = 153.936 kg.

zirāʿ see *arşun*

BIBLIOGRAPHY

Hinz, Walther (1955). *Islamische Masse und Gewichte umgerechnet ins metrische System*, Leiden.

İnalcık, Halil (1982). "Rice cultivation," *Turcica*, XIV, 69–141.

(1983). "Introduction to Ottoman metrology," *Turcica*, XV, 311–48.

(1984). " *Yük (Himl)* in the Ottoman silk trade, mining and agriculture," *Turcica*, XVI, 131–56.

GLOSSARY

These terms apply primarily to the period 1300–1600. They are listed here without transliteration as found in the text, and then in their original form in the transliteration alphabet used in *Encyclopaedia of Islam*, 2nd edition. Terms whose meaning is clear in the text or are to be found in an English dictionary are not included.

ABBREVIATIONS

A Arabic
G Greek
It Italian
L Latin

P Persian
Sl Slavic
Sp Spanish
T Turkish

ahdname (P. *'ahdnāma*): A written pledge under oath by the sultan granting a privilege, immunities or authority to a community, ruler or person.

akça or *akçe* (T): Ottoman silver coin, see volume 2, part V.

askeri (A. *'askarī*): (1) Literally "of the military class"; (2) All those groups belonging to the military or religious elite with complete tax exemption; a non-Muslim, when granted such a status by a royal diploma also becomes an *askeri*.

avarız (A. *'awāriḍ*): Extraordinary levies or services introduced by the state on emergency situations, mostly to support the navy; a certain number of households of *reaya* is registered as *avarız* tax units (*hane*).

azeb (A. *'azab*): (1) An unmarried young man; (2) An auxiliary footman recruited for the imperial army, whose expenses were met by the local people under the *avarız* system; (3) Fighting man in the navy.

bac (P. *bādj*): Market or transit dues taken on goods for sale per container.

barca or *barça* (Old Venetian:*barca*): Large ships with a capacity of 600 × 8 tons, equipped with guns.

bashtina (Sl): A peasant family farm in the Balkans corresponding to the Ottoman *raiyyet çiftlik*. The Ottomans retained the Slavic term with groups whose pre-Ottoman status and services were maintained.

bayt al-mal (A. *bayt al-māl*): (1) The public treasury; (2) An inheritance without heir, hence belonging to the public treasury.

bedestan or *bedesten* (T. from P. *bezzāzistān*): Synonym of *ḳayṣariyya*, or Roman *basilica*, a covered strong stone building in the center of a bazaar, where imports such as precious textiles, jewelry and arms are stored and sold; the leading merchants have shops, and trust money is preserved in a *bedestan*.

beg or *bey* (T): (1) Ruler in central Asian Turkish states and in the early Ottoman centuries; (2) Commander; (3) Title of the governor-commander of a *sancak*, or of a *ziamet*.

beglerbegi or *beylerbeyi* (T): Synonym of *mīrmīrān*: it designates the governor-general of a *beglerbegilik*.

beglerbegilik (T): Synonym of *eyālet* or *vilāyet*; all these terms stand for the Ottoman province, the largest administrative unit under a *beglerbegi*.

berat (A. *berāt*): A sultanic diploma bearing his official seal, *tughra*; also called *manshūr*.

bogasi or *bohassi* (T): A fine cotton textile manufactured in large quantities in Hamid-eli and exported to the Balkans, the Crimea, Hungary and other European countries.

Boz-Ulus (T): Turcoman tribal confederation in eastern Anatolia.

cebelü (T): A fully armed retainer of a *timar*, *ziamet* or *hass* holder.

Celali (T): Mostly *sekban* and *saruca* mercenary bands, which turned into bandit gangs when unemployed; they infested Anatolia during the period 1596–1610.

cihad (A. *djihād*): Islamic Holy War.

cizye (A. *djizya*): Islamic poll-tax imposed upon a non-Muslim male adult, originally at the rate of 12, 24 or 48 *dirhem* of silver according to his means; the three categories are: working poor man, those of medium income and the well-to-do in the tax registers; however, the Ottomans mostly levied the tax per household uniformly, at the rate of one gold, or its equivalent in silver *akça*.

çift-hane system: Under this system the state organized rural society and economy by appropriating grain-producing land and distributing it under the *tapu* system to peasant families (*hane*). Each family in theory in possession of a pair of oxen was given a farm (*çiftlik*) sufficient to sustain the family and to meet its tax obligations. This was the basic fiscal unit which the state endeavored to maintain. Families with less than half a *çift* or *çiftlik*, or unmarried peasants, were separately categorized as *bennak* and *mücerred* (or *kara*), and subjected to lower rates of *çift*-tax.

çiftlik (T): (1) Land workable by a pair (*çift*) of oxen, or a farm in which the fields make up a unit workable with a pair of oxen by a peasant family within the *çift-hane* system; (2) A big farm consisting of several *raiyyet çiftliks* under the control of an absentee landlord; (3) Any plantation-like agricultural exploitation.

çift-tax (T): A tax under the *çift-hane* system, assessing a peasant's labor capacity in combination with the land in his possession.

devşirme (T): Levy of boys from Christian rural population for services at the palace or the divisions of the standing army at the Porte; also see *kul*.

divan (P. *dīwān*): (1) Imperial council which functioned as the government and the supreme court in İstanbul: (2) The government; (3) The state treasury.

dolab (P. *dōlāb*): (1) A turning device; (2) Water wheel; (3) A vortex of affairs, bank.

Eflaks (Ottoman name for Vlachs): In the fifteenth century Vlachs, mostly pastoralist nomads, were organized for military or other public services under the Ottomans.

ekinlik (T): See *mezra'a*

emin (A. *amīn*): (1) A man of trust, a superintendent; (2) An agent of the sultan appointed to carry out a public work with financial responsibility; (3) The head of an office in the palace or government responsible to provide provisions, etc., or to supervise a public work.

eşkünci (T): (1) "Campaigner"; (2) Those *timar*-holders assigned to take part in military expeditions, or *eşkün*.

fay' (A. *fay'*): The inalienable property (land) of Muslims as a community, or of the Islamic state.

faytor (Sp. *feitor*): The representative in Basra of the Portuguese *capitaō* of Hormuz in the sixteenth century.

ferag (A. *farāgh*): Legal transfer of property or possession of rights in it.

fetva (A. *fatwā*): Formal written legal opinion by an authority in Islamic Law.

gaza (A. *ghazā*): Fighting for the cause of Islam, Holy War against the infidels.

gazi (A. *ghāzī*): A Muslim warrior fighting for Islam.

gulam (P. *ghulām*): See *kul*.

hane (P. *khāna*): (1) A house; (2) A family; (3) A household as tax unit.

harac (A. *kharādj*): (1) *Djizya*; (2) A combined land–peasant tax levied from a non-Muslim possessor of state-owned agricultural land; (3) Tribute in general; (4) a Tribute paid by a non-Muslim state to an Islamic state.

haraci land: In early Islam those state-owned agricultural lands left in the possession of non-Muslim farmers in return for a higher rate of tithes.

hasil (A. *ḥāṣil*): (1) Product, total revenue or income; (2) In the *tahrir* registers the total sum of the revenues estimated for a village or other units.

hass or *hassa* (A. *khāṣṣ*): (1) Belonging to a member of the elite or to the sultan; (2) Those prebends pertaining to the elite or to the sultan; (3) A farm or vineyard assigned to the direct control of a *timar*-holder.

havass-i humayun (A. *khawāṣṣ-i humāyūn*): Sources of revenue in the *timar* system reserved for the sultan, actually for the central state treasury; *havass* are collected directly by the sultan's agents or through tax-farms.

hawala (A. *ḥawāla*): An assignation of a fund from a distant source of revenue by a written order, used in both state and private finances.

hayduk or *haydud*: (1) Originally a Hungarian irregular foot-soldier; (2) A brigand.

hutba (A. *khutba*): Sermon delivered in the mosque by the *khaṭīb* or leader of the community at the Friday service or at religious festivities; the custom was established to mention the name of the ruling sovereign at the prayer; Ottoman sultans appointed shaykhs of religious orders as *khaṭīb*s to major mosques; the mentioning of the name became a symbol of the recognition of the legitimacy of his sovereignty.

icaratayn (A. *idjāratayn*): The "dual" lease system in which the tenant of a
    vakf property paid, first, an immediate substantial amount to dispose of the
    property and then a second monthly rent; under the system the renter
    enjoyed extensive possession rights on the property.

imam (A. *imām*): (1) Prayer leader; (2) A successor of the Prophet, Caliph; (3)
    The chief of a Muslim state.

imaret (A. ʿimārat): Soup kitchens attached to *vakf* complexes.

irsalat or *irsaliyye* (A. *irsālāt, irsāliyya*): (1) Goods destined for the consumption
    of military units, or shipments belonging to the state; (2) Revenue in cash
    sent to the central treasury from the surplus of a province.

ispence (originally Sl, *jupanića*): Poll-tax paid to feudal lord in pre-Ottoman
    Serbia; continued under the Ottomans as a customary tax, it is mostly
    included in *timar* revenue.

istimalet (A. *istimālat*): Literally to make someone inclined to accept; an Ottoman
    term for winning over the population in conquered lands or enemy territory.

kapan (A. *ḳabbān*): (1) A large public weighing device; (2) Caravanserai or mart
    in which such a device is placed to weigh goods and collect dues.

kaza (A. *ḳādā*): (1) Jurisdiction of a kadi; (2) An administrative unit correspond-
    ing to the kadi's jurisdiction in a province.

Kara-Ulus (T): A Kurdish tribal confederation in eastern Anatolia.

kethüda (P. *katkhudā*): (1) A steward; (2) The head or member of the governing
    body of a military, professional or social group, elected by the group and
    certified by the local kadi or the sultan.

kılıç (T): (1) A sword; (2) Registered *timar* unit, not to be divided and assigned
    in parts.

kirbas (Sanskrit *karpassa*): A coarse cotton cloth manufactured in various regions
    in Asia Minor and exported to the Balkans and Black Sea countries in great
    quantities.

kışlak (T): Winter pastureland.

Kızılbaş (T): (1) Literally "red-head," it designated Turcoman soldiers in Anatol-
    ian emirates who wore red caps; (2) A member of the sect in central and
    eastern Anatolia, mostly of Turcoman origin, following heteredox beliefs,
    often rebellious against the centralist and orthodox Sunni policy of the Otto-
    man state.

kul (T): (1) A slave; (2) A tax-paying subject of the state (cf. *reaya*); (3) *kuls*
    (plural) designate the sultan's servants and soldiery at the Porte.

kulluk (T): (1) The state of a slave; (2) Labor service, or its monetary compensa-
    tion, which an Ottoman subject owes to the state (cf. *çift*-tax); (3) Special
    services and dues a peasant with state-owned land had to give to the state
    or *timar*-holder (cf. *çift resmi*).

levend (P. *lawand*): Privateers who joined the Ottoman navy with their ships
    when their services were needed.

liva (A. *liwā*): see sancak

maktu (A. *maḳṭūʿ*): A lump sum agreed upon for payment of rent or taxes.

malikane (P. *mālikāne*): Belonging to a landlord.

martolos: A pre-Ottoman group of militia maintained by the Ottomans, mostly
    serving on the frontier for raids and intelligence in the neighboring country.

mashlah (A): A large cloak of camel wool made in Arabia.

mevat (A. *mawāt*): Legal term for "dead" land; a "dead" land is either one abandoned and left uncultivated for a long time or wastelands such as deserts, forests or marshes.

mezra'a (A. *mazra'a*): (1) A field under cultivation; (2) A large farm with no permanent settlement; it may be originally a deserted village or land reclaimed by a nearby village.

millet (A. *milla*): A community, the religious autonomous organization of which is formally recognized by the Islamic state; *millets* in the Ottoman Empire obtained their own charters in the reform period in the 1860s, which extended their autonomous status and gave their organization a formal secular character.

miri (P. *mīrī*): Belonging to the ruler or to the state.

muaf (A. *mu'āf*): Exempt from taxation.

mudaraba (A. *mudāraba*): Corresponding to the Western *commenda*, *mudaraba* is a contract between a person providing capital and a caravan trader; they shared the profit equally.

muhtesib (A. *muhtasib*): An inspector helping the kadi of a town to see that the Muslims' conduct in their public lives and transactions conformed to the prescriptions of Islamic Law; he was particularly active in the bazaar area, inspecting weights and measures, prices and the quality of goods.

mukataa (A. *mukāta'a*): (1) A renting contract, tax-farm; (2) The rent itself; (3) A source of revenue estimated and entered into the registers of the finance department as a separate unit.

mukataalu (T): State-owned land leased under the *mukataa* system.

mukus (A. *mukūs*): (1) Customs or excise duty; (2) All kinds of small dues and taxes outside those approved by Islamic Law.

mülk (A. *mulk*): Freehold ownership as opposed to state ownership; see *miri*.

müsellem (A. *musallam*): (1) Exempt from taxation; (2) A group of militia of *reaya* origin, enjoying various tax exemptions in return for military service.

musha' (A. *mushā'*): (1) Collective ownership; (2) Communal land.

narh (P. *narkh*): The maximal price list on necessities, periodically established by the local kadi.

nişancı (T): A member of the imperial council responsible for the chancery, checking all diplomas and putting the imperial seal (*nishan*) on them; responsible in particular for the administration of *miri* land and the *timar* system.

nüzul (A. *nuzl*): (1) Food served to a guest; (2) A tax, mostly in kind, imposed upon the fiscal units of households for provisioning the army or navy, see also *avarız*.

ocak (T): (1) Hearth; (2) The unit of households in military organizations such as *yaya* or *voynuk*; (3) Corps or the whole body of a military organization such as *Yeniçeri Ocağı*.

ortakçılık (T): Sharecropping; as opposed to *reaya* in possession of land under the *tapu* system, a sharecropper cultivates land belonging to another person who as a rule supplies means of production and sometimes also shelter, and shares the product equally; an *ortakçı kul* is a slave working for his owner on the same basis.

paroikoi (G): A dependent peasant, serf; in Turkish texts *parikoz*, in Italian *parici*.

pishkesh (P. *pīshkesh*): A gift presented to a superior as a symbol of recognition of his authority and protection.

poliçe (It. *polizza*): A letter of credit.

proniar (G): Provincial military elite in the Byzantine Empire, enjoying a prebend in return for military or administrative service, as in the Ottoman *timar* system.

raiyyet (A. *raʿiyya*): See *reaya*.

rakaba (A. *raḳaba*); (1) Eminent domain; (2) *proprietas nuda*; (3) State ownership (of land); see also *miri*.

reaya (A. *raʿāyā*): All those groups, Muslim or non-Muslim, outside the *askeri* elite, engaged in economic activities and thus subject to taxes.

rikab (A. *riḳāb*): See *rakaba*.

salgun (T): See *avarız*.

sancak (T): A sub-province; administrative unit under a *sancak-begi* (*beyi*); a *beglerbegilik* is divided into several *sancaks*.

sekban (P. *sagbān*): (1) Literally a keeper of hounds; (2) In the Janissary army: divisions originally of the keepers of the sultan's hounds, who were incorporated to the corps of Janissaries under Mehmed II; (3) A particular mercenary organization, equipped with muskets, organized as companies of 50 to 100 under a Janissary officer; in the sources, usually mentioned together with a similar group called *saruca*.

serbestiyet (P. *sarbastiyyet*): (1) Freedom, full immunity; (2) Full immunity from government control in *vakf* and *temlik* lands.

Shi'i (A. shīʿī): As opponents of the Sunni, the Shi'is follow the *shīʿa*, claiming that the legitimate imamate or the religio-political leadership belonged after the death of Muhammad to ʿAlī, the cousin and son-in-law of the Prophet, and to his descendants. In general, Shi'is believe that with the Shi'i Imam divine revelation and mediation between God and His creatures continues, and until the day the Mahdi, or the hidden Imam, reappears the *mudjtahids*, as spokesmen of the hidden Imam, have the supreme religio-political authority over the Islamic community. In Iran, with the accession of the Safavids in 1501, such a regime was believed to be achieved. This gave the old rivalry between the Ottoman state and Iran a religio-ideological character as a fight between Sunnis and Shi'is. The rivalry became particularly fierce when the Safavids were supported by the Kızılbash Turcomans of Asia Minor throughout the sixteenth century.

simsar (L. *censarii*): The head of brokers in a bazaar.

sipaşı (P. *sipāhī*): (1) A mounted soldier; (2) A member of the noble class; (3) A member of the cavalry divisions at the Porte; (4) The lowest rank in the provincial *timariot* (see *timar*) army.

sipahi-oğlanları (T): The top division among the six salaried cavalry divisions at the Porte.

subaşı (T): (1) Commander, originally a compound of *sü*, soldier and *bash*, head; (2) In the Ottoman provincial administration it designates a commander in the *timariot* army above *sipahi* and below *sancak-begi*; (3) An agent appointed by a governor to take care of the collection of his revenues and other resposibilities; see *voyvoda* and *ziamet*.

Sunni (A. sunnī) or *ahl al-sunna*: Those Muslims who refrain from deviating from the *Sunna*, or the dogma and practice as established by the Prophet, the companions (*aṣḥāb*) and the traditions of the community. Sunnis consider Shi'is as heretics deviating from the *Sunna*. Turkish states, including the Ottoman state, made Sunnism a state policy, which entailed serious social and political consequences and brought the government into a fierce struggle with the Turcoman Kızılbash sect in Asia Minor in the sixteenth century.

sürgün (T): (1) A term for the Ottoman method of relocation or forcibly deporting and settling population from one region to another; (2) An individual subjected to this operation.

tafviz (A. *tafwīḍ*): (1) To give full power and authority; (2) Full possession rights entrusted to a peasant on state-owned land.

tahrir (A. *taḥrīr*): (1) Enregisterment; (2) Ottoman system of periodical surveying of population, land and other sources of revenue. Survey registers called *defter-i khākānī* were of two kinds: *mufassal*, registering the sources of revenue "in detail," and *idjmāl* that register only their distribution among the military.

tahtacı (T): A generic name for the Yörük Turcoman tribes on the Taurus mountain range who were occupied with cutting and trading in timber (*tahta*); in eastern Asia Minor they are known as *ağaç-eri* or "woodmen."

taife (A. *ṭā'ifa*): See *millet*.

tamga: See *bac*.

Tanzimat (A. *Tanzīmāt*): (1) Reforms; (2) Radical Ottoman westernizing reforms introduced in the period 1839–76.

tapu (T): (1) An act of homage; (2) Permanent patrilineal lease of state-owned land to a peasant family head in return for his pledge to cultivate it continuously and meet all the obligations in tax or services; (3) The title deed certifying *tapu* rights.

tapulu (T): A state-owned farm leased to a peasant family head under the special conditions of the *tapu* system.

tasarruf (A. *tasarruf*): (1) Free disposal; (2) The exercise of actual possession rights on state-owned land.

temlik (A. *tamlīk*): Sultan's grant to a member of the elite of state-owned land as freehold property with complete tax immunity and autonomy.

timar (P. *tīmār*): (1) Any kind of care; (2) A prebend acquired through a sultanic diploma, consisting as a rule of state taxes in return for regular military service, the amount of which conventionally was below 20,000 *akça*: also see *sipahi, hass* and *ziamet*.

ulufe (A. *'ulūfa*): Salary in cash paid, as a rule, to the military.

umma (A. *umma*): The Muslim community as a whole.

urfi or *örfi* (A. *'urfī*): (1) Customary; (2) Based on the sultan's command; (3) State taxes mostly based on pre-Ottoman dues confirmed by the sultan, as in the term *rusum-i 'urfiyya* or *takalif-i urfiyya*.

uthmani (A. *'uṣmānī*): (1) Of the Ottoman sultan; (2) The Ottoman silver coin *akça* or *akçe*, as called in Arab lands.

vakf (A. *wakf*, plural *awḳāf*): Synonym of *hubs*, namely a pious foundation or an endowed thing, as a rule real estate, but sometimes also an amount of cash, which "while retaining its substance yields a usufruct and of which the owner has surrendered his power of disposal with the stipulation that the yield is used for permitted good purposes" (*Shorter Encyclopaedia of Islam*, p. 624).

valā' (A. *walā'*): (1) Legal control; (2) A master's legal rights on the inheritance of a manumitted slave.

vekil (A. *wakīl*): (1) An agent; (2) A proxy.

voynuk or *voynug* (Sl. *voynik*, warrior, soldier): A pre-Ottoman militia from the peasant population of Slavic states in the Balkans, maintained by the Ottomans.

voyvoda or *voyvode* (Sl): (1) Slavic title for prince, used in particular for the rulers of Wallachia and Moldavia; (2) A military agent appointed by a governor to take care of the collection of his revenues in the *kada* area; the title *subaşı* is sometimes used instead.

yasakiyye (T): Fee for Janissary in charge of enforcing law.

yaya (T): (1) Footman; (2) Peasant militia organized in *ocak*.

Yörüks: A bureaucratic name for Turcoman pastoralist nomads when they came in the territories controlled by the Ottomans, mostly in western Anatolia and the eastern Balkans.

yurt (T): An area reserved for a pastoralist nomadic group with summer and winter pasturelands.

Ziamet (A. *ziʿāmat*): (1) Military leadership; (2) A prebend bestowed by a sultanic diploma to the commander of *timariot sipahi*s in a district, conventionally from 20,000 to 100,000 *akça*; synonym of *subaşılık*.

ं

INDEX

In the organization of this index, the modern Turkish alphabet is followed, according to which ç comes after c, ş after s, ü after u, and ö after o.

Abbas, shah of Iran (1588–1629) 22, 223, 227–28, 230, 245–50, 351, 353, 377
Abdülhamid II (1876–1909) 21
Abu'l Barakat, sherif of Mecca 322
Abussu'ud Efendi, Sheyhülislam 111–14, 148
Abyssinia, 29, 321, 324
Acre 225, 369
Aden, India trade 320, 321, 323–27, 329, 332–36, 347
administration:
    imperial 45–48, 77–79, 88–95, 103–18, 132–42, 195–208
    provincial 84–88
    beglerbegilik 13, 115, 304, 337
    sancak 13, 14, 34, 63, 92, 115, 138, 141, 172, 291, 294, 305, 335, 337
    kada/kaza 138, 141, 171
    sale of offices 74–75
local dynasts 74, 155
Adrianople 11, 19, 262, 301
    see also Edirne
Adriatic Sea
    silk trade 232, 242, 243
    Balkan trade 256, 261 263–69
Aegean Sea 192, 245
agriculture 103-8, 120-30, 131–42, 143–53, 155–57
tools 297, 317
field system 155–57
cereal farming and trade 30, 71, 95–98, 106, 108, 110, 113, 130, 135, 138, 160, 162, 164, 167,171–72, 176, 179–83, 185–86, 206, 243, 257, 272, 273, 295, 308, 351
    see also peasant
ahdname, see capitulations
Ahyolu (Anchialos) 62, 211, 212
Akdağ, Mustafa 30, 183–84
akıncı 22; *see also* military organization

Akkerman (Moncastro) 56, 275, 291–93
    settlement 169–70
    sancak of 294–95
    transit center 179, 185, 186, 275, 291–93
    silk trade 228, 235
    Lwow route 276-78, 285–91
Akkoyunlu 21, 252
Akşehir 317
alaca 56; *see also* cotton: cloth
Albania 32, 113, 184, 229, 230, 258, 366
    Ottoman conquest 12, 13, 17
    trade 265, 268
Aleppo 353
    provisioning 161
    silk trade 224, 244–45, 248–50, 355
    spice trade 239, 317, 344–47, 348, 351
    India trade 338–40, 356, 359
    English trade 365, 367–68, 370
    Dutch trade 373, 375
    foreign merchant communities 191
    state revenue 56–57, 73
    mints 57
    population movements 166
Alexandretta (Iskenderun) 219, 349
Alexandria (Iskenderiye) 180, 235, 246, 277, 368, 376
    naval base 88, 94
    spice trade 315–17, 319, 329, 341, 343, 344, 347, 348, 355, 356, 358
Algeria 84, 94
Algiers 375 *see also* administration: local dynasts
alum 38, 40, 341, 365; *see also* textile
Amasra 56
Amasya 32, 127, 129, 135, 223, 229
    silk industries 219, 229
Amir b. Dawud, sultan of Adem 326
Amsterdam 357
Ana 339
Anazeh tribes 32; *see also* tribes

animal husbandry 37–38, 40–41, 155, 309
  sheep breeding 37, 38, 57, 160, 161, 163,
    166, 170, 292, 293, 295, 352
  stock breeding 64
  cattle 125, 166, 169, 170, 204, 288, 292,
    293, 295, 304, 310
Ankara 12, 32, 34, 96, 198, 223, 235, 246
  mohair industry 240
Antakya (Latakia-Antioch) 347
Antalya 26, 34, 39, 95, 197, 219, 222, 315,
  317, 319
Antwerp 233, 348, 364, 365, 366, 373–74
appanage 141–42
Arabian peninsula 352
Armenian community 18, 224
  in Istanbul 274
  in Crimea 288
  merchants 278, 286, 291, 304, 365, 371
army, *see* military organization
arpalık, 141–42
artisan, *see* craftsmen
askeri 16, 17; *see also* military organization
  and administration
astar 275; *see also* cotton: cloth
astarhal 309; *see also* woolen cloth
Astrakhan 222, 229, 280, 315, 330
Aşık Paşazade, historian 95
Athens 187, 369
Atjeh 20, 327–31, 345–47
Augsberg 355–57
Austria
  Ottoman wars 23, 24
  trade 188, 298, 303, 304, 307–11
  Levant Company 304
  see also Habsburg Empire
avarız-i divaniyye 16, 24, 98, 113, 135,
  154 n 16
  houses (*avarızhane*) 101 n 56
  see also taxes: extraordinary *and*
    imperial campaign(s)
Avlona (Vlorë) 232, 233, 238, 239, 242,
  256, 265, 266–69, 345
ayan 155; *see also* administration: local
  dynasts
Ayas (Layas) 315
Ayasoluk (Altoluogo-Ephesus) 193, 223,
  315
Aydın 32, 34, 40, 63, 195, 257
azeb/azab 89, 92–93, 101 n 34, 306
Azemini 227, 243, 345; *see also* Iran
Azerbaijan 22, 24, 40, 96, 224, 230, 353
Azov (Tana) 180, 182, 219, 222, 276, 278,
  315, 317, 375

Bab al-Mandab 320, 321, 323, 324
Babur 321
bac 198, 201, 204; *see also* market: dues

Baghdad 73, 84, 219, 315, 332, 336
  taxation 97
  Iranian occupation 248–49
  trade 248, 339
  India trade 350–53
Bahadur Shah, sultan of Gujerat 325–26
Bahrain 206, 246, 315, 350–52
  Portuguese–Ottoman conflict 336–38
Balat (Palatia-Milet) 38, 223, 264
Balkan peninsula 71, 79, 156, 194, 242,
  307, 316
  conquest 11–16
  population movements 26, 27, 32, 35
  trade 232, 256–69
Banat 304
Bandar-Abbas 246, 249, 351, 353
banking 48, 66, 213–14; *see also* credit *and*
  loans
Bantam 347
Banyas 347
Barkan, O. L. 27–29, 35, 106, 207
başbakıkulu 64; *see also* tax collection
bashtina 136, 148; *see also* peasant: farm
Basra 84, 201, 327
  Portuguese–Ottoman struggle 336–40
  spice trade 57, 346, 347–55
Bayezid I (1389–1402) 12, 16, 18, 39, 93
Bayezid II (1481–1512) 19–20, 92, 194,
  197, 228, 232
bazaar 18, 46, 85, 175, 307, 340; *see also*
  market
bazdar 91; *see also* military organization:
  auxiliary troops
bedel 73; *see also* military organization
bedestan 79, 98, 265, 274; *see also* market
Bedouin 156, 165, 339
  settlement 156
begler-begi 13, 84, 121
  spice trade 315, 316, 341, 343, 344
  trade 364, 376
Belgrade 13, 18, 98, 185, 304, 306
  trade center 265–66
  population movements 165
bennak 149–50; *see also* taxes: land
berat 75; *see also* merchant
Bessarabia 169
Bilecik 229
Birecik (al-Bira) 339
biro 306; *see also* administration, local
Bitlis 68
  trade 224
Black Sea 35, 52, 79, 179, 181, 192, 212
  trade zone 55, 57, 95, 156, 182, 185–87,
    197, 375
  Eastern Europe 271–311
  silk trade 230, 239
  spice trade 315, 316, 342

boğası 275, 297; *see also* cotton: cloth
Bohemia 277
Bolu 34
Bosnia 26
  conquest 13, 17, 73–74, 307
  gold and silver mines 58–60, 256,
    258–60
  landholding 73–74, 113, 164
  trade 226, 230, 231, 243, 268
  commercial rise 265–66
Bozcaada (Tenedos) 424
Boz-Ulus 32, 36
Brăila 180, 186, 296, 299
Brașov 289, 296, 298–303
Braudel, Fernand 28, 30, 341, 354
brigandage 41, 159
Bruges 218
Buda(pest) 304, 305, 306, 308–9
budget: imperial 77–79
  deficits 98–100
  provincial 83–88
  pious foundations 79–83
Bulgaria
  trade 257
  industry 264
  annexation 299
bullion 44
  flow 52, 58, 198, 338, 342, 354; *see also*
    money
Bursa 19, 53, 160
  sericulture 19, 50, 179
  Iranian silk 56
  trade 196–98, 200, 202, 203, 206, 208,
    218–30, 243–50, 265, 267, 277, 278,
    369
  Florentines in 230–43
  Brașov route 295–99
  Hungary pepper route 299–304
  Lwow route 285–91
  India trade 317, 319, 339, 341, 343, 345,
    355
Byzantine Empire 11, 32, 163, 190, 195,
    198, 210, 230, 257, 272, 316
  influence 95, 103, 105, 167, 188, 199
  Ottoman conquest 11–13, 15
  landholding and taxation 16, 70, 71, 91,
    121, 164
  control of the Black and Aegean Seas
    271–74

caba 149, 150; *see also* land: taxes
Cadiz 356
Caffa (Kefe) 32, 55, 56, 196
  trade 179, 180, 198, 200, 203
  silk trade 222, 223, 225, 226, 228, 235,
    272

Crimean khanate 275–79
  Black Sea trade 280–83, 286–88, 290,
    296
  India trade 315, 317, 375
  Kiev–Muscovy route 276–85
Cairo 32
  Mamluks 20, 87
  trade 86, 191, 249
  India trade via 315, 316, 319, 335, 341,
    354
  spice trade 345–47, 355
Calicut 319, 329, 339, 341, 346–47
camel: transport 38–39, 62–63, 345
  hair 351–52
canbaz 91; *see also* military organization:
  auxiliary troops
Candarids 17; *see also* Turcoman:
  principalities
Cape of Good Hope 341, 371–72
capitulations 48, 50–52, 188–91, 192, 199,
  222, 224, 225, 232–33, 242, 245, 269,
  273, 274, 304, 344, 348, 355, 365–75
  history 192–95
  ahdname 189
caravan trade 39, 195, 219, 222–24, 237,
  242, 246, 256, 261, 262, 265, 276, 277,
  286, 296, 317, 319, 338–40, 351–52,
  369
  see also transportation
caravanserai 79, 83, 191, 196, 202, 219, 317
carpets 38, 43 n 51, 364
  and rugs 38, 240
Casa da India 357, 358
Caspian Sea 219, 222, 229, 330
Caucasus 23, 275–76
cavalry 65, 68, 73, 90–91, 93, 127, 141
  see also sipahi
Cebele 347
cebelü 88–90; *see also* military
  organization: auxiliary troops *and*
  sipahi
Celali rebellions 24, 30–32, 96, 281; *see*
  also migration: "great flight"
Cenghis Khan(ids) 95, 272
Cephalonia 364
cere-hor 93; *see also* military organization
Chayanov, A.V. 143–45, 147
China 38
  imports from 57, 315
  silk 218, 222
Chios 225, 356
  trade 37, 55, 197, 245, 287, 347, 356
  silk trade 226, 239, 241, 245, 364, 365,
    369
  Genoese entrepôt 271, 272, 278, 372
Christians in the Ottoman Empire 41, 75,
  94, 164, 267

Christians in the Ottoman Empire –
  (*contd.*)
  reaya 16–17, 268
  militia 26, 93
  population 25–29, 30, 280
  poll-tax 66–69
  levy of children 16, 27
  corsairs 192, 261
  merchants and trade 246, 252
  exemption from taxes 306
Cilicia 28, 37; *see also* Çukurova
Circassia 31
cizye 24, 25, 68–69, 104, 152; *see also*
  poll-tax
Cochin 319
coffee
  colonial production 353
  trade via Cairo 359
commenda partnership 47, 48, 209; *see
  also mudaraba*
Comeni 272
Constanţa (Galatz) 180
Constantinople 12, 15, 17, 18, 32, 195,
  224, 231, 237, 258, 272–74; *see also*
  Istanbul
consul 190–92, 231, 244, 303, 364, 373,
  374, 377; *see also* merchant
  communities
Cook, Michael 30
copper 55, 56, 299, 311, 329, 370
  mines 55
  mint 57
Coron 325, 377
corsair 188, 375, 376–77; *see also* trade
Cossacks 291, 293–95
cotton: production 38, 161–62, 171
  trade 40, 63, 223, 297, 299, 317, 340,
    347–56, 359, 364, 365, 370, 375
  raw 37, 49, 86, 126, 350, 353, 356
  cloth 50, 55, 56, 240, 275, 296, 297, 351,
    353, 354, 356
  yarn 352, 370, 375
craftsman 16, 32, 47, 53, 94, 329, 370; *see
  also* guilds *and* manufacturing
credit 48, 51, 64, 66, 204, 207–8, 226, 235,
  236, 241, 247, 268, 288
  letter of 208
  see also money: usury
Crete 113, 212, 230, 364, 369, 376
Crimea, Khanate 18, 32, 63, 195, 271, 285,
  288, 291, 330
  and the Genoese 275–78
  refugees 31
  Tatars 95, 293
Crusaders 12, 13, 34
currants 364, 377
customs: regulations 51, 237, 277, 317

zones 66, 195–204, 210, 347
houses 86, 209, 211
registers 228, 298
duties 49, 56, 58, 64, 65, 85, 222, 238,
  246, 247, 251, 259, 260, 268, 303, 304,
  324, 333, 335, 348, 350, 375
gümrük 198
rüsum 70, 135
tariff 199, 201, 268, 343
toll 352
and capitulations 187–95, 368, 375
see also taxes *and* trade *and bac*
Cyprus 113, 133, 194, 225, 347

Çanakkale 197
Çepni 32; *see also* Turcoman
çift-hane system 30, 45, 107, 108, 110, 125,
  138, 139, 145–49, 156, 157, 159, 161,
  168, 172, 174, 185
  historical perspective 143–45
  fiscal basis 149–53
  subdivision of *çift* units 30
  see also landholding
çift-resmi 70, 108; *see also* taxes: land
çiftlik 91, 92, 108, 109, 111, 135, 136, 140,
  157, 164, 166, 168–71, 184
  size 146–48
  indivisibility 148–49
  see also peasant farm
Çorum 275
Çukurova 161, 162

Dalmatia 26, 79, 265, 297
Damascus 196, 201
  revenues 65, 73, 85
  tribes 161, 165
  silk trade 224, 236
  spice trade 236, 239, 301, 316, 317, 319,
    340, 345, 347, 348, 351
damga, see tamga
Damietta 88, 180, 319, 376
Dan II, Wallachian Voyvode 286, 298
Danishmendlü 160; *see also* tribes
Danube basin 12–14, 18, 26, 39, 79, 84,
  180, 196, 286, 356, 369
  ports 64, 169, 185, 228, 306
  provisioning 98, 182, 186, 239, 290
  trade 296–99, 300, 304–5
  transportation 308, 356
Dardanelles 11, 34, 197
Daurak 350, 351
defterdar 77, 84
Denizli 34, 219, 223
derbendci 175
dervish 14, 83, 123, 127, 168, 169, 175
deştiban 177
devşirme 16; *see also* administration *and*
  military organization

Diu (Bender-i-Türk) 20, 323, 325, 326
divan 303, 326
divan 163; *see also* land: periodic
   settlements
divani malikane 126–30; *see also* land:
   possession outside the *miri* system
Diyarbekir 224
   population movements 27, 28
   manufacture 219
Djezayir 350–52
Dnieper 276
Dobruja 36, 40, 180, 264, 275, 291, 293–95
dolab 48, 214; *see also* banking
duaguyan 47
Dubrovnik 59, 84, 189, 242, 243, 256ff,
   343, 345, 355
   Balkan trade 256–69
Dutch East India Company 358
dyes and dyestuff 38, 57, 317, 340, 351,
   359, 365, 370

East India Company 354, 358, 371
Edirne 19, 53, 210
   trade 232, 233, 235, 242, 341
   Balkan trade 256, 262, 264, 265
   Black Sea trade 278, 289, 296, 299
   cloth industry 374
   see also Adrianople
Egypt 12, 17, 20, 38, 98, 103
   trade 50, 94, 95, 194, 199, 219, 224, 228,
      247, 298, 315, 317, 368, 375–77
   state revenues 56–57, 65, 73, 79, 84,
      86–88
   agriculture 156
   provisioning by 180, 181, 186
   pilgrimage 196
   India trade 319–25, 329, 331–35, 342,
      343, 354, 356, 359
ekinlik 162; *see also* land: periodic
   settlements *and mezraa*
El Dorado 52
Elizabeth I 244, 366, 367
emin 65, 79; *see also* taxes
England 264
   capitulations 21, 189–91, 194, 195, 234
   silk trade 228, 229, 233, 237, 244,
      247–49
   Mediterranean trade 95, 241, 268, 269,
      364, 365–67, 369, 370, 374, 376–77
   woolen cloth 238, 288, 303
   India trade 229, 316, 342, 343, 345, 348,
      349, 353–59, 364, 365–67, 369, 370,
      374, 376–77
   Levant Company 249, 368, 370, 371
   Turkey Company 368
Ephesus, *see* Ayasoluk
epidemic 159, 165, 232

Erivan (Revan) 246
Erzincan 219, 223
Erzurum 40, 73, 98, 123, 246
Estado da India 351
Estergon 306
eşkünci 36, 90; *see also* sipahi
eşraf, see administration, provincial
Euphrates 12, 18, 27, 36, 39, 84, 339
Evliya Çelebi 171, 307–8

factory 348; *see also* workshop
fairs 233, 243, 303, 306, 345; *see also* trade
Falluja 339
famine 184, 185
ferag 111, 112; *see also* land: *miri*
fetva 23, 112; *see also* Sheyhülislam *and*
   Islamic Law
fey land 11, 103, 111; *see also* land: *miri*
Filibe (Plovdiv) 14, 62, 242, 264
firewood 71
fiscalism 44, 50, 58, 72
Flanders 303, 342, 364, 373
flax 127, 235, 355, 356
fleet, *see* navy
Florence 199, 218, 227, 230–34, 235–43,
   263, 267, 288
Foçalar (Phocaeas) 32, 180, 197, 264, 265
Fojnica, silver mines 59
France 230, 233, 367
   capitulations 21, 50, 189–91, 194, 234
   silk trade 236, 243, 245, 248
   woolen cloth 238
   Mediterranean trade 268, 372–77
   India trade 343, 347, 348, 355, 356–59
fruits, *see* horticulture
Fuggers 355, 357, 358

Galata 31, 48, 66, 93, 94, 191, 209, 211,
   224, 225, 231–32, 235, 242, 264, 267,
   271, 274, 287, 288, 369, 373, 374; *see
   also* Pera
Gallipoli (Gelibolu) 11, 19, 93, 195, 197,
   210, 233, 235
gall-nuts 38, 349
gardens, vegetable 108, 136, 155, 171, 177
Gaza 56
gaza 11, 20, 21, 193
gazi 19, 193, 307; *see also* military
   organization
gedik 93; *see also* guilds
Gelibolu, *see* Gallipoli
Genoa 19, 38, 190, 198, 199, 209
   capitulations 193, 194
   silk trade 50, 218, 219, 222, 224–27, 229,
      230, 232, 235, 236, 241, 244
   colonies and the Black Sea trade 271–80,
      285–88, 290
   India trade 315–17, 341, 343, 355

Georgia 113, 138, 156, 229
Germany 287, 296–98, 303, 308–10, 343,
    369
  spice trade 250, 342, 355–59
Gilan 219, 222, 223, 226, 230
Giresun 187
Giurgiu (Yergögü) 64, 286, 290, 296, 298
Goa 357
Godinho, V. M., *see* Magalhães, G.-V.
gold 49, 56, 64, 87, 246–48, 324, 331
  mines 58, 59, 210
  monies 65, 69, 189, 257, 288–89, 375
Golden Horde 222, 275–76, 278, 293, 315
gönüllü 22; *see also* military organization
Gördes 38
Great Britain, *see* England
Greek community and Greece 18, 26, 32,
    38, 58, 63, 66, 79, 123, 133, 160, 167,
    186, 209–16, 271, 272, 274, 369, 370,
    377
  merchants 236, 241, 243, 277, 288, 304,
    345, 371
  shipping 181, 209–12, 224
Greek Patriarchate of Istanbul 18, 75
guilds 51, 52, 107, 236; *see also, gedik,*
    manufacturing, labor *and* workers
Gujerat 319, 321, 323, 325–28, 335, 339,
    346
gulam 90; *see also sipahi and* military
    organization
Güçer, Lütfi 30
gümrük, see customs: tariff

Habsburg Empire 14, 22, 301–5
Hadramawt 323, 329
hajj, see pilgrimage
hali land 120
Hamid (Isparta) 34
hane 25–29; *see also* household
Hanseatic 356, 358
haracı land 103, 111, 113; *see also* land:
    miri
haraç 103, 104m, 113, 152; *see also* land:
    taxes
Al-Hasa 29, 337, 351, 352
Haskovo 36
hass 55, 66, 69, 73, 90, 133, 141, 166, 172;
    see also land
havale 208
Hejaz 29, 87, 88, 322, 331
Herzegovina 17, 259, 260, 265
Heyd, Wilhelm 3, 214, 295–96
hides 38, 40, 49, 171, 181, 185, 186, 235,
    240, 260, 264, 266–68, 272, 288, 303,
    351
  skins 263, 264, 267, 511; *see also* animal
    husbandry

hiref-i hassa 47; *see also* craftsmen
hisar-eri 90; *see also sihapi*
Hit 339
Holland 233, 237, 242, 268, 303, 366
  capitulations 21, 189, 191, 192, 194, 195
  silk trade 244–49
  India trade 330, 347, 351, 353–55,
    357–59
  Mediterranean trade 95, 372–77
  revolt 373
Holy Cities 20, 87; *see also* Mecca *and*
    Medina
Hormuz 219, 246, 248, 327, 335–40, 343,
    350, 351, 353, 354, 356
horticulture: fruits 38, 40, 63, 171, 172,
    185, 186, 187, 266
  vegetables 108, 155, 171, 172
Hotin 303
household 25–29, 30, 34, 47, 66–69, 73, 85,
    92, 97, 136, 143, 157, 161, 163
hukuk taxes 70; *see also* Islamnic Law *and*
    taxes
Humayun, Moghul emperor 325
Hungary 12–14, 15, 21, 26, 29, 57, 58, 68,
    69, 73, 84, 89, 119, 124, 137, 138, 156,
    168, 169, 185, 256, 258, 259, 286, 289,
    290, 296–97, 327
  campaign 95–96, 98
  eastern European trade 303–11
  pepper route 299–304
  slave trade 307–8
Hüdavendigar 93, 118; *see also* Bursa

Ibn Kemal, historian 19
icaratayn 106
ifraz 137
ihtisab 180–81; *see also* market: dues
iki baştan 128; *see also* land: possession
    outside the *miri* system
iltizam 55; *see also* tax-farm
imam 104, 172, 174, 175
imaret 47; *see also* pious endowment
imperial campaign(s) 39, 64, 65, 71, 73, 88,
    91, 92, 95–98, 100, 133, 168, 182, 228,
    242, 258, 286, 289, 293, 326, 330, 331,
    334, 336, 367
India 20, 38, 52, 107, 371, 373
  trade 57, 85, 86, 179, 197, 219, 224, 229,
    239, 246–49, 300, 315, 319–59
  see also Mughal Empire
Indian Ocean 85, 88, 246–49, 319–31, 334,
    337, 338, 340, 341, 346, 353, 358
Indonesia 371
Iran 17, 21, 22, 23, 32, 44, 52, 75, 95, 96,
    98, 100, 167, 367, 379
  trade 57, 197, 364, 365
  silk 57, 196, 202, 203, 206, 218, 219,

222–24, 226–30, 235, 236, 237, 241,
244–47, 248, 249, 370, 372, 373
spice trade 315, 317, 320, 330–31,
336–38, 345, 347–49, 349–52, 354, 359
azemini 227, 243, 345
Iraq 29, 31, 37, 38, 89, 103, 121, 138, 156,
315, 336
India trade 338, 350, 352, 353
irsalat (irsaliyye) 201; *see also* provisioning
Isfahan 226
Islamic Law 14, 47–48, 103, 110, 111, 128,
188, 192, 201, 373
ispence 69, 76 n 15, 152; *see also jupaniéa*
and poll tax
İstanbul 19, 23, 32, 39, 48, 53, 56, 63, 95,
137, 165, 168, 176, 195, 219, 335, 348
provisioning 161, 169–70, 179–82,
182–87, 256, 272, 275, 292, 295
customs zone 197, 200
Greeks and Jews 209–16
silk trade 219, 223, 241–43
trade 277, 278, 285–91, 303, 317, 319,
343
Golden Horn 231, 272
see also Constantinople
İstanköy (Cos) 187
istiglal 106; *see also* land: *miri*
Italy, republic(s) of 31, 38, 49, 53, 58, 256,
257, 272, 273
silk trade 18, 218, 219, 223, 227, 228,
229, 230–37, 243–44, 367, 372
merchant community 48, 209, 267
trade 182, 184, 185, 227, 228, 229, 262,
264, 265
woolen cloth 237–39
Black Sea trade 277, 287, 303
India trade 316, 317, 341, 343, 345, 356,
357, 359
Ivan III, prince of Muscovy 277
İzmir 34, 316, 370, 377
port of 63, 180, 196, 264
rise 245–46, 359, 365
merchant communities 191, 192, 368
Iranian silk via 372
İzmit 94, 187

Janissary 12, 15, 18, 19, 24, 25, 72, 133,
306, 321, 326, 335
uprising 25
agriculture 173
merchants and craftsmen 183
clothing 48
Jerusalem 161
Jews in the Ottoman Empire 189, 212–14,
366, 374
communities 18, 26, 274

population movements 27, 29, 31, 32,
224, 242
financier 66
tax-farmers 209–10, 212
and banking 213–14
merchants 226–27, 235, 241, 243, 251,
263, 264, 266–69, 277, 278, 285,
287–88, 301, 302
Jidda 316, 333, 346
jupaniéa 69, 76 n 15; *see also* poll-tax

kadi
responsibilities 46, 65, 84, 94, 97, 109,
112, 134–36, 138, 173–76, 208, 236,
265
courts 71–72, 84, 94, 110, 121, 130, 203,
206, 227, 235, 346
court records 71, 109–11, 121, 188, 208,
223, 225, 227, 237, 267, 278, 287, 288,
345
Kaminiec 138, 369
Kandehar 353
Kanuni Süleyman, *see* Süleyman I
kanunname 136; *see also* administration
kapan (kabban) 198, 204; *see also* taxes
kapıkulu 133; *see also* military
organization
kapitane 74; *see also* administration: local
dynasts
kapu-resmi 69; *see also* poll-tax
Karaman 55, 73, 163
Karamanids 18, 20; *see also* Turcoman,
principalities
Karatova, *see* Kratova
Kara-Ulus 35; *see also* Turcoman
Karbela 339
Kars 246
karziya 309, 369–70; *see also* woolen cloth
Kasim Shirvani 322
Kassa (Kaschau) 300
kassabiyye 251; *see also* taxes
Kastamonu 17
Al-Katif 337, 350, 352
Kavala (Kephalia) 94, 258
Kayseri 135, 159, 160
Kazan 330
kethüda 74, 162, 172, 174–75; *see also*
sipahi and guilds
Khwarezm 276, 330
Kiev 276–80
Kilia 180, 256, 278, 286, 287, 289, 291–93,
296
Kınalızade, historian 44, 45
kır-bekçisi 177; *see also* village
kirbas 275; *see also* cotton: cloth
Kirkkilise 62, 369
kışlak 170; *see also* pasture

Kızılbaş 34, 40; *see also* nomads
Kocaeli 30
Konya 34, 38, 127, 166, 219, 223, 317
Kopan 306
Kossovo-Polje, battle of 12
Kratova 36, 59
Kresovo, silver mines of 59
kul 16, 68, 71, 73, 116, 202; *see also* administration
Kula 38
kulluk 71, 150; *see also* labor; services
kulluk akçası 150; *see also* land: taxes
Kurds 32, 156
Kurnah 352
Kutna-Hora 298
Küre (Kastamonu) 55; *see also* mining
Kütahya 32, 34, 91, 317

labor: coerced 16
  services 71, 72, 150
Lala Mustafa Pasha 213
land: categories 139–42
  miri (state-owned) 23, 66, 105–8, 110–13, 117, 118 n 9, 120–26, 127, 129, 130, 139, 140, 155, 181, 187
  origin 103–7
  types of possession 108–10
  nature of possession 110–14
  timar system 114–17
  hassa çiftlik 117–18
  possession outside the *miri* system 120–26
  surveying 132–39
  deserted 162–67
  imperial grant 120–26
  extension of state ownership 126–30
  taxes 70, 86, 103, 104, 108, 113, 149–50, 152
  dead 120–26
  settlement 155–57
  reclamation 167–71
  periodic settlements 113, 120, 135, 140, 158–62, 162–67, 167–71, 176
  landholding 30, 48, 105–7, 112, 125, 139, 155, 173, 185, 318
  dual tenancy 106; *see also* çiftlik and tax-farm
Lane, Frederick 341
Languedoc 309
Lanzan 243, 345
leather 186, 206, 235, 256, 260, 264, 307, 316, 375
Lebanon 347
Leghorn 239, 245, 357, 372, 377
Leipzig 304
Lemberg, *see* Lwow

Lepanto 24, 94, 184, 213, 330, 334, 337, 365, 366
levend 261; *see also* military organization
Licostomo 272
Lisbon 319, 320, 327, 336, 338, 342, 343, 346, 348, 356–58
loans 227
  merchant 98, 241
London 218, 247, 248, 365, 367, 371
londra/londrina 309, 369; *see also* woolen cloth
Lopez, Roberto 218, 296, 341
Low Countries 53, 298, 365, 367, 372
Lübeck 357
luxury goods 46
Lwow (Lemberg) 189, 276–78, 285, 287–90, 303, 343, 364, 365, 369, 372
Lybyer, H. O. 79, 341

Macedonia 13, 14, 24, 184, 258
Magalhães, G.-V. 338, 341, 344
maktu 68, 108; *see also* taxes *and* tax-farm
Malabar 319, 320, 347
Malacca 328, 330
Maldive Islands 328, 329
malikane 128; *see also* tax-farm
Malowist, Marion 276–77, 296
Mamluks 19, 20, 87, 162, 181, 194, 319–23, 325
Ma'n, Fahreddin 349
manufacturing 219
Maraş 73, 319
Mardin 219, 224
Maritsa 32, 36
Marj Dabik 20, 322
market; rural periodic 71
  inspector 53, 309
  dues 180–81, 204–6, 224
  see also fairs *and* trade
Marmara, Sea of 160, 182, 184–87, 197
Marseilles 356, 358
martolos 17; *see also* military organization
Mazandaran 219
Mecca 20, 87, 196, 316, 317, 320, 322, 326, 333, 338, 345, 352
Medici 234, 235
Medina 20, 87, 320, 322
Mehmed I (1413–21) 12, 129, 194, 286
Mehmed II (the Conqueror) (1451–81) 13, 17–19, 50, 58, 65, 69, 95, 106, 111, 130, 162, 167, 177, 194, 196–97, 199, 209, 226, 228, 230–31, 258–59, 261, 273, 275, 278, 289–90
Menteşe 34, 63
menzil-hane 98
mercantilism 45, 48–52, 364, 369, 372
merchant 48, 62, 72, 94, 185, 189–92, 196,

198, 201, 202, 203, 206, 210, 225, 227, 228, 234–36, 241, 243, 256, 259, 263, 266, 268, 276, 287, 298, 299, 302, 304, 311, 315, 321, 322, 327, 338, 345–47, 350, 352, 355, 368
  foreign 190, 192, 373
  indebtedness 191, 236, 240, 356
merchant communities 285, 328
millet 190–91
mevat 120, 140–41; *see also* land
mezraa 114, 120 135, 140, 159, 161, 162–67, 176
  settlement 158–62, 167–71
  see also land: periodic settlements
Michael the Brave 64, 186
migration 29, 32, 34, 35, 40, 165, 346
  to frontier zones 14
  emigration 30, 37
  immigration 14, 26, 34, 158, 369
  "great flight" after Celali rebellions 32, 40, 96, 134, 159, 165–66, 274
military organization 16, 17, 18, 89, 91, 92–93, 101 n 34, 122, 304, 306
  standing army 133
  incorporation of pre-Ottoman military groups 16, 117, 167
  frontier forces 13–14, 22, 72
  volunteers 22, 72
  privateers 261
  enrollment of man of *reaya* origin 22
  enrollment of mercenaries 24, 116, 166
  auxiliary troops 41, 91, 128
  auxiliary troops of nomadic origin 34, 91–93
  militia of Christian troops of nomadic origin 34, 91–93
  militia of Christian origin 93
  irregular forces 89, 92–93, 101 n 34, 306
  expenditures for the army 88–93
  see also Janissary, cavalry, *sipahi and askeri*
millet, see merchant communities
mines 55
  Serbia and Bosnia 58–60, 65, 66, 107, 136, 175, 209–11, 224, 256, 258, 260
  mining 41, 53, 58, 60
  salt 60–64, 93, 258, 359
Mir Ali Bey 331
miri, see land
Mısr (Old Cairo) 87
Mocha (al-Mukha) 85, 334, 335, 346, 359; *see also* coffee
Modon 316, 377
Mogadishu 331
mohair 50, 240, 268, 297, 317, 359
  cloth 924
Moldavia (Boğdan) 14, 95, 185, 256, 271,

276, 278, 285–89, 291, 292, 293, 294, 299, 301–3, 304, 369
Mombasa 331
money 206–9
  depreciation 64
  devaluation 68, 100
  coin 56, 57, 289
  counterfeit 24
  dinar 222, 260
  dirhem 68, 98, 250
  para 57, 85–88, 335
  usury 72; *see also* bullion
Mongols 12, 20, 95, 218, 219, 222, 224, 315
Morea 12, 17, 32, 211, 229, 230, 325, 366, 377
Morocco 20
Moscow 229, 247, 276; *see also* Muscovy
Mosul 339
Mudanya 186, 197
mudaraba 48, 209; *see also* commenda partnership
Mughal Empire 107, 321, 325; *see also* India
muhtesib 46, 52; *see also* market: inspector
mukataa 55, 57, 65, 66, 72, 86, 88, 108, 139–40, 170–71; *see also* tax-farm
Murad I (1362–89) 12, 58, 93, 130, 194, 224, 273
Murad II (1421–44, 1446–51) 12, 13, 92, 114, 194, 224, 258
Murad III (1574–95) 98
Muscat 353
Muscovy 179, 213, 276, 277, 376; *see also* Moscow
mushaa 156, 176; *see also* landholding
al-Mutahhar, Zaydi Iman 333–34
müccerid 149; *see also* land: taxes
mülazemet 115; *see also* timar
mülk 23, 79, 104, 128, 140; *see also* landholding
müsselem 34, 91, 92; *see also* military organization; auxiliary troops of nomadic origin

Nagyszeben (Sibu) 299
Nagyvarad 290, 300
Naima, historian 355
narh 46
navi 95; *see also* transportation: shipping
navruz 47
navy 20, 24, 93, 94, 181, 192, 247, 263, 286, 304, 319–23, 325–31, 337, 338, 346, 358, 367, 374, 377
  expenditures for 93–95
  galley 94, 652
Nicopolis (Niğbolu) 12, 64, 185, 211, 256, 296, 298

Niksar 168, 350
Nile River 86, 324, 325
Niş 13
nişancı 105; *see also* land: *miri*
Nogay Tatars 295
nomads 14, 29, 32–41, 158–62, 163, 169
  transhumance 170
  nomadic populations 32–41
  settlement of 158–62
  see also tribes
North Africa 354, 366, 377
Nova (Hercegnovi) 94, 256, 261, 268
Novibazar 265, 266
Nubia 325
nüzul 96–97; *see also* taxes: extraordinary
  and imperial campaign(s)

oba 163; *see also* land: periodic settlements
olive: groves 157, 164, 187
  oil 187, 198, 271, 317, 348, 364, 370,
    374, 377
Orhan (1324–62) 11, 222
ortakçı kul 152; *see also* sharecropping
ortakçılık 167; *see also* sharecropping
Osman Gazi (d. 1324) 17, 95
Osmancık 223

ören 163; *see also* village: abandoned *and*
  mezraa
öşür 113; *see also* tithe
özengilik 141; *see also* appanage
Özü (Cankerman) 196, 292, 293

Pach Z. P. 296
Palestine 28, 68, 138, 157, 159, 163, 164,
  166, 196
Papacy 21, 259, 330
Pasai 328, 347
paşmaklık 141; *see also* appanage
pasture 37, 40, 155, 164, 176, 177, 296,
  306; *see also* nomads
Patras 264, 368
  currant trade 377
peasant 24, 25, 30, 31, 40, 44, 48, 60, 69,
  71, 74, 77, 91, 96, 100, 104–6, 108,
  110, 111, 123, 124, 126–30, 133–37,
  139, 141, 147, 157, 159, 164–70,
  172–74, 176, 317
  farm 30, 55, 60, 66, 73, 74, 92, 106, 108,
    109, 122, 123, 126, 135, 136, 156, 157,
    191, 211, 212
  size of farm 30, 146–48
  taxation 69–72
Pera 194, 222, 223–27, 230–37, 241–42,
  271–75, 277, 278, 285, 287, 289, 296,
  317

Persia 17, 95, 105, 244, 246–49; *see also*
  Iran *and* Safavids
Persian Gulf 57, 84, 224, 247–49, 315, 316,
  321, 327–28, 335–40, 344, 349–51,
  353, 356, 359, 372
Peter of Wallachia 64
Philip II 195, 357, 365, 367, 372
Philippopolis 13; *see also* Filibe
pilgrimage 20, 87, 196, 317, 322, 328, 329
  pilgrims 330
pious endowment/foundation 19, 79, 98,
  105, 111; *see also* vakıf
pişkeş 47, 57, 74–75
plague 53, 232, 241; *see also* epidemic
Poland 40, 138, 179, 194, 212, 214, 256,
  276, 277, 286, 287–89, 291, 292, 296,
  298, 303, 357, 369, 372
poliçe 208
poll-tax 24, 25, 26, 55, 66–96, 74, 75 n 15,
  104, 123, 152, 211, 213
Polyani, Karl 47
population, overall 25, 28–29
  Christian 26–27, 30
  Muslim 27
  movements 30–32
  nomadic 32–37, 137
  pressure 22, 29–30, 51, 183, 185
  density 161
Porte, Sublime, *see* administration,
  imperial
Portugal 19–20, 31, 195, 247–49, 267, 300,
  319–25, 325–31, 335–47, 350, 351,
  353, 355, 356, 357, 358, 365, 366
Poszony (Pressburg) 300, 301, 304
Praca, iron mines 59
Preveza 21
Prizren 229
pronia 117, 167
Provence 199, 343
provisioning 39, 50, 63, 95, 96, 181, 182,
  209, 210, 294
  foodstuffs 96, 98, 171, 179, 206, 256,
    257, 273, 304, 351

Ragusa, *see* Dubrovnik
railways 39
rakaba/rikab 104, 106, 107, 129, 130; *see*
  also land: *miri*
Ramazanids 20; *see also* Turcoman:
  principalities
reaya 16, 17, 22, 23, 25, 70, 71, 74, 91, 93,
  108, 109, 121, 132, 134–37, 164, 168,
  172, 173, 259; *see also* craftsmen,
  merchant *and* peasant
Recanati 345
Red Sea 20, 192, 219, 247–49, 344–46, 354,
  358, 359